JOURNAL FOR THE STUDY OF THE NEW TESTAMENT
SUPPLEMENT SERIES
162

Executive Editor
Stanley E. Porter

Sheffield Academic Press

Example Stories

Perspectives on Four Parables in the Gospel of Luke

Jeffrey T. Tucker

Journal for the Study of the New Testament
Supplement Series 162

For
Jessica Marie Tucker and
Samuel Jefferson Tucker
With whom I am well pleased and
in whom I delight

Copyright © 1998 Sheffield Academic Press

Published by Sheffield Academic Press Ltd
Mansion House
19 Kingfield Road
Sheffield S11 9AS
England

Typeset by Sheffield Academic Press
and
Printed on acid-free paper in Great Britain
by Bookcraft Ltd
Midsomer Norton, Bath

British Library Cataloguing in Publication Data

A catalogue record for this book is available
from the British Library

ISBN 1-85075-897-2

CONTENTS

PREFACE

This book is a revision of my dissertation, which was written under the direction of Professor Mary Ann Tolbert.[1] The title of this work in its present form denotes the subject of concern, while the subtitle connotes a certain slant. If I were to punctuate the title to suggest my take on the topic, it would read 'Example Stories' to serve as a visable indication that I consider the categorization of four parables in the Gospel of Luke as such to be problematical.

Indeed, the name for that category is not without its problems. First, 'example story' is a rather inexact translation of *'Beispielerzählung'*, Adolf Jülicher's designation for a category of Jesus' parables. While 'example narrative' is a more precise translation, I have retained the more familiar rendering 'example story' since that is commonly regarded as the English equivalent of the German term in New Testament scholarship, particularly in parable scholarship. I do, however, use both terms interchangeably throughout this study. Secondly, scholars before Jülicher placed the same four parables in a group, but they did not call them by the same name. Thus, in a discussion of how scholars who antedate Jülicher treated that group of four parables, any reference to them as 'example stories' is, technically speaking, an anachronism.

The category 'example story', in my opinion, presents problems of more moment than simply how we should refer to it. The ensuing chapters make manifest my reasons for challenging the categorization of four parables in the Gospel of Luke as 'example stories' and for wanting to do away with the term. Still, I needed to use the term 'example story' in order to discuss the group of four parables called by that name. I avoided the temptation to imitate Jacques Derrida's graphic gesture of placing the term under erasure.[2] Had I decided in

1.   'Four Parables in the Gospel of Luke: Perspectives on the Example Narratives' (PhD dissertation, Vanderbilt University, 1994).
2.   See Derrida's use of this gesture in, among other places, *Of Grammatology*

favor of that ploy, I would have written the term 'example story' and then crossed it out. Such a gesture would make the term legible since it is necessary, but would also be an initial move toward striking the term since it is inaccurate. Moreover, such a gesture would make us mindful that even if irrefutable evidence could be produced to prove that the four parables in question are not 'example stories', the term has been inscribed in New Testament scholarship, and the trace of it will always be present. The advantages of putting 'example story' under erasure notwithstanding, I decided against employing that gesture because my aim is not to deconstruct, in the strictest philosophical sense, the term or the category. Nevertheless, even though the term 'example story' cannot be erased, my intent is to call the category into question.

One gesture I would be remiss to forgo is the giving of thanks to those whose significant acts of kindness and generosity enabled me to complete this project. I remain indebted to those whom I acknowledged in the dissertation, and I reaffirm my gratitude to all of them, especially the readers on my dissertation committee, Professors Daniel Patte, Fernando F. Segovia, Peter J. Haas and F. Carter Philips. I am profoundly indebted to my adviser, Professor Mary Ann Tolbert, who has always been gracious to me, constantly offering encouragement, and I will continue to owe her more than she knows for that. I must express my appreciation to Vanderbilt University for allowing me to continue my research at the Alexander and Jean Heard Library. The fine people at Sheffield Academic Press deserve special mention, for without their efforts and considerable patience, the publication of this work in its present form would not have been possible; in particular, I thank Professor Stanley E. Porter, Jean R.K. Allen, Ailsa Parkin and Vicky Acklam for all that they have done for me. Above all others, I thank my lovely wife, Allison, who has ceaselessly given me more than I expected to receive from anyone, who gave me her hand and two wonderful children, my treasures, thanks to whom I have experienced incredible moments of sudden joy and through whom I have been blessed. I dedicated the dissertation to her; I dedicate this book to our children.

In several places throughout this study, I have reproduced passages from various texts—several of which are scarce, and many of which have not appeared in English—in their original language so that the

(trans. Gayatri Chakravorty Spivak; Baltimore: The Johns Hopkins University Press, 1976).

nuance of an important point will not be lost in translation.[3] Unless explicitly stated otherwise, all translations are my own.

3. Those who would like to read the words of several scholars in their own language (especially in Chapters 2, 3 and 4) may wish to consult my dissertation, for here I have either translated or omitted altogether a number of passages.

ABBREVIATIONS

AB	Anchor Bible
AJP	*American Journal of Philology*
AnBib	Analecta biblica
ANQ	*Andover Newton Quarterly*
ANRW	Hildegard Temporini and Wolfgang Haase (eds.), *Aufstieg und Niedergang der römischen Welt: Geschichte und Kultur Roms im Spiegel der neueren Forschung* (Berlin: W. de Gruyter, 1972–)
ATDan	Acta theologica danica
BAGD	Walter Bauer, William F. Arndt, F. William Gingrich and Frederick W. Danker, *A Greek–English Lexicon of the New Testament and Other Early Christian Literature* (Chicago: University of Chicago Press, 2nd edn, 1958)
BETL	Bibliotheca ephemeridum theologicarum lovaniensium
BEvT	Beiträge zur evangelischen Theologie
BGBE	Beiträge zur Geschichte der biblischen Exegese
BibLeb	*Bibel und Leben*
BJRL	*Bulletin of the John Rylands University Library of Manchester*
BTB	*Biblical Theology Bulletin*
BWANT	Beiträge zur Wissenschaft vom Alten und Neuen Testament
CBQ	*Catholic Biblical Quarterly*
CBQMS	*Catholic Biblical Quarterly*, Monograph Series
CJT	*Canadian Journal of Theology*
ConNT	*Coniectanea neotestamentica*
CTM	*Concordia Theological Monthly*
ETR	*Etudes théologiques et religieuses*
ExpTim	*Expository Times*
FRLANT	Forschungen zur Religion und Literatur des Alten und Neuen Testaments
IDB	George Arthur Buttrick (ed.), *The Interpreter's Dictionary of the Bible* (4 vols.; Nashville: Abingdon Press, 1962)
Int	*Interpretation*
JBL	*Journal of Biblical Literature*
JR	*Journal of Religion*
JSNTSup	*Journal for the Study of the New Testament*, Supplement Series

JSOT	*Journal for the Study of the Old Testament*
JTS	*Journal of Theological Studies*
LB	*Linguistica biblica*
LCL	Loeb Classical Library
LCM	Loeb Classical Monographs
LQ	*Lutheran Quarterly*
LSJ	H.G. Liddell, Robert Scott and H. Stuart Jones, *Greek–English Lexicon* (Oxford: Clarendon Press, 9th edn, 1968)
NovT	*Novum Testamentum*
NovTSup	*Novum Testamentum*, Supplements
NTAbh	Neutestamentliche Abhandlungen
NTS	*New Testament Studies*
PTMS	Pittsburgh Theological Monograph Series
RGG	*Religion in Geschichte und Gegenwart*
RSV	Revised Standard Version
SBLBMI	SBL The Bible and its Modern Interpreters
SBLDS	SBL Dissertation Series
SBLSS	SBL Semeia Studies
SBS	Stuttgarter Bibelstudien
ST	*Studia theologica*
TDNT	Gerhard Kittel and Gerhard Friedrich (eds.), *Theological Dictionary of the New Testament* (trans. Geoffrey W. Bromiley; 10 vols.; Grand Rapids: Eerdmans, 1964–)
TRu	*Theologische Rundschau*
WUNT	Wissenschaftliche Untersuchungen zum Neuen Testament
ZNW	*Zeitschrift für die neutestamentliche Wissenschaft*
ZST	*Zeitschrift für systematische Theologie*
ZTK	*Zeitschrift für Theologie und Kirche*

Chapter 1

INTRODUCTION: PERSPECTIVES ON THE EXAMPLE STORIES

'...[W]e stand here before the heritage of Adolf Jülicher. It is a heritage
worth preserving and, contrary to dissentient voices, defending.'

Hans-Josef Klauck,
'Adolf Jülicher: Leben, Werk und Wirkung'

The parables of the Gospel of Luke occupy a prominent place in the
history of parable scholarship. To those interested in the parables of
Jesus, the Gospel of Luke is an invaluable resource not only because of
the quantity of parables it records,[1] but because it alone furnishes the
record of several famous parables attributed to Jesus. If not for the
efforts of the third evangelist, parables such as The Good Samaritan,
The Prodigal Son, The Rich Man and Lazarus, The Unjust Judge, and
The Pharisee and the Tax Collector, to name a few by their traditional
titles, would be unknown.[2] However, four parables found in the third

1.   There is no consensus on the number of parables in the Gospel of Luke (or,
for that matter, the other synoptic gospels). For instance, Warren S. Kissinger lists
40 parables in the third Gospel (*The Parables of Jesus: A History of Interpretation
and Bibliography* [American Theological Library Association Bibliography Series,
4; Metuchen, NJ: Scarecrow Press, 1979], pp. xxii-xxiv), whereas Jan Lambrecht
counts 31 (*Once More Astonished: The Parables of Jesus* [New York: Crossroad,
1981], pp. 18-20). According to Lambrecht, 'the third evangelist has preserved the
greatest number of parables' (p. 24).

2.   For a list of parables found only in the Gospel of Luke, commonly
described as belonging to Luke's *Sondergut* (or 'L'), see Gerhard Sellin, 'Lukas als
Gleichniserzähler: Die Erzählung vom barmherzigen Samariter (Lk 10 25-37)',
ZNW 65 (1974), pp. 166-89 (176); John Drury, *The Parables in the Gospels: History and Allegory* (New York: Crossroad, 1985), p. 112; Lambrecht, *Once More
Astonished*, pp. 18-20. The propriety of including The Foolish Rich Man (Lk.
12.16-21) in 'L' depends, of course, upon what is meant by 'L'. If 'L' is conceived
of as 'material peculiar to the Gospel of Luke alone', then The Foolish Rich Man
should not be included in 'L' since another version of it appears also in the Gospel

Gospel have posed problems to those who wish to interpret the parables
of Jesus.

The Problem: Example Stories

Four parables recorded in the Gospel of Luke—known traditionally as
The Good Samaritan (Lk. 10.30-35), The Rich Fool (Lk. 12.16-20),
The Rich Man and Poor Lazarus (Lk. 16.19-31) and The Pharisee and
the Tax Collector (Lk. 18.9-14)—have received the special attention of
parable scholars in this century largely as a consequence of their
classification as 'example narratives' (*Beispielerzählungen*) by Adolf
Jülicher.[3] Those four parables, which have shared the bond of a
common Gospel context for nearly two millennia, have been bound to
each other by category for over a century. Thanks to the category they
are said to constitute, those four Lukan parables, quite apart from the
Gospel context in which they appear, have a checkered past, especially
in the century of parable research since Jülicher. Those parables and
that category are the subjects of interest in this study.

The four parables in question have captured the imagination of generations of readers. The third evangelist has Jesus tell those parables in
this way:[4]

---

of Thomas; if 'L' is conceived of as 'a private source containing material not found
in the other synoptic gospels', then The Foolish Rich Man can be included there.
For a discussion of the 'L' source, a list of all 'L' passages in the Gospel of Luke,
and a brief treatment of the relation of the third Gospel to the Gospel of Thomas,
see Joseph A. Fitzmyer, *The Gospel According to Luke (I–IX): Introduction, Translation, and Notes* (AB, 28; Garden City, NY: Doubleday, 1981), pp. 83-87. For an
insightful analysis and interpretation of the parables in 'L', see Bernhard Heininger,
*Metaphorik, Erzählstruktur und szenisch-dramatische Gestaltung in den Son-
dergutgleichnissen bei Lukas* (NTAbh, NS 24; Münster: Aschendorff, 1991).

3.   Adolf Jülicher, *Die Gleichnisreden Jesu* (Zwei Teile in einem Band; Nachdruck der Ausgabe Tübingen 1910; Darmstadt: Wissenschaftliche Buchgesellschaft, 1963), I, p. 112. On the publication history of *Die Gleichnisreden Jesu*,
see p. 45 n. 1 below.

4.   The following are my translations based upon the text of *Novum Testa-
mentum Graece* (eds. Barbara Aland, Kurt Aland *et al.*; Stuttgart: Deutsche
Bibelgesellschaft, 27th rev. edn, 1993). Unless stated otherwise, all citations of
New Testament documents will be from this text and all translations will be my
own.

The Merciful Samaritan

Jesus replied and said: 'A certain man was going down from Jerusalem to Jericho and he fell among robbers who, having both stripped him and beat him, went away, leaving him half-dead. And by chance a certain priest was going down that road, and having seen him, he passed by on the opposite side. And likewise a Levite who was happening toward the place, having come and having seen, passed by on the opposite side. And a certain Samaritan who was travelling went toward him, and having seen, he had compassion, and having approached, he bound up his wounds, pouring olive oil and wine, and having mounted him upon his own animal, he brought him to an inn and took care of him. And the next day he took out and gave two denarii to the innkeeper and said, "Take care of him, and whatever you might spend in addition, I will give back to you upon my return."'

The Foolish Rich Man

And he told a parable to them, saying: 'The land of a certain rich man yielded plentifully, and he was thinking to himself, saying, "What shall I do, because I have nowhere to gather my fruit?" And he said, "I will do this: I will tear down my storehouses, and I will build greater ones, and there I will gather all my wheat and goods, and I will say to my soul, 'Soul, you have many goods lying for many years; rest yourself, eat, drink, and be merry.'" And God said to him, "Fool, this very night they are demanding from you your soul. And the things you have prepared, whose will they be?"'

The Rich Man and Poor Lazarus

'And there was a certain rich man who dressed himself in a purple garment and fine linen, being merry all day, splendidly. And a certain beggar named Lazarus, who was covered with sores and who desired to be fed from the things that fell from the table of the rich man, was laid in front of his gate; not only this, the dogs who came were licking his sores. And it happened that the beggar died and was carried by the angels to Abraham's bosom; and the rich man died and was buried. And in Hades, having lifted up his eyes, being in torment, he sees Abraham in the distance and Lazarus in his bosom. And he, having cried out, said, "Father Abraham, have mercy on me and send Lazarus so that he might dip the end of his finger in water and cool my tongue, because I am in anguish in these flames." But Abraham said, "Child, remember that you received your good things in your life, and Lazarus likewise the bad things; and now he is being comforted here, but you are in anguish. And in all these things between us and you a great chasm has been fixed, so that the ones wishing to cross from here to you might not be able, nor might they cross over from there to us." But he said, "Then I ask you, Father, that you might send him to my father's house, for I have five brothers, so that he might warn them in order that they might not also come to this place of torment." But Abraham says, "They have Moses and the prophets; let them hear them." But he said, "No, Father Abraham, but if someone from the dead might go to them, they will repent." But he said to him, "If they do not hear Moses and the prophets, not even if someone from the dead might be raised will they be persuaded."'

The Pharisee and the Toll Collector

And he also told this parable to certain ones who have been persuaded in themselves that they are righteous and who despise others: 'Two men went up to the temple to pray, the one a Pharisee and the other a toll collector. The Pharisee, having stood to himself, prayed these things, "God, I give thanks to you that I am not like other people, rapacious, unjust, adulterers, or even like this toll collector; I fast twice a week, I tithe of everything that I acquire." But the toll collector, having stood in the distance, was not willing even to lift up his eyes to heaven, but beat his chest, saying, "God, be propitiated to me, the sinner." I tell you, this one went down to his house having been justified rather than that one; because all those who lift themselves up will be made low, but all those who make themselves low will be lifted up.'

At first glance, these four parables seem innocuous enough, but the category to which they are said to belong has captured the attention of parable scholars, some of whom are at odds with each other over the viability of that very category. The debate among those scholars revolves around the issue of whether the parables classified as 'example stories' are anomalous or clearly different from all the other parables told by Jesus. Thus, these four parables have become embroiled in a controversy that has, at times in this century, taken on a life of its own. This study contains the story of that debate, and it begins *in medias res*.

Adolf Jülicher's Famous Proposal

As every student of the parables knows, Jülicher divided Jesus' parables into three categories—*Gleichnisse*, *Parabeln* and *Beispielerzählungen*—which in English are commonly called 'similitudes', 'parables' and 'example stories'.[5] Those categories are ingrained in parable

---

5.   A problem in translation, one which is addressed more fully in Chapter 3

scholarship; indeed they have become codified as form-critical *Gattungen* (genres) in sectors of New Testament scholarship.[6] As Madeleine Boucher remarks, 'It was Jülicher, of course, who proposed the classification of the parables which has remained standard in the scholarly literature'.[7] Nevertheless, Jülicher's classification of four parables as example stories has not carried the day with all parable scholars.

The magnitude of the controversy surrounding the category *'Beispielerzählung'* is proportionate to the stature of the scholar who made that category famous. Few scholars have had such an impact on a specific area of inquiry in New Testament scholarship as has Adolf Jülicher on the study of the parables of Jesus.[8] Since Jülicher published the first part of his two-volume work over a century ago, scarcely a single book written on the parables has failed to mention his *Die Gleichnisreden Jesu*. To anyone interested in the parables of Jesus, Jülicher has bequeathed a lasting legacy. The program for interpreting Jesus' parables Jülicher set forth in his first volume is a powerful synthesis of critical insights which has produced terms and principles that,

(see pp. 100-101 n. 114), confronts us here. The English renderings of these German words differ among scholars, a point which is not without significance for an understanding of Jülicher's categories.

6.   This is the case especially in introductory texts; see, e.g., Hans Conzelmann and Andreas Lindemann, *Interpreting the New Testament: An Introduction to the Principles and Methods of N.T. Exegesis* (trans. Siegfried S. Schatzmann; Peabody, MA: Hendrickson, 1988), pp. 74-75.

7.   Madeleine Boucher, *The Mysterious Parable: A Literary Study* (CBQMS, 6; Washington, DC: Catholic Biblical Association, 1977), p. 3.

8.   Jülicher's sphere of influence in New Testament studies extends beyond the study of Jesus' parables. For a biographical sketch of Jülicher, a description of his collective work, a discussion of the effective-history of his research, and a complete bibliography, see Hans-Josef Klauck, 'Adolf Jülicher: Leben, Werk und Wirkung', in Georg Schwaiger (ed.), *Historische Kritik in der Theologie: Beiträge zu ihrer Geschichte* (Studien zur Theologie und Geistesgeschichte des neunzehnten Jahrhunderts, 32; Göttingen: Vandenhoeck & Ruprecht, 1980), pp. 99-150. Klauck suggests that Jülicher's *Einleitung in das Neue Testament*, which went through several revisions and seven reprints, also helped establish his reputation as a leading figure in the field: '...it can be said without exaggeration that Jülicher's introduction was the exegetical textbook of a whole generation of students' (p. 104). Jülicher's *Einleitung* has been translated into English; see *An Introduction to the New Testament* (trans. Janet Penrose Ward; London: Smith, Elder & Co.; New York: Putnam's Sons, 1904).

even if modified, are still encountered today. Familiar technical terms
(such as *Bildhälfte, Sachhälfte, tertium comparationis*) and familiar
tenets of interpretation (that the parables of Jesus must be critically
reconstructed, that the parable effects a comparison, that the parable has
one point of application, that the parable impels the hearer to make a
judgment, that Jesus employed the parables to teach about the kingdom
of God) find their places there. Thus, we can begin to understand the
lofty praise of Jülicher's work and the repeated warnings that *Die
Gleichnisreden Jesu*, even today, must not be ignored. As Geraint
Vaughan Jones puts it,

> Jülicher was not without his opponents, and a just assessment of his
> work must take into account the contentions of his critics; yet it is no
> exaggeration to say that a study of the parables which does not reckon
> with it can be no other than grossly inadequate.[9]

As a matter of fact, Wolfgang Harnisch describes parable research in
this century as the history of the critical reception of the insights formulated by Jülicher.[10]

The sole purpose of this study is not to provide a 'just assessment' of
Jülicher's work; rather, the aim of this study is to provide a 'just
assessment' of a variety of views advanced by scholars about a particular group of parables that have come to be known, due in large part to
the influence of Jülicher's work, as 'example stories'. The contentions
of Jülicher's critics will be taken into account, but this study will not
simply chronicle the debate conducted by scholars who accept or reject
his classification of the example stories. Indeed, prior to a discussion of

---

9.   Geraint Vaughan Jones, *The Art and Truth of the Parables: A Study in their
Literary Form and Modern Interpretation* (London: SPCK, 1964), p. 3. Kissinger
(*The Parables of Jesus*, p. 77) echoes Jones on this point. Two prestigious parable
scholars offer counsel to those who would ignore Jülicher's work: see Norman
Perrin, 'The Modern Interpretation of the Parables of Jesus and the Problem of
Hermeneutics', *Int* 25 (1971), pp. 131-48 (131-32), and Robert W. Funk, *Lan-
guage, Hermeneutic, and Word of God: The Problem of Language in the New
Testament and Contemporary Theology* (New York: Harper & Row, 1966), p. 127.

10.   Wolfgang Harnisch, 'Vorwort', in *idem* (ed.), *Gleichnisse Jesu: Positionen
der Auslegung von Adolf Jülicher bis zur Formgeschichte* (Wege der Forschung,
366; Darmstadt: Wissenschaftliche Buchgesellschaft, 1982), p. x. David M.
Granskou (*Preaching on the Parables* [Philadelphia: Fortress Press, 1972], p. 16)
would concur: 'The history of the interpretation of the parables has been advanced
only by way of technical corrections of Jülicher'.

the debate that has ensued, it will be necessary to give Jülicher's conception of the category *Beispielerzählung* full consideration on its own, because unrecognized misconceptions about his view of the example stories have informed some of the questions scholars have raised about the example stories in the century of parable research since Jülicher's renowned work was published. Some of those misconceptions can be attributed to an inadequate appreciation of the context in which Jülicher proposed the classification of Jesus' parables and the significance of that classification within the overall argument of *Die Gleichnisreden Jesu*. A preview of one assumption about Jülicher's view of the example stories will indicate what is at stake for some scholars who participate in the debate, especially those who contest the classification of the four Lukan παραβολαί (parables) known as example stories.

A Preview of the Debate: 'Parables versus Examples' or 'Parables of Jesus versus Parables of Luke'

A rather common assumption about Jülicher's conception of the example stories is that he considered them to be different in kind from the other two groups of Jesus' parables; that is to say, he maintained that the example stories are not parables. Such an assumption is understandable since Jülicher placed four παραβολαί into a separate category with its own name—and unbeknownst to many parable scholars, Jülicher made remarks in the first edition of *Die Gleichnisreden Jesu* that lend credence to such an assumption. However, in the only edition of that work known to most scholars of this century, the second, Jülicher offered a revised position on the example stories, and a thorough reading of the chapter in which Jülicher treats the example stories reveals a more nuanced stance. If Jülicher's classification of Jesus' parables is situated within his argument about the essence of Jesus' parables, it becomes evident that the example stories are a group of παραβολαί similar in many respects to the narrative parables (*Parabeln*).

Jülicher, in the first volume of *Die Gleichnisreden Jesu*, issued a public declaration: The method of interpreting Jesus' parables that has prevailed for generations is deficient and defective. The impetus behind Jülicher's manifesto was his furious ambition to extirpate any vestige, any tincture, of allegory from the parables of Jesus so that it would be untoward for any serious scholar to engage in allegorical interpretations of Jesus' parables. According to Jülicher, the parables of Jesus are not in essence allegories: Among Jesus' parables, we may find *Gleichnisse*, *Parabeln* and *Beispielerzählungen*, but we will not find allegories. So forceful was Jülicher's attack against allegory that for years many scholars denied that any of Jesus' genuine parables partake of allegory. The trend of refusing to acknowledge that there is a scintilla of allegory in Jesus' parables may no longer be de rigueur, but Jülicher's assault on allegory is still celebrated as his enduring contribution to parable scholarship.[11] An interesting development in recent parable scholarship is that while Jülicher claimed that Jesus told no allegories, now some scholars tolerate the notion that Jesus did tell (some) allegories; yet another is that while Jülicher claimed that Jesus did tell some example stories, some scholars now resist the notion that Jesus told any example stories. The latter development stands squarely within the purview of this study.

The focus of this study, then, will be upon the problems, real and perceived, posed by a group of four parables in the Gospel of Luke, specifically, The Merciful Samaritan, The Foolish Rich Man, The Rich Man and Poor Lazarus, and The Pharisee and the Toll Collector.[12]

11. Among those who hold such a view are: Joachim Jeremias, *Die Gleichnisse Jesu* (Göttingen: Vandenhoeck & Ruprecht, 8th edn, 1970), pp. 14-15 (cf. *The Parables of Jesus* [trans. S.H. Hooke; New York: Charles Scribner's Sons, 2nd rev. edn, 1972], pp. 18-19); Friedrich Hauck, 'παραβολή', *TDNT*, V, p. 753 n. 66; Klyne Snodgrass, *The Parable of the Wicked Tenants: An Inquiry into Parable Interpretation* (WUNT, 27; Tübingen: J.C.B. Mohr [Paul Siebeck], 1983), p. 3; and Herman Hendrickx, *The Parables of Jesus* (Studies in the Synoptic Gospels; London: Geoffrey Chapman; San Francisco: Harper & Row, rev. edn, 1986), p. 13. Bernard Brandon Scott (*Hear Then the Parable: A Commentary on the Parables of Jesus* [Minneapolis: Fortress Press, 1989], p. 43) has written, 'The abiding significance of Jülicher's attack is his rejection of the existing allegories of Jesus' parables as products of the early church, and his arguments remain the rock that breaks those who would counterattack in favor of allegory'.

12. These titles are slight variations of the traditional titles given those narratives. For the purposes of this study, I translate and retain the titles by which Jülicher referred to the *Beispielerzählungen* (see *Die Gleichnisreden Jesu*, II, pp. viii, 585-641). I have not endeavored to make the titles given the parables in other studies conform to my preference; as a rule, when discussing a particular study of the parables, I refer to the parables by the titles given them by the author of that study. All titles appended to the parables jade interpretation, and any title, traditional ones included, can be deemed unsatisfactory in light of how one understands the parable. Scott (*Hear Then the Parable*, p. 4) recognizes that 'the

Given the large number of sayings that are included in the canon of Jesus' parables, the breadth of this study is already narrowed considerably in that it is devoted to a relatively small group of four παραβολαί.[13] The main interest will be with what is written about the example stories in the secondary literature, that is, the issues put forward for discussion by scholars who have participated in the debate on the status of the '*Beispielerzählungen*'. In order to focus on the problems associated with a specific group of four parables, the scope of this study must be delimited carefully because a number of important issues dealt with by parable scholars in this century impinge upon the subject of concern. Obviously, it will not be possible to deal comprehensively with the plethora of issues and problems, interrelated as they are, that have surfaced in the century of parable research since the publication of Jülicher's first volume, for an attempt to do so would entail writing a

title unconsciously and unknowingly provides the reader with a definite perspective on the parable', and so he chooses to rename the parables in a 'neutral' way by deriving the title from the first words of the parable. Charles W. Hedrick, 'Parables and the Kingdom: The Vision of Jesus in Fiction and Faith', in Kent Harold Richards (ed.), *Society of Biblical Literature 1987 Seminar Papers* [Atlanta: Scholars Press, 1987], p. 375 n. 16) maintains that 'the whole issue of titles for the parables should be rethought in the light of a literary/critical analysis of the structure of the parables'.

13. The canon of the historical Jesus' parables is neither fixed nor stable. There is a wide range in the number of entries included in the different versions of that canon; while one scholar may regard as few as 12 to be authentic parables of the historical Jesus (James Breech, *The Silence of Jesus: The Authentic Voice of the Historical Man* [Philadelphia: Fortress Press, 1983], p. 66), another may consider as many as 120 to be authentic (L. Castellani, cited in Hans-Josef Klauck, *Allegorie und Allegorese in synoptischen Gleichnistexten* [NTAbh, NS, 13; Münster: Aschendorff, 1978], p. 1). As Stephen L. Wailes (*Medieval Allegories of Jesus' Parables* [Berkeley: University of California Press, 1987], p. 3) puts it, 'There is no full agreement among modern scholars on the canon of Jesus' parables'. For a sample of the different number of parables included in some versions of that canon, see Jülicher, *Die Gleichnisreden Jesu*, I, pp. 28-29 (he approves of C.E. van Koetsveld's total of 79, but he himself exposits 53 in the second volume); Jones, *The Art and Truth of the Parables*, p. 141, cf. p. 144; and A.M. Hunter, *Interpreting the Parables* (London: SCM Press, 1960), p. 11, cf. pp. 121-22. Jeremias refers to '41 Gleichnissen Jesu' in the opening sentence of his famous book on the parables (*Die Gleichnisse Jesu*, p. 7; oddly, this part of that sentence does not appear in the English translation [cf. *The Parables of Jesus*, p. 11]). That there has been disagreement over the canon of Jesus' parables since the first century CE is evident in that even the synoptic evangelists record different parables.

history of parable scholarship, a task which has already been carried out admirably by others.[14] Nor will it be possible to treat at length specific

14. A reading of the following would provide a comprehensive history of parable research covering nearly every major parable interpreter, the significant issues involved in parable interpretation, and the various interpretive methods applied to the parables: Jülicher, *Die Gleichnisreden Jesu*, I, pp. 203-322; Jones, *The Art and Truth of the Parables*, pp. 3-54; E.C. Blackman, 'New Methods of Parable Interpretation', *CJT* 15 (1969), pp. 3-13; Jack Dean Kingsbury, 'Ernst Fuchs' Existentialist Interpretation of the Parables', *LQ* 22 (1970), pp. 380-95; *idem*, 'Major Trends in Parable Interpretation', *CTM* 42 (1971), pp. 579-96; *idem*, 'The Parables of Jesus in Current Research', *Dialog* 11 (1972), pp. 101-107; Perrin, 'The Modern Interpretation of the Parables', pp. 131-48; *idem*, *Jesus and the Language of the Kingdom: Symbol and Metaphor in New Testament Interpretation* (Philadelphia: Fortress Press, 1976), pp. 89-193; Klauck, *Allegorie und Allegorese*, pp. 4-31; *idem*, 'Neue Beiträge zur Gleichnisforschung', *BibLeb* 13 (1972), pp. 214-30; Wilfred J. Harrington, 'The Parables in Recent Study (1960–1971)', *BTB* 2 (1972), pp. 219-41; Charles E. Carlston, 'Changing Fashions in Interpreting the Parables', *ANQ* 14 (1974), pp. 227-33; M. Mees, 'Die moderne Deutung der Parabeln und ihre Probleme', *Vetera Christianorum* 11 (1974), pp. 416-33; James C. Little, 'Parable Research in the Twentieth Century. I. The Predecessors of J. Jeremias', *ExpTim* 87 (1976), pp. 356-60; *idem*, 'Parable Research in the Twentieth Century. II. The Contributions of J. Jeremias', *ExpTim* 88 (1976), pp. 40-44; *idem*, 'Parable Research in the Twentieth Century. III. Developments since J. Jeremias', *ExpTim* 88 (1976), pp. 71-75; Robert Morris Johnston, 'Parabolic Interpretations Attributed to Tannaim' (PhD dissertation, The Hartford Seminary Foundation, 1977), pp. 1-123; Hans Weder, *Die Gleichnisse Jesu als Metaphern: Traditions- und redaktionsgeschichtliche Analysen und Interpretationen* (FRLANT, 120; Göttingen: Vandenhoeck & Ruprecht, 1978), pp. 11-98; Kissinger, *The Parables of Jesus*, pp. 1-230, Robert H. Stein, *An Introduction to the Parables of Jesus* (Philadelphia: Westminster Press, 1981), pp. 42-71; Mogens Stiller Kjärgaard, *Metaphor and Parable: A Systematic Analysis of the Specific Structure and Cognitive Function of the Synoptic Similes and Parables qua Metaphors* (ATDan, 29; Leiden: E.J. Brill, 1986), pp. 133-97; Brad H. Young, *Jesus and his Jewish Parables: Rediscovering the Roots of Jesus' Teaching* (New York: Paulist Press, 1989), pp. 20-54; William A. Beardslee, 'Recent Literary Criticism', in Eldon Jay Epp and George W. MacRae (eds.), *The New Testament and its Modern Interpreters* (SBLBMI, 3; Atlanta: Scholars Press, 1989), pp. 177-83; and Craig L. Blomberg, *Interpreting the Parables* (Downers Grove, IL: InterVarsity Press, 1990), pp. 29-163. To compile a complete bibliography of parable research conducted in this century would be an ambitious endeavor. Some of the more comprehensive bibliographies of parable research can be found in John Dominic Crossan, 'A Basic Bibliography for Parables Research', *Semeia* 1 (1974), pp. 236-73; Hendrickx, *The Parables of Jesus*, pp. 256-91; Kissinger, *The Parables of Jesus*, pp. 231-415; and Klauck, *Allegorie*

aspects of Jülicher's work on Jesus' parables which, though not completely unrelated to the topic of concern, have been subjected to critique.

The program for interpreting Jesus' parables propounded in the first volume of *Die Gleichnisreden Jesu* has spawned debate on a number of issues, and that debate has advanced parable scholarship in this century. Some scholars, in reaction to Jülicher's treatment of the משל (*mashal*) as it appears in the Jewish scriptures, have produced studies in which there is a more deliberate examination of Jesus' parables in light of his own scriptural heritage.[15] Others, reacting to Jülicher's treatment of the משלים (*meshalim*) in rabbinic literature, have provided studies in which Jesus' parables are investigated vis-à-vis those of his (near) contemporaries.[16] Some scholars have questioned Jülicher's conception of

und Allegorese, pp. 363-95; cf. also Klaus Berger, 'Hellenistische Gattungen im Neuen Testament', *ANRW*, 25.2, pp. 1110-11.

15. See, e.g., Birger Gerhardsson, *The Good Samaritan—The Good Shepherd?* (*ConNT*, 16; Lund: C.W.K. Gleerup, 1958); *idem*, 'The Narrative Meshalim in the Synoptic Gospels: A Comparison with the Narrative Meshalim in the Old Testament', *NTS* 34 (1988), pp. 339-63; Drury, *The Parables in the Gospels*, pp. 7-20; Claus Westermann, *Vergleiche und Gleichnisse im Alten und Neuen Testament* (Calwer Theologische Monographien, Series A, 14; Stuttgart: Calwer Verlag, 1984), translated into English as *The Parables of Jesus in the Light of the Old Testament* (trans. Friedemann W. Golka and Alastair H.B. Logan; Minneapolis: Fortress Press, 1990). Funk critiques Gerhardsson and puts into question the relationship between scripture and parable (*Language, Hermeneutic, and Word of God*, pp. 199-222; cf. pp. 201, 206). Boucher is more confident about that relationship: '...the ancestors of the NT *parabolai* are to be found in the OT'. She does not 'deny that there could have been a Greek influence on the Semitic writings...But the Synoptic speeches trace their lineage directly to the OT and Jewish literature, and if they are related to the Greek literature at all, it is only indirectly through these' (*The Mysterious Parable*, p. 13).

16. Early on, Paul Fiebig raised his voice in opposition to Jülicher's maltreatment of the rabbinic parables; among his several contributions, see *Altjüdische Gleichnisse und die Gleichnisse Jesu* (Tübingen: J.C.B. Mohr [Paul Siebeck], 1904) and *Die Gleichnisreden Jesu im Lichte der rabbinischen Gleichnisse des neutestamentlichen Zeitalters: Ein Beitrag zum Streit um die 'Christusmythe' und eine Widerlegung der Gleichnistheorie Jülichers* (Tübingen: J.C.B. Mohr [Paul Siebeck], 1912). More recent studies investigate the rabbinic parables and their implications for the study of Jesus' parables: see David Flusser, *Die rabbinischen Gleichnisse und der Gleichniserzähler Jesus. I. Das Wesen der Gleichnisse* (Judaica et Christiana, 4; Bern: Peter Lang, 1981); Johnston, 'Parabolic Interpretations Attributed to Tannaim'; Young, *Jesus and his Jewish Parables*; and Philip L.

allegory and have contributed studies that yield a more precise understanding of Jesus' parables and their relation to allegory.[17] Still others have questioned Jülicher's position on the nature of Jesus' parables and their relationship to metaphor, arguing against Jülicher that the parables are indeed metaphorical.[18] Those scholars, while certainly not always in agreement with the specifics of Jülicher's position on the various issues, share with him a common interest: the form of the parables spoken by Jesus. It soon becomes apparent that many scholars—from different perspectives, directly or indirectly— have debated Jülicher's classification of Jesus' parables, a classification which, like almost every other aspect of his program, has met with opposition. However, the concern here is with a single category.

To reiterate, Jülicher's identification of a particular group of four

Culbertson, *A Word Fitly Spoken: Context, Transmission, and Adoption of the Parables of Jesus* (Albany, NY: State University of New York Press, 1995). A literary-rhetorical study of selected rabbinic *meshalim* is provided by David Stern, 'Rhetoric and Midrash: The Case of the Mashal', *Prooftexts* 1 (1981), pp. 261-91; *idem*, *Parables in Midrash: Narrative and Exegesis in Rabbinic Literature* (Cambridge, MA: Harvard University Press, 1991).

17. Klauck's *Allegorie und Allegorese* is an important study on this issue. Recently, Blomberg (*Interpreting the Parables*, pp. 29-69) has argued that Jesus' parables are allegories. See also Gerhard Sellin, 'Allegorie und "Gleichnis": Zur Formenlehre der synoptischen Gleichnisse', *ZTK* 75 (1978), pp. 281-335 (repr. in Wolfgang Harnisch [ed.], *Die neutestamentliche Gleichnisforschung im Horizont von Hermeneutik und Literaturwissenschaft* [Wege der Forschung, 575; Darmstadt: Wissenschaftliche Buchgesellschaft, 1982], pp. 367-429; all references will be to the reprint edition); Matthew Black, 'The Parables as Allegory', *BJRL* 42 (1960), pp. 273-87; Raymond E. Brown, 'Parable and Allegory Reconsidered', *NovT* 5 (1962), pp. 36-45; Charles E. Carlston, 'Parable and Allegory Revisited: An Interpretive Review', *CBQ* 43 (1981), pp. 228-42; Philip Barton Payne, 'The Authenticity of the Parables of Jesus', in R.T. France and David Wenham (eds.), *Gospel Perspectives II* (Sheffield: JSOT Press, 1981), pp. 329-44.

18. The literature on the relationship of parable and metaphor, especially with regard to the parables of the historical Jesus, is extensive. A partial list of influential studies would include: Funk, 'The Parable as Metaphor', in *Language, Hermeneutic, and Word of God*, pp. 133-62; *idem*, *Parables and Presence: Forms of the New Testament Tradition* (Philadelphia: Fortress Press, 1982), pp. 29-34; John Dominic Crossan, *In Parables: The Challenge of the Historical Jesus* (New York: Harper & Row, 1973), esp. pp. 7-22; Paul Ricoeur, 'Biblical Hermeneutics', *Semeia* 4 (1975), pp. 29-148; Perrin, *Jesus and the Language of the Kingdom*; Weder, *Die Gleichnisse Jesu als Metaphern*; Sellin, 'Allegorie und "Gleichnis"', esp. pp. 404-17; and cf. Kjärgaard, *Metaphor and Parable*.

parables in the Gospel of Luke as 'example stories' has sparked controversy. Some scholars question its value, some reject it altogether, some
scholars accept it without change, some modify or refine it. John
Dominic Crossan succinctly describes one moment in the debate on the
Beispielerzählungen in this way:

> Segments of American parable research deliberately and provocatively
> chose The Good Samaritan as a paradigmatic case of parable as
> metaphor, thereby simultaneously opposing Jülicher's claims that para-
> ble was not metaphor but comparison and that The Good Samaritan was
> not parable but example story.[19]

A particular issue that must be addressed directly in this study is, in
Crossan's words, 'the problem of parables versus examples'.[20] This
study of the example stories, even if it does not offer a solution to that
problem satisfactory to all, should clarify some of the issues of the
debate.

A certain tension, already evident in the subtitles Jülicher gave the
two parts of his study of *Die Gleichnisreden Jesu*, complicates any
study of the example stories. Jülicher entitled the first volume, in which
he constructed his program, *The Parable Speeches of Jesus in General*
(*Die Gleichnisreden Jesu im Allgemeinen*); the second volume, in
which he provided an exposition of the individual parables, *Exposition
of the Parable Speeches of the First Three Gospels* (*Auslegung der
Gleichnisreden der drei ersten Evangelien*). Of course, Jülicher's desire
was to examine the parable speeches of *Jesus*, not the parable speeches
of the synoptic gospels. The problem he confronted was that the parables of Jesus are recorded in three separate Gospel narratives, each with
its own particular traits and character. Therefore, Jülicher labored to
reconstruct the genuine parables of Jesus by peeling away layers of
tradition. However, when one focuses on the category 'example story',
a category of parables recorded *tout ensemble* in the Gospel of Luke,
the tension in the line of choice between 'parables of Jesus' and
'parables of the gospels' increases.

That all of the four example stories appear in the Gospel of Luke has

---

19. John Dominic Crossan, review of *Metaphor and Parable: A Systematic
Analysis of the Specific Structure and Cognitive Function of the Synoptic Similes
and Parables qua Metaphors* (ATDan, 29; Leiden: E.J. Brill, 1986), by Mogens
Stiller Kjärgaard, in *JBL* 108 (1989), p. 150.

20. Crossan, *In Parables*, p. 56.

not gone unnoticed. Crossan, among others, has observed that '...it must be noted, even in passing, that all these are found only in Luke'.[21] Crossan's passing glance should be transformed into a sustained gaze. While 'parables' (*Gleichnisse*) and 'parables in the narrower sense' (*Parabeln*) can be found in all three synoptic gospels, the 'example narratives' (*Beispielerzählungen*) *in toto* can be found in one alone, the third Gospel.[22] This datum would suggest that in a study of the *Beispielerzählungen* two lines of research, parable scholarship and Lukan scholarship,[23] intersect, which makes it imperative that the scope

21. Crossan, *In Parables*, p. 56. Crossan here makes reference to Rudolf Bultmann's list of *Beispielerzählungen*, which is sometimes represented as containing other narratives found in the Gospel of Luke but not in Jülicher's group of four (on this, see p. 155 n. 25 below). Johnston ('Parabolic Interpretations Attributed to Tannaim', p. 189 n. 2) notes that Bultmann's list includes two additional Lukan narratives and remarks, 'It is curious that this phenomenon appears to be exclusively Lucan'. Breech (*The Silence of Jesus*, pp. 160-61), speaking of the four narratives in Jülicher's category, makes a similar observation and offers an explanation: 'All of the example stories which occur in the synoptic tradition, both positive and negative example stories, appear only in Luke's gospel...Luke had a particular interest in communicating the moral behavior appropriate to the Christian life through the use of example stories, the most probable explanation being that he wrote for a specifically Gentile audience'. According to Hedrick, however, example stories also appear in the Gospel of Matthew ('Parables and the Kingdom', pp. 378, 391).

22. A version of The Foolish Rich Man also occurs in the *Gospel of Thomas* (Logion 63), a Gospel discovered over half a century after Jülicher first published his work on the parables; see 'The Gospel of Thomas', in James M. Robinson (ed.), *The Nag Hammadi Library: In English* (San Francisco: Harper & Row, 1981), p. 125 (all references to the Gospel of Thomas will be to this edition). We will see that the Lukan version of The Foolish Rich Man differs in a notable way from that of the Gospel of Thomas (see p. 253 n. 356 below). For a treatment of both versions, see Charles W. Hedrick, *Parables as Poetic Fictions: The Creative Voice of Jesus* (Peabody, MA: Hendrickson, 1994), pp. 142-63.

23. Several sources can be consulted for bibliographies of modern research on the Gospel of Luke and the Acts of the Apostles; see François Bovon, *Luc le théologien: Vingt-cinq ans de recherches (1950–1975)* (Neuchâtel: Delachaux & Niestlé, 1978); Earl Richard, 'Luke—Writer, Theologian, Historian: Research and Orientation of the 1970s', *BTB* 13 (1983), pp. 3-15; Martin Rese, 'Das Lukas-Evangelium: Ein Forschungsbericht', *ANRW*, 25.3, pp. 2258-328; Günther Wagner (ed.), *An Exegetical Bibliography of the New Testament*. II. *Luke and Acts* (Macon, GA: Mercer University Press, 1985); Frans Van Segbroeck, *The Gospel of Luke: A Cumulative Bibliography 1973–1988* (BETL, 88; Collectanea Biblica et Religiosa

of this study be carefully delimited.

There is a temptation to invoke the heuristic stratagem of viewing the example stories only as parables of the Gospel of Luke so that some of the problematical issues can be disentangled. However, this examination of the example stories will prove true Hans-Josef Klauck's assertion that as one pursues an investigation of the effective history of Jülicher's work, a portion of the *Nachleben* of Jesus research comes into view simultaneously: 'For whoever deals with the parables will sooner or later come to speak on the question of the historical Jesus'.[24] No willful act of force can completely remove 'the historical Jesus' from a study of the example stories; that historical figure will continue to hover in the background. As a consequence, other complications arise.

The manner in which several issues in parable research have become superimposed upon each other can be illustrated by recalling Crossan's words on 'the problem of parables versus examples' and his description of how 'segments of American parable research' have opposed 'Jülicher's claims that parable was not metaphor but comparison and that The Good Samaritan was not parable but example story'. That opposition is exemplified in a section of the published report of The Jesus Seminar where the 'Marks of the Genuine Parables of Jesus' are detailed. When the authenticity of some parable is disputed—that is, there is disagreement over whether a parable represents the words of the historical Jesus, 'what he really said'—the following 'final test' for evaluating the evidence is advanced:

> ...[C]an one read or interpret this parable in a way that coheres with other authentic (or inauthentic) parables in the tradition?...For example, if the parable of the Good Samaritan...is an example story that illustrates what it is like to be a good neighbor, it is probably not a parable of Jesus. But if it is a metaphor that hints at what it is like to receive help from an alien, from an enemy, then it is metaphorical and may be a

Antiqua, 2; Leuven: Peeters, 1989); A.J. Mattill and Mary Bedford Mattill, *A Classified Bibliography of Literature on the Acts of the Apostles* (Leiden: E.J. Brill, 1966); Ward Gasque, *A History of the Criticism of the Acts of the Apostles* (BGBE, 17; Tübingen: J.C.B. Mohr [Paul Siebeck], 1975); Erich Grässer, 'Acta-Forschung seit 1960', *TRu* 41 (1976), pp. 141-94; *idem*, 'Acta-Forschung seit 1960', *TRu* 42 (1977), pp. 1-68; and Watson E. Mills, *A Bibliography of the Periodical Literature on the Acts of the Apostles 1962–1984* (Leiden: E.J. Brill, 1986).

24. Klauck, 'Adolf Jülicher', p. 113. Hedrick ('Parables and the Kingdom', p. 368) maintains a similar position.

genuine parable. The modern reading of the Samaritan has convinced
many scholars that it is a genuine parable.[25]

This reasoning can be stated in the form of a syllogism, with The Good
Samaritan synecdochically representing the category 'example story':

Major Premise: All the parables of the historical Jesus are metaphors.
Minor Premise: The Good Samaritan is a metaphor.
Conclusion: Therefore, The Good Samaritan is a parable of the
                 historical Jesus.

Such a logical move is praiseworthy if one's goal is to retrieve a group
of narrative parables apparently banished from the realm of Jesus'
authentic parables. We shall see, however, that in the second edition of
Die Gleichnisreden Jesu Jülicher himself did not exclude the example
stories from among Jesus' parable speeches.

That 'the problem of parables versus examples' has become for some
'a problem of authentic parables of Jesus versus inauthentic parables' is
nonetheless clear. The solution offered above to both problems rests
upon an a priori assumption that the historical Jesus' parables were
metaphors.[26] However, the fact that all four example stories under

---

25. Robert W. Funk, Bernard Brandon Scott and James R. Butts, *The Parables
of Jesus: Red Letter Edition: A Report of the Jesus Seminar* (The Jesus Seminar
Series; Sonoma, CA: Polebridge Press, 1988), p. 18. This test is a variation of the
criterion of multiple attestation, as Scott points out elsewhere (*Hear Then the
Parable*, p. 29; his emphasis): 'Usually four Lukan parables are classified as
example stories...That all four occur *only* in Luke should arouse suspicions about
the proposed genre. No serious challenge has been laid to the authenticity of three
of the four stories, but the criterion of multiple attestation raises questions about
whether the genre of example story belongs among those genres used by Jesus.
This criterion maintains that genuine genres will be found among the several
Gospels and traditions that have preserved the sayings of Jesus'. It appears to me
that this criterion and this logic could just as easily be used to support the position
that these four stories are not authentic to Jesus, but that is beside the point. I will
not deny the authenticity of these stories, nor will I argue that they are not parables.
The issue of concern here is the conclusion that the example stories are not
'example stories', but metaphors and therefore parables. See Funk's statement of
the case: 'The view advocated here is that the Good Samaritan is metaphorical and
therefore not an example story...' (*Parables and Presence*, p. 29).

26. Hedrick ('Parables and the Kingdom', pp. 391-93; 391), with reference to
an article by Bernard Brandon Scott ('Essaying the Rock: The Authenticity of the
Jesus Parable Traditions', *Forum* 2.1 [1980], pp. 3-53 [4]), makes this remark: 'But

consideration are to be found in the Gospel of Luke will not be ignored in this study. Thus, the figure of the historical Jesus and the issue of the authentic parables of Jesus as metaphors will be moved from the center of focus to the periphery. Mark well that this study will neither challenge nor refute the claim that the authentic parables of the historical Jesus are metaphors, and studies making that claim will not be denigrated.[27] The concern here, quite simply, is not with the problem of the authentic parables of Jesus versus the inauthentic parables. Support for delimiting the scope of this study in such a manner can be had by appealing to the arguments promulgated by central figures in 'segments of American parable research'.

An intriguing aspect of the debate among some American parable scholars over Jülicher's category 'example story' is this: There is little disagreement that, within the context of the Gospel of Luke, Jülicher's four example stories are in fact example stories. Bernard Brandon Scott's remark is representative: 'These parables are examples for Luke, but do they formally demand such a reading?'[28] The response expected is, 'As parables of Jesus, no'. Scott sides with Crossan and Robert W. Funk, who provide just such a response and who suggest that Luke (mis)understood those metaphorical parables of Jesus in a moralistic or literal fashion.[29] Since the Lukan narrative context exerts such a considerable influence on the narratives in this group, seeming to demand that The Merciful Samaritan in particular be viewed as an

it should be noted that he *assumes* that these stories have metaphorical quality' (Hedrick's emphasis).

27. Indeed, some of the more innovative studies of the parables in this half of our century arise from the hermeneutical endeavor of defining the parable spoken by the historical Jesus as metaphor. I concur, however, with John R. Donahue's prudent suggestion that 'while reflection on the parable as metaphor continues, a number of cautions are in order' (*The Gospel in Parable: Metaphor, Narrative, and Theology in the Synoptic Gospels* [Philadelphia: Fortress Press, 1988], p. 10; cf. pp. 10-11). Mary Ann Tolbert (*Perspectives on the Parables: An Approach to Multiple Interpretations* [Philadelphia: Fortress Press, 1979], pp. 40-49) offers a critique of the position that equates parable and metaphor; see also Heininger, *Metaphorik*, pp. 21-30.

28. Scott, *Hear Then the Parable*, p. 29; see also Breech's conclusion that Luke understood The Good Samaritan as an example story (*The Silence of Jesus*, p. 159).

29. Funk, *Language, Hermeneutic, and Word of God*, pp. 158, 211 n. 52; and Crossan, *In Parables*, pp. 56, 64. This is a simplification of the opinions espoused by Funk and Crossan; for a more complete discussion, see Chapter 4.

'example story', some scholars interested in the parables of the historical Jesus advocate rejecting completely the narrative context of the
example stories.[30] Crossan's remark is representative: '...[W]e are
interested in the historical Jesus and not in the creative genius of
Luke'.[31] Thus, 'the problem of parables versus examples' becomes 'the
problem of the parables of Jesus versus the parables of Luke'.

Again, however, it is not insignificant that the example stories one
and all appear in the Gospel of Luke. Hence, this study will approach
the problems surrounding the classification of the example stories without excluding 'the creative genius of Luke'.[32] We do not possess verbatim transcripts of the example stories as spoken by the alluring but
elusive 'historical Jesus'; rather, the example stories as we now have
them are Lukan (re)productions spoken by another Jesus, the main protagonist in the Gospel of Luke. Therefore, in this study there will be no
rejection of the narrative context of the example stories. On the contrary, this study will show that an appreciation of the narrative context
in which those four parables appear can provide insight on some of the
issues raised in the debate about Jülicher's classification of them as
example stories.

Approaches to the parables of Jesus which situate them either within
a reconstructed historical context in his ministry and message or within
a hermeneutical context have not yet yielded answers to some of the
questions raised in the debate about the example stories. One need not
be skeptical about the value of a historical approach to the parables
which situates them within a setting in Jesus' life or ministry to recog-

---

30. For example, both Breech (*The Silence of Jesus*, p. 161) and Bernard Brandon Scott (*Jesus, Symbol-Maker for the Kingdom* [Philadelphia: Fortress Press,
1981], pp. 25-26) advocate disregarding the Lukan context of The Good Samaritan
for this reason.

31. Crossan, *In Parables*, p. 56.

32. As a convenience and by convention, I use the name 'Luke' to refer to the
author of the third Gospel without issuing any judgment about the identity of its
'real' author. The classic discussion of the external and internal evidence that is
available to those who seek to establish the identity of the real author of the Gospel
of Luke and the Acts of the Apostles is to be found in F.J. Foakes-Jackson and
Kirsopp Lake (eds.), *The Beginnings of Christianity*. Part 1: *The Acts of the
Apostles* (5 vols.; London: Macmillan, 1922), II, pp. 205-359; for further discussion, see Fitzmyer, *The Gospel According to Luke (I–IX)*, pp. 31-33; *idem*, 'The
Authorship of Luke–Acts Reconsidered', in *Luke the Theologian: Aspects of his
Teaching* (Mahwah, NJ: Paulist Press, 1989), pp. 1-26.

nize the validity of examining the parables within their Gospel con-texts.[33] A reasonable assumption, given the impact that a parable's context has upon its interpretation and given the fact that the parables which Jülicher identified as example narratives all appear in the Gospel of Luke, is that it is time to look carefully at the example stories within their narrative context for possible answers to some of the questions raised about their classification, for, as Susan Wittig claims, 'the para-bles as we have them are embedded narratives, and our perception of them is largely ordered by the context—the Gospel context—in which they are set'.[34] Indeed, to pare away the putative 'Lukan accretions' in an investigation of the example stories would in effect obscure the object of study. An approach to the example stories as embedded narra-tives which permits them to flourish within their narrative context in the Gospel of Luke will provide a more stable foundation for an assessment

33. Susan Wittig ('A Theory of Multiple Meanings', *Semeia* 9 [1977], pp. 75-103 [77]; cf. pp. 93-94) and Drury (*The Parables in the Gospels*, pp. 2-4) are among those who offer bleak judgments of such a historical approach to the para-bles of Jesus; consequently, they argue for an approach which respects the narrative settings of the parables in their respective Gospels. Dan Otto Via, Jr (*The Parables: Their Literary and Existential Dimension* [Philadelphia: Fortress Press, 1967], pp. 21-25) negatively critiques 'the severely historical approach' to the parables of Jesus, as does John W. Sider ('Rediscovering the Parables: The Logic of the Jeremias Tradition', *JBL* 102 [1983], pp. 61-83), who asserts that 'it is time for a new examination of the genre of the parable *in the gospel texts*' (p. 64; his empha-sis). Although I am sympathetic with those who recognize the enormous difficulties confronting one who would attempt to situate the parables in a historical setting in Jesus' life and ministry, I wish to avoid what Carlston ('Changing Fashions in Interpreting the Parables', p. 233) terms 'the non-contextual aestheticism of much contemporary interpretation' of the parables: 'To say that the original context of particular parables has been irrevocably lost to us—an insight that form-critical studies have made abundantly plain—is by no means to say that the context is irrel-evant or that we may treat the parables as if they originally did not have one' (pp. 232-33). For a recent study that situates Jesus' parables within his life and ministry, see Georg Baudler, *Jesus im Spiegel seiner Gleichnisse: Das erzählerische Lebenswerk Jesu—Ein Zugang zum Glauben* (Stuttgart: Calwer Verlag; Munich: Kösel, 1986).

34. Wittig, 'A Theory of Multiple Meanings', p. 101 n. 11. Her assertion cor-roborates, from a different angle, the opinion mentioned earlier that within their Lukan context the four 'parables' identified by Jülicher as *Beispielerzählungen* appear to be 'examples'.

of their common characteristics, as well as their similarities to *and* differences from other parables.

Nevertheless, a clash of cultures complicates this study of the example stories. To claim that some of the questions raised about the example stories can be answered from a perspective which emphasizes their narrative context in the Gospel of Luke does not mean that the historical context of the example stories is insignificant, because the Gospel of Luke itself, like every text, is a narrative embedded within a historical context of significance—its cultural context. Parable scholars since Jülicher have, in fact, stressed the importance of establishing the cultural context for a study of the parables, but they have argued about which cultural context is most suitable. Again, the distinction between approaching the parables as parables of Jesus or parables of the Gospels[35] not only plays a crucial role in the determination of a cultural context for a study of the parables, but it can also clarify some of the issues in the debate.

Those interested in the parables of the historical Jesus have claimed that his parables must be understood and interpreted in light of the proper cultural context, 'their original Jewish milieu'.[36] Although there is sometimes disagreement over whether the delimitation of that original Jewish milieu should give priority to the rabbinic parables or the parables in the Jewish scriptural tradition as the background against which Jesus' parables should be read,[37] there is usually agreement that Jülicher's use of Aristotle's *Rhetoric* was misguided.[38] As Joachim Jeremias puts it, 'To force the parables of Jesus into the categories of

35. Tolbert delineates two major streams of parable research since Jülicher: 'Scholars have chosen to concentrate on the parables either as parables *of Jesus* or as parables *of the gospels*' (*Perspectives on the Parables*, pp. 18-30; 18 [her emphasis]). We will see that Jülicher himself already made that distinction (see pp. 73-74, 79, 87 below).

36. See, e.g., Young, *Jesus and his Jewish Parables*, pp. 2-3.

37. See the studies cited earlier on pp. 23-24 nn. 15 and 16.

38. See, e.g., Christian August Bugge, *Die Haupt-Parabeln Jesu* (Giessen: J. Ricker'sche Verlagsbuchhandlung, 1903), pp. xi, 11-13; Fiebig, *Die Gleichnisreden Jesu*, pp. 119-32, esp. pp. 126-27; Eberhard Jüngel, *Paulus und Jesus: Eine Untersuchung zur Präzisierung der Frage nach dem Ursprung der Christologie* (Tübingen: J.C.B. Mohr [Paul Siebeck], 3rd edn, 1967), pp. 88-102; and Drury, *The Parables in the Gospels*, pp. 8, 20. Sellin ('Allegorie und "Gleichnis", pp. 369-75) summarizes the criticisms of several who reproach Jülicher for applying Aristotelian rhetorical categories to the synoptic parables.

Greek rhetoric is to impose upon them an alien law'.[39] Indeed, Robert
H. Stein goes so far as to suggest that '...a classical or even a koine
Greek dictionary will not define for us what a "parable" signified for
Jesus' because '...Jesus did not live in a primarily Greek-speaking
environment!'[40] A.M. Hunter summarily states a commonly accepted
assessment of Jülicher's 'error': '...the antecedents of Christ's parable
must be sought not in Hellas but in Israel; not in the Greek orators but
in the Old Testament prophets and the Jewish Fathers'.[41] Thus, according to those who hold that opinion, it would be best to attempt to
understand Jesus' view of 'parable', as well as his parables, in light of
his native language.[42] This distrust of Greek rhetoric may be seen as a
contributing factor to the view of Jesus as a 'poet' and his parables as
'aesthetic' or 'literary' objects.[43] While it may be conceded that

39. Jeremias, *The Parables of Jesus*, p. 20; cf. Culbertson, *A Word Fitly Spoken*,
pp. 8-9.
    40. Stein, *An Introduction to the Parables of Jesus*, p. 16; cf. pp. 54-55.
    41. Hunter, *Interpreting the Parables*, p. 8; cf. p. 113.
    42. Jeremias is a staunch proponent of this view: 'Hence the retranslation of the
parables into the mother-tongue of Jesus is perhaps the most important aid to the
recovery of their original meaning' (*The Parables of Jesus*, p. 25). The task of
retranslating the parables is problematical at the outset because there are strong
differences of opinion about the language(s) Jesus spoke. Jeremias, who holds the
widely accepted view that Jesus' native language was Aramaic, is critical of
H. Birkeland's claim that Jesus spoke Hebrew (p. 25; cf. his n. 25). Young, who
argues that Jesus spoke Hebrew, critiques Jeremias in turn (*Jesus and his Jewish
Parables*, pp. 40-42). Max Wilcox ('Jesus in the Light of his Jewish Environment',
ANRW, 25.1, p. 146) suggests that Jesus may have been bilingual, even trilingual:
'...there is indeed very good reason for supposing that he spoke both Greek and
Aramaic (and perhaps also Hebrew)...' For a helpful treatment of the problems
associated with determining which language(s) Jesus spoke, as well as a good
summary of the main positions taken by various scholars, see Philip Edgcumbe
Hughes, 'The Languages Spoken by Jesus', in Richard N. Longenecker and Merrill
C. Tenney (eds.), *New Dimensions in New Testament Study* (Grand Rapids: Zondervan, 1974), pp. 127-43. Based upon his stylistic analysis of several narrative
parables in the synoptics, Funk reaches the intriguing conclusion that those parables
were composed in Greek; however, he refuses 'to attribute the narrative parables in
their Greek form to Jesus', although he does not rule out such an attribution
(*Parables and Presence*, p. 28).
    43. C.H. Dodd (*The Parables of the Kingdom* [New York: Charles Scribner's
Sons, rev. edn, 1961], p. 157) makes what has become a familiar claim about Jesus'
parables: 'The parables, however, have an imaginative and poetical quality. They
are works of art, and any serious work of art has significance beyond its original

Jülicher erred in appealing to Greek rhetoric in order to classify and interpret *Jesus'* parables, it is altogether a different question whether it is legitimate to draw upon Greek rhetoric in order to classify and interpret the parables recorded in the Gospel of Luke in *its* cultural context.

To examine the example stories as parables of the Gospel of Luke and not as the parables of the historical Jesus implies a different cultural context—that of the Gospel of Luke. The case could be made that the cultural context most suitable for an understanding of the example stories is that of the narrative in which they are embedded. The Gospel of Luke can be located—with confidence—within the Greco-Roman cultural milieu of the first century CE. That the author of the Gospel of Luke wrote his narrative in koine Greek (ἡ κοινὴ διάλεκτος) indicates that he intended to communicate to a Greek-speaking audience; for him to communicate effectively would require not only that he employ the common language of his readers, but also common conventions readily

occasion'. Dodd suggests that this view might assuage those who may feel that his 'severely historical treatment of the parables robs them of universal and contemporary interest' (pp. viii-ix). This has become, for some, the hermeneutical key to unlock the relevance of the parables; unchained from the manacles of a localized and particular meaning for those in the past, the parables are deemed free to communicate an understanding of human existence to those in the present. Jones develops the view of Jesus' parables as literary art (*The Art and Truth of the Parables*, pp. 110-66). Via (*The Parables*, pp. 26-107) is an influential proponent of the view of Jesus' parables as aesthetic objects. Funk (*Parables and Presence*, pp. 26-107) and Crossan (*In Parables*, pp. 10-22), because of the radical new vision of experience expressed in Jesus' parables, regard them as a type of poetic language. Yet another view of Jesus' parables as poetry is proffered by Kenneth E. Bailey, *Poet and Peasant: A Literary-Cultural Approach to the Parables in Luke* (Grand Rapids: Eerdmans, 1976), pp. 47-75. Jeremias would demur: '...the parables of Jesus are not—at any rate primarily—literary productions...' (*The Parables of Jesus*, p. 21). Against such a claim as that of Madeleine Boucher (*The Parables* [New Testament Message, 7; Wilmington, DE: Michael Glazier, rev. edn, 1983], p. 15), who states that 'even today parables, and in particular those of Jesus, remain among the most beautiful and memorable works in the history of literature', A.T. Cadoux (*The Parables of Jesus* [New York: Macmillan, 1931], p. 11) offers a more balanced assessment: 'The parable is unquestionably a form of art, though not one of its highest forms'. Jülicher's opinion (see Chapter 3) is similar to that of Cadoux in that both view Jesus' parables as superior to all others. Jülicher and Cadoux and all others who view Jesus' parables as high art subscribe to what Sellin aptly describes as 'a genius-Christology of an aesthetic sort' ('Lukas als Gleichniserzähler', p. 167).

accessible to his public.[44] A number of recent studies have made it abundantly clear that this cultural milieu and its discourse, both its literature and its oratory, were informed and shaped by the rhetorical tradition.[45] Since almost all public discourse of that period was couched thoroughly in rhetoric, one needs to know something of that era's rhetorical practice.[46] 'Indeed', according to Mary Ann Tolbert, 'the Hellenistic period was, above all, the age of rhetoric'.[47]

44. What George A. Kennedy says of the New Testament in general is applicable to the Gospel of Luke in particular: 'The New Testament lies on the cusp between Jewish and Greek culture; the life and religious traditions it depicts are Jewish, its language is Greek' (*New Testament Interpretation through Rhetorical Criticism* [Chapel Hill, NC: University of North Carolina Press, 1984], p. 8). It is well known in Lukan research that the author of the third Gospel made extensive use of the Septuagint (LXX); thus, we cannot remain oblivious to the Jewish religious and literary traditions reflected in the Gospel of Luke. Not to be overlooked, however, is that since the LXX is a Greek translation of the Jewish scriptures, it too is designed to communicate to a Greek-speaking audience.

45. Studies which address this issue as it pertains to the documents of the New Testament include Kennedy, *New Testament Interpretation*; *idem*, *Classical Rhetoric and its Christian and Secular Tradition from Ancient to Modern Times* (Chapel Hill, NC: University of North Carolina Press, 1980), pp. 125-32; Burton L. Mack, *Rhetoric and the New Testament* (Guides to Biblical Scholarship Series; Minneapolis: Fortress Press, 1990); Burton L. Mack and Vernon K. Robbins, *Patterns of Persuasion in the Gospels* (Foundations and Facets: Literary Facets; Sonoma, CA: Polebridge Press, 1989); Mary Ann Tolbert, *Sowing the Gospel: Mark's World in Literary-Historical Perspective* (Minneapolis: Fortress Press, 1989), pp. 41-46; Paul J. Achtemeier, '*Omne verbum sonat*: The New Testament and the Oral Environment of Late Western Antiquity', *JBL* 109 (1990), pp. 3-27. Berger ('Hellenistische Gattungen im Neuen Testament', pp. 1031-432) provides copious documentation with respect to the influence of the Greek rhetorical tradition evident in New Testament literature.

46. See Achtemeier's description of 'the oral environment in late antiquity' ('*Omne verbum sonat*', esp. pp. 9-19). With regard to Paul and the Gospel writers, Kennedy writes: 'He and the evangelists as well would, indeed, have been hard put to escape an awareness of rhetoric as practiced in the culture around them, for the rhetorical theory of the schools found its immediate application in almost every form of oral and written communication: in official documents and public letters, in private correspondence, in the lawcourts and assemblies, in speeches at festivals and commemorations, and in literary composition in both prose and verse' (*New Testament Interpretation*, p. 10).

47. Tolbert, *Sowing the Gospel*, p. 41; cf. *idem*, 'The Gospel in Greco-Roman Culture', in Regina M. Schwartz (ed.), *The Book and the Text: The Bible and Literary Theory* (Oxford: Basil Blackwell, 1990), pp. 258-75.

The pervasive influence of rhetoric in the culture and society of the Hellenistic milieu necessitates an approach to the literature of that period, including the New Testament, which takes into account the rhetorical patterns and conventions that would be easily recognized by the inhabitants of that epoch.[48] George A. Kennedy provides the rationale: 'Classical rhetoric was one of the constraints under which New Testament writers worked...'[49] An approach to the Gospel of Luke which situates it within its cultural context, its literary milieu, is especially appropriate because, as Thomas Louis Brodie states, 'there is, first of all, considerable evidence not only that Luke was a litterateur but also that he employed specifically Hellenistic modes of writing, including various techniques of Hellenistic rhetoric'.[50] That the author

48. The formal dissemination of rhetorical theory in Greece and Rome was accomplished in the educational system; the rhetorical practice of those formally trained contributed to the pervasiveness of rhetoric in Hellenistic culture. As Kennedy (*New Testament Interpretation*, p. 5), Tolbert (*Sowing the Gospel*, pp. 41-46), and Achtemeier (*'Omne verbum sonat'*, pp. 9-19) make clear, even for those in late antiquity who had no formal training in rhetoric—including the illiterate—rhetorical patterns and conventions facilitated the comprehension of public discourse (oral and written). The standard texts on educational practices in Greece and Rome are: Henri-Irénée Marrou, *Histoire de l'education dans l'antiquité* (Paris: Seuil, 3rd edn, 1955), which has been translated into English (*A History of Education in Antiquity* (trans. George Lamb; New York: Sheed and Ward, 1956); and Donald L. Clark, *Rhetoric in Greco-Roman Education* (New York: Columbia University Press, 1957); see also James L. Kinneavy, *Greek Rhetorical Origins of Christian Faith: An Inquiry* (Oxford: Oxford University Press, 1987), pp. 56-100. For bibliographical information on other important studies pertaining to the educational systems of Greece and Rome in antiquity, see Tolbert (*Sowing the Gospel*, pp. 36, 41) and William S. Kurz, 'Hellenistic Rhetoric in the Christological Proof of Luke-Acts', *CBQ* 42 (1980), pp. 171-95 (192-95). William V. Harris provides a reassessment of the educational systems in Greco-Roman antiquity that should temper any facile view of the ubiquity of educational practices in Greece and Rome; see *Ancient Literacy* (Cambridge, MA: Harvard University Press, 1989), pp. 16-17, 116-46, 233-48.

49. Kennedy, *New Testament Interpretation*, p. 160.

50. Thomas Louis Brodie, 'Greco-Roman Imitation of Texts as a Partial Guide to Luke's Use of Sources', in Charles H. Talbert (ed.), *Luke–Acts: New Perspectives from the Society of Biblical Literature Seminar* (New York: Crossroad, 1984), p. 33. That the author of the Gospel of Luke and the Acts of the Apostles wrote in the popular literary style of his day is shown by Stephen P. Schierling and Marla J. Schierling, 'The Influence of the Ancient Romances on *Acts of the Apostles*', *The Classical Bulletin* 54 (1978), pp. 81-88. Several of the motifs and traits which they

of the Gospel of Luke extensively and felicitously used rhetorical conventions is demonstrated by William S. Kurz.[51] Therefore, to examine the example stories within their narrative context and, in turn, to situate the Gospel of Luke within its cultural context legitimates, even demands, an approach that draws upon Greek rhetoric. Viewed from this perspective, Greek rhetoric is no 'alien law'. That being said, however, the important points to be underscored here are that (1) some parable scholars have indeed analyzed and categorized the parables of Jesus in light of the ancient rhetorical tradition, and (2) some of their conclusions are unsatisfactory. Consequently, what the ancient rhetoricians had to say about parables and examples will need to be re-examined.

This study of the example stories is complicated further by the fact that a multitude of methodologies, some of which are highly technical, have been employed advantageously by scholars to analyze and interpret the parables recorded in the synoptic gospels. Hans Weder, in his account of modern parable research, identifies four methodological approaches and some representative practitioners dominant in parable exposition since the time of Jülicher: the form-critical (Rudolf Bultmann), the historical-critical (C.H. Dodd, Joachim Jeremias and Eta Linnemann), the hermeneutical (Ernst Fuchs and Eberhard Jüngel) and the literary-critical (Robert W. Funk and Dan Otto Via, Jr).[52]

---

identify in the Acts of the Apostles—i.e. travel, idealized heroes, miracles, apparent deaths, dreams and oracles, trials and sorcery—also occur in the Gospel of Luke. Another study which investigates the relationship of the Gospel of Luke and the Acts of the Apostles to the ancient romance is provided by Susan Marie Praeder, 'Luke–Acts and the Ancient Novel', in Kent Harold Richards (ed.), *Society of Biblical Literature 1981 Seminar Papers* (Chico, CA: Scholars Press, 1981), pp. 269-92.

51. Kurz, 'Hellenistic Rhetoric', esp. pp. 184-95. For evidence that Luke made use of classical rhetorical conventions, see Philip E. Satterthwaite, 'Acts Against the Background of Classical Rhetoric', in Bruce W. Winter and Andrew D. Clarke (eds.), *The Book of Acts in its First Century Setting*. I. *The Book of Acts in its Ancient Literary Setting* (Grand Rapids: Eerdmans, 1993), pp. 337-79; cf. Robert Morgenthaler, *Lukas und Quintilian: Rhetorik als Erzählkunst* (Zürich: Gotthelf Verlag, 1993).

52. Weder, *Die Gleichnisse Jesu als Metaphern*, pp. 19-57. Perrin (*Jesus and the Language of the Kingdom*, pp. 89-193) and Beardslee ('Recent Literary Criticism', pp. 177-183) also offer descriptions of various methodological approaches to the parables.

Other methodological approaches can be added to Weder's list: redaction-critical,[53] semiological or structural,[54] psychoanalytical,[55] rhetorical[56] and sociological.[57] The array of methods invoked by

53. See, e.g., Weder, *Die Gleichnisse Jesus als Metaphern*; Donahue, *The Gospel in Parable*; Jack Dean Kingsbury, *The Parables of Jesus in Matthew 13: A Study in Redaction-Criticism* (Richmond, VA: John Knox Press, 1969); Charles E. Carlston, *The Parables of the Triple Tradition* (Philadelphia: Fortress Press, 1975); Gerhard Schneider, *Parusiegleichnisse im Lukas-Evangelium* (SBS, 74; Stuttgart: Katholisches Bibelwerk, 1975).

54. Semiological or structural studies abound; in addition to those studies listed in Crossan, 'A Basic Bibliography for Parables Research', pp. 272-73, see Daniel Patte, 'An Analysis of Narrative Structure and the Good Samaritan', *Semeia* 2 (1974), pp. 1-26; *idem*, 'Structural Analysis of the Parable of the Prodigal Son: Towards a Method', in *idem* (ed.), *Semiology and Parables: An Exploration of the Possibilities Offered by Structuralism for Exegesis* (PTMS, 9; Pittsburgh: Pickwick Press, 1976), pp. 71-149; Georges Crespy, 'La parabole dite: "Le bon Samaritan": Recherches structurales', *ETR* 48 (1973), pp. 61-79 (cf. 'The Parable of the Good Samaritan: An Essay in Structural Research' [trans. John Kirby], *Semeia* 2 [1974], pp. 27-50); Robert W. Funk, 'Structure in the Narrative Parables of Jesus', *Semeia* 2 (1974), pp. 51-73; Groupe d'Entrevernes, *Signes et paraboles: Sémiotique et texte évangélique* (Paris: Seuil, 1977; cf. *Signs and Parables: Semiotics and Gospel Texts* [trans. Gary Phillips; PTMS, 23; Pittsburgh: Pickwick Press, 1978]); Susan Wittig, 'Meaning and Modes of Signification: Toward a Semiotic of the Parable', in Patte (ed.), *Semiology and Parables*, pp. 319-47; *idem*, 'A Theory of Multiple Meanings', pp. 75-103; Erhardt Güttgemanns, 'Narrative Analyse synoptischer Texte', *LB* 25/26 (1973), pp. 50-72 (repr. in Harnisch [ed.], *Die neutestamentliche Gleichnisforschung*, pp. 179-223; cf. 'Narrative Analysis of Synoptic Texts' [trans. William G. Doty], *Semeia* 6 [1976], pp. 127-79); Bernard Brandon Scott, 'The Prodigal Son: A Structuralist Interpretation', *Semeia* 9 (1977), pp. 45-73; *idem*, *Jesus, Symbol-Maker for the Kingdom*. Additional structural analyses of the *Beispielerzählungen* are discussed in Chapter 4.

55. See, e.g., Dan Otto Via, Jr, 'The Parable of the Unjust Judge: A Metaphor of the Unrealized Self', in Patte (ed.), *Semiology and Parables*, pp. 1-32; *idem*, 'The Prodigal Son: A Jungian Reading', *Semeia* 9 (1977), pp. 21-43; Mary Ann Tolbert, 'The Prodigal Son: An Essay in Literary Criticism from a Psychoanalytic Perspective', *Semeia* 9 (1977), pp. 1-20.

56. See, e.g., Berger, 'Hellenistische Gattungen im Neuen Testament', pp. 1110-24; William R. Farmer, 'Notes on a Literary and Form-Critical Analysis of Some of the Synoptic Material Peculiar to Luke', *NTS* 8 (1962), pp. 301-16; Burton L. Mack, 'Teaching in Parables: Elaboration in Mark 4.1-34', in Mack and Robbins, *Patterns of Persuasion in the Gospels*, pp. 143-60.

57. See Scott, *Hear Then the Parable*; and most recently, William R. Herzog, II, *Parables as Subversive Speech: Jesus as Pedagogue of the Oppressed*

interpreters of the parables demonstrates not only the high regard still given to the words of a particular first-century parabler, but also the resiliency of the parables themselves. Such methodological diversity should not bewilder or dismay, rather it should be celebrated as a sign of the ingenuity of interpreters and their delight in the act of interpretation.[58] Moreover, the proliferation of methodological approaches to the parables has enhanced our understanding of the parable form and has produced fascinating, if sometimes fanciful, interpretations of the individual parables. The results obtained by the application of several modern methodologies in analyzing the example stories will be examined and evaluated in this study. However, what Wayne C. Booth refers to as 'the gaps of conventions' that occur 'when older classics meet modern readers' must be taken into account.[59] That there are 'gaps of conventions' to be reckoned with in this study can be demonstrated by a simple observation: Some parable scholars bristle when any parable attributed to Jesus is (for whatever reason) classified as an 'example' because such a classification is perceived negatively ('Jesus' parables are not "mere" examples'); yet according to some ancient rhetorical treatises, if a parable were to be classified as an 'example' (for any reason), that classification would be received positively because examples were highly esteemed rhetorical devices. Indeed, one may well wonder whether some perspectives on the example stories are skewed as a result of a mismatch of conventions.

The fact that the various methodological approaches just mentioned have yielded a variety of classification schemes for the parables,[60]

(Louisville, KY: Westminster/John Knox Press, 1994).

58. If, as Wittig ('A Theory of Multiple Meanings', p. 87) and Tolbert (*Perspectives on the Parables*, pp. 49-50) both argue, the parable compels the perceiver to interpret—the parable demands interpretation—then the multiplicity of interpretations can be said to arise from a faithful adherence to the intentionality of the parable.

59. Wayne C. Booth, *The Rhetoric of Fiction* (Chicago: University of Chicago Press, 2nd edn, 1983), p. 434.

60. Parable scholars acknowledge that some of the parables recorded in the synoptic gospels exhibit different features. As Scott states, 'There are obvious formal differences between parables in the synoptic tradition. How to classify those differences on the basis of objective criteria has been a perplexing problem ever since Jülicher's pioneering attempts' (*Jesus, Symbol-Maker for the Kingdom*, p. 65). Some of the more familiar classification schemes of Jesus' parables come from the form critics, even though their categories differ (see Rudolf Bultmann,

although different from Jülicher's, confirms one of his conclusions: that is, despite the differences among the parables, some parables do exhibit enough common features to permit their being grouped together as a type of parable. In this study, then, and in accord with a host of parable scholars, Jeremias's judgment that the endeavor to classify the parables is 'a fruitless labor in the end' will not be accepted.[61] On the contrary, while admitting that a certain lack of precision is inherent in any attempt to classify the parables[62] and while acknowledging that the malleability of the name and phenomenon παραβολή precludes any 'reduction to hard and fast categories',[63] it can still be granted that groups of synoptic parables manifest enough identifiable common characteristics to warrant their being viewed as particular types of parables. The specific question to be addressed in this study is whether Jülicher's classification of four Lukan parables as example stories is justified.

Parable scholars in this century have paused to reflect upon the legacy that Jülicher, whose contributions to New Testament scholarship are many, left behind to subsequent generations. Klauck's words in the epigraph to this chapter suggest that Jülicher's life-work is a valuable legacy that is worth preserving and defending despite dissent. *Die Gleichnisreden Jesu* indeed represents a sizeable devise of Jülicher's bequest to subsequent generations of parable scholars. Certain reappraisals of *Die Gleichnisreden Jesu* have resulted in a depreciation or

History of the Synoptic Tradition [trans. John Marsh; New York: Harper & Row, rev. edn, 1963], pp. 166-205; Martin Dibelius, *From Tradition to Gospel* [trans. Bertram Lee Woolf; Cambridge: James Clark and Co., 1971], pp. 249-65; and, most recently, Klaus Berger, *Formgeschichte des Neuen Testaments* [Heidelberg: Quelle and Meyer, 1984], pp. 25-62). G.J. Jordan ('The Classification of the Parables', *ExpTim* 45 [1933–34], pp. 246-51) gives a brief survey of attempts to categorize Jesus' parables, but he excludes the form critics. Johnston ('Parabolic Interpretations Attributed to Tannaim', pp. 151-59, 508-26) describes the different criteria employed in defining separate groups of *meshalim*. Blomberg (*Interpreting the Parables*, pp. 290-96) provides a helpful discussion of the problems involved in attempting to classify the parables.

61. Jeremias, *The Parables of Jesus*, p. 20. For similar judgments, see Georg Eichholz, *Gleichnisse der Evangelien: Form, Überlieferung, Auslegung* (Neukirchen–Vluyn: Neukirchener Verlag, 1971), p. 13; and Tolbert, *Perspectives on the Parables*, pp. 16-17.

62. In agreement with Dodd, *The Parables of the Kingdom*, p. 7.

63. In agreement with Funk, *Language, Hermeneutic, and Word of God*, p. 126.

outright rejection of particular parts of Jülicher's interpretive program, while certain re-evaluations of it have yielded an appreciation of the lasting value of some of his contributions to the study of the parables. Although some scholars may be reluctant, others selective, legatees, few would underwrite a complete divestiture of the heritage descended from Jülicher. John R. Donahue writes that Jülicher 'bequeathed to scholarship the descriptive categories' known as 'similitude', 'parable' and 'example story', categories that have certainly had a lasting influence in parable scholarship.[64] In this study, the intent is to ascertain whether a particular portion of our inheritance from Jülicher, the category 'example story', against which several students of the parables have voiced dissent, merits defense and preservation.

The Purpose of This Study

The purpose of this study, then, is to mount a sustained, focused and detailed examination of the category of παραβολή that has been labelled 'example story'. This study of the example stories will not be limited to Jülicher's formulation of that category, for questions have been raised about The Merciful Samaritan, The Foolish Rich Man, The Rich Man and Poor Lazarus, and The Pharisee and the Toll Collector as a group before and since the publication of *Die Gleichnisreden Jesu*. Therefore, a number of perspectives on the example stories will be introduced and evaluated. The main concern of this study, however, will be with the debate over the categorization of those parables conducted by parable scholars in the twentieth century. Because in more recent parable research the category 'example story' is sometimes defined and delineated in different ways, the permutations of that category will also need to be assessed.

Even though all four of the parables usually included in the category 'example story' are to be found in the Gospel of Luke, as has been observed, the main goal of this study is not to interpret those parables in their narrative context. Moreover, the goal of this study is neither to forge a definition of 'parable' which encompasses all of the parables attributed to Jesus in the synoptic gospels,[65] nor to formulate a

64. Donahue, *The Gospel in Parable*, p. 8.
65. Funk is of the opinion that 'even if the term is confined to the parable as used by Jesus, and the Synoptic parables (i.e. leaving John out of account) reduced to a list universally agreed upon, it would still be difficult to bring all the parables

definition of the category 'example story'. On the contrary, the goal of this study is far more modest—and somewhat more subversive.

The main goal of this study is to determine whether the classification of The Merciful Samaritan, The Foolish Rich Man, The Rich Man and Poor Lazarus, and The Pharisee and the Toll Collector as *Beispielerzäh-lungen* holds up under scrutiny. This investigation of the category 'example story' will be guided by a set of questions: When the state-ment is made that a parable is, or is not, an 'example story', what is meant by 'example'? Upon what basis is the determination made that the four specified Lukan parables are 'example stories'? Do the exam-ple stories manifest an aggregate of formal characteristics which unifies them as a peculiar group of parables? If so, are those formal character-istics unique to that group? If so, does the manifestation of any one of the formal characteristics said to be peculiar to that group lead ineluctably to the conclusion that they are 'examples'?

If this study can provide answers to those questions, then the ramifications for what Crossan has called 'the problem of parables versus examples' will be obvious. We will discover that the categorical distinction between parable and example story is problematic for a number of reasons. The results of this investigation will be in accord with a conclusion advanced by Ernst Baasland, who has produced one of the most comprehensive studies of the *Beispielerzählungen* since Jülicher. Within a framework of an accidence of the parables in the synoptic gospels, we can speak only of the 'relative peculiarity of the example narratives'.[66] However, if the category 'example narrative' is examined rigorously from a variety of angles, we may find that the 'relative peculiarity of the example narratives' is relativized even further, that the categorical distinction between *Parabel* and *Beispiel-erzählung* does not withstand scrutiny, that the conception of the cate-gory 'example story' as advanced by several parable scholars is otiose.

This study of the example stories will be organized along the follow-ing lines. Jülicher's treatment of the example stories is pivotal, and an extensive examination of it will be provided for several reasons. Jülicher's classification of the παραβολαί *Jesu* as proposed in the

under one formal definition' (*Language, Hermeneutic, and Word of God*, p. 126).

66. Ernst Baasland, 'Zum Beispiel der Beispielerzählungen: Zur Formenlehre der Gleichnisse und zur Methodik der Gleichnisauslegung', *NovT* 28 (1986), p. 219.

second edition of *Die Gleichnisreden Jesu* brought the *Beispielerzäh-lungen* to prominence, and his conception of that category has engen-dered much of the debate on 'the problem of parables versus examples'. Since *Die Gleichnisreden Jesu* remains untranslated[67] and thus inacces-sible to some students of the parables, and since some of Jülicher's views on the example stories have been distorted in the history of their transmission, an exposition of his classification scheme of Jesus' para-bles, carefully contextualized within the overall argument of the first volume, will be provided in Chapter 3.

Modern parable scholars who debate the status of the example stories not infrequently take as their point of departure the second edition of *Die Gleichnisreden Jesu* because that is where, so the assumption goes, Jülicher argued that the example stories should be separated into a class unto themselves since they are not parables. However, this study of the example stories will not begin with Jülicher, for he was not the first to gather the four parables in question into a group. Because *Die Gleich-nisreden Jesu* is considered to be the *fons et origo* of so many tenets of modern parable interpretation, the assumption that Jülicher originated the category 'example story' is understandable. Nevertheless, a more expansive reading of parable scholarship proves that assumption false. Scholars before Jülicher grouped together The Merciful Samaritan, The Foolish Rich Man, The Rich Man and Poor Lazarus, and The Pharisee and the Toll Collector, and then attempted to articulate their rationale for separating those parables as a group from the other parables of Jesus. Both the notion that those four parables belong together in a dis-tinct group and the designation of that group as 'examples' predate Jülicher. Knowledge of the questions raised about that group of para-bles by other scholars before Jülicher may shed light on his treatment of the example stories as a category of Jesus' parables. In Chapter 2, therefore, some of what was written about that group of four parables before the publication of the second edition of *Die Gleichnisreden Jesu* will be examined summarily.

67. This can be regarded as a serious deficiency in American parable scholar-ship, one that should be redressed. Blomberg writes: 'The lack of any English translation of this work is one of the strangest omissions in modern biblical scholarship' (*Interpreting the Parables*, p. 32 n. 6). Carlston, however, holds a different view: 'Yet on balance, given the Anglo-Saxon penchant for moralism, it is perhaps a mercy that the work was never translated' ('Changing Fashions in Interpreting the Parables', p. 228).

Chapter 4 will provide a survey of research on the example stories conducted by scholars who succeed Jülicher. There, attention will be focused on several of the more important studies of the example stories that have been published in this century. The debate on 'the problem of parables versus examples' will be assessed in light of the questions previously enunciated. During the course of that chapter, we will learn that another formulation of the category '*Beispielerzählung*', that of Rudolf Bultmann, has had a significant impact on the manner in which the example stories have been received by modern parable scholars.

Because several parable scholars, including Jülicher and Bultmann, have appealed to the ancient rhetorical tradition in their treatment of the example stories, Chapter 5 will offer an exposition of what five ancient rhetoricians had to say about parables and examples. There, we will want to discern whether what some modern parable scholars present as the position of the ancient rhetorical tradition on parables and examples is congruent with what the ancient rhetoricians themselves wrote about parables and examples. In addition, a number of features that have been identified in the example stories and regarded as peculiar to them by parable scholars will be evaluated in light of the precepts issued by several ancient rhetoricians with respect to parable and example. In that chapter we will find that the categorical distinction between parable and example story is increasingly suspect.

A study of the example stories conducted in this manner should bring into clearer focus some of the complicated, and sometimes confused, issues surrounding the categorization of four parables found in the third Gospel as '*Beispielerzählungen*', a categorization which has been a fixture in parable scholarship for over a century. If this study provides satisfactory answers to some of the questions raised about the example stories in the past, and if those answers call into question the category itself, we will then be left to ponder the future of these four parables in the Gospel of Luke.

Chapter 2

THE EXAMPLE STORIES BEFORE *DIE GLEICHNISREDEN JESU*

'Indeed...some in all seriousness raised the question...''parable or story?'''

C.E. van Koetsveld,
De Gelijkenissen van den Zaligmaker

The history of the category 'example story' does not begin with the publication of Adolf Jülicher's *Die Gleichnisreden Jesu* in 1886.[1] Jülicher, in fact, did not create *ex nihilo* the category '*Beispielerzählung*', comprised of The Merciful Samaritan, The Foolish Rich

---

1. We can trace what Klauck aptly calls 'the complicated publication history' of *Die Gleichnisreden Jesu* (see 'Adolf Jülicher', p. 102 n. 12). The first volume appeared under the title *Die Gleichnisreden Jesu. Erste Hälfte: Allgemeiner Theil* (Freiburg i.B.: J.C.B. Mohr [Paul Siebeck], 1886). This first volume, with the omission of the subtitle and with the addition of a table of contents, foreword, index and corrigenda, was published two years later in an emended, not revised, edition (*Die Gleichnisreden Jesu* [Freiburg i.B.: J.C.B. Mohr (Paul Siebeck), 1888]). Eleven years after that, the second volume appeared for the first time under the title *Die Gleichnisreden Jesu. Zweiter Teil: Auslegung der Gleichnisreden der drei ersten Evangelien* (Freiburg i.B.: J.C.B. Mohr [Paul Siebeck], 1899). That same year, the first volume was revised and issued separately as *Die Gleichnisreden Jesu. Erster Teil: Die Gleichnisreden Jesu im Allgemeinen* (Freiburg i.B.: J.C.B. Mohr [Paul Siebeck], 2. bearb. Aufl., 1899). The version most familiar to scholars of this century is the unaltered (except for the correction of typographical errors and the addition of a brief foreword by Jülicher) reprint in which both parts are collected in one volume under the main title *Die Gleichnisreden Jesu* (Zwei Teile in einem Band; Tübingen: J.C.B. Mohr, 1910). The subtitles of the two parts remain unchanged. Three photocopy reprints of the 1910 Tübingen edition have been issued subsequently by Wissenschaftliche Buchgesellschaft in 1963, 1969 and 1976. All quotations in this study, unless specified otherwise (in which case the full title and date of the version cited will be given), come from *Die Gleichnisreden Jesu* (Zwei Teile in einem Band; Nachdruck der Ausgabe Tübingen 1910; Darmstadt: Wissenschaftliche Buchgesellschaft, 1963).

Man, The Rich Man and Poor Lazarus, and The Pharisee and the Toll Collector. Thus, the notion that Jülicher was the first to claim that the example stories belong in a class unto themselves is a scholarly myth.[2] If this point is significant, it is not because it counts as a mark against Jülicher but because it counts as a contribution to the history of parable scholarship, for if one subscribes to the commonly held notion that with the appearance of *Die Gleichnisreden Jesu* came the definitive break with the allegorical method of interpreting the parables which prevailed, almost without exception, from the time of the church fathers until the end of the nineteenth century,[3] then one might naturally surmise that prior to Jülicher's formulation of the category '*Beispielerzählung*' the four parables in that group were always perceived and interpreted in the same way as all the other parables attributed to Jesus in the synoptic gospels. That, however, is not the case.

Not all of the example stories were interpreted allegorically. Stephen L. Wailes furnishes evidence to indicate that some of the earliest parable exegetes were more interested in extracting lessons in morality, or moral theology, from some of these very parables (especially The Foolish Rich Man, The Rich Man and Poor Lazarus, and The Pharisee and the Toll Collector) than in developing intricate allegorical interpretations of them, although there was some of that with respect to a particular favorite (The Merciful Samaritan).[4] Indeed, Wailes scours his sources and finds that they 'contain no thorough allegory' for The Foolish Rich Man.[5] At a very early date, then, questions were raised about the parables Jülicher designated as *Beispielerzählungen*.

---

2.   This chapter was presented, in a slightly altered form, as 'A Class unto Themselves: The Scholarly Myth of Adolf Jülicher's Example Narratives' (Paper delivered at the annual meetings of the Society of Biblical Literature, New Orleans, November 1996). I would like to express my appreciation to Professor John A. Darr, co-chair of the Synoptic Gospels Section, for the opportunity to participate in those meetings.

3.   See, e.g., Kissinger's expression of this view: 'Jülicher definitely imparted a new direction to parabolic interpretation, for he broke decisively with the allegorical exegesis which, with few exceptions, had predominated since the patristic period' (*The Parables of Jesus*, p. 77; cf. p. xiii). The validity of this notion is not in question here.

4.   Wailes, *Medieval Allegories of Jesus' Parables*, pp. 209-14, 219-20, 253-60, 264-66.

5.   Wailes, *Medieval Allegories of Jesus' Parables*, p. 220.

Jülicher himself gave two responses to some of the questions raised about this group of parables, one virtually unknown response given in the first edition of *Die Gleichnisreden Jesu* (1886), and another famous response given in the revised edition of *Die Gleichnisreden Jesu* (1899). Although Jülicher's treatment of the example narratives in the revised edition of *Die Gleichnisreden Jesu* is the one most well known to modern parable scholars, that was not the first attempt, by Jülicher or anyone else, to delimit and define the category of four parables in the Gospel of Luke he called *Beispielerzählungen*. Therefore, it is entirely appropriate that we investigate what was said about the example stories before Jülicher published his revision of *Die Gleichnisreden Jesu* in 1899.

This investigation of the example stories before *Die Gleichnisreden Jesu* need not be exhaustive, however. Although several scholars who antedate Jülicher gathered the same four parables into a group and attempted to articulate what, if anything, distinguishes them from the other parables, consideration will be given here to the works of three scholars whose examinations of the example stories precede Jülicher's and whom Jülicher himself cites throughout *Die Gleichnisreden Jesu* (though not in his section on the *Beispielerzählungen*[6]): C.E. van Koetsveld, Bernhard Weiss and Siegfried Göbel. In addition, the work of another scholar, Immanuel Stockmeyer, will be included because Jülicher cites him specifically with reference to the *Beispielerzählungen* in the revised edition of *Die Gleichnisreden Jesu*. The intent here is to provide a representative sample of opinions penned by scholars who wrote before *Die Gleichnisreden Jesu* with respect to the issue of whether the example stories are a specific category of parable distinct from all the others.

C.E. van Koetsveld: De Gelijkenissen van den Zaligmaker

We learn from C.E. van Koetsveld that long before the appearance of *Die Gleichnisreden Jesu* some or all of the four parables which later came to be known as *Beispielerzählungen* gave pause to the church fathers (*kerkvaders*) and gave rise to the question, as formulated by van

---

6.   No indictment against Jülicher for dissimulation is intended by this. The canons of modern scholarship obviously differ from those of his era. Therefore, it would be rash to accuse Jülicher of being disingenuous.

Koetsveld, 'Do we have in view here a parable or a story?'[7] Van
Koetsveld indicates that three of the example stories—The Merciful
Samaritan, The Rich Man and Poor Lazarus, and The Pharisee and the
Toll Collector—continued to perplex parable interpreters, who prof-
fered various responses to the question of whether they are a 'parable or
story'.[8] Van Koetsveld gives notice of his opinion at the very beginning
of his two-volume work on *The Parables of the Savior*: The Merciful
Samaritan, The Rich Man and Poor Lazarus, and The Pharisee and the
Toll Collector are mentioned among 'the fine parables of the savior'.[9]
Although van Koetsveld is somewhat ambivalent with regard to these
parables in the Gospel of Luke, it is obvious nonetheless that he considers them to be parables.

Van Koetsveld is not unaware of attempts to distinguish between
various forms of Jesus' parables, but he does not employ the 'form' of
the parable as the controlling standard for interpreting them. The
premise that lies at the foundation of van Koetsveld's plan for
interpreting Jesus' parables is this: The main content of Jesus'
parables—indeed, the *tertium comparationis* of all Jesus' parables—is
'the kingdom of heaven'.[10] Given that, van Koetsveld prefers to divide

7.   C.E. van Koetsveld, *De Gelijkenissen van den Zaligmaker* (2 vols.; Utrecht:
A.H. Ten Bokkel Huinink, n.d.), II, p. 22: '"Hebben wij hier eene gelijkenis of eene
geschiedenis voor oogen?"' Copies of van Koetsveld's work—first published in the
Netherlands for a limited number of subscribers including King Willhelm III and
Queen Emma, of the House of Orange—are extremely rare in the United States.
According to Jülicher (*Die Gleichnisreden Jesu*, I, p. 314), the first issue appeared
in 1854. A second edition with two volumes (the one cited most often by scholars)
was published some 15 years later: *De Gelijkenissen van den Zaligmaker*
(Schoonhoven: 1869). The edition available to me, and from which all citations will
come, has a different place of publication and no date of publication; the two
volumes are bound together, with the first volume subtitled *Het Koninkrijk der
Hemelen*, and the second *Het Evangelie des Koninkrijks*. Judging from some of van
Koetsveld's remarks—that he has expanded his collection of parables beyond the
original number of 66 (I, p. vii)—and the inclusion of a list of errata (I, p. ii), it can
be surmised that this edition of *De Gelijkenissen van den Zaligmaker* is either a
reprint or an expansion of the Schoonhoven edition.
8.   Van Koetsveld, *De Gelijkenissen van den Zaligmaker*, II, p. 435; cf. II,
p. 436 n. 1. Van Koetsveld states later (II, p. 435) that he does not attach much
significance to the question '"Gelijkenis of geschiedenis?"' often raised with reference to the parables.
9.   Van Koetsveld, *De Gelijkenissen van den Zaligmaker*, I, p. iii.
10.   Van Koetsveld, *De Gelijkenissen van den Zaligmaker*, I, pp. vii, xxxiv, l.

Jesus' parables into two main groups. In the first volume of *De Gelijkenissen van den Zaligmaker*, van Koetsveld treats the briefer parables, 'the parables of God's kingdom', by means of which Jesus offered representations of the kingdom of heaven; in the second volume, he treats the longer parables by means of which Jesus announced 'the gospel in parables'.[11] Each of the four *Beispielerzählungen* are included among the latter by van Koetsveld.[12] This, then, is how van Koetsveld chooses to differentiate among Jesus' parables, but he is keenly aware that several problematical issues encroach upon that choice.

One of the first problems that confronts one who wishes to interpret Jesus' parables, according to van Koetsveld, is the definition of the word 'parable', for that definition will influence the determination of what items from among Jesus' figurative language (*beeldspraak*) are to be treated and thus the number of parables to be treated. As he puts it, every endeavor to express clearly and briefly the basic character of the parables illuminates the difficulties in giving a precise definition of 'parable' because no two interpreters seem to agree on what the Gospels themselves name as 'Parabel'.[13] In order to avoid unnecessarily restricting the scope of Jesus' parables, van Koetsveld opts for a wider concept of the term 'parable'.[14] From among a number of definitions proposed by scholars, van Koetsveld favors one of the

11. Van Koetsveld, *De Gelijkenissen van den Zaligmaker*, I, p. vii. Van Koetsveld uses the words 'Gelijkenis' and 'Parabel' interchangeably throughout both volumes. In some places, however, he gives indication that 'Gelijkenis' in the strictest sense of the word is reserved for the briefer parables in which there is a 'representation of the kingdom of heaven' and that 'Parabel' is used for the more 'developed' parables (see, e.g., p. xxx).

12. The *Beispielerzählungen* are dealt with in the second volume along with other 'parables of the gospel of the kingdom'. The Rich Fool and The Rich Man and Poor Lazarus appear among the parables of 'sin and grace' (*De Gelijkenissen van den Zaligmaker*, II, pp. 11-20, 21-53), The Merciful Samaritan among the parables dealing with 'Christian life' (pp. 277-96), and The Pharisee and the Toll Collector among the parables having to do with 'prayer' (pp. 435-52).

13. Van Koetsveld, *De Gelijkenissen van den Zaligmaker*, I, p. vi; cf. p. xxvii. Van Koetsveld notes (p. xxix) that neither the Dutch word 'Gelijkenis' nor the Greek word 'Parabel' shed much light on the subject.

14. Van Koetsveld, *De Gelijkenissen van den Zaligmaker*, I, pp. vi, ix. This wider understanding of the word 'parable', in van Koetsveld's opinion, is consonant with the first three evangelists' usage of the term (p. xxx).

briefest: 'The parable is an earthly story with a heavenly meaning'.[15]

Comfortable with an expansive understanding of the concept 'parable', van Koetsveld does not exercise himself unduly in attempting to delimit the forms of Jesus' parables because, from the simple proverb to the developed parable, the various forms run almost imperceptibly into each other.[16] This does not mean that van Koetsveld makes no effort to differentiate certain forms said to lie within the parameters of an expansive understanding of the term 'parable'— indeed, he wants to distinguish Jesus' parables from fables and allegories.[17] However, van Koetsveld takes umbrage with modern critics who, based upon their view of the essence of Jesus' parables, would exclude from among Jesus' parables some of the parables found only in the Gospel of Luke. He rehearses the problem posed by the parables exclusive to the third Gospel in the 'General Introduction' (volume 1), and revisits it in the 'Epilogue' (volume 2). With this, we come to van Koetsveld's treatment of the parables later known as *Beispielerzählungen*.

In the 'General Introduction', van Koetsveld addresses the issue of whether the *Beispielerzählungen*, among other Lukan parables, are a different form of parable. According to van Koetsveld, all interpreters who seek to describe the essence of the parable meet with a particular sort of parable which is Luke's own and which one scholar called, not unjustly, 'parables in the manner of instructive narratives'.[18] Here, van Koetsveld makes a preliminary observation: In all the parables (*Gelijkenissen*) of the Gospel of Matthew that are also found in the

---

15. Van Koetsveld, *De Gelijkenissen van den Zaligmaker*, I, p. xxxii: '"De Parabel is eene aardsche historie, met eene hemelsche bedoeling"'. Van Koetsveld lists several of what he considers to be the most important definitions of 'parable' given by interpreters (pp. xxvii-xxix).

16. See *De Gelijkenissen van den Zaligmaker*, I, p. xxxiii. Van Koetsveld states that sometimes certain Greek and Latin writers did not distinguish a parable from an 'image, example or simile', and that other 'secular writers' did not sharply separate the parable as a genre from 'fable' or 'myth' (p. xxix). Although he mentions Cicero, Quintilian and Aristotle (p. xxix n. 2), van Koetsveld does not appeal to ancient rhetoric in order to define the term 'parable' or to describe the forms of the parables.

17. See, e.g., Van Koetsveld, *De Gelijkenissen van den Zaligmaker*, I, pp. xiv-xvi, xxxi-xxxiv, xlv-lvi.

18. Van Koetsveld quotes the words of his teacher, J.H. van der Palm; see *De Gelijkenissen van den Zaligmaker*, I, p. xxxii and II, p. 11.

Gospel of Mark and the Gospel of Luke, the emblematic (*zinne-beeldige*) is clearly in view. However, in the parables that are exclusive to the Gospel of Luke (such as The Prodigal Son), which sketch the deity's manner of action and the audience's vocation in human figurative language, more care is spent on the images (*beelden*) themselves, which are to function as an example (*voorbeeld*) for the audience and not solely as an emblem (*zinnebeeld*).[19] Van Koetsveld wishes to delay a decision on the matter until after all the parables have been interpreted and the synoptic gospels have been compared with respect to their origin and purpose. Now he will only provisionally point to The Rich Fool, The Rich Man and Poor Lazarus, The Pharisee and the Toll Collector, and The Merciful Samaritan as character depictions rather than emblems, and to The Prodigal Son and The Unjust Judge as susceptible to a figurative understanding only with respect to the main idea expressed in them.[20] These Lukan parables, then, present a problem to van Koetsveld's plan of interpreting all of Jesus' parables as emblems of the kingdom of heaven.

'It is indubitable', van Koetsveld asserts, 'that Jesus sometimes by design described the kingdom of heaven in parables...', but van Koetsveld knows that disputes arise over whether 'all the parables are images of God's reign'.[21] The main content of Jesus' parables, the kingdom of heaven, is either made explicit by the introductions to many of the parables or is suggested by the context in which the parables are spoken in the Gospels.[22] However, questions are raised about some of the parables peculiar to the Gospel of Luke, parables which van Koetsveld refers to as 'moral parables'. These 'moral parables', concedes van Koetsveld, 'are never placed in a definite relation to the kingdom of God'.[23] He conjectures that if a rabbi other than Jesus had sketched The Rich Fool as a example of a man rich in the world and not rich toward God, or had pursued beneficence through the picture of the Unjust Steward, we would not suspect in the least that such 'pure moral sketches' stood in a particular relation to an expectation of the approach

---

19. Van Koetsveld, *De Gelijkenissen van den Zaligmaker*, I, p. xxxii.
20. Van Koetsveld, *De Gelijkenissen van den Zaligmaker*, I, p. xxxiv.
21. Van Koetsveld, *De Gelijkenissen van den Zaligmaker*, I, p. xliii.
22. Van Koetsveld compares the introductions to the parables and the contexts of the parables as given in the synoptic gospels; see, e.g., *De Gelijkenissen van den Zaligmaker*, I, pp. xl-xliv.
23. Van Koetsveld, *De Gelijkenissen van den Zaligmaker*, I, p. xliii.

of the already established reign of God.[24] Van Koetsveld warns that to
bring such 'moral sketches' into a forced relation to the reign of God
can lead interpreters astray from simple and sound expositions, and he
wants to avoid fanciful allegorical interpretations or dogmatic theological interpretations while disallowing a view of these parables as literal
stories or stories of real events.[25] Reiterating that such 'moral sketches'
occur mostly in the Gospel of Luke, van Koetsveld allows that if one
were to confine the definition and the number of Jesus' parables within
the narrowest of limits, then these parables that stand in no historical
connection to the establishment and development of the reign of God—
as well as all proverbs, similes and allegories—would have to be
excluded.[26]

That being said, however, van Koetsveld does not exclude all such
forms from among Jesus' parables. He aligns his work with those who
bring all the parables into a certain relation to the kingdom of heaven
and who interpret all Jesus' parables from that point of view.[27] For van
Koetsveld, the problem posed by the parables peculiar to the Gospel of
Luke is not that they have 'moral content', for the aim of Jesus' parables is 'didactic and moral';[28] nor is the problem that these Lukan
parables are stories of real events. Rather, the problem is that a clear

24. Van Koetsveld, *De Gelijkenissen van den Zaligmaker*, I, p. xliv.

25. Van Koetsveld, *De Gelijkenissen van den Zaligmaker*, I, p. xliv. Van
Koetsveld wants to avoid placing too much emphasis on the putative significance of
details found in the parables, as if the details had a meaning independent of their
context in the parables. Thus, for example, van Koetsveld disallows making the
Samaritan into an image of Christ (I, p. lv), and he asserts that the significance of
the foolish rich man is nothing other than a foolish rich man, that the significance of
Lazarus is nothing other than a poor man (II, pp. 11-12). As we have seen, however, van Koetsveld does not regard these as stories of real events.

26. Van Koetsveld, *De Gelijkenissen van den Zaligmaker*, I, p. xliv. Van
Koetsveld claims that there is only one developed *Gelijkenis* in the Gospel of
Matthew, The Unmerciful Servant (18.23-35), which could be put on the same
level as the 'moral sketches' in the Gospel of Luke, but that even this parable
begins with the usual Matthean introduction which brings it into direct relation to
the kingdom of heaven (Mt. 18.23).

27. Van Koetsveld, *De Gelijkenissen van den Zaligmaker*, I, pp. xliii-xliv.

28. See *De Gelijkenissen van den Zaligmaker*, I, p. liii. Van Koetsveld says
elsewhere that Jesus' parables 'have above all a general religious content' and that
'the Christian religion is the only thing' which is directly propagated in the parables
(p. xxxi). Indeed, van Koetsveld claims that the singular meaning of 'the kingdom
of heaven' is 'Christianity' (p. xlii).

relation to the main content of Jesus' customary teaching, the kingdom of heaven, is lacking in the parables found only in Luke's Gospel. If one adheres to some basic principles for interpreting the parables, then van Koetsveld is not opposed to including the Lukan parables among the parables of Jesus.[29] Van Koetsveld concludes that even the parables exclusive to the Gospel of Luke, which are said to have a less emblematic content and a more definite moral content—such as The Merciful Samaritan, The Rich Man and Poor Lazarus, The Foolish Rich Man, and The Pharisee and the Toll Collector—rightfully belong in the second volume of his collection of *De Gelijkenissen van den Zaligmaker*.[30]

Bernhard Weiss: 'Ueber das Bildliche im Neuen Testamente'

A quarter of a century before the publication of *Die Gleichnisreden Jesu*, the four parables now known as *Beispielerzählungen* received special comment in a published lecture on the expansive topic of 'pictorial language' (*Bildersprache*) in the New Testament delivered by

29. See van Koetsveld's chapter 'Eerste Grondslagen voor de Verklaring der Gelijkenissen', *De Gelijkenissen van den Zaligmaker*, I, pp. lvi-xlv. We have encountered two principles for interpreting the parables as specified by van Koetsveld: that the *tertium comparationis* of all Jesus' parables is the kingdom of heaven; and that the aim of Jesus' parables is didactic and moral. A brief summary of other principles is provided by Jones, *The Art and Truth of the Parables*, pp. 11-14. Against Jones (p. 11), however, I cannot find where van Koetsveld explicitly classifies any of Jesus' parables as 'exemplary stories'. I use the term here as a matter of convenience.

30. In the Epilogue, van Koetsveld returns to the issue of the form of Jesus' parables (*De Gelijkenissen van den Zaligmaker*, II, pp. 485-89). He places riddles in the foreground of the parables. The Foolish Rich Man is included among *Gelijkenissen* (p. 486), while The Merciful Samaritan and The Pharisee and the Toll Collector are found among *Parabelen* (p. 487). Van Koetsveld mentions The Rich Man and Poor Lazarus, The Unfruitful Fig Tree (Lk. 13.6-9), and Going to the Judge (Mt. 5.25-26//Lk. 12.58-59) as *Gelijkenissen* that stand 'unexplained and unmotivated' in their Gospel contexts and which must be considered 'in connection with Jesus' common instruction', the kingdom of heaven (p. 487). Of the remaining parables, van Koetsveld says: 'All the others already of their own accord have a direction, whether in the context or as emblems of the reign of God [*zinnebeelden van 't Godsrijk*], which conveys to us their explanation—unless one is not willing to believe the Evangelist in this' (p. 487).

Bernhard Weiss, one of Jülicher's teachers.[31] Although Weiss cata-
logues and describes several kinds of pictorial speech (*Bilderrede*)
employed by popular speakers and found in the New Testament, the
focus here will be on what Weiss says about the parables spoken by
Jesus.[32]

Weiss includes the four example stories among a set of *Gleichniserzählungen* (narrative parables) which are customarily called, in the
narrower sense, *Parabeln*.[33] According to Weiss, these 18–20 narratives—which are sometimes sketched roughly, sometimes executed in
detail—can be distinguished from the *Gleichnisse* (parables) in this
way: A standing relation or necessary law lies at the foundation of the
Gleichnisse, whereas a single event that happens under completely
concrete circumstances lies at the foundation of the *Parabeln*.[34] Thus,
in the *Parabeln* 'that which happened once under certain circumstances' is used as a means of representing a 'higher wisdom', not 'that

---

31. Bernhard Weiss, 'Ueber das Bildliche im Neuen Testamente', *Deutsche
Zeitschrift für christliche Wissenschaft und christliches Leben* NS 4 (1861), pp. 309-
31. Klauck correctly notes that Jülicher doubtlessly owed much to Weiss, who was
one of Jülicher's teachers in Berlin, for his book on the parables ('Adolf Jülicher',
p. 101). The profound influence that another scholar, G.E. Lessing, had upon the
thought of Jülicher is documented by Hans Gunther Klemm, 'Die Gleichnisauslegung Ad. Jülichers im Bannkreis der Fabeltheorie Lessings', *ZNW* 60 (1969),
pp. 153-74 (repr. in Harnische [ed.], *Gleichnisse Jesu*, pp. 343-68; all references
will be to the journal article).

32. By 'Bildersprache' Weiss means, in broad terms, a manner of speech in
which a subject matter (*Sache*) or thought (*Gedanken*) is expressed by means of a
picture (*Bild*); on this, see his 'Ueber das Bildliche im Neuen Testamente', pp. 309-
10. Among the types of *Bilderrede* treated by Weiss are hyperbole (p. 311),
illustrative examples (pp. 311-13), emblematic speech (pp. 315-18), *Gleichnisse*
(pp. 318-24) and *Gleichniserzählungen* (or *Parabeln*; pp. 324-31). According to
Weiss, emblematic speech (*sinnbildlicher Rede*) is the *Grundtypus* of the collective
Bildersprache in the New Testament (pp. 315-16).

33. Weiss, 'Ueber das Bildliche im Neuen Testamente', p. 324. This usage of
the word 'Parabel' does not, according to Weiss, correspond to the New Testament
concept. Weiss does not restrict his use of the term 'Gleichnis' to a set of brief narratives found only in the synoptic gospels; rather, he opts for an extremely broad
understanding of 'Gleichnis' which allows him to include material from the synoptics, the fourth Gospel and several epistles (see pp. 318-24). Note also that Weiss
sometimes uses the words 'Gleichnis' and 'Parabel' interchangeably. He does not
employ the term *Beispielerzählung*, although I do so for the sake of convenience.

34. Weiss, 'Ueber das Bildliche im Neuen Testamente', p. 324.

which takes place always and everywhere' as in the *Gleichnisse*.[35] Weiss asserts that even though 'Christ himself almost everywhere indicates' the meaning of his parables, that does not remove all difficulties and differences from the exposition of his parables.[36]

The variety of fields of life from which the *Parabelerzählungen* (narrative parables) are derived occasions some of the difficulties that arise in attempts to interpret them. In some instances, Weiss explains, *Parabeln* are drawn from circumstances which—like the other '*Gleichnisreden Christi*'—already have something representative or emblematic about them.[37] An interpretive difficulty is posed by another kind of *Parabel* which obviously has an allegorical character because its individual features are not drawn only from a living reality, but are intentionally fabricated and arranged to have an analogy to the concrete circumstances to which they refer.[38] Another interpretive difficulty is posed by four parables which derive their matter from fields so closely related to each other that the parables *appear* to be 'mere examples' of the truth intended by them.[39] As Weiss states,

> In the *Parabel* of the Pharisee and Toll Collector, humility and pride before God already stand out directly; the Merciful Samaritan is a living

35. Weiss, 'Ueber das Bildliche im Neuen Testamente', p. 324. Echoes of this can be heard in *Die Gleichnisreden Jesu*.

36. Weiss, 'Ueber das Bildliche im Neuen Testamente', p. 324. According to Weiss, only the 'Gleichnissen' of The Lost Son and The Rich Man and Poor Lazarus lack such an application, but that is probably because they undergo a double application. Weiss refers to the 'Parabel' of The Rich Fool as a place in which Jesus shows directly the point of his teaching (p. 325); he also mentions The Pharisee and the Toll Collector in this regard.

37. Weiss, 'Ueber das Bildliche im Neuen Testamente', p. 325.

38. Weiss, 'Ueber das Bildliche im Neuen Testamente', p. 326. For Weiss, some attempts to provide an allegorizing interpretation of Jesus' parables are harmless (p. 326); most other attempts, however, run into 'insurmountable difficulties' (p. 327).

39. Weiss, 'Ueber das Bildliche im Neuen Testamente', p. 327. I italicize 'appear' because in a later writing Weiss emphatically states with regard to The Pharisee and the Toll Collector and The Foolish Rich Man that neither is a 'mere example', and suggests with regard to The Rich Man and Poor Lazarus and The Merciful Samaritan that each is more than an 'illustrative narrative' or 'explanatory narrative' (see *The Life of Christ* [3 vols.; trans. M.G. Hope; Edinburgh: T. & T. Clark, 1894], II, pp. 134, 251 n. 1, 293, 359).

example of love of neighbor; the narratives of the Rich Man and Poor
Lazarus as well as the Foolish Rich Man unveil directly the deceit of
riches.[40]

However, Weiss does not view these four narratives as less than *Parabeln* because of that. Indeed, these four parables partake of the same
'captivating spell, the triumphant power' as do the other *Parabeln*.[41]
All of the '*Parabelerzählungen Christi*' obtain their power through the
potency of the accomplished fact, the potency of the example (*Macht
des Beispiels*) and the potency of contrast; and, in giving evidence of
that power, Weiss cites all four of the example stories among the other
Parabeln.[42]

Siegfried Göbel: Die Parabeln Jesu methodisch ausgelegt

Several years before Jülicher published *Die Gleichnisreden Jesu*,
Siegfried Göbel provided an interpretation of *Die Parabeln Jesu* in
which his stated intent was to redress the problem of an exegetical
excess that treats Jesus' parables with 'unbounded arbitrariness', an
excess by which interpreters impute to his parables 'all imaginable
relations and comparisons'.[43] Göbel seeks to determine 'more definite
norms for the interpretation of the *Gleichnisse*' in order to lay a secure
foundation for interpreting them.[44] Prior to that, however, Göbel delim-

---

40. Weiss, 'Ueber das Bildliche im Neuen Testamente', p. 327: 'In der Parabel
vom Pharisäer und Zöllner tritt bereits die Demuth und der Hochmuth vor Gott
unmittelbar hervor, der barmherzige Samariter ist ein lebendiges Beispiel der Näch-
stenliebe, die Erzählungen vom reichen Mann und armen Lazarus sowie vom
thörichten Reichen enthüllen den Betrug des Reichthums unmittelbar'. Weiss contrasts these four parables to others which, being drawn from a thoroughly heteroge-
neous field of life, have a special persuasive force, and which—like The Unjust
Householder (Lk. 16.1-9)—derive their matter from the area of worldly life.
41. Weiss, 'Ueber das Bildliche im Neuen Testamente', p. 328.
42. See Weiss, 'Ueber das Bildliche im Neuen Testamente', pp. 328-30.
43. Siegfried Göbel, *Die Parabeln Jesu methodisch ausgelegt* (2 vols; Gotha:
Friedrich Andreas Perthes, 1879), pp. v-vi. One may wish to consult the English
translation entitled *The Parables of Jesus: A Methodological Exposition* (trans.
Professor Banks; Edinburgh: T. & T. Clark, 1883). All translations here are my
own.
44. Göbel, *Die Parabeln Jesu*, pp. 29, 32; see pp. 29-32 for Göbel's outline of
methodological principles (or for a brief summary, see Jones, *The Art and Truth of
the Parables*, pp. 14-16).

its the boundaries of the material upon which he will fix his interpretive gaze, and that is the point of interest here.

Göbel is aware that the word παραβολή when applied to the speeches of Jesus has a considerably wider sense than is customary in modern ecclesial usage when reference is made to the *Gleichnisse* or *Parabeln* of Christ.[45] Rather than treat all of Jesus' utterances that fall under the broad category of *Parabel* as comparative, pictorial speech, Göbel wants to limit the material to the '*Parabeln* in the narrower sense'.[46] He identifies the 'narrative form' as the distinguishing factor constitutive of the concept '*Parabel* in the narrower sense'.[47] Thus, Göbel will treat as *Parabeln* only those sayings which exhibit 'the character of the self-contained pictorial story or narrative'.[48] He gives this general definition of the concept *Parabel*:

> It is a narrative moving in the field of natural or human life which does not intend, however, to communicate an event that really happened, rather, which is expressly invented with the aim of representing in a vivid picture a truth belonging to the field of religion, therefore referring to the relation of human beings or humankind to God.[49]

Göbel identifies 27 such narratives as *Parabeln Jesu*.

With regard to the kind and manner of representation, however, Göbel claims that there is an 'essential difference' among the *Parabeln Jesu* as they appear in the Gospels: there are 'either *symbolic* (emblematic) or *typical* (exemplifying) *Parabeln*'.[50] The general background for Göbel's claim is the presupposition that there is a continuous harmony between two fields—the collective field of life that encompasses both the visible world of nature and natural human life, and the higher field of life that embraces the relation of human beings to God. By virtue of this divinely established harmony, the states and circumstances, the incidents and activities belonging to the former field mirror something of the same kind in the latter field.[51] Thus, on the basis of that prevailing inner coherence, and not chance similarity, 'the visible is an emblem for the invisible, the earthly for the heavenly, the temporal for

---

45. Göbel, *Die Parabeln Jesu*, p. 1.
46. Göbel, *Die Parabeln Jesu*, p. 3: 'Parabeln im engeren Sinne'.
47. Göbel, *Die Parabeln Jesu*, pp. 4-5.
48. Göbel, *Die Parabeln Jesu*, p. 4.
49. Göbel, *Die Parabeln Jesu*, p. 5; Göbel's emphasis.
50. Göbel, *Die Parabeln Jesu*, p. 5; Göbel's emphasis.
51. Göbel, *Die Parabeln Jesu*, pp. 5-6.

the eternal'.[52] Proceeding from this standpoint, Göbel states that

> the symbolic parable is such that brings to pictorial representation the
> truths belonging to the religious field that it intends to illustrate in a nar-
> rative freely composed out of emblematically significant circumstances,
> incidents and activities of natural or human life.[53]

There are, according to Göbel, 23 symbolic parables.

The only four parables in the group Göbel designates as 'typical
Parabeln' are the example stories. Göbel's description of the typical
parables is admirable in its precision and clarity; because it prefigures
much of what has been said about the example stories in this century,
the entire section will be quoted in full.

> Alongside these symbolic *Parabeln*, however, we find in addition a
> number of others which we have called *typical*, τύπος here nevertheless
> not taken in the specific sense of Rom. 5.14 as a foreboding advance-
> representation of a future thing, rather in the usual sense of *exemplum*,
> whether now a model summoning to imitation (e.g. Phil. 3.17; 1 Tim.
> 4.12), whether a warning and deterrent (e.g. 1 Cor. 10.6; 11). These are
> the ones which demonstrate graphically the teaching that they wish to
> give, not by the way of emblematic clothing, but by that of direct exem-
> plification. Such are the *Gleichnisse* of The Merciful Samaritan, The
> Rich Fool, The Rich Man, and The Pharisee and Toll Collector (Lk. 10,
> 12, 16, 18). In all these *Parabeln* a παραβάλλειν, a comparative juxta-
> position takes place only insofar as the author draws near a definite, par-
> ticular case to be developed into an invented story for the comparison
> with the general truth to be taught, at which it proves effective so that
> now in this story, as in a striking example (*Beispiel*), the relevant reli-
> gious truth is intuitively perceived. Thus, the narratives themselves as
> such already, then, bear the religious character. Their main personages,
> after whom they are named, are not emblematic portrayals, rather they
> are themselves already the typical representatives of an ethical-religious
> disposition. And, on the other hand, the name and person of God can
> appear directly in the narrative without pictorial clothing; divine acts,
> which are withdrawn from inspection, can form an essential component
> of the action (both in the *Gleichnisse* of The Rich Fool and The Pharisee
> and Toll Collector), or, as in the *Parabel* of The Rich Man, the story of
> human personages is pursued into the hereafter—all of which is impos-
> sible in the symbolic parable in accordance with its nature. Here, what is
> necessary first in order to express the didactic content of the narrative is

52. Göbel, *Die Parabeln Jesu*, p. 6.
53. Göbel, *Die Parabeln Jesu*, p. 6.

not the interpretation of an emblem, rather only the generalized application of what has been said about, or what has been narrated in a definite, particular case to all similar cases so that the special occurrences of the narrated story are led back to the generally valid law fulfilled in them and to the generally valid truth proven effective in them.[54]

Göbel, after having defined the concept '*Parabel* in the narrower sense', does not devote a separate inquiry into the purpose of the parabolic teaching form, for the purpose of the *Parabel* lies in its essence: The purpose of the *Parabel* is to represent a religious truth directly in a vivid picture, either in a concrete picture of the particular case (typical *Parabel*), or in an emblem taken from the world of nature and the human world (symbolic *Parabel*).[55] The didactic matter of the New Testament *Parabeln*, which is always religious truth, not their form, is what allows Göbel to differentiate the *Parabeln* from the *Fabeln* of 'profane literature'.[56] Moreover, Göbel deems the distinction between '*Parabel* (παραβολή) and *Fabel* (λόγος)' made by Aristotle in his *Rhetoric* to be of little relevance, and certainly incapable of marking a difference between *Parabel* in the narrower sense and *Fabel*.[57]

Although Göbel strives to state succinctly his reasons for distinguishing between the symbolic *Parabeln* and the typical *Parabeln*, the classification of the parables he constructs as the framework for his interpretation is not based upon the form of the parables. While Göbel remains wary of classifications of Jesus' parables based upon their content, he offers one in which the parables are divided into two groups: those which describe the 'essence and development of the kingdom of God' and those which deal with the 'right conduct of associates of the kingdom'.[58] It should come as no surprise that Göbel includes the example stories among the latter since the typical *Parabeln* are said to be '*exempla*' which provide models either for imitation or deterrence. However, a number of the symbolic *Parabeln* are said to have a reference to the conduct of associates of the kingdom, either as an

54. Göbel, *Die Parabeln Jesu*, pp. 7-8; Göbel's emphasis.
55. Göbel, *Die Parabeln Jesu*, p. 18. He concludes that 'the *Parabel* is therefore essentially visual instruction' (or 'object lesson', *Anschauungsunterricht*).
56. Göbel, *Die Parabeln Jesu*, pp. 8-11.
57. Göbel, *Die Parabeln Jesu*, p. 8 n. 1.
58. Göbel, *Die Parabeln Jesu*, pp. 26-27. Göbel concedes that many *Parabeln* lack a direct reference to the kingdom of God, but he retains the kingdom of God as the 'central concept' of the *Parabeln* since it is the 'central concept' of the teaching of Jesus in general (see pp. 25-26).

exhortation to what is right or as a warning against the opposite.[59] That notwithstanding, Göbel clearly regards the example stories, which he designates as typical *Parabeln*, as '*Parabeln* in the narrower sense'. Therefore, those four parables have a rightful place among *Die Parabeln Jesu*.

Adolf Jülicher: The First Edition of Die Gleichnisreden Jesu

As we have seen, questions were raised about four parables peculiar to the Gospel of Luke prior to the publication of the first edition of *Die Gleichnisreden Jesu* in 1886. Some scholars collected those four parables—The Merciful Samaritan, The Foolish Rich Man, The Rich Man and Poor Lazarus, The Pharisee and the Toll Collector—into a group and attempted to discern in what way, if indeed at all, these parables were to be distinguished from the other parables recorded in the synoptic gospels. Jülicher continued that trend. He pondered the questions raised about these parables—referred to variously as 'moral parables' or 'examples' or 'typical parables'—and offered a response in his chapter on 'The Essence of the Parable Speeches of Jesus' in the section where he defines and describes the category *Beispielerzählung*.[60] Jülicher's initial solution to the problem posed by the example narratives was not his last, for he reformed some of his opinions about the *Beispielerzählungen* at some point between the first issue of *Die Gleichnisreden Jesu* in 1886 and the publication of the revised edition in 1899. Although Jülicher does not alter significantly his formal definition of the category *Beispielerzählung*, he does change his views

59. Göbel, *Die Parabeln Jesu*, p. 26. The *Beispielerzählungen* are listed under the heading applied to the second group of *Die Parabeln Jesu*, 'Von dem rechten Verhalten der Reichsgenossen' (p. 27); thus the Pharisee and the Toll Collector, The Treasure in the Field, The Costly Pearl, The Importunate Friend, and The Unjust Judge all have to do with 'the right conduct of associates of the kingdom toward God'. The Merciful Samaritan, The Unmerciful Servant, The Lost Sheep, The Lost Coin, and The Lost Son treat 'the right conduct of associates of the kingdom toward the world', and in particular with regard to human beings, while The Rich Fool, The Rich Man [and Poor Lazarus], and The Unjust Householder deal with 'the right conduct of associates of the kingdom toward the world', and in particular with regard to earthly goods.

60. See Jülicher's chapter 'Das Wesen der Gleichnisreden Jesu', in *Die Gleichnisreden Jesu. Erste Hälfte: Allgemeiner Theil* (1886), pp. 24-121, esp. pp. 117-19.

of some of the implications of that definition.[61] The aim here is to highlight Jülicher's initial assessment of the ramifications issuing from his
definition of that category in his first treatment of the example
narratives.

According to Jülicher, the *Beispielerzählungen* are narratives which
must be counted among the 'παραβολαί *Jesu*', but which are neither
Gleichnisse nor *Parabeln* as Jülicher defines those terms.[62] Like the
Gleichnisse and *Parabeln*, the example narratives are not narrated for
their own sake in order to enrich the hearer in historical knowledge;
like the *Gleichnisse* and *Parabeln*, the example narratives are freely
invented, they serve a religious-ethical purpose, and they intend to
promote the subject matter of the kingdom of heaven. As Jülicher puts
it, 'What distinguishes them is only that they already move in the
higher field which exclusively dominates Jesus' interest'.[63] Unlike the
Parabeln (in Mt. 13–25, for instance), which introduce the reader to
earthly circumstances, 'those four pieces present to us events which
refer to religious things and can only be comprehended from this standpoint'.[64] Jülicher amplifies that point: 'The story does not unwind in a
different field, as our "parable" definition demands, rather in the same
[field], in that [field] in which is located the proposition to be secured;
in other words, the story is there an example [*Beispiel*] of the proposition to be asserted'.[65] For this reason, Jülicher feels compelled to call
this category '*Beispielerzählung*', which he defines formally as follows:
'The third category of "παραβολαί Jesu" are therefore example narratives; that is, narratives *which bring forward a general proposition of
religious-ethical character in the dress of a particular case*, "the general truth confirmed by the evidentness of the act"'.[66] The example

61. In the foreword to the revised edition, Jülicher gives little notice that he
makes changes with respect to the *Beispielerzählungen* (see *Die Gleichnisreden
Jesu*, I, p. [ix] v).

62. Jülicher, *Die Gleichnisreden Jesu. Erste Hälfte: Allgemeiner Theil* (1886),
p. 117.

63. Jülicher, *Die Gleichnisreden Jesu. Erste Hälfte: Allgemeiner Theil* (1886),
p. 117.

64. Jülicher, *Die Gleichnisreden Jesu. Erste Hälfte: Allgemeiner Theil* (1886),
p. 117. Jülicher refines this sentence in the revised edition.

65. Jülicher, *Die Gleichnisreden Jesu. Erste Hälfte: Allgemeiner Theil* (1886),
p. 117.

66. Jülicher, *Die Gleichnisreden Jesu. Erste Hälfte: Allgemeiner Theil* (1886),
p. 119 (Jülicher's emphasis): 'Diese dritte Kategorie von παραβολαί Jesu sind also

narratives may be called 'pictorial speech' because they are intended
for the senses, because they paint a law (as it were) before the eyes.
Jülicher emphasizes that this type of speech is not to be interpreted
allegorically; but a comparison of the details in the story makes no
sense either.[67] On these points Jülicher remains firm, for the most part,
in the revised edition of *Die Gleichnisreden Jesu*.

Jülicher's first impression of the *Beispielerzählungen* disposes him to
argue that they are inferior to the other parables, especially the *Parabeln*. He bases his judgment on the comparative character of the example narratives vis-à-vis the other parables. In the *Beispielerzählung* 'the
soil of the ὅμοιον is actually abandoned'.[68] Here, the narrator has not
engaged in a comparative activity and the hearer should not either.[69]
According to Jülicher, it suffices if the hearers sense the general rule
disclosed in 'these unassuming stories', and then subject their lives to
that rule in the future. Nevertheless, 'in persuasive power' and 'in
rhetorical value', the example narratives are not able to compete with
the other παραβολαί.[70] He explains:

> One cannot prove a subject matter with itself; the means of proof, the
> κοιναὶ πίστεις must be borrowed from elsewhere. One cannot illuminate a topic with its own light; it becomes brighter around it only when a
> foreign body of light is used for that purpose. The 'so also' of the *Gleichnis* and *Parabel* has no more place here. This speech form wins no
> unbelievers; it will at most support the believers, the already won...
> Strictly speaking, these pericopae no longer belong in the circumference

Beispielerzählungen, d.h. Erzählungen, *die einen allgemeinen Satz religiös-sittlichen Charakters in dem Kleide eines Einzelfalles vorführen*, "durch die Evidenz
der That die allgemeine Wahrheit bestätigen"'. In the revised edition, Jülicher
added modifiers so that the 'Einzelfalles' becomes an 'especially impressively
shaped particular case' (see below, p. 127).

67. Jülicher, *Die Gleichnisreden Jesu. Erste Hälfte: Allgemeiner Theil* (1886),
p. 117.

68. Jülicher, *Die Gleichnisreden Jesu. Erste Hälfte: Allgemeiner Theil* (1886),
pp. 117-18: 'Der Boden des ὅμοιον ist eigentlich verlassen'. In the revised edition
'eigentlich' is changed to 'beinahe'.

69. Jülicher, *Die Gleichnisreden Jesu. Erste Hälfte: Allgemeiner Theil* (1886),
p. 118: 'Eine vergleichende Thätigkeit hat weder der Erzähler geübt noch soll der
Hörer sie üben'.

70. Jülicher, *Die Gleichnisreden Jesu. Erste Hälfte: Allgemeiner Theil* (1886),
p. 118.

of the *mashal*, for its basic concept—that of the comparative speech—is not suited to them.[71]

Jülicher asserts that another disadvantage of the example narratives is that 'whoever does not acknowledge the authority of the narrator will never submit himself to the authority of such a narrative'.[72] He doubts that a Pharisee would believe Jesus' statement that the Pharisee in Lk. 18.9-14 went down to his house less justified than the toll collector; and Jülicher imagines that a Sadducee, one who denies a future life, would have laughed at The Rich Man and Poor Lazarus. Such disadvantages are avoided by 'the genuine *"Parabel"*'.[73] The *Parabeln* play out a struggle 'on neutral soil, where the opponent decides impartially about true and untrue, right and wrong, and, after he has decided that, [the *Parabeln*] compel him for the sake of honor to decide according to the same principle on the contested soil'.[74] A *Beispielerzählung* may hold a mirror before people so that they must notice their imperfections, but of course stubborn people who will not see their deficiencies cannot be subdued even with a mirror because they simply shut their eyes when confronted. The *Parabel*, in Jülicher's view, proceeds in a more clever fashion: It holds before obstinate people a thing that they look at with interest and without suspicion; when they become aware, at the moment when they become convinced of their imperfections, it is too late.[75]

This, then, is the view of the *Beispielerzählungen* promulgated by Jülicher in his 1886 edition of *Die Gleichnisreden Jesu*. The example

71. Jülicher, *Die Gleichnisreden Jesu. Erste Hälfte: Allgemeiner Theil* (1886), p. 118. Jülicher claims that the 'two-memberedness' (*Zweigliedrigkeit*) evident in both the *Gleichnisse* and the *Parabeln* is present in the *Beispielerzählungen* only in passing. For instance, when Jesus narrates The Pharisee and the Toll Collector, as Lk. 18.9 says, to an audience made up of some who are not fully aware of their conceit and disdain of others, then certainly those hearers will compare their activity to that sketched in the story; but there can be no talk of wider similarity.

72. Jülicher, *Die Gleichnisreden Jesu. Erste Hälfte: Allgemeiner Theil* (1886), p. 118: 'Wer die Autorität des Erzählers nicht anerkennt, wird sich der Autorität solcher Erzählungen nie unterwerfen...'

73. Jülicher, *Die Gleichnisreden Jesu. Erste Hälfte: Allgemeiner Theil* (1886), pp. 118-19.

74. Jülicher, *Die Gleichnisreden Jesu. Erste Hälfte: Allgemeiner Theil* (1886), p. 119.

75. Jülicher, *Die Gleichnisreden Jesu. Erste Hälfte: Allgemeiner Theil* (1886), p. 119.

narratives are 'παραβολαί *Jesu*', to be sure, but they do not measure up to the *Gleichnisse* and the *Parabeln*. As we will see in Chapter 3, Jülicher ameliorates his harsh assessment of the *Beispielerzählungen* in the 1899 revision of *Die Gleichnisreden Jesu*, where he omits some of what we just read, subtly changes some sentences and adds fresh material. Jülicher also adds a citation that refers to another understanding of the example stories, that of Immanuel Stockmeyer.

Immanuel Stockmeyer: Exegetische und praktische Erklärung ausgewählter Gleichnisse Jesu

Two years before Jülicher issued his revised edition of *Die Gleichnisreden Jesu*, Immanuel Stockmeyer's rather large volume, in which he provides an 'exegetical and practical exposition of selected parables of Jesus', was published.[76] Jülicher, in his revised treatment of the example stories, cites Stockmeyer's nomenclature for those four παραβολαί, and it is no mystery why Jülicher is so moved: Stockmeyer's classification of the *Gleichnisse Jesu* bears such a striking resemblance to Jülicher's that one could almost substitute Stockmeyer's 'analogized description' for Jülicher's *Gleichnis*, Stockmeyer's *Parabel* for Jülicher's *Parabel*, and Stockmeyer's '*Exempel*' or '*Hypotypose*' for Jülicher's *Beispielerzählung*.[77] Before Stockmeyer's conception of the '*Exempel*' or '*Hypotypose*' is examined, a brief summary of how he justifies his selection of the *Gleichnisse Christi* is in order.

Stockmeyer begins his introduction by making a few remarks about the use of the word παραβολή in the New Testament, where the term is employed in such an expansive manner that within the scope of the concept παραβολή lies nearly every saying on the lips of Jesus that is alloyed with 'more or less parabolical or pictorial elements'.[78] For

---

76. Immanuel Stockmeyer, *Exegetische und praktische Erklärung ausgewählter Gleichnisse Jesu* (ed. Karl Stockmeyer; Basel: Verlag von R. Reich, 1897). Stockmeyer's volume was edited by his son and published posthumously.

77. Presumably, Stockmeyer's is an independently constructed classification schema. As far as I can determine, Stockmeyer makes no specific reference to Jülicher. It is quite possible that there is a mediating figure of whom I remain unaware.

78. Stockmeyer, *Exegetische und praktische Erklärung*, p. 3. Stockmeyer asserts that the term παραβολή can be applied to the briefest of gnomic utterances, both to those with a comparative character (e.g. Lk. 6.39) and to those without a hint of comparison about them (e.g. Mk 7.15//Mt. 15.11). The word παραβολή is

Stockmeyer, the term *'Gleichnis'* corresponds to the more expansive usage of παραβολή in the New Testament. He prefers, however, to limit himself to a consideration of a smaller number of *Gleichnisse*, which he differentiates into three classes according to their 'formal difference'.[79]

Stockmeyer wishes to fix his attention, first and foremost, on the *Parabeln* 'in the fullest and strictest sense of the word'.[80] The name 'Parabel' refers to a *Gleichnis* in its most developed shape.[81] According to Stockmeyer, the *Parabel* is a fictitious narrative whose material is taken from either circumstances in nature or circumstances in ordinary human life that could happen at any time. The narrative of a *Parabel* serves not only to tell a story, but also to illustrate a circumstance which, in an analogous manner, is found in a 'higher supernatural field', a field which is, in the *Parabeln Christi*, always the 'religious-ethical field'.[82] By means of 'illustrative individualization', the 'actual *Parabel*' intends to make a teaching more lively and impressive.[83]

Stockmeyer treats another form of *Gleichnis*, which he refers to as 'allegorical descriptions' or, more precisely, 'analogized descriptions' *(analogisierende Schilderungen)*.[84] Here, the circumstance that serves as a comparison is not individualized in a narrative, but is sketched from the circumstance of a generally valid description which is applied (or is left to the hearer to apply) to a higher field.[85] Frequently, but not always, the 'analogized descriptions', which relate a normal or customary course of events taken from nature or human life, are employed as a means of inductive proof.[86]

Stockmeyer chooses to include for treatment in his study a third form which is sometimes called a παραβολή or a *Gleichnis*, but which, in his

---

applicable to the latter in that it is a graphic manner of speech which gives concrete expression to an abstract thought (see p. 1).

79. Stockmeyer, *Exegetische und praktische Erklärung*, p. 6; cf. p. 3.

80. Stockmeyer, *Exegetische und praktische Erklärung*, p. 3.

81. Stockmeyer, *Exegetische und praktische Erklärung*, p. 3.

82. Stockmeyer, *Exegetische und praktische Erklärung*, p. 3; cf. p. 5.

83. Stockmeyer, *Exegetische und praktische Erklärung*, p. 4. The Prodigal Son, for instance, is a *Parabel*.

84. Stockmeyer, *Exegetische und praktische Erklärung*, p. 4. Mt. 13.32 and 13.47 are cited as specimens.

85. Stockmeyer, *Exegetische und praktische Erklärung*, pp. 4-5.

86. Stockmeyer, *Exegetische und praktische Erklärung*, pp. 4-5.

view, is neither a *Gleichnis*, nor a *Parabel*, nor a comparison.[87] The Foolish Rich Man, The Merciful Samaritan, The Rich Man and Poor Lazarus, and The Pharisee and the Toll Collector are manifestations of this third form and are referred to alternatively as '*Hypotypose*' (hypotyposis), '*anonyme Beispiel*' (anonymous example) and '*Exempel*'.[88] According to Stockmeyer, a '*Hypotypose*' is an illustrative analogy for the circumstances of a higher field, a field which moves about on the same field as its application. The *Parabel* is a circumstance of a higher field illustrated analogously by a circumstance from a lower field.[89] That is to say, in a *Hypotypose* the teaching moves wholly on the same field as does the story. With respect to The Merciful Samaritan, Stockmeyer writes: 'The teaching is not symbolized, rather exemplified; the narrative is a fictitious example, no actual *Parabel*, altogether like Luke 12.16-21 and 18.9-14'.[90]

Stockmeyer explains his notion of *Hypotypose* with reference to Lk. 12.16-21. The Foolish Rich Man would be a comparison (*Vergleichung*) if it told of a rich man who had committed some folly in the field of agriculture and because of that folly had suffered an economic loss, which story was then applied to the religious-ethical field to the effect that so it goes with people who make poor use of their lives, their gifts, their energies, their goods and who lose everything and have nothing in the end. But that is not the case: 'The ἀφοσύνη [foolishness] of the πλούσιος [rich man] moves directly on the religious-ethical field...'[91] The Foolish Rich Man, then, is not a comparison, but an example of an anonymous rich man taken from real life.

Nevertheless, Stockmeyer will not disallow the use of the word παραβολή with reference to The Foolish Rich Man; indeed, it can be

87. Stockmeyer states this view with specific reference to The Foolish Rich Man (*Exegetische und praktische Erklärung*, p. 1) and The Merciful Samaritan (pp. 7, 221).

88. See Stockmeyer, *Exegetische und praktische Erklärung*, pp. 1-3, 7; cf. pp. 221, 364.

89. Stockmeyer, *Exegetische und praktische Erklärung*, pp. 221, 364.

90. Stockmeyer, *Exegetische und praktische Erklärung*, p. 221; cf. p. 364, where Stockmeyer says of The Rich Man and Poor Lazarus: 'For it is not a *Parabel*; it does not illustrate the relation of a higher sphere through an analog of a lower [sphere]; it is a *Hypotypose*, like the Merciful Samaritan (Lk. 10), The Landowner with Full Barns (Lk. 12.16), and The Pharisee and the Toll Collector in the Temple (Lk. 18.9ff.)'.

91. Stockmeyer, *Exegetische und praktische Erklärung*, pp. 1-2.

justified for two reasons. First, The Foolish Rich Man is a 'juxtaposition': It is placed beside a teaching, not as an analogy from a different field, but as an example (*Beispiel*) from the very field of concern. Secondly, the example (*Beispiel*) is supposed to accomplish the same thing that is otherwise accomplished by the comparison, 'namely, it is supposed to represent concretely the abstract teaching, to make it more vivid and more forceful'.[92] What he says of The Foolish Rich Man is extended to the other three παραβολαί which share that form:

> It is what is called in rhetoric hypotyposis. The teaching is illustrated by a 'sketch', only the sketch is not taken from an analogical field; rather, the teaching is demonstrated in a concrete example, and thus is not an actual *Parabel*, but a sketch which serves the very same purpose, a model [*Vorbild*] set up for imitation or warning.[93]

For all of that, however, Stockmeyer does not wish to offend his readers in his treatment of some of the individual παραβολαί of this class, and so he will not focus on the question 'parable [Gleichnis] or example [Beispiel]?' And Stockmeyer himself will refer to The Merciful Samaritan, for instance, as a *Parabel* or *Gleichnis*.[94]

Comments and Conclusions

A fascination with the parables of Jesus flourished in the nineteenth century. Scholars were already engaged in earnest endeavors to identify the form or forms of Jesus' parables decades before Jülicher arrived on the scene. This chapter provides only a glimpse of the scholarly activity devoted to the parables of Jesus taking place on the continent[95] during

92. Stockmeyer, *Exegetische und praktische Erklärung*, p. 2.
93. Stockmeyer, *Exegetische und praktische Erklärung*, pp. 2-3.
94. See Stockmeyer, *Exegetische und praktische Erklärung*, p. 221.
95. If we may look to the books written by R.C. Trench (first edition published in 1841) and A.B. Bruce (first edition published in 1882) as representatives of English scholarship on the parables in the period before *Die Gleichnisreden Jesu*, then it appears that the distinction between *Parabel* and *Beispiel* was either of little concern or minimal consequence. Richard Chenevix Trench (*Notes on the Parables of Our Lord* [New York: D. Appleton & Co., 8th edn, 1856]) pauses to distinguish the parable as spoken by Jesus from those forms with which it is most likely to be 'confounded'; thus, he notes what makes Jesus' parables different from fable, *mythus*, proverb and allegory (pp. 8-16). Trench makes no attempt to differentiate between parable and example; indeed, he offers no classification of Jesus' parables. Alexander Balmain Bruce (*The Parabolic Teaching of Christ: A Systematic and*

the era in which Jülicher began his study of *Die Gleichnisreden Jesu*, but enough evidence has been furnished to dispel the myth that Jülicher created the category '*Beispielerzählung*'. Clearly, Jülicher was not the first to claim that the example stories comprise a class unto themselves.

The classification of Jesus' parables into three categories—*Gleichnis*, *Parabel*, 'Example'—existed in nascent form within the realm of common knowledge shared by scholars before Jülicher published his first edition of *Die Gleichnisreden Jesu*. We have learned that some

Critical Study of the Parables of Our Lord [New York: Armstrong & Son, 3rd rev. edn, 1898], pp. 3-4) divides Jesus' parables into three classes: theoretic parables (which contain 'the general truth, or what has been called the "metaphysic" of the Divine kingdom'); parables of grace (which are 'evangelic'—'their burden being grace, the mercy and the love of God to the sinful and the miserable'); and parables of judgment (which are 'prophetic'—'not in the predictive so much as in the ethical sense, to convey the idea that in this class of parables Jesus, as the messenger of God, spoke words of rebuke and warning to an evil time'). Interestingly, Bruce places three of the *Beispielerzählungen*—The Pharisee and the Publican, The Good Samaritan, and Dives and Lazarus—in the second class, not the third, as one might have expected. Bruce knows of Göbel's distinction between parable and example (see p. 344 n. 1) as it pertains to certain Lukan parables. In his section on The Good Samaritan, Bruce remarks: 'But the present parable is one of those peculiar to Luke, in which the vehicle of instruction is not a type taken from the natural sphere to teach a truth in the spiritual, but an *example* of the very action recommended' (p. 344; his emphasis). A similar comment is made with reference to The Pharisee and the Publican (p. 312), but not with reference to Dives and Lazarus. Bruce excludes other 'parabolic utterances' of Jesus from his study, i.e. certain metaphors and 'similitudes', among which he lists The Rich Fool (p. 9). He states his rationale in this way: 'The parables we propose to consider have all this in common, that they embody truths deep, unfamiliar or unwelcome—"mysteries of the kingdom". Such a parable as that of the Rich Fool, on the other hand, conveys no new or abstruse lesson, but simply teaches in concrete lively form a moral commonplace. Parabolic utterances of that description were not distinctive of Christ as a Teacher: they were common to Him with the Jewish Rabbis. He spake these merely as a Jewish moralist; but the parables now to be studied were uttered by Him as the Herald of the kingdom of heaven' (p. 9). Both Trench and Bruce subscribe to the familiar view that there is a harmony between the natural world and the spiritual world and that Jesus' parables express a spiritual truth by means of a comparison or analogy appropriated from the world of nature or the world of humans which is based not upon mere resemblance but inward necessity (see, e.g., Trench, *Notes on the Parables of Our Lord*, pp. 18-22; Bruce, *The Parabolic Teaching of Christ*, pp. 9, 312, 344); Trench, however, does not conclude that such a view requires a distinction among Jesus' parables.

scholars already distinguished between *Gleichnis* and *Parabel*, and that some scholars consulted ancient rhetoric in order to enhance their understanding of the *Parabeln*. Moreover, some scholars were already formulating responses to questions raised about four parables peculiar to the Gospel of Luke, which, thanks to Jülicher, we now know as example stories. The Merciful Samaritan, The Foolish Rich Man, The Rich Man and Poor Lazarus, and The Pharisee and the Toll Collector were grouped together years before Jülicher did so. As was the case with the *Parabeln*, some scholars turned to ancient rhetoric in order to describe these four parables. Jülicher inspected carefully the work of his predecessors, and it remained for him to synthesize the results of their studies.

Jülicher, then, was not the first to ponder the distinction between *Parabel* and *Beispielerzählung*. Others before him grappled with the problems posed by those four parables. Early on, if we may take van Koetsveld as representative, the question raised about each of the example stories was 'parable or story?' Later, if we may take Stockmeyer as representative, the question became 'parable or example?' It is instructive to note that the scholars dealt with in this chapter, who attempt to specify in what way, if at all, the example stories are to be distinguished from the *Parabeln*, do not differentiate *Beispielerzählungen* from *Parabeln* primarily because the *Beispielerzählungen* alone, in contradistinction to all the other parables, have a 'religious-ethical' concern.

We have examined Jülicher's first response to the problem posed by the example stories, a response that is virtually unknown to twentieth-century scholars. It should be kept in mind that Jülicher's definition of the example story as a category and his assessment of the members of that category are part of a larger plan. Although Jülicher alters his formal definition of the category *Beispielerzählung* in only a minor way, he revises his assessment of that category so that its members appear in a more favorable light. That revision, however, will not disrupt in the least Jülicher's greater purpose in *Die Gleichnisreden Jesu*. The reasons or factors lying behind Jülicher's decision to review and revise his evaluation of the example stories remain unknown and need not be known, for it is his revised view of the category which is most familiar to modern parable scholars and which has shaped the modern understanding of the example stories.

Jülicher did more than merely pass on what was handed down to him

with respect to the *Beispielerzählungen*. Like many tradents, he put his
own stamp on the tradition, and Jülicher's stamp remains firmly
imprinted upon the example stories. The effects of his definition of that
category are far-reaching, as we will see in Chapter 4. Even if it is true
that Jülicher did not originate the category of παραβολή that includes
The Merciful Samaritan, The Foolish Rich Man, The Rich Man and
Poor Lazarus, The Pharisee and the Toll Collector; even if it is true that
Jülicher was not the first to call the members of that category
'examples'; and even if it is true that Jülicher was not the first to impart
a definition of that category, it is true, nonetheless, that the treatment of
the example stories advanced in the revised edition of *Die Gleichnisreden Jesu* has exerted a powerful influence upon parable scholarship in
this century. And it is to Jülicher's treatment of the example stories
within the context of the most famous edition of *Die Gleichnisreden
Jesu* that attention is now directed.

Chapter 3

THE EXAMPLE STORIES ACCORDING TO *DIE GLEICHNISREDEN JESU*

> '...[A]ll four pieces of this class of example narratives have many rela-
> tions, and almost with equal right the title could be set above them all: τὸ
> ἐν ἀνθρώποις ὑψηλὸν βδέλυγμα ἐνώπιον τοῦ θεοῦ. With its warning
> against the excesses of sagacity and against the omniscience of an art
> which has at hand a solution for every riddle, it is also the suitable
> inscription underneath the attempt of an exposition of the already a thou-
> sand times exposited *Gleichnisreden Jesu*.'
>
> Adolf Jülicher,
> *Die Gleichnisreden Jesu*

This chapter begins with an ending: The conclusion to the second
volume of Jülicher's extensive examination of the parables of Jesus,
where Jülicher reaffirms his contention that the four narrative pieces in
the class he calls 'example narratives' share many affinities, is cited in
the epigraph. Jülicher may not have been the progenitor of the category
he designated as '*Beispielerzählung*', but he certainly was its popular-
izer. If participants in the debate over 'the problem of parables versus
examples' trace the origin of that problem to Jülicher's classification of
four parables as such, then before that debate is reviewed it is quite
appropriate that we should learn what Jülicher himself said about the
example narratives. A preview of how Jülicher approached the
Beispielerzählungen was provided in the preceding summary of his
formal definition, delimitation and description of that category in the
first edition of *Die Gleichnisreden Jesu*. As interesting and illuminating
as it may be, however, Jülicher's first treatment of the example narratives has not had a formative influence on modern parable research.

The purpose of this chapter, then, is to provide an account of
Jülicher's description and definition of the example narratives as given
in the revised edition of *Die Gleichnisreden Jesu*, and that purpose will
be accomplished in the following fashion. In order to guard against
misrepresentation, it is necessary to situate the category 'example

narrative' within its context in the classification of Jesus' parable speeches constructed by Jülicher. Therefore, a rather detailed exposition of the second chapter of *Die Gleichnisreden Jesu* must be provided, for it is there that Jülicher laid out his classification of the parable speeches of Jesus. It will become apparent that Jülicher proposed that tripartite classification as part of his understanding of the essence of Jesus' parable speeches. Furthermore, it will become obvious that for Jülicher the problem was not one of 'parables versus examples', but of 'parables versus allegories'. The entire first volume of *Die Gleichnisreden Jesu*, in fact, contains the record of Jülicher's solution to that problem as he conceived it. A deeper appreciation of Jülicher's formulation of the category 'example narrative' can be had by locating its place both within the classification scheme he proposed and within the overall argument he advanced in that first volume. A summary statement of the contours of Jülicher's argument will enable us to situate the example narratives within the context of *Die Gleichnisreden Jesu*.

A *Summary of* Die Gleichnisreden Jesu

Jülicher expresses the purpose of his enterprise in the first chapter, 'The Genuineness of the Parable Speeches of Jesus'; namely, '...to meet Jesus himself in his parables'.[1] One who would attempt such an under-taking, Jülicher candidly admits, is confronted with a substantial, though not insurmountable, problem at the start, for the parables of Jesus are found in sources—the synoptic gospels—that do not agree about the number, setting or wording of the parables themselves. Two approaches to that problem Jülicher deems equally unacceptable: the first simply assumes that the synoptists faithfully recorded verbatim Jesus' words as he actually spoke them; the second contends that the synoptists actually invented the words they recorded as Jesus' own.[2]

---

1.   Jülicher, *Die Gleichnisreden Jesu*, I, p. 11.

2.   A more acceptable position to Jülicher would be a synthesis of the two, one which recognizes that in the synoptic gospels there is an admixture of ἱστορία and ποίησις (see *Die Gleichnisreden Jesu*, I, p. 4). Jülicher's first chapter can be divided into two parts: in the first part (pp. 1-11), he addresses those who see too much ἱστορία in the Gospels, against whom he argues that 'the genuineness of the Gospel parables [*Parabeln*] is no absolute' (p. 11); in the second part (pp. 11-24), Jülicher addresses those who see too much ποίησις in the Gospels, arguing against their view that the synoptists fabricated the words they attribute to Jesus. He ends

Jülicher attempts to navigate a critical course between the Scylla of
hypocriticism and the Charybdis of hypercriticism by maintaining that
one should be neither excessively sanguine nor skeptical in weighing
the evidence appertaining to the genuineness of Jesus' parables.

Jülicher's critical course involves a crucial distinction: He stresses
that '...*the parables of the Gospels are not to be equated
unconditionally with the ones spoken by Jesus*' because the free activity
of the evangelists, patently evident when one compares the parables in
the synoptic gospels, obviates such an uncritical assumption.[3] Indeed,
as he states, '...the parables of the different Gospels exhibit distinctly
the character of the evangelists'.[4] Thus, in Jülicher's opinion, there can
no longer be an exegesis of the parables of Jesus without criticism; that
is, without a differentiation of the original from the addition.[5] He will
not concede, however, that the different renderings of the parables in
the parallel synoptic passages are evidence against their genuineness in
general; rather, those deviations are evidence that the synoptists transmitted the parabolic material out of a conservative historical interest.[6]
Striving to guard against both a superficially uncritical approach and a
severely critical approach to the parables, Jülicher posits:

> Thankfully, our enterprise—to meet Jesus himself in his parables
> [*Gleichnissen*]—is not hopeless. We find no reason to deny altogether
> the genuineness of the Gospel parables [*Parabeln*]; on the contrary, we
> see ourselves compelled to grant them a relative authenticity. Almost
> without exception, they have a genuine core going back to Jesus him-
> self.[7]

Nonetheless, throughout the entirety of *Die Gleichnisreden Jesu*
Jülicher insists that 'the parables of the Gospels' must be distinguished

this chapter by saying that 'only the self-willed can deny... [that] the Gospel parable speeches go back to Jesus himself' (p. 24).

3.   Jülicher, *Die Gleichnisreden Jesu*, I, p. 2; Jülicher's emphasis. He submits
several observations as evidence to support this claim (see pp. 2-7).

4.   Jülicher, *Die Gleichnisreden Jesu*, I, p. 7. Subsequent to his demonstration
that the synoptists altered the parables according to their tastes, Jülicher remarks:
'Still more important than all of this is the fact that the *Gleichnisse* of the different
Gospels exhibit distinctively the character of the evangelists' (p. 7). Jülicher
devotes attention to the characteristics of the parables as they appear in the
respective synoptic gospels (see pp. 183-202, esp. pp. 194-202).

5.   Jülicher, *Die Gleichnisreden Jesu*, I, p. 5.

6.   See Jülicher, *Die Gleichnisreden Jesu*, I, pp. 20-22.

7.   Jülicher, *Die Gleichnisreden Jesu*, I, p. 11.

from 'the parables of Jesus'.[8] Jülicher specifies the ramifications of this distinction in the chapters to follow; for now, in his view, it is sufficient to say that he does not approach the synoptic parables with exaggerated expectations, but with a good bias, because even if it can be shown that the synoptists had a false conception of the essence and purpose of Jesus' parable speeches, the parable speeches as found in the synoptics belong to the most secure and best transmitted of the traditions of Jesus' words that we possess. Behind the 'emended' shape of the synoptic parables, there shines through an archetype whose creator was Jesus himself.[9]

The next two chapters in *Die Gleichnisreden Jesu* are integrally related, for Jülicher contends that 'in a speech form the purpose must be knowable out of the essence'.[10] The urgent impetus behind his insistence that the parables of the Gospels must not be equated with the parables of Jesus, that they must be distinguished from each other, becomes apparent. Simply stated, Jülicher argues that the evangelists had a false conception of Jesus' parables (in Chapter 2, 'The Essence of the Parable Speeches of Jesus'), as well as a false conception of the purpose of Jesus' parables (in Chapter 3, 'The Purpose of the Parable Speeches of Jesus'). He describes the evangelists' theory of the essence of Jesus' parables in this way: According to the evangelists, Jesus' parables are in essence dark, obscure sayings which veil a deeper meaning and therefore require interpretation; in short, the evangelists conceive of Jesus' parables as allegories. Thus, Jülicher contends,

---

8.   On the first page of *Die Gleichnisreden Jesu*, Jülicher makes this distinction in his criticism of Göbel, who had written the (then) most recent work on the parables of Jesus, because Göbel promised to provide an exposition of the parables of *Jesus* ('Parabeln *Jesu*') but exposits only the parables of the *evangelists* ('Parabeln der *Evangelisten*'), and thus deceives his readers (Jülicher's emphasis). About this distinction Jülicher writes later: 'The misunderstanding of Jesus by the evangelists must be admitted, the *Parabeln* of the Gospels must be distinguished from the *Parabeln Jesu*, if both parts shall have their due: the break with any dogma of inspiration must be openly and unrestrictedly executed before we can hope to interpret justly both Jesus as well as the evangelists' (p. 194).

9.   Jülicher, *Die Gleichnisreden Jesu*, I, p. 24.

10.   Jülicher, *Die Gleichnisreden Jesu*, I, p. 118: '...bei einer Redeform muss der Zweck aus dem Wesen erkennbar sein'. Since a detailed exposition of Jülicher's chapter on 'The Essence of the Parable Speeches of Jesus' will soon be provided (pp. 81-127), I focus here on Jülicher's understanding of the purpose of Jesus' parable speeches.

according to the theory of the evangelists the purpose of Jesus' parables is to conceal their meaning, to hide the truth, and thus to bring about the obduracy of the masses.[11] If the evangelists misunderstood the essence of Jesus' parable speeches, it follows that they were mistaken about the purpose of his parable speeches.[12] Jülicher vehemently opposes the evangelists' theory about the essence and purpose of Jesus' parables and advocates that it be abandoned altogether.

Jülicher, in turn, puts forward his own theory about the essence and purpose of Jesus' parable speeches. He posits that the evangelists made a categorical error: *Die Gleichnisreden Jesu* do not partake of the essence of allegory, rather they partake of the essence of comparison (*Vergleichung*). Based upon his examination of Jesus' parable speeches, in the course of which he maintains that those parables admit of a clear understanding, Jülicher asks:

> ...[W]hat are the parables, the parables in the narrower sense—one and all—except a means of demonstration and conviction? What can they have intended, then, except *to demonstrate*, except to procure the σαφές of the high, divine truths, and *to win* souls over to them?[13]

Jülicher can agree with the evangelists that the parables of Jesus deal with the kingdom of God, but he rejects their notion that Jesus' parables are mysterious speech.[14] Repeatedly, Jülicher states that Jesus

11. Jülicher asserts that Mark created the parable chapter (Mk 4) in order to ameliorate the embarrassment caused by the desertion of Jesus by his followers, and thus to explain the obduracy of the masses; the other synoptists adopted this view more or less intact (see *Die Gleichnisreden Jesu*, I, pp. 120-37).

12. In a candid moment, Jülicher admits that the synoptists might reciprocate by rejecting his theory: 'The correct hermeneutical theory is inseparable from a resolute criticism; if I demand the concession that Jesus' parables have nothing to do with allegory, then I myself must concede that Jesus' parables are not present intact in the Gospels, and that the evangelists surely would have no more acknowledged my theory [than I theirs]' (*Die Gleichnisreden Jesu*, I, p. 193).

13. Jülicher, *Die Gleichnisreden Jesu*, I, pp. 118-19; Jülicher's emphasis: '...[W]as sind die Gleichnisse, die Parabeln samt und sonders als Veranschaulichungs- und Ueberführungsmittel? Was können sie denn gewollt, als *veranschaulichen*, als das σαφές der hohen Gotteswahrheiten besorgen und die Gemüter dafür *gewinnen*?'. Elsewhere, he contends that the 'summa lex of parabolical speech on all levels is vividness...' and that at this Jesus excelled above all others (pp. 157-58).

14. Jülicher (*Die Gleichnisreden Jesu*, I, pp. 119-48) takes issue not only with the evangelists, but also with his contemporaries who suggest that Jesus' parables

employed parables as a means of creating clarity, not as a means of obfuscating his meaning.[15] 'If Christ looked upon κηρύσσειν [proclaiming] and διδάσκειν [teaching], ζητεῖν [seeking] and εὑρίσκειν [finding] as his life-work, then he cannot have spoken in parables [*Parabeln*] with that intention—to come to be not understood by any of his hearers'.[16] Rather, according to Jülicher, Jesus employed parables in his speeches and sermons in order to heighten the clarity and persuasive power of his thoughts.[17] Jesus used the parables for the same general purpose as did other orators, '...namely, in order to demonstrate the unknown in the generally known, in order to lead upwards gently from the easy to the difficult'.[18] Jesus, however, made more specific use of the parables: '...the son of Galilee clothed his thoughts in the garb of his homeland and led his faithful followers with a sure hand from the known to the unknown, from the material world to the kingdom of heaven'.[19] The parables, then, are a means of teaching employed by the one who taught about the kingdom of God. It is within the context of his refutation of the evangelists' theory about the essence and purpose of Jesus' parable speeches that Jülicher issues his famous ultimatum:

> Either—or: Either solely the hardening [or 'obduracy'] purpose vis-à-vis the masses and also the reliability of the synoptists on this question, or an erroneous inference by them because of an error in the premises, and the same purpose which the parables usually [serve], as everyone feels, those [parables] of the Lord also serve. This either—or goes deep: Either the evangelists, or Jesus.[20]

conceal (to everyone), or that they conceal (to the masses) and reveal (to the disciples and the faithful).

15. Although Jülicher persistently argues in favor of *one* purpose for Jesus' parables (see *Die Gleichnisreden Jesu*, I, pp. 118, 137, 146), he allows that Jesus sometimes spoke in parables for other reasons: e.g. when he found it necessary to defend his honor, piety and life, and when he had need to attack the vanity, self-seeking and malice of his opponents (p. 145).

16. Jülicher, *Die Gleichnisreden Jesu*, I, p. 143.

17. Jülicher, *Die Gleichnisreden Jesu*, I, p. 146.

18. Jülicher, *Die Gleichnisreden Jesu*, I, p. 146. Here, Jülicher is arguing that it does not desecrate Jesus to suggest that he employed the same speech form as did the 'profane' orators and for the same reason as they did.

19. Jülicher, *Die Gleichnisreden Jesu*, I, p. 145. Prior to this statement, Jülicher holds forth against the views that Jesus spoke parables to bring about the judgment of God or to conceal the gospel among unbelievers; Jülicher's claim is that the parables flowed freely and spontaneously from Jesus' lips.

20. Jülicher, *Die Gleichnisreden Jesu*, I, p. 148.

Jülicher's choice is manifest in the title of his book.[21]

'The Value of the Parable Speeches of Jesus', the topic Jülicher addresses in his next chapter (4), arises from the relationship of the parables to their creator.[22] The parables comprise a significant portion of the words spoken by Jesus and preserved in the synoptic gospels.[23] The value of the parables for our knowledge of Jesus is not confined to their sheer quantity, rather the parables deserve careful scrutiny because 'they are an irreplaceable part of his teaching in which we see him deepest in the heart'.[24] The value of the parables, then, is difficult to overestimate:

> They are concerned with, in large part, the kingdom of heaven, this fundamental and main concept in Jesus' world of thoughts, which recently, then, is also moved into the center of the 'doctrine system' of Jesus; if the parables were missing to us, we would see only poorly from a different source how Christ had imagined the kingdom of God to himself.[25]

21. However, recall my remark earlier (p. 25) that a certain tension is evident in the subtitles of the first and second volumes of *Die Gleichnisreden Jesu*.

22. Jülicher begins his Chapter 4 by stating that we can speak of a relative value and an absolute value of Jesus' parables. A relative value might be claimed for Jesus' parables as products of world literature; these parables meet all the requirements of excellence with regard to the demands made of the speech form in the aesthetic-rhetorical sphere (*Die Gleichnisreden Jesu*, I, pp. 153-64)—indeed, Jesus is a 'master' and second to no one, his parables 'masterpieces' and second to none. (Jülicher bases this conclusion on his comparison of Jesus' parables with Jewish [Old Testament and rabbinic] parables and Buddhist parables [see pp. 165-82].) An absolute value is due Jesus' parables within the overall effectiveness of their speaker; thus, the absolute value of the parables of Jesus, upon which I have focused attention here, issues from the personality of their author (cf. p. 182).

23. Jülicher, *Die Gleichnisreden Jesu*, I, p. 148. Thus, to Jülicher, the value of the parables for our knowledge of Jesus is due first of all to their sheer number, for parables comprise a significant part of all of Jesus' words recorded in the synoptic gospels.

24. Jülicher, *Die Gleichnisreden Jesu*, I, pp. 148-49.

25. Jülicher, *Die Gleichnisreden Jesu*, I, p. 149. Jülicher explores further the intimate relationship between Jesus and his parables, suggesting that 'the new time is already there, everything is already prepared' in his parables. Moreover, although Jesus himself did not differentiate between his words and his work, what Jesus preached was salvation, not the savior. History made Jesus into the savior because for us his gospel is inseparable from his personality. In a striking phrase, Jülicher asserts, 'He became the redeemer...'(p. 152). It is but a short step from Jülicher's paragraph to Rudolf Bultmann's proposition that 'the proclaimer became the one proclaimed' (see 'The Primitive Christian Kerygma and the Historical Jesus', in

What Jesus taught and how he taught it are revealed most faithfully in his parables.[26] Still more important to Jülicher is this: '...we find before us Jesus himself alive in his words'.[27]

To the history of Jesus' parables Jülicher directs his full attention in the remaining chapters. That history, in his view, falls quite naturally into two unequal periods, which he designates as 'the record of the parable speeches of Jesus' and 'the exposition of the parable speeches of Jesus'. Although one period flows into the other, the border between the two became distinct at the moment when the synoptic gospels attained canonicity, for then the text was fixed and the early church, unlike the first generation of interpreters who could alter the text, had to make do with explanation or exegesis of the text.[28] Accordingly, the first period ('the record', *die Aufzeichnung*) is that in which the parables were being written down by the evangelists, when the possibility of altering the parables considerably still existed. The second period ('the exposition', *die Auslegung*) began after the synoptics were established as canonical and continues even to this day. Jülicher examines the history of Jesus' parables chronologically. In his fifth chapter, 'The Record of the Parable Speeches of Jesus', Jülicher's concern is to see how, in their various relations and from various points (that is, in the synoptics), Jesus' παραβολαί are viewed. His concern in Chapter 6, 'History of the Exposition of the Parable Speeches of Jesus', is evident in the chapter's title.

Jülicher, in his chapter on 'The Record of the Parable Speeches of Jesus', reinforces his earlier claim that the parables of the evangelists must not be considered as coterminous with the parables of Jesus. Because each evangelist narrated the parables as he thought best, Jülicher cannot regard the synoptists as 'helpless compilers'.[29] Based upon his comparison of the parables preserved in the multiple redactions, Jülicher thinks it possible to perceive two directions in which the parables of Jesus were reshaped. In one direction, the evangelists added color and detail to the parables, drew thicker lines and sharper contrasts in the parables; in brief, the evangelists expanded the parables, adding

---

Carl E. Braaten and Roy A. Harrisville [trans. and eds.], *The Historical Jesus and the Kerygmatic Christ* [Nashville: Abingdon Press, 1964], p. 30, cf. p. 38).

26. See Jülicher, *Die Gleichnisreden Jesu*, I, p. 150.
27. Jülicher, *Die Gleichnisreden Jesu*, I, p. 153.
28. Jülicher, *Die Gleichnisreden Jesu*, I, p. 183.
29. Jülicher, *Die Gleichnisreden Jesu*, I, p. 195.

to them and making them more elaborate.[30] In the other direction, the evangelists inserted into the parables features which seemed to recommend an allegorical interpretation, or they added allegorical interpretations directly to the parables (for instance, The Parable of the Sower).[31] An awareness of the tendencies of the evangelists in either direction provides criteria by which one may assess the genuineness or authenticity of the parable traditions.[32] Therefore, Jülicher considers it extremely important to grasp the literary peculiarities of each evangelist. Appropriately, then, he concludes this chapter by drawing a picture of each evangelist as 'parable narrator' in which he characterizes, in a general way, the renderings of the parables speeches of Jesus in each of the synoptic gospels.[33]

In his final chapter, Jülicher chronicles the approach to Jesus' parables that has prevailed since the writing of the Gospels. The 'History of the Exposition of the Parable Speeches of Jesus' is, in Jülicher's view, a history of the allegorizing interpretation of Jesus' parables. Only a

30. Jülicher refers to this direction as *ausmalende*, *Ausmalung* or *Ausmalen* (*Die Gleichnisreden Jesu*, I, pp. 183, 184, 188), and he provides an apt description of it (pp. 184-86). I find it difficult to translate these words into English because the literal meaning 'to paint' for *ausmalen* does not capture the nuance of 'to complete the painting' implied, it seems to me, by Jülicher.

31. This direction is referred to as *ausdeutende* (*Die Gleichnisreden Jesu*, I, p. 183), and sometimes as the more familiar *Allegorisierung* or *allegorisieren* (pp. 190-91). *Ausdeuten*, literally 'to interpret', is another word difficult to render in English. For Jülicher, *ausdeuten* seems to imply 'to complete the signification'. At any rate, this is where the two periods in the history of Jesus' παραβολαί overlap: The period of allegorizing Jesus' parables began in those accounts in which Jesus' parables are retold—that is, in the Gospels (p. 190).

32. Jülicher, *Die Gleichnisreden Jesu*, I, pp. 187-88. See, e.g., Jülicher's discussion of the natural inclination toward *die ausmalende* expansion, which leads him to conclude that whenever two or three parallel references confront us, 'the briefest almost always lies nearest to the authentic' (p. 188).

33. Jülicher, *Die Gleichnisreden Jesu*, I, pp. 194-202. In addition, Jülicher is concerned with the 'appealing task' of delineating the position of the individual evangelists in the gradually progressing process of the recording of the parables, which is, at the same time, a process of parable recreation (p. 194). Due to the enormous problems of determining the relations among the synoptic gospels and among their sources, Jülicher eschews that task in favor of giving a general impression of the characteristics of each synoptist as a *Gleichniserzähler*. The task of writing a history of the parables within the development of the synoptic tradition was even more appealing to one of Jülicher's students, Rudolf Bultmann.

few—John Maldonatus, John Calvin, M. Butzer, C.E. van Koetsveld and Bernhard Weiss—struggled, in varying degrees, to break with the allegorizing method of interpreting Jesus' parables and moved toward a more historically and critically sound method of exposition.[34] Jülicher situates his own work among that of these five men, unpretentiously claiming that if he has gone beyond them, he still does not feel that he laid out a newly broken ground by himself.

> Everything which I maintained has been maintained already by others; my task was merely to bring into relation the, in my opinion, sound insights of a few men with respect to our subject, to remove the vestiges of a more irrational tradition which were noticeable everywhere, to develop clearly—for the sake of the subject matter, in the strongest opposition to the hitherto prevailing theories—a uniform conception of Jesus' parables according to essence and purpose, and, finally, to produce evidence, through a careful exposition of the parabolic texts of our Gospels, that the representatives of the more recent conception are quite far removed from doing violence to the speeches of Jesus, rather they are disposed to help them to their right, to free them from all additions, even the most ancient.[35]

Jülicher closes the first volume of his study of *Die Gleichnisreden Jesu* by suggesting that without the fundamental distinction between the parables of Jesus and the parables of the evangelists, the anti-allegorical method of exposition will not become pervasive.[36] Thus, he continues the struggle against the allegorical method of interpretation under the banner '*simplex sigillum veri*'.[37]

'*The Essence of the Parable Speeches of Jesus*'

One of the most significant chapters in the first volume of *Die Gleich-*

---

34. On Maldonatus, Calvin and Butzer, see *Die Gleichnisreden Jesu*, I, pp. 259-77. Jülicher mentions van Koetsveld and Bernhard Weiss throughout the first volume, but see esp. pp. 226-29, 314-20.

35. Jülicher, *Die Gleichnisreden Jesu*, I, p. 320.

36. Jülicher, *Die Gleichnisreden Jesu*, I, p. 322. Jülicher ends this volume as he began it—insisting that the parables of Jesus be differentiated from the parables of the evangelists.

37. Jülicher, *Die Gleichnisreden Jesu*, I, p. 322: 'a simple sign of truth'. Jülicher states that he will be satisfied with the effects of his work if allegorists of all stripes are routed and if, in all theological camps, only a retreat to an interpretation of the main points of the parables is sanctioned (even if these 'main points' are strongly influenced by dogmatic tastes).

nisreden Jesu, perhaps in the history of parable scholarship, is the second, which is entitled 'Das Wesen der Gleichnisreden Jesu'. It is here that Jülicher vigorously argues that Jesus' παραβολαί are not in essence allegories, and it is here that he lays out his classification of Jesus' parable speeches. We will want to proceed deliberately through Jülicher's chapter for the obvious reason that he here furnishes his understanding of the nature of Jesus' parable speeches, distinguishing among them three sorts of παραβολαί. Special attention must be given to Jülicher's description of a particular type of *Gleichnisreden Jesu*— the *Beispielerzählung*, the category of interest in this study. A careful reading of Jülicher's characterization of the example narratives will indicate that at least on one point he has been misunderstood by some American parable scholars: Nowhere does he claim that a *Beispielerzählung* is not a παραβολή. Jülicher's definition of the example narrative occurs near the end of his second chapter, but the salient points of his argument leading up to that definition ought to be noted.[38]

The Scope of Jesus' παραβολαί
Jülicher begins his investigation of the essence of Jesus' parables with an attempt to establish the extent of the material to be treated. Observing that all three synoptists depict Jesus as having a predilection for parable speech (*Parabelrede*), and that all three synoptists provide definite examples of this manner of speaking or teaching (*Rede-[Lehr-]weise*) employed by Jesus, Jülicher calculates the number of parables explicitly labelled παραβολή, excluding parallels, in the synoptic gospels to be 20.[39] However, Jülicher reasons, since the synoptists did not overtly identify each and every parable spoken by Jesus as παραβολή, the undisputed list of parables can be supplemented with other sayings not identified by the word παραβολή, but which are in fact parables. For instance, if Luke identified the saying (*Wort*) of The New Patches (5.36) as a παραβολή, then the saying (*Wort*) of The New Wine (5.37-39) must be recognized as a παραβολή. If Luke considered the narrative (*Erzählung*) of The Lost Sheep (15.3) as a parable (*Parabel*), then he did not think otherwise about The Lost Penny (15.8-10) and The Lost Son (15.11-32). Even The Unjust Householder

38. The subheadings that appear in this chapter are my own; Jülicher himself provides no headings or subtitles in any of his chapters.
39. For the specifics of Jülicher's algorithm, see *Die Gleichnisreden Jesu*, I, pp. 25-26.

(16.1-8) and The Rich Man and Poor Lazarus (16.19-31) belong in the same category.[40] Thus, an expanded list of synoptic parables would include about 60.[41] Nonetheless, Jülicher insists that the selection of material to be considered should not be made according to a preconceived notion of what a parable (*Parabel*) is, but according to the claims of the text.[42] Further, he asserts that we should refrain from all modern definitions of παραβολή and let the sources themselves determine that definition.

A Preliminary Definition of παραβολή
Jülicher admits that the sources in which we find Jesus' parable speeches nowhere define παραβολή, but he contends that the name παραβολή is not so opaque. He begins his assay of παραβολή by giving its etymology:

> παραβολή is derived from παραβάλλειν, and that means to throw alongside, to put next to (especially similar things for the purpose of comparison), interchanged with ὁμοιοῦν and συγκρίνειν, so that it can be expected that παραβολή, when applied to a speech form, will designate such that has been produced by means of a comparison of two quantities.[43]

40. Jülicher, *Die Gleichnisreden Jesu*, I, p. 27. Note that Jülicher mentions The Rich Man and Poor Lazarus in conjunction with other *Parabeln*.
41. Jülicher, *Die Gleichnisreden Jesu*, I, p. 27. Jülicher assesses the lists of parables proposed by his contemporaries—some of whom, he feels, include too few; others too many—and concludes that van Koetsveld's number of 79 is correct. Those who include more than that confuse altogether 'Parabel und bildliche Ausdruckswcisc' (p. 28).
42. Jülicher critiques his contemporaries (Göbel, D.T.K. Drummond, G.C. Diffenbach) whose concepts of 'parable' have been determined by ecclesiastical or religious usage of the term (*Die Gleichnisreden Jesu*, I, pp. 29-30). He contends that in the German literature some things are considered a parable (*Parabel*) that do not fit the New Testament parables (*Parabeln*). In that literature, a sensed distinction is made between *Gleichnis* and *Parabel*. 'By "Parabel" they think about, in all circumstances, a fictitious narrative which conceals behind its simple words a deeper sense, while they expect nothing from the "Gleichnis"; however, what we today understand under "Parabel", in German or other modern languages, certainly cannot be foisted authoritatively upon the New Testament parable concept—not now, not ever' (pp. 30-31).
43. Jülicher, *Die Gleichnisreden Jesu*, I, p. 31: 'παραβολή ist abgeleitet von παραβάλλειν, und das bedeutet nebenwerfen, danebenlegen (besonders Gleichartiges zum Zweck der Vergleichung), wechselt mit ὁμοιοῦν und συγκρίνειν, sodass

Jülicher notes that the synoptists employ the word παραβολή as an established coinage; it is a word which for centuries belonged to the Greek language and had a fixed meaning. Nothing, then, justifies the conclusion that the synoptists gave a new conception of παραβολή or that they used the word for an entirely new speech form that 'was exclusively peculiar to the Lord'.[44] Since the synoptists do not give the faintest hint that the παραβολή would be a foreign or new teaching form to the disciples—rather they call attention to the fact that the disciples recognize and describe Jesus as speaking or teaching in parables—Jülicher concludes that the παραβολή as spoken by Jesus was readily recognizable to his hearers.[45] This compels Jülicher to raise the question: 'Now from where are the disciples able to know such a teaching method except from their life experience or from the Old Testament?'[46] Thus, he proceeds to the Jewish scripture tradition in order to determine whether the manner of teaching in parables one finds there can shed light on Jesus' parables.

sich erwarten lässt, παραβολή werde, wenn auf eine Redeform angewandt, eine solche bezeichnen, die durch Vergleichung zweier Grössen entstanden ist'.

44. Jülicher, *Die Gleichnisreden Jesu*, I, p. 31. In order to argue against the view that Jesus' parables were an utterly new and unique teaching form, Jülicher quotes F.L. Steinmeyer, who holds that view. Jülicher goes on to add that the synoptists' use of the word παραβολή 'shows that they by no means caught sight of a theophany in every *Parabel* as such' (p. 32). Later, he cautions that there should be no excessive zeal in the claims made for Jesus' parables, e.g. that his parables are 'masterpieces of popular poetry' (p. 155). Perceptively, Jülicher notes that 'it is common among theological and aesthetic writers to praise the *Parabeln Jesu* as models. The majority of what one reads about them is panegyric...' (p. 153). Jülicher is not threatened by claims that Jesus' parables are not great works of art; and he views the demand that the parable must be the domain of the son of God as a modern development (p. 164). Although Jülicher states that Jesus did not invent the parable as an entirely new genre, which is evident in the fact that we encounter parables in other literatures, he does defend Jesus' originality both in the manner in which he employed the parable speech form and the content of those parables (cf. pp. 164-81). While he would demand a more limited praise for Jesus' parables (p. 155), Jülicher himself—in his desire to argue that Jesus neither copied someone's model nor stole anyone's material—elevates Jesus' parables above all others, and thus joins in the panegyric (see p. 182).

45. Jülicher, *Die Gleichnisreden Jesu*, I, pp. 31-32.

46. Jülicher, *Die Gleichnisreden Jesu*, I, p. 32.

The Antecedents of Jesus' παραβολαί

According to Jülicher, the Greek translation of the Jewish scriptures, the Septuagint (LXX), is the main document 'in Hellenism' that can illuminate the New Testament concept of parable (*Parabelbegriff*).[47] It is apparent to him that the synoptists or their sources intended with a Greek word, παραβολή, to render an Aramaic or Hebrew word which perhaps Jesus and his associates already used to describe the conspicuous formal aspect of his speeches.[48] The Greek word παραβολή corresponds to the Hebrew word משל (*mashal*) throughout most of the LXX.[49] In dialogue with his contemporaries, Jülicher then attempts to ascertain the meaning of the Hebrew משל and to discern the characteristic features of that form of speech.[50] While Jülicher's discussion is insightful, his argument at times intricate, only his conclusions will be summarized here.[51]

Given the multifarious types of material identified as משל, Jülicher is able to discover a certain unity among the *meshalim* only when the notion of comparison, or similarity, constitutes the basis of the word.[52]

47. Jülicher, *Die Gleichnisreden Jesu*, I, p. 33.

48. On the basis of Mt. 13.35 (where Ps. 78.2 is quoted), Jülicher contends that the first evangelist, at least, considered the *Parabeln Jesu* to be identical in form to the παραβολαί of the LXX (see *Die Gleichnisreden Jesu*, I, pp. 32-33). He adds: 'Consequently, the evangelists intended to designate Jesus' "Gleichnisreden" as *meshalim*, we have no basis to take their will as arbitrary...' (p. 33).

49. Jülicher is aware of exceptions where other Greek words are used to translate משל, but he regards them as insignificant given the preponderant number of cases in which משל is replaced with παραβολή (*Die Gleichnisreden Jesu*, I, p. 33). He gives attention to Hebrew terms almost synonymous with משל, as well as to the Greek words used to render those terms (see pp. 33-35).

50. Jülicher, *Die Gleichnisreden Jesu*, I, pp. 34-35; see especially his critique of F. Delitzsch.

51. Jülicher's expertise in the Jewish scriptures should not be underrated; his dissertation was, after all, an investigation of the sources of Exod. 1.1–7.7. For bibliographical information, as well as a description of Jülicher's educational formation, see Klauck, 'Adolf Jülicher', pp. 100-102.

52. Jülicher, *Die Gleichnisreden Jesu*, I, p. 36. He supports this claim with his observation that even when the LXX employs words other than παραβολή to translate משל, the notion of comparison remains. Why? 'The comparative כ played a leading role in that...' According to Jülicher, proverbs, people, even allegories, are correctly called a משל in the Jewish scriptures (see pp. 36-37).

Accordingly, משל would be a speech form which is brought about by juxtaposition of the alike, by comparison, or is based thereupon.[53]

Although neither the length nor the brevity of the saying makes the *mashal*, the parallelism of members in a *mashal* indicates such a juxtaposition of the similar or alike. However, Jülicher emphasizes that in the Jewish scriptures the משל is always a speech that contains a comparison or provokes one,[54] and he stresses that a משל is a comparative *speech* and not a *part* of speech (for instance, a metaphor).[55] Finally, Jülicher contends that to the Hebrew people the *mashal* is considered a product of Wisdom, but not necessarily prophetic Wisdom alone because the present and past shape the content of a *mashal* more frequently than does the future.[56]

Having examined the *mashal* in the Jewish scriptures, Jülicher considers it necessary to investigate the apocryphal literature in order to discern possible influences upon the New Testament understanding of the παραβολή. Based upon a brief treatment of the παραβολαί in Sirach and the Apocalypse of Enoch, Jülicher states that an interesting development has taken place: The concept of παραβολή is more closely identified with the riddles spoken by wise men. Obscurity and difficulty are now deemed essential to the concept of παραβολή, so much so that the epigones no longer search for all sorts of deep mysteries in the parables as enigma, but transfer the essence of Wisdom to unintelligibility.[57] This, he concludes, is the prevailing view of the 'Maschal-Parabel' in Hellenistic Judaism.

Jülicher emphasizes, nevertheless, that this Hellenistic Jewish view

53. Jülicher, *Die Gleichnisreden Jesu*, I, p. 36: 'Demnach wäre משל eine Redeform, die durch Nebeneinanderstellung von Gleichem, durch Vergleichung zu Stande kommt oder darauf beruht'.

54. See Jülicher, *Die Gleichnisreden Jesu*, I, p. 37.

55. Jülicher, *Die Gleichnisreden Jesu*, I, p. 38: 'Doch ich betone ausdrücklich: eine vergleichende *Rede* ist der Maschal: ein Rede*teil*, eine Metapher z.B. könnte nicht so heissen, immer sind die Meschalim vollständige Sätze; Gedanken, nicht blosse Begriffe' (Jülicher's emphasis). He makes this point after his discussion of the relationship between the *mashal* and the riddle, in which he states that any riddle might arise from a comparison, but that riddles have a closer relationship to metaphor.

56. Jülicher, *Die Gleichnisreden Jesu*, I, p. 38.

57. Jülicher locates this development at a discrete moment; see *Die Gleichnisreden Jesu*, I, pp. 39-40. The school of the scribes, according to Jülicher, monopolized Wisdom for themselves at that time.

of the 'Maschal-Parabel' cannot predetermine the view which Jesus attached to the word.[58] Still, Jülicher posits that the concept of 'Maschal-Parabel' prevalent in Hellenistic Judaism did influence the tradents of Jesus' παραβολαί: They simply viewed Jesus' parables through the then current conception of משל or παραβολή. As with those who propagated the oral traditions of Jesus' parables, even so with the evangelists:

> Unfortunately, scarcely a doubt remains that the evangelists—and already their sources—confused the παραβολή of Hellenistic scribal learning, as we know it from Sirach, the twin sister of αἴνιγμα, with the mashal of scripture in all its breadth and naturalness, which at the same time had been the mashal of Jesus. Or, more carefully expressed, their parable concept, insofar as they have one at all, is just as obviously the one of Jewish-Hellenistic literature. They understood under παραβολή not simply *a comparative speech*, rather *one which*, in addition, *is obscure*, which requires interpretation.[59]

The Evangelists' Conception of Jesus' παραβολαί

At this point, Jülicher pauses to give scrupulous attention to the evangelists' conception of the essence of the παραβολή. As he stated at the outset, Jülicher thinks it crucial to distinguish between the parables of Jesus and the parables of the evangelists; accordingly, the parables of the Gospels must not be equated unconditionally with the parables

58. Jülicher, *Die Gleichnisreden Jesu*, I, p. 40. Jülicher goes on to argue that Jesus' concept of the word παραβολή did not correspond to that of the scribes; rather, he had a clearer and broader conception of the משל than they, for Jesus did not seek Wisdom in unclarity (pp. 40-41).

59. Jülicher, *Die Gleichnisreden Jesu*, I, p. 42; Jülicher's emphasis: 'Leider bleibt kaum ein Zweifel übrig, dass die Evangelisten—und schon ihre Quellen—die παραβολή der hellenistischen Schriftgelehrsamkeit, wie wir sie aus Sirach kennen, die Zwillingsschwester des αἴνιγμα, mit dem Maschal der Schrift in all seiner Weite und Natürlichkeit, der zugleich der Maschal Jesu gewesen sein wird, verwechselt haben. Oder, vorsichtiger ausgedrückt, ihr Parabelbegriff, soweit sie überhaupt einen haben, ist wie selbstverständlich der der jüdisch-hellenistischen Litteratur. Sie verstehen unter παραβολή nicht blos *eine vergleichende Rede*, sondern *eine, die* ausserdem *dunkel ist*, der Deutung bedarf'. Jülicher is not sure that the evangelists were aware that their understanding of παραβολή differed from Jesus' conception and use of the *mashal*; if they were, they did not call attention to it for the benefit of their readers. As 'naïve writers' are wont to do, the evangelists molded the stuff (material), Jesus' parable speeches, according to their judgment.

spoken by Jesus.[60] The rationale underlying this position will now become clear: Jülicher argues that three moments constitute the evangelists' understanding of παραβολή. The first two he will accept as constitutive of Jesus' παραβολαί as well, but the third he will roundly reject, contending that in this regard the evangelists have misunderstood the essence of Jesus' parable speeches. Having claimed that the evangelists' conception of παραβολή is that of Jewish-Hellenistic literature, one which views the parable not simply as a comparative speech, but as an obscure speech that requires interpretation, Jülicher continues:

> Correspondingly, three moments constitute their παραβολή; it must be *a complete thought*, a speech *of comparative character*, and, finally, one which veils *a deeper sense*.[61]

The first moment of the evangelists' conception of παραβολή is, according to Jülicher, consonant with that of Jesus. 'Indisputably', Jülicher states, 'every παραβολή of Jesus is a rounded, thoroughly independent whole'.[62] Although 'roundedness does not mean length', Jülicher is adamant that 'nowhere is a sentence *part* called "a parabolical or pictorial element" by the evangelists'.[63] Thus, again, Jülicher finds reason to exclude metaphor from among Jesus' παραβολαί.[64]

Jülicher states that the second moment of the evangelists' conception of παραβολή, its comparative character, is also in accord with Jesus'.[65] He cites numerous instances where the synoptists ceremoniously introduce Jesus' parables with ὁμοιοῦν or ὅμοιος; indeed, 'Luke declares the ὅμοιον to be the root of the parable [*Parabel*]'.[66] Elsewhere in the synoptic gospels, instead of ὅμοιος we find οὕτως ὡς, ὡς, ὥσπερ, οὕτως καί or merely καί.[67] The comparative character of the parable

---

60. See above, p. 74 n. 8; cf. *Die Gleichnisreden Jesu*, I, p. 194.

61. Jülicher, *Die Gleichnisreden Jesu*, I, p. 42; Jülicher's emphasis: 'Drei Momente konstituieren demgemäss ihre παραβολή, *ein vollständiger Gedanke* muss es sein, ein Rede *von vergleichendem Charakter*, und endlich eine, die *tieferen Sinn* verhüllt'.

62. Jülicher, *Die Gleichnisreden Jesu*, I, p. 42.

63. Jülicher, *Die Gleichnisreden Jesu*, I, p. 42; Jülicher's emphasis.

64. Therefore, in Jülicher's opinion, Göbel, Stockmeyer and G. Volkmar erred in including metaphors among Jesus' παραβολαί (*Die Gleichnisreden Jesu*, I, p. 43).

65. Jülicher, *Die Gleichnisreden Jesu*, I, p. 43: 'Nicht minder fest steht für alle παραβολαί Jesu das zweite, der vergleichende Charakter'.

66. Jülicher, *Die Gleichnisreden Jesu*, I, p. 43.

67. Jülicher approvingly cites Clement of Alexandria, who refers to the particle

does not rest solely upon the appearance of these narrative introductions. According to Jülicher,

> Where, in the Gospels, perchance all these instructions for how to com-
> pare are missing, there the context urges the reader to notice a compari-
> son as having been executed or to undertake the comparison himself.[68]

Overt in some parables, less so in others, the comparative character of
the παραβολή is never missing entirely.[69]

Jülicher posits that the third moment of the evangelists' conception
of παραβολή, its secretiveness, represents a misunderstanding of the
essence of Jesus' parables. To the synoptists, in Jülicher's opinion, the
παραβολαί are opaque and furtive sayings that conceal a deeper
meaning, much like the παροιμία in the Gospel of John.[70] Thus, in
order to be understood, the παραβολή requires interpretation; if it is
not interpreted properly—and by one with the proper insight—the
παραβολή remains a mystery, a riddle, an enigma. To the synoptists,
the parables succeed only on the basis of a new hearing, an interpreta-

---

ὡς as a παραβολῆς δηλωτικόν (*Die Gleichnisreden Jesu*, I, p. 43).

68. Jülicher, *Die Gleichnisreden Jesu*, I, p. 43: 'Denn wo in den Evangelien
etwa alle diese Anleitungen zum Vergleichen fehlen, da hält doch der Zussamenhang den Leser an, eine Vergleichung als vollzogen zu bemerken oder diese
Vergleichung selber vorzunehmen'.

69. Jülicher, *Die Gleichnisreden Jesu*, I, p. 44. Jülicher takes issue with alleged
exceptions, proposed by Göbel and Stockmeyer, where the comparative character
of the parable is said to be lacking. His defense of The Foolish Rich Man as
exhibiting a comparative character is interesting from the point of view of this
study. Jülicher claims that even if the merry-making rich man, to whom Lk. 12.16-
20 is addressed, is not exactly portrayed photographically in the story, still a figure
is held up to the readers, to whom they have good reason to compare their attitude
and views. We will return to this later (see below, pp. 123-27).

70. Here, Jülicher makes a surprising and curious, though revealing, move in
his argument. Whereas in his consideration of the first two moments of the synoptists' conception of the παραβολαί Jülicher treats only the synoptic gospels, he now
appeals to the Gospel of John to adduce evidence in support of his claim that the
synoptists view Jesus' παραβολαί as veiled speeches that conceal deeper truths. He
surmises '...John designated with παρομία = Mashal what his predecessors designated with παραβολή = Mashal' (*Die Gleichnisreden Jesu*, I, p. 44). He states, furthermore: 'John's view differs...little from the synoptists' view of the *Parabeln*'
(p. 45). He maintains that Jn 10.6 and 16.25, 29 correspond to Mk 4.13. In the
main, the oldest and the youngest evangelists agree that in order to be understood
the *Parabeln* and the *paroimiai* of Jesus require a solution (p. 46). The first and the
third evangelists hold to the same opinion since they simply copied Mark.

tion (λύσις). The Parable of the Sower in each of the synoptic gospels (Mk 4; Mt. 13; Lk. 8) remains obscure, mysterious and difficult to understand without its interpretation. Although that parable apparently deals with a farmhand and the conditions of sowing, the true subject of the parable is the mystery of the kingdom, the mystery being what kind of reception the word of God finds. Thus, 'the seed' is not really 'seed' but, for those with insight, 'the word'; 'the seed which fell on the road' are those hearers of the word who immediately afterward have the word taken away from them by Satan; 'the seed sown on rocky soil' are those hearers who receive the word but who, in tribulation and persecution, turn their backs on the word; and so forth.[71] On the basis of his consideration of this parable, Jülicher concludes:

> We now know why the *Parabeln* are so obscure and 'require interpretation': because all the main concepts in them, instead of their ordinary meaning, are intended to be understood in an entirely different sense because the hearer, in order to attain σύνεσις, must insert in place of the ἀκουόμενα other concepts (νοούμενα) indeed somehow similar, but pertaining to another field; which field that would be and which concepts must be discovered by him—until then the *Parabel* is a riddle...As the evangelists conceive of the *Parabel*, it is a *speech unit* whose essential component *conceals* remote and lofty, recumbent topics behind familiar words, however topics which in the *simile* with its covering prove themselves as resembling the same.[72]

Although Jülicher acknowledges that the three constitutive moments of the synoptists' parable concept are compatible in theory,[73] he will not concede that the third moment, the putative secretiveness of the παραβολή, has anything to do with Jesus' parables in reality. He states emphatically:

> As far as I see, we have no choice but to pronounce the evangelists' sense and understanding of the essence of Jesus' parables to be a misunderstanding. The distinction can be formulated, in a word, thus:

71. See Jülicher, *Die Gleichnisreden Jesu*, I, pp. 46-47. Soon (p. 50) Jülicher contends that although the evangelists did not employ the name ἀλληγορία, they treated the παραβολαί as a 'Hellenistic theologian' treated allegories (e.g. in Mt. 13.37 the field is the world, and so on).

72. Jülicher, *Die Gleichnisreden Jesu*, I, pp. 47-48; Jülicher's emphasis. He does not suggest that the relationship is arbitrary; rather, '...the λαλούμενον is always comparable with its νοούμενον...'

73. See Jülicher, *Die Gleichnisreden Jesu*, I, p. 48.

> *According to the theory of the evangelists, the* παραβολαί *are allegories,*
> *therefore non-actual speech that, to a certain extent, require translation;*
> *in reality they are—or they were before the hand of a zealous revisor*
> *came upon them—quite various things indeed: parables, fables, example*
> *narratives, but always actual speech.*[74]

The defense of this thesis occupies Jülicher's attention for the remainder of the chapter.[75]

Two Types of Pictorial Speech: Allegory and Parable
In substantiating his thesis, Jülicher decides to forgo, as much as possible, the use of technical terms drawn from rhetoric;[76] but since his is a rhetorical classification of the parables, some rhetorical terms are necessary. Jülicher declares that he will not employ modern definitions of

---

74. Jülicher, *Die Gleichnisreden Jesu*, I, p. 49; Jülicher's emphasis: 'Soviel ich sehe, können wir nicht umhin, den Sinn und Verstand der Evangelisten vom Wesen der Parabeln Jesu für Missverstand zu erklären. Der Unterschied lässt sich mit einem Worte so formulieren: *Nach der Theorie der Evangelisten sind die* παραβολαί *Allegorien, also uneigentliche, gewissermassen der Uebersetzung bedürftige Rede, in Wirklichkeit sind sie—resp. waren sie, ehe die Hand eifriger Ueberarbeiter an sie kam—recht Verschiedenes zwar, Gleichnisse, Fabeln, Beispielerzählungen, aber immer eigentliche Rede'*. The translation of the antithetical *eigentlich* and *uneigentlich* into English presents a problem. Literally, *eigentlich* means 'actual', 'proper' or 'real'; thus, *uneigentlich* means 'non-actual', 'non-proper' or 'non-real'. I retain 'actual' and 'non-actual' as the primary meanings of this pair because other words can be used to express 'proper' and 'real', and their opposites, in German. Since it can be assumed that Jülicher knew the word for 'literal', I prefer not to translate *eigentliche Rede* as 'literal speech' and *uneigentliche Rede* as 'non-literal [i.e. figurative] speech'—although, certainly, this connotation obtains here—or, as some have done, 'direct speech' and 'indirect speech', for there are other phrases in German that indicate these more precisely. John W. Sider, however, argues in favor of translating this tandem as 'literal' and 'figurative' because of the confusion that has arisen among many scholars who understand these words to mean 'authentic' and 'inauthentic'; see *Interpreting the Parables: A Hermeneutical Guide to their Meaning* (Grand Rapids: Zondervan, 1995), pp. 247-50.

75. Crossan reverses Jülicher's claim that the παραβολαί are 'various things' (*Verschiedenes*); see below, pp. 168-69.

76. Jülicher, *Die Gleichnisreden Jesu*, I, p. 49. Jülicher does so in order to avoid confusion. He thinks that his contemporaries misunderstood his position, as advanced in the first edition of *Die Gleichnisreden Jesu*, because he used too many technical rhetorical terms; see his responses to G. Gerber and G. Runze (pp. 49-50).

rhetorical concepts, rather he will appeal to the ancient usage and understanding of rhetorical terms.[77]

Because he wants to take part in the struggle against the allegorizing exposition of Jesus' parables, Jülicher's main concern now is to circumscribe precisely the meaning of the word 'allegory'.[78] He writes:

> ἀλληγορεῖν is ἑτέρως νοεῖν, is to understand in other than the actual sense, ἀλληγορεῖσθαι is to be subject to such a *different* understanding or to provoke it...ἀλληγορία is the object of such an explanation.[79]

The constitutive element in the concept of allegory is this: ἄλλο λέγον τὸ γράμμα καὶ ἄλλο τὸ νόημα. Here, Jülicher is careful not to equate allegory with metaphor.[80] Appealing to Cicero, Jülicher restricts the concept of allegory to a 'form composed of metaphors';[81] that is, the rudiment of allegory is the metaphor. He continues:

77. Jülicher, *Die Gleichnisreden Jesu*, I, p. 50.

78. Jülicher, *Die Gleichnisreden Jesu*, I, p. 50. Jülicher's bellicose language belies his passionate disdain of the allegorical interpretation of Jesus' parables: 'The sense of the word "Allegorie" must above all be circumscribed precisely because it is the battle against the allegorizing exposition [*allegorisierende Auslegung*] of Jesus' "Parabeln" which I would like to take part in with this work, a battle which these past several generations have waged with varying degrees of energy. One must know the enemy if one wishes to annihilate him'. Here, Jülicher tacitly equates 'Allegorie' and 'allegorisierende Auslegung'; his assumption seems to be that if he can prove that the parables of Jesus are *not* allegories, then they ought not be interpreted allegorically. As Klauck points out (*Allegorie und Allegorese*, pp. 4-12), Jülicher fails to distinguish properly between *Allegorie* and *Allegorese*.

79. Jülicher, *Die Gleichnisreden Jesu*, I, p. 51: 'ἀλληγορεῖν ist ἑτέρως νοεῖν, in einem andern als dem eigentlichen Sinn verstehen, ἀλληγορεῖσθαι solchem *andern* Verständnis unterliegen oder es herausfordern... ἀλληγορία ist das Objekt solcher Erklärung'. Two subtle shifts—from the active voice to the passive voice of the Greek verb ἀλληγορεῖν, and from the verb form to the noun form ἀλληγορία— make explicit Jülicher's equation of *Allegorie* and *Allegorese*.

80. Suidas, according to Jülicher, does so in his definition (*Die Gleichnisreden Jesu*, I, p. 51).

81. Jülicher, *Die Gleichnisreden Jesu*, I, p. 51. Jülicher regards a letter written by Hieronymous, and interpreted by Augustine, as the model example of what he means by 'allegory'. That letter contains the three moments which, according to Jülicher's representation of the evangelists' conception, are essential to Jesus' παραβολαί. Thus, Jülicher reasons, if we follow the evangelists' prescription, we would have to interpret Jesus' παραβολαί like Augustine interpreted the letter written by Hieronymous.

> A metaphor is a word that must be replaced by another one similar to it, and with that the reader grasps completely the context in which he finds the metaphor; a metaphor is formed so that a concept is not produced in the form of a word circulating for it, rather in the form of another word only related to the represented concept.[82]

At this point, Jülicher arrives at a crucial moment in his extended argument about the essence of Jesus' parable speeches. While Jülicher acknowledges that 'the metaphor is the base-form of the "pictorial" manner of speech in the full sense', he adds immediately that 'there is also, of course, a broader sense of pictorial speech'.[83] His intent is to differentiate two types of pictorial speech: One type of pictorial speech, the allegory, has its roots in metaphor and is that in which the words do not mean in their literal sense; another type of pictorial speech, the parable (specifically, Jesus' parable), has its roots in simile and is that in which the words do mean in their literal sense. Jülicher's first step, then, is to make an essential distinction between metaphor and simile, and he strives to do so by appealing to Aristotle's *Rhetoric*.

> What Aristotle in his *Rhetoric* called specifically the image (ἡ εἰκών) is essentially—to be sure, he said μικρόν (*Rhet.* 3.4)—distinguished from the metaphor. We designate this 'image' best as *simile*.[84]

82. Jülicher, *Die Gleichnisreden Jesu*, I, p. 52: 'Eine Metapher ist ein Wort, das durch ein andres ihm ähnliches ersetzt werden muss, damit der Leser den Zussamenhang, in dem er die Metapher findet, ganz erfasse; man bildet eine Metapher, indem man einen Begriff nicht in Gestalt des für ihn kursierenden Wortes vorführt, sondern in Gestalt eines andern, nur einen verwandten Begriff darstellenden Wortes'.

83. Jülicher, *Die Gleichnisreden Jesu*, I, p. 52. The nuance of Jülicher's argument is lost in translation: 'Die Metapher ist die Grundform der in vollem Sinn "bildlichen" Redeweise. Es giebt nämlich auch einen weiteren Sinn von bildlicher Rede...' Observe below that Jülicher renames Aristotle's 'Bild' as 'Vergleichung'. It is interesting, if not a bit ironic, that Jülicher marginalizes metaphor in his definition of parable, whereas many modern parable scholars choose to marginalize simile in their definition of parable (see, e.g., Funk, *Language, Hermeneutic, and Word of God*, p. 136).

84. Jülicher, *Die Gleichnisreden Jesu*, I, p. 52; Jülicher's emphasis. I translate 'Vergleichung' here as 'simile' because it is apparent that Jülicher refers to a technical rhetorical term known in English by that name. However, I do not rule out the meaning 'comparison' for 'Vergleichung' since Jülicher does use 'Vergleich' elsewhere when referring to 'simile'. The German original reads: 'Was ARISTOTELES in seiner Rhetorik speziell das Bild (ἡ εἰκών) nennt, ist von der Metapher wesentlich—er sagt zwar Rhet. III 4 μικρόν—unterschieden. Wir

Jülicher cites the well-known samples of a simile and a metaphor produced by Aristotle: An εἰκών is when one says of Achilles ὡς δὲ λέων
ἐπόρουσε [he rushed forth like a lion]; a metaphor is when one says
with reference to Achilles λέων ἐπόρουσε [a lion rushed forth].
According to Jülicher, Aristotle makes two main points about simile
and metaphor: Although the simile and metaphor share in common the
ὅμοιον, they differ in that 'the simile [*Vergleichung*] remains absolutely on the soil of actual speech [*eigentlichen Rede*], whereas the
metaphor forms the fundamental element of non-actual speech
[*uneigentlicher Rede*]'.[85] Thus, in the simile 'Achilles rushed forth like
a lion' the words mean literally what they say, but in the metaphor 'a
lion rushed forth' the words do not mean literally because by a
process of transference (that is, one must think something like 'both
Achilles and a lion are brave') Achilles is called a lion, and therefore
the metaphor must be translated as 'the courageous Achilles rushed
forth'.[86] Jülicher explicates the difference between simile and metaphor
in this way:

> In the εἰκών something similar is moved beside (παραβάλλεται) the
> subject matter or person about whom the speech is in order to animate
> the perception or to guide correctly the perception of the hearer; in the
> μεταφορά the subject matter or person about whom the speech is disap-
> pears in the expression behind something similar that appears in its
> place: through a thought-process, if even the most extremely simple one,
> the hearer must first substitute the concept which is meant for that which
> is named.[87]

Jülicher contends that the simile and the metaphor are fundamental
concepts in rhetoric and that no orator, Jesus included, does without them entirely. He illustrates the difference between simile and

bezeichnen dieses "Bild" am besten als *Vergleichung*'.
    85. Jülicher, *Die Gleichnisreden Jesu*, I, p. 52.
    86. Jülicher, *Die Gleichnisreden Jesu*, I, p. 52. Jülicher claims that Aristotle's
remarks about both speech forms indicate that he regards the metaphor as something more than a mere abbreviated simile that lacks the comparative particle ὡς.
    87. Jülicher, *Die Gleichnisreden Jesu*, I, p. 52: 'In der εἰκών wird neben die
Sache oder die Person, von denen die Rede ist, etwas ähnliches gerückt
(παραβάλλεται), um die Anschauung des Hörers zu beleben oder richtig zu leiten,
in der μεταφορά verschwindet im Ausdruck die Sache oder die Person, von denen
die Rede ist, hinter etwas ähnlichem, das direkt an ihrer Stelle auftritt: durch
einen, wenn auch meist höchst einfachen Denkprozess muss der Hörer erst den
Begriff, der gemeint ist, für den, der genannt wird, einsetzen'.

metaphor by adducing samples of each attributed to Jesus in the synoptic gospels.[88] For instance, Jesus utters a memorable simile in Lk. 13.34: 'Jerusalem, Jerusalem...How often would I have gathered your children like a hen gathers her brood under her wings, but you would not'; an equally memorable metaphor is recorded in Mk 8.15: 'Beware the leaven of the Pharisees'. Jülicher argues that the simile has two prominent features. First, the simile—by means of the comparative word, either ὡς or ὥσπερ—compels the hearer to consider simultaneously both items that are named and said to be similar. Secondly, the simile is comprised of actual (*eigentliche*) speech; that is, each word in the simile means the same thing as it customarily means. Thus, with regard to the preceding sample of a simile, 'Jerusalem is Jerusalem, but even the hen, the chicks, the wings mean the same thing that they would mean in a book about chicken farming'.[89] The converse is the case with metaphor. It is obvious, in Jülicher's view, that in Jesus' warning about Pharisaism 'leaven' is not to be taken literally, and thus the hearer must rely upon her or his acumen to discover the reality or subject matter described as 'leaven'.[90] 'Consequently, the *metaphor* is *non-actual* speech [*uneigentliche* Rede]; something is said, but something other is meant; what this other might be emerges simply through μεταφέρειν, or by discovering the word whose concept can be transferred to the word that is written down'.[91]

Jülicher concludes that although both the simile and the metaphor are based upon the ὅμοιον, they are in fact contrary speech forms.[92] His description of each speech form can be summarized in oppositions:

88. Jülicher, *Die Gleichnisreden Jesu*, I, pp. 53-56.

89. Jülicher, *Die Gleichnisreden Jesu*, I, p. 54.

90. Jülicher, *Die Gleichnisreden Jesu*, I, pp. 55-56. Jülicher suggests that only those who are already acquainted with Pharisaism, whom he calls adepts or initiates, would understand this metaphor. He points out that the author of the Gospel of Luke attempted to ensure that the hearer would understand this metaphor by adding ἥτις ἐστὶν ὑπόκρισις (Lk. 12.1). Jülicher's point here is that metaphors require interpretation.

91. Jülicher, *Die Gleichnisreden Jesu*, I, p. 55; Jülicher's emphasis.

92. Jülicher is aware that 'Aristotle praises the metaphor' in his *Rhetoric* and *Poetics*, but he claims that Aristotle does not speak of the metaphor alone (else such praise would be comical); rather, Aristotle is said to perceive 'that in the metaphor is disclosed the source of all skill with respect to words, the capability to see the similar' (*Die Gleichnisreden Jesu*, I, p. 157).

Whereas the simile is instructive and informative, requiring no interpretation, the metaphor is interesting and necessitates interpretation; whereas the simile is direct and literal, the metaphor is indirect and figurative; whereas the simile demonstrates, the metaphor intimates.[93]

> The simile offers the ὅμοιον to a ὄν in order to help those who do not understand; the metaphor offers a ὅμοιον instead of a ὄν, but only to those who understand. The former is intended for children or the uninformed, the latter for the informed or adults; the former has a didactic feature, the latter a confidential feature.[94]

The difference between simile and metaphor, Jülicher suggests, becomes acute for those who wish to exposit ancient literary texts, in which case the difference amounts to this: The simile aids interpretation, whereas the metaphor not only impedes interpretation, it requires interpretation itself.[95]

The ramifications of Jülicher's conclusions about simile and metaphor become apparent immediately. The essential distinction now made between simile and metaphor, Jülicher is poised to execute his second step in differentiating two types of pictorial speech, the allegory and the parable, a step which he initiates by positing that what applies to simile and metaphor applies also to their higher forms, which he designates as parable (*Gleichnis*) and allegory, 'for as the parable [*Gleichnis*] is the simile extended into a whole proposition, so is the allegory the metaphor extended into a whole proposition'.[96] Prior to a

---

93. See *Die Gleichnisreden Jesu*, I, pp. 56-57. Jülicher adds: 'Indeed, the metaphor occupies the νοῦς, which the simile intends to awaken' (p. 58).

94. Jülicher, *Die Gleichnisreden Jesu*, I, p. 57.

95. Jülicher, *Die Gleichnisreden Jesu*, I, p. 57.

96. Jülicher, *Die Gleichnisreden Jesu*, I, p. 58: 'Was aber von Vergleichung und Metapher gilt, dasselbe gilt von ihren höheren Formen, die ich als Gleichnis und Allegorie bezeichne. Denn wie das Gleichnis die auf ein Satzganzes erweiterte Vergleichung, so ist die Allegorie die auf ein Satzganzes erweiterte Metapher'. Elsewhere, Jülicher writes: 'The parable, in fact, is an amplified comparison' ('Parables', in T.K. Cheyne and J. Sutherland Black [eds.], *Encyclopædia Biblica* [4 vols.; New York: Macmillan, 1902], III, p. 3565). Unfortunately, an original German edition of this article does not exist, but I think it can be assumed that Jülicher himself did not write the English version. There is no indication of who translated the article into English. Wolfgang Harnisch has translated Jülicher's article into German ('Gleichnisse', in his *Gleichnisse Jesu*, pp. 1-10). In her criticism of Jülicher's definition of allegory, Boucher (*The Mysterious Parable*, pp. 4, 20, 23) fails to make reference to his claim that the allegory is an extended metaphor,

description of the parabolic type of pictorial speech, Jülicher fixes his gaze upon the allegorical.

According to Jülicher, when in a sentence a single word is used metaphorically, it is to replace another similar thing; however, when in a sentence more than one word is used metaphorically, which then necessitates the exchange of all controlling concepts for others similar to them, there exists no longer simply a metaphor, but an allegory. He points out that an allegory is not comprised of arbitrary metaphors, rather an allegory is a type of speech whose constitutive elements are clear metaphors that are connected to each other and taken from the same field.[97] Thus, 'the ideal of allegory is to report something which corresponds to the thing actually meant so excellently that whoever has recognized the thing meant at one point of the report can immediately undertake the transposition of the whole to the higher position'.[98] The continuity and inner uniformity of the metaphors within the allegory permit a great freedom of movement to the allegory as an art form: An allegory may be as short as a sentence or as long as a book; an allegory may have ethical, historical or didactic content; an allegory may proceed in the perfect, present or future tenses; and an allegory may deal with lasting conditions or single occurrences. In Jülicher's view, allegory exists whenever a complete speech leads to true understanding only through a transference of all its main concepts to another field.[99]

In light of this description of allegory, Jülicher is prepared to state more fully the reasons why Jesus' παραβολαί should not be considered allegories. To begin with, asserts Jülicher, the putative principle that Jesus' parables require allegorical interpretation, as it is apparently

---

although she does mention his claim that the parable is an extended simile (which she deems 'inadequate'). Boucher's own definition of allegory rests upon the tenet that allegory is '*an extended metaphor in narratory form*'(p. 20, her emphasis). As will become evident, there is more to Jülicher's understanding of allegory than is acknowledged by Boucher, who reduces it to a claim that allegory is a 'series' or 'sequence' of metaphors and then calls it 'inaccurate'.

97. Jülicher, *Die Gleichnisreden Jesu*, I, p. 58. This is where Jülicher explains the relationship between metaphor and allegory by employing mathematical terminology drawn from geometry.

98. Jülicher, *Die Gleichnisreden Jesu*, I, p. 58. Moreover, Jülicher claims that in an allegory there is a precise one-to-one correspondence between the number of images and the concepts that they depict (see p. 59).

99. Jülicher, *Die Gleichnisreden Jesu*, I, p. 59; my paraphrase. Samples of allegories written by D.F. Strauss, Ebrard and F. Rückert are provided (see pp. 59-60).

advanced in the interpretation of The Parable of the Sower, is not normative for all the remaining parables quite simply because none of the
synoptists themselves consistently adheres to this principle. Not only
do the synoptists leave many parables unexplained, but readers are able
to understand the main points of the parables without ἐπίλυσις.[100]
Jülicher contends that this situation presents a dilemma that cannot be
avoided: Either the parables as allegories require an ἐπίλυσις, but since
we have only two such interpretations transmitted, then the remaining
parables are closed to us; or we understand the parables even without a
transmitted interpretation, which means that an interpretation was never
unconditionally necessary and that the parables are not allegories.
Jülicher's position is obvious in his claim that one does not have to be
an initiate or an adept to understand correctly the sense of a parable
speech (*Gleichnisrede*) such as The Merciful Samaritan, The Pharisee
and the Toll Collector, The Impetuous Pleading Friend or The Unfaithful Servant.[101] Thus, he writes, 'Despite the authority of so may centuries, despite the greater authority of the evangelists, I cannot regard
the *Parabeln Jesu* as allegories'.[102]

In a more speculative vein, Jülicher considers it improbable that
Jesus would have been so exceedingly fond of allegory 'because allegory is one of the most artificial of speech forms'.[103] Allegory is elaborate and calculated, requiring considerable attention and concentration
on the part of the hearer or reader to decipher it successfully. Not only
does allegory demand intellectual agility on the part of its reader or
hearer, it demands even more agility and diligence on the part of its
maker, and Jülicher deems it improbable that Jesus, who had so much
to say, would have had the leisure to reflect upon how he could speak in
so intricate and polished a speech form as allegory.[104]

100. Jülicher, *Die Gleichnisreden Jesu*, I, p. 61. Jülicher states further that the
evangelists neither interpreted nor explained everything, which means that they
understood those things as we do—'*eigentlich*'.

101. Jülicher, *Die Gleichnisreden Jesu*, I, p. 62. I point out in passing that
Jülicher quite clearly includes two *Beispielerzählungen* among the *Gleichnisreden*
he mentions here.

102. Jülicher, *Die Gleichnisreden Jesu*, I, p. 61. Later, Jülicher adds that the allegorical method of interpreting the parables is suspect because it has produced various interpretations that are contradictory (p. 63); he furnishes evidence to back up
this assertion in his second volume.

103. Jülicher, *Die Gleichnisreden Jesu*, I, p. 63.

104. Jülicher, *Die Gleichnisreden Jesu*, I, p. 64. Jülicher's assumption here is

More concretely, Jülicher claims that 'Jesus' parables [*Parabeln*] positively oppose' identification with allegory because the customary introductory formula of the most famous parables reads 'the kingdom of heaven is like'—a king, a householder, a mustard seed, and so on. Such an introduction invites the reader or hearer to compare two different things between which a similarity is said to exist. The allegory, conversely, does not desire the reader or hearer to gaze upon the similarity between words and thoughts, rather to hear through the words the thoughts. Whereas a parable holds up two planes that are to be compared, an allegory requires that one plane be replaced by the other.[105]

Jülicher now identifies what to him is the main characteristic of allegory: '...every allegory points beyond itself because its wording does not satisfy'.[106] That is to say, an allegorical narrative taken literally does not satisfy the reader or hearer that it has been narrated for its own sake.[107] Emphatically, Jülicher asserts:

> I maintain that *it must be noted in every sentence, especially every story, whether it ought to be understood actually or non-actually.*[108]

that Jesus did not write out or construct his speeches in advance. Later, he suggests that Jesus did not prepare his parables like a modern preacher prepares sermons, carefully weighing each word (p. 109).

105. Jülicher, *Die Gleichnisreden Jesu*, I, p. 65. Here, again Jülicher describes the difference between parable and allegory in terms of opposition.

106. Jülicher, *Die Gleichnisreden Jesu*, I, p. 65.

107. Jülicher illustrates this point by referring to the allegory in Ezek. 17.

108. Jülicher, *Die Gleichnisreden Jesu*, I, p. 66; Jülicher's emphasis: 'Ich behaupte, *man muss es jedem Satze, zumal jeder Geschichte anmerken, ob sie eigentlich verstanden werden soll oder uneigentlich*'. He formulates a canon for distinguishing between the parabolic and allegorical types of pictorial speech: 'This canon will hardly mislead competent orators: if in wording their pictorial speeches [*Bildreden*] yield a fully satisfying sense, then they are to be received as they are read, they are meant actually [*eigentlich*]; however, if they are not satisfying in and of themselves, appear either empty and insignificant or improbable and disconnected, then they are intended to represent something other than what the words describe, thus one must transfer them—probably as a rule—to a higher region in order to discover amply the missing depth and meaning, consistency and good development. *To treat something as allegory because it pehaps could be is an arbitrary action; this holds true only for what cannot at all be taken actually* [*eigentlich*]: as long as a speech, it may sound as pictorial [*bildlich*] as it wants, admits another version than the allegorical, the privilege is due this other version so long as this is the case; also, we are permitted to recognize Jesus' *Parabeln* as

Based upon this fundamental criterion, Jülicher concludes that Jesus'
parables predominantly give the impression that they are to be understood actually (*eigentlich*).[109] Most of his parables distinguish themselves with natural colors, vividness, liveliness, offering little to suggest that they are mere coverings to conceal a kernel of a different
sort.[110] The parables of Jesus can be viewed as allegories only when
every actual (*eigentlich*) understanding is cut off from them. This,
insists Jülicher, is not the case.

> On the contrary, as soon as we move away from the wrong track, which
> the 'interpretations' in Mt. 13 showed us, the parables by themselves and
> without any coercion take their place in a different class of speech form,
> namely in the one whose lowest level we have discussed in more detail
> above, the simile.[111]

Since he considers it highly probable that the synoptists transported
certain prejudices from their cultural circles to the parables of Jesus—
prejudices from which Jesus himself was completely free—Jülicher
chooses to submit himself only to the parables of Jesus and not what
the synoptists say about them.[112] Accordingly, Jülicher states that he
will abandon 'the subjective standpoint of the evangelists' and examine
the parables themselves alone. If he cannot agree with the synoptists'

---

allegories only when we see that every actual [*eigentliche*] understanding of them is
cut off' (pp. 67-68; Jülicher's emphasis).

109. Jülicher, *Die Gleichnisreden Jesu*, I, p. 66; cf. also pp. 68, 194.

110. Jülicher, *Die Gleichnisreden Jesu*, I, p. 66; my summary. Among the samples of Jesus' *Parabeln* cited to substantiate this point, Jülicher includes The
Pharisee and the Toll Collector and The Foolish Rich Man.

111. Jülicher, *Die Gleichnisreden Jesu*, I, p. 68: 'Im Gegenteil, sobald wir uns
von der falschen Fährte entfernen, die die "Deutungen" in Mt 13 uns wiesen, reihen
die Parabeln sich ganz von selber und ohne allen Zwang in eine andre Klasse von
Redeformen ein, in die nämlich, deren unterste Stufe wir oben genauer besprochen
haben, die Vergleichung'. As a warrant for this step, Jülicher refers again to the
elasticity of the *mashal*.

112. Summarized from *Die Gleichnisreden Jesu*, I, pp. 68-69. Jülicher notes that
the synoptists elsewhere have Jesus say things that 'he decidedly had not spoken',
e.g. the passion predictions. Nevertheless, he concedes that the '*Parabel*' of The
Wicked Tenants (Mk 12.1-11 and parallels) can be cited as evidence that Jesus did
not disdain allegorical speech entirely. Jülicher does not dispute that this pericope
is an allegory; rather, he does not dare ascribe it to Jesus because it is one of the
most 'suspect' of all Jesus' speeches in the synoptic gospels in that it refers to the
murder of Jesus, before the fact, as a matter of fact (see p. 116).

conception of the parables, it remains for Jülicher to develop his own view of the essence of the parables speeches of Jesus.[113]

The Classification of Jesus' παραβολαί
Having expended considerable effort to show that the synoptists' conception of the παραβολαί as allegories rests upon a misunderstanding, Jülicher propounds his own understanding of the essence of Jesus' παραβολαί, arguing that among the synoptic 'parables' it is possible to distinguish three classes of παραβολαί, namely the parable (*Gleichnis*), the parable in the narrower sense (*Parabel*) and the example narrative (*Beispielerzählung*).[114] Thus, that part of Jülicher's chapter on 'The

---

113. Jülicher, *Die Gleichnisreden Jesu*, I, p. 69. Later, Jülicher suggests that the motive behind the evangelists' allegorizing Jesus' parables was an immense reverence for Jesus and his words (pp. 190-91): '"Nihil otiosum": this war-cry of reverence explains to us thoroughly the evangelists' propensity toward *Allegorese*' (p. 191).

114. The important issues of translation and terminology can be addressed here. I strictly follow Jülicher's terms for the three classes of παραβολαί. Note that the second of the three (*Parabel*), and not the first (*Gleichnis*), is the one to which Jülicher refers as 'the parable in the narrower sense' (cf. *Die Gleichnisreden Jesu*, I, p. 117). Others have represented Jülicher as designating the *Gleichnis* as 'the parable in the narrower sense' (see, e.g., Sellin, 'Lukas als Gleichniserzähler', p. 176: 'Jülicher divides them into *Gleichnisse* [in the narrower sense], *Parabeln*, and *Beispielerzählungen*'; cf. also Berger, *Formgeschichte des Neuen Testaments*, p. 45). Some confusion, or at least inconsistency, still exists among English-speaking scholars with regard to the translation of Jülicher's terms. When reference is made to Jülicher's classification of Jesus' παραβολαί, some choose to translate *Gleichnis* as 'similitude' despite the fact that they translate the same word as 'parable' (or incorrectly as 'parabolic') when it appears elsewhere, such as in the title of Jülicher's work (see, e.g., E.P. Sanders and Margaret Davies, *Studying the Synoptic Gospels* [London: SCM Press; Philadelphia: Trinity Press International, 1989], pp. 176-77). Nevertheless, two reasons could be given to justify translating 'Gleichnis' as 'similitude': first, Jülicher himself uses 'eine παραβολή, *eine similitudo, ein Gleichnis*' in the same sentence (*Die Gleichnisreden Jesu*, I, p. 70); secondly, Jülicher claims that the parable (*Gleichnis*) is an amplified simile or comparison (Ver*gleich*ung). However, it is equally clear that Jülicher uses 'Gleichnis' in a broader sense to denote what we in English call 'parable', as the title of his work indicates (*Die Gleichnisreden Jesu*, which I translate as *The Parable Speeches of Jesus*). Many German scholars employ the word 'Gleichnis' to translate the Greek word παραβολή; Jeremias, for instance, consistently uses 'Gleichnis' for παραβολή, and his term is translated into English as 'parable'. It is misleading, in my opinion, to render 'Gleichnis' as 'similitude' when translating

Essence of the Parable Speeches of Jesus' which is of particular importance in this study is at hand. The primary concern here will be to point out the prominent features of each class of παραβολή as delineated by Jülicher. In what follows, every attempt will be made to provide a faithful account of Jülicher's classification of *Die Gleichnisreden Jesu*.[115]

The Gleichnisse. One division of the παραβολαί, according to Jülicher, consists of 'Gleichnisse', parables. Jülicher begins his description of this class of parable by stating that with the word 'Gleichnis' he incorporates the sense which Aristotle assigned to the παραβολή in his *Rhetoric*.[116] Then Jülicher reiterates and amplifies the thesis that the parable and the simile are closely related:

Jülicher and then to render 'Gleichnis' as 'parable' when translating Jeremias (and others)—as if Jülicher is speaking of an entirely different entity. (On the usage of 'Gleichnis' in the German language and literature, consult Jacob Grimm and Wilhelm Grimm, *Deutsches Wörterbuch* [ed. Deutschen Akademie der Wissenschaften zu Berlin; Leipzig: Verlag von S. Hirzel, 1849], IV.I.4, pp. 8183-204.) Therefore, I translate 'Gleichnis' (literally, 'likeness') as 'parable' in order to make clear that Jülicher is, in fact, referring to the parable (παραβολή). I should mention that Jülicher himself adds to the confusion because he sometimes employs 'Gleichnis' and 'Parabel', the German transliteration of παραβολή, interchangeably (see n. 123 below for a telling instance). This confusion is compounded by the article written by Jülicher, which originally appeared in English, where the παροιμία *as well as* some παραβολαί are referred to as 'similitudes' ('Parables', pp. 3564-65). Thus, I provide the specific German word in brackets or parentheses throughout this study. Finally, although various English translations have been given for 'Beispielerzählung' (e.g. 'example story', 'exemplary story', 'example', 'illustrative story' or 'illustration'), in this chapter I translate this word as 'example narrative' because, as we shall see, Jülicher argues that the narrative form is one of the distinguishing features of the *Beispielerzählung*.

115. Some criticisms levelled against Jülicher for his classification of the παραβολαί are unwarranted and unfounded because insufficient attention has been given to the omissions and accretions that have occurred in the tradition-history of parable scholarship. Thus, I think it is important to strive to hear Jülicher in his own terms, not to rely upon hearsay. To be sure, it is imperative that we attend to Jülicher's description of each class of παραβολή as carefully and thoroughly as possible; however, the constraints of space and time prohibit the inclusion of every detail of his argument in this section of his chapter.

116. This provides evidence that Jülicher's term 'Gleichnis' can be translated as 'parable'.

The 'parable' is the simile at a higher level, the demonstration of a proposition by means of [the] placing-beside of another similar proposition.[117]

The matter of fundamental importance in the parable (*Gleichnis*), Jülicher emphasizes, is the relationship of the concepts embodied in it, and not simply the similarity of the concepts.[118]

In order to understand a parable, therefore, one must not track down similarities between the individual concepts of the parable, rather one must discern the *similarity between the relation of the concepts* of one side and that of the concepts on the other side. The parable intends to illuminate *one* thought by means of a ὅμοιον, as does the simile *one* word; that is why one also speaks of only one *tertium* comparationis in it and not of several *tertia*. [119]

Accordingly, Jülicher posits that the parable (*Gleichnis*) necessarily consists of two components: a proposition the writer regards as standing in need of demonstration, which Jülicher designates as the 'subject matter' (*Sache*), and a proposition the writer develops for the purpose of such demonstration, which he designates as the 'picture' (or 'image',

117. Jülicher, *Die Gleichnisreden Jesu*, I, p. 69: 'Das "Gleichnis" ist die Vergleichung auf höherer Stufe, die Veranschaulichung eines Satzes durch Nebenstellung eines andern ähnlichen Satzes'. 'Veranschaulichen' is difficult to render into English. Usually, the translations given for this verb are 'to illustrate' or 'to demonstrate', even though there are other German verbs for both of those words ('illustrieren' and 'demonstrieren', respectively). Since the verb 'veranschaulichen' is formed by adding the prefix 'vor-' to the adjective 'anschaulich' (literally, 'visual'), perhaps it could be translated 'to visualize'—a meaning not entirely inconsistent with Jülicher's position. I translate the noun 'Veranschaulichung' as 'demonstration' and not as 'illustration' in order to indicate that Jülicher attempts to describe the rhetorical effect of the *Gleichnis*. He has been criticized unduly as speaking of the *Gleichnis* as 'mere illustrations' of a proposition.

118. Jülicher explains the relationship between *Gleichnis* and simile by employing mathematical terminology; see *Die Gleichnisreden Jesu*, I, pp. 69-70.

119. Jülicher, *Die Gleichnisreden Jesu*, I, p. 70; Jülicher's emphasis: 'Um ein Gleichnis zu verstehen, darf man also nicht Aehnlichkeiten zwischen den einzelnen Begriffen des Gleichnisses aufspüren, sondern muss die *Aehnlichkeit zwischen dem Verhältnis der Begriffe* der einen Seite und dem der Begriffe der andern Seite erkennen. Das Gleichnis will, wie die Vergleichung *ein* Wort, so *einen* Gedanken durch ein ὅμοιον beleuchten, daher man auch bei ihm nur von einem *tertium* comparationis redet, nicht von mehreren *tertia*'. Cf. p. 74: '...for the observer ought to draw from the *Gleichnisse* only *one* thought; the allegory occupies him constantly, gives him in some new steps a new work of translating'.

Bild).[120] The subject matter (*Sache*) and the picture (*Bild*) are combined by means of the comparative particle, which invites the reader or hearer to seek the point in which the two propositions coincide.[121]

Jülicher now expounds upon the function of the parable (*Gleichnis*), demonstrating his points by making repeated and detailed references to a παραβολή cited by Aristotle.[122] Jülicher's conclusions can be summarized as follows. He states that Aristotle classifies the parable (*Parabel*) among the means of proof (κοιναὶ πίστεις) beside the fable and the historical example.[123] Jülicher describes the function of the parable (*Gleichnis*) by comparing it to the simile: '…what the simile [*Vergleichung*] affords to the individual concepts—namely to support, to enliven, to refine the representation of the [concepts] by means of foreign help—that the parable [*Gleichnis*] affords to the propositions, to the judgment *that indeed each proposition contains*; it supports this judgment and makes it obvious'.[124] The propositions, the subject matter (*Sache*) and the picture (*Bild*), are specimens of the same species; that is, the similarity upon which the propositions are based is the general

120. Jülicher, *Die Gleichnisreden Jesu*, I, p. 70. Jülicher contends that it is erroneous to think of the *Bild* alone as the parable: 'Improperly, one sometimes hears only the latter proposition [*Satz*], the *Bild*, the simile, called "*Gleichnis*", a habit which must be warned against as the source of numerous errors, for this simile is in and of itself unstable and worthless; a παραβολή, a *similitudo*, a *Gleichnis* arises when one complete in itself proposition [*Satz*] is moved beside another similar one…' He makes clear that there is an enormous variety of *Gleichnisse*; therefore, although it is possible to detect the character of the form, he will not advance a rigid schema that does not admit of variety.

121. Jülicher, *Die Gleichnisreden Jesu*, I, p. 70.

122. Jülicher, *Die Gleichnisreden Jesu*, I, p. 70. This παραβολή, which Aristotle attributes to Socrates, can be found in *Rhetoric* 2.20.4. Based upon his analysis of this parable (see pp. 70-73), Jülicher offers concrete evidence for his conclusions, which I have gleaned and present in generalized form.

123. Jülicher, *Die Gleichnisreden Jesu*, I, p. 71: 'ARISTOTELES rechnet die Parabel unter die *Beweismittel* (κοιναὶ πίστεις) neben Fabel und geschichtlichem Beispiel' (Jülicher's emphasis). Here, Jülicher refers to *Rhetoric* 2.20.1-3. We shall have occasion to return to this section of Aristotle's *Rhetoric*, for what Jülicher fails to mention here is that Aristotle classifies the παραδείγματα—of which he identifies two types, τὸ λέγειν πράγματα προγεγενημένα and τὸ αὐτὸν ποιεῖν, the παραβολαί and λόγοι being types of the latter—among the common proofs. Note that Jülicher employs the German transliteration of παραβολή (*Parabel*) in referring to the *Gleichnis*. Cf. p. 110 n. 150 below.

124. Jülicher, *Die Gleichnisreden Jesu*, I, p. 71; Jülicher's emphasis.

law or principle of which both propositions are outward manifestations. This general law is the *tertium comparationis*. A thesis can be disputed or defended by producing a case or instance intended to induce a similar judgment or opinion and thus lead to the acceptance of the desired general truth or principle that both propositions, *Sache* and *Bild*, manifest.

The parable (*Gleichnis*), according to Jülicher, is a type of popular argumentation, a means of proof that draws its material from daily life or common experience, that can produce the desired effect on the highly educated as well as the uneducated; it is not a form of rigorous argumentation that moves from the universal to the particular.

> Truth is mightier in more concrete form than in abstract form; hence, the might of the parable. It is a proof from concession to the not yet conceded similarity.[125]

The clever orator can make a thesis acceptable, a fact plausible, by the presentation of a case or instance, drawn from daily life or common experience, against which no opposition is expected.[126]

Having compared the parable (*Gleichnis*) to the simile in order to elucidate the parable's characteristic features, Jülicher now contrasts the parable to allegory in order to demonstrate the parable's distinctiveness and to show how far removed those two forms are. He repeats his assertion that allegory is 'non-actual speech [*uneigentliche Rede*] that does not mean what it says' and that the parable (*Gleichnis*) is 'actual [*eigentliche (Rede)*] speech that intends to be taken as it presents itself'.[127] The allegory obscures, the parable (*Gleichnis*) illuminates. Indeed, as Jülicher puts it, 'To illustrate is the intention of the *Gleichnisse*; only the thing illustrated, which really stands *in luce*, can

125. Jülicher, *Die Gleichnisreden Jesu*, I, p. 72. Jülicher also points out that the *Gleichnis* appeals to the passion of the hearer; it does not demand a rigorous logical activity on the part of the hearer. The *Gleichnis*, a means of proof that submits a particular case or instance of a law or principle which no one disputes, thus can create the mood for the acceptance of a thesis or fact.

126. Jülicher, *Die Gleichnisreden Jesu*, I, p. 73: 'One reports a simple state of affairs that might come as a surprise to those present. For this reason, one places beside it a similar case, against which no opposition is expected—thus, the doubter notices that what might feel unheard of to him is familiar to him elsewhere, and the quotidian helps him to recognize the unusual and to add to his treasure of knowledge'.

127. Jülicher, *Die Gleichnisreden Jesu*, I, p. 73.

overcome the reluctant mind by means of the mind'.[128] The pictorial
elements of the allegory should be interpreted; however, the pictorial
element in the parable (*Gleichnis*) should make clearer, or illuminate,
the subject matter. 'For this reason, the picture-half of a parable must
not only be drawn from the generally accessible fields of perception
and experience, but also must be protected from any ornament that
impedes comprehension; e.g. to employ a metaphor in it is not recommended'.[129] Jülicher maintains that in order to be compelling,
'everything in the picture-half must be familiar, clear, free from any
objection'.[130] Unlike the picture-half of the allegory, which must be
understood non-actually, the picture-half of the parable is to be understood actually.[131] The two forms, he concludes, are opposites: Allegory
and parable should not be identified with each other, nor should there
be any admixture of those two forms of speech.[132]

128. Jülicher, *Die Gleichnisreden Jesu*, I, p. 73.

129. Jülicher, *Die Gleichnisreden Jesu*, I, pp. 73-74. Jülicher is aware, nevertheless, that metaphors do appear in the parables of Jesus as recorded by the synoptists
(see p. 83). Here, Jülicher goes on to stress that one should not compare the contents of the *Sachhälfte* and *Bildhälfte* in the *Gleichnis*, rather one should compare
the relationships of the two fields (p. 75). The context makes manifest the point
of coincidence, the *tertium comparationis*, between the *Sachhälfte* and *Bildhälfte*
(p. 77). Moreover, Jülicher insists that the meanings of particular words or concepts
in a *Gleichnis* emanate from their context within that *Gleichnis*. He considers it a
gross error to ascribe to particular concepts within a parable (*Parabel*) the
metaphorical meanings that they might have elsewhere in the scriptures. For
instance, he deems it 'a monstrosity' that Steinmeyer 'dismisses as "capricious" the
traditional "interpretation" of The Parable of the Leaven because it forgets that
ζύμη [leaven] is employed without exception elsewhere in the Bible as an image
for a *res culpabilis*...' (p. 77; cf. p. 84, where Jülicher quotes Steinmeyer's own
words against this type of exegesis). Jülicher's point is that the meaning of a word
used figuratively in a parable cannot be determined simply by accumulating parallels from the Jewish scriptures and the New Testament. He, as a result, would
understand ζύμη literally in this particular context (p. 78). For a recent interpretation of The Parable of the Leaven that not only views ζύμη as a metaphor, but also
appreciates the negative and scandalous associations of ζύμη, see Scott, *Hear Then
the Parable*, pp. 321-29.

130. Jülicher, *Die Gleichnisreden Jesu*, I, p. 74.

131. Jülicher, *Die Gleichnisreden Jesu*, I, p. 76: 'Die Bildhälfte im Gleichnis
muss, um zu etwas zu dienen, eigentlich verstanden werden, die Allegorie
uneigentlich'.

132. For the sake of brevity, I have telescoped Jülicher's conclusions: 'Nicht nur
vor Identifikation von Allegorie und "Gleichnis", sondern auch vor Vermischung

The culmination of Jülicher's protracted argument about the disparity of parable and allegory is near. The lines of that argument converge in his formal definition of those two divergent speech forms:

> I define the *parable as that figure of speech in which the effect of a proposition* (thought) *is to be secured by a placing-beside of a similar proposition which belongs to another field, whose effect is certain.* Precluded thereby is any mingling and mixing with the *allegory as that figure of speech in which a connected series of concepts* (a proposition or proposition complex) *is represented by means of a connected series of similar concepts from another field.*[133]

Immediately, Jülicher concedes that these two figures of speech share a relationship in what constitutes the essential elements of the 'Mashal-concept'; that is, a certain independence and the ὅμοιον are the foundation of both the parable (*Gleichnis*) and the allegory. Moreover, both the allegory and the parable are permitted a great freedom of movement respective to the wealth of material with which they deal and the wealth of forms in which they can appear, and both require as necessary for their realization a picture-proposition (*Bildsatz*) and a principal-proposition (*Hauptsatz*). Apart from that, however, Jülicher avows that

---

beider Redeformen müssen wir uns hüten' (*Die Gleichnisreden Jesu*, I, p. 74); 'Dieser Gegensatz verträgt keine Vermischung der Arten' (p. 76). In all fairness to Jülicher, I should point out that his argument is more involved than is indicated here. To bolster his claims that the *Gleichnis* should not be defined in terms of allegory and that exegetes should not proceed as if the *Gleichnisse* were 'allegorische Gleichnisse', Jülicher posits that the allegory is a more elaborate and developed form of speech, while the *Gleichnis* is a more compact and concise form. The former occupies the observer with new steps of translating, the latter yields one thought. Within this framework, Jülicher pens the now often quoted similes in which he compares the allegory to a string of pearls and the *Gleichnis* to a chain (p. 74). To support his conclusion that the allegory and the *Gleichnis* are contrary speech forms that should not be intermixed, Jülicher provides analyses of *Gleichnisse* from various authors, ancient and modern, such as Aristotle, E.L.T. Henke, M. Lazarus and G.E. Lessing (see pp. 73-80).

133. Jülicher, *Die Gleichnisreden Jesu*, I, p. 80; Jülicher's emphasis: 'Ich definiere *das Gleichnis als diejenige Redefigur, in welcher die Wirkung eines Satzes* (Gedankens) *gesichert werden soll durch Nebenstellung eines ähnlichen, einem andern Gebiet angehörigen, seiner Wirkung gewissen Satzes.* Ausgeschlossen ist damit jede Verwechslung und Vermengung mit der *Allegorie als derjenigen Redefigur, in welcher eine zusammenhängende Reihe von Begriffen* (ein Satz oder Satzkomplex) *dargestellt wird vermittelst einer zusammenhängenden Reihe von ähnlichen Begriffen aus einem andern Gebiete'.*

parable and allegory are absolute opposites. The main difference between allegory and parable is this: In the former, the picture-proposition (*Bildsatz*) is inextricably intertwined with the principal-proposition (*Hauptsatz*), and after the *Bildsatz* has been interpreted, it is of no use; in the latter, conversely, the picture-proposition and the principal-proposition stand side by side with equal right, both retaining their actual meaning (*eigentlichen Bedeutung*), both intending to be viewed and remembered. 'The allegory is more an ornament, the parable a means of might'.[134] Thus, there can be no talk of interpreting a *Gleichnis*, for nothing enigmatic or puzzling is allowed to be in it.[135]

Jesus, according to Jülicher, told many parables (*Gleichnisse*) which conform to the definition given. 'The repeatedly mentioned παραβολή of the Fig Tree (Mk 13.28-29) is the paragon of such a parable'.[136] Jülicher then provides cursory analyses of this and several other *Gleichnisse*, endeavoring to demonstrate that they embody the characteristic features of the parable (*Gleichnis*) as he defines it.[137] Although the specifics of Jülicher's analyses of these *Gleichnisse* cannot be dealt with here, a particular issue that surfaces there is noteworthy.

Jülicher has insisted repeatedly that neither a parable (*Gleichnis*) nor its *Bildsatz* are to be interpreted. He now adds a new tenet to that dictum:

> The parable-picture does not intend to be *interpreted*, rather *applied*; thus, it is sufficient for the learning of something (μάθετε, Mk 13.28) because it induces the hearer to elevate the reigning law from the thought-kernel of something well known to him, and to apply this without prejudice to the circumstance, the field, which was unclear to him until now.[138]

134. Jülicher, *Die Gleichnisreden Jesu*, I, p. 81.
135. Jülicher, *Die Gleichnisreden Jesu*, I, pp. 80-81; my summary.
136. Jülicher, *Die Gleichnisreden Jesu*, I, p. 82.
137. See *Die Gleichnisreden Jesu*, I, pp. 82-92. The *Gleichnisse* that receive Jülicher's attention can be found in Lk. 12.39-40, Lk. 5.36-39, Lk. 4.23, Lk. 6.39, Mk 3.22-27, Lk. 14.28-33. Observe that again Jülicher uses the words 'Gleichnis' and 'Parabel' interchangeably: e.g. he refers to Mk 13.28-29 first as a 'Gleichnis' (p. 82), then as a 'Parabel' (p. 83); similarly, he refers to Lk. 5.36-39 as a 'Gleichnis' and a 'Parabel' (p. 86).
138. Jülicher, *Die Gleichnisreden Jesu*, I, p. 87; Jülicher's emphasis: 'Nicht *gedeutet* will das Parabelbild werden, sondern *angewendet*; dadurch reicht es etwas zum Lernen (μάθετε Mc 13.28) hin, weil es den Hörer veranlasst, aus irgend einem ihm wohlbekannten Satz den Gedankenkern, das regierende Gesetz zu erheben and

Jülicher anticipates that an objection may be raised at his point. If Jesus' parables were unmistakable and clear, meant to be applied and not interpreted, then why is it difficult to ascertain the meaning of many Gospel parables?[139]

Jülicher's resolution of this problem hinges upon the distinction he makes between the parables of the synoptic gospels and the parables of Jesus. In Jülicher's opinion, Jesus' parables were clear and unambiguous; however, we possess Jesus' parables only in mutilated and fragmentary form (for instance, the *Sachhälfte* may have been omitted completely). That most of Jesus' parables have been preserved without a context or in a false connection presents a formidable problem since the *Gleichnis* obtains clarity from the context in which it is placed. Jesus did not utter his parables in isolation; rather, 'Jesus' parables [*Gleichnisse*], as even the evangelists still convey, were spoken for the most part within larger speeches, with specific causes for offensive or defensive purposes...'[140] It is a great misfortune, then, that Jesus' parables (*Parabeln*)—which 'were intended for immediate effect, plunged deeply into the peculiarity of the present'—have been handed down to us in mutilated and fragmentary form by the tradition.[141] Exegetes can proceed on firmer ground and with less uncertainty if they remain aware of the true occasion and purpose of Jesus' parables.[142] There are, in Jülicher's estimation, about 30 *Gleichnisse* in the synoptic gospels.[143] The circle of Jesus' παραβολαί, however, extends further.

dies vorurteilslos auch auf das Verhältnis, das Gebiet anzuwenden, welches ihm bisher noch unklar war'. He soon expands this tenet beyond the *Parabelbild* to the παραβολή: 'The παραβολή in Lk. 4.23 demands application, not interpretation'. Jülicher will clarify later what he means by 'interpretation' (see below, p. 117).

139. Jülicher, *Die Gleichnisreden Jesu*, I, pp. 90-92; my summary.

140. Jülicher, *Die Gleichnisreden Jesu*, I, p. 91. The echo of this claim reverberates in the thought of Jeremias. For a brief description of the effect that Jülicher had on Jeremias, see Klauck, 'Adolf Jülicher', pp. 122-24; for a comparison of some aspects of Jülicher's and Jeremias's work on the parables, see Eichholz, *Gleichnisse der Evangelien*, pp. 43-47.

141. Jülicher, *Die Gleichnisreden Jesu*, I, p. 91.

142. Although it sounds odd coming from him, Jülicher suggests yet another way of dealing with the lacunae in the tradition: 'Only through a loving immersion in the spirit of Jesus, by a cautious illumination of the pale, are we able in some measure from the remaining light to fill up the gaps which the tradition left and thus recover the full value of the relics of Jesus' *Gleichnissen*' (*Die Gleichnisreden Jesu*, I, p. 92).

143. Jülicher, *Die Gleichnisreden Jesu*, I, p. 92. In the second volume of *Die*

The Parabeln. Some of the most famous of the synoptic παραβολαί, Jülicher writes, are to be distinguished from the actual parables (*eigentlichen Gleichnissen*) as a particular class. Although Jülicher explicitly states that 'to be sure the boundaries are fluid' between the *Gleichnisse* and this other class of παραβολή, there is nevertheless a peculiarity which 20–25 of the remaining synoptic παραβολαί share in common, namely, 'the *narrative* form'.[144] This category of παραβολή is designated as 'Parabeln', '"*parables*" in the narrower sense'.[145]

In order to highlight some of the characteristic features of the *Parabeln*, Jülicher compares them to the *Gleichnisse*. In the *Gleichnisse*, as we have seen, the *Bild* (picture, image) and the *Sache* (subject matter) share the same verb tense; further, the *Bild* is drawn from everyday reality accessible to everyone and points to circumstances which must be acknowledged.[146] In the *Parabeln*, however, the homogeneity between the verb tenses in the *Bild* and *Sache* disappears: 'The picture [*Bild*] always lies in the past, the subject matter [*Sache*] does not'.[147] Moreover, in the *Parabeln* a story—freely invented by Jesus—is narrated, a story which does not tell what someone does that cannot be otherwise, rather a story which tells what someone once did. Nonetheless, Jülicher emphasizes that the *Parabeln* and the *Gleichnisse*, both species of the *mashal*, are closely related speech forms; indeed, the *Parabel* is a *Gleichnis* raised to a higher power.[148]

Since the most obvious distinguishing feature between the *Gleichnis*

Gleichnisreden Jesu, Jülicher provides his exposition of 28 *Gleichnisse*.

144. Jülicher, *Die Gleichnisreden Jesu*, I, p. 92; Jülicher's emphasis. He mentions Mt. 7.24-27 and Lk. 11.5-8 as samples of παραβολαί that could perhaps be regarded as *Gleichnisse* or *Parabeln* (he himself includes them among the latter). In the second volume of *Die Gleichnisreden Jesu*, Jülicher provides his exposition of 21 *Parabeln*.

145. Jülicher, *Die Gleichnisreden Jesu*, I, p. 101; Jülicher's emphasis. Although I anticipate the discussion to come, in which Jülicher struggles with the name for this class of παραβολή, I choose to reveal his decision now for the sake of clarity.

146. Jülicher, *Die Gleichnisreden Jesu*, I, p. 93. The *Gleichnis*, Jülicher observes, prepares for its effect by appealing to the unassailable obviousness of a τίς ἐξ ὑμῶν, a μήτι or an οὐδείς.

147. Jülicher, *Die Gleichnisreden Jesu*, I, p. 93. That the *Sache* does not lie in the past is an important point for Jülicher, especially since he understands the *Sache* of most, if not all, *Parabeln* to be the kingdom of God.

148. See *Die Gleichnisreden Jesu*, I, pp. 93-94. Here, Jülicher treats the relationship between *Parabel* and *Gleichnis* in craftily fashioned rhetorical questions.

and the *Parabel* is the respective length of each—the former, a sentence; the latter, a narrative—Jülicher suggests that we might manage with the name 'narrative parable' (*Gleichniserzählung*) for the παραβολή of the second class.[149] Yet, he continues, this genus of speech form has been known for a long time by another name: the fable. Jülicher points out that Aristotle mentions the fable in conjunction with the παραβολή as types of rhetorical examples.[150] In order to describe how the fable functions, Jülicher provides analyses of fables cited by Aristotle in his *Rhetoric*.[151] Jülicher's conclusions can be summarized as follows.

The orator, according to Jülicher, creates the fable in order to induce the auditors to pass the same judgment on the affairs put before them for deliberation that they must pass concerning the affairs submitted in the form of a fable.[152] 'He can count on success because the one *case* is similar to the other'.[153] The particulars of both cases need not correspond exactly to each other; rather, the overall state of affairs in both cases are similar.[154] 'Therefore', Jülicher states, 'as with the parable [*Gleichnis*], in the fable there is only *one* tertium comparationis, which one discovers when one recognizes, or at least senses, the law that governs in both parts of the fable'.[155] Again, there is no non-actual speech (*uneigentlicher Rede*) in the fable. The fable functions only as a whole;

---

149. Jülicher, *Die Gleichnisreden Jesu*, I, p. 94.

150. Jülicher, *Die Gleichnisreden Jesu*, I, p. 94: 'Aristotle (*Rhet.* 2.20) mentions in the same breath together with the παραβολή a kind of rhetorical example constituted by the fables, Aesopic and Libyan'. This representation of Aristotle's *Rhetoric* is an improvement over the earlier reference (see above, p. 103 n. 123). Jülicher states that Aristotle called the fables λόγοι, as well as μῦθοι and αἶνοι, known in Latin as *apologi, fabulae* and *fabellae*. As I will point out in Chapter 5, several parable scholars, including Jülicher, have an insufficient appreciation of this aspect of Aristotle's view of parable and example.

151. See *Rhetoric* 2.20.5-6; Aristotle attributes the first fable to Stesichorus, the second to Aesop.

152. This paragraph is my summary of *Die Gleichnisreden Jesu*, I, pp. 95-96. Jülicher reiterates that the parables elicit a judgment from the audience; see pp. 162, 189.

153. Jülicher, *Die Gleichnisreden Jesu*, I, p. 95; Jülicher's emphasis.

154. Jülicher, *Die Gleichnisreden Jesu*, I, p. 95. Jülicher's concern here is to obviate any allegorizing interpretation of the fable. He reinforces this point by making specific reference to the fable of Aesop quoted by Aristotle.

155. Jülicher, *Die Gleichnisreden Jesu*, I, p. 95; Jülicher's emphasis.

the fable's application to a present question should come only from its kernel of thought, and no transference must take place except from the impression of the completed event depicted in the fable to the one now in question.

Jülicher pauses to enunciate the similarities that the *Gleichnis* and the *Fabel* share in common and to elucidate the differences that exist between the two speech forms.[156] To begin with, Jülicher claims, the fable performs quite like the parable (*Gleichnis*). The fable, classed among the κοιναὶ πίστεις by Aristotle, is a means of attestation not bound to a specific genre of rhetoric.[157] Since the fable affects the will of the auditor due to the fact that it disperses clarity upon the subject it treats, the fable's use is not confined solely to persuasion. Accordingly, the result of the fable is just as manifold as that of the *Gleichnis*, for fables 'enrich knowledge, rectify a sentiment, determine the will'.[158] Like the parable (*Gleichnis*), the fable addresses common sense, although the fable—the narrative involving an individual case—has the advantage of vividness because the subject matter (*Sache*) develops step by step and thus intensifies the interest of the hearer.[159] In order to obtain the consent of the hearer, it is imperative, for both the *Gleichnis* and the fable, that no objection, no opposition to the picture-half (*Bildhälfte*) be possible.

There are, however, differences between the *Gleichnis* and the fable:

> ...only the λόγος seeks to obtain the same aim in a different way than the Aristotelian παραβολή our 'parable'. The parable cites that which is generally valid, the fable that which occurred once.[160]

156. Jülicher, *Die Gleichnisreden Jesu*, I, pp. 96-98; my summary.

157. Jülicher, *Die Gleichnisreden Jesu*, I, p. 96. Jülicher states that the fables adduced by Aristotle belong to political and judicial oratory.

158. Jülicher, *Die Gleichnisreden Jesu*, I, p. 96. This constitutes, in Jülicher's view, the power of this popular form of proof. Jesus' parable speeches are compelling because they do not appeal to the mind alone, but to the total person—senses, experience, emotions and conscience (p. 162; cf. p. 182).

159. Jülicher, *Die Gleichnisreden Jesu*, I, pp. 96-97. Jülicher himself uses visual imagery: 'And the narrative of an individual case has the considerable advantage of vividness; the interest becomes more rapt, and if the subject matter develops step by step before the eyes, then one is overwhelmed by its force. In the *Gleichnis*, e.g., "No one sows a patch from a new cloth onto an old garment", the mind only gives its affirmation; in the *Fabel* the mind and the eyes [give their affirmation]'.

160. Jülicher, *Die Gleichnisreden Jesu*, I, p. 97: '...nur sucht der λόγος das gleiche Ziel auf anderm Wege als die aristotelische παραβολή, unser "Gleichnis",

Other differences between the two can be identified. On the one hand, the figures in the *Gleichnis* are timeless; by means of an οὐδείς, a μήτι, a πᾶς ἄνθρωπος or a 'whenever', the *Gleichnis* attempts to overwhelm the hearer with the force of an 'in general'.[161] The *Gleichnis* seeks to obviate any opposition by speaking of the indubitable, by presupposing the authority of that which is generally known and generally acknowledged. On the other hand, specific figures appear in the fable—such as κριτής τις, δέκα παρθένοι, ἵππος, ἔλαφος, ἀλώπηξ, or merely a τις— and bear the plot.[162] The fable attempts to avoid opposition by narrating an enthralling account of an action completed in the past and by granting a semblance of reality to its 'mythos'. In Jülicher's opinion, the fable is superior to the *Gleichnis* because it is more refined and objective; more refined in that its intention is less noticeable, more objective in that the opinions and sentiments of the narrator are less evident.[163] Jülicher strives to buttress his estimation of the fable by contrasting it to the *Gleichnis* and the historical example: The fable, a well-invented story, creates the impression of a law to which one must submit more certainly than both the *Gleichnis*, which prescribes a law to which everyone must conform under certain circumstances, and the historical example, in which chance reigns.[164]

zu erreichen. Das Gleichnis beruft sich auf Allgemeingiltiges, die Fabel auf einmal Vorgekommenes'.

161. Jülicher, *Die Gleichnisreden Jesu*, I, p. 97.

162. Jülicher, *Die Gleichnisreden Jesu*, I, p. 97.

163. Jülicher, *Die Gleichnisreden Jesu*, I, p. 97. Jülicher has a rather optimistic, if not idealistic, view of the 'objectivity' of the narrator. While some interpreters informed of modern literary theory would cede to Jülicher that, as he puts it, 'The *Fabel* is superior because it is more refined, the intention shown less', few would grant to him the following: 'The *Fabel* disdains the tutelage of the hearers— through "no one", "whoever had not", etc.—in the *Gleichnisse*; the individual steps before the eyes of the hearers in flawless objectivity, the narrator never permits himself with his judgment, his sentiment, to peep through the interstices of his nets'.

164. This is my summary of an important moment in Jülicher's argument, for here is the first indication that he will not follow Aristotle's delineation of the παραδείγματα in his own classification and description of the *Beispielerzählungen*. Of the fable vis-à-vis the *Gleichnis*, Jülicher writes: '...a well-invented story [*Geschichte*] produces more surely the impression of a law to which one must submit than if it is just announced in advance: According to law, everyone has to act like that under those circumstances' (*Die Gleichnisreden Jesu*, I, pp. 97-98); of the historical example vis-à-vis the fable, he writes: 'Even historical examples

Jülicher proceeds to bring the results of his preliminary discussion of the fable to bear on the parables of Jesus. He posits that 'the majority of Jesus' παραβολαί that bear the narrative form are fables like those of Stesichorus and Aesop'.[165] He then offers his definition of the fable:

> I can only define the *fable* as the *figure of speech in which the effect of a proposition* (thought) *is to be secured by a placing-beside of a fictitious story which unwound in a different field, whose effect is certain, whose thought-framework is similar to the one of that proposition.*[166]

Jülicher hastens to indicate that the fable is comprised of two members, as is the parable (*Gleichnis*). He contends that this cannot really be denied with respect to the *Parabeln* which begin with the introduction 'the kingdom of heaven is like' because such an introduction makes sense only if one talks about two different objects.[167]

At this juncture, Jülicher anticipates objection, conceding that some would deny that the fable is comprised of two parts and would therefore protest against his identification of the Gospel *Parabeln* with the fable.[168] His response unfolds along the following lines.

One is led astray about the essence of the fable if one's understanding of that essence is based upon a later fable collection.[169] Jülicher

[*geschichtlichen Beispiele*] (πράγματα προγεγενημένα in Aristotle *Rhet.* 2.20 is regarded first as εἶδος παραδείγματος, second as the παραβολή, third and last as λόγος) cannot compete with the fable in force: "What has never and nowhere come to pass, that alone is truly eternal". In history [*Geschichte*] an unpredictable chance frequently rules, in fiction the ought to [rules], and to the spirit the latter is superior: Nowhere is the δέον perceived as strongly as in that which has been as it ought to be' (p. 98).

165. Jülicher, *Die Gleichnisreden Jesu*, I, p. 98.

166. Jülicher, *Die Gleichnisreden Jesu*, I, p. 98; Jülicher's emphasis: 'Ich kann die *Fabel* nur definieren als die *Redefigur, in welcher die Wirkung eines Satzes* (Gedankens) *gesichert werden soll durch Nebenstellung einer auf anderm Gebiet ablaufenden, ihrer Wirkung gewissen erdichteten Geschichte, deren Gedankengerippe dem jenes Satzes ähnlich ist*'.

167. Jülicher, *Die Gleichnisreden Jesu*, I, p. 98. Jülicher maintains that one should not press the letter of this introductory formula because the kingdom of heaven, in all seriousness, cannot be equated with a man going on a journey, or ten virgins (five of whom are foolish); rather, 'it perhaps means: In the kingdom of heaven it comes to pass like in the following story; or in the kingdom of heaven it will be according to the same law which governs in the following narrative'.

168. Jülicher, *Die Gleichnisreden Jesu*, I, pp. 98-101; my summary.

169. Jülicher, *Die Gleichnisreden Jesu*, I, p. 98. Jülicher suggests that Lessing erred in this way.

grounds his argument on the premise that 'the fable does not owe its origin to the poets, rather to the orator'.[170] The most ancient of fables, according to Jülicher, were neither sung nor written down, but were spoken in a moment and for the moment; they were not spoken in order to expound vividly a rule of wisdom or an ethical precept, but to elucidate a precarious situation in which the orator found himself—they were spoken to secure the understanding and judgment desired by the orator. The fables suffered the same fate as Jesus' parables: They were ripped from their context and transmitted in a defective manner, with the picture-half (*Bildhälfte*) circulating by and for itself. Thus, when the picture-half alone was transmitted, it was natural to search for the general law manifest in it, and then to formulate that law in the form of a 'frigid' epimythium appended to the fable.[171] 'The more rhetoric declined and paranetic speech, the mother of the parables [*Gleichnisse*] and fables, disappeared behind the encomiastic, the more the fable was alienated from its origin and soon could be tended to entirely for itself (more precisely, its "pictorial" half) as an independent speech—or genus of fiction.'[172] The last step on the way to the dissolution of the fable, Jülicher states, was the development of the animal fable. Here, the interest in form almost consumed the contents, with the parley in the animal world being developed for humorous effect to the extent that the didactic motive was discarded. The original intent of the fable, however, was this: instruction.[173]

Jülicher maintains that if one acknowledges these observations about the fable, then one can no longer oppose the equation of Jesus' narrative παραβολαί with fables. He is aware, nonetheless, that serious objections to such an equation arise from theological motives. For instance, some may depreciate the fable because it displays the grossest impossibility (for instance, the personification of animals), whereas the parable never transgresses the limits of possibility;[174] or some may

170. Jülicher, *Die Gleichnisreden Jesu*, I, p. 98.

171. Jülicher, *Die Gleichnisreden Jesu*, I, p. 99. In constructing this developmental trajectory of the fable, Jülicher refers to specific fables recorded in a variety of ancient sources (e.g. Herod1tus, Livy, Hesiod and Judg.).

172. Jülicher, *Die Gleichnisreden Jesu*, I, p. 99. He adds that fable poets succeeded the generation of fable orators.

173. Jülicher, *Die Gleichnisreden Jesu*, I, p. 99.

174. Jülicher, *Die Gleichnisreden Jesu*, I, p. 100. Jülicher remarks that this view fails to appreciate the rhetorical value of *prosopopoia*.

want to dissociate the fable from the parable because the tone of the former often lapsed into the comical or burlesque, whereas Jesus' parables were always serious and noble.[175] More importantly, whereas the parables have in view circumstances that have to do with the religious-ethical life, which they attempt to illuminate by a drawing-near of similar circumstances from lower (or baser) fields, the fables have in view circumstances of the earthly-social life, which they do not exactly fulfill with the most elevated of sentiments. In light of these objections, Jülicher is willing to refrain from calling the narrative παραβολαί 'fables'; he proposes that these narrative parables (*Gleichniserzählungen*) be called '*"parables" [Parabeln] in the narrower sense*'.[176]

In the ensuing treatment of the 'parables in the narrower sense' (hereafter, simply called '*Parabeln*'), Jülicher does not provide an exposition of the individual *Parabeln* (that comes in the second volume of *Die Gleichnisreden Jesu*); rather, in a section that is quite diffuse, Jülicher confronts what he regards as two misguided approaches to the exposition of Jesus' *Parabeln*, providing evidence from specific synoptic *Parabeln* to support his argument. The first approach can be characterized as that which ignores (for different reasons) the details of the narrative; the second approach, as that which reads too much into the details of the narrative.[177] Jülicher does not feel compelled to subscribe to either approach.

Jülicher reproaches adherents of the first approach because they undervalue the narrative part (*Bild*) of the *Parabeln*. Some regard the narrative part (*Bild*) as unattractive, as failing to allure because the individual features of the narrative are contrived and deceptive due

---

175. Jülicher, *Die Gleichnisreden Jesu*, I, p. 101. Jülicher admits that these objections may be sufficient to justify distinguishing the *Parabeln Jesu* from the fable, although he adds that the worthiness or unworthiness of contents and tone is not very suitable for the determination of rhetorical or poetical forms. A recent study foregrounds what is considered to be burlesque aspects of Jesus' parables; see Tim Schramm and Kathrin Löwenstein, *Unmoralische Helden: Anstössige Gleichnisse Jesu* (Göttingen: Vandenhoeck & Ruprecht, 1986).

176. Jülicher, *Die Gleichnisreden Jesu*, I, p. 101; Jülicher's emphasis: '...ich schlage vor, diese Gleichniserzählungen Jesu "*Parabeln*" *im engeren Sinne* zu nennen'.

177. The following represents my understanding of a rather oblique part of Jülicher's argument about Jesus' narrative parables (*Die Gleichnisreden Jesu*, I, pp. 101-11).

to the fact that they are tailored to the case in question.[178] The circumstances described in the parable narrative are said to contravene the natural process; thus, the *Parabel* is considered arbitrary, artificial, incredible. Against this position, Jülicher argues that in general the narrative part of Jesus' *Parabeln* are of a great natural truth, that the events depicted therein possess a higher degree of verisimilitude than is admitted, and that these *Parabeln* are less arbitrary and artificial than other famous fables.[179] Compared to other fabulists, Jülicher contends, Jesus narrated 'an event taken *out of* daily life certainly not to while away the hearer's time, rather *from* life with a stricter observance of verisimilitude'.[180] Jülicher voices his disapproval of those who treat the narrative part (*Bild*) of the *Parabel* as if it were mere ornamentation, as if it were a worthless shell to be discarded once one arrives at either the main point or the application (epimythium). He rejects this position, claiming, on the one hand, that each feature of the narrative contributes to the fundamental thought, causes it to emerge more clearly and vividly, and therefore serves the comprehension of the subject matter,[181] and, on the other hand, that the epimythien appended to the parables are sometimes misplaced or misleading.[182]

Jülicher's strictures against adherents of the second approach, whom he calls 'allegorizing misinterpreters of the parables of Jesus',[183] should be familiar by now. About such (mis)interpreters he writes, 'They themselves, to be sure, praise the putative ambiguity of the parables

178. Jülicher, *Die Gleichnisreden Jesu*, I, p. 101. Jülicher names G. Gerber as one who holds this view.

179. These conclusions are excerpted from *Die Gleichnisreden Jesu*, I, pp. 101-102. Jülicher does admit that some 'parabolic picture-narratives' (*parabolischen Bilderzählungen*) exhibit violations of the natural process (e.g. Mt. 22.6-7, 13; 25.21-24), but states that these are scarce (cf. pp. 102-103).

180. Jülicher, *Die Gleichnisreden Jesu*, I, p. 103; Jülicher's emphasis.

181. Jülicher, *Die Gleichnisreden Jesu*, I, p. 101-102. Cf. pp. 109-10, where Jülicher anticipates and rebuts the objection to his formulation of the parable (*Parabel*) as fable. He acknowledges that it might be perceived as a debasement of Jesus to posit that '...he narrated lengthy stories [*Geschichten*] in order to teach only *one* thought...As if a good *Fabel* contained ornament, as if the details of a *Parabel* were merely poetic covering! Each feature which contributes to make the fundamental thought emerge clearer, more vivid, is therefore not intended for embellishment, rather it serves the subject matter and its comprehension' (Jülicher's emphasis).

182. Jülicher, *Die Gleichnisreden Jesu*, I, p. 104.

183. Jülicher, *Die Gleichnisreden Jesu*, I, p. 101.

[*Parabeln*] and are delighted about the abundance of thoughts that they dig out there...'[184] Jülicher reiterates that to interpret fables and parables feature by feature is a hopeless enterprise: 'There can be no talk of interpretation in the *Parabeln*?'[185] Why? To understand that, one must know what Jülicher means by 'interpretation'.

> 'To interpret' means to indicate, instead of the apparent signification of a word, the correct [signification of a word]; this we must never promise or permit in a fable or parable, for every word of its narrative must signify that which it appears to signify, and nothing else.[186]

In Jülicher's opinion, everything in the *Parabel* (its fictitious story) corresponds precisely to simple reality, and the more detailed a picture-speech (*Bildrede*) becomes, the less likely is it possible for it to be at once actual (*eigentlich*) and non-actual (*uneigentlich*), true and satisfying.[187] Moreover, unlike the allegory, which builds up pictures (*Bilder*),

> the fable-parable builds up *one picture* [*Bild*]; there is *one* thought that the author embodies in it in order to forge it into the soul of his hearer. The ὅμοιον is its aim, not ὅμοια.[188]

Jülicher concurs with Bernhard Weiss that 'the parable intends to prove', and, according to Jülicher, one can prove only one thing at time.[189] Thus, he insists—as if it needed repeating—that the *Parabel*

184. Jülicher, *Die Gleichnisreden Jesu*, I, pp. 101-102. Jülicher even wishes to do away with multiple meanings: 'And hopefully for us the double literary sense is a banished ghost' (p. 106). These remarks lead one to suspect that Jülicher would disdain the modern view which valorizes the polyvalence of the parables. In this regard, Snodgrass (*The Parable of the Wicked Tenants*, p. 29; emphasis his) writes: 'Particularly in America, the term "polyvalence" has frequently been associated with parable research. The idea in the use of this term is that parables are not to be confined to *a* meaning, but by their very nature open up the reader to various meanings or levels of meanings. It seems to me that this is an unfortunate turn of events that leads back to the very abuse of the parables against which Jülicher was reacting'.

185. Jülicher, *Die Gleichnisreden Jesu*, I, p. 103.

186. Jülicher, *Die Gleichnisreden Jesu*, I, p. 106: '"Deuten" heisst: statt der scheinbaren Bedeutung eines Wortes die richtige angeben; dies dürfen wir nie in einer Fabel oder Parabel versprechen resp. gestatten; denn jedes Wort ihrer Erzählung muss das bedeuten, was es zu bedeuten scheint, und sonst nichts'.

187. Jülicher, *Die Gleichnisreden Jesu*, I, p. 105.

188. Jülicher, *Die Gleichnisreden Jesu*, I, p. 105; Jülicher's emphasis.

189. Jülicher, *Die Gleichnisreden Jesu*, I, p. 105. Jülicher approvingly quotes Bernhard Weiss again, faulting him only for his use of the word 'interpretation'

is not an allegory and should not be approached as if it were an allegory.[190]

Throughout the course of his descriptions of the improper approaches to the *Parabeln Jesu*, Jülicher delineates, in piecemeal fashion, his understanding of the proper approach. A pastiche of quotations will serve to provide a sufficient summary of Jülicher's view.

As we have seen, Jülicher contends that Jesus, in his parables (*Parabeln*), narrated—with a high degree of verisimilitude—an event taken from daily life. The narrative part of the parable was not spoken simply to entertain the hearer, and it should not be regarded as mere ornamentation. As Jülicher explains,

> Now in each correctly comprehended incident in life a law becomes evident, a firm relationship, and the hearer ought to notice this law, this order, in order to discern it also in a higher field—that of the religious, inner life—and to act according to it.[191]

Again, Jülicher rejects the notion that we should interpret the parable narrative; instead, 'we should place ourselves quite completely in the situation which is drawn before us' and then recall the introductory formula, 'the kingdom of God is like', so that we can become aware that incidents in the kingdom of heaven are similar to the one narrated.[192] Although many parables in the synoptic gospels are preceded by the introductory formula 'the kingdom of heaven is like' (the *Sachhälfte*), frequently only half the parable, the picture-half (*Bildhälfte*), has been preserved in the tradition. Even if only the *Bildhälfte* of the *Parabel* survives, there is nothing for one to *interpret*; rather, one is to seek the field to which the fundamental thought in the *Bildhälfte* is to

(*Deutung*), which suggests to Jülicher the old view which treated the *Parabel* as '*uneigentliche Rede*'. The quote belies Jülicher's indebtedness to his teacher: ' "The interpretation of the *Parabel* can only lie in *one general truth*, which results from the transference of the represented rule to the area of the religious-moral life, to the order of the kingdom of God" ' (the emphasis appears in Jülicher's citation).

190. The Parable of the Sower receives considerable mention as Jülicher strives to denounce the error of approaching a *Parabel* as if it were an allegory (see *Die Gleichnisreden Jesu*, I, pp. 106-11). Although the particulars of Jülicher's treatment of this parable cannot be included in this study, it can be mentioned that he takes issue with the view of Johannes Weiss that The Parable of the Sower is 'half *Parabel*, half *Allegorie*' (cf. p. 108).

191. Jülicher, *Die Gleichnisreden Jesu*, I, p. 103.

192. Jülicher, *Die Gleichnisreden Jesu*, I, pp. 103-104.

be *applied*.[193] Unfortunately, in Jülicher's opinion, we cannot be certain of the situation in which Jesus found himself when he invented his parables, and the applications (epimythien) appended to the parables in the synoptic gospels are poor replacements for that lost context. We can endure the loss of *Sachhälfte* and context because, as Jülicher claims,

> Christ narrated at least part of his parables just as the fables were origi-
> nally narrated. At a specific occasion, where his kingdom-of-heaven-
> companions showed ignorance of their duty, he wanted to set straight
> their judgment, and thereby their conduct, first of all with respect to the
> present case, by bringing forward to them a fictitious story drawn from a
> field of lower life thoroughly accessible to them (in characteristic fash-
> ion, predominantly from the domestic, the family life—the persons who
> appear are masters, slaves, house-servants, family friends… fathers and
> children…), where their judgment cannot falter, where they found every-
> thing in order, in order to say to them, 'Now in the case which occupies
> us at the present time the same order is in force, for there you find the
> same circumstances'.[194]

He continues:

> …[W]e know that Jesus' every word concerned the education for the
> kingdom of heaven, and wherever he taught and as [he taught], he dis-
> pensed instruction about circumstances of the kingdom of heaven. Of
> course, to him the point was not to describe in pictorial form a few
> topics from the kingdom of heaven to his own people, rather [it was] to
> win them—for even in the friends there remained enough to conquer—to
> captivate their mind and thereby their will, their strength. Certain pre-
> suppositions entail certain consequences—he showed that to them in
> vivid examples [*anschaulichen Beispiele*] from the circumference of
> their experiences. Must not similar presuppositions entail similar conse-
> quences in the world above?[195]

Jesus, then, employed his parables toward a didactic end—to teach about the kingdom of God.[196] Perhaps we can now understand

193. Jülicher, *Die Gleichnisreden Jesu*, I, pp. 105-106; Jülicher's emphasis.

194. Jülicher, *Die Gleichnisreden Jesu*, I, p. 104. This is a rough translation of a tortuous section. The ellipses within the parentheses indicate that I have omitted citations of specific parables.

195. This is a rather loose translation of *Die Gleichnisreden Jesu*, I, pp. 104-105. Note that Jülicher's discussion of the *Parabeln* here includes mention of them as 'vivid examples'.

196. Jülicher expounds more fully upon this in his chapter 'Der Zweck der Gleichnisreden Jesu'; see especially *Die Gleichnisreden Jesu*, I, pp. 126-27, 145-46, and cf. pp. 155, 163.

more clearly the impetus behind Jülicher's repeated claim, formulated once in a memorable sentence: 'The parable interprets, it cannot be interpreted'.[197]

Jülicher ends his section on the *Parabeln* with a brief apology. He asserts that simply because his theory of the *Parabeln* and their proper exposition excludes the approach that squeezes out too much from the particulars of the narrative, his theory degrades neither the *Parabeln* nor the one who spoke them. On the contrary, his theory assigns a value to the *Parabeln* that is not simply aesthetic, but didactic and deeply moral.[198]

The Beispielerzählungen. This is the category in Jülicher's classi-fication of Jesus' parables that is of particular interest in this study. Although Jülicher's treatment of the *Beispielerzählungen*, in contrast to the *Gleichnisse* and *Parabeln*, is less expansive (he devotes just over three pages to the example narratives in this chapter), this section will

197. Jülicher, *Die Gleichnisreden Jesu*, I, p. 106. Although this statement sounds strikingly similar to one that has become familiar in the thought of several scholars belonging to the interpretive movement known as 'The New Hermeneutic', Jülicher's claim is neither identical to theirs, nor is it as far-reaching as theirs. Sallie McFague (*Speaking in Parables: A Study in Metaphor and Theology* [Philadelphia: Fortress Press, 1975], p. 71) subscribes to what she calls the 'watchword of the new hermeneutic': '...we do not interpret the parables, but the parable interprets us'. The origin of this dictum is traced to Ernst Fuchs and Gerhard Ebeling by Funk in his chapter, 'Language as Event: Fuchs and Ebeling', in *Language, Hermeneutic, and Word of God*, pp. 47-71. Funk's formulations of said 'watchword' are as follows: 'Modern man is to be interpreted by the text, not the text by modern man' (p. 50); 'The parable does not require interpretation or application; it *is* interpreta-tion in that it interprets its hearers' (p. 196; his emphasis). Tolbert pointedly rebuffs McFague's assertion, and, in so doing, that of The New Hermeneutic as well (*Perspectives on the Parables*, pp. 41-42). Perrin (*Jesus and the Language of the Kingdom*, pp. 107-27) describes the influence of The New Hermeneutic, including two of Fuchs's students, Eta Linnemann and Eberhard Jüngel, upon modern parable interpretation and critiques their understanding of the parable as 'language event'. Kingsbury ('Ernst Fuchs' Existentialist Interpretation of the Parables', pp. 383-85, 393-94) shows the strong influence that Jülicher had upon the thought of Fuchs (who studied under Bultmann, who studied under Jülicher). Berger (*Formgeschichte des Neuen Testaments*, pp. 34, 41) critiques the view that parables or metaphors are 'language events', concluding that 'language event is not subject matter event'.

198. Jülicher, *Die Gleichnisreden Jesu*, I, p. 111; cf. his chapter on 'Der Wert der Gleichnisreden Jesu'.

proceed slowly and deliberately because Jülicher's formulation of that category has been sometimes misunderstood, sometimes misrepresented in the history of parable scholarship. Here, Jülicher's definition and description of the example narratives will be given in his own terms. One fact will become certain at the outset; namely, Jülicher himself regards the example narratives as παραβολαί.

The categories *Gleichnis* and *Parabel*, according to Jülicher, do not exhaust the riches of Jesus' παραβολαί. There are still four narratives which, though neither parables (*Gleichnisse*) nor parables in the narrower sense (*Parabeln*) as defined earlier, must nonetheless be counted among Jesus' παραβολαί: The Pharisee and Toll Collector, The Rich Man and Poor Lazarus, The Foolish Rich Man, and The Merciful Samaritan.[199] Although the *Beispielerzählungen* do share features in common with the *Parabeln*, the two categories are not coterminous. Jülicher notes the affinities of the *Parabeln* and the *Beispielerzählungen*, then their differences.

The example narratives, like the *Parabeln*, are narratives that have not been narrated for the hearers' enrichment in historical knowledge; rather, the example narratives, like the *Parabeln*, are freely invented, they serve a religious-ethical purpose, and they are intended to advance the subject matter of the kingdom of heaven.[200] There is only one thing, Jülicher maintains, that differentiates the *Beispielerzählung* from the *Parabel*; with reference to the example narratives, he states that 'what distinguishes them is only that they already move in the higher field which exclusively dominates Jesus' interest'.[201] The difference is explained in this manner:

> Whereas the fables and the parables [in the narrower sense] in Matthew 13–25, without exception, introduce the reader to earthly circumstances —banquets, domestic and professional work, negotiations between masters and slaves—those four pieces present to us events which belong

199. Jülicher, *Die Gleichnisreden Jesu*, I, p. 112.

200. Jülicher, *Die Gleichnisreden Jesu*, I, p. 112: 'They are narratives, and also like the ones discussed so far, such which for their own sakes have not been narrated for the hearers' enrichment in historical knowledge, likewise freely invented, which serve a religious-moral purpose, entirely like the others intended to promote the subject matter the kingdom of heaven'. At this point, it becomes apparent that Jülicher intentionally dissociates the *Beispielerzählung* and the 'historical example'. Conspicuous in its absence throughout the entire discussion of the example narratives is any reference at all to Aristotle or his *Rhetoric*.

201. Jülicher, *Die Gleichnisreden Jesu*, I, p. 112.

directly to the religious-ethical sphere and do not become usable for this field only by a comparison with higher things.[202]

This differentia, Jülicher contends, has significant ramifications for the *Beispielerzählungen*:

> The story does not unwind in a different field, as our 'parable' definition demands, but in the same [field], in that [field] in which is located the proposition to be secured; in other words: The story is an example of the proposition to be asserted. I can really call this category nothing else but example narratives—Stockmeyer says, p. 7: 'example or hypotyposis'.[203]

Jülicher makes reference to the example narratives both to substantiate his claim that 'the story is an example of the proposition to be asserted' and to intimate the proper approach to the example narratives. As he puts it, 'In the example of the Samaritan in Lk. 10.30ff., the proposition that genuine, joyfully sacrificed love is bestowed the highest nobility in heaven and on earth is demonstrated, just as in Lk. 18.9ff., in the example of the Pharisee and the toll collector, [the proposition] that a proud prayer is humbled in God's eyes, on the other hand [that] a humble [prayer] is exalted [is demonstrated].'[204] Any attempt,

---

202. Jülicher, *Die Gleichnisreden Jesu*, I, p. 112: 'Während die Fabeln und die Parabeln in Mt 13-25 samt und sonders den Leser in irdische Verhältnisse, Gastereien, haüsliche und Berufsarbeit, Verhandlungen zwischen Gebietern und Hörigen hineinführen, stellen jene vier Stücke uns Ereignisse vor, die ohne weiteres der religiös-sittlichen Sphäre angehören und nicht erst durch Vergleichung mit Höherem für dies Gebiet nutzbar werden'.

203. Jülicher, *Die Gleichnisreden Jesu*, I, p. 112: 'Die Geschichte laüft nicht, wie unsre "Parabel"-Definition es forderte, auf anderm Gebiete ab, sondern auf demselben, auf dem der zu sichernde Satz liegt, mit andern Worten: Die Geschichte ist ein Beispiel des zu behauptenden Satzes. Ich kann denn auch diese Kategorie nicht anders als Beispielerzählungen—STOCKMEYER sagt S. 7: "Exempel oder Hypotyposen"—nennen'.

204. Jülicher, *Die Gleichnisreden Jesu*, I, p. 112: 'An dem Beispiel des Samariters in Lc 10.30ff. wird der Satz veranschaulicht, dass echte, opferfreudige Liebe den höchsten Adel verleiht im Himmel und auf Erden, ebenso Lc 18.9ff. an dem Beispiel des Pharisäers und des Zöllners, dass ein hochmütiges Gebet in Gottes Augen erniedrigt, ein demutsvolles dagegen erhöht'. Jülicher clearly accepts the epimythium found in Lk. 18.14 as a trustworthy indicator of the proposition (*Satz*) of this example narrative. Curiously, instead of referring to the *story* as an example, Jülicher now refers to the *characters* as examples. One could infer that the characters within the *Beispielerzählungen* constitute the 'example' part of the 'example

in his view, to declare the toll collector to be anything other than a poor sinner, or to declare the foolish rich man to be anything other than a foolish rich man, does not succeed; thus, the method of allegorical parable exposition is foiled again.[205] Additionally, Jülicher suggests that it makes no sense to compare the individual features of the characters in the story as if an individual were to be compared to the genus to which he or she belongs. In his words, 'A comparison of the individual features also makes no sense at all; for if one describes the Pharisee as the picture of all arrogance, can one in all seriousness compare *all* arrogant people with *one* arrogant person, therefore the genus with the individual belonging to it?'[206] Thus, it remains for Jülicher to specify the manner in which the *Beispielerzählung* evokes a comparison.

That the example narrative, like the *Gleichnis* and the *Parabel*, provokes a comparison is beyond question. Jülicher, however, does not utilize the same terms to describe the comparison mechanism in the *Beispielerzählung*. In contradistinction to the *Gleichnis* and the *Parabel*, there is no assertion that the example narrative is two-membered,[207] no mention of a *tertium comparationis*. Indeed, as Jülicher states with respect to the example narrative:

> The soil of the ὅμοιον is nearly abandoned. Such a story has originated not as the result of seeking a similar circumstance or incident on other soil. The narrator has not exercised a comparative activity as he drafted such a παραβολή; the hearer ought to exercise it by measuring his previous behavior, his principles, against the behavior and sentiments of the persons who confront him in this unpretentious story, and—either deeply attracted to or deterred by their model—resolve to arrange his life in

narrative', especially in light of his subsequent query: 'The priest and the Levite in Lk. 10, the notorious Pharisee in Lk. 18, the rich man in Lk. 16—are they not far from having become the *mashal* in the sense of Ps. 68 (69).12?' (p. 113).

205. Jülicher, *Die Gleichnisreden Jesu*, I, p. 112: 'The method of allegorical parable exposition has always run aground on this cliff; it does not turn out well to declare the foolish rich man to be something other than a foolish rich man and the toll collector to be more than a poor sinner; here that interpretation has been made much too difficult'.

206. Jülicher, *Die Gleichnisreden Jesu*, I, p. 112; Jülicher's emphasis. He reinforces his point by raising the same type of question with regard to the priest, Levite and Samaritan in Lk. 10.30-37 (pp. 112-13).

207. Jülicher is more direct about the 'two-memberedness' of the example narratives in his first edition of *Die Gleichnisreden Jesu* (see above, p. 62).

such a way that he completely resembles these people or has nothing at all in common with them any longer.[208]

According to Jülicher, then, the hearer is to compare herself or himself to the characters in the example narrative, as is confirmed by his subsequent remarks.

> Such a speech cannot even seem non-actual [*Uneigentlich*] any longer. It remains a picture-speech [*Bildrede*] because it is meant to affect the senses; it paints before the eyes, as it were, the law in the brightest colors of reality. Also, it remains a *mashal*, provided that we rightly defined this ...as a speech which contains a comparison [*Vergleichung*] *or provokes one*. The priest and the Levite in Luke 10, the notorions Pharisee in Luke 18, the rich man in Luke 16—are they not far from having become a *mashal* in the sense of Ps. 68(69).12?[209]

208. Jülicher, *Die Gleichnisreden Jesu*, I, p. 113. Recall that in the first edition of *Die Gleichnisreden Jesu*, Jülicher states, 'The soil of the ὅμοιον is actually abandoned', and contends that the hearer should not exercise a comparative activity (see above, p. 62). Now Jülicher allows for a minimal degree of comparison in the example narratives, although he shifts the responsibility for making the comparison to the hearer. This is the closest Jülicher comes to claiming that the example narratives offer examples to be imitated.

209. Jülicher, *Die Gleichnisreden Jesu*, I, p. 113; Jülicher's emphasis. Observe that here Jülicher alters his earlier assertion that the *Beispielerzählungen* 'no longer belong within the circumference of the *mashal*' (see above, p. 62). That Jülicher came to regard the *Parabeln* and the *Beispielerzählungen* as closely related is confirmed here; however, in an article written later ('Parables', p. 3566) Jülicher reiterates some of the notions about the *Beispielerzählungen* expressed in the first edition of *Die Gleichnisreden Jesu* and combines them with the notions he expresses now in the revised edition: 'A special variety of this second form of parable [narrative parable] is represented in four examples in Lk.: the Good Samaritan (10.30ff.), the Foolish Rich Man (12.16ff.), the Rich Man and Lazarus (16.19ff.), the Pharisee and the Publican (18.9ff.). Like the others they are narratives; but here the narrative moves from the beginning on the higher religious and ethical plane, the laws of which are to be set forth; the story is itself an instance of the proposition to be demonstrated. Here there is neither comparison nor allegory, there is no "laying alongside" of two things that they may be compared; if we are precluded from using the word "parable" we must call them illustrative instances which establish an abstract religious or ethical truth by the evidence of a concrete case. But any one finding parabolic stories in which the comparison with the higher reality was entirely left to the imagination of the readers placed in close juxtaposition with illustrative instances which in outward form are not distinguishable from them (cp. Lk. 15.11-32 and Lk. 18.9ff.) might very easily regard the two sorts as identical'.

Here, Jülicher is not far from affirming that the characters in the narrative constitute the *Beispiel* in the *Beispielerzählung*.

A comparison of the example narratives and the *Parabeln* affords Jülicher the opportunity to amplify several points. He contends that an appraisal of the status of the example narratives vis-à-vis the *Parabeln* does not necessarily result in a devaluation of 'the παραβολαί of this class', the example narratives.[210] Although the fundamental thoughts in the example narratives are more tightly enclosed, more unified than those of the *Parabeln*, the former are not inferior to the latter; while the persuasive power of the example narratives, and consequently their rhetorical value as a means of evidence, rests upon other grounds than the fable, that does not mean that their value is less than the *Parabel*, or that they derive their authority from the narrator.[211] This claim leads Jülicher to explain his previous contention that, unlike the *Parabel*, the story in the example narrative does not transpire in other fields, but in the very field in which the proposition to be secured is located.

> To be sure, in the fable-parable the conflict is played on neutral soil; the opponent must first decide completely impartially about true and untrue, right and wrong, in order to be compelled, after that, to the acknowledgment of his decision now also on the soil in dispute. The example narrative forgoes that—to enter first a neutral soil with the opponent; it presents to him immediately the subject matter itself [*Sache selber*], but not as a pale formula, rather demonstrated in a particular case which the composer skillfully selected so that all disturbing moments, as they continuously push into life, remain excluded and the idea alone acquires currency most forcibly and unmistakably.[212]

210. Jülicher, *Die Gleichnisreden Jesu*, I, p. 113. Jülicher excludes Lk. 16.27-31 from consideration because there 'a supplementer has played his evil game'.

211. Jülicher, *Die Gleichnisreden Jesu*, I, p. 113: 'An straffer Geschlossenheit, an Einheitlichkeit des Grundgedankens stehen die παραβολαί dieser Klasse hinter denen der vorigen nicht zurück—die Ausnahme Lc 16.27ff. kommt nicht in Betracht, da dort ein Ergänzer sein übles Spiel getrieben hat—, und ihre Ueberzeugungskraft, somit ihr rednerischer Wert als Beweismittel ruht zwar auf anderm Grunde als bei der Fabel, braucht aber nicht geringer zu sein, und ist unabhängig von der Autorität der Erzählers'. Compare this to his remark in the first edition of *Die Gleichnisreden Jesu* that 'whoever does not acknowledge the authority of the narrator will never submit himself to the authority of such a narrative' (see above, p. 63).

212. Jülicher, *Die Gleichnisreden Jesu*, I, p. 113; cf. II, p. 585, where Jülicher describes the *Beispielerzählungen* as narratives which do not encourage the transference of a thought obtained in a different field to the religious field, rather the

That the example narrative is able to present the subject matter itself, the idea alone, is due in large part to the characters who appear in the narrative. Thus, the importance of the characters who people the example narratives comes to the fore again in Jülicher's understanding of this class of παραβολή. The characters are inextricably related to the subject matter: '...the figures in Jesus' example narratives are in their own way perfect, absolutely pure types of the idea to be represented, and nothing in them draws the attention away from this main point'.[213] That being so, our judgment can only be like that of the narrator: 'What a fool indeed is the rich man (Lk. 12.16ff.)! Justified in God's eyes must be the toll collector gone down to his house, not the Pharisee (Lk. 18.9ff.)!'[214] Jülicher can now develop his claim that one who hears the example narrative should compare herself or himself to the characters in the narrative:

> And the generalization of this judgment, the application to us, the—perhaps only instinctive—formation of the general law out of the particular case in which we view it effective does not fail to take place. One must show the Good in all its goodness, beside it the Evil in all its unveiled and unalloyed wickedness, so that the hearer will no longer require further proof of Good and Evil; he sees here—as he had been compelled to acknowledge it in the parables [*Parabeln*] through a process of inference—τί τὸ ἀγαθὸν καὶ εὐάρεστον καὶ τέλειον, and after hearing such a παραβολή, in his heart he involuntarily chimes in also: οὕτως καὶ οὐ.[215]

His brief examination of the four example narratives complete, Jülicher furnishes his formal definition of the *Beispielerzählung*:

> This third category of Jesus' παραβολαί are therefore example narratives; that is, narratives *which bring forward a general proposition of religious-ethical character in the dress of an especially impressively shaped particular case*, 'the general truth confirmed by the evidentness of the deed'. They do not tolerate interpretation; they are as clear and transparent as possible; they desire practical application. If a mirror is

Beispielerzählungen '...illustrate a religious thought in its unassailable general validity in the form of an especially suitably selected individual case'.

213. Jülicher, *Die Gleichnisreden Jesu*, I, pp. 113-14. In the space marked by the ellipsis, Jülicher contrasts the figures in the *Beispielerzählungen* to cases in real life which represent, in his view, an impure alloy of 'the repulsive and the impressive, the edifying and the trivial'.

214. Jülicher, *Die Gleichnisreden Jesu*, I, p. 114.

215. Jülicher, *Die Gleichnisreden Jesu*, I, p. 114.

held up to someone, as the example narrative does, so that he perceives his ugliness or smudges that disfigure him, then no further explanatory words are required in addition to that; the mirror indicates even better how it stands in truth than might be achieved with the lengthiest of descriptions.[216]

Jülicher is quick to admit that the example narrative cannot force the stubborn hearer to look in the mirror. However, that remark does not apply only to the example narratives; even the fable (parable) does not have an absolutely irresistible effect because the unwilling can disavow or ignore the similarity between themselves and that which is held up before them.[217]

Jülicher terminates his treatment of the *Beispielerzählungen* with remarks that obtain for all categories of *Die Gleichnisreden Jesu*:

> In order to teach, the κοιναὶ πίστεις of all sorts rely upon the good will of the hearer; they are powerless vis-à-vis the resolute ἀπιστία. In short, Jesus' parable speeches have an altogether wonderful effect on the portion of humankind who possess an organ for his spirit, even today as on the first day.[218]

---

216. Jülicher, *Die Gleichnisreden Jesu*, I, p. 114; Jülicher's emphasis: 'Diese dritte Kategorie von παραβολαί Jesu sind also Beispielerzählungen, d.h. Erzählungen, *die einen allgemeinen Satz religiös-sittlichen Charakters in dem Kleide eines besonders eindrucksvoll gestalteten Einzelfalles vorführen*, "durch die Evidenz der That die allgemeine Wahrheit bestatigen". Sie vertragen keine Deutung, sie sind so klar und durchsichtig wie möglich, praktische Anwendung wünschen sie sich. Wenn man, wie die Beispielerzählung thut, jemandem einen Spiegel vorhält, dass er seine Hässlichkeit oder Schmutzflecke, die ihn entstellen, wahrnehme, so bedarf man dazu keines weiteren erklärenden Wortes; der Spiegel deutet eben besser, wie es in Wahrheit steht, als man es mit den längsten Beschreibungen zu Stande brächte'.

217. Jülicher, *Die Gleichnisreden Jesu*, I, p. 114: 'Der Widerwillige, der ahnungslos aufmerksam das fremde Bild betrachtet hat, das ihm da vorgehalten wurde, wird gegenüber dem plötzlich auf ihn eindrängenden οὕτως καὶ νῦν um Ausreden nicht verlegen sein; er wird die Aehnlichkeit ableugnen oder ignorieren'.

218. Jülicher, *Die Gleichnisreden Jesu*, I, p. 115. After this section on the three classes of παραβολαί *Jesu*, Jülicher turns his attention to other pictorial speeches ascribed to Jesus in the New Testament. He considers two παροιμία in the Gospel of John (10.1-16; 15.1-11), as well as the pericope of the evil tenants (Mk 12.1-11 and parallels), to be allegorical and inauthentic, although he contends that a few simple parables (*Gleichnisse*) in the fourth Gospel can be traced back to Jesus (see pp. 115-16). He makes one observation here that will be of interest later: 'The exposition will show that Lk. 14.7ff. must not be named as a parallel' (p. 115).

Jülicher's Summary of Results

Jülicher ends his lengthy chapter on 'The Essence of the Parable Speeches of Jesus' by recapitulating the conclusions drawn throughout the course of his investigation of the pictorial speeches attributed to Jesus in the New Testament. Since Jülicher's prose is trenchant here, there is little need for anything other than a translation of his words.

> The results of our examination are: What the synoptists call παραβολή is a genus of picture-speech [*Bildreden*] that is almost completely lacking in the fourth Gospel. The παροιμία of John are related to the synoptic παραβολαί least of all. The evangelists' conception of the essence of these speeches is untenable. They are by no means λόγοι σκοτεινοί which constantly require a special λύσις. If something in them remains unclear to us now, then the defective, disjointed, fragmentary tradition solely bears the blame. A properly and completely preserved παραβολή requires no interpretive words, tolerates not even one, for everything in it is distinct. Particularly in the pictorial part, i.e. the one which is created by the fantasy of the speaker or which is drawn near, every word is to be understood actually [*eigentlich*]. The παραβολαί are rhetorical, not poetic forms. Three classes are to be distinguished among the synoptic 'parables' [*Parabeln*], two of which offer a freely invented narrative, one a generally acknowledged experience from the field of daily life. The latter is the parable [*Gleichnis*], the others are the parable in the narrower sense [*Parabel im engeren Sinne*], i.e. the fable in the service of religious ideas, and the example narrative [*Beispielerzählung*]. The basic form of them all, likewise with Jesus, is the non-rare comparison [*Vergleichung*]. As each παραβολή makes up a unified, enclosed whole, each also intends only *one* proposition, *one* thought, be it to fortify by a support fetched from foreign soil, be it to demonstrate and impress by individualization. Jesus, in these παραβολαί, did not devise by himself a peculiar manner of teaching or manner of speaking; countless analogues to each of the aforesaid kinds lie before us from all literatures, and no mystical vapor is suitable to veil his parable speeches [*Parabelreden*]. Not in some sort of form [*Formellen*], rather in the content lies the domain of the son of God; he has not dowried us with new leather skins, rather new wine. His pictures move about in the field of daily life, are not afraid to utilize the lowly, the sinful; 'all things are yours' runs the tenet. In order to pour out clarity about the lofty and divine, about affairs and laws of the kingdom of God, in order to make the heavenly accessible to his sense-partial hearers, he kindly led them from the generally-known upwards to the unknown; on the bands of similarity he pulled up their souls from the common to the eternal. With regal magnanimity, he took into his service the whole world, even the worldly in it, in order to

overcome the world; he beat it with its own weapons. No means he left untried, no means of words, in order to bring the word of his God to and into the hearts of his hearers; only the allegory—which does not proclaim, rather veils; which does not disclose, rather closes up; which does not combine, rather separates; which does not persuade, rather rejects—this speech form the clearest, the mightiest, the plainest of all orators could not employ for his purposes.[219]

Comments and Conclusions

In this chapter the concern has been to contextualize Jülicher's formulation of the category *Beispielerzählung*, and an attempt was made to do so by locating the place of that category within the tripartite classification scheme of Jesus' parable speeches and by situating that classification scheme within the overall argument articulated in the revised version of *Die Gleichnisreden Jesu*. The classification scheme proposed by Jülicher is central to his understanding of the essence of Jesus' parable speeches, and above all else Jülicher strives to make it exceedingly clear that Jesus' parables are not in essence allegories. To be sure, Jülicher maintains that Jesus' parables are pictorial speeches which come in the forms of *Gleichnis*, *Parabel* and *Beispielerzählung*, which are rooted in simile, which are *eigentliche Rede* that need to be applied. He denies that Jesus' parables are pictorial speeches which come in the form of allegory, which is rooted in metaphor, *uneigentliche Rede* that must be translated or interpreted. By defining precisely the essence of Jesus' parables as *eigentliche Rede* of a comparative nature, by carefully delimiting the sphere or field to which Jesus' parables refer, Jülicher strives to demolish the very foundation of the allegorizing approach to Jesus' parables. If the parables of Jesus are not in essence allegories, then it should follow logically that Jesus' parables should not be allegorized. This is the context of the *Beispielerzählungen* within *Die Gleichnisreden Jesu*, and it matters not which version—the first or the revised edition—of *Die Gleichnisreden Jesu* is consulted: Jülicher emphasizes that the *Beispielerzählungen*, a third category of 'παραβολαί Jesu', are not allegories and should not be allegorized.

In light of that context within the overall argument of *Die Gleichnisreden Jesu*, Jülicher's handling of one *Beispielerzählung*, The Merciful Samaritan, is intriguing. The Merciful Samaritan throughout

---

219. Jülicher, *Die Gleichnisreden Jesu*, I, pp. 117-18; Jülicher's emphasis.

the history of its interpretation has been regularly subjected to some of
the most elaborate and fanciful allegorized interpretations, according to
which, for instance, the Samaritan is equated with Christ, the robbers
with the rulers of darkness, the Priest with the Law, the Levite with the
prophets, the wounds with sin, the inn with the church, and so on.[220]
Jülicher placed The Merciful Samaritan in a category of 'παραβολαί
Jesu' least susceptible to allegorized interpretations, the *Beispielerzählungen*, a category in which the field of reference is more narrowly
limited than all the other 'παραβολαί Jesu': The Merciful Samaritan
and the other members of this category move directly on the same field
as the proposition to be asserted. Consequently, this lessens further the
need for a transference of some sort, which can lead us down the
wicked path of allegorized interpretation. In this way, Jülicher rescues
The Merciful Samaritan and the other example narratives from the
clutches of interpreters who delight in arabesque allegorized interpretations of Jesus' parable speeches. Again, this obtains for either edition of
Die Gleichnisreden Jesu.

As we observed earlier, Jülicher modified his appraisal of the
Beispielerzählungen in the revised edition of *Die Gleichnisreden Jesu*,
and for good reason. In the first edition of that book, Jülicher came per-
ilously close to giving cause for the removal of the example narratives
from among the genuine parables of Jesus. There, it will be recalled,
Jülicher asserted that the *Beispielerzählungen*—in which 'the soil of the
ὅμοιον is actually abandoned', and which are removed from the circumference of the *mashal*—lack a comparative character of the same
magnitude as the other categories of the 'παραβολαί Jesu', an assertion
which is inconsistent with the tenet that the 'παραβολαί Jesu', being
rooted in simile, are of a comparative nature. Such a claim does not
damage his argument that the *Beispielerzählungen* are not allegories,
but it does open a window of opportunity for the charge that the example narratives are mere stories, or worse, stories of 'real' events, and
not παραβολαί. In this connection, it becomes apparent why Jülicher
might have wanted to avoid any correlation of the *Beispielerzählungen*

220. For specific details on such allegorized interpretations of The Merciful
Samaritan, see Werner Monselewski, *Der barmherzige Samariter: Eine ausle-
gungsgeschichtliche Untersuchung zu Lukas 10, 25-37* (BGBE, 5; Tübingen: J.C.B.
Mohr [Paul Siebeck], 1967), pp. 18-62; see further Hans Gunther Klemm, *Das
Gleichnis vom barmherzigen Samariter: Grundzüge der Auslegung im 16./17.
Jahrhundert* (BWANT, 3; Stuttgart: W. Kohlhammer, 1973).

and the 'historical examples': to rule out the already common notion held by some interpreters, if we may accept van Koetsveld's testimony, that the example narratives are not 'parables' but 'stories'.

Jülicher, in revising his initial treatment of the *Beispielerzählungen*, was among the first to critique his appraisal of the example narratives in the 1886 edition of *Die Gleichnisreden Jesu*. Jülicher certainly wanted no part of any approach that disfigured the parables of Jesus by treating them as allegories; neither did he want to be a party to the debasement of some of Jesus' παραβολαί. Without redefining the category *Beispielerzählung*, Jülicher discovered a way in which he could revise his assessment of the example narratives and thus secure their proper place among the genuine parables of Jesus. In the revised edition of *Die Gleichnisreden Jesu*, Jülicher affirms the comparative character of the *Beispielerzählungen*, thereby rooting them a bit deeper in the simile and, as a result, allowing them to partake more fully of the essence of Jesus' parable speeches. The example narratives, now included within the circumference of the *mashal*, are more in line with the comparative character of the *Gleichnisse* and the *Parabeln*; and the authority of the *Beispielerzählungen* is now more like that of the *Parabeln*. Jülicher can still dissociate the example narratives from the historical examples in order to fend off a view that the *Beispielerzählungen* are stories of real events; and he can offer a more positive appraisal of the *Beispielerzählungen* without marring his argument that they are not allegories. Indeed, Jülicher's shrewd and strategic reappraisal of the example narratives, in which he is careful to stress that they are not inferior to the *Parabeln*, makes his argument more consistent. By removing a reason to doubt that the *Beispielerzählungen* should remain among the genuine 'παραβολαί Jesu', Jülicher buttresses his argument that the example narratives, like the *Gleichnisse* and the *Parabeln*, are not allegories. However, these speculative musings about why Jülicher reevaluated his treatment of the *Beispielerzählungen* and published a revised view of them in 1899 should not distract us, for the treatment of the example narratives in the revised edition of *Die Gleichnisreden Jesu* is the one of import in modern parable scholarship, and thus the one dealt with in this chapter.

The preceding summary and exposition of *Die Gleichnisreden Jesu* should make manifest the magnitude of the debt parable scholars owe to Jülicher. Although Jülicher's program has not met with universal acceptance or unqualified acclaim, certain themes become apparent in the homage paid to Jülicher by New Testament scholars, both those who were his contemporaries and those who succeed him by decades.

Soon after its publication, *Die Gleichnisreden Jesu* began to secure a place in the history of parable scholarship.[221] At the close of the last century, Jülicher's work received some favorable reviews in English;[222] at the beginning of the present century, his study garnered more notice, with some scholars more appreciative, some less.[223] However, it is no exaggeration to state that, among a number of English-speaking scholars, Jülicher's two-volume work has not received the serious attention it deserves, most probably because it remains untranslated to this day.[224]

221. The second volume of *Die Gleichnisreden Jesu*, in which Jülicher provides his exposition of the parable speeches of Jesus, has been less influential, at least in this country. Perrin ('The Modern Interpretation of the Parables', pp. 132-33) relates that after his reading of Jülicher's second volume he '...began to realize that one could put together Jülicher's interpretations of the various parables and come up with a manifesto of nineteenth-century German theological liberalism'. Johnston ('Parabolic Interpretations Attributed to Tannaim', pp. 7-8) observes that '...while the second volume, containing the author's reconstructed interpretations of the parables as teaching general moral points, has been generally ridiculed and repudiated, the first volume, consisting of prolegomena, remains important for debate'. Werner Georg Kümmel (*The New Testament: The History of the Investigation of its Problems* [trans. S. Maclean Gilmour and Howard Clark Kee; Nashville: Abingdon Press, 1972], p. 433 n. 246) holds a different view: 'The second volume, which appeared in 1898, offered a detailed "Exposition of the parables of the first three Gospels" which has not been surpassed to the present day'.

222. See, e.g., David Eaton, 'Professor Jülicher on the Parables of Jesus', *ExpTim* 10 (1898–99), pp. 539-43; *idem*, 'Jülicher on the Parables', *ExpTim* 11 (1899–1900), p. 300.

223. As a representative of the former, see G.W. Stewart, 'Jülicher on the Nature and Purpose of the Parables', *The Expositor* 1 (1900), pp. 232-40, 311-20, 461-72. As a representative of the latter, see W. Sanday, 'A New Work on the Parables', *JTS* 1 (1900), pp. 161-80. Johannes Weiss, although he makes no mention of Sanday, rebuts almost every charge Sanday levels against Jülicher; see his review 'Jülichers "Gleichnisreden Jesu"', *TRu* 4 (1901), pp. 1-11 (repr. in Harnisch [ed.], *Gleichnisse Jesu*, pp. 11-19).

224. According to Kingsbury ('Major Trends in Parable Interpretation', p. 587): 'The English world of scholarship took relatively little notice of Jülicher's parable theory when it was first propounded and therefore did not actively participate in the ensuing debate it generated on the Continent'. Stewart ('Jülicher on the Nature and Purpose of the Parables', p. 231) wrote at the turn of the century: 'Long as the book has been before the world, it is questionable if it is so well known to English

Some modern biblical scholars have expressed high opinions of the significance of Jülicher's *Die Gleichnisreden Jesu* for the study of the parables. Harnisch writes that Jülicher's work is, without doubt, fundamental for the modern history of parable interpretation.[225] *Die Gleichnisreden Jesu* is hailed as a 'pioneering work'[226] because in it Jülicher constructs a forceful case against the method of parable interpretation that prevailed from the time of the early church, to the Church Fathers, through the Middle Ages, to the Reformation, even until today: the allegorical interpretation of Jesus' parables. The immensity of this feat is heralded again and again. Several scholars credit Jülicher with inaugurating a 'new day'[227] in the study of the parables, or with initiating the modern critical approach to the study of the parables.[228] Funk states that 'Adolf Jülicher's work represents the watershed between pre-modern (allegorical) interpretation of the parables and the modern, historical-critical approach'.[229] While it would be an overstatement to assert that Jülicher was the solitary harbinger of a new era of parable interpretation[230] (for he did not construct his program in a vacuum, as

theologians as it should be; and even at this late date it may not be inopportune to direct attention to a work whose importance, as a contribution to the literature of the subject, is beyond all question'. Years later, Granskou (*Preaching on the Parables*, p. 11) is led to suspect 'that not all of the critics of Jülicher have read Jülicher'.

225. Harnisch, 'Vorwort', in his *Gleichnisse Jesu*, pp. ix-x. Rudolf Bultmann also refers to Jülicher's work as 'grundlegenden' in *Die Geschichte der synoptischen Tradition* (FRLANT, 29; Göttingen: Vandenhoeck & Ruprecht, 8th edn, 1970), p. 184 n. 1 (cf. *History of the Synoptic Tradition*, p. 170 n. 1).

226. See, e.g., Jones, *The Art and Truth of the Parables*, pp. 16-17, cf. p. 11; Klauck, *Allegorie und Allegorese*, p. 1.

227. See, e.g., Tolbert, *Perspectives on the Parables*, p. 24; Kissinger, *The Parables of Jesus*, p. xiii.

228. See, e.g., Bailey, *Poet and Peasant*, p. 16; Young, *Jesus and his Jewish Parables*, p. 21; Scott, *Hear Then the Parable*, p. 42.

229. Robert W. Funk, 'Foreword', in Kissinger's *The Parables of Jesus*, p. v. Granskou (*Preaching on the Parables*, p. 16) makes a similar remark.

230. Kingsbury ('Major Trends in Parable Interpretation', p. 579) makes the more reasoned assertion: 'By the compelling force of his scholarship, complemented as it was by the considerable weight of his tomes (two volumes totalling 971 pages!), Jülicher almost singlehandedly inaugurated a new era in the history of parable interpretation'. As we have seen, Jülicher acknowledges his debt to Bernhard Weiss and C.E. van Koetsveld. Jones (*The Art and Truth of the Parables*, pp. 11-14) provides a summary statement of the scope and significance of van

was evidenced in Chapter 2), many scholars consider *Die Gleichnis-reden Jesu* to be the 'turning point'[231] which marks the advent of a new epoch[232] in the history of the interpretation of Jesus' parables. Commonly, those who provide a history of parable interpretation either begin with Jülicher or, like Jones, divide that history into two periods— 'Before and After Jülicher'.[233] The author and his book have almost attained the status of legend: *Die Gleichnisreden Jesu* is said to be 'the most famous book on the parables in this century',[234] and the author's name is said to 'loom large'[235] in the history of the interpretation of Jesus' parables. It comes as no surprise that Jülicher has been called 'the father of modern parable research'.[236]

Koetsveld's two-volume work on the parables, *De Gelijkenissen van den Zalig-maker*. Jones writes: 'Had he written in German instead of in Dutch, van Koetsveld would have doubtless acquired a prestige equal to that of Jülicher, whose admiration for him was by no means exaggerated…Indeed, much of the work done by Jülicher and regarded as original by those unfamiliar with that of van Koetsveld had been done by the latter who had already discussed the literary forms of the parables and classified them according to type and form' (p. 14). Klauck ('Adolf Jülicher', p. 114), after providing details of specific contributions made by Jülicher's forerunners and the impact they had on his work, states: 'Indeed, all these insights really gained currency only in the precise, carefully thought out form which Jülicher gave them'. While some of the individual insights may not be original to Jülicher, his contribution is a synthesis of insights into a comprehensive program (see Jülicher's own remarks to this effect, p. 80 above).

231. See, e.g., Funk, *Language, Hermeneutic, and Word of God*, p. 147; Johnston, 'Parabolic Interpretations Attributed to Tannaim', pp. 6-7.

232. Among those who refer to *Die Gleichnisreden Jesu* as 'epoch-making' are B.T.D. Smith, *The Parables of the Synoptic Gospels: A Critical Study* (London: Cambridge University Press, 1937), p. 23; Kingsbury, 'Ernst Fuchs' Existentialist Interpretation of the Parables', p. 383; Perrin, *Jesus and the Language of the Kingdom*, p. 92; and Weder, *Die Gleichnisse Jesu als Metaphern*, p. 11.

233. I quote the title of Jones's chapter on the history of parable interpretation in his *The Art and Truth of the Parables*, pp. 3-40. Admittedly, I have followed a similar tack in this study.

234. Hunter, *Interpreting the Parables*, p. 37.

235. Granskou (*Preaching on the Parables*, p. 10) introduces Jülicher by saying, 'This is the name that looms large in any history of the exegesis of Jesus' parables'. The import of Jülicher's name is heightened by Kissinger (*The Parables of Jesus*, pp. 71-72): 'The name of Adolf Jülicher looms like a colossus in the history of interpretation of Jesus' parables'.

236. Tolbert, *Perspectives on the Parables*, p. 16; Perrin, 'The Modern Interpretation of the Parables of Jesus', pp. 131-32.

Jülicher, however, has not lacked critics. Despite the lofty praise lavished upon *Die Gleichnisreden Jesu*, which sometimes approaches the encomiastic, Jülicher's work has engendered negative responses, which sometimes approach the invective. It is not uncommon for Jülicher's critics who are interested in pursuing a particular issue with respect to Jesus' parables to focus their attention on a specific aspect of Jülicher's program and subject it to critique. If, for instance, one is investigating the relationship of Jesus' parables to rabbinic parables, then Jülicher's treatment of the rabbinic parables is criticized;[237] or if one is advancing the view that Jesus' parables are metaphors or allegories or analogies, then Jülicher's understanding of the essence of Jesus' parables comes under review and is revised or refuted.[238] This study is no different and will follow suit: Since the object of interest here is the *Beispielerzählungen*, Jülicher's formulation of that category will be critiqued. Given the narrow focus of this study, all of the criticisms levelled against Jülicher's work need not, and cannot, be dealt with thoroughly, although a catalogue of some of the more typical can be provided.

Several tenets of Jülicher's theory have been called into question and subsequently modified or rejected.[239] Jülicher has been criticized for:

—his application of categories taken from ancient Greek rhetoric to Jewish speech forms; and, consequently, for
—his classification of Jesus' parables based upon the *Rhetoric* of Aristotle;[240]

237. See the studies previously mentioned (pp. 23-24 n. 16).

238. For studies which propound the view that the parables are metaphors, see p. 24 n. 18; several studies which claim Jesus' parables are allegories have already been cited (see p. 24 n. 17). John W. Sider argues that Jesus' parables are proportional analogies, suggesting that as such—and in light of Jülicher's definition of allegory—they are allegories ('Proportional Analogies in the Gospel Parables', *NTS* 31 [1985], pp. 1-23 [22]); see also his *Interpreting the Parables*, pp. 18-23.

239. The list of criticisms that follows has been compiled from Berger, *Formgeschichte des Neuen Testaments*, pp. 40-41; Klauck, 'Adolf Jülicher', pp. 113-24; and Sellin, 'Allegorie und "Gleichnis"', pp. 369-76.

240. Interestingly, although Jüngel (*Paulus und Jesus*, p. 95) reproaches Jülicher for projecting an Aristotelian logic and ontology onto the parables of Jesus, he approves of Jülicher's classification of Jesus' παραβολαί because, in his opinion, Jülicher draws upon Aristotle's *Rhetoric* to define the essence of Jesus' parables and not to classify them. I offer a different view of Jülicher's use of Aristotle's *Rhetoric* as a means of classifying Jesus' παραβολαί (see Chapter 5, pp. 314-17).

—his assertion that Jesus' parables have an argumentative function;
—his treatment of the rabbinic parables;
—his definition of allegory, including both his statement of the relationship between allegory and metaphor, parable and simile, and his failure to differentiate adequately between '*Allegorie* as a text-producing, poetical-rhetorical procedure and *Allegorese* as a text-expositing, exegetical-hermeneutical method';[241]
—his separation of *Bildhälfte* and *Sachhälfte* within the parable;
—his insistence that a parable intends to illustrate a general, moral (or abstract) truth;[242]
—his contention that a parable has only one *tertium comparationis*;
—his failure to take seriously the narrative form in his distinction between *Gleichnis* and *Parabel*;
—his understanding of the meaning and mode of the kingdom of God;[243]
—his critical reconstruction of Jesus' parables.

To be sure, these criticisms merit attention and should not be slighted; yet, a consideration of the debate surrounding each of them lies beyond the purview of this study.

However, 'the contentions of [Jülicher's] critics' must nonetheless be taken into account with respect to those issues which have a more direct bearing on the example narratives. Thus, one task that remains is to provide an account of the critiques of Jülicher's conception of the category *Beispielerzählung* that have been advanced by scholars in the century following the publication of his opus (see Chapter 4). Prior to that undertaking, but toward that end, attention will be given to those aspects of Jülicher's program in general that should inform a study of the example narratives, and then to those aspects of his formulation of the *Beispielerzählung* as a category of παραβολή that invite further study.

241. On the distinction between 'Allegorie' and 'Allegorese,' see Klauck, *Allegorie und Allegorese*, pp. 4-12; this quote comes from his article, 'Adolf Jülicher', p. 117.

242. John W. Sider, 'Nurturing our Nurse: Literary Scholars and Biblical Exegesis', *Christianity and Literature* 32 (1982), pp. 15-21 (17): 'The one-point theory is the most influential and the most pernicious part of Jülicher's legacy to a century of interpretation'. See what Granskou (*Preaching on the Parables*, pp. 11, 14-15) has to say with regard to the carping about the so-called 'one-point theory'.

243. Jülicher's assertion that the kingdom of God is of central interest in Jesus' parables is seldom disputed; his description of Jesus' conception of the kingdom of God is frequently criticized.

Jülicher knew well that the parables ascribed to Jesus within each of the synoptic gospels bear the unmistakable imprints of the hand of the respective evangelists, that the synoptic parables exhibit the character of the Gospel in which they appear, and that each evangelist manifests peculiarities as a parable narrator. These assertions warrant unqualified assent, as anyone casually acquainted with redaction criticism would agree. Jülicher knew equally well that the four example narratives as a group can be found in only one Gospel, the Gospel of Luke.[244] Interestingly, Jülicher's closing remarks in the second volume of *Die Gleichnisreden Jesu* (see the epigraph of this chapter) suggest that all four example narratives share a similar stance that can be placed under a title which he excerpts from the third Gospel (Lk. 16.15). However, his decision to excise all of Jesus' parable speeches from their Gospel contexts and to remove all 'accretions' (based upon his conclusion that the evangelists had a false conception of the essence, and therefore the purpose, of Jesus' parables) is a factor that may have prevented him from realizing fully some of the characteristic features of the example narratives and how those features might be understood in light of their specific narrative context. In this study, the example stories will be given consideration mainly as parables of the Gospel of Luke, and in response to Jülicher's 'either—or', a particular evangelist will be chosen.

Choosing to view the *Beispielerzählungen* as parables of the Gospel of Luke, as opposed to parables of Jesus, does not necessarily entail the conclusion that they (and any or all of the other parables) are allegories, as Jülicher's 'either—or' would seem to mandate. If it is true that Jülicher overstated his case *against* conceiving of *any* of the parables as allegory, it is also true that others overstate their case *for* conceiving *all* the parables as allegories.[245] It seems more prudent to maintain that some parables are allegories, while others exhibit allegorical features, and still others none.[246] Indeed, one assumption underlying Jülicher's classification of Jesus' parable speeches is that the παραβολή is not μία, but πολλαί. Although one may well question Jülicher's essential

---

244. See Jülicher, *Die Gleichnisreden Jesu*, II, pp. 2, 585.

245. Some critics have failed to observe that Jülicher readily admits that some of the parables in the synoptic gospels are indeed allegories. However, the *raison d'être* of *Die Gleichnisreden Jesu* is to show that the parables of *Jesus* are not allegories.

246. In agreement with Boucher, *The Mysterious Parable*, pp. 22, 24.

distinction between metaphor and simile (both of which, he admits, share in common the ὅμοιον)[247]—and, for this reason, wish to jettison his insights about the example narratives—Jülicher's formulation of the example narrative as a category of παραβολή does not stand or collapse on the basis of his definition of allegory.

Jülicher, in his attempt to discern the essence and purpose of Jesus' parables, stipulated that we should refrain from all modern definitions of the parable, as if modern definitions can adequately account for the ancient form παραβολή. Moreover, he judiciously recommended that we should resist foisting modern definitions of rhetorical concepts upon the ancients. Above all else, Jülicher desired to understand the parables of Jesus within their own distinctive historical milieu. The problem said to confound Jülicher's theory, that he applied Greek rhetoric to Jesus' Jewish parables, does not necessarily confront those who wish to apply insights drawn from ancient Greek rhetoric to the parables recorded in ancient Greek texts (the synoptic gospels). Stated another way, the strictures that may apply to Jülicher for his definition and classification of Jesus' parables, most probably spoken in Aramaic, based upon distinctions found in the ancient Greek rhetorical tradition, do not hold the same force against a study of the parables of the Gospel of Luke, parables written in Greek and embedded within a larger narrative also written in Greek. Critics should recognize that Jülicher, who eschewed attempts to reconstruct an *Ur*-parable in Jesus' native tongue, did deal with the παραβολαί in their Greek form, as they are recorded in the synoptic gospels. Therefore, there exists no absolute incongruity in Jülicher's rationale, that is, bringing ancient Greek rhetoric to bear upon parables recorded in Greek. However, the manner in which Jülicher implemented that rationale will need to be inspected closely. A

247. That Jülicher waffles a bit in his attempt to draw hard and fast distinctions between parable and allegory, simile and metaphor, must be acknowledged. For example, he contends, on the one hand, that the allegory requires a substitution of concepts while, on the other hand, the parable requires a transference, but then he speaks of a transference in the functioning of metaphor, which he claims is the rudiment of allegory (see above, pp. 90-98). As is well known, in contrast to Jülicher, a number of modern parable scholars view metaphor as the rudiment of parable, while appealing to Jülicher as a warrant for the assertion that parables are not allegories. Berger (*Formgeschichte des Neuen Testaments*, p. 41) observes that many of the traits which the simile exhibits according to Jülicher are now assumed for the metaphor.

particular aspect of Jülicher's classification of the παραβολαί, based upon a particular rhetorician, is open to question.

Jülicher, as we have seen, appealed to Aristotle's *Rhetoric* in his attempt to separate the παραβολαί into three categories. Recall that Jülicher regarded the *Gleichnis* as corresponding to Aristotle's παραβολή, the *Parabel* as corresponding to Aristotle's λόγος. Jülicher's reading of Aristotle needs to be re-evaluated for two reasons. First, he gave insufficient attention to the fact that Aristotle regards the παραβολή *and* the fable (λόγος) as types of παραδείγματα. If one takes seriously Aristotle's rhetorical classification, then Jülicher's *Gleichnis* and *Parabel* should also be regarded as examples (παραδείγματα), and not simply the *Beispielerzählung* alone. Secondly, Jülicher departed from Aristotle's treatment of the παραδείγματα in his attempt to define the example narrative; specifically, he omitted any reference to 'historical examples', preferring instead to speak of the *Beispielerzählung* in more general terms as a 'means of proof' (κοιναὶ πίστεις). Although, as mentioned earlier, Jülicher resisted making the example narratives equivalent to historical examples, there may be reason to reconsider the 'example narratives' in light of the 'historical example'.[248] Other scholars have criticized Jülicher's equation of *Parabel* and *Fabel*; I will focus my criticism upon his formulation of the category *Beispielerzählung*.[249]

248. Reference has already been made to Jülicher's use of Aristotle's *Rhetoric*. One of the first things Jülicher says about the *Beispielerzählungen* is that they, like the *Parabeln*, have not been narrated in order to enrich the hearer in historical knowledge. The impetus behind this remark remains a curiosity until later, when Jülicher emphasizes that nothing—neither the form of the parable itself, nor the picture produced, nor even the desire to know details about the subsequent fate of the characters in a parable—should divert attention away from the content, the subject matter, the ethical-religious core of the parable (see *Die Gleichnisreden Jesu*, I, pp. 159-61). Jülicher then defends Jesus' parables against the reproach that they are arbitrary fairy tales since they do not provide more information about the characters (his specimen: the Samaritan). In addition, by insisting that the *Parabeln* and the *Beispielerzählungen* are freely invented by Jesus, perhaps Jülicher attempts to safeguard the creativity of Jesus, which would be attenuated if the *Beispielerzählungen* were merely narratives of events that had actually transpired in history—but this is pure speculation.

249. Jülicher anticipated criticism of his decision to correlate the *Parabeln Jesu* and the *Fabeln*, as we saw earlier. He was not to be disappointed. P. Dionisio Buzy, in a discussion informed by the works of several ancient rhetoricians, argues against equating the synoptic parables and ancient fables; see *Introduction aux*

Another result of Jülicher's research on the parables deserves affirmation; namely, his conclusion that the παραβολή is comparative in character. Insightfully, Jülicher contended that even when the obvious narrative introductions to the parables, introductions containing a comparative particle or phrase, are absent in the Gospels, the context urges the readers to notice that a comparison has been executed, or to make the comparison themselves: Overt in some παραβολαί, less so in others, the comparative character of the παραβολαί is never missing entirely. The comparison, Jülicher argued persuasively, underlies all three categories of παραβολαί; and, as we have seen, he located the foundation of the comparative character of the παραβολή, its essence, in the ὅμοιον. However, in the example narratives, according to Jülicher, 'the soil of the ὅμοιον is nearly abandoned'. Although the presuppositions that fund this statement—that all parables advance the subject matter 'the kingdom of God'; that all parables depict earthly circumstances drawn from daily life (the 'neutral soil') which have an application to matters in the religious-ethical sphere, but with the tacit assumption evidenced in his definition of the *Beispielerzählung* that 'daily life' excludes things religious and moral—invite further inquiry, such a statement suggests that an attempt to describe the comparative character of the example narratives in terms of the ὅμοιον alone is inadequate. The ancient rhetorical tradition knew of more than one way to effect a comparison, and Jülicher himself, in his definition of παραβολή, mentioned one in passing: σύγκρισις.[250]

paraboles évangéliques (Paris: J. Gabalda, 1912), pp. 2-26, 170-182. Stern (*Parables in Midrash*, p. 5) has this to say about one of the most notable aspects of the fable: 'A fable utilizes anthropomorphic animals or plants to portray the particularly theriomorphic or phytomorphic features of human behavior'. Young (*Jesus and his Jewish Parables*, pp. 5-6) acknowledges the close relationship between the fable and the parable, but wants to maintain a distinction between the two. Berger ('Hellenistische Gattungen im Neuen Testament', pp. 1116-20) gives a more favorable review of Jülicher's correlation of parable and fable, pointing out that fables do share several affinities with parables.

250. See above, p. 82. Jülicher's focus on the ὅμοιον is due in part to his desire to argue that the parable intends *one tertium comparationis*, not *tertia*. However, his exposition of the *Beispielerzählungen* indicates that a type of comparison other than the ὅμοιον alone might be taking place. For instance, he notes that in The Pharisee and the Toll Collector the prayer of the Pharisee is juxtaposed to the prayer of the toll collector, just as in The Merciful Samaritan the priest's and the Levite's treatment of the man left half-dead are juxtaposed to that of the Samaritan

That Jülicher attempted to describe and to define the parables of Jesus as recorded in the synoptic gospels from a rhetorical perspective is praiseworthy. It can be regarded as one of the inexplicable curiosities of scholarship that although Jülicher's treatment of the Jewish (rabbinic and scriptural) antecedents of Jesus' parables has been subjected to review in numerous studies, his treatment of the parables in light of the writings of the ancient rhetoricians is sometimes questioned, but rarely scrutinized. However, as has been intimated, certain aspects of Jülicher's rhetorical approach to defining and classifying the parables call for further study.[251] In that regard, two tasks must be accomplished (in Chapter 5). First, Aristotle's classification of the παραδείγματα as given in his *Rhetoric* must be reviewed in order to discern the concord and discord between it and Jülicher's use of it in his classification of the παραβολαί *Jesu* in general, the example narratives in particular. Secondly, the example narratives must be reassessed in light of other ancient rhetoricians, for Aristotle did not have the first word about παραβολαί, παραδείγματα, or comparisons, nor did he have the last.

Jülicher, whose aim was to examine the speech of a particular

(*Die Gleichnisreden Jesu*, II, p. 605). Moreover, he observes that The Rich Man and Poor Lazarus, as well as The Merciful Samaritan and The Pharisee and the Toll Collector, invites the auditor to offer a judgment about the fortune of the characters depicted in those stories (p. 635). We will see in Chapter 5 that παραβολή and σύγκρισις are mentioned together in some rhetorical treatises. While an examination of the possible relationships between παραβολή and σύγκρισις might yield interesting results, we will not be able to give the matter the attention it deserves. For more on σύγκρισις, see Christopher Forbes, 'Comparison, Self-Praise and Irony: Paul's Boasting and the Conventions of Hellenistic Rhetoric', *NTS* 32 (1986), pp. 1-30.

251. As Jülicher himself states, his is an attempt at a *rhetorical* classification of Jesus' παραβολαί (see above, p. 91). Thus, Scott misses the mark somewhat in his remark that a disadvantage of Jülicher's treatment of the parables 'is that he has classified the parables under form-critical categories that do not adequately account for the material' (*Hear Then the Parable*, pp. 72-73). In addition, it is anachronistic to call Jülicher's categories 'form-critical', even though one of his own students, Bultmann, adopted these same categories in the famous form-critical study, *History of the Synoptic Tradition*. Moreover, not only did Jülicher's classification of the parables have an impact on later form-critical studies, but his conception of the traditioning process did as well; however, Jülicher himself, according to Klauck, 'resisted being included in the gallery of ancestors of form criticism' ('Adolf Jülicher', p. 111). For more on Jülicher's influence on form criticism and redaction criticism, see Klauck, 'Adolf Jülicher', pp. 111-12.

historical figure, reached the conclusion that 'the παραβολαί are rhetorical, not poetic forms'. While Jülicher's assertion that the parables attributed to Jesus are neither 'high literature' nor 'poetry' should command attention,[252] an approach to the parables from a rhetorical perspective alone is insufficient because (1) the longer parables, including the *Beispielerzählungen* (example *narratives*), are *narrative* parables (*Gleichniserzählungen*), and (2) the example narratives are parts of a larger narrative.[253] Thus, literary aspects of the *Beispielerzählungen* should not go unappreciated, for the example narratives are rhetorical devices embedded within the Gospel of Luke.

An appreciation of the literary aspects of the example narratives and the rhetorical aspects of the example narratives offers the potential for an added degree of precision in the evaluation of features purported to distinguish them from the other παραβολαί. Jülicher made observations which seem to suggest that the *Beispielerzählungen* differ from the *Gleichnisse* in form rather than content, and from the *Parabeln* in content rather than form. Both the *Beispielerzählungen* and the *Parabeln*, unlike the *Gleichnisse*, are narrative in form; but the *Beispielerzählungen*, as opposed to the *Gleichnisse* and *Parabeln*, have as content circumstances or incidents that already belong to the religious-ethical sphere.[254] Moreover, we have seen that Jülicher descried a similarity in theme (content) among the example narratives, for which he proposed a Lukan title.

Still, one may rightfully wish that Jülicher had provided more

252. Certainly, Jülicher would have no truck with some of the more recent views of the parables as self-enclosed, autonomous aesthetic objects or parables as poems, even parables as ballads. Against Bailey (*Poet and Peasant*, pp. 72-75), the parables are not 'ballads' in the strictest formal sense of the word.

253. If one wishes to interpret the parables in their Gospel contexts, there should be no false bifurcation between the 'rhetorical' and the 'poetical'—or better, 'literary'—in the narrative parables, for it is not a matter of 'rhetoric versus poetry', as Jülicher would have it; rather, it is a matter of 'rhetoric in narrative'. Boucher sorts out some of the issues involved in a consideration of the parable as 'literature'; see *The Mysterious Parable*, pp. 14-17.

254. The distinguishing feature of the example narratives, according to Jülicher, is *not* that they alone among the three types of παραβολαί are intended to have an affect on the hearer's conduct, or that they alone are concerned with things religious and ethical. The *Parabeln* also are designed to have an affect on the judgment and conduct of the auditor, and they serve a religious-ethical purpose (see above, pp. 109-20).

tangible evidence to support his decision to differentiate between *Parabel* and *Beispielerzählung*. He did not identify any specific formal aspects, literary or rhetorical, exhibited by the *Beispielerzählungen* that may be said to unite them as a group. Nor did he identify any such aspects 'peculiar' to the *Beispielerzählungen* that may be said to differentiate them clearly from the *Parabeln*. Yet some of Jülicher's insights become increasingly important. For instance, in his exposition of the *Beispielerzählungen*, Jülicher noted that the example narratives depict an 'exceptional case',[255] or an 'individual case',[256] or a 'marked case', and he goes so far as to call this 'the law of such example narratives'.[257] In addition to that, he made observations about setting and character—which can be regarded as important formal features of a narrative—in the example narratives. Among all the parable speeches of Jesus in the synoptics, according to Jülicher, a definite indication of the setting is provided in only two, both *Beispielerzählungen*: The Merciful Samaritan and The Pharisee and the Toll Collector exhibit a certain 'local coloring' in that the environs of Jerusalem figure in the setting of the stories.[258] Even more remarkable than that, to Jülicher, is the naming of the poor man in The Rich Man and Poor Lazarus.[259] Thus, the increased specificity with regard to setting and character are contributing factors to 'the law of such example narratives'—their movement toward the exceptional, individual or marked case—and lend depth to Jülicher's remarks that the example narratives adhere strictly to the soil of reality, and that they demonstrate and impress through individualization.[260]

255. Jülicher, *Die Gleichnisreden Jesu*, II, p. 617.

256. Jülicher, *Die Gleichnisreden Jesu*, II, pp. 585, 615.

257. Jülicher, *Die Gleichnisreden Jesu*, II, p. 636.

258. Jülicher, *Die Gleichnisreden Jesu*, II, p. 608. Jülicher contends that these two example narratives therefore exhibit a formal relationship and belong together as a pair. More will be said later about setting in the *Beispielerzählungen* (see Chapter 4, pp. 249-52).

259. Jülicher, *Die Gleichnisreden Jesu*, II, p. 586; cf. p. 621. That characters or groups of characters are specifically identified in the other example narratives went unnoticed by Jülicher, perhaps as a result of his focus on content as the most important distinguishing feature of the *Beispielerzählungen*. Recall that Jülicher states that the figures in the *Gleichnis* are timeless, the figures in the *Parabel* are specific, the figures in the *Beispielerzählung* are pure types of the idea to be represented.

260. See Jülicher, *Die Gleichnisreden Jesu*, I, pp. 117-18, 162. Jülicher himself apparently did not correlate these insights; at the very least, he did not state the

Nevertheless, Jülicher neither demonstrated that these features are manifest in all of the *Beispielerzählungen*, nor did he show that these features are not exhibited by other *Parabeln*. He left us with rather vague assertions that the *Beispielerzählungen* are different from the *Parabeln* because the *Beispielerzählungen* 'present to us events which belong directly to the religious-ethical sphere', or because in the *Beispielerzählungen* 'the *Sache* itself' is demonstrated in a particular case. Are we to infer, then, that the difference between the *Parabeln* and the *Beispielerzählungen* is that the latter have 'religion' as their content? We will see that these issues resurface repeatedly in the work of other scholars who have devoted their attention to the *Beispielerzäh-lungen*.

Jülicher's insights about the example narratives serve as an excellent point of departure for any study of these four παραβολαί, individually or collectively. Jülicher's critics, whose contentions we must now take into account, have discounted some of his conclusions about the features that relate the example narratives to each other and have identified other features that went unnoticed by him. One astute student of the parables has noticed that a characteristic of the decades of parable research since Jülicher is 'the acceptance, modification, or supplementation of his famous parable theory'.[261] We shall see that this certainly holds true with respect to the example stories. In the next chapter, which records the debate surrounding the example stories, we will want to discover what has been added to our understanding of that group of παραβολαί by scholars who refine and scholars who reject Jülicher's identification of them as example narratives. We have been attentive to Jülicher's claims about the *Beispielerzählungen*. To Jülicher's critics we now turn.

relationship among them in this fashion.
261. Kingsbury, 'Major Trends in Parable Interpretation', p. 579.

Chapter 4

AFTER *DIE GLEICHNISREDEN JESU*: THE EXAMPLE STORIES IN MODERN PARABLE SCHOLARSHIP

'The current classification of the narrative parables goes back to Jülicher... This division is today almost a genre-critical dogma.'

Gerhard Sellin,
'Lukas als Gleichniserzähler'

The classification of Jesus' parables promoted by Jülicher a century ago still receives mention—pervasively, if sometimes perfunctorily—in studies of the New Testament parables. Gerhard Sellin's remark cited in the epigraph, as is commonly the case with generalities, is generally true.[1] However, only a superficial reading of the history of parable scholarship could give rise to the conclusion that Jülicher's classification of *Die Gleichnisreden Jesu* has enjoyed the unanimous approbation of parable scholars. While some scholars have questioned the value of drawing such distinctions among the synoptic parables, and

---

1. Sellin, 'Lukas als Gleichniserzähler', p. 176 (and see his n. 52). Given the fact that all four of the *Beispielerzählungen* identified by Jülicher appear in the Gospel of Luke, it is easy to understand why this group of παραβολαί might have attracted the notice of Lukan scholars; nevertheless, the most interesting investigations of the example stories, ones that have yielded the most intriguing insights about that category, have taken place within the context of parable scholarship, a scholarly tradition that is, by and large, concerned with the parables as spoken by the 'historical' Jesus. It should come as no surprise that studies devoted to the parables of the Gospel of Luke are heavily influenced by studies of Jesus' parables. For instance, Heininger, in an insightful study of the parables peculiar to Luke, draws conclusions about the example stories which echo the remarks of scholars whose main interest is in Jesus' parables. Heininger maintains that in light of a theory of the parables as extended metaphors, which are told in the context of the rule of God, the *Beispielerzählungen*—unlike the other parables in Luke's special source—are not parables (*Gleichnisse*) of God's rule (*Metaphorik*, pp. 29-30; cf. pp. 217-18, 221-23).

some have called into question the putative difference between 'parable' (*Gleichnis*) and 'parable in the narrower sense' (*Parabel*), it is perhaps the distinction between *Parabel* and 'example narrative' (*Beispielerzählung*) that is the most controversial to some parable scholars.[2] Sellin's 'almost' suggests consensus, but hints at dissent; thus, this 'almost' marks the space in which the critical reception of a particular aspect of Jülicher's parable theory—namely, his classification of four Lukan παραβολαί as 'example narratives'—will be interrogated in this chapter.

The discussion among modern parable scholars regarding the category 'example story' is the topic of concern here. Although many scholars have tendered their opinions about that category, this chapter will not provide an exhaustive annal including every scholar who has mentioned the example stories; instead, the concern here will be with those who have provided specific analyses of the example stories and who have thereby influenced or advanced our understanding of that group of parables.[3] To be sure, both the category 'example story' itself

2.   Among those who do not find the classification scheme proposed by Jülicher and then adopted by Bultmann to be of much use are Jeremias (*The Parables of Jesus*, p. 20), Norman Perrin (*Rediscovering the Teaching of Jesus* [New York: Harper & Row, 1967], p. 87), Tolbert (*Perspectives on the Parables*, pp. 16-17), and Blomberg (*Interpreting the Parables*, p. 75). Other scholars may object to one or another category; e.g. Johnston ('Parabolic Interpretations Attributed to Tannaim', p. 636) holds that 'the distinction between similitude (*Gleichnis*) and parable, stressed by Bultmann, cannot be maintained', while Sellin ('Lukas als Gleichniserzähler', pp. 176-77 n. 53) deems Jülicher's division between those categories 'unsatisfactory' because a uniform type of parable, the 'τίς-ἐξ-ὑμῶν-parables', is partitioned into two separate categories (Lk. 17.7-10 appears with the *Gleichnisse*, Lk. 11.5-8 with the *Parabeln*). Both Johnston and Sellin, nonetheless, retain the category *Beispielerzählung*. Baudler (*Jesus im Spiegel seiner Gleichnisse*, pp. 58-79) suggests a distinction between the shorter parables (which he calls 'Vorgangsgleichnisse') and the longer narrative parables (which he calls 'Handlungsgleichnisse') based upon, he insists, different formal criteria than those underlying Jülicher's division between *Gleichnisse* and *Parabeln*, although he emphatically rejects the category *Beispielerzählung*. Similarly, Scott (*Jesus, Symbol-Maker for the Kingdom*, pp. 23-93) allows for a distinction between narrative parables and 'one-liner parables', but disallows the category example story (see pp. 24-26).

3.   Some interpreters of the parables ignore the example story altogether without offering a rationale. Dodd, one of the most influential parable scholars of this century, refuses to mention the category 'example story' and provides no

and the four παραβολαί that Jülicher placed in it have been repeatedly examined within the context of parable scholarship; yet, of the profusion of issues and problems that have captivated the attention of parable scholars in the century since Jülicher, only those issues and problems that have a direct bearing on an understanding of the example stories will be addressed here. Therefore, this chapter will furnish a selective, but comprehensive survey of how modern parable scholars have dealt with the example stories.

The following discussion will not be a chronological account of the critical reception of the category 'example story' among parable scholars after Jülicher; rather, it will be arranged largely according to topic, that is, according to the particular traits or features said to distinguish the example stories from all the other synoptic parables. This 'history of research' on the *Beispielerzählungen* will be used as a means of

---

substantive treatment of any of the four example stories. In the place where he makes reference to Bultmann's classification of the parables (*The Parables of the Kingdom*, pp. 6-7), Dodd names only 'figurative sayings, similitudes, and parables proper... Bildwörter, Gleichnisse, and Parabel' [*sic*] (cf. p. 7 n. 1). Presumably, Dodd effaces the example stories from 'the parables of the kingdom' to avoid any suggestion that Jesus espoused merely moral or ethical principles in his parables (see pp. 12-13). Other interpreters base their conclusions about the category example story upon an examination of one member of that group without considering the other three narratives placed in the same group. Llewellyn Welile Mazamisa (*Beatific Comradeship: An Exegetical-Hermeneutical Study on Lk 10:25-37* [Kampen: Kok, 1987], pp. 87-89) roundly rejects the category example story, describing it as one of the major problems confronting exegetes of a particular parable: 'Categorizing the parable of the Good Samaritan as an examplary [*sic*] story has the tendency of trivializing the subtle and complex hermeneutical function of this parable, and obscures its urgent message' (p. 88). Mazamisa offers general reasons to support his attack of this category (e.g. Jülicher's classification 'lacks consistency and clarity; it has an inherent categorical overlap'; The Merciful Samaritan 'bears the characteristics of all other parables, namely profanity... opening up of history, destabilization and universality'; Jesus' parables belong more in the tradition of rabbinic and 'Old Testament' parables than that of the classical parables; Luke 'maintained the pith and marrow of rabbinic interpretation' [see pp. 88-89]), yet he does not attempt to determine whether *all* the example stories share any feature(s) in common that might validate their being grouped together or that might have contributed to their being classified together in the category example story. In this chapter, I will be more interested in studies that have added to our knowledge of the category *Beispielerzählung* by taking into account all of the narratives which comprise that category.

identifying the characteristics of the example stories which scholars have regarded as peculiar to that group, and I will show that other scholars find many of those same characteristics in other parables. This section begins with a particular formulation of the category *Beispielerzählung* that has had a significant impact on current under-standings of the example stories.

From Rhetoric to Form Criticism: The Example Stories According to Rudolf Bultmann

Rudolf Bultmann's conception of the category 'example story' occu-pies a place of considerable prestige in modern parable research, espe-cially among American scholars.[4] It is widely known that Bultmann subsumes the three categories of παραβολαί postulated by his teacher, Jülicher, into his own classification of Jesus' sayings; however, although the pupil appears to repeat the views of his teacher concerning the *Beispielerzählungen*, there are certain nuances that are not without significance in Bultmann's treatment of the example narratives.[5] One of the more subtle differences between the two is that whereas Jülicher strives overtly to base his classification of the synoptic parables upon categories drawn from Greek rhetoric, Bultmann does not.[6] Before any

4.   The ascendancy of Bultmann's conceptualization of the *Beispielerzählun-gen* over Jülicher's in some segments of American parable scholarship can be attributed, in part, to the fact that *Die Geschichte der synoptischen Tradition*, unlike *Die Gleichnisreden Jesu*, has been translated into English. Unfortunately, the English translation of *Die Geschichte der synoptischen Tradition* is often inconsis-tent and misleading (see Perrin's assessment of it in *Rediscovering the Teaching of Jesus*, p. 251); therefore, all references in this study will be to the eighth German edition, and all translations will be my own. The work of another important form critic, Martin Dibelius, has had much less impact in the discussion about the example stories among American parable scholars.

5.   As Baasland ('Zum Beispiel der Beispielerzählungen', p. 196) has correctly noted. Some scholars seemingly remain unaware that there are, in fact, differences between Jülicher and Bultmann with regard to the example narratives (see, e.g., Mazamisa, *Beatific Comradeship*, pp. 87-88). Erhardt Güttgemanns points out some of the differences in the classifications of the parables proposed by Jülicher and Bultmann; see 'Die linguistisch-didaktische Methodik der Gleichnisse Jesu', in *idem, Studia linguistica neotestamentica: Gesammelte Aufsätze zur linguistischen Grundlage einer neutestamentlichen Theologie* (BEvT, 60; Munich: Chr. Kaiser Verlag, 1971), pp. 125-37.

6.   Indeed, Bultmann judges the synoptic tradition of Jesus' sayings, when seen

additional remarks are made about aspects of Bultmann's form-critical classification of the synoptic parables, attention must be given to his description of the example stories.

Bultmann does not tarry long in his treatment of the example stories. Prior to his analysis of the individual example stories themselves, where his concern is to determine the original form of each by distinguishing the secondary accretions attributed to the redactor, Bultmann states without much ado:

> A strong formal relationship to the parables have the *example narratives*, which for this reason must also be treated here, though in them every element of the pictorial is missing.[7]

Then, in what may be one of the most influential footnotes in modern parable scholarship, Bultmann adds:

> The genre of the '*example narratives*' of the synoptists is different from the *paradigms* of ancient rhetoric...not only by their compass, insofar as no historical exempla belong to it (as perhaps Lk. 13.3f.; Acts 5.34-37), but also conceptually. The paradigms are exempla that illustrate, make vivid some sort of thought; the 'example narratives' offer examples=models for the right conduct. The concept paradigm in M. Dibelius corresponds to the ancient concept. Naturally, in particular cases a narrative can be a 'paradigm' in the one sense as in the other.[8]

as a whole, to be 'unhellenistisch' (*Die Geschichte der synoptischen Tradition*, p. 179).

7. Bultmann, *Die Geschichte der synoptischen Tradition*, p. 192; Bultmann's emphasis: 'Starke formale Verwandtschaft mit den Parabeln haben die *Beispielerzählungen*, die deshalb auch hier behandelt werden müssen, wenn ihnen auch jedes Element des Bildlichen fehlt'. This point marks another difference between Jülicher and Bultmann with respect to the *Beispielerzählungen*. Jülicher is somewhat ambiguous about the *Bildliche* in the example narratives, but Bultmann is not. However, nowhere does Jülicher state that in the *Beispielerzählungen* 'every element of the *Bildliche* is missing'.

8. Bultmann, *Die Geschichte der synoptischen Tradition*, p. 192 n. 1; Bultmann's emphasis: 'Von den *Paradigmen* der antiken Rhetorik (vgl. K. Alewell, Über das rhetor. παράδειγμα, Diss. Kiel 1913 u. E. Fascher, Die formgeschichtl. Methode S. 191-195) ist die Gattung der "*Beispielerzählungen*" der Synoptiker nicht nur durch ihren Umfang verschieden, insofern keine historischen Exempla zu ihr gehören (wie etwa Lk 13,3f.; Act 5,34-37), sondern auch begrifflich. Die Paradigmen sind Exempla, die irgend einen Gedanken illustrieren, anschaulich machen; die "Beispielerzählungen" bieten Beispiele=Vorbilder für das rechte Verhalten. Der Begriff Paradigma bei M. Dibelius entspricht dem antiken Begriff.

The description proper of the example narratives ends here. Although it seems relatively straightforward, Bultmann's treatment of the example narratives is more complex, even confusing, than it appears. Several observations can be made in order to thicken the texture of Bultmann's conception of the example narratives and thus bring into relief certain of its finer points.

Bultmann locates the *Beispielerzählungen* and other forms of the παραβολαί in the tradition of Jesus' sayings, and he divides the tradition of the sayings of Jesus into two major groups, apophthegms (*Apophthegmata*) and dominical sayings (*Herrenworte*). The latter are subdivided into three main groups: logia in the narrower sense, or wisdom sayings; prophetic and apocalyptic sayings; legal sayings and community rules.[9] The I-sayings and parables belong to each of these three groups of dominical sayings, although both are also discussed in separate sections.[10] The 'parables and cognates' are deemed to require independent treatment because of their form.[11]

In the section where he devotes attention to the 'parables and cognates' (*Gleichnisse und Verwandtes*), Bultmann distinguishes several forms: picture sayings (*Bildworte*), actual parables (*eigentliche Gleichnisse*), parables (*Parabeln*), and example narratives (*Beispielerzählungen*).[12] The synoptic parable tradition, according to Bultmann,

In einzelnen Fällen kann natürlich eine Erzählung ein "Paradigma" im einen wie im andern Sinne sein'. In an early (1928) article, this is what Bultmann has to say about the example narratives: 'In Luke a few example narratives are found as well…which, however, differ from the others in that nothing is compared in them, rather a good or bad example is presented. For this reason, it is customary to designate them as *Beispielerzählungen*' ('Gleichnis und Parabel. II. In der Bibel', *RGG*, 2nd rev edn, II, p. 1241).

9. Bultmann, *Die Geschichte der synoptischen Tradition*, p. 73.

10. Bultmann, *Die Geschichte der synoptischen Tradition*, p. 73. For the section on the I-sayings, see pp. 161-79; for the section on the parables, see pp. 179-222.

11. Bultmann, *Die Geschichte der synoptischen Tradition*, p. 73: '…and finally I append an independent treatment of the *Gleichnisse* and related pieces, which demand this because of their form, even if because of their content they also could be distributed among the first three groups'. Prior to that independent treatment, Bultmann discerns the basic forms of the 'Old Testament and Jewish' *mashal* in the logia: Some sayings exhibit the form of a one-membered *mashal*, others the form of a two-membered *mashal* (p. 84); other developments of these forms are noted as well (pp. 84-85).

12. On the *Bildworte*, see Bultmann, *Die Geschichte der synoptischen Tradition*, pp. 181-84; on the *eigentliche Gleichnisse*, see pp. 184-88; on the *Parabeln*,

exhibits all of these forms of the *mashal*; moreover, 'especially characteristic is the use of similes and pictures in each form'.[13] Thus, although
it would be erroneous to conclude that Bultmann excludes the example
narratives from among the *meshalim* or παραβολαί, he himself—as we
have just witnessed—excludes the 'Bildliche' from the example narratives; in fact, that is how he characterizes the differentia of the *Parabeln* and the *Beispielerzählungen*, two forms that manifest a strong
formal relationship. Before we ponder this curiosity in Bultmann's
handling of the example narratives, it can be indicated rather easily how
similar the *Parabeln* and *Beispielerzählungen* are to him.

Bultmann states clearly that the example narratives are closely related to the *Parabeln*: 'Starke formale Verwandtschaft mit den Parabeln
haben die Beispielerzählungen ...' ('A strong formal relationship to the
Parabeln have the *Beispielerzählungen* ...). The strength of that formal
relationship becomes evident in Bultmann's observations about the
construction of the parables,[14] yet the similarity between the example
narratives and the *Parabeln* becomes most evident in his analysis of
style, especially when he describes the technique of the parable
narrative, for the example narratives exhibit nearly every characteristic
feature identified in the *Parabeln*.[15] Bultmann indicates explicitly that
the *Parabeln* and the example narratives share in common the
following: only the necessary persons appear in the story; groups are

see pp. 188-92; on the *Beispielerzählungen*, see pp. 192-93.

13. Bultmann, *Die Geschichte der synoptischen Tradition*, p. 181. Bultmann
discusses simile and metaphor chiefly in relation to the *Bildworte* and *eigentliche
Gleichnisse* (see pp. 181-88).

14. See Bultmann, *Die Geschichte der synoptischen Tradition*, pp. 195-203.
E.g. the verb tense suitable to the narrative character of the *Parabeln* and the
Beispielerzählungen is the preterit (p. 196); within the parables (*Gleichnisse*) and
one example narrative (Lk. 18.14), the point is accentuated by (ἀμὴν) λέγω ὑμῖν
(see p. 197); some *Parabeln* end with a question directed to the hearer, as does The
Merciful Samaritan (p. 197); it is common for an application to be appended to the
parable (*Gleichnis*) by οὕτως, as is the case in The Foolish Rich Man (p. 199);
some *Parabeln* and example narratives have applications given in the form of a
logion (pp. 200-201).

15. See Bultmann, *Die Geschichte der synoptischen Tradition*, pp. 203-208.
Bultmann's analysis of the technique of the parable narrative, as is widely known,
is based upon Axel Olrik's famous essay 'Epische Gesetze der Volksdichtung',
Zeitschrift für deutsches Altertum 51 (1909), pp. 1-12, which has been translated
into English as 'Epic Laws of Folk Narrative', in Alan Dundes (ed.), *The Study of
Folklore* (Englewood Cliffs, NJ: Prentice–Hall, 1965), pp. 129-41.

treated as one person and are differentiated only as necessary; some persons are characterized in the judgment of other persons who appear in the narrative; the feelings and motives of characters are mentioned only when it is essential for the plot and the point; subordinate persons are characterized only as necessary; motivations are missing in the exposition; some pieces lack a conclusion; incidents and actions are described with economy; there is an abundant use of direct speech and soliloquy; phrases and actions are repeated ('the law of repetition'); the most important things are described last ('the law of end-stress'); the hearer is provoked to make a judgment; types of characters are contrasted.[16] These are similar forms indeed. How, then, do the *Parabeln* and *Beispielerzählungen* differ?

To discover how Bultmann distinguishes the *Beispielerzählungen* from the *Parabeln*, we must return to the oft quoted sentence: 'A strong formal relationship to the parables have the *example narratives...* though in them every element of the pictorial [*Bildliche*] is missing'. There is a nuance in Bultmann's use of 'Bildliche' that can go unrecognized if the term is understood to mean only 'figurative'.[17] In a fashion reminiscent of Jülicher, Bultmann speaks of 'picture' (*Bild*) and 'subject matter' (*Sache*) being juxtaposed in the picture sayings (*Bildworte*) and the parables (*Parabeln*).[18] The *Gleichnisse* and *Parabeln*, in addition, are said to require the transference of a judgment

16. Although not specified by Bultmann, the example narratives also exhibit 'the law of stage duality' ('das Gesetz der *szenischen Zweiheit*') and 'directness, or single-strandedness of narrative' ('*Gradlinigkeit bzw. Einsträngigkeit der Erzählung*'); on this, see *Die Geschichte der synoptischen Tradition*, p. 204 (Bultmann's emphasis).

17. Cf. *History of the Synoptic Tradition*, pp. 177-78 (emphasis in the translation): '*Exemplary stories* have a striking formal relationship to parables, and must therefore be discussed here, even if they have no figurative element at all'.

18. This aspect of Bultmann's treatment of the parables will forever remain unknown if one relies on the English translation. With regard to the picture sayings, Bultmann writes: 'Indeed, in the *meshalim* of the Old Testament the form I designate as *Bildwort* appears with extraordinary frequency in such a way that *Bild* and *Sache* are juxtaposed without comparative particle...' (*Die Geschichte der synoptischen Tradition*, p. 181; his emphasis). With regard to the *Parabeln*: 'Jülicher rightly distinguishes the *Gleichnis* from the *Parabel*, which does not juxtapose two circumstances, rather converts the circumstances serving as a *Gleichnis* into narrative, or as the case may be, presents as *Bild* not a typical situation or a typical or regular incident, rather an interesting individual case' (p. 188).

obtained in neutral material (the *Bild*) to a different field under discussion (the *Sache*).[19] The implication this has for the example narratives would seem to be that they lack the *Bild(hälfte)*.[20] This does not mean that the sole difference between the example narratives and the *Parabeln* is that the former *alone* provoke a moral judgment in contradistinction to the latter, for Bultmann asserts that in some parables the moral quality of the characters is not the issue of concern; nonetheless

> In other cases, however, the *moral* judgment about an action is provoked not only in the example narratives (except Lk. 16.19ff.), but also in the parables of The Lost Son, The Entrusted Money, The Unmerciful Servant, The Two Sons, where precisely the point drives at this judgment. Of course, a judgment is provoked *in general* by *all* parables, and the argumentative character indeed, as shown, is often expressed in the form.[21]

If, then, the example narratives lack 'every element of the pictorial' and provoke a 'moral judgment about an action', does this mean that for Bultmann the *Beispielerzählungen* are *exempla*? Strangely enough, the answer is 'No'.

Bultmann, as we have seen, differentiates between the example narrative and the *exemplum* (*Paradigma*), and he gives two reasons for so doing. The synoptic example narratives are said to differ from the *Paradigmen* of ancient rhetoric (1) in compass because 'no historical

19. Bultmann, *Die Geschichte der synoptischen Tradition*, p. 214. Bultmann makes this point in his argument that the parables are not allegory (in agreement with Jülicher). Unlike allegory, the *Gleichnis* and the *Parabel* express a correspondence or relation between *Bild* and *Sache* (see pp. 214-15). Even if the correspondence between *Bild* and *Sache* is expressed in simple assertions of identity, and even if metaphors are employed, that does not yet constitute allegory in Bultmann's opinion (see pp. 214-15; cf. p. 202 n. 2).

20. This is my own inference. Bultmann does speak of the 'Bildhälfte' of the *Bildworte* (*Die Geschichte der synoptischen Tradition*, p. 181) and *Gleichnisse* (p. 184). It will become clear immediately that the *Beispielerzählungen* do evoke a judgment of a sort.

21. Bultmann, *Die Geschichte der synoptischen Tradition*, p. 208; Bultmann's emphasis: 'In anderen Fällen aber wird das *moralische* Urteil über eine Handlung herausgefordert, nicht nur in den Beispielerzählungen (außer Lk 16,19ff.), sondern auch in den Parabeln vom verlorenen Sohn, von den anvertrauten Geldern, vom unbarmherzigen Knecht, von den beiden Söhnen, wo eben die Pointe auf dies Urteil hinaus will. Ein Urteil *überhaupt* wird natürlich durch *alle* Gleichnisse herausgefordert, und der argumentative Charakter kommt in der Form ja, wie gezeigt, oft zum Ausdruck'.

exempla' belong to them, and (2) in concept because the 'paradigms are *exempla* that illustrate, make vivid some sort of thought: the "example narratives" offer examples=models for the right conduct'.

Some of the assertions made by Bultmann in that footnote must be called into question.[22] Bultmann explicitly excludes the synoptic *Beispielerzählungen* from among the *Paradigmen* because that group (that is, the example narrative) does not include historical examples; here, he implicitly equates 'Paradigmen' and 'historischen Exempla'—which is a dubious maneuver in light of the fact that some ancient rhetoricians speak of several types of παραδείγματα. Moreover, as Bultmann would have it, the example narratives are not παραδείγματα (*exempla*) that serve to illustrate or make vivid some thought; rather, the example narratives serve to provide 'Beispiele' (examples), which he equates here with 'models for the right conduct'. However, it must be noted that providing 'examples' is not a function peculiar to the example narratives alone, as becomes evident later:

> More frequently, two contrary types are juxtaposed in two independently lapsing descriptions, so that a kind of double-*Gleichnis* arises; thus, the *Gleichnis* of The House Building (Mt. 7.24-27 par.), The True and Untrue Servant (Lk. 12.42-46), and the formally related pieces of The Banquet Speech (Lk. 14.7-11, 12-14), which in a positive and negative half produce example and counterexample [*Beispiel und Gegenbeispiel*].[23]

By now it should be apparent that Bultmann's conception of the category 'example narrative' is more complex than is sometimes realized. Despite the fact that Bultmann's definition of *Beispielerzählung* is not grounded in ancient rhetoric, his understanding of the παραδείγματα still stands in need of revision.[24]

That some of the subtleties in Bultmann's conception of the form 'example narrative' have gone unnoticed is unfortunate given its imposing influence upon subsequent generations of parable scholars. In order

22. In agreement with Sellin, 'Lukas als Gleichniserzähler', p. 178 n. 56. The treatment of the παραδείγματα in the ancient rhetorical tradition will be dealt with in Chapter 5.

23. Bultmann, *Die Geschichte der synoptischen Tradition*, p. 208.

24. The vague caveat issued by Bultmann at the end of the footnote quoted above does not rehabilitate his position on the παραδείγματα. His understanding of the παραδείγματα is odd, given his citation of Erich Fascher, because it is precisely Fascher's contention that the Lukan *Beispielerzählungen* are παραδείγματα (see below, pp. 159-61).

to avoid perpetuating misconceptions about Bultmann's treatment of the *Beispielerzählungen*, several points need to be stressed. First, Bultmann does not provide a definition of the category 'example narrative' based upon ancient rhetoric; rather, he provides his own form-critical definition of the *Gattung* 'example narrative', in which he restricts their function to offering 'models for the right conduct'. Secondly, the example narratives, according to Bultmann, are not *exempla*. Thirdly, the example narratives are not the only kind of parable that offer 'examples'. Fourthly, although the example narratives offer 'examples=models for the right conduct', the example narratives are not unique in that they alone among all the other parables provoke the hearer to make a moral judgment about an action. Fifthly, Bultmann includes among the *Gattung* '*Beispielerzählung*' the same four narratives as did Jülicher.[25] Some of the blame for any misconceptions about

25. Bultmann unequivocally regards The Merciful Samaritan, The Foolish Rich Man, The Rich Man and Poor Lazarus, and The Pharisee and the Toll Collector as *Beispielerzählungen* (see *Die Geschichte der synoptischen Tradition*, pp. 192-93). It is often claimed that he also considers Lk. 14.7-11 and Lk. 14.12-14 to be example narratives (see, e.g., Jones, *The Art and Truth of the Parables*, p. 43), which is not quite the case. Bultmann's position on these two pericopes is ambiguous. At the end of the section on the example narratives he writes: 'Like the *Gleichnisse* are to the *Parabeln* as their preliminary stage [*Vorstufe*], so are the two following pieces to the *Beispielerzählungen*...' Then he cites Lk. 14.7-11 and Lk. 14.12-14. But he continues: 'Their stylistic relationship to the *Gleichnisse* and *Parabeln* is obviously small; they are in truth only rather elaborated exhortations [*Mahnworte*]' (p. 193). Bultmann first mentions these two pieces under 'Exhortations' [*Mahnworte*] (p. 81); he classifies them there due to their imperative form (cf. p. 74 for his list of criteria for classification). Later, he considers these two pieces in a brief discussion of how the *meshalim* can be enlarged by adding descriptions in which direct speech appears (p. 85). Still later, he lists these two logia among the profane (or secular) *meshalim* that the tradition probably made into Jesus-sayings (p. 107). Finally, he mentions these two pieces in his description of a kind of double-parable in which contrasting types are juxtaposed (as we have seen). We can conclude, perhaps, that Bultmann considers Lk. 14.7-11 and 14.12-14 to be some kind of παραβολή, but that they are not example narratives proper. Compare what Jülicher says of Lk. 14.7-11, 12-14: 'Consequently, we possess nothing in Lk. 14.7-14 that we could call a "*Gleichnis*"; it requires nothing to be transferred from a lower field to a higher: a sort of synecdoche is present, which in the proverbial saying and in Sirach is chosen with preference in the formulation of moral rules; the *Beispielerzählungen* are related most closely to sayings of this sort; Lk. 14.8-11 and 12-14 are to the *Gleichnisse* 14.28-32 as the *Beispielerzählung* Lk. 18.9-14 is to the *Parabel* Lk. 18.1-8' (*Die Gleichnisreden Jesu*, II, pp. 253-54).

the nature of the example narratives as expounded in *Die Geschichte der synoptischen Tradition* must rest upon Bultmann himself, for he does not render 'clarity of concept' in his discussion of that form.[26] His analysis of style, however, is commendable because the strong formal relationship that exists between the *Parabeln* and the *Beispielerzählungen* is made manifest, and that remains Bultmann's lasting contribution to the understanding of the example narratives.

Beyond Bultmann: The Example Stories in Recent Parable Research

A detailed examination of Bultmann's conception of the example narrative reveals that both he and Jülicher concur on one important point: The example narratives and the *Parabeln* are closely related groups of parables. This conclusion is to be affirmed, and subsequent studies of the parables corroborate it again and again. However, to classify the four mentioned Lukan παραβολαί as a group of 'example narratives' separate from the 'narrative parables' implies that formal differences do, in fact, exist between the *Parabeln* and the *Beispielerzählungen*. Endeavors to account for those differences do not result in unanimity of opinion, as the preceding review of two prominent formulations of that category has suggested, and as the following survey of that category in recent parable research will reveal.

Some of the developments in the understanding of the example stories in recent parable research can be better understood if it is kept in mind that Jülicher and Bultmann do not express identical views of the *Beispielerzählungen*. Whereas Jülicher strives to classify and describe the παραβολαί on the basis of Aristotle's rhetorical categorization of the παραδείγματα, but departs from it in his classification of the example narratives, Bultmann makes a patent shift away from a rhetorical understanding of the παραβολαί—indeed, for him the example narratives are not παραδείγματα. Although Jülicher and Bultmann appear to agree that one of the peculiar features of the example narratives is the apparent lack of a *Bildhälfte* (Jülicher) or any 'element of the pictorial' (Bultmann)—and this putative lack makes these narratives *Beispielerzählungen*, not *Parabeln*—the teacher and his pupil express the

---

26. Bultmann himself demands 'clarity of concept' of those who dispute Jülicher's conception of allegory (*Die Geschichte der synoptischen Tradition*, p. 214).

significance of that differently: according to the former, the example narrative therefore provides an 'example of the proposition to be asserted'; according to the latter, the example narratives therefore 'offer examples=models for the right conduct'. Time has not eroded the imprints made by Jülicher and Bultmann upon scholarly understanding of the example stories; on the contrary, the issues they raised and the conclusions they reached are etched in the ensuing discussion.

Nevertheless, there is still no consensus among modern parable scholars about what, if anything, constitutes the singularity of the example stories. Thus, the task to be undertaken in the remainder of this chapter is to describe how modern parable scholars have dealt with the category *Beispielerzählung*. The characteristic features of the example stories purported to be peculiar to this group of παραβολαί will be specified. Attention will be focused on the criteria invoked as a means of differentiating between *Beispielerzählung* and *Parabel*, the criteria used as a means of establishing the putative peculiarity of the example stories, and the formal elements manifest in the example stories said to distinguish them from all other parables in the synoptic gospels.

The 'Example' in the Example Stories

Familiar by now is the tenet that The Merciful Samaritan, The Foolish Rich Man, The Rich Man and Poor Lazarus, and The Pharisee and the Toll Collector are—in contradistinction to all the other synoptic parables—'examples'. We can gain access to some of the more common conceptions of the category 'example story' in recent parable scholarship by attempting to discover what is meant by 'example' with respect to these four Lukan παραβολαί; yet, we will not be granted an easy access because the word 'example' has a history and has been used in a variety of ways.[27] Broadly speaking, however, it seems to be the case that with reference to the example stories parable scholars have employed the word 'example' either in a more technical, restricted sense to mean 'rhetorical example' (παράδειγμα or *exemplum*), or in a more general, looser sense to mean 'moral example'. These do not hold

27. John D. Lyons, in his review of the historical and theoretical background of the terms 'exemplum' and 'example', documents the various meanings, both technical and vernacular, assigned to those words from ancient to modern times (in the Romance languages); see *Exemplum: The Rhetoric of Example in Early Modern France and Italy* (Princeton, NJ: Princeton University Press, 1989), pp. 3-25.

as hard and fast distinctions, for the two senses are sometimes com-
mingled, as we will soon see.

The example stories as rhetorical examples. One might assume that
recourse to the ancient rhetorical tradition in order to define 'example'
would lead to a uniform or, at least, a consistent view of the category
'example story'. That, however, is not the case. Neither clarity nor concord necessarily issues from an appeal to ancient rhetoric as a means of
defining and delimiting either 'example' or 'example story'.[28] We have
already encountered studies in which the rhetorical tradition, mainly
Aristotle's *Rhetoric*, is consulted in order to elucidate and describe the
characteristics of the example stories as 'examples'.[29] Yet, we have also
seen that Bultmann refers to the ancient rhetorical tradition, via Karl
Alewell, in order to argue that the example narratives are neither
'Paradigmen' nor 'Exempla'. The question naturally arises: How are
the example stories and the παραδείγματα related? Or we might ask:
Are the example stories παραδείγματα (*exempla*) or are they not? My
intent at this juncture is not to adjudicate these matters; it is, rather, to
introduce the judgments of others who have formed their opinions on
the basis of a consideration of the example stories in light of the ancient
rhetorical tradition.[30] An overview of selected studies will indicate the

28.   Disagreement about the synoptic parables also arises in studies that
approach the category 'example' from broader perspectives. Susan Suleiman considers many of the synoptic parables to be 'exempla', and she treats several,
namely, The Sower (Mt. 13.3-9), The Wise and Foolish Virgins (Mt. 25.1-13), and
The Prodigal Son (Lk. 15.11-31)—none of which are usually included in the category example story by parable scholars (see 'Le récit exemplaire', *Poétique* 32
[1977], pp. 468-89; cf. '"Exemplary" Narratives', in *idem, Authoritarian Fictions:
The Ideological Novel as a Literary Genre* [New York: Columbia University Press,
1983], pp. 25-61). Lyons questions Suleiman's use of biblical parable as a basis for
her definition of exemplary narrative (*Exemplum*, p. 250 n. 45): 'The choice of
parable as starting point for the study of example leads to many problems. Chief
among these is the allegorical nature of most parables. Short of equating example
and allegory, most New Testament parables would fail to qualify as example
because of their replacement of the literal sense of their constitutive terms'.
      29.   Aristotle's classification of the παραδείγματα is thought to inform
Jülicher's conception of the category example narrative; to a lesser extent, the
ancient rhetorical tradition contributes to Stockmeyer's understanding of that category.
      30.   The term 'paradigm' with reference to the parables has been employed by
others, but in either a more modern sense or an idiosyncratic sense. For instances of

breadth of issues involved in defining the example story from the perspective of the ancient rhetorical tradition.[31]

Erich Fascher contends without reservation that the narrative pieces designated by Jülicher as 'Beispielerzählungen' are 'Paradigmen'.[32]

the former, see Funk, *Language, Hermeneutic, and Word of God*, p. 193 (emphasis his): 'The parable is a (double) *paradigm of reality*... It is a paradigm (model or declension) of reality'; and Timothy Polk, 'Paradigms, Parables, and *Mĕšālîm*: On Reading the *Māšāl* in Scripture', *CBQ* 45 (1983), pp. 564-83: 'Put another way, telling a parable is a matter of presenting to others an imaginatively shaped paradigm (a model of reality, a description of experience) and asking that they recognize it as somehow true' (p. 573). For instances of the latter, see Ernst Lohmeyer ('Vom Sinn der Gleichnisse Jesu', *ZST* 15 [1938], pp. 319-46), who uses 'paradigmatische' to describe the peculiarity of the Lukan parable tradition (that Luke is more interested in the parables as a means of religious instruction to train human hearts) vis-à-vis the Matthean (Matthew tends to employ parables as a means toward the end of the eschatological revelation of the kingdom of God); and John Dominic Crossan, 'Structuralist Analysis and the Parables of Jesus: A Reply to D.O. Via, Jr., "Parable and Example Story: A Literary-Structuralist Approach"', *Semeia* 1 (1974), pp. 192-221 (213-14): 'The paradigm parables ["the Treasure, the Pearl, the Great Fish"] show the code of the entire parabolic system of Jesus at its most obvious' (p. 214 n. 2). Jones (*The Art and Truth of the Parables*, p. 86) contends that not all 'parables of comparison' are 'paradigmatic'—'(i.e. they are not examples for imitation but statements about God or human life)'—but later asserts that '...many of the parables are descriptions of people in a particular life-situation; hence their permanent value and significance as positively or negatively paradigmatic types, in so far as they show the kind of behaviour which is or is not required of a man' (p. 157). While I do not rule out that parables are indeed concerned with action or behavior, I would not concede that parables are 'paradigmatic' only when they evince a 'moral' concern or offer 'examples to imitated'.

31. Any view of the *Beispielerzählungen* as 'metaphor', 'synecdoche' or 'metonymy' might be labelled 'rhetorical'—in the liberal sense of the word—in that rhetorical tropes are employed as models. Here, I restrict myself to those studies which refer specifically to the ancient rhetorical tradition.

32. Erich Fascher, *Die formgeschichtliche Methode: Eine Darstellung und Kritik: Zugleich ein Beitrag zur Geschichte des synoptischen Problems* (Beihefte zur Zeitschrift für die neutestamentliche Wissenschaft und die Kunde der älteren Kirche, 2; Giessen: Alfred Töpelmann, 1924), p. 192. Fascher's remarks occur in his critique of the definition of the form 'Paradigma' as proposed by Dibelius; he concludes that from the perspective of philological research, Dibelius's use of the term is incorrect (see pp. 191-96). Fascher's position provides quite a contrast to Bultmann's, especially since they both derive their understanding of the παράδειγμα in ancient rhetoric from a common source: Karl Alewell, 'Über das rhetorische ΠΑΡΑΔΕΙΓΜΑ: Theorie, Beispielsammlungen, Verwendung in der

The term 'Paradigma', according to Fascher, is not intended to designate a particular form because an example can be a story or even a reference to a historical event; rather, 'Paradigma' denotes a speech technique in which an example serves as an elucidation (*Verdeutlichung*) or as a proof (*Erweis*) of an assertion.[33] He notes that Aristotle divided examples (*Paradigmen*) into two kinds—the freely invented and the historical. Later, the freely invented examples came to be called παραβολαί or even εἰκόνες, while the term 'Paradigmen' came to be reserved for historical examples.[34] Fascher concludes that 'paradigm and parable are therefore originally the same: rhetorical means for the elucidation of a thought'.[35] Having granted that, he then attempts to make a finer distinction between example story and parable as types of παραδείγματα.

Fascher maintains that Jülicher's definition of example story, which pertains to a group that conspicuously appears only in the Gospel of Luke, corresponds to Aristotle's prescriptions about the use of 'Paradigmen': namely, they either take the place of lacking evidence (*Beweise*), or instead—as do selected examples—play the role of a witness (or testimony; 'Zeugnisses').[36] The latter is the case with The Merciful Samaritan and, by implication, the other example stories. Jesus' parables (*Gleichnisse*), however, bear a somewhat different aspect in that they do not serve as proof (*Erweis*) for just any assertion, rather they serve as elucidation (*Verdeutlichung*) for religious thoughts. Practically observed, Jesus' parables (*Gleichnisse*) are παραβολαί in the technical sense given earlier: 'namely, freely invented stories...that

römischen Literatur der Kaiserzeit' (PhD dissertation, University of Kiel, 1913).

33. Fascher, *Die formgeschichtliche Methode*, p. 191: 'Die Form dieses Beispiels ist dabei ganz gleichgültig'; cf. p. 194.

34. Fascher, *Die formgeschichtliche Methode*, pp. 191-93. Here, again, Fascher relies upon Alewell. Later I review the issue of whether the term παράδειγμα was restricted 'exclusively' to mean only 'historical example' in the ancient rhetorical tradition (see Chapter 5). At any rate, Fascher finds evidence of both kinds of examples in the New Testament. He considers all παραβολαί to be freely invented examples. Fascher identifies historical examples in Lk. 13.1-5, 17.20-36; Acts 5.34-39; and in sections of Heb. 11–12.

35. Fascher, *Die formgeschichtliche Methode*, p. 192: 'Paradigma und Parabel sind also ursprünglich dasselbe, rednerische Hilfsmittel zur Verdeutlichung eines Gedankens'.

36. Fascher, *Die formgeschichtliche Methode*, p. 192.

he used in his speeches for demonstration [*Veranschaulichung*]'.[37] Based upon his observation that 'Paradigmen' are not only means of proof, but also ornaments of speech, Fascher asserts that the (Lukan) *Beispielerzählungen* are means of proof, while the *Gleichnisse* of Jesus are ornaments of speech.[38] Thus, according to Fascher, there are Lukan example stories and there are parables (*Gleichnisse*) of Jesus, but both are types of παραδείγματα.

Sellin, who also refers to the ancient rhetorical tradition in his treatment of the example stories, would agree with Fascher on at least one point; that is, many different forms (such as quotations, historical examples, literary examples, parables, fables) can serve as 'Paradigmen'.[39] Therefore, 'Paradigma' does not name a 'form', rather it designates a 'function'. Sellin posits that within their narrative context, where the subject matter becomes evident, the example narratives serve as rhetorical paradigms, as didactic models: 'By way of an individual case, they are supposed to effect a conviction in a subject matter to be thoroughly distinguished from the individual case; therefore, they have a *paradigmatic function*'.[40] This is not true of the example narratives alone, however, but for all the narrative parables in the Gospel of Luke because they, too, are context-dependent.[41] Sellin points out that other parables perform a paradigmatic function, but—unlike Fascher—he does not claim that all (synoptic) parables are παραδείγματα.[42] Sellin

37. Fascher, *Die formgeschichtliche Methode*, p. 192. Fascher does not cite any *Gleichnisse Jesu* as evidence for his claims.

38. Fascher, *Die formgeschichtliche Methode*, p. 194 n. 1.

39. Sellin, 'Lukas als Gleichniserzähler', pp. 168 n. 13, p. 178 n. 56.

40. Sellin, 'Lukas als Gleichniserzähler', p. 178 (Sellin's emphasis): 'Sie dienen also innerhalb dieses Kontextes als rhetorisches Paradigma, als didaktisches *Modell*: Sie sollen an einem Einzelfall eine Überzeugung in einer vom Einzelfall durchaus zu unterscheidenden Sache bewirken, haben also eine *paradigmatische Funktion*'.

41. Sellin, 'Lukas als Gleichniserzähler', p. 178: 'As a consequence, they are dependent upon the context. It appears, however, that this is not true for the *Beispielerzählungen*, but for all the narrative parables in Luke'. Elsewhere, Sellin states: 'The "*Parabel*" in Luke, accordingly, would be a subclass of the paradigmatic narrative, to which even the *Beispielerzählungen* also belong' ('Gleichnisstrukturen', *LB* 31 [1974], pp. 89-115 [113]).

42. For instance, Sellin ('Lukas als Gleichniserzähler', pp. 179-81) states that two other parable forms can serve a paradigmatic function; namely, the 'τίς-ἐξ-ὑμῶν-Gleichnisse' and the 'exemplarischen Rechtsentscheid' (such as Lk. 7.41-43, 10.30-37; Mt. 21.28-31a; 2 Sam. 12.5ff.; *b. 'Abod. Zar.* 54b-55a). On the 'τίς-ἐξ-

concludes that the example narratives cannot be classified as such on the basis of their paradigmatic function, for the function of a narrative can be a secondary element.[43] As we will soon see, Sellin invokes another criterion as a means of differentiating between *Parabeln* and *Beispielerzählungen*.

Klaus Berger makes it clear that neither the ancient rhetoricians nor those who study the ancient rhetorical tradition (be they classicists or biblical scholars) speak with one voice concerning the various genres (*Gattungen*) that can be collected under the term 'parable' (*Gleichnis*).[44] A few of Berger's findings that are pertinent to this study of the example stories will be excerpted here.

In ancient rhetoric, according to Berger,

> …parables serve as means of proof (related to the historical example) or as demonstration. As a means of proof, they illustrate rational arguments.[45]

Familiarity with the various attempts at organizing and classifying the παραβολαί in ancient rhetoric leads to the realization that the same term, 'parable', is used to cover a variety of genres (*Gattungen*). Berger himself crafts a classification scheme of the *Gattung* '*Gleichnis*', which he divides into four subgenres: (1) *exempla* (παραδείγματα), which here means 'historical examples'; (2) parables (*Gleichnisse*) in the narrower sense (παραβολαί); (3) fictional narratives which obtain their character as parables through their context; and (4) allegories.[46]

ὑμῶν-Gleichnisse', see below, pp. 209-16, 239 n. 310.

43. Sellin, 'Lukas als Gleichniserzähler', p. 179.

44. My statement of the situation is an expansion of Berger's; see 'Hellenistische Gattungen im Neuen Testament', p. 1112: 'Both in ancient rhetoric and in New Testament criticism widespread unclarity prevails about the various *Gattungen* which can be collected under the generic term "*Gleichnis*"'.

45. Berger, 'Hellenistische Gattungen im Neuen Testament', p. 1112: 'In der Rhetorik dienen Gleichnisse als Beweismittel (dem historischen Beispiel verwandt) oder zur Veranschaulichung. Als Beweismittel illustrieren sie Vernunftgründe'.

46. Berger, 'Hellenistische Gattungen im Neuen Testament', p. 1113. Berger states that his schema is a modification of the outline proposed by Heinrich Lausberg in *Handbuch der literarischen Rhetorik: Eine Grundlegung der Literaturwissenschaft* (2 vols.; Munich: Hueber, 1960), I, pp. 227-35. Berger's is a substantial alteration, in my opinion, because Lausberg (a classicist) divides the category 'Exempla' into five subgroups (*res gesta, commemoratio, inductio, similitudo* and *auctoritas*), while Berger (a biblical scholar) divides the category 'Gleichnis' into four subgroups. Berger offers a somewhat different classification in

Although he prefers to reserve the term 'Gleichnis' for the second sub-genre, Berger notes: 'All four subgenres have been designated by the title παραβολή/*similitudo* in antiquity (and later)'.[47] Berger's reading of the ancient rhetorical tradition does not compel him to make a distinction between those texts Jülicher calls '*Parabeln*' and those Jülicher calls '*Beispielerzählungen*'; instead, Berger regards both the *Parabeln* and the *Beispielerzählungen* as 'narrative parables' (*Gleichniserzählungen*) because both are fictional narratives of an individual case.[48] More needs to be said, nonetheless, about the relationship between narrative parables and *exempla*.

One of Berger's outstanding contributions to the study of the rhetoric of the New Testament, one that can palliate some of the confusion about the rhetoric of the example stories, is his demonstration that a number of rhetorical genres (*Gattungen*) share in common certain rhetorical devices or features.[49] This is the case with the *exemplum* and the narrative parable. Both the *exemplum* and the narrative parable stand in a larger literary or pragmatic context, and both name an actuality—real or fictional—which is distinguished from that context.[50] For Berger, the manner in which that reality relates to its context is important. In the *exempla*, the event or action is of the same kind as that of the surrounding context; in the narrative parables, the action is not of the same kind as that of the surrounding context—*except* in the four narrative parables Jülicher identified as *Beispielerzählungen*.[51] Those four narrative parables, according to Berger, stand in closest proximity to the *exempla*.[52] Further, he suggests that all of the narrative parables,

Formgeschichte des Neuen Testaments (see pp. 25-62), where *exempla* and narrative parables are included among a number of 'analogische und bildhälfte Texte'.

47. Berger, 'Hellenistische Gattungen im Neuen Testament', p. 1113.

48. Berger, 'Hellenistische Gattungen im Neuen Testament', p. 1114. Berger lists the παραβολαί that he regards as 'Gleichniserzählungen' in *Formgeschichte des Neuen Testaments*, p. 51.

49. During the course of his treatment of 'Gleichnisgattungen' ('Hellenistische Gattungen im Neuen Testament', pp. 1112-24), Berger indicates that the narrative parable shares features in common with fable (pp. 1116-20), *narratio* (pp. 1114-15, 1120-22), *chria* (pp. 1117-18), *protreptikos* (p. 1117) and 'model cases' (or 'paradigmatischer Rechtsentscheid'; pp. 1121-23).

50. Berger, 'Hellenistische Gattungen im Neuen Testament', p. 1113.

51. Berger, *Formgeschichte des Neuen Testaments*, pp. 45, 56; cf. p. 28.

52. Berger, *Formgeschichte des Neuen Testaments*, p. 56. Berger explicitly

especially The Merciful Samaritan, perhaps have affinities to moral examples.[53]

Berger does differentiate, then, between types of *exempla* (παραδείγματα) and types of parables.[54] With reference to the *exempla* and the narrative parables, the event or happening that occurs in each becomes important. One of the characteristic features of the *exempla* is that they depict a past happening—a happening that can be mythical, but is more commonly historical—while one of the characteristic features of the narrative parables is that they depict a fictional matter or happening.[55] The narrative parables, however, have to do with a type of judgment, and it is this 'judgment structure' which distinguishes the *Gleichniserzählungen* from the *exempla* in questionable cases.[56] Thus, while Berger maintains a (sub)categorical distinction between narrative parable and *exemplum*, at the same time he also shows that the narrative parables—in particular, the *Beispielerzählungen*—have affinities with the *exempla*.[57]

Certain distinctions among the synoptic παραβολαί have been validated by alternative readings of the ancient rhetoricians. These three more recent studies of the *Beispielerzählungen* by Fascher, Sellin and Berger provide a marked contrast to some of the earlier studies of the example stories which also refer to the ancient rhetorical tradition. In contradistinction to the analyses of Stockmeyer and Jülicher, which

states that The Merciful Samaritan, The Foolish Rich Man, and The Rich Man and Poor Lazarus depict actions that are of the same sort as those in their individual surrounding contexts; he implies that the same is true of The Pharisee and the Toll Collector. Yet now the difference between these narrative parables and the *exempla* is the fictional character of the former.

53. Berger, *Formgeschichte des Neuen Testaments*, p. 30. Berger's label 'moralische Beispiele' issues from his understanding of the function of those *exempla* in their contexts (see pp. 29-31); it does not come directly from ancient rhetorical handbooks.

54. This is evident in Berger's separate treatment of *exempla* and *Gleichnisse*; see 'Hellenistische Gattungen im Neuen Testament', pp. 1110-24, 1145-48, and *Formgeschichte des Neuen Testaments*, pp. 28-31, 40-56 (cf. also pp. 322-23, where he discusses 'Beispielerzählungen aus dem Jüngerkreis').

55. Berger, 'Hellenistische Gattungen im Neuen Testament', p. 1145; *Formgeschichte des Neuen Testaments*, p. 56.

56. Berger, *Formgeschichte des Neuen Testaments*, pp. 52-53.

57. Besides those affinities already mentioned, Berger notes that both the *exempla* and the narrative parables sometimes appear in series (*Formgeschichte des Neuen Testaments*, pp. 28, 55).

imply that the ancient rhetoricians can be invoked in order to uphold a categorical distinction between example narrative and narrative parable (*Beispielerzählung* and *Parabel*, or *Gleichniserzählung*), the analyses of Fascher, Sellin and Berger suggest that such a distinction cannot be grounded soundly in the ancient rhetorical tradition. The findings of Fascher, Sellin and Berger converge to indicate that the synoptic παραβολαί, among which the example narratives belong, and the παραδείγματα are closely related. Indeed, a reasonable conclusion would seem to be this: Viewed from the perspective of the ancient rhetorical tradition, the dichotomy between 'example narrative' as παράδειγμα (or *exemplum*) and 'narrative parable' as παραβολή, as it is advanced or implied in some studies of the parables, is untenable. This conclusion needs to be defended; thus, more attention must be given to how the παράδειγμα and παραβολή are viewed in the ancient rhetorical tradition (see Chapter 5).

Other issues that need to be investigated more fully have arisen in this overview of studies of the example stories informed by ancient rhetoric. As the studies mentioned here suggest, there are a variety of παραδείγματα discussed in the ancient rhetorical tradition and evidenced in New Testament documents—among which must be listed the synoptic παραβολαί, including the four so-called example stories.[58] Thus, one question that remains to be addressed is whether παράδειγμα and παραβολή are employed as 'form' designations by the ancient rhetoricians. Correspondingly, it needs to be determined whether or not παράδειγμα means *solely* 'historical example' in ancient rhetoric.[59] Moreover, the studies mentioned above have shown not only that the synoptic παραβολαί, including the four that have been called 'example stories', belong among the παραδείγματα, and thus that the *Beispielerzählungen* and *Parabeln* (or *Gleichniserzählungen*) share features or

58. See Berger, 'Hellenistische Gattungen im Neuen Testament', pp. 1113, 1145-48; and *Formgeschichte des Neuen Testaments*, pp. 28-31, 56, 322-23. The use of παραδείγματα in epistolary texts has been examined by Benjamin Fiore, *The Function of Personal Example in the Socratic and Pastoral Epistles* (AnBib, 105; Rome: Biblical Institute Press, 1986); on the Pauline letters, see pp. 164-90, and on the pastorals, see pp. 22-25, 191-231. For an analysis of Paul's use of example in a section of Romans (3.27–4.25), see Stanley Kent Stowers, *The Diatribe and Paul's Letter to the Romans* (SBLDS, 57; Chico, CA: Scholars Press, 1981), pp. 155-74.

59. Bultmann, as we have seen, makes this claim. Baasland ('Zum Beispiel der Beispielerzählungen', p. 198; cf. his n. 23) also subscribes to this view.

functions in common, but also that both the παραβολαί and the παραδείγματα have affinities to other '*Gattungen*' mentioned in the ancient rhetorical tradition. An examination of the rhetorical strategies apparent in the example stories with those findings in mind will better enable us to discern whether the *Beispielerzählungen* are a unique category of synoptic παραβολή. We have seen how some scholars view the example stories as rhetorical examples. Now yet another understanding of the category 'example story' must be pursued.

The example stories as moral examples. The notion that the example stories present 'moral examples' is encountered in studies of the parables more frequently than the notion that the example stories represent a type of rhetorical example. As it appears variously in modern parable scholarship, the view that the example stories are 'moral examples' is commonly based upon Bultmann's contention that the *Beispielerzählung* is a form to be distinguished from the *Parabel* because the example narratives lack any 'element of the pictorial' and, consequently, 'offer models for the right conduct'.[60] An adequate appreciation of the conception of the example stories as 'moral examples' can be gained from a small sample of the many scholars who underwrite Bultmann's definition of that 'form'.

A leading American parable scholar, Dan Otto Via, Jr, explicitly adopts Bultmann's definition of the form 'example story', as can be seen in his claims that '...in an example story the symbolic, figurative, or indirect element is missing', and that 'the behavior and attitude sketched in The Good Samaritan and The Rich Fool (example stories) are not comparable to or analogous to what a man should do or avoid but are exactly what he should do or avoid'.[61] Via chooses to exclude the example stories from his study of Jesus' parables, to quote words he later uses to reiterate his rationale, '...*because* they can only be read

---

60. So familiar is Bultmann's definition of the example narrative that it is often projected onto Jülicher's. Baasland ('Zum Beispiel der Beispielerzählungen', p. 198; cf. his n. 24) does so when he states, 'By "example" the research means, on the other hand, "a model for the right conduct"'and in the corresponding footnote cites Jülicher at the beginning of a list of scholars who purportedly accept this definition, a list that fails to include Bultmann. See also Heininger, *Metaphorik*, p. 7; and James M. Robinson, *A New Quest of the Historical Jesus* (Philadelphia: Fortress Press, 1983), p. 197.

61. Via, *The Parables*, p. 12.

morally or are not genuine metaphors, as the case may be, and are not parables'.[62]

To those who regard Jesus' parables as metaphors, this last remark might prove especially disquieting. Other prominent American parable scholars have an appreciation of Bultmann's definition of the example narrative and its consequent implication, but that appreciation gives way to apprehension. Three students of the parables—Funk, Crossan and Scott—acknowledge the applicability of Bultmann's definition of the *Gattung 'Beispielerzählung'* to the Gospel of Luke, only to disavow its suitability to the parables of Jesus.

Funk is the first to advocate the view that The Good Samaritan as spoken by Jesus '...is metaphorical and therefore not an example story'.[63] With The Good Samaritan in view, Funk—conflating Jülicher and Bultmann—defines the *Beispielerzählung* is this way:

> An exemplary story does not draw its pictorial element from a sphere other than the one to which its *Sache* belongs; it has no figurative element at all. 'The "exemplary stories" [*Beispielerzählungen*] offer examples=models of right behavior.' The exemplary story does not, therefore, call for a transference of judgment as do the parables proper. The Samaritan is just an example of a true neighbor (or, to follow the prevailing view, of the true love of one's neighbor), nothing more.[64]

Funk names three factors that have contributed to the understanding that The Good Samaritan offers a moral example, or that it should be given a moral reading: the first, and here he follows Jeremias, is 'the pronounced tendency of the tradition to convert parables with eschatological horizons into hortatory material'; the second is the definition of

62. Dan Otto Via, Jr, 'A Response to Crossan, Funk, and Petersen', *Semeia* 1 (1974), pp. 222-35 (227; emphasis his); cf. *The Parables*, p. 13.

63. Robert W. Funk, 'The Good Samaritan as Metaphor', *Semeia* 2 (1974), pp. 74-81 (74) (cf. *Parables and Presence*, p. 29). Funk argues this view in a study which antedates Via's book; see 'The Old Testament in Parable: The Good Samaritan', in *Language, Hermeneutic, and Word of God*, pp. 199-222. Contra Baasland ('Zum Beispiel der Beispielerzählungen', p. 197), Funk was the first to criticize the conception of the category *Beispielerzählung* based upon a view of 'parable as metaphor' (see the bibliography Funk provides in *Parables and Presence*, pp. 29, 189).

64. Funk, *Language, Hermeneutic, and Word of God*, p. 211. Bultmann does not state explicitly that the example narratives do not 'call for a transference of judgment'; Funk infers this from remarks Bultmann makes elsewhere (see *History of the Synoptic Tradition*, p. 198).

'Beispielerzählung' itself; the third is the Lukan context, which terminates the narrative with the exhortation, 'Go and do likewise'.[65] Funk
contends that when the literal and non-literal (that is, metaphorical)
meanings of The Good Samaritan are grasped concomitantly, then it is
allowed to function as a parabolic metaphor, a language event that dis-
closes Jesus' view of 'world'.[66] Read literally, The Good Samaritan
remains what Luke understood it to be—an example story.

Crossan's tack is similar to Funk's inasmuch as he, too, posits that
the stories called 'example stories' as told by Jesus are really metaphorical parables.[67] Such a generalization, however, glosses over the distinctiveness of Crossan's ideas about the example stories. In his well-
known essay, 'Parable and Example in the Teaching of Jesus', Crossan
addresses the issue of whether Bultmann's form-critical class
'exemplary story' is fitting for that group of authentic parables as
uttered by the historical Jesus.[68] While he concedes that Bultmann's
classification is correct for those stories as they now stand in the Gospel
of Luke, Crossan argues that '...they were changed into examples by

65. Funk, *Language, Hermeneutic, and Word of God*, p. 211; cf. n. 52. Elsewhere, Funk describes the common understanding (Luke's included) of The Good
Samaritan as example story: 'The parable therefore makes the Good Samaritan an
example of what it means to be a neighbor. There is no figurative element in the
parable, and the parable is taken as commending this kind of behavior' (*Parables
and Presence*, p. 31).

66. Funk, *Language, Hermeneutic, and Word of God*, pp. 214-21. For a more
complete description of how Jesus' parables function, see his famous exposition of
'The Parable as Metaphor', *Language, Hermeneutic, and Word of God*, pp. 133-62.

67. Crossan has written extensively on the parables told by Jesus (and those told
by others), and he has developed and refined his view of Jesus' parables—including, as we will see, the example stories. Although it does not do justice to Crossan's
expansive interests, I have decided to condense several sources and to limit the discussion to those places where he treats the example stories. For a description of the
development of Crossan's thought on the parables, see Frank Burch Brown and
Elizabeth Struthers Malbon, 'Parabling as a *Via Negativa*: A Critical Review of the
Work of John Dominic Crossan', *JR* 64 (1984), pp. 530-38; and Lynn M. Poland,
Literary Criticism and Biblical Hermeneutics: A Critique of Formalist Approaches
(American Academy of Religion Academy Series, 48; Chico, CA: Scholars Press,
1985), pp. 108-20.

68. John Dominic Crossan, 'Parable and Example in the Teaching of Jesus',
NTS 18 (1972), pp. 285-307 (repr. in *Semeia* 1 [1974], pp. 63-104; page references
are to the reprint edition).

the tradition and/or the evangelists'.[69] Such a transformation is understandable, Crossan suggests, because '...when Jesus tells parables
whose content is not some morally neutral activity such as sowing or
harvesting but involves a morally significant action it may not be at all
so clear if he is giving examples (act/do not act like this) or telling
parables'.[70] As parables of Jesus, all of the stories purported to be
'example stories' are poetic metaphors;[71] more specifically, all but The
Rich Fool are 'parables of reversal'.[72] Given the purpose of this study,
the focus will be on what Crossan has to say about the example stories
as (Lukan) example stories.

Crossan appropriates Bultmann's definition of the category
'exemplary story', as well as his specification of the stories which
comprise that category. He gives Bultmann's definition and then
modifies it so that now, according to Crossan, exemplary stories are
'models of right and/or wrong behavior'.[73] From Bultmann's definition
Crossan deduces that—in contradistinction to 'metaphors', 'similitudes' and 'parables'—'...examples are essentially different in that, as
Bultmann noted, they may "have no figurative element at all"'.[74]
Crossan continues: 'They are stories of how one should or should not
behave in certain situations and, while being also paradigmatic for
other cases, these stories could be actually lived out in practice...'[75]
The imprint of Bultmann's definition can be seen in other places where
Crossan mentions the example stories. If the stories told by Jesus are
viewed as examples and not parables, then they are read as 'storied
models of conduct or storied warnings against misconduct'.[76] Indeed,

69. Crossan, 'Parable and Example', p. 63; cf. pp. 77, 85-86. Here, Crossan
argues in favor of a view that is the inverse of Jülicher's position (see above, p. 90).

70. Crossan, *In Parables*, p. 56.

71. Crossan, 'Parable and Example', p. 88; cf. *In Parables*, pp. 10-22.

72. Crossan, *In Parables*, pp. 53-78. Note that The Prodigal Son (Lk. 15.11-32)
also belongs to this group of parables; moreover, certain 'servant parables' exhibit
the structure of reversal (see also 'Structuralist Analysis and the Parables of Jesus',
p. 214).

73. Crossan, 'Parable and Example', pp. 63, 64.

74. Crossan, 'Parable and Example', p. 64. The subjunctive 'may' was not
penned by Bultmann; it does not appear in either *Die Geschichte der synoptischen
Tradition* or the English translation.

75. Crossan, 'Parable and Example', pp. 64-65.

76. John Dominic Crossan, *Raid on the Articulate: Comic Eschatology in Jesus
and Borges* (New York: Harper & Row, 1976), pp. 99-100.

with respect to the group of parables called 'example stories', Crossan contends that '...the tradition has consistently asked us to read them as examples, as stories of how one should or should not act and how God approves or disapproves such action'.[77] For Crossan, then, to read the *Beispielerzählungen* as 'moral example-stories' is to read them as Luke accepted them—that is, as 'actual examples of good and/or bad ethical action'.[78]

Scott also regards the *Beispielerzählungen* in the Gospel of Luke as 'moral examples'. Echoes of Bultmann can be heard in his terse statement: 'An example story has no figurative element but offers an example of correct behavior or of negative behavior to avoid'.[79] Like Funk and Crossan before him, Scott holds that the *Beispielerzählungen* as found in the Gospel of Luke are example stories, but that those stories as Jesus told them are parables—indeed, a specific type of parable: metonymic parables.[80]

The view of the example stories as 'moral examples', which, in its recent renditions, emanates primarily from Bultmann, seems to discomfort its advocates. We have encountered two remedies for relieving the discomfort: exclusion of the example stories or rehabilitation of the example stories. If one opts for the former, then like Via one cedes that the example stories are 'moral examples' and as such are not to be counted among the authentic parables of the historical Jesus, who did not utter mere examples. If one opts for the latter, then like Crossan and Scott (and to a lesser extent, Funk), one can affirm that the example stories in the Gospel of Luke are 'moral examples' but then argue that they were originally metaphorical or metonymic, and thus authentic, parables of the historical Jesus, who did not utter mere examples. The obvious benefit of following the second approach is that Bultmann's definition of the form 'example narrative' can be accepted without

---

77. Crossan, *Raid on the Articulate*, p. 107. Elsewhere, Crossan argues that this is precisely what the parables are not: 'The parables of Jesus are *not* historical allegories telling us how God acts with mankind; neither are they moral example-stories telling us how to act before God and towards one another' (*The Dark Interval: Towards a Theology of Story* [Allen, TX: Argus Communications, 1975], pp. 121-22; emphasis his).

78. Crossan, *In Parables*, p. 56.

79. Scott, *Hear Then the Parable*, p. 29.

80. Scott, *Hear Then the Parable*, pp. 29-30. Scott here draws upon a development in Crossan's understanding of the example stories, one which will be discussed in the next section.

extirpating the narratives which comprise that class from among the authentic parables of Jesus.[81]

Interestingly, common ground can be found to exist among proponents of both remedies. Via, Funk, Crossan and Scott agree on at least two points: (1) that example stories as a category (or 'form') offer 'moral examples'; and (2) that category (or 'form') does not apply to Jesus' parables because his parables do not offer 'moral examples'. The 'moral content' or 'moral purpose' of the example stories, then, is at the same time both the unsettling issue in the dispute and the means for differentiating between 'parable' (of Jesus) and 'example story' (of the Gospel of Luke).

Other scholars are not greatly troubled by the 'moral content' or 'moral purpose' of the example stories, for they do not regard this as unique to that group of παραβολαί alone. David Flusser, for instance, states that 'exempla are instructive, autonomous stories to which a moral teaching can be attached'.[82] Unlike anecdotes, to which the

---

81. Stein (*An Introduction to the Parables of Jesus*, p. 20) presents another alternative. He includes the example stories among the parables of Jesus, but with a twist. Stein provides his own terminology to represent the received distinction, which he draws from Eta Linnemann, between *Parabeln* and *Beispielerzählungen*; the former Stein calls 'story parables', the latter 'example parables'. He adds, 'It is primarily these two types of parables which come to mind when we think of the parables of Jesus'. Both types, according to Stein, are 'single extended metaphors', although the 'example parable' is said to serve 'primarily as a model for behavior'. Stein lists among the 'example parables' Lk. 10.29-37, 12.16-21, 14.7-14, 16.19-31, 18.9-14, and Mt. 18.23-25.

82. Flusser, *Die rabbinischen Gleichnisse und der Gleichniserzähler Jesus*, p. 69. Flusser does not refer directly to the ancient rhetorical tradition to define the term 'exempla', although his claim that exempla are 'narratives of past events that really happened or were freely invented' (p. 57) seems to echo Aristotle. Later, Flusser states that the *exemplum* often has a real event as its background (p. 60; cf. p. 58). He stresses that an important aspect of the fable (Flusser means by 'fable' stories like those told by Aesop) and the parable is that they recount events in such a way as to give the impression that the events really happened (pp. 32-34, 54-60). Unlike the fable and the parable, however, the *exemplum* is said to be autonomous; i.e. it can be understood by itself (p. 69). In Flusser's view, all three *Gattungen*— fable, parable, *exemplum*—are closely related, which is as it should be given his dependence upon 'Lessings Fabeltheorie'. Flusser notes that 'all of Jesus' exempla occur only in Luke' (p. 57)—and he includes The Lost Son (Lk. 15.11-32) in the group—and later adds that they belong to Luke's *Sondergut* (p. 69). He points out

exempla are otherwise closely related, the *exempla* are told not to entertain, but to teach a moral.[83] The realization that *exempla* are narrated to
teach a moral lesson does not suffice, in and of itself, to differentiate
them from parables, for the parables also evince moral decisions.
According to Flusser, 'the majority of Jesus' parables had the purpose
to make clear to simple people a general moral teaching by means of a
parable'.[84]

Providing instruction for action, in Claus Westermann's opinion, is
not the sovereign domain of only the example stories. He does categorize the *Beispielerzählungen* among the parables of Jesus that, according to their structure, provide 'instruction [*Weisung*] for a present
action';[85] however, other parables not commonly designated as
'example narratives' (for instance, Lk. 17.7-10) appear in that group or
have 'instruction' as a subordinate motif.[86] Still other parables (for
instance, in Mt. 24–25) are said to provide 'instruction for a future
action'.[87]

The thesis that Jesus' parables in general have to do with action, or
behavior, is advanced forcefully by Jacques Dupont.[88] The parables,
Dupont contends, should not be reduced to general or abstract truths,

(p. 57) that such stories occur also in rabbinic literature and are there called
'stories' (ma'asîm).

83. Flusser, *Die rabbinischen Gleichnisse und der Gleichniserzähler Jesus*,
p. 295.

84. Flusser, *Die rabbinischen Gleichnisse und der Gleichniserzähler Jesus*,
p. 14: 'Die meisten Gleichnisse Jesu hatten den Zweck, den einfachen Menschen
eine allgemeine moralische Lehre durch ein Gleichnis klarzumachen'; cf. pp. 53-
55, 58-60.

85. Westermann, *Vergleiche und Gleichnisse*, pp. 123, 126-28; my translation.
(One may consult the English translation, *The Parables of Jesus in the Light of the
Old Testament*, pp. 184, 189-91. All subsequent page references will be to the
German edition.) Interestingly, Westermann includes The Pharisee and the Toll
Collector among a group of parables that involve God's merciful acceptance of sin-
ners (p. 124).

86. Westermann, *Vergleiche und Gleichnisse*, p. 127.

87. Westermann, *Vergleiche und Gleichnisse*, pp. 128-29. Moreover, Westermann maintains that according to their function many similes (*Vergleichen*) form
part of an instruction for action, occur in such instruction, or occur as such instruction (see pp. 130-32).

88. Jacques Dupont, *Pourquoi des paraboles? La méthode parabolique de
Jésus* (Lire la Bible, 46; Paris: Cerf, 1977). Dupont's view is endorsed by Boucher
(*The Parables*, p. 41) and Hendrickx (*The Parables of Jesus*, pp. 3-10).

for '...the true terrain of the parables is that of behavior, of praxis'.[89]
This contention is based upon the observation that only meager details
about the characters are provided in the parables; thus, attention is
drawn to the actions of the characters. As a result, '...one takes interest
in what they [the characters] do, in their conduct, in the manner in
which they behave with others'.[90] Dupont divides the parables into two
groups, depending upon whether the concern is with the behavior of the
auditors, or whether the concern is with the behavior of Jesus or God.[91]
The example stories obviously fall into the former group. Some of the
parables of that group commend a specific conduct, whereas others
warn against conduct that would have disastrous consequences. About
the 'récits exemplaires', Dupont writes succinctly:

> ...no transposition is necessary in order to disengage the lesson. An
> example to follow is offered in the story of the Good Samaritan...one
> not to follow in the stories of the Rich Fool...the Rich Man and Poor
> Lazarus...and the Pharisee and the Publican.[92]

However, to reiterate, it is not just the example stories that treat human
behavior. The parables of Jesus, to paraphrase Dupont, meet human
beings in their concrete situations; the parables allure by means of a
dialogue that appeals to a lived experience; the parables want to lead
their auditors to change their manner of seeing, their attitudes, their
behavior.[93] Dupont's thesis that Jesus' parables in general have to do

---

89. Dupont, *Pourquoi des paraboles?*, p. 41: '...le véritable terrain des
paraboles est celui des comportements, de la praxis' (cf. p. 15). Dupont devotes an
entire chapter to 'Le terrain des comportements' (pp. 19-41).

90. Dupont, *Pourquoi des paraboles?*, p. 24: 'Ces personnages, on ne les décrit
pas tels qu'ils sont, on ne leur demande pas de belles idées ou de profondes
réflexions théologiques; on s'intéresse à ce qu'ils font, à leur conduite, à la manière
dont ils se comportent avec les autres' (cf. p. 20).

91. Dupont, *Pourquoi des paraboles?*, pp. 25-26. Even if the parable concerns
God, the parable does not illustrate God's attributes; rather, the concern is with how
God acts and what that might entail for human behavior (p. 24; cf. p. 40).

92. Dupont, *Pourquoi des paraboles?*, p. 26: '...aucune transposition n'est
nécessaire pour dégager la leçon. Un exemple à suivre est proposé aux auditeurs
dans l'histoire du Bon Samaritain (Lc 10, 30-37), à ne pas suivre dans les histoires
du Riche insensé (Lc 12, 16-20), de l'Homme riche et du pauvre Lazare (Lc 16, 19-
31), du Pharisien et du publicain (Lc 18, 9-14)'.

93. Dupont, *Pourquoi des paraboles?*, p. 105: 'Toujours collées à la vie, les
paraboles de Jésus rejoignent l'homme dans ses situations concrètes, l'entraînent
dans un dialogue qui fait appel à une expérience vécue, voulant ainsi le conduire à

with action, or behavior, serves as a foil to the view that only the example stories depict 'moral behavior'.

Is it possible to isolate specific formal features evident in the example stories to support the view that they alone are 'moral examples'? To elevate the 'moral or pious conduct' within the example stories, as Baasland suggests, to the status of a formal criterion for differentiating between *Beispielerzählung* and *Parabel* is a dubious procedure because 'exemplary or non-exemplary conduct' also occurs in parables.[94] Perhaps, Baasland continues, the 'example' in the example narrative is not to be located within the narrative itself, but can be shifted to the application.[95] However, it must be asked whether there exists in the applications of the example stories a formal element, such as an imperative verb, to indicate that these narratives alone issue a challenge to action.[96] With respect to the example stories, only after The Merciful Samaritan does Jesus admonish his hearer to 'do likewise', with the verb ποιεῖν (do) in the imperative.[97] Interestingly, two other parables in the Gospel of Luke conclude with applications containing the verb ποιεῖν in the

changer ses manières de voir, ses attitudes, son comportement. Les paraboles s'intéressent aux comportements bien plus qu'aux idées'.

94. Baasland, 'Zum Beispiel der Beispielerzählungen', pp. 198-99: 'In the majority of the *Handlungsgleichnissen* exemplary or non-exemplary conduct occurs, perhaps in Mt. 13.44-46; 21.28ff; 22.1ff; 24.43ff; 25.1ff etc.'. Baudler (*Jesus im Spiegel seiner Gleichnisse*, pp. 58-78, 117-28) offers an exposition of the *Handlungsgleichnisse*, among which he includes (see pp. 64-65): 'Velorenes Schaf (Mt 18, 12-13; Lk 15, 4-6), Barmherziger Vater (Lk 15, 11-32), Gütiger Arbeitsherr (Mt 20, 1-15), Barmherziger Samariter (Lk 10, 30-35), Betrügerischer Verwalter (Lk 16, 1-7), Unfairer Knecht (Mt 18, 23-33), Großes Gastmahl (Lk 14.16-24 [verändert Mt 22, 2-10]), Zehn Jungfrauen (Mt 25, 1-10), Anvertraute Gelder (Mt 25, 14-28 [in veränderter Form Lk 19, 12-24]), Mord im Weinberg (Mk 12, 1b-8; Mt 21, 33-39; Lk 20, 9-15), Pharisäer und Zöllner (Lk 18, 10-14a), Reicher Prasser (Lk 16,19-31 [V 19-26 vorjesuanische Überlieferung]), Reicher Kornbauer (Lk 12, 16-20)'.

95. Baasland, 'Zum Beispiel der Beispielerzählungen', p. 199. Baasland thinks of Jülicher's definition of *Beispielerzählung* as being nuanced more toward the application than is Bultmann's.

96. Baasland ('Zum Beispiel der Beispielerzählungen', p. 199) points out that only The Merciful Samaritan ends with both a question and imperative addressed to the hearer; other parables end with either questions or imperatives.

97. See Lk. 10.37. The context of Jesus' remark that the lawyer should 'go and do likewise' (πορεύου καὶ σὺ ποίει ὁμοίως) clearly suggests that the lawyer should 'do mercy'.

imperative.[98] Moreover, other synoptic *Gleichnisse* and *Parabeln* have imperative verbs in their applications, as Bultmann has already noted.[99] Indeed, Susan Suleiman regards conclusions that take the form of an injunction as 'an essential element of Jesus' parabolic discourse'.[100] Therefore, an explicit or implied imperative in the application does not appear to be unique to the example stories and should not be adduced as a characteristic feature in order to distinguish them as a particular genre (*Gattung*) of παραβολή.[101]

Although the notion that the example stories are a separate type of παραβολή because they provide 'moral examples' is almost a commonplace in sectors of parable scholarship, several of the assumptions made to support such a notion do not withstand scrutiny. The question bears repeating: Are there any formal characteristics in the *Beispielerzählungen* that can be identified and adduced as evidence to prove the claim that the example stories alone offer 'moral examples', and hence are not *Parabeln*? Until now in this survey of recent research on the *Beispielerzählungen*, the example stories as a group have not been shown to manifest enough common formal features to warrant differentiating them from the *Parabeln*. The recognition that the example stories exhibit a concern for the behavior they depict does not necessarily make them 'moral examples' and thus different from the *Parabeln*. Recall Bultmann's indication that some *Gleichnisse* also produce

98. See Lk. 4.23 (ποίησον) and Lk. 16.9 (ποιήσατε).

99. Bultmann, *Die Geschichte der synoptischen Tradition*, pp. 197, 200.

100. Suleiman, *Authoritarian Fictions*, p. 31. Even if an explicit injunction is missing, according to Suleiman, it is implied and must be provided by the hearer (pp. 36-37); these pragmatic injunctions, in turn, produce rules of action (see pp. 30-36, 46, 54). Lyons (*Exemplum*, pp. 20-25) argues against Suleiman's claim that injunction is a necessary component of the *exemplum*. For more discussion of Suleiman's view of the example, see Alexander Gelley's article, 'The Pragmatics of Exemplary Narrative', in *idem* (ed.), *Unruly Examples: On the Rhetoric of Exemplarity* (Stanford, CA: Stanford University Press, 1995), pp. 143-46, 156-61.

101. In agreement with Baasland, 'Zum Beispiel der Beispielerzählungen', p. 199. Johnston ('Parabolic Interpretations Attributed to Tannaim', p. 579) regards applications with explicit or implied imperative verbs as 'characteristic of the typical example story', although he is aware that only Lk. 10.37 'has a clearly imperative application' (pp. 521-22 n. 1). Lambrecht (*Once More Astonished*, p. 7) writes that there are moralizing applications appended to parables (e.g. Mk 13.33-37), and thus a moralizing application '...in itself is not sufficient to categorize the narratives in question as exemplary stories'.

'example and counterexample', and that a '*moral* judgment about an action is provoked not only in the example narratives', but also in some *Parabeln*. Furthermore, recall Dupont's postulation that 'the true terrain of the parables is that of behavior, of praxis'. Claims such as these, if there is any merit to them, increase the difficulty of maintaining a categorical distinction between *Parabel* and *Beispielerzählung*, and the ramifications of these claims extend to both the *Parabeln* and the *Beispielerzählungen*. Seen in this light, 'moral concerns' cannot be expunged from the *Parabeln* and reserved for the *Beispielerzählungen* alone.[102] Although it is convenient to do so, it seems to beg the question to claim that the example stories as they appear in the Gospel of Luke are 'moral examples', but that as authentic parables of Jesus they are not. Birger Gerhardsson's observation provides a compelling explanation that accounts for some of the discontent about the example stories: 'The work done on the parables by recent generations shows us that one after another must be divested of their moralistic, parænetic significance in order to reveal their original, eschatological meaning'.[103]

The economy of narrative details evident in the παραβολαί draws attention to what the characters do, their actions. This is no less true of the *Parabeln* than of the *Beispielerzählungen*. Does this mean, then, that both the narrative parables (*Parabeln*) and the example narratives serve only to 'offer models for the right conduct' or 'examples to be imitated'? One problem with answering in the affirmative is that the *Parabeln* and the *Beispielerzählungen* would then be read as if they

---

102. Polk ('Paradigms, Parables, and *Měšālîm*', pp. 565-70) argues that the *mashal* serves a 'behavior-affecting function': '...[I]n terms of purpose and function the *māšāl*, *qua* genre, might well be construed as designating a device for involving the reader in a process of cognitive assent to its claims and moral self-evaluation in the light of those claims' (p. 565 n. 5). 'Relatedly, like the parable the *māšāl* has the marked ability to involve its addressee, or target, in a self-judgement' (p. 570).

103. Gerhardsson, *The Good Samaritan—The Good Shepherd?*, p. 8. Gerhardsson refers here to Jeremias and, by extension, to those who follow him. It was Jeremias who formulated ten 'laws of transformation' to explain how the early church effected changes upon Jesus' parables. Pertinent here is 'law six', by which Jeremias identifies 'an increasing shift of emphasis to the hortatory aspect, especially from the eschatological to the hortatory' (*The Parables of Jesus*, p. 113; cf. pp. 42-48). Funk observes that with Jeremias (and Dodd), 'Jülicher's moral *point* of broadest possible application has become the eschatological *point* of particular historical application' (*Language, Hermeneutic, and Word of God*, p. 148 [his emphasis]; cf. pp. 147-49).

were 'literally literal'.[104] There is another problem with conceiving of
the example stories, or any of the παραβολαί, exclusively as 'models
for the right conduct' or 'examples to be imitated'. While it is certainly
correct that the example stories draw attention to the behavior or action
of the characters—be it virtuous, noble, ignominious or wretched—to
apply the example stories as they appear in the Gospel of Luke, or any
of the synoptic παραβολαί for that matter, directly to the living of life
in the present is to leap too quickly from the text in which they are
embedded to reality outside the text. As Sellin puts it, the example
stories 'are therefore by no means simply directly applicable parane-
sis'.[105] Both the *Parabeln* and the *Beispielerzählungen* may have
'ethical implications', but neither comprise an 'ethics'.[106]

To think that the example stories communicate values is not entirely
inappropriate, but they do so as parts of a larger narrative, and that
larger narrative—the Gospel of Luke—*as a whole* reflects an ideology.
This study, then, will challenge the view that the example stories in the
Gospel of Luke are merely 'actual examples of good and/or bad ethical
actions', nothing more than 'moral examples'. In addition, this study
will suggest that the example narratives are narrative παραβολαί, that
the example narratives are embedded narrative texts, which would, in
turn, suggest that the example narratives function to support the ideology of the Gospel of Luke.

The Comparative Mechanism of the Example Stories: Metaphor, Synecdoche and Metonymy

A perusal of parable scholarship in the twentieth century leaves the
impression that if any consensus is to be found among scholars about
the form and function of the παραβολαί, such solidarity revolves
around the conclusion that the parable involves comparison, or effects
the act of comparing. As Via states:

> It is generally agreed by New Testament scholarship that comparison
> lies at the heart of a parable. Parables are in various ways elaborated

104. Funk, *Parables and Presence*, p. 30; cf. *Language, Hermeneutic, and Word
of God*, pp. 214-15.
105. Sellin, 'Lukas als Gleichniserzähler', p. 178 (see also his n. 57).
106. See Gerhardsson, 'The Narrative Meshalim in the Synoptic Gospels', p. 362
(his emphasis): 'That the narrative meshalim in the gospels even have ethical
implications in many cases and also *consequences* for social, economic, and political issues, is another matter'.

comparisons, and this is a feature which Jesus' parables share with some
of the *meshalim* of the Old Testament and, also, with the parables of the
Greek tradition.[107]

Irrespective of the term or model used to describe the manner in which
a παραβολή effects a comparison—and several have been proposed,
such as analogy, simile, metaphor—not infrequently a corollary conclusion is tendered: The 'comparative mechanism' of the *Parabel* (that
is, the means by which it effects a comparison) is different from that of
the *Beispielerzählung*.[108] An examination of the various explications of
the comparative mechanism operative in the example narratives will
illuminate further the reasons given for either choosing to distinguish
between narrative parable (*Gleichniserzählung*, or *Parabel*) and example narrative (*Beispielerzählung*), or refusing to do so.

A familiar means of describing the putative singularity of the example stories is founded upon an understanding of the relationship or connection between *Bildhälfte* and *Sachhälfte* in a παραβολή. The manner
in which these two members (or fields, or spheres or planes) are related
constitutes the 'comparative mechanism' of the παραβολή. In order to

---

107. Via, *The Parables*, p. 11. The following is a sample of scholars who emphasize the comparative aspect of the parable: Dodd, *The Parables of the Kingdom*,
p. 7; Hunter, *Interpreting the Parables*, p. 8; Jones, *The Art and Truth of the
Parables*, p. 63; Hauck, 'παραβολή', pp. 745-53; Funk, *Language, Hermeneutic,
and Word of God*, pp. 136-37; Perrin, *Jesus and the Language of the Kingdom*, p. 6;
Boucher, *The Mysterious Parable*, p. 25; Tolbert, *Perspectives on the Parables*,
pp. 43-48; Westermann, *Vergleiche und Gleichnisse*, p. 10; Young, *Jesus and his
Jewish Parables*, pp. 4-6; Granskou, *Preaching on the Parables*, pp. 1-3. The
etymology of παραβολή (see p. 206 below) would seem to preclude dissent.
Hedrick, the etymology of παραβολή notwithstanding, questions the traditional
view that Jesus used parables to make comparisons ('Parables and the Kingdom',
pp. 388-89, 391; see also *Parables as Poetic Fictions*, pp. 7-35, esp. p. 28).

108. For instance, John W. Sider ('The Meaning of *Parabole* in the Usage of the
Synoptic Evangelists', *Bib* 62 [1981], pp. 453-70 [468]) describes the 'center of the
field of meaning' of '*parabole*' as 'illustration by analogy'. He distinguishes
between analogies of equation, evident in *Gleichnisse* and *Parabeln*, and analogies
of example, evident in *Beispielerzählungen* (see pp. 460-66). In a subsequent
article, Sider refers to the *Gleichnisse* and *Parabeln* as 'proportional analogies', the
Beispielerzählungen as 'non-proportional analogies' ('Proportional Analogies in
the Gospel Parables', pp. 8, 23). Sider repeats his position in *Interpreting the
Parables* (pp. 18-26; cf. pp. 254, 257), but he goes on to show that the example
stories exhibit many of the same features as the other parables (see pp. 101, 107,
109-10, 116-18, 130-31, 134-35).

facilitate a deeper appreciation of the discussion about the comparative mechanism of the example stories, some terms need to be clarified. Since Jülicher popularized the terminology used to characterize the comparative mechanism of the παραβολή, it may be helpful to review how he describes it and how that is then brought to bear upon the example stories.[109]

As we have seen, Jülicher regards the παραβολή as a type of pictorial speech in which two quantities are moved side by side for the sake of comparison. The παραβολή, which has its roots in the simile and is always actual speech, is comprised of two members: a proposition in need of demonstration, the *Sache* (or *Sachhälfte*), and a proposition developed for the purpose of such demonstration, the *Bild* (or *Bildhälfte*). The similarity upon which both propositions are based is a general law or principle, the *tertium comparationis*. Jülicher identifies three types of παραβολαί in the synoptic gospels—*Gleichnisse, Parabeln* and *Beispielerzählungen*. He argues that all three types of παραβολαί advance the subject matter 'the kingdom of God'; are related to the 'religious-ethical' sphere or field; serve a 'religious-ethical' purpose; and that both the *Parabeln* and the *Beispielerzählungen* influence conduct. While the *Gleichnis* introduces an everyday reality accessible to everyone, the *Parabel* and the *Beispielerzählung* are freely invented narratives which relate a particular incident or occurrence. The *Parabel* brings forward an earthly circumstance in the *Bildhälfte* (the 'neutral soil') that is to be compared to the religious-ethical sphere in the *Sachhälfte*. The *Beispielerzählung*, however, already belongs to the religious-ethical sphere. In the example narrative, the story does not transpire in another field, as it does in the *Parabel*, but in the field in which the proposition to be secured is located. 'The story is an example of the

---

109. This summary is taken from the section in the preceding chapter (pp. 80-127) in which a detailed explication of Jülicher's view of the essence of Jesus' parable speeches—as presented in the revised edition of *Die Gleichnisreden Jesu*—is given. I repeat that this summary is based upon the revised edition because, as was indicated earlier, Jülicher changed his view of the *Beispielerzählungen* on several points. With that in mind, it will become apparent that Boucher's representation of Jülicher's position on the example narratives is not entirely accurate. Citing the 1899 (2nd, or revised) edition of *Die Gleichnisreden Jesu*, Boucher writes: 'In addition, Jülicher distinguished four parables, all Lukan, to which he gave the name *exemplary story*...This type differs from the first two in that it presents, not a comparison, but an example to be imitated' (*The Mysterious Parable*, p. 3; her emphasis).

proposition to be asserted.' The example narrative forgoes entering a
'neutral soil' first; rather, it presents immediately the subject matter
(*Sache*) demonstrated in a particular case. Thus, Jülicher emphasizes
that the difference between the *Parabeln* and the *Beispielerzählungen*
has to do with the greater or lesser proximity of the circumstance narrated in each to the religious-ethical sphere, or—to put it another
way—the greater or lesser immediacy of the *Sache*.[110]

Many scholars concur with Jülicher that the comparative mechanism
operative in the *Beispielerzählungen* is different from the comparative
mechanism operative in the *Parabeln*, and more often than not that
difference is articulated in terms appropriated from Jülicher or in terms
correlative to his. Although few contend overtly that the example stories do not effect a comparison at all,[111] many conclude that there is

110. As we now know, Jülicher resists speaking of the *Bild* or *Bildhälfte* with
regard to the example narratives, preferring rather to speak of the 'story' and its
relation to the *Sache*. Jülicher's use of the terms *Bildhälfte* and *Sachhälfte* to label
the components of the παραβολή and thereby to describe the functioning of the
παραβολή has been criticized severely, especially in recent years. Drawing upon
the results of current studies of metaphor, Ricoeur ('Biblical Hermeneutics', pp. 90-
92), Weder (*Die Gleichnisse Jesu als Metaphern*, pp. 64-67, 97), Westermann
(*Vergleiche und Gleichnisse*, p. 116), and Baudler (*Jesus im Spiegel seiner Gleichnisse*, pp. 41-57) recommend abandoning the differentiation between *Bildhälfte* and
Sachhälfte. Berger (*Formgeschichte des Neuen Testaments*, pp. 32-35, 41-45) and
Sellin ('Allegorie und "Gleichnis"', pp. 370-76, 387-88, 404-406), both apprised of
the new developments in the study of the parables in light of theories of metaphor,
agree that while Jülicher's terminology is unfortunate, the distinction—given certain modifications—can be upheld as useful. Berger (pp. 42-45) suggests the terms
Bildebene and *Ausgangsebene* as alternatives to *Bildhälfte* and *Sachhälfte*, respectively. Sellin (pp. 387-88) correlates *Bildhälfte* and *Sachhälfte* with other terms
from metaphor research. In order to avoid confusion, I will retain the terms *Bildhälfte* and *Sachhälfte* in this section on the comparative mechanism of the example
stories.

111. Bultmann (see pp. 149-50 n. 8 above) and Lambrecht are among the few.
Lambrecht (*Once More Astonished*, pp. 7-8), who regards the example story as an
'illustration', writes: '...we can conclude that the subject matter of an exemplary
story is taken from the reality with which one is concerned. There is no comparison
or image, but only a "specimen," a sample taken from real life. Consequently, no
transfer is needed from image to reality. The illustration selected and narrated
already belongs to the intended sphere, namely, the moral and religious world'. See
also M.D. Goulder, 'Characteristics of the Parables in the Several Gospels', *JTS* 19
(1968), pp. 51-69 (60-61): 'Indeed four of the "L" parables are not parables at all in

something peculiar enough about the comparative mechanism of the example stories to warrant either identifying them as a separate type of παραβολή or regarding them as something other than παραβολαί. Having reviewed how Jülicher accounts for the peculiarity of the example stories, we can direct attention to how others have done so.

Eta Linnemann owes much to Jülicher for her understanding of the example stories.[112] Linnemann asserts that while the *Parabeln* and *Beispielerzählungen* are similar in that both are invented stories, subject to the same narrative laws, and both are intended to be a means of proof (*Beweismittel*),[113] there is a difference between the two resulting from their manner of operation.

> The narrative parable produces a correspondence (analogia) to the subject matter, the example narrative a model case (exemplum). The parable obtains its cogency from the fact that what is acknowledged in the one case can be ill-contested in one corresponding exactly to the other. The example narrative operates by this means, that the reality itself, following the testimony of the model case, appears to acknowledge the narrator right in the subject matter.[114]

the sense of offering some *tertium comparationis*...[they] are actual live illustrations of the point at issue'.

112. Eta Linnemann, *Gleichnisse Jesu: Einführung und Auslegung* (Göttingen: Vandenhoeck & Ruprecht, 4th edn, 1966). References here will be to this German edition; all translations are my own. (There is an English translation of the 3rd edition of Linnemann's *Gleichnisse Jesu*; see *Parables of Jesus: Introduction and Exposition* [trans. John Sturdy; SPCK Large Paperbacks, 25; London: SPCK, 1966].) Linnemann adopts Jülicher's classification system intact (see pp. 13-15), and documents her indebtedness (p. 137).

113. Linnemann's understanding of the category *Beispielerzählung* could be considered 'rhetorical', especially since she refers to it as 'exemplum'; however, because the ancient rhetorical tradition, primarily Aristotle, is mediated to her through Jülicher, I have chosen not to include Linnemann among those who view the example stories as rhetorical examples.

114. Linnemann, *Gleichnisse Jesu*, pp. 14-15 (Linnemann's emphasis): 'Die Beispielerzählungen haben mit den Parabeln gemein, dass sie erfundene Geschichten sind und denselben Erzählungsgesetzen unterliegen. Ebenso wie jene wollen auch sie Beweismittel sein. Aber die Wirkungsweise ist verschieden. *Die Parabelerzählung bringt eine Entsprechung (analogia) zur Sache, die Beispielerzählung einen Musterfall (exemplum).* Die Parabel gewinnt ihre Beweiskraft daraus, dass man das, was man in dem einen Falle anerkennt, in einem genau entsprechenden anderen schlecht abstreiten kann. Die Beispielerzählung wirkt dadurch, dass die Wirklichkeit selber, nach dem Zeugnis des Musterfalles, dem

In order to explain more clearly the difference between narrative parable and example narrative, she adduces specimens of each. Referring to The Unjust Householder (Lk. 16.1-8, a *Parabel*) and The Foolish Rich Man (Lk. 12.16-21, a *Beispielerzählung*), Linnemann continues:

> The parable presents the conduct that the situation requires in a corresponding (analogous) conduct from economic life. The example narrative produces a model case appertaining to the subject matter. In the parable, the valuation toward which the narrative compels ought to be transferred to another plane (from 'picture' [*Bild*] to 'subject matter' [*Sache*]). In the example narrative, it [the valuation toward which the narrative compels] refers directly to the subject matter [*Sache*] and only needs generalization.[115]

Linnemann, in her treatment of the category 'example narrative', reinforces, but does not simply restate, Jülicher's conclusions. Although the *Parabeln* and the *Beispielerzählungen* are similar, Linnemann maintains that it is possible to distinguish between them on the basis of their narrative content and the relationship of that content to the subject matter. The narrative parable produces a case which has a correspondence (analogy) to the subject matter (*Sache*), and its narrative (*Bild*) compels a valuation which is transferred to the plane of the subject matter (*Sache*); the example narrative produces a model case (*exemplum*) which appertains to the subject matter (*Sache*), and its narrative compels a valuation which refers directly to the plane of the subject matter (*Sache*), thus needing only to be generalized.[116] Although Linnemann's description of the narrative content of the example narrative and its relationship to the plane of the *Sache* remains rather indistinct, she does suggest perhaps even more strongly than Jülicher—that the example narrative relates to only one plane. The discussion about the narrative content of the example story and its relation

Erzähler in der Sache Recht zu geben scheint'.

115. Linnemann, *Gleichnisse Jesu*, p. 15: 'Die Parabel führt das Verhalten, das die Situation erfordert, an einem entsprechenden (analogen) Verhalten aus dem Wirtschaftsleben vor. Die Beispielerzählung bringt einen zur Sache gehörenden Musterfall. Bei der Parabel soll die Wertung, zu der die Erzählung nötigt, auf eine andere Ebene (vom "Bild" auf die "Sache") übertragen werden. Bei die Beispielerzählung bezieht sie sich direkt auf die Sache und bedarf nur der Verallgemeinerung'.

116. Others restate her conclusions; see, e.g., Stein, *An Introduction to the Parables of Jesus*, p. 20, and Jindřich Mánek, *...Und brachte Frucht: Die Gleichnisse Jesu* (trans. Joachim Dachsel; Stuttgart: Calwer Verlag, 1st edn, 1977), p. 8.

to the plane of the *Sache* is moved forward by others.

Flusser argues, even more distinctly than Jülicher or Linnemann, that the example story has a connection to a single plane. In terms correlative to Jülicher's, Flusser states that the distinction between the 'sphere of the *sujet*' and the 'sphere of the moral theorem [*Lehrsatzes*]' belongs to the essence of both the *Gleichnis* and the *Fabel*.[117] In the *Gleichnis* and the *Fabel*, the cases narrated are not on the same plane as the moral theorem (*moralische Lehrsatz*). 'The lower plane is that of the sujet, whereas the higher plane is the ethical teaching deducible from the sujet'.[118] Flusser contends that while both *exempla* and fables can conclude with a moral theorem, in rabbinic *Gleichnisse* and in Jesus' *Gleichnisse* there is a wider cleft between the *sujet* and the application than in the fable. The content of the fable and its moral application stand in a more transparent relationship to each other; however, the plane of the *sujet* and the application are different in the *Gleichnis*: '...the plane of the sujet is daily life, whereas the plane of the application is a religious truth'.[119] Flusser is convinced that 'precisely the tension between the profane content and the religious sphere of the solution belongs to the essence of the parable'.[120] Although, as we have seen, Flusser contends that both parables and *exempla* are intended to provide moral teaching, there is a difference:

> In contradistinction to a parable, however, there are not two planes in an exemplum. The sujet of a parable and some of its motifs have correspondences to the moral plane, whereas the exemplum is simply a didactic moral story.[121]

117. Flusser, *Die rabbinischen Gleichnisse und der Gleichniserzähler Jesus*, p. 59. For Flusser's understanding of 'sujet', see pp. 20 and 53. Certain parallels between Flusser's view of the *exemplum* and Jülicher's view of the *Beispielerzählung* arise because both Flusser and Jülicher appeal to Lessing's fable theory. Unlike Jülicher, however, Flusser does not equate *Fabel* and narrative parable (Jülicher's *Parabel*).

118. Flusser, *Die rabbinischen Gleichnisse und der Gleichniserzähler Jesus*, p. 60: 'Die niedrigere Ebene ist die des Sujets, während die höhere Ebene die aus dem Sujet deduzierbare sittliche Lehre ist'.

119. Flusser, *Die rabbinischen Gleichnisse und der Gleichniserzähler Jesus*, p. 60.

120. Flusser, *Die rabbinischen Gleichnisse und der Gleichniserzähler Jesus*, p. 60.

121. Flusser, *Die rabbinischen Gleichnisse und der Gleichniserzähler Jesus*, p. 295: 'Im Unterschied zu einem Gleichnis gibt es aber bei einem Exemplum nicht

Flusser is concise on the relation of the narrative content to the plane of the *Sache* in an example story, but he is not as precise about the narrative content of the example stories.[122]

Some scholars express their conclusions on the supposed uniqueness of the *Beispielerzählungen* vis-à-vis the *Parabeln* in terms of their understanding of the parable as metaphor. Even if the terms *Bildhälfte* and *Sachhälfte* are eschewed, important issues similar to those just encountered come to the foreground, only now in sharper focus. Before going further, however, an issue that has remained in the background needs to be addressed. If the example story is not comprised of two planes (or fields, or spheres), as is the *Parabel*—that is, if the example story does not have a *Bildhälfte* and a *Sachhälfte*—does it, as does the *Parabel*, effect a comparison? The answer would have to be negative if 'to effect a comparison' means to establish correspondences that are to be transferred from one plane (or field, or sphere) to another, or to put it another way, are to be transferred from *Bild* to *Sache*. This, in turn, leads to another question: Is the example story 'pictorial' speech or literal speech? The same issues are discussed, albeit with different terminology, by those who view the parable as metaphor. The question now becomes: Does the example story, as does the parable, effect a comparison by means of metaphor? And that question also leads to another: Is the example story 'figurative' speech or literal speech? Responses to the last two questions can be grouped broadly as follows: (1) the example stories are either figurative or metaphorical and are therefore parables; (2) the example stories are neither figurative nor metaphorical and are therefore not parables; (3) the example stories are figurative and therefore parables, but they are synecdochical parables or metonymical parables rather than metaphorical parables.

Funk, as we saw earlier, conceives of the comparative mechanism of Jesus' parables as being metaphorical in nature. Since the comparative mechanism in a particular so-called 'example story' (The Good Samaritan) is the same as that operative in other authentic parables (as uttered by Jesus), Funk concludes that The Good Samaritan as spoken by Jesus

zwei Ebenen. Das Sujet eines Gleichnisses und einige seiner Motive haben Entsprechungen in der Moralebene, während das Exemplum einfach eine lehrhafte moralische Geschichte ist'.

122. Flusser does state that 'all exempla in the Gospels are directed against human arrogance, self-satisfaction, and heartlessness' (*Die rabbinischen Gleichnisse und der Gleicniserzähler Jesus*, p. 69).

is metaphorical and therefore a parable.[123] Although Funk challenges
the validity of the distinction between example story and parable, what
is of interest in this section are his remarks about how the dynamics of
the example stories have been characterized. Funk makes two important
observations about the example stories that can help explain why
scholars have judged them to be a different type of parable. The first
has to do with their comparative mechanism, the second with their narrative content.

Funk, following Bultmann and Dodd, contends that the parable leads
the hearer to specify the application by means of a transference of
judgment.

> The application is not specified until the hearer, led by the 'logic' of the
> parable, specifies it for himself. This goes together with Dodd's further
> observation that the parable is argumentative, inducing the listener to
> make a judgment upon the situation set out in the parable and to apply
> that judgment, either explicitly or implicitly, to the matter at hand. The
> parable thus involves what Bultmann calls a transference of judgment.
> This would not seem to be the case with the so-called 'exemplary-
> stories,' where the application is evident in the example.[124]

Why is there no transference of judgment in the example stories? Why
is its application evident in the example? The reason Funk gives, citing
Bultmann, is because 'an "exemplary-story" (*Beispielerzählung*) is a
parable involving no figurative element at all...'[125] There may yet be
another reason, one which involves the content of the example stories.

Funk provides a clue about how the narrative content of the example
stories is thought to differ from that of the *Parabeln*. He gives consideration to the way in which Dodd, Jeremias and Amos Wilder have
described the 'realism' or 'authenticity' or 'everydayness' of Jesus'
parables.[126] While discussing what he regards as the vivid, yet strange,
realism of the parables, Funk writes:

123. Funk, *Language, Hermeneutic, and Word of God*, pp. 199-222, esp. pp.
210-15. As I indicated earlier, Funk intimates that the version of The Good Samaritan as it is found in the Gospel of Luke is a 'moral example'.

124. Funk, *Language, Hermeneutic, and Word of God*, pp. 133-34.

125. Funk, *Language, Hermeneutic, and Word of God*, p. 134 n. 5 (Funk's
emphasis). Funk states the case more emphatically in his treatment of The Good
Samaritan (see p. 211).

126. Funk, *Language, Hermeneutic, and Word of God*, pp. 152-58; see also
pp. 194-95.

> Wilder ventures to speak of the secularity of the parables. The parables
> rarely take up explicitly 'religious' themes. Is this because, in wishing to
> speak about *A* (religion), Jesus directs attention to *B* (a secular image), as
> is the case with metaphorical and symbolic language generally, in that
> they look away from the subject-matter?[127]

What of the example stories? Funk notes that the example stories have
been said to have 'religious content'.[128] The significance of that observation deserves further consideration.

Funk's comments afford us the opportunity to gain insight about
some of the previous claims regarding the peculiarity of the example
stories, claims made by others that may have seemed vague. If, using
Funk's language, it is true that the example stories have religious content, this would mean that the example stories speak about *A* (religion)
by directing attention to *A'* (a religious image). This formulation helps
us better understand: (1) Jülicher's assertions that in the example stories there is no 'neutral soil', that the example stories do not narrate an
'earthly circumstance' (in a *Bildhälfte*) to be compared to the
'religious-ethical sphere' (the *Sachhälfte*), that the example stories present the subject matter (*Sache*) directly in a particular case; (2) Bultmann's claim that there is no pictorial element in the example stories,
and Funk's inference that the example stories do not require, therefore,
a transference of judgment; (3) Linnemann's statements that 'the
example story produces a model case appertaining to the subject
matter', and that the valuation which the example story compels 'refers
directly to the *Sache*'; and (4) Flusser's suggestion that there is no tension between profane content and the religious sphere in an example
story, and his comment that 'there are not two planes' in an example
story. Although this extension of Funk's observations about the religious content of the example stories does add clarity to what other

127. Funk, *Language, Hermeneutic, and Word of God*, pp. 153-54. According to
Funk, '…the language of the parable is metaphorical, in the sense that it talks about
B when *A* is intended…' (p. 193; his emphasis); for a more complete discussion of
metaphor ('To say *A is B* is a metaphor…' [p. 136; his emphasis]) and parable as
metaphor, see pp. 136-62.

128. Funk, *Language, Hermeneutic, and Word of God*, p. 211 n. 57. Funk
(p. 204) refers to an article by Lucetta Mowry ('Parable', in *IDB*, III, pp. 649-54
[650]), in which she states that 'in these [the narrative] parables the subject is, with
four exceptions (the rich fool, the rich man and Lazarus, the publican and the
Pharisee, and the good Samaritan), secular, and the story as a whole makes its own
point'.

scholars have said, Funk himself circumspectly questions the assumption that the example stories have 'religion' as their content.[129]

Funk is not persuaded that the example stories are anything other than parables. For him it is not the case that the example stories are in essence more direct and therefore more literal than the parables (which are more indirect and therefore figurative), neither is it the case that the example stories have only 'one plane'; rather, the problem is that the 'metaphorical horizon' of all the parables, especially the example stories, has been lost.[130] Funk contends that in metaphorical language, due to its nature, literal and non-literal meanings can bear various relations to each other. He argues that the parable is a type of metaphorical language in which the literal and non-literal (metaphorical) meanings are interwoven, or are concomitant.[131] To understand the significance of a parable, then, one needs to grasp the concomitant meanings.[132] Failure to do so results in one of two types of 'literal' interpretations, what Funk calls reading a parable as 'literally literal' or reading it as 'literally figurative'.[133] In the latter type of reading, some parables—'nature parables and certain others drawn from the sphere of human life'—are read as de-emphasizing the literal meaning and prioritizing the metaphorical, with the result that the parables are viewed as allegories.[134] In the former type of reading, conversely, some parables—the 'exemplary-stories'—are read as de-emphasizing the metaphorical meaning and prioritizing the literal, resulting in the view that these are 'examples'. A depreciation of the metaphorical horizon of any of the so-called 'exemplary-stories' will result in its being perceived as an 'example' and not as a parable. Thus, according to Funk, the 'example

129. Funk, *Language, Hermeneutic, and Word of God*, p. 204 n. 15: 'It might be inquired whether the "religious" content of these four parables is really religious, or whether it is religion viewed as a secular phenomenon'. Funk makes this point concretely with respect to The Good Samaritan (p. 213). Going beyond Funk, let us assume for a moment that 'religion' is, in fact, the content of the *Beispielerzählungen*. Then we could pose this question: Is it possible to use 'religion' in a 'figurative' way?

130. Funk, *Parables and Presence*, p. 30.

131. For a more complete presentation of Funk's explication of 'concomitant meanings', see *Language, Hermeneutic, and Word of God*, pp. 136-52, 213-14.

132. Funk, *Language, Hermeneutic, and Word of God*, p. 174.

133. See Funk, *Language, Hermeneutic, and Word of God*, p. 174 n. 57; *Parables and Presence*, pp. 29-30.

134. Funk, *Language, Hermeneutic, and Word of God*, p. 158.

stories' are actually metaphorical parables whose literal and metaphorical meanings must be grasped concomitantly, Funk is not the only proponent of the view that the 'example stories' are in essence metaphorical parables.

Crossan, among others, also views the example stories as metaphorical parables.[135] We have already seen that Crossan acknowledges the distinction between example story and parable, only to deny that such a distinction holds true for the authentic versions of those parables as uttered by Jesus. That is to say, according to Crossan, the example stories as they appear in the Gospel of Luke are in fact example stories, but as spoken by Jesus they are parables. Thus, Crossan marks a point of transition between a view of the example story as a literal 'normative example' and a view of the example story as a metaphorical 'figurative parable'.[136]

Crossan distinguishes between example story and parable on the basis of what has been called here the comparative mechanism of the parable. However, instead of 'two planes' or 'two spheres', Crossan speaks of 'two points' and 'two levels'.

> One knows that in parables there is, to put it very simply, a literal level and a metaphorical level. There is a literal point which stems from the surface level of the story, and a metaphorical one which lives on a much deeper level and appears in a mysterious dialectic with the former point. In distinction to this, of course, example has only one, literal level.[137]

Crossan argues that every example story '...is actually a parable whose literal level has been taken as a moral injunction (do/do not do like this man) and whose metaphorical challenge has been ignored'.[138] He thinks the likelihood that a parable's metaphorical level will be ignored increases when the parable does not involve 'the "amoral" world of

---

135. For the views of others who contend that (all of the, or some of) the example stories are in some way metaphorical parables, see Ricoeur, 'Biblical Hermeneutics', pp. 117-18; Mowry, 'Parable', pp. 650-52; and Scott, *Jesus, Symbol-Maker for the Kingdom*, pp. 25-32.

136. Crossan, 'Parable and Example', p. 72: 'The classification and interpretation of the Good Samaritan as exemplary story (*Beispielerzählung*), as a normative example rather than as a figurative parable, is completely correct as far as the tradition and the redaction are concerned'.

137. Crossan, *In Parables*, p. 64; see 'Parable and Example', p. 73: 'In distinction to this an example works on only one level and has only one point'; cf. p. 87.

138. Crossan, 'Parable and Example', p. 74.

agriculture', but involves the moral or immoral actions of the characters. Moreover, the tendency in the tradition and among interpreters to confuse the literal and metaphorical levels increases significantly when the parable, on its literal level, depicts the protagonist doing a morally good action.[139]

The tradition, the third evangelist and parable interpreters erred, in Crossan's opinion, by focusing on the literal level of the example stories and ignoring their metaphorical level, an error so pervasive that it eventually resulted in a classification of these erstwhile parables as 'example stories'. As he states, 'the presence of the class of developed example stories in the teaching of Jesus and the ease in mistaking parables for examples (and seeing example within other parables?) denotes a serious misunderstanding of the nature and function of parable'.[140] As parables of Jesus, the example stories are really parables, poetic metaphors, which were later, as we have heard Crossan say, 'changed into examples by the tradition and/or the evangelists'. There is a figurative element, which Crossan refers to as 'metaphorical', in these example stories. We will see soon, however, that while Crossan consistently views the so-called 'example stories' as figurative, he himself begins to regard the 'example stories' as something other than poetic metaphors.

Funk and Crossan represent the view that the example stories are figurative or metaphorical and therefore parables. Since the example stories have concomitant literal and non-literal (metaphorical) meanings, they are parables (Funk); since the example stories (as Jesus spoke them) have two levels and give rise to a literal point and a metaphorical point, they are parables (Crossan). On this Funk and Crossan agree: The comparative mechanism operative in the example

139. Crossan, 'Parable and Example', pp. 73-74; *In Parables*, p. 65.
140. Crossan, 'Parable and Example', pp. 87-88. Thus, Boucher errs when she cites Crossan as one who is guided by the misconception that parable is 'tropical' while example story is literal (see *The Mysterious Parable*, p. 22 n. 14). Crossan holds that the example stories as found in the Gospel of Luke are rightly regarded as example stories; however, he exerts considerable energy in arguing that the example stories as spoken by Jesus are in fact parables. Therefore, with regard to the *Beispielerzählungen* in their authentic versions—as told by Jesus—Crossan quite clearly does not *adopt* Bultmann's view 'that exemplary stories differ from other parables in that they alone are not "figurative" (i.e., tropical)', as Boucher states; rather, Crossan argues *against* Bultmann's view of the example narratives.

story is the same as that operative in the parable; the authentic *Beispiel-erzählungen*, like the authentic *Parabeln*, effect a comparison by means of metaphor or the metaphorical process. Another scholar argues the counterview: The example stories are neither figurative nor metaphorical and therefore are not parables.

Via is a staunch proponent of the view, to repeat his words, that the example stories 'are not genuine metaphors' and thus 'are not parables'.[141] In *The Parables*, Via expresses his opinion that the example stories are not parables in terms of his understanding of the parable as 'aesthetic object'. Accepting the classification system descended from Jülicher and Bultmann, and acknowledging that many of the formal characteristics of a parable also belong to the example story, he writes:

> ...in an example story the symbolic, figurative, or indirect element is missing. In a parable we have a story which is analogous to, which points to but is not identical with, a situation or world of thought outside of the story. In an example story, on the other hand, the meaning or thought or reality with which the story is concerned is not pointed to but is present in the story. The story is an example of it directly and only needs to be generalized.[142]

The example stories, rather than depicting something analogous to what one should do or avoid doing, describe directly what one should do or avoid doing; rather than symbolizing God and God's actions toward human beings, the example stories directly describe them. According to Via, the example stories 'lack the development in plot and in dramatic encounter', and 'they also lack that "distance" from their meaning, or point, or from the world of thought outside the story', both of which are characteristics in many of the parables.[143] For these reasons, Via is

141. Others who regard the example stories, because they are not metaphors, as a distinct group apart from the parables include Amos N. Wilder (*Early Christian Rhetoric: The Language of the Gospel* [Cambridge, MA: Harvard University Press, 2nd edn, 1971], p. 72) and Kjärgaard (*Metaphor and Parable*, pp. 215-16).

142. Via, *The Parables*, p. 12. Via identifies the formal characteristics of the parable, in contrast to the similitude, as follows: 'In a parable we have, not the relating of a typical, recurring incident, but a freely invented story told with a series of verbs in a past tense. The parable is not concerned with what everyone typically does but narrates a particulate thing in which some person or persons were once involved. The similitude gets its force from its appeal to what is universally acknowledged, while the parable achieves its power by making the particular credible and probable' (pp. 11-12).

143. Via, *The Parables*, p. 13.

content to exclude the example stories from his analyses of the parables of Jesus.

In a later article, Via reaffirms his conclusion that the example stories are not parables, but this time he does so on the basis of his 'literary-structuralist analysis' and within the framework of his understanding of the parable as metaphor.[144] Via remains convinced that a 'lack of distance', now termed 'semantic tension or distance', is what distinguishes example story from parable. He states his position in this way:

> The narrative parables are metaphors of the kingdom of God: they give a new vision of everyday existence as transected by the surprising incursion of the transcendent. The metaphoric tenor is the kingdom of God (heaven), and the vehicle is the narrative. Sometimes the tenor is explicitly mentioned (Mt. 20.1—The Workers in the Vineyard), and sometimes it is not (The Prodigal Son; The Unjust Steward). But whether or not the kingdom (tenor) is explicitly mentioned, it is always represented implicitly and subsidiarily in the story by the king-master-father figure who is the *actantiel* ordainer. The king-master-father figure in the story is involved in a dramatic encounter with a son-servant-subordinate figure who is the *actantiel* subject...The important point to remember is that the parable is a *metaphor* of the kingdom of *God* because the semantic distance and tension between the divine and the human is supported by the distance between ordainer (king-father) and the subject (servant-son) who are always separate and distinct characters.[145]

What of the example stories? According to Via:

> To be a metaphor of the kingdom of God the semantic tension would have to be between ordainer and subject, but in The Good Samaritan those actants are identical...There is not enough semantic tension or distance to be overcome between the two [literal and metaphorical] levels for the [other example story] texts to be regarded as metaphors. Therefore, they are not parables. They remain illustrative examples of what one is to do or not to do.[146]

144. The technical details of Via's sequential analysis and actantial analysis cannot detain us now, although they do inform his statements on the parable as metaphor (as we will soon see); for the specifics of his analysis of the example stories, see Dan Otto Via, Jr, 'Parable and Example Story: A Literary-Structuralist Approach', *Semeia* 1 (1974), pp. 105-33.
145. Via, 'Parable and Example Story', p. 118; Via's emphasis. Cf. his article, 'A Response to Crossan, Funk, and Petersen', p. 226.
146. Via, 'Parable and Example Story', p. 119. Via allows that The Good Samaritan does contain 'enough semantic distance to make the story a metaphor', but he adds this qualification: '...this narrative is a metaphor which gives a new

For Via, then, there are narrative parables of Jesus, which are metaphors of the kingdom of God, and there are example stories, which are not metaphors of the kingdom of God. Whether the parables are viewed as aesthetic objects or as metaphors, in Via's opinion, the example stories exhibit features substantial enough to justify maintaining their classification as a group separate from the parables. The example stories are too direct, they lack a figurative element, they are not metaphors, they are not parables.

Yet another option remains. There are those who would concur with Funk and Crossan that the example stories are figurative, but who would agree with Via that the example stories are not metaphors. For some scholars, the example stories are figurative indeed, but they are said to have their basis in a rhetorical figure other than metaphor.

Sellin endorses Jülicher's classification of the synoptic parables after making what he regards as the necessary corrections, the salient one being that Sellin defines the *Gleichnis* and the *Parabel* on the basis of a semantics of metaphor, not simile.[147] All three subgroups—*Gleichnis*, *Parabel* and *Beispielerzählung*—are, according to Sellin, models (*Modelle*), all three have a paradigmatic function in their contexts, and all three are comprised of a *Bildhälfte* and a *Sachhälfte*.[148] Nevertheless, distinctions can be made between the three subgroups: While the *Gleichnis* is a metaphor expanded into a sentence, the *Parabel* and the *Beispielerzählung* are narrative parables (*Gleichniserzählungen*); but

meaning to the responsibilities of neighborliness but is not a metaphor of the kingdom of God, and on this ground is not a parable'.

147. Sellin reviews and revises Jülicher's program in a 1978 study entitled 'Allegorie und "Gleichnis"', pp. 367-76. As the title of his essay suggests, Sellin—like Jülicher—draws a distinction between allegory and parable; however, Sellin argues that allegory is based upon a semantics of the symbol (see pp. 389-403), whereas the parable has its foundation in a semantics of the metaphor (see pp. 376-89, 404-17). In a 1974 study Sellin offers reasons for calling into question Jülicher's distinction between *Parabel* and *Beispielerzählung* (see below, pp. 212-16).

148. These points are dispersed throughout Sellin's essay 'Allegorie und "Gleichnis"': For the contention that *Gleichnisse*, *Parabeln* and *Beispielerzählungen* are models (*Modelle*), see pp. 407-409; for a description of the 'paradigmatische Funktion' of *Gleichnisse*, *Parabeln* and *Beispielerzählungen*, see pp. 403, 407-409, 425-26; for a discussion of the *Bildhälfte* and *Sachhälfte* in *Gleichnisse*, *Parabeln* and *Beispielerzählungen*, see pp. 387-88, 405-408, 410, 416-17, 421-25.

while the *Parabel* is a 'narrated *metaphor*' ('erzählte *Metapher*'), the *Beispielerzählung* is 'nonmetaphorical'.[149] The specifics of Sellin's disposition concerning the example stories can be summarized as follows.

Sellin contends that even though the example stories are very similar to the *Parabeln* in construction[150] and function, and for this reason are correctly counted among the parables, the *Beispielerzählungen* and *Parabeln* are nonetheless to be distinguished from each other due to a difference in their semantics. The *Parabeln* have their basis in a semantics of metaphor; since the *Beispielerzählungen* have no metaphorical features, they are 'actually not parables any longer'.[151] Sellin explains the semantic distinction between *Parabel* and *Beispielerzählung* in terms of the functioning of *Bildhälfte* and *Sachhälfte*:

> In the *Parabel* as metaphor, the *Bildhälfte* and *Sachhälfte* intersect (the intersection quantity between topic-concept and predicate as analogy or *tertium comparationis*); in the *Beispielerzählung*, the *Bildhälfte* lies completely in the field of the *Sachhälfte* (partial quantity). Consequently, it lacks the distance typical for the *Parabel* and *Gleichnis*.[152]

Sellin then makes finer points about the *Bildhälfte* and the *Sachhälfte* in the example narrative.

According to Sellin, in the example narrative the *Sachhälfte* consists of the situation—the context, the frame—of the example (*Beispiel*).[153] Here, in a way different than in the metaphor and hence the *Parabel*, the *Sachhälfte* can be conceived as the sum of all possible examples (*Beispiele*).

> The example [*Beispiel*] condenses, concretizes, works like a focal point, so that the structure of the *Sachhälfte* becomes obvious, the problem solvable. Then the *Sachhälfte* would be the quantity of daily experience.

149. Sellin, 'Allegorie und "Gleichnis"', pp. 404, 417, 422, 426; Sellin's emphasis. Sellin also observes that distinctions can be made between the *Gleichnisse* and *Gleichniserzählungen* on the basis of verb tense (see pp. 417-19).

150. Sellin, e.g., remarks that The Prodigal Son 'structurally in its internal construction hardly differs' from the *Beispielerzählungen* ('Allegorie und "Gleichnis"', p. 424); indeed, without its context (Lk. 15.1-3), this *Parabel* would 'lose its metaphorical reference and be turned into an example of inter-human conduct' (p. 423 n. 163).

151. Sellin, 'Allegorie und "Gleichnis"', p. 424; cf. p. 367 n. 1.

152. Sellin, 'Allegorie und "Gleichnis"', p. 425.

153. Sellin, 'Allegorie und "Gleichnis"', p. 425. Sellin revises the concept of *Sachhälfte*, arguing contra Jülicher that the *Sachhälfte* is not propositional truth (see pp. 376, 405-406).

It appears in the context of the narrative as: the problem 'Who is my neighbor?'; self-righteousness and disdain of others; poverty and wealth; *securitas* of material goods.[154]

Thus, Sellin posits that the *Beispielerzählungen* are, like the *Parabeln*, models (*Modelle*), narratives that represent vis-à-vis their narrative frame, a change in narrative level.[155] In addition, like the *Parabeln*, the *Beispielerzählungen* have a paradigmatic function in their context, except that they are more concrete as example (*Exempel*): 'The everyday offers itself one example [*Beispiel*] as model [*Modell*] of the truth'.[156]

154. Sellin, 'Allegorie und "Gleichnis"', p. 425; Sellin's emphasis. Sellin makes some suggestive comments about the relationship between the *Bildhälfte* and *Sachhälfte* in the *Gleichnis* vis-à-vis *Allegorie* and *Beispielerzählung* (p. 410). The *Gleichnisse* do not objectify God, and they deal only with the profane: 'They leave completely uncolored in the *Bildhälfte* the matter of importance to them in the *Sachhälfte*. Therein lies their plainly hostile character to allegory, but also an essential difference to the example narrative...There is no ladder which leads from the *Bildhälfte* up to religion, the *Sachhälfte*'. Everything that happens in the *Gleichnisse* takes place totally on the human side. However, the *Sachhälfte* of the *Gleichnisse* assume, as Sellin puts it, 'the experience of the in-breaking of God's rule'. Sellin's comments here intimate that the *Bildhälfte* of the example narratives deal directly with religion, thus the 'lack of distance' from the *Sachhälfte* (religion). Yet, as we have seen, Sellin maintains that in the example narratives 'the everyday offers itself one example as model of truth', and that the example concretizes the *Sachhälfte* so that 'the *Sachhälfte* would be the quantity of daily experience'. Let us note, then, that there is some tension in Sellin's comments on the *Sachhälfte* in the *Beispielerzählungen*.

155. Sellin, 'Allegorie und "Gleichnis"', pp. 425-26. Recall, however, that Sellin earlier (1) redefines the *Sachhälfte* as the context (or situation) in which the *Bildhälfte* is located, and (2) states that the *Sachhälfte* of the *Beispielerzählung* lacks the distance typical for the *Parabel* and *Gleichnis*. The level change between *Bildhälfte* and *Sachhälfte* in the *Parabel* and the *Gleichnis*, which corresponds to the relationship of the topic-concept and predicate in the metaphor, is one marked by more distance.

156. Sellin, 'Allegorie und "Gleichnis"', p. 426. Sellin resists speaking of the *Beispielerzählung* as a moral example. Against Bultmann, Sellin contends that the example narratives do not simply offer 'models for the right conduct': 'The story is not the *Sache* itself, rather precisely a model, indeed only a particularized [model]'. Moreover, Sellin states that there is a transfer from one level to another even in the *Beispielerzählung*. Thus, the example narrative (The Merciful Samaritan) does not prescribe simple imitation. Although Sellin concurs with Berger that the 'exemplarischen Rechtsentscheid', which deals with a weighing out in the area of

Sellin defines the *Beispielerzählung*, then, as 'narrated *example*' ('erzähltes *Exempel*').[157] Accordingly, the *Beispielerzählungen* have their basis in a semantics of the example (*Exempel*), which, Sellin insists, is not simply a semantics of nonmetaphorical predication.[158] The example (*Exempel*) obtains its signifying function between the poles of the general and the individual. Whereas the metaphor brings about meaningful signification through the tension of two incompatible fields, meaningful signification happens in nonmetaphorical assertions by means of the claim to state the general or by means of the claim to represent exemplarily the general in the particular.[159] Therefore, Sellin concludes that 'the rhetorical figure to which the example [*Exempel*] corresponds is the *synecdoche* (pars pro toto)'.[160]

Like Via, then, Sellin is emphatic in his assertion that the example narratives are not metaphors. Unlike Via, however, Sellin implies that the example stories are figurative since they have their basis in a semantics of the example (*Exempel*), which in turn corresponds to synecdoche. Others more overtly make the claim that the *Beispielerzählungen*, though they are not metaphors, are figurative indeed.

Boucher, even though she shuns the term 'figurative', contends that the synoptic parables are characterized by 'tropical meaning', which is to say that each parable has two levels of meaning, a direct or literal meaning and an indirect or tropical meaning.[161] Boucher regards

ethical norms, lies behind The Merciful Samaritan, Sellin holds that the main issue is the decision itself, not exemplary conduct (see pp. 428-29 n. 171).

157. Sellin, 'Allegorie und "Gleichnis"', p. 426; Sellin's emphasis.

158. Sellin, 'Allegorie und "Gleichnis"', p. 427.

159. Sellin, 'Allegorie und "Gleichnis"', p. 427; my paraphrase.

160. Sellin, 'Allegorie und "Gleichnis"', p. 428 n. 171 (Sellin's emphasis): 'Die rhetorische Figur, die dem Exempel entspricht, ist die *Synekdoche* (pars pro toto)'.

161. See Boucher, *The Mysterious Parable*, pp. 17-25. Boucher (p. 17) claims that literature can be classified according to the form and mode of meaning (both of which are based upon the structure of meaning), and genre (which is based upon the nature of meaning). The second taxon, mode of meaning, is especially important to Boucher: 'There are only two modes of meaning: direct or literal meaning; and indirect or tropical meaning (usually but inaccurately called figurative), an example of which is allegory' (p. 17). Boucher's choice of the term 'tropical' over against 'figurative' results from her desire to maintain a fixed distinction between rhetorical figures and rhetorical tropes (see pp. 17-18). Among rhetoricians a more common distinction is usually made between 'schemes' and 'tropes', both being 'figures of words' as opposed to 'figures of thought'. As Richard A. Lanham points out, in a source to which Boucher herself refers, theorists differ among themselves as to how

herself as 'a radical critic of Jülicher's theory', yet she accepts his classification of the synoptic parables into three groups.[162] In Boucher's view, various figures or tropes may provide the framework or basis of a parable: Some synoptic parables are based on the simile, others on the metaphor, but most of them are allegories because 'any parable which has both a literal and a metaphorical meaning is an allegory'.[163] Thus, according to Boucher, the 'similitudes' (which narrate a 'typical occurrence in real life') and the parables (which narrate 'a fictitious event') are allegories because they have both a literal and a metaphorical meaning.[164] The 'exemplary stories' are set apart as different because they are not allegories, or 'extended metaphors'.[165] Boucher maintains that the 'exemplary story is distinguished from the other two insofar as it is composed of extended synecdoche (rather than allegory)'.[166]

Boucher explains her position on the example stories in this way:

> What we have in these parables is something akin to synecdoche, the name of the part for the whole, or the one for the many. They are not extended metaphors; rather they present one particular example to

they define and categorize those terms (*A Handlist of Rhetorical Terms: A Guide for Students of English Literature* [Berkeley, CA: University of California Press, 1968], pp. 101, 116) .

162. Boucher, *The Mysterious Parable*, pp. 1, 22. Boucher severely criticizes Jülicher's concept of allegory (see pp. 1, 4, 20, 23), arguing that allegory is extended metaphor, not a series of metaphors (but see my comment on her critique of Jülicher on this point [pp. 95-96 n. 96 above]). Moreover, against Jülicher, Boucher argues that not all parables are based upon simile, and that no parable is 'literal speech' (see p. 33). She also questions aspects of Jülicher's thesis concerning the genuineness of Jesus' parables (pp. 4-5, 38). Perhaps her most 'radical' counterarguments against Jülicher are her contentions that all similitudes and parables are allegories, and that those types of parables are indeed 'mysterious speech' (see pp. 4, 42-63, 83-84).

163. Boucher, *The Mysterious Parable*, p. 21; cf. p. 22.

164. Boucher, *The Mysterious Parable*, p. 23. Note Boucher's claim that even parables based mostly on simile (a 'figure', not a trope, according to her) can also be 'tropical' and thus 'result in allegory' (see pp. 21-22).

165. Boucher, *The Mysterious Parable*, p. 22. Boucher is aware that her reasons for distinguishing between 'similitude and parable', on the one hand, and 'exemplary story', on the other, are alien to Jülicher, who 'held that *all* parables (similitudes, parables, and exemplary stories) are literal speech, and that it is precisely this which distinguishes them from allegory' (p. 22 n. 14; her emphasis).

166. Boucher, *The Mysterious Parable*, p. 23. Boucher states much the same about the 'exemplary stories' in her book *The Parables*, pp. 22, 32-33.

illustrate a general principle, and so might be called extended synec-doches.[167]

Simply because the 'exemplary stories' are not extended metaphors, Boucher insists, does not mean that they are not 'tropical'. She continues:

> A current misconception is that exemplary story and parable are distin-guished by this, that the exemplary story is strictly literal while the parable is tropical. In fact, however, the exemplary story (an extended synecdoche) is as much a tropical composition as the parable (an extended metaphor or an allegory). This is because synecdoche and metaphor are equally tropes. No exemplary story is intended to be taken only literally.[168]

If the 'exemplary stories' are not literal, they are nevertheless more transparent than the other two types of parable. Boucher explains that 'this is so because in synecdoche there is more similarity than dis-similarity between the two things compared, whereas in metaphor there is more dissimilarity than similarity'.[169]

167. Boucher, *The Mysterious Parable*, p. 22. One may accept Boucher's definition of synecdoche, but resist her assertion that the *Beispielerzählungen* are extended synecdoches because 'they present one particular example to illustrate a general principle'. Compare this understanding of synecdoche to what Aristotle says at one point in his *Rhetoric* (2.23.13): enthymemes can '...come from example by induction of what is like, whether one thing or more, whenever a general statement is made and then supported by a particular instance...' Aristotle and his *Rhetoric* are treated more fully in Chapter 5.

168. Boucher, *The Mysterious Parable*, p. 22; cf. p. 33: 'The parable that has only a literal level of meaning does not exist'. To Boucher, tropical meaning consti-tutes the essence of a parable for, as she writes, 'the double-meaning effect is a *sine qua non* of the parable' (p. 22). Johnston ('Parabolic Interpretations Attributed to Tannaim', p. 186) would beg to differ. Of the example stories, which he contends are formally *me'aśim* rather than *meshalim*, Johnston writes: 'Most important, that which corresponds to the *Bildhälfte* itself is not tropic; it stands for nothing other'. He identifies a type of rabbinic parable similar to the example story, but which is actually a 'sample-*mashal*' (see pp. 520-22). The following remark made by John-ston provides an interesting contrast to Boucher: 'There is really nothing tropic about the example story, but the "sample-parable" is at least semi-tropic in that a part stands for the whole, as in synecdoche, but as a representative of the total number' (p. 521).

169. See Boucher, *The Mysterious Parable*, p. 37; cf. p. 19, where she gives the specifics of synecdoche as follows: 'Synecdoche, another kind of trope, is also the substitution of the name of one thing for the name of another, in this case of the

We have now encountered several attempts to account for the figurative element in the example stories. Still another option exists: The example stories can be described as figurative because they have their basis in the rhetorical figure metonymy.

Crossan, as we saw earlier, argues that the example stories are in fact, like the other parables of Jesus, poetic metaphors and thus are comprised of both a literal level and a metaphorical level. In a later work on parables, Crossan still maintains that the so-called example stories, like other authentic parables, are figurative—and therefore are not to be read or heard only literally as moral injunctions—but he does so in different terms. Crossan now defines 'parable' in this way:

> The term *parable*, then, should be used technically and specifically, from ancient to contemporary example, for *paradoxes formed into story by effecting single or double reversals of the audience's most profound expectations*. The structure of parable is a deliberate but comic reversal of the expected story.[170]

The parable can effect reversals whether it is based on metaphor or metonymy. As Crossan states,

> The paradoxicality of linguistic world can be shown either in metaphoric or metonymic parables. Metonymic parables will take real or representative *parts-of-world* in order to reduce that world to paradox. Metaphoric parables will do the same but with *miniworlds* or model and miniature worlds.[171]

Three of the example stories—The Good Samaritan, The Pharisee and the Toll Collector, and The Rich Man and Poor Lazarus—are metonymic parables because, according to Crossan, they use 'parts-of-world' in the story to bring about the reversal of the audience's expectations.

What Crossan means by 'parts-of-world' and its function in

---

part for the whole, the singular for the plural, the individual for the species, the species for the genus—or the reverse of all these. We employ synecdoche when we say "hands" to mean workmen, "sails" to mean ships, and "our daily bread" to mean our daily sustenance. In synecdoche there is more similarity than dissimilarity between the two things compared'.

170. Crossan, *Raid on the Articulate*, p. 98; his emphasis.

171. Crossan, *Raid on the Articulate*, p. 108; Crossan's emphasis. Several scholars speak only of the example stories as being models; Sellin speaks of all synoptic parables as being models. Although Crossan's use of the term 'model' in association with the metaphorical parables is intriguing, it should not be pressed too far.

metonymic parables can be described as follows. The Good Samaritan subverts the social and religious world of Jesus' audience because in the appearance of a priest, a Levite and a Samaritan, parts of the audience's real world now appear in the story world, and when 'parts-of-world' are subverted in the story world, then the whole (the real world) is attacked. Because The Pharisee and the Toll Collector involves Pharisees and toll collectors, parts of the real world of Jesus' audience, and the judgment of their prayers, then 'Jesus' story was a shocking, radical, and double reversal of the metonymic poles of his contemporary ethical world'.[172] In The Rich Man and Poor Lazarus, the fates of the two main characters is an attack on the economic world of Jesus' contemporaries since the rich man and Lazarus are given as metonyms of that economic world.[173]

Crossan's new position, that these three example stories are metonymic rather than metaphoric parables, represents a change of opinion. Whereas earlier Crossan argued that these three example stories were poetic metaphors and functioned like the other authentic parables of Jesus, here Crossan tacitly acknowledges that there is something different about these three vis-à-vis the other parables. However, Crossan insists that these three example stories—now metonymic parables, in which 'parts-of-world' are employed to 'reduce that world to paradox'—are still figurative nonetheless.

The views of the example stories espoused by Boucher and Crossan have garnered the notice of Craig L. Blomberg and Scott. Because in their separate discussions both Blomberg and Scott broach the same issue, that of the characters who appear in the example stories, their comments will receive brief mention here. A more complete treatment of the issue of character will be reserved until the formal aspects of the example stories come under consideration.

Blomberg provisionally commends Boucher's understanding of the example stories as extended synecdoche, but he does not provide the specific details as given by her; rather, he states that at least two of the example stories, The Foolish Rich Man and The Pharisee and the Toll Collector, are extended synecdoches because '...the main characters are representative of an entire class of *similar* people'.[174] Blomberg soon revises this notion of the example stories in favor of another

172. Crossan, *Raid on the Articulate*, p. 109.
173. See Crossan, *Raid on the Articulate*, pp. 109-10.
174. Blomberg, *Interpreting the Parables*, p. 43; emphasis his.

'...since exemplary characters in the parables (for example, the rich man and Lazarus) are not really parts of some larger whole but examples of a particular category of people'.[175] Blomberg's comments about character, an issue never raised by Boucher with regard to the example stories, intimate that the example stories are different from the other narrative parables because of the types of characters appearing in them.

Scott unhesitatingly endorses Crossan's conception of the example stories as metonymic parables. Scott begins by making a remark that highlights one of Crossan's contentions about the example stories: 'These four parables exhibit metonymic characters'.[176] However, Scott does not elaborate; instead, he gives a definition of metonymy and then brings it to bear upon the example stories:

> Although recent parable research has identified the figurative element [in the parables] with metaphor, metaphor is only one pole of figurative possibility. The other pole is metonymy, which 'may be defined as a linguistic substitution in which a thing is named not directly but by way of something adjacent to it either temporally or spatially.' Metonymy implies or suggests that a real relationship exists between the thing and that which is adjacent to it. The basic difference between metonymic and metaphoric parables is that the former use real 'parts-of-the world' for their figure whereas the latter create 'mini-worlds.' An alternative to Jülicher's example story may be formulated: the issue of transference revolves not around behavior to be imitated or avoided (example story) but around the question of what part of the real world something is adjacent to.[177]

This alternative, which holds that the example stories are figurative, still implies that the parables and the example stories are not figurative in the same way.

---

175. Blomberg, *Interpreting the Parables*, p. 46. Blomberg considers Sider's formulation of the example story as 'example' (or 'non-proportional analogy' [see p. 135 n. 238 above]) to be an improvement over Boucher's 'extended synecdoche'.

176. Scott, *Hear Then the Parable*, p. 29. I cannot rule out the possibility that the word 'characters' here should read 'character'. In any case, Scott does not develop the idea that the characters in the example stories are 'metonymic'. It should be pointed out that Crossan himself names only three of the 'example stories' as metonymic parables. The Foolish Rich Man is not included; in fact, it does not receive mention in *Raid on the Articulate*.

177. Scott, *Hear Then the Parable*, pp. 29-30. The definition quoted by Scott comes from J. Hillis Miller (see Scott's n. 107 on p. 29).

The preceding array of attempts to account for the peculiarity of the example stories is testimony to the conviction held by many that the comparative mechanism of the *Beispielerzählungen* is somehow different from that of the *Parabeln*. While few choose the position held by Via, who argues that because the comparative mechanism of the example stories does not operate by way of metaphor they are not parables, the supposition that the comparative mechanism of the example stories is peculiar still lingers. Some who contend that the so-called 'example stories' as spoken by Jesus are metaphorical and therefore not unlike his other parables will nevertheless allow that the *Beispielerzählungen* as recorded in the Gospel of Luke are 'examples' and therefore unlike other authentic parables. Even those who claim that the example stories are not to be read literally as moral or normative examples but figuratively as synecdochical or metonymical parables nonetheless tacitly admit that the comparative mechanism of the *Beispielerzählungen* differs from that of the metaphorical *Parabeln*. Although few assert baldly that the example stories do not have a *Bildhälfte*, some approximate that assertion by stating that the example stories do not have two planes (Flusser), or that the Lukan example stories have only one literal level (Crossan). For most, then, a perceived difference in the degree of immediacy or distance between the *Bildhälfte* and the *Sachhälfte* of the example stories vis-à-vis the *Parabeln* becomes the basis for an assertion that the example stories and the narrative parables differ in kind, and it is this perceived difference in the comparative mechanism of the *Beispielerzählungen* which commonly informs the decision that the example stories are to be read literally as moral examples. This point is corroborated by some of Baasland's observations about the example stories.

Baasland states that 'the research since Jülicher has viewed the peculiar connection between *Bildhälfte* and *Sachhälfte* as characteristic for the so-called example narratives'.[178] Baasland haltingly concedes that the close association or identical nature of *Bildhälfte* and *Sachhälfte* in the example narratives is a characteristic feature that may permit the retrieval of this group as *Beispielerzählungen*, but he struggles to keep that concession in check.[179] After claiming that, in

---

178. Baasland, 'Zum Beispiel der Beispielerzählungen', p. 217. As we have seen, some interpreters before Jülicher held the same view.

179. Baasland ('Zum Beispiel der Beispielerzählungen', p. 209) acknowledges the influence of Güttgemanns, who extols the *Beispielerzählungen* as the most

general, the narrative parables (*Gleichniserzählungen*), which depict certain actions opposite other actions, presuppose a conclusion *a minore ad majus*—from the action of humans to that of God or Jesus— Baasland contends that the *Beispielerzählungen*, which depict deficient or flawed actions (such as egoism, self-satisfaction), permit no conclusion *a minore ad majus*. Thus, he writes, 'no correspondence to the "transcendent" plane is suggested or at all possible'.[180] In these cases, rather, the egoistical action is opposed to God's or Jesus' judgment of that action, a judgment which lies outside the narrative proper (that is, in the 'application'). For this reason, negative examples predominate in the *Beispielerzählungen*. The only positive examples, according to Baasland, are the Samaritan and the toll collector.[181]

Baasland surmises that the positive examples provided by the Samaritan and the toll collector, coupled with the positive judgment of their actions given after the narratives in which they appear, provide the basis for talk of the identical nature of *Bildhälfte* and *Sachhälfte* in the example narratives and thus of what he calls their 'synekdotischen [*sic*] Charakter':

> These narratives recount a 'particular case' (Jülicher), an 'ideal case' (Linnemann/Sellin and others), a 'model case' (Eichholz), a particular case 'which only needs to be generalized' (Via and others). In fact, it appears that with the synecdochical character one can salvage the example narrative as example narrative: In *one* very concrete example the actions of *one* Samaritan/one toll collector are exemplary.[182]

effective of the *Gleichnisgattungen* because of their pragmatic aspect. According to Güttgemanns, the *Beispielerzählungen* do not persuade indirectly by means of thought and logical conclusions; rather, they persuade directly by means of direct representation. In the *Beispielerzählungen*, the *Bildhälfte* confronts the hearer directly with the *Sachhälfte*, and the fictionally represented requisite conduct compels the hearer to the immediate recognition of the self-evident (see Güttgemanns, 'Die linguistisch-didaktische Methodik der Gleichnisse Jesu', pp. 122-23).

180. Baasland, 'Zum Beispiel der Beispielerzählungen', p. 209.

181. Baasland, 'Zum Beispiel der Beispielerzählungen', pp. 209-10.

182. Baasland, 'Zum Beispiel der Beispielerzählungen', p. 210; Baasland's emphasis: 'Diese Erzählungen berichten von einem "Einzelfall" (Jülicher), "Musterfall" (Linnemann/Sellin u.a.), "Modellfall" (Eichholz), einem Einzelfall, der "nur noch verallgemeinert zu werden braucht" (Via u.a.). In der Tat scheint man mit dem synekdotischen [*sic*] Charakter die Beispielerzählung als Beispiel- erzählung retten zu können: In *einem* sehr konkreten Beispiel sind die Handlungen *eines* Samariters/eines Zöllners exemplarisch'. More than the other example narra- tives, according to Baasland, The Merciful Samaritan and The Pharisee and the Toll

However, and despite that, Baasland gives two reasons to explain why neither the identical nature of *Bildhälfte* and *Sachhälfte* nor the 'synecdochical character' of the *Beispielerzählungen* can be elevated to the status of a criterion to decide the genre (*Gattung*) of these narratives: first, other parables share these features—that is, other parables afford positive or negative '*exempla*', or 'exemplary actions', or Jesus' or God's judgment of actions given in the 'application';[183] secondly, none of these traits are formal features in the strictest sense.[184]

The preceding survey of attempts to distinguish between the *Parabeln* and *Beispielerzählungen* in terms of a perceived difference in their comparative mechanisms demonstrates that such a distinction is rendered problematical. No formal features have been identified in the four example narratives, and in those four alone, to substantiate either the claim that they do not make a comparison or the claim that the comparative mechanism operative in the example narratives is different from that of the *Parabeln* to such an extent that the example narratives are no longer 'parabolical' or figurative.[185] If no formal features in the

Collector thematize 'love of God and love of neighbor'. In this sense, then, Baasland submits that the '*Sache*' is in the example narrative, which gives rise to the view that in an example narrative 'the *Bildhälfte* lies completely in the field of the *Sachhälfte*' (here Baasland quotes Sellin [see p. 217 n. 88]). Sellin himself does not mention the thematization of 'love of God, love of neighbor' in the example narratives, and holds that the *Beispielerzählungen*, as well as other parables, are *Modelle*.

183. Baasland, 'Zum Beispiel der Beispielerzählungen', pp. 199, 210, 217-18. To Baasland, all of these features are closely associated. In addition, Baasland's view of the example narrative as synecdoche is related to what I have referred to as the example story as 'moral example'; see esp. p. 218, where he writes: 'Synekdote [*sic*] (Exemplum als Aufforderung nur in Luk. 10:37; positive und negative Exempla auch in den Verwaltungs- und Einsatzgleichissen)'.

184. Baasland, 'Zum Beispiel der Beispielerzählungen', pp. 197, 199, 217. Sellin also questions this—the distinction between *Parabeln* and *Beispielerzählungen* on the basis of the overlapping of *Bildhälfte* and *Sachhälfte* in the latter—as a meaningful trait for the purposes of classification since it is not a formal feature (see 'Lukas als Gleichniserzähler', p. 179); however, in a later study ('Allegorie und "Gleichnis"', pp. 425-29) Sellin is not reluctant to uphold that distinction and Jülicher's classification of the synoptic parables.

185. This is the gist of Wilder's remarks when, commenting on the variety of parables in the Gospels, he writes: 'Some of the parables are straight narratives about a given individual case, ending with an application: the Good Samaritan, the Rich Fool; or sometimes about more than one person, as for example the Pharisee

Beispielerzählungen can be specified to ground those claims, one may with good reason begin to doubt the basis upon which those claims rest.

In several of the various studies of the example stories reviewed throughout this study, one presupposition remains rather constant: The parables spoken by Jesus—either the Jesus of history or the Jesus(es) of the synoptic gospels—are about the kingdom of God. The *Sache* of these parables is therefore fixed, although minimal allowances for diversity are made for their *Bildhälfte*: The narrative of a parable depicts some aspect of daily life (the *Bildhälfte*) in order to reference the kingdom of God (the *Sachhälfte*). Or put another way, one plane of the parable has to do with the profane, things of the human order; the other plane of a parable has to do with the sacred, things of the divine order. Thus, according to this scheme, 'daily life' excludes 'religion'. With thick lines drawn so rigidly between the two 'planes' (or spheres, or fields or levels) of a parable, it is easy to see how the alleged 'religious' content of the four so-called example stories gives pause to interpreters. If there is to be 'semantic tension' or distance between the divine and the human, the sacred and the profane, in the *Sachhälfte* and the *Bildhälfte* of a parable, then when 'religion' is espied in the *Bildhälfte* of each of the four Lukan parables in question there seems to be less 'semantic tension' or distance between their *Bildhälfte* and *Sachhälfte*. Consequently, it is often said that the parables are indirect—by means of *B* they speak of *A*—and that the example stories are direct—by means of *A'* they speak of *A*. The former are to be read as figurative, the latter as literal. It is but a small step from there to the conclusion that the example stories do not have 'two planes', do not have a 'neutral soil', do not effect a comparison in the same way as do the *Parabeln*. Would the same line of reasoning hold for two *Parabeln* in which there is mention of things 'religious'? Does the mention of 'heaven' in The Prodigal Son (Lk. 15.18, 21) and the mention of 'God' in The Unjust Judge (Lk. 18.2, 4) make them 'examples'? Is it possible that 'religion' is used 'figuratively' in these instances?

Leaving aside the issue of whether or not all of the synoptic parables

and the Publican. Here we have "example-stories", not symbolic narrative. The point is in these cases that we should go and do likewise, or take warning by the given example. But in the parable of the Lost Sheep, on the other hand, the upshot is not that we should or should not go and do likewise. We have rather an extended image—the shepherd's retrieval of the lost sheep and his joy—a narrative image which reveals rather than exemplifies' (*Early Christian Rhetoric*, p. 72).

reference the kingdom of God,[186] Funk's query about the putative narrative content of the *Beispielerzählungen* asserts itself: Is the 'religious content' of the example stories really 'religious'? One could also ask: Do each of the four example stories have 'religion' as their content?[187]

Doubts naturally arise about the adequacy of the familiar model of a parable as composed of two planes (spheres, fields, levels), and the attendant assumptions about those two planes, to describe the comparative mechanism of the παραβολαί.[188] At the very least, the suitability of

186. The longstanding consensus that all of the parables of Jesus give reference to the kingdom of God is being challenged. Earl Breech ('Kingdom of God and the Parables of Jesus', *Semeia* 12 [1978], pp. 15-40) questions the axiom that 'the Kingdom of God is the ultimate referent of the parables of Jesus' (p. 15). Hedrick ('Parables and the Kingdom', pp. 368-93) reappraises the relationship between Jesus' parables and the kingdom, and he concludes that 'these stories should not be initially approached with the assumption that they are symbols for the Kingdom of God, or some other cryptic reality' (p. 393). James Breech (*The Silence of Jesus*, pp. 36-39, 66-74, 216-22), who questions whether Jesus himself prefixed his parables with the phrase 'the kingdom of God is like', offers yet another re-evaluation of the relationship between Jesus' parables and the kingdom of God. Correspondingly, the view that all the parables of the Gospels refer to the kingdom of God has not gone unchallenged. Berger (*Formgeschichte des Neuen Testaments*, p. 41) states that not all parables of the synoptic gospels are about the kingdom. Sellin ('Gleichnisstrukturen', pp. 113-15) also contends that the kingdom of God should not be a presupposition underlying the interpretation of every parable (e.g. the *Beispielerzählungen* and others) unless specific mention is made of the kingdom. Elsewhere ('Lukas als Gleichniserzähler', p. 175), Sellin endorses the observation made by Goulder ('Characteristics of the Parables in the Several Gospels', p. 65) that 'none of the "L" parables begins, "The kingdom of God is like…"'

187. Admittedly, the strongest case for an example story having 'religion' as its content can be made for The Pharisee and the Toll Collector, in which a Pharisee and a toll collector appear in the temple, a religious location, at prayer, a religious act (see Lk. 18.9-14). What is it about the other three example stories that could give rise to the conclusion that they have 'religion' as their content? The appearance of a priest and a Levite in the Merciful Samaritan (Lk. 10.30-35)? The appearance of God in The Foolish Rich Man (Lk. 12.16-20)? The mention of Hades and 'Moses and the prophets' in The Rich Man and Poor Lazarus (Lk. 16.19-31)? Even if it is certain that these four example stories have religion as their content, is that what makes them examples rather than parables?

188. Klemm observes that it is Jülicher's distinction between *Bildhälfte* and *Sachhälfte* that moves the *Beispielerzählungen* to the periphery; and he suggests

that model as a criterion for demarcating the difference between *Parabel* and *Beispielerzählung* must be pondered because the differentia remains rather intangible. Moreover, that familiar model limits the range of possibilities—or better, restricts the understanding—of how a παραβολή might effect a comparison.

The Greek word παραβολή itself does not authorize a definitive model of a singular comparative mechanism operative in all narratives called by that name. Although the word παραβολή does not literally mean 'comparison', few would deny that a parable effects a comparison. While constructing an elaborate model of the comparative mechanism of the synoptic parables, or even the Lukan parables, is well beyond the purview of this study—indeed, that is not necessary here—the etymology of the word παραβολή does suggest a simple means of envisioning the comparative mechanism of those parables. Derived from παραβάλλειν, which means 'to cast, or to put (βάλλειν) along [side] (παρά)', παραβολή could be rendered into English as 'juxtaposition'.[189] Understanding παραβολή as juxtaposition encourages readers or hearers to consider what is being set side by side, by what means and for what reasons. In addition, envisioning the comparative mechanism of a παραβολή as juxtaposition admits the possibility of comparison, an investigation along the isotopy of similarity or resemblance, as well as the possibility of contrast, an investigation along the isotopy of contrariety or contradiction.[190] To propose 'juxtaposition' as the term for the comparative mechanism of a parable, then, does not have as its advantage neutrality, but flexibility; it does not rigidify the means by which a comparison can be made so that some narratives explicitly called παραβολή in the Gospel of Luke would be excluded on that basis.

that Jülicher could have avoided problems had he examined further the sharp differentiation between *Bildhälfte* and *Sachhälfte* (see 'Die Gleichnisauslegung Ad. Jülicher's im Bannkreis der Fabeltheorie Lessings', pp. 170-72; cf. p. 159).

189. As is well known, the English word 'parable' is merely a transliteration, not a translation, of the Greek word παραβολή. On the etymology of παραβολή, see Hauck, 'παραβολή', pp. 744-46; Young, *Jesus and his Jewish Parables*, pp. 4-11; and Scott, *Hear Then the Parable*, pp. 7-21.

190. For a discussion of comparison and contrast from a semiotic perspective, see Daniel Patte, *The Religious Dimensions of Biblical Texts: Greimas's Structural Semiotics and Biblical Exegesis* (SBLSS; Atlanta: Scholars Press, 1990), pp. 14-15, 80, 226.

Conceiving of the comparative mechanism of the παραβολή as jux-taposition may prove especially beneficial to studies in which an attempt is made to understand and appreciate parables in their narrative context in a specific synoptic gospel. Although Sellin makes a case for revising the terms *Bildhälfte* and *Sachhälfte* to mean the plane of the narrative world of the parable itself and the plane of its narrative con-text, respectively, those terms carry such weighty baggage from over a century of use that it may be better to relinquish them.[191] For the pur-poses of this study, therefore, I am content with a description of the comparative mechanism of the παραβολή as follows: The παραβολή is an embedded narrative which effects a comparison within its larger narrative context by means of juxtaposition.

This section has provided a survey of attempts to specify the particu-larity of the example stories on the basis of a difference in their com-parative mechanism. Nevertheless, that distinction remains rather impalpable as long as no formal features of the example stories are identified to bolster the claim that they are categorically different from the other narrative parables. This observation is borne out by those who argue that the example stories, like the other parables, are metaphorical, which means that the comparative mechanism of the example stories is no different than that of the *Parabeln*. Still, the perceived difference between the *Beispielerzählungen* and the *Parabeln*, articulated in terms of the peculiar proximity of *Bildhälfte* and *Sachhälfte* in the example stories, may be a function of a tangible formal aspect of the example stories. Before I focus on that, however, consideration must be given to studies in which attempts are made to identify formal aspects of the example stories purported to be unique to that category of synoptic parable.

Formal Aspects of the Example Stories: Plot, Character, Structure
In the determination of a *Gattung*, formal criteria are usually of prime importance, yet it is often the case, as Baasland correctly observes, that some views about the contents of the *Beispielerzählungen* are accentu-ated in deciding the question of the uniqueness of the example sto-ries.[192] As we have seen in the preceding sections of this chapter, the

---

191. See Sellin, 'Allegorie und "Gleichnis"', pp. 376, 387-88, 405-10, 416-25.
192. Baasland, 'Zum Beispiel der Beispielerzählungen', p. 179. For a more complete discussion of the factors involved in an attempt to fix *Gattungen*, see Berger, 'Hellenistiche Gattungen im Neuen Testament', pp. 1036-48; and *idem*,

judgment that the *Beispielerzählungen* are a different kind of παραβολή than are the *Parabeln*—or that the example stories are 'examples' and not parables—is sometimes based upon views that the example stories, unlike the other narrative parables, have 'moral behavior' or 'religion' as their content. Proponents of those views, however, provide no definitive evidence, such as formal elements manifest in the example stories, to uphold the claim that the *Beispielerzählungen* are 'moral examples' and thus different in kind from the *Parabeln*. This section will be guided by a particular question: Is it possible to mount a defense for the uniqueness of the example stories based upon specific aspects of their design and construction? It must now be determined what, if any, formal characteristics of the example stories can be adduced to sustain the verdict that they are 'examples' and that as such they are different in kind from the *Parabeln*.

Framing the issue in this way does not necessarily imply that the 'content' of any example story, or any parable—or, for that matter, any narrative—is separable from its 'form'. Indeed, in a study of narrative, no absolute distinction between the form of a narrative and its content ought to be assumed; rather, it ought to be axiomatic that the form of a narrative is inseparable from its content.[193] Mindful of that tenet, however, it is possible to focus attention on either the form of a narrative or the content of a narrative. Focusing on the formal aspects of a narrative is nothing more than a heuristic strategy which enables interpreters to identify and to appreciate the manner in which the narrative material is organized into a whole. As a corollary, it ought to be stressed that the formal 'elements' of narrative are inextricably interrelated and virtually inseparable. Although different components of a narrative can be distinguished (for instance, plot and character), no single component can

Formgeschichte des Neuen Testaments, pp. 16-22. We have seen that both Jülicher and Bultmann invoked a criterion based upon narrative contents and not narrative components as a means of differentiating *Beispielerzählung* and *Parabel*. Jülicher did not involve himself in a sustained effort to identify formal narrative elements in the *Beispielerzählungen*. Bultmann did, in his analysis of style, show that the *Beispielerzählungen* have 'a strong formal relationship' to the *Parabeln*, but he distinguished between the two primarily on the basis of the content of the example narratives, which 'offer examples=models for the right conduct'.

193. In agreement with Tolbert, *Perspectives on the Parables*, p. 71. For more on the unity of form and content in the parables, see Dan Otto Via, Jr, 'The Relationship of Form to Content in the Parables: The Wedding Feast', *Int* 25 (1971), pp. 171-84, esp. p. 174.

be divorced from the others (for instance, plot cannot be sundered from character). Devoting attention to particular formal elements of a narrative provides a perspective by which specific aspects of that narrative can be illuminated. The integrity of narrative—that is, the unity of its form and content, as well as the interrelationship of its formal elements—now affirmed, it must be acknowledged that there are various and varied approaches to treating the formal aspects of narrative. Let us consider for a moment a relatively simple approach to identifying formal characteristics of the parables.

Some scholars contend that certain formal characteristics discovered in the introductory sentences of the synoptic parables offer a means of classifying those parables. Jeremias concludes that Jesus' parables have 'two basic forms': those that begin with a noun in the nominative case—'a simple narrative without any introductory formula'; and those that begin with a dative—a narrative introduced by some sort of comparative formula.[194] The first of these 'basic forms', according to Jeremias, can be found in all three of the synoptic gospels and the *Gospel of Thomas*, although he notes 'this is the form most commonly found in Luke'.[195] Indeed, all four of the example stories are to be found in this group. There is, however, yet another characteristic in the introductory sentences of some of the synoptic parables that has been discerned and used as the basis for identifying a specific type of parable. Heinrich Greeven observes that the introductions to several synoptic parables contain the phrase τίς ἐξ ὑμῶν. He argues that since these parables share a similar introductory formula and other characteristics in common, they should be regarded as a particular form of parable.[196]

194. Jeremias, *The Parables of Jesus*, p. 100; cf. pp. 101-103.

195. See *The Parables of Jesus*, p. 100, where Jeremias lists parables beginning with a noun in the nominative. Funk (*Language, Hermeneutic, and Word of God*, p. 146) expresses his reticence to define the nature of Jesus' parables on the basis of the distinction made by Jeremias by citing one of the very 'principles of transformation' formulated by Jeremias: 'Since, however, there is a tendency to prefix the comparative formula in the process of transmission, it would be premature to rest a substantive distinction on the introductory phrase'.

196. Heinrich Greeven, '"Wer unter Euch...?"', *Wort und Dienst* NS 3 (1952), pp. 86-101; repr. in Harnisch (ed.), *Gleichnisse Jesu*, pp. 238-55 (all references are to the reprint edition). For Greeven's list of five parables belonging to this group, as well as those parables closely related to them, see pp. 238-40. Contra Greeven's claims for the uniqueness of this *Gleichnisform* (see pp. 254-55), Berger shows that this type of parable can be found in other hellenistic literature, particularly in the

Even though the introductory sentences of the synoptic parables may display formal characteristics sufficient to warrant grouping them according to shared features, the *Parabeln* and the *Beispielerzählungen* cannot be distinguished from each other on that basis. In order to prove that the distinction between *Parabeln* and *Beispielerzählungen* is justified because they have different formal characteristics, more sophisticated methods of analysis must be employed to identify those formal characteristics.

Parable scholars, as was mentioned earlier, have availed themselves of nearly every known methodological approach in order to analyze the παραβολαί. It is possible, of course, to isolate a specific formal aspect of narrative and then examine the parables to discover how that aspect is manifested in them, but it is more commonly the case that scholars search for aggregates of formal characteristics in the parables in order to discern organizational patterns or structures, with some scholars analyzing 'surface structures' (usually by means of an approach that utilizes an apparatus provided by literary criticism) and others analyzing 'deep structures' (usually by means of an approach that utilizes an apparatus provided by structuralism). To answer the question raised in this section, consideration must be given, without prejudice toward method, to the results of several studies in which formal characteristics of the example stories have been identified. Although studies of the formal aspects of the parables frequently give rise to classification schemes different from the one under consideration here (*Gleichnis, Parabel, Beispielerzählung*), such studies cannot be passed over in silence because they heighten the suspicion that the *Beispieler-*

'popular philosophical tradition' (see 'Materialien zu Form und Überlieferungs-geschichte neutestamentlicher Gleichnisse', *NovT* 75 [1973], pp. 1-37). An interesting avenue of investigation from a literary-critical perspective would be to subject the synoptic parables to analysis in terms of point of view. In the τίς-ἐξ-ὑμῶν parables, Jesus begins his narration in the second person, not the third person characteristic of most other narrative parables, including the *Beispielerzählungen*. The τίς-ἐξ-ὑμῶν in these parables addresses the characters in the Gospel narrative(s), but that 'you' functions also to address hearers or readers of the larger Gospel narrative(s). Thus, it would appear that if the hearer or reader of a parable is expected to compare her or his behavior directly to the behavior depicted in any parable, it would be the case with the τίς-ἐξ-ὑμῶν parables more than with the *Beispielerzäh-lungen* (against Jülicher). For descriptions of the types of responses the τίς-ἐξ-ὑμῶν parables evoke, see Greeven, '"Wer unter Euch…?"', pp. 242-45; and Berger, *Formgeschichte des Neuen Testaments*, pp. 45-46.

zählungen and the *Parabeln* are more alike than not.[197] However, attention will be given mainly to those studies of the formal aspects of the parables which have a direct bearing on the example stories.

A number of technical studies proffer analyses in which an attempt is made to identify formal aspects of the synoptic parables in order to determine whether they exhibit common patterns or organizational structures. Among the formal aspects of narrative that come into consideration—simultaneously, serially or singularly—in enterprises intent on discerning such patterns or structures, character and plot are two which figure prominently. For instance, with regard to character, the parables have been grouped according to the number of principal characters and according to the types of characters depicted in them; with regard to plot, the parables have been grouped according to the overall plot movement, according to the number of actions or events, and according to the sequence of narrative events or actions evident in them. This section will begin with those studies in which the parables are grouped mainly according to an index based on character and then move on to those studies which group the parables mainly according to an index based on plot.

197. Even as highly idiosyncratic a study of organizational patterns in the parables as the one proposed by Bailey serves to indicate that the *Beispielerzählungen* and the *Parabeln* share substantial similarities. Bailey (*Poet and Peasant*, pp. 72-74) defines the 'form' of parable found in the Gospel of Luke—the 'seven stanza parabolic ballad'—and finds that both *Beispielerzählungen* and *Parabeln* (e.g. 10.30-35, 14.16-23, 16.1-8, 18.9-14) exhibit that 'form' (pp. 86-110; cf. *idem*, *Through Peasant Eyes: More Lukan Parables, their Culture and Style* [Grand Rapids: Eerdmans, 1980], pp. 33-56, 88-113, 142-56). For a more viable approach to identifying organizational patterns in the parables formed by the repetition of words and phrases, see Tolbert, *Perspectives on the Parables*, pp. 78-82. Breech (*The Silence of Jesus*, p. 66) provides a novel categorization of Jesus' parables (or more correctly, Breech's reconstruction of Jesus' parables) according to whether they depict what people do, the 'photodramatic parables', or whether they depict what people do and say, the 'phonodramatic parables'. The former group includes The Sower, The Mustard Seed, The Leaven, The Hidden Treasure, The Pearl, The Lost Sheep, and The Lost Coin; the latter, The Unjust Steward, The Great Supper, The Labourers in the Vineyard, The Prodigal Son, and The Good Samaritan. Although the phonodramatic group of parables includes one *Beispielerzählung*, Breech explicitly excludes two others, The Rich Fool, and The Rich Man and Lazarus, because they do not exhibit 'the same stylistic, formal, and functional characteristics as do the five core phonodramatic parables of Jesus' (p. 160; see pp. 125-28).

Sellin's study of the formal features of the Lukan parables vis-à-vis other synoptic parables in his essay 'Lukas als Gleichniserzähler' is an interesting starting point because in an earlier study Sellin upheld Jülicher's distinction between *Parabeln* and *Beispielerzählungen* due to a difference in their semantics; however, in this later study Sellin promotes a classification scheme of the parables which differs from Jülicher's.[198] Sellin now posits that a meaningful classification scheme should not be based upon whether a parable has a paradigmatic function since all Lukan parables have such a function; rather, it should be based upon the formal features of the parables.[199]

Sellin allows that a possibility for classifying the parables arises from features in their introductory sentences, and his analysis of stylistic features in their introductory phrases yields three types of parables: the τίς-ἐξ-ὑμῶν parables (Mt. 7.9-11//Lk. 11.11-13; Mt. 18.12-13// Lk. 15.4-7; Lk. 11.5-8, 14.28-30, 14.31-33, 15.8-10, 17.7-10); the ἄνθρωπός-τις parables (Mt. 21.28-31; Lk. 7.41-43, 10.30-35, 12.16-21, 15.11-32, 16.1-9, 16.19-31, 18.9-14); and the ἄνθρωπος parables (Mk 12.1-10//Mt. 21.33-46//Lk. 20.9-19; Mt. 22.1-10//Lk. 14.16-24; Mt. 25.14-30//Lk. 19.12-27; Mt. 18.23-35, 20.1-16, 21.28-31, 25.1-13).[200]

---

198. It should be reiterated that I have drawn from more than one article authored by Sellin. In his 1974 study, 'Lukas als Gleichniserzähler', Sellin presents his own classification scheme of the παραβολαί based upon their structure. While Sellin does not reject Jülicher's categorization in that study, he does point out some of its shortcomings. In his 1978 study, 'Allegorie und "Gleichnis"', Sellin—with the revisions he deems necessary—offers a defense of Jülicher's categorization of the παραβολαί (see above, pp. 192-95). We can observe that for Sellin the structure of the παραβολαί is the main index for classification in the earlier study, while the semantics of the παραβολαί becomes the main index in the later study.

199. Sellin, 'Lukas als Gleichniserzähler', pp. 178-79. Sellin's chief interest here, as his title indicates, is the parables in the Gospel of Luke, specifically those in 'Lk–Sonderguts'. However, he does treat other synoptic parables in order to show how they compare with those in 'L' (see pp. 184-89).

200. Sellin, 'Lukas als Gleichniserzähler', pp. 184-85, 188-89. Sellin expands upon an observation made by Goulder ('Characteristics of the Parables in the Several Gospels', p. 65), who writes: 'None of the "L" parables begins, "The kingdom of God is like...". They all begin with τίς interrogative or τις indefinite'. Sellin accepts Greeven's results on the construction of the τίς-ἐξ-ὑμῶν type of parable. The parables in the Gospel of Luke (and one from Mt.) that begin with τις (usually ἄνθρωπός τις) comprise the group Sellin calls the ἄνθρωπός-τις type of parable (see p. 179).

This alone, Sellin suggests, is enough to challenge Jülicher's categorization of the parables because the τίς-ἐξ-ὑμῶν type of parable includes both *Gleichnisse* and *Parabeln*, and because the ἄνθρωπός-τις type of parable includes both *Parabeln* and *Beispielerzählungen*.[201] However, dividing the parables into groups according to introductory phrases remains rather arbitrary, Sellin avers, unless corresponding distinctions among those groups can be made according to their structure, and Sellin occupies himself with the task of showing that such distinctions can be made.[202] Since Sellin's interest lies with the ἄνθρωός-τις parables in 'Lk-Sonderguts ("L")', and since all four of the example stories can be found in that group, the focus will be on the formal characteristics of that group as identified by Sellin.

Sellin states that the ἄνθρωπός-τις parables are structured according to a particular constellation of characters, which he refers to as a 'three person scheme'.[203] The typical 'three person parables in Lk-Sonderguts' (10.30-35, 15.11-32, 16.19-31) are constructed according to this scheme, which can be described as follows. These parables open with ἄνθρωπός τις, or with a variation of that phrase.[204] In the beginning of these narratives, two persons appear who are equal in status ('twins': two travellers, two sons, two people in Hades), but who come to form a contrast.[205] An important feature of these narratives is that the plot is dramatically developed by a genuine interaction of the plots of two free and equal individuals in which the initiative mainly proceeds from one of the 'twin figures'.[206] The contrast formed between these two 'twin characters' is essential to the point of the parable; thus, the second of these 'twins' (the Samaritan, the older brother, the rich man)

201. Sellin, 'Lukas als Gleichniserzähler', pp. 176-77 n. 53, 178-80.
202. Sellin, 'Lukas als Gleichniserzähler', pp. 179-84.
203. Sellin, 'Lukas als Gleichniserzähler', p. 181.
204. Sellin, 'Lukas als Gleichniserzähler', p. 179. Sellin will later leave aside 13.6-9 and 18.1-8 as exceptions even though they begin with this type of phrase (see p. 184).
205. Sellin, 'Lukas als Gleichniserzähler', p. 181. Sellin points out that by 'travellers' he means 'the pair clerics-Samaritan' (p. 181 n. 73). While it is true that the priest and the Levite form a contrast to the Samaritan, and that the priest and the Levite perform the same action, a strict count of characters in this parable would yield five, not three.
206. Sellin, 'Lukas als Gleichniserzähler', p. 181. On the basis of this feature, Sellin regards Lk. 7.41-43 as an 'outline' (*Skizze*) of the ἄνθρωπός-τις type of parable (see p. 180).

is essential to the content. To this pair of 'antithetical twins' is added a third character, who represents a sort of authority. This third figure is the 'formal main character', but remains a background figure (the wounded man, the father, Abraham). This 'formal main character' in terms of status is usually a 'king-father-master figure', while the main character with regard to content is usually a 'son-slave figure'.[207] These three characters, the two 'twin' characters and the 'formal main character', form a 'dramatic triangle'.[208]

Sellin includes other parables in the ἄνθρωπός-τις group, but they are 'two person narratives' in which only the 'antithetical twins' appear (Lk. 12.16-21, 16.1-9, 18.1-8).[209] He finds it striking that in each of these three narratives one of the two characters has a monologue which is essential to the plot of the story.[210] Sellin suggests that the monologue represents a third person, or better, that one of the characters takes on two plot functions. If that is so, then the 'dramatic triangle' is also present in the 'two person narratives'.[211] The contrast, which is represented by the plots of the 'antithetical twins' in the 'three person parables', now takes place between the plot elements 'apparent solution' and 'astonishing solution' in the 'two person parables'.

Sellin recognizes The Pharisee and the Toll Collector as a special case. In Lk. 18.9-14 only the 'antithetical twins' (two people at prayer in the temple) seem to appear. The 'formal main character' is only

207. Sellin, 'Lukas als Gleichniserzähler', p. 181. Sellin adopts this distinction from Via (p. 181 n. 76), but it should be noted that Via uses this very distinction to demarcate the line between example story and parable (see below, pp. 226-32).

208. Sellin, 'Lukas als Gleichniserzähler', p. 184; cf. p. 180.

209. Sellin, 'Lukas als Gleichniserzähler', p. 182. The Unjust Judge (Lk. 18.1-8), Sellin indicates, does not correspond exactly to the 'dramatic triangle' scheme (see p. 182 n. 79). Because Lk. 16.1-9, according to Sellin, shares the very same structure as The Rich Fool, he suggests that it is also a *Beispielerzählung*, albeit a negative one (see p. 182 n. 77). Note that here the index upon which Sellin bases his decision is structure, not semantics. In his 1978 article, 'Allegorie und "Gleichnis"', Sellin does not mention Lk. 16.1-9 in his treatment of the *Beispielerzählungen* (see pp. 424-29).

210. Sellin, 'Lukas als Gleichniserzähler', p. 182. It is perhaps more accurate to say that in each of these three narratives a character has an 'interior monologue', or soliloquy. On the soliloquy as a characteristic of the parables peculiar to Luke, see Heininger, *Metaphorik*, esp. pp. 31-37; see also Philip Sellew, 'Interior Monologue as a Narrative Device in the Parables of Luke', *JBL* 111 (1992), pp. 239-53.

211. Sellin, 'Lukas als Gleichniserzähler', p. 182.

apparently missing; the 'formal main character' is transposed into the narrative by means of the 'instance of justification' pronounced by Jesus (v. 14a). Correspondingly, Sellin submits that the act of prayer itself assumes the hidden presence of God, and thus the third character.[212]

Sellin contends that the principle of revaluation (*Umwertung*) underlies all of the ἄνθρωπος-τις parables structured by a 'dramatic triangle', a principle which is crucial for the transition to the content plane of interpretation.[213] Each of these parables begins with one of the two 'twin figures' depicted in a positive light (the debtor with few debts, the priest and the Levite, the son who remained home, the rich man, the Pharisee), but at the end of the narrative the apparently negative person proves to be preferred (the debtor with many debts, the despised Samaritan, the lost son, the poor man, the toll collector). This is even true of The Foolish Rich Man, in which the apparent solution is destroyed by God.[214]

The ἄνθρωπός-τις parables, Sellin concludes, show enough formal features in common to be regarded as a special class of parable, their essential feature being the structure he calls the 'dramatic triangle' (three characters, or two characters and monologue).[215] Thus, it is possible to distinguish the ἄνθρωπός-τις parables from the τίς-ἐξ-ὑμῶν parables and the ἄνθρωπος parables, groups which have their own set of characteristic features.[216]

Two dimensions of Sellin's analysis need to be highlighted. First, according to Sellin's inventory of formal features, the *Beispielerzählungen* belong to the same group as do a number of *Parabeln*. Like the

212. Sellin, 'Lukas als Gleichniserzähler', p. 181.
213. Sellin, 'Lukas als Gleichniserzähler', p. 183.
214. Sellin, 'Lukas als Gleichniserzähler', p. 183.
215. Sellin, 'Lukas als Gleichniserzähler', p. 184.
216. On the ἄνθρωπος parables, see 'Lukas als Gleichniserzähler', pp. 185-88. Sellin posits that the majority of the ἄνθρωπος parables have a uniform structure, which he refers to as 'monarchic' (p. 185). The 'structural' (or formal) features of these parables as given by Sellin are: (1) the 'formal main character' is usually at the same time the 'main character according to content'; (2) the antagonists usually form a group (e.g. slaves, hosts, workers, tenants, maidens) and are differentiated in a variety of ways (e.g. by the 'law of three', repetition, contrast); (3) the main character shows his sovereign might before the end of the narrative; (4) closely related to that, the main character almost always has an allegorical reference to God or Jesus (pp. 187-88; cf. p. 185).

Parabeln in Sellin's ἄνθρωπός-τις group of parables, the example stories are structured by means of a 'dramatic triangle', with a principle of
revaluation underlying the depiction of the 'antithetical twins'. However, it must be acknowledged that not all of the example stories are
entirely alike. Secondly, the *Beispielerzählungen* and the *Parabeln*
which comprise the ἄνθρωπός-τις parables manifest formal features
that seem to have a Lukan, though not exclusively Lukan, hue.[217] Nevertheless, the example stories share formal features in common with
other parables in the synoptic gospels, as a number of studies have
demonstrated.

Character is the formal feature of narrative prioritized by Blomberg
in his classification of Jesus' parables. Blomberg's focus on the number
and nature of main characters in the parables as the criteria for categorizing them yields three groups—triadic parables, dyadic parables and
monadic parables.[218] Since the example stories do not occur among the
monadic parables, the concern here will be with the triadic parables and
the dyadic parables.[219]

Blomberg divides the triadic parables into two subgroups. The simple
triadic parables have three main characters, an authority figure of some
sort and two subordinate figures. According to Blomberg,

> The authority figure, usually a king, father or master, typically acts as a
> judge between the two subordinates, who in turn exhibit contrasting
> behavior...These have been called *monarchic* parables, since in each

217. Sellin must acknowledge that Mt. 21.28-31 is 'completely identical' in its
structure to Lk. 7.41-43 (see 'Lukas als Gleichniserzähler', p. 187) and that other
parables share affinities with the ἄνθρωπός-τις parables (p. 188). He asserts that
Matthew prefers the narrative parables with a monarchic structure, while Luke
prefers narrative parables with a dramatic triangle structure.

218. Blomberg, *Interpreting the Parables*, p. 148; cf. pp. 171-288. One of
Blomberg's main contentions against Jülicher is that a parable can—indeed, most
parables do—have more than one 'point' (see pp. 21, 69, 163-66). Blomberg asserts
that a 'main point' is tied to each of the main characters in a parable; thus, he alternatively refers to the triadic parables as 'three-point parables', the dyadic parables
as 'two-point parables', the monadic as 'one-point parables'.

219. On the monadic parables, see Blomberg, *Interpreting the Parables*, pp. 278-
88. The monadic parables are brief narratives that focus on a single protagonist
(p. 278). This group includes four of what Blomberg calls 'brief similes' (The
Hidden Treasure, The Pearl of Great Price, The Mustard Seed, The Leaven) and
two of what he recognizes as τίς-ἐξ-ὑμῶν parables (The Warring King and The
Tower Builder).

case the central or unifying character (the character who directly relates to each of the other two) is the master or king figure. Often the particular underling, a servant or son, who would have seemed to a first-century Jewish audience to have acted in a praiseworthy manner, is declared to be less righteous than his apparently wicked counterpart.[220]

Blomberg identifies the following as simple triadic parables: The Prodigal Son, The Lost Sheep, The Lost Coin, The Two Debtors, The Two Sons, The Faithful and Unfaithful Servants, The Ten Virgins, The Wheat and the Tares, The Dragnet, The Rich Man and Poor Lazarus, and The Children in the Marketplace.[221]

The complex triadic parables have the same 'triangular structure' as the simple triadic parables, but the former have more than three main characters or groups of characters. Further, the good or bad subordinate roles may be filled by 'multiple examples'.[222] Other parables in this group, while exhibiting the triadic structure apparent in the simple triadic parables, are not 'monarchic' because, as Blomberg states, 'the unifying character is not an authority figure, and there is no contrast between equally matched subordinates'.[223] Blomberg puts the following into the group of complex triadic parables: The Talents, The Laborers in the Vineyard, The Sower, The Good Samaritan, The Great Supper, The Unforgiving Servant, The Unjust Steward, and The Wicked Tenants.[224]

220. Blomberg, *Interpreting the Parables*, pp. 171-72 (his emphasis). Blomberg adopts from Sellin the appellation 'monarchic' to refer to parables in which an authority figure (king, father, master) appears; he adapts that insight further in light of Funk's analysis (see p. 171 n. 1; cf. pp. 148-49). Other aspects of Sellin's study (e.g. the inauthenticity of 'L' parables) receive more stringent comment (see pp. 146-47).

221. Blomberg, *Interpreting the Parables*, pp. 171-211. All of the simple triadic parables are found in Matthew or Luke; the scripture references for these parables in order of mention are: Lk. 15.11-32; Lk. 15.4-6; Lk. 15.8-9, cf. Mt. 18.12-14; Lk. 7.41-43; Mt. 21.28-32; Lk. 12.42-48//Mt. 24.45-51; Mt. 25.1-13; Mt. 13.24-30; Mt. 13.47-50; Lk. 16.19-31; Lk. 7.31-35//Mt. 11.16-19.

222. Blomberg, *Interpreting the Parables*, p. 213. On the complex triadic parables, see pp. 213-53.

223. Blomberg, *Interpreting the Parables*, p. 213. This is the case with The Unforgiving Servant and The Unjust Steward. Blomberg later states: 'It is perhaps better to speak of a unifying figure and two additional individuals with whom he interacts' (p. 251).

224. The complex triadic parables can be found in each of the synoptic gospels; the scripture references in order of mention are: Mt. 25.14-30, cf. Lk. 19.12-27; Mt.

The dyadic parables have only two main characters (or objects). Blomberg observes that in some of the dyadic parables there may be a contrast between the actions of the two main characters, as in The Pharisee and the Tax Collector and The Two Builders; or there may be an interaction between an authority figure and one subordinate (with no contrasting subordinate), as in The Unprofitable Servant, The Rich Fool, and The Unjust Judge; or agricultural imagery may take the place of a human subordinate, as in The Seed Growing Secretly and The Barren Fig Tree.[225] Rounding out the group of dyadic parables are The Friend at Midnight and The Householder and the Thief.[226]

In summary, Blomberg types two of the example stories as triadic parables and two as dyadic parables: The Rich Man and Lazarus is one of several simple triadic (monarchic) parables; The Good Samaritan is one of several complex triadic parables; The Rich Fool and The Pharisee and the Tax Collector are two of many dyadic parables. According to Blomberg's classification of Jesus' parables, the example stories are parables, but all four example stories neither belong to the same category of parable, nor do they constitute a unique group of parables.[227]

The two preceding studies, in which the parables found in the synoptic gospels are categorized initially by means of an index based on the number of characters depicted in them, do not point to the uniqueness of the example stories. If Sellin's analysis emphasizes that the example stories share formal features (such as introductory phrases, contrasting characters, revaluation) in common with other Lukan parables, then Blomberg's indicates that the example stories share formal features (such as contrasting characters and reversal) in common with other synoptic parables. Discrepancies between Sellin's and Blomberg's findings aside, both studies show that the four example stories do not

20.1-16; Mk 4.3-9//Mt. 13.3-9//Lk. 8.4-8; Lk. 10.30-35; Lk. 14.15-24, cf. Mt. 22.1-14; Mt. 18.23-25; Lk. 16.1-13; Mk 12.1-12//Mt. 21.33-43//Lk. 20.9-18.

225. Blomberg, *Interpreting the Parables*, pp. 256, 258-59; 260, 266, 271; 263, 268. On the dyadic parables, see pp. 255-78.

226. Dyadic parables can also be found in all three synoptic gospels; the scripture references in order of mention are: Lk. 18.9-14; Mt. 7.24-27//Lk. 6.47-49; Lk. 17.7-10; Lk. 12.16-21; Lk. 18.1-8; Mk 4.26-29; Lk. 13.6-9; Lk. 11.5-8; Mt. 24.43-44//Lk. 12.39-40.

227. This remark must be tempered with statements in which Blomberg allows that both The Rich Fool and The Pharisee and the Toll Collector are 'as close as one comes to finding a pure example story' (*Interpreting the Parables*, p. 266; cf. p. 257).

exhibit uniformity in the number of characters which they depict.[228] The issue of character as a peculiar formal feature of the example stories will resurface. For the moment, however, let us move on to studies of the parables in which character is considered in tandem with another formal feature of narrative, that of plot.

Funk subjects the major narrative parables in the Jesus tradition to analysis with the intent of formulating a more precise grid for the definition of 'parable'.[229] He focuses on two of what have been referred to here as 'formal aspects' of narrative, specifically, character and plot. The initial criterion for a 'narrative parable' stipulated by Funk is that it must have at least three major participants.[230] He lists the following as

228. One difference between the two studies is the manner in which the number of characters is calculated. Sellin recognizes that The Foolish Rich Man and The Pharisee and the Toll Collector are 'two person parables', but he regards them as having the 'dramatic triangle' structure for reasons already given, whereas Blomberg counts them both as dyadic parables. A more important difference has to do with what is meant by 'monarchic' parable. For Sellin, while a parable may contain a 'formal main character' who is an authority figure (king, master, father)—as do the ἄνθρωπός-τις parables—a parable is 'monarchic' (an ἄνθρωπος parable) when the 'main character according to content' and the 'formal main character' are identical in the same character, and when that main character (king, master, father)—usually with an allegorical reference to God or Jesus—exercises his authority. For Blomberg, a parable is monarchic (simple triadic) when the central or unifying character is an authority figure (king, master, father) who judges between two subordinates. Only two of Blomberg's monarchic (simple triadic) parables (Mt. 21.28-31, 25.1-13) correlate to Sellin's monarchic (ἄνθρωπος) parables; the remainder of Sellin's ἄνθρωπος parables are considered by Blomberg to be complex triadic parables. Four of Sellin's ἄνθρωπός-τις parables, including one *Beispielerzählung* (Mt. 21.28-31; Lk. 7.41-43, 15.11-32, 16.19-31), are found among Blomberg's simple triadic (monarchic) parables. Finally, Sellin leaves the τίς-ἐξ-ὑμῶν parables intact as a distinct group, while Blomberg distributes them among the simple and complex triadic parables, the dyadic parables and the monadic parables.

229. See Funk, *Parables and Presence*, pp. 19, 35. As a reminder, this citation refers to versions of two previously published essays, 'The Narrative Parables: The Birth of a Language Tradition' (pp. 19-28) and 'Participant and Plot in the Narrative Parables of Jesus' (pp. 35-54).

230. Funk, *Parables and Presence*, p. 35. Funk notes that this criterion excludes parables with two participants (e.g. 'Unjust Judge, Servant's Wages, Pharisee and Publican') and those with one participant (e.g. 'Lost Coin, Lost Sheep, Sower'). He observes further: 'To this list could be added the Two Sons (Matt 21:28-31a...), which, if a narrative at all, is a narrative only in the most skeletal form' (p. 36).

parables with three major participants: Laborers in the Vineyard (Mt. 20.1-15), Talents (Mt. 25.14-40//Lk. 19.12-27), Ten Maidens (Mt. 25.1-13), Great Supper (Lk. 14.16-24//Mt. 22.1-10), Good Samaritan (Lk. 10.30-35), Prodigal (Lk. 15.11-32), Unjust Steward (Lk. 16.1-9), Unmerciful Servant (Mt. 18.23-34), Wicked Tenants (Mk 12.1-9//Mt. 21.33-41//Lk. 20.9-16), and Rich Man and Lazarus (Lk. 16.19-31).[231] A second criterion for Funk's definition of narrative parable is that 'a narrative parable must have at least two scenes'.[232] This criterion, which according to Funk eliminates Wicked Tenants and Rich Man and Lazarus from the list, limits the major narrative parables to the first eight.[233] Funk then groups those parables based upon his observations of their characteristics relating to participant (character) and plot.

Funk divides the major narrative parables into two distinct groups on the basis of the formal function of the three principal participants in the narrative. In Group I—Laborers in the Vineyard, Talents, Ten Maidens, Great Supper, Good Samaritan, Prodigal—one principal participant functions as the 'determiner' (D) who establishes or determines the situation that gives rise to the action(s) in the narrative (the 'focal actuality'), and the other two principals function as 'respondents' (R1 and R2) who give contrasting responses to the situation established by the determiner (D). The determiner (D), then, is the mediating principal between the other two participants (R1 and R2).[234] In Group II—Unjust Steward and Unmerciful Servant—a determiner (D) also 'initiates or evokes the action' in the narrative, but here there is one principal respondent (R) and a second subordinate principal (r). In this group, the principal respondent (R) and the subordinate principal (r) do not give contrasting responses to the action initiated by the determiner (D); 'rather', as Funk states, 'r provides the occasion for development in the

231. Funk, *Parables and Presence*, pp. 35-36. Funk counts groups of characters as a single participant 'if members of the group act in concert' (even if there is a change of scale within the narrative) and he does not count subordinate characters as principal participants (p. 36).

232. Funk, *Parables and Presence*, p. 36.

233. Funk does not explain why he thinks that both Wicked Tenants and Rich Man and Lazarus do not have two scenes. Although these two parables are excluded, Funk has more to say about their idiosyncrasies later (cf. *Parables and Presence*, pp. 53-54).

234. For Funk's discussion of these technical terms and his identification of the principal participants in Group I, see *Parables and Presence*, pp. 37-39.

relation of R to D'.[235] The subordinate principal (r) is the foil to the principal respondent (R). The principal respondent (R), then, is the mediating or unifying principal in Group II parables. The relation of the principal participants to the plot of the narrative receives Funk's attention next.

Funk investigates the plot of the major narrative parables from two angles, first with regard to the 'narrative line' of the parables and then with regard to their 'episode patterns'. The results of his analysis lead him to conclude that the parables in Group I can be subdivided into Group Ia (Laborers in the Vineyard, Talents, Ten Maidens) and Group Ib (Great Supper, Good Samaritan, Prodigal).[236] In Group Ia, the two respondents (R1 and R2) make contrasting responses to the situation created by the determiner (D) and then witness the fate of their counterpart, with the fate of the first respondent (R1) turning downward (tragic) and that of the second respondent (R2) turning upward (comic). In Group Ib, the two respondents confront their respective fates (R1 meets with tragic fate, R2 with comic fate) separately, or in isolation from their counterpart.

In terms of how the principal participants relate to the narrative line of the parable, Funk explains the difference between the subgroups in Group I this way: '...in Ia the sets of relationships between D and R1/R2 are intertwined on the narrative line; in Ib the two sets of relationships are discrete'.[237] The parables in Group II exhibit another relation of principal participants to narrative line: '...the determiner appears at the beginning of the narrative, sets the stage by encountering R, then drops out of the narrative during R's encounter with r, until the denouement'.[238]

The episode patterns of each group are described by Funk as follows:

235. Funk, *Parables and Presence*, p. 39. Given these distinctions with regard to the 'narrative contact' (=surface structure) between principal participants, Funk submits the 'possibility' that Wicked Tenants belongs to Group II and the 'probability' that Rich Man and Lazarus belongs to Group I (pp. 39-40). He makes further observations about the 'fundamental relationships' (=deep structure) between principal participants in both groups that need not detain us here (see pp. 39-41).

236. Funk, *Parables and Presence*, pp. 42-46. Funk is careful to point out that some of the parables in each subgroup (e.g. especially Prodigal), while exhibiting comparable plot structures, also exhibit significant differences (cf. pp. 42, 45-46).

237. Funk, *Parables and Presence*, p. 43.

238. Funk, *Parables and Presence*, p. 43.

the parables in Group Ia follow the pattern 'action/crisis/ denouement'; those in Group Ib follow the pattern 'crisis/response 1/ response 2' (which serves as the denouement); and those in Group II follow the pattern 'crisis/response/denouement'.[239] Having grouped the major narrative parables according to similarities relating to their participants and plots, Funk strives to determine more specifically how the principal participants function as actants.

Funk defines four actantial functions in the major narrative parables.[240] One actantial function is performed by those participants who exhibit the 'justified response' (the expected or appropriate response 'in accordance with the canons of everydayness') to events unfolding in the narrative, and who are superior in status to the other respondent; those participants who give the justified response, labelled RJ, never attain what they desire, and their fortune 'invariably turns downward (tragic)'.[241] In contrast, another actantial function is performed by those participants who are 'pleasantly surprised by the way things turn out' in that they get what they do not deserve; these participants, labelled RG ('recipients of grace'), have a fate that regularly turns upward (comic).[242] In several narrative parables, Funk states, the fortunes of the actants RG and RJ are 'reversed in relation to expectations'.[243] A third actantial function is performed by the principal participant who 'dispenses grace or justice (IG/J=instrument of grace or justice)'.[244] The actantial functions of RJ and RG are usually filled by R1 and R2 (Group I) or may be combined in R (Group II); the actantial role of IG/J is regularly, but not always, filled by the determiner (D), who is usually an authority figure.[245] A fourth actantial function is performed by the

239. Funk, *Parables and Presence*, pp. 44-45. The Prodigal, due to its 'episodic nature', can be read in three ways and thus, according to Funk, can be assigned to Group Ia or Ib, or even Group II (see pp. 45-46).

240. Funk, *Parables and Presence*, p. 46. By 'actant' Funk means 'function, role, status'.

241. Funk, *Parables and Presence*, pp. 47-48.

242. Funk, *Parables and Presence*, p. 48.

243. Funk, *Parables and Presence*, p. 49. This happens, according to Funk, in six narrative parables: Laborers in the Vineyard, Great Supper, Good Samaritan, Prodigal, Unjust Steward, Unmerciful Servant.

244. Funk, *Parables and Presence*, p. 48: 'The instrument of grace is he who receives, admits, rewards, helps; as instrument of justice he excludes, pays what is due, rebukes, refuses aid'.

245. Funk, *Parables and Presence*, p. 48. Funk notes that 'the actants IJ/G, RJ,

participant who certifies and sanctions the reversal of fortunes (of RJ and RG) in the narrative; this actantial role, labelled as C, is preeminently—but, again, not always—filled by the determiner (D).[246]

Funk concludes that if six of the narrative parables—those which share a 'common deep structure' (Laborers in the Vineyard, Great Supper, Good Samaritan, Prodigal, Unjust Steward, Unmerciful Servant)—'are taken as indicative of the "message" of Jesus, it may be said that Jesus announces a fundamental reversal of the destinies of men'.[247] He continues:

> This reversal is related to expectations as informed by the received or everyday world. Further, this reversal is a perpetual state of affairs in the kingdom: whatever man comes to expect as owed to him is perpetually refused, but to him who expects nothing, the kingdom arrives as a gift.[248]

Funk's study indicates that eight narrative parables recorded in the synoptic gospels[249] share a substantial number of similarities with respect to the formal features of character and plot. If Funk's findings are considered with respect to the subject of concern in this study, the example stories, the following becomes evident. Funk includes at least one example story, The Good Samaritan, among the major narrative parables; indeed, The Good Samaritan shares a 'common deep structure' with six narrative parables 'indicative of the "message" of Jesus'.[250] Funk is less confident about another example story: Since The

---

and RG are thus mapped onto the formal structure of the parables of Group II in a way which differs from any of the options finding expression in Group I' (p. 49; see the table on p. 51).

246. Funk, *Parables and Presence*, pp. 49-50. The exception occurs in Good Samaritan, where, according to Funk, the determiner (D) is the man robbed and left in the ditch (cf. pp. 38, 48, 50-51).

247. Funk, *Parables and Presence*, p. 51.

248. Funk, *Parables and Presence*, p. 51. This confirms Funk's previous contention that the major narrative parables are 'double paradigms or declensions of reality' (see p. 52).

249. Actually, these eight narrative parables are to be found in the first and third Gospels: three appear only in the Gospel of Matthew (Laborers in the Vineyard, Ten Maidens, Unmerciful Servant), three only in the Gospel of Luke (Good Samaritan, Prodigal, Unjust Steward), and two are found in both Gospels (Talents, Great Supper).

250. It should be noted that another parable elected to this prestigious group by Funk, Great Supper, is also considered to be an example story by many parable

Rich Man and Poor Lazarus exhibits a number of idiosyncracies, Funk does not include it among the major narrative parables in the Jesus tradition.[251] Two of the example stories, The Foolish Rich Man and The Pharisee and the Toll Collector, are completely excluded from Funk's group of major narrative parables. Thus, according to Funk's analysis of 'Participant and Plot in the Narrative Parables of Jesus', one example story exhibits the same formal characteristics found in other narrative parables, but the four example stories do not manifest enough collective formal characteristics to warrant classifying them as a unique group of parables. A study conducted by one of Funk's contemporaries, who employs a similar methodology, does exclude each of the example stories from among the narrative parables of Jesus.

Via argues that there are compelling reasons for regarding the *Beispielerzählungen* as 'example stories' rather than narrative parables.[252] Utilizing a 'literary-structuralist methodology', Via identifies the formal characteristics of the 'genre narrative parables of Jesus' and then proceeds to show why the example stories do not belong to that 'genre'.[253] He performs an analysis of 14 narrative texts attributed to Jesus in the synoptic gospels. After making a distinction between story and discourse in narrative, Via identifies two levels of the story— specifically, a sequential level (plot) and an actantial level—that have a direct bearing on the 14 narratives under consideration.[254]

scholars influenced by a traditional reading of Bultmann (see p. 155 n. 25 above).

251. Although Funk thinks it 'probable' that Rich Man and Lazarus belongs to Group I in terms of its surface structure (see p. 221 n. 235 above), two idiosyncracies preclude it from being counted among the major narrative parables in the Jesus tradition: (1) it does not have the requisite two or more scenes; (2) its surface structure does not match its deep structure (see *Parables and Presence*, p. 41).

252. Via, 'Parable and Example Story', p. 106.

253. Norman R. Petersen ('On the Notion of Genre in Via's "Parable and Example Story: A Literary-Structuralist Approach"', *Semeia* 1 [1974], pp. 134-81) discusses the issue of genre in some detail, concluding that Via is incorrect to claim that there is a genre 'narrative parable of Jesus' (cf. pp. 136-41). Via, according to Petersen, has produced rather a *'typology of Jesus' utterances'* (p. 139; emphasis his). Via partially agrees with Petersen's critique, and provisionally accepts the term 'type' as a designation for Jesus' narrative parables, although that does not change his position on the example stories (see 'A Response to Crossan, Funk, and Petersen', pp. 229-33, esp. p. 230).

254. On the distinction between story and discourse in narrative, see Via, 'Parable and Example Story', p. 107. Via analyzes plot in terms of the overall plot movement (falling [tragic] and rising [comic]) and the sequence of episodes (crisis,

Based upon his sequential and actantial analyses of several narratives ascribed to Jesus, Via chooses 16 textemes and orders them into eight binary pairs of oppositions.[255] Via asserts that eight narratives which manifest a similar surface structure comprise the 'genre narrative parables of Jesus': Talents, Ten Maidens, Wedding Guest, Wicked Husbandmen, Workers in Vineyard, Unforgiving Servant, Unjust Steward, and Prodigal Son.[256] Via regards another narrative—Wedding Feast—as a 'modified' parable, and five other narratives—Good Samaritan, Rich Fool, Pharisee and Publican, Lazarus and Rich Man, Wedding Guest—as 'example stories'.[257] The reasons given by Via to support his conclusions warrant further consideration.

Via contends that he is justified in maintaining that there is a 'genre narrative parables of Jesus' because those eight narratives consistently display five textemes, with three of the eight narratives varying only with respect to three textemes.[258] Indeed, Via states, 'five of these eight

response, denouement) in the 14 narratives attributed to Jesus (see pp. 107-108, 122-23). Via employs the actantial scheme widely accepted in structural analysis at that time, according to which: '...a subject (S) desires to possess an object (O) or communicate it to a recipient (R), the object proceeding from an ordainer (Or). In this effort the subject may be aided by a helper (H) or impeded by an opponent (Op)' (p. 108).

255. Via, 'Parable and Example Story', pp. 108-109: 'The eight binary oppositions are as follows: (1) falling (tragic) plot movement/rising (comic) plot movement (a/b) [;] (2) episode pattern: action-crisis-denouement/episode pattern [:] crisis-response-denouement (c/d) [;] (3) subject receives object/subject does not receive object (e/f) [;] (4) subject desires to possess object (intends to be recipient)/subject desires to communicate object (does not intend to be recipient) (g/h) [;] (5) causal connection between events/chronological connection between events (i/j) [;] (6) subject unifies action/subject is only part of action (k/l) [;] (7) subject distinguished from ordainer/subject identified with ordainer (m/n) [;] (8) subject and ordainer are related as inferior to superior (employee to master)/subject and ordainer are equal or the relation is undefined or the distinction is based on a local circumstance (o/p)'.

256. Via, 'Parable and Example Story', p. 114; cf. 'Figure 1', p. 127.

257. Via, 'Parable and Example Story', pp. 115-19. Via follows the traditional reading of Bultmann in identifying The Wedding Guest (Lk. 14.7-11) as an example story.

258. Via, 'Parable and Example Story', p. 114. The constant textemes manifested by all eight narrative parables of Jesus are g, i, k, m, o; the narrative parables of Jesus may vary as to whether they manifest textemes a or b, c and d, e or f. According to Via, 'the formula a/b+c/d+e/f+g+i+k+m+o represents the "inter-

narratives have, in fact, the same surface structure'.[259] This group is
divided into the subgenres 'comic and tragic' narrative parables of
Jesus.[260]

With regard to the actants in the 'narrative parables of Jesus', Via
makes several observations.

> These eight narrative parables do not have two protagonists. The protag-
> onist (whose action or fate shapes the plot) is always the *actantiel*
> subject who is represented by a servant-son-subordinate figure. The
> *actantiel* ordainer is not the protagonist.[261]

Later, Via reveals that in the narrative parables of Jesus the ordainer is
always a 'king-master-father figure'.[262]

Having stated the results of his analysis of the 'genre narrative parables of Jesus', Via explains why he continues to exclude the example
stories from that genre. The Good Samaritan, according to Via, does
not display the five textemes found to be constants in the narrative
parables of Jesus, and thus does not belong to that group.[263] The Good
Samaritan has a plot that is not 'organically united':

> In the narrative parables the figure who is present in all of the episodes
> and gives the plot its shape is the *actantiel* subject. But in The Good
> Samaritan the figure who is present throughout and who gives the plot its
> shape is the victim, the *actantiel* recipient, while the *actantiel* subject,
> the Samaritan, appears only in the last episode. That is why the plot
> lacks organic *unity*.[264]

mediate" structure which is the genre, narrative parable of Jesus...' (p. 109).

259. Via, 'Parable and Example Story', p. 114. The five narrative parables with
the same surface structure referred to by Via here are Talents, Ten Maidens,
Wedding Garment, Wicked Husbandmen, and Workers in the Vineyard.

260. According to Via, the parable is comic if the subject successfully possesses
or communicates the object he or she intends to possess or communicate, tragic if
the subject is prevented from possessing the object she or he intends to possess (see
'Parable and Example Story', pp. 114-15).

261. Via, 'Parable and Example Story', p. 114; his emphasis. Via states that in
the comic narrative parables the ordainer may also fill other actantial roles, but that
'in all of the parables with a tragic plot, however, the ordainer is identical with the
opponent: he prevents the subject from possessing the object which he intends to
possess'.

262. Via, 'Parable and Example Story', p. 118.

263. Via, 'Parable and Example Story', pp. 115-17.

264. Via, 'Parable and Example Story', p. 115.

What is more, Via contends, the roles of the ordainer and subject are filled by the same figure, the Samaritan.[265] In addition, the denouement of this narrative is flawed; and rather than sequential causality, this narrative manifests psychological causality.[266] In terms of Via's analysis, then, the surface structure of The Good Samaritan diverges significantly from that of the other narrative parables of Jesus.

The variations exhibited by the remaining example stories may be fewer in number, but they are nonetheless of enough significance to convince Via to uphold his decision to exclude them from the 'genre narrative parables of Jesus'. The Rich Man and Poor Lazarus has a variation important to Via:

> Lazarus and the Rich Man has the same surface structure as the first five narrative parables, but there is philosophical as well as sequential causality. The rich man, who seeks relief from his torment, cannot obtain it because his former manner of life is now being requited (sequential) but also because there is an impassible gulf between the saved and the damned (philosophical). Thus the transcendent world is directly represented in a mythological way.[267]

The Pharisee and the Publican manifests the same surface structure as one of the narrative parables of Jesus, that of The Prodigal Son, but it has a flawed plot in that the crisis of the actantial subject, the Pharisee, and the denouement both belong to the discourse rather than the story.[268] Further, Via observes that God is addressed directly in the story instead of being represented by a human figure.[269] The Rich Fool diverges from the textemes constant in the narrative parables of Jesus with respect to its crisis and denouement:

265. Via, 'Parable and Example Story', p. 119.

266. Via, 'Parable and Example Story', pp. 115-16. Via insists that the narrative parables of Jesus have an 'expressed denouement'; that is, the actions in the story have consequences in the story: 'Thus it would seem that in Jesus' narrative parables it is a generic principle that the denouement, the end, is expressed; the close of the narrative is stated; the goal's being reached or not being reached comes to explicit narrative expression' (p. 123; cf. 125). Via points out that all of the narrative parables of Jesus have sequential causality, although that may be moderated with psychological causality (p. 116).

267. Via, 'Parable and Example Story', p. 117.

268. Via, 'Parable and Example Story', p. 117. Another narrative deemed by Via to be an example story, The Wedding Guest, also displays the same surface structure as The Prodigal Son (see p. 118).

269. Via, 'Parable and Example Story', p. 117.

...the crisis is no more than suggested by the term 'Fool.' God again appears as a character in the story but not so mythologically as in Lazarus and the Rich Man. The rich man's anticipated death in the end is not so much the consequence of his previous life as the standpoint from which it must be evaluated. Hence the denouement is again discourse.[270]

Via, despite criticisms concerning his selection and definition of textemes, is confident that his analysis 'empirically' demonstrates that the eight narrative parables of Jesus 'are formally quite distinct from the alleged example stories'.[271] Via's study suggests that most of the significant formal differences between the example stories and the narrative parables do not have to do with plot, but with actants: Of the eight binary oppositions of textemes identified by Via, three—a/b, c/d, i/j—deal directly with plot, while five (four of which contain the constant textemes found in all eight narrative parables)—e/f, g/h, k/l, m/n, o/p—specifically involve actants.[272] Via makes the strongest case that an example story is 'formally quite distinct' from the narrative parables with regard to The Good Samaritan because, according to his analysis, it manifests none of the five constant textemes found in the narrative parables, which would indicate that The Good Samaritan diverges widely from the narrative parables in terms of actants. However, that case appears less than hermetic in light of the fact that no less than five other scholars fill out the actantial scheme of The Good Samaritan differently than does Via, which would, in turn, have an impact upon four of the five constant textemes and would thus necessitate a re-evaluation of those textemes.[273]

270. Via, 'Parable and Example Story', p. 117. It must be observed that nowhere in Lazarus and the Rich Man does God appear as a character. Perhaps Via has conflated his previous remarks about Lazarus and the Rich Man ('Thus the transcendent world is directly represented in a mythological way') and The Pharisee and the Publican ('...but God is directly addressed in prayer in the story rather than being imaged by a human figure').

271. Via, 'A Response to Crossan, Funk, and Petersen', p. 230. As noted above, Petersen critiques Via's notion of genre; Funk ('Critical Note', *Semeia* 1 [1974], pp. 182-91) and Crossan ('Structuralist Analysis and the Parables of Jesus', pp. 192-206) offer criticisms of Via's choice and definitions of textemes. Sellin reviews and critiques the exchange between Via and Crossan ('Gleichnisstrukturen', pp. 89-115).

272. Via does, as we have seen, point to plot 'flaws' in three of the example stories—The Good Samaritan, The Rich Fool, and The Pharisee and the Publican.

273. See Crossan, 'Structuralist Analysis and the Parables of Jesus', pp. 193-202,

Even if the parameters set by Via in his formal analysis (the configuration of textemes manifest in the surface structure of the narratives attributed to Jesus) are left intact, his conclusion that the example stories are 'formally quite distinct' from the narrative parables is tenuous for several reasons. According to Via's own analysis, two of the example stories cannot be distinguished from the narrative parables on the basis of surface structure. To repeat Via's words: 'Lazarus and the Rich Man has the same surface structure as the first five narrative parables'; 'The Pharisee and the Publican has the same surface structure as The Prodigal Son'.[274] Furthermore, and contrary to what might be expected, the example stories do not manifest the same surface structure among themselves. Indeed, the surface structure of The Good Samaritan differs from the other example stories no less than it does from the narrative parables.[275] The example stories do not exhibit a set of constant textemes; in fact, only one texteme (c) is manifest an all four example stories.[276] Via, in his sequential and actantial analyses, then, neither produces conclusive evidence to substantiate the claim that the example stories are 'formally quite distinct' from the narrative parables, nor uncovers readily distinguishable formal attributes that unite the example stories as a discrete group of narratives. On the contrary, Via's literary-structuralist analysis shows that the example stories

198; Patte, 'An Analysis of Narrative Structure and the Good Samaritan', pp. 18-19; Crespy, 'The Parable of the Good Samaritan', pp. 40-46; Scott, *Jesus, Symbol-Maker for the Kingdom*, p. 100; Pheme Perkins, *Hearing the Parables of Jesus* (New York: Paulist Press, 1981), p. 119; cf. John Dominic Crossan, 'The Good Samaritan: Towards a Generic Definition of Parable', *Semeia* 2 (1974), pp. 82-112 (90-93).

274. Since Via counts The Wedding Guest among the example stories, three of his example stories have the same surface structure as narrative parables: 'The Wedding Guest displays the same surface structure as The Prodigal Son...' ('Parable and Example Story', p. 118). The only two example stories that do *not* exhibit all five constant textemes found in the narrative parables are The Good Samaritan and The Rich Fool (see p. 127).

275. The Good Samaritan differs from Lazarus and the Rich Man and The Pharisee and the Publican in terms of six textemes; The Good Samaritan shares only four textemes in common with The Rich Fool (see Via, 'Parable and Example Story', p. 127).

276. This same texteme can be found in The Wedding Guest (see 'Parable and Example Story', p. 127), and consequently in all five of the narratives Via considers example stories.

do share formal features in common with the narrative parables.[277]

To be sure, Via advances quite a different assessment of his findings on the formal features characteristic of the narrative parables as opposed to those characteristic of the example stories.[278] Via, it will be recalled, turns to metaphor as a means of expressing his view that there is a fundamental difference between the narrative parables and the example stories, a difference which concerns textemes m and n, o and p. According to Via, the narrative parables are metaphors of the kingdom of God, and he explains this in terms of the relationships between actants defined in textemes m and o, which are two of the constant textemes displayed in all eight narrative parables:

> In order to clarify that the parable itself...is a metaphor, it is necessary to identify the metaphoric tenor (authority figure) and the metaphoric vehicle (the servant-son figure) as both being within the story. And if the parable is to be taken as a parable of the kingdom of God (a new picture of human existence transected by the divine) then the ontological difference between God and man must be supported by the structural distinction between the king-father figure (ordainer) and the servant-son (subject). Or to speak more inductively, that is the way it in fact is in the eight narrative parables.[279]

The example stories are not narrative parables, Via surmises, because in them there is a lack of semantic tension or not enough semantic distance between the divine and the human. The example stories as a

---

277. The same can be said of the structural analysis of the parables performed by Erhardt Güttgemanns ('Narrative Analyse synoptischer Texte', pp. 179-223 [German repr. edn]). Güttgemanns identifies and defines 16 (positive and negative) motifemes. His matrix of motifemes (pp. 220-21) indicates that the motifemes manifest in the *Beispielerzählungen* are also manifest in the *Parabeln*, and that none of the *Beispielerzählungen* exhibits the same pattern, or combination, of motifemes. Indeed, at one point (p. 219) Güttgemanns speaks of the motifeme sequence which is 'text-constitutive' for the genre 'metaphorical narrative' and mentions both *Gleichnis* and *Beispielerzählung* in the same parenthesis ('Für das Genre der metaphorischen Erzählung [*Gleichnis, Beispielerzählung*]...'). Sellin ('Lukas als Gleichniserzähler', pp. 172-73) criticizes Güttgemanns' study, concluding that 'Weder Typisches noch spezifisches der Texte lässt sich mit dieser formalistischen Methode erklären' ('neither the typical nor the specific [attributes] of texts can be explained with this formalistic method'; p. 173).

278. Via, 'A Response to Crossan, Funk, and Petersen', p. 227: 'Therefore, my final conclusion is that the only strong reason for holding The Good Samaritan and its companions to be parables, and not example stories, is the wish that it were so'.

279. Via, 'A Response to Crossan, Funk, and Petersen', p. 226.

group, then, should manifest textemes n and p instead of m and o, but that is not the case. Via identifies textemes n and p in only two example stories, The Good Samaritan and The Rich Fool.[280] Explicitly and repeatedly, Via maintains The Good Samaritan lacks semantic tension between the divine and the human because in it the subject and the ordainer are identical, or are the same figure (texteme n)—the Samaritan.[281] However, Via attenuates the strength of his position with respect to those textemes when he allows that The Wedding Feast is a 'modified' parable even though it manifests textemes n and p, the ordainer and the subject being identical in the figure of the king.[282] Moreover, Via identifies textemes m and o, which are constant textemes in the eight narrative parables, in two of the example stories, The Pharisee and the Publican and Lazarus and the Rich Man.[283] Hence, the example stories as a group show no uniformity among themselves by consistently manifesting textemes n and p, textemes so important to Via's argument that the example stories are not metaphors of the kingdom of God and thus are not parables.

Obviously, Via's literary-structuralist analysis informs his argument that the narrative parables are metaphors of the kingdom of God, but it

280. See Via, 'Parable and Example Story', p. 127. On textemes m and n, o and p, see p. 109.

281. Via, 'Parable and Example Story', pp. 112, 115, 118-19; see also 'A Response to Crossan, Funk, and Petersen', p. 126. Sellin ('Gleichnisstrukturen', p. 114) is of the opinion that Via's argument about The Good Samaritan—that since it has no king or father figure it is not a kingdom of God parable—is the strongest. However, Sellin points out that the relationship of subordination between ordainer and subject is not exclusive to the *Parabeln*; it can be found, Sellin asserts, in three *Beispielerzählungen* (Lk. 12.16-21, 16.19-31, 18.10-14) and in Russian folktales. Sellin suggests that this relationship of subordination between ordainer and subject as such has nothing to do with the kingdom of God since it evidently belongs to the structure of such narratives (tales, sagas, anecdotes) in general. He thinks it probable that in narratives of this sort, which reach back to the mythical, an ancient religious structural principle (God as ordainer, human being as hero) glimmers through.

282. Via, 'Parable and Example Story', p. 115. Additionally, Via notes that this 'modified' parable manifests only two of the five textemes constant in the narrative parables.

283. Via, 'Parable and Example Story', p. 127. Indeed, Lazarus and the Rich Man has a subject who is a son-subordinate figure—the rich man, whom Abraham calls 'child' (τέκνον; Lk. 16.25)—and an ordainer who is a father-figure—Abraham, whom the rich man call 'father' (πάτερ; Lk. 16.24, 27).

should be noted that he must sometimes go outside his inventory of strictly formal features—that is, his analysis of the surface structure, or combinations of textemes—manifest in the narrative parables vis-à-vis the example stories to bolster his claim that the example stories do not evidence as much semantic tension between the divine and the human as do the narrative parables, and it is precisely this lack of semantic tension which makes it exceedingly difficult for Via to conceive of the example stories as metaphors of the kingdom of God.[284] One may well wish to ask whether the direct mention of 'heaven' in The Prodigal Son—which Via deems to be a parable—represents a decrease in, or lack of, semantic tension between the divine and the human. It is readily apparent that Via excludes three example stories—The Rich Fool, The Pharisee and the Publican, Lazarus and the Rich Man—from among the parables because in these narratives there is either a direct appearance by God, or a direct appeal to God, or the 'transcendent world is directly represented in the story', which, in Via's estimation, effectively decreases the semantic tension or distance between the divine and the human characteristic of the narrative parables. Nonetheless, these observations do not lie within the domain of formal features Via establishes in his sequential and actantial analyses and then uses to differentiate the example stories from the narrative parables.

Via strives to identify the formal characteristics in the example stories to substantiate his claim that they are not parables, but he does not succeed in showing that the example stories manifest a peculiar set of formal features (textemes) that both unifies them as a distinctive group of narratives and also distinguishes them from the narrative parables. The decisive warrant invoked by Via as a means of differentiating the example stories from the narrative parables is his definition of the narrative parables as metaphors of the kingdom of God, a definition which

284. Via goes well beyond his sequential and actantial analyses to argue the point that The Wedding Guest is an example story: 'The Wedding Guest displays the same surface structure as The Prodigal Son, and in conformity with the narrative parables God does not appear as a character. However, the indicative modal nuance of the narrative parables has been replaced by the imperative. This means that whereas discourse is subordinate in the narrative parables to story, in The Wedding Guest the story has been absorbed in discourse' ('Parable and Example Story', p. 118). The imperative mood is not one of Via's 16 textemes. Would the appearance of the imperative in a *Gleichnis* (Mt. 5.25//Lk. 12.58) make it an 'example story'?

Crossan calls 'a crucial prescriptive claim'.[285] Unlike Funk and Crossan, among others, Via cannot allow that the example stories have metaphorical qualities of that sort, and therefore he concludes that the example stories are not parables. Via may show to his satisfaction that the example stories are not metaphors and thus are not parables, but is it necessary to deduce from that the conclusion that the example stories are 'moral examples'? Via's deduction will appear to be a non sequitur until formal features are identified in the example stories to indicate that they and they alone, among all the synoptic parables, are 'moral examples'.

Crossan, as we have seen, has no qualms about viewing the example stories as metaphorical parables.[286] Based upon his 'structuralist analysis' of Jesus' parables, Crossan contends that because the example stories manifest a formal feature—a specific texteme—that is fundamental in the deep structure of Jesus' parabolic system, then they quite properly belong among Jesus' parables. Crossan is convinced that '...many of Jesus' parables intend an attack on the UP/DOWN or GOOD/BAD basis of normalcy and that falling or rising plot is secondary to this first purpose'.[287] Accordingly, Crossan defines the elemental texteme of Jesus' parables in this way: '...up/down or good/bad categories of existence are accepted or rejected (y/z)'.[288] He labels the parables of Jesus that manifest texteme y/z as 'parables of reversal', a group which includes The Good Samaritan (Lk. 10.30-35), The Pharisee and Publican (Lk. 18.10-14), The Rich Man and Lazarus (Lk. 16.10-31), The Prodigal Son (Lk. 15.11-32), The Great Feast (Mt. 22.1-10//Lk. 14.16-24//*Gos. Thom.* 81.28–82.3), The Places at Table (Lk. 14.8-10) and The

285. Crossan, 'Structuralist Analysis and the Parables of Jesus', p. 202.
286. This statement must be qualified with several points borne in mind from the previous treatment of Crossan. First, Crossan regards the so-called 'example stories' in their original form in the Jesus tradition as metaphorical parables; he cedes that those narratives in their Lukan form are 'example stories'. Secondly, Crossan later modifies his position and comes to regard those narratives as metonymical parables. Finally, Crossan separates The Rich Fool (a parable of action) from the other example stories (parables of reversal).
287. Crossan, 'Structuralist Analysis and the Parables of Jesus', p. 204. According to Crossan, this texteme is absent in Via's structural analysis and that contributes to the divergences in their studies, especially their opposing views in 'the whole parable versus example discussion' (see pp. 202-203; cf. p. 205).
288. Crossan, 'Structuralist Analysis and the Parables of Jesus', p. 205.

Vineyard Workers (Mt. 20.1-13).[289] As Crossan explains:

> In all these cases we are dealing with parables in which the binary oppo
> sitions of certain positions (Clergy/Samaritan; Pharisee/Publican; Rich
> & healthy/Poor & afflicted) or certain actions (Prodigal Son/Dutiful Son;
> First-seated/Last-seated) or certain situations (Invited Guests/Uninvited
> Guests; First-hired/Last-hired) would be expected to beget certain results
> or conclusions and beget instead the exact opposite, a double and indeed
> a polar reversal.[290]

Even though the parables of reversal as a group do not share exactly
the same actantial structure, according to Crossan, the attack on the
common expectations of normalcy held by Jesus' hearers is still evidenced in the respective actantial structures of these parables because
Jesus consistently fills the actantial roles of giver (G+ and G- in The
Good Samaritan) or receiver (R+ or R- in the remaining parables of
reversal) in polar opposition to what the hearers expect.[291] Thus, it can
be concluded that for Crossan the actantial structure of the parables of
reversal is secondary to the texteme y/z.[292] Since the example stories
(except The Rich Fool) manifest the texteme y/z, they too are parables
of reversal. In Crossan's view, the attack on the deep structure of the
hearer's expectations of normalcy—an attack which profoundly
unnerves the hearer and casts doubts upon her or his principles of

---

289. Crossan, 'Structuralist Analysis and the Parables of Jesus', p. 205. According to Crossan, a group of 'servant parables' also challenges the accepted view of
world (or normalcy) 'postulated by the genre of master/servant stories among
Jesus' rabbinical contemporaries' (p. 211) and is thus found among the parables of
reversal (see p. 214).

290. Crossan, 'Structuralist Analysis and the Parables of Jesus', p. 205.

291. Crossan, 'The Good Samaritan', p. 99. Based upon his modification of the
actantial grid, Crossan makes this point explicitly with regard to the parables of
reversal that have one giver and two receivers (R+ and R-), an actantial structure he
designates as F3 (see pp. 93, 99): 'If we think of R+ and R- as empty slots to be
filled with a story-person, Jesus has consistently filled them in *polar opposition* to
the hearer's expectation' (p. 99; his emphasis). All of the parables of reversal
except The Good Samaritan have structure F3. The Good Samaritan has two givers
(G+ and G-) and one receiver, an actantial structure designated by Crossan as F2.
We can extrapolate from Crossan's analysis of The Good Samaritan that the roles
of G+ and G- are filled in 'polar opposition to the hearer's expectation' (see pp. 96-
98).

292. Again, The Rich Fool is a 'parable of action'.

security, and thereby opens the hearer to the 'possibility of transcendence'[293]—effected by the deep structure of Jesus' parables is what makes them 'metaphors' of the kingdom of God.[294]

The example stories are indeed parables according to Crossan's analysis. They share formal features—most notably, texteme y/z—in common with other parables of reversal. However, the example stories as a group do not manifest the same actantial structure: The Good Samaritan exhibits an actantial structure different from the other parables of reversal, and The Rich Fool is not a parable of reversal.[295] Thus, Crossan's actantial analysis contrasts with Via's: Whereas Via excludes the example stories from among the narrative parables of Jesus because the former, in their actantial structure, do not manifest a relationship of subordination between ordainer and subject (or worse, because several directly represent either the transcendent world or God), Crossan includes the example stories among the parables of Jesus because, regardless of whether or not they have an identical actantial structure, they have actantial roles filled in a fashion contrary to the hearer's expectations of normalcy. The issue of importance for Crossan with regard to the example stories is not whether the transcendent world is somehow directly represented in them, but whether their actantial structure—which actualizes the deep structure—opens the hearers to the 'possibility of transcendence'.

Prior to an examination of Baasland's study of the example stories, in which he devotes himself to the task of providing a comprehensive inventory of the formal characteristics exhibited by the example stories, it may be helpful to pause momentarily and reflect upon some of the

---

293. Crossan, 'The Good Samaritan', p. 82; cf. pp. 98-105. In this article, Crossan wants to give a definition for the genre 'parable' that would also include parables such as the book of Jonah, as well as the parables of Kafka and Brecht. He writes: 'Like all these, the Good Samaritan attacks the hearer's deep structure of expectation and thereby and therein opens one to the possibility of transcendence' (p. 82).

294. Crossan, 'Structuralist Analysis and the Parables of Jesus', p. 216. Crossan's own words to explain the difference between his view of parable and example and that of Via are more precise: '...(i) it is the *structure* of Jesus' parabolic system which is a metaphor for the *structure* of the Kingdom of God, and (ii) this is to be read ontologically and not morally' (pp. 216-17; emphasis his).

295. The Rich Fool, then, shares formal features in common with other parables of action (see 'Structuralist Analysis and the Parables of Jesus', pp. 214-15 n. 3; *In Parables*, pp. 79-120, 85).

findings obtained in this review of several studies in which formal
characteristics of the example stories have been identified. Regardless
of the position advanced by the respective analysts with regard to the
status of the *Beispielerzählungen* as 'example stories' or 'parables', the
preceding analyses suggest at least two things: first, that the four example stories as a group do not manifest identical formal characteristics;
secondly, that this group of four narratives share formal characteristics
in common with other *Parabeln*. Tangentially, we have observed that
when the formal characteristics of this group of four narratives are
evaluated in terms of a view of the 'parable as metaphor', some—or all
four—resist being identified as 'metaphorical parables'.[296] Baasland's
analysis, which at almost every turn issues a challenge to the claim that
the *Beispielerzählungen* are 'formally quite distinct' from the *Parabeln*,
corroborates these findings.

Baasland is determined to decide the issue of the status of the
Beispielerzählungen as a special genre (*Gattung*) not on the basis of
whether they are or are not 'metaphorical parables', but on the basis of
whether they exhibit enough common formal characteristics to demonstrate that they share a common formal structure.[297] Baasland contends
that formal criteria are normally decisive in attempts to establish the
existence of a genre; 'however', he asserts, 'a common formal structure
cannot be demonstrated in the example narratives'.[298] Thus, Baasland
rejects the thesis that the *Beispielerzählungen* comprise a special genre.
He does concede that there are certain features, or aspects of narrative
technique, characteristic to the 'so-called example narratives', but he
stipulates that a consideration of the accidence of the synoptic parables

296. This is the case with four studies we have reviewed in which some sort of
view of the parable as metaphor is advanced. For Funk, The Good Samaritan is
clearly a metaphorical parable; he does not vigorously argue that the remaining
Beispielerzählungen are metaphorical parables. Crossan does maintain that all of
the so-called *Beispielerzählungen* (as spoken by Jesus) are poetic metaphors and
thus parables, although he later claims that the *Beispielerzählungen* (as spoken by
Jesus) are metonymical parables. Sellin contends that the *Beispielerzählungen* are
parables, but that they are 'no longer metaphorical'. Via forcefully posits that the
Beispielerzählungen are not metaphorical and thus are not parables.

297. Baasland ('Zum Beispiel der Beispielerzählungen', p. 205 n. 48) overtly
avoids a view of the parable as metaphor.

298. Baasland, 'Zum Beispiel der Beispielerzählungen', p. 197: 'Für eine Gattung sind normalerweise formale Kriterien ausschlaggebend; eine gemeinsame
formale Struktur lässt sich in den Beispielerzählungen aber nicht nachweisen'.

provides the proper frame of reference for viewing those characteristic features.[299] In order to make his case, Baasland constructs a new classificatory grid, an accidence of the synoptic parables, based upon the formal features of plot and character, which then becomes the vantage point from which he assesses the propriety of one familiar category of parable accepted widely by parable scholars, the *Beispielerzählungen*.

Baasland begins his analysis proper by identifying the plot patterns (*Handlungsmuster*) manifest in the synoptic parables.[300] He labels the four plot patterns found in the narrative parables as follows: (1) 'sow-grow-harvest' (or 'fish-catch'), (2) 'commission-stewardship-reckoning', (3) 'plans made-plans accomplished', and (4) 'need-call for help-outcome'.[301] While the first and second plot patterns exhibit a rather uniform 'thematic', growth and stewardship, respectively, the third and fourth plot patterns exhibit a wider variety of thematics.[302] According to Baasland, the *Beispielerzählungen* bear the imprint of the 'need-call for help-outcome' plot pattern in that either a need in relation to God or a

299. Baasland, 'Zum Beispiel der Beispielerzählungen', p. 200.

300. With limited explanation, Baasland ('Zum Beispiel der Beispielerzählungen', p. 202) distinguishes between plot (*Handlungsmuster*) and sujet, or narrative framework (*Erzählgerüst*). He remains convinced that the *Erzählgerüst* is an important factor for the classification of the parables (contra, he claims, Funk and Via [see pp. 202, 211]), but that it is important to consider the *Erzählgerüst* when interpreting the parables. For a brief, clear statement on the difference between *Handlungsmuster* and *Erzählgerüst*, see Erhardt Güttgemanns, 'Introductory Remarks Concerning the Structural Study of Narrative', *Semeia* 6 (1976), pp. 23-33, esp. p. 100 n. 5 (William G. Doty's translation of 'Einleitende Bemerkungen zur strukturalen Erzählforschung', *LB* 23/24 [1973], pp. 2-47).

301. For references to specific parables, see Baasland, 'Zum Beispiel der Beispielerzählungen', pp. 202-204. Additionally, Baasland identifies the plot of the shorter parables which are not made into narratives as 'activity—an expected reaction/action' (see p. 204).

302. Baasland, 'Zum Beispiel der Beispielerzählungen', pp. 202-204. According to Baasland, the plot pattern 'plans made-plans accomplished' can have to do with: meals and weddings, thus the thematic 'invite-celebrate'; or something valuable, like a treasure or pearl, and thus the thematic 'seek-find'; or building a home, a tower, a storehouse; or actions against other people; or problems relating to debts and money (p. 203). The plot pattern 'need-call for help-outcome' can also have to do with the need imposed by a situation involving debt, or one involving something lost (p. 204). He later (pp. 206-207) utilizes the 'thematic' of the various plot patterns to discuss the variations in narrative frameworks (*Erzählgerüsts*).

neighbor's need serve as the point of departure or aim of the narratives, although he points out that a clear situation of need is presupposed only in two (Lk. 16.19-31 and 10.30-37).[303]

Baasland then examines the actors (*Akteure*) who appear in the synoptic parables. He affirms the assumption that Jesus, in constructing his parables, drew upon certain biblical images or metaphors for God and the Jewish people, images that would have been readily understood by Jesus' audience.[304] Baasland states that interpreters ought to be cognizant of the content of the metaphors in Jesus' parables by investigating the connotations they evoke in relation to the biblical tradition and to reality; however, he posits that certain metaphors are simply more suitable to a particular plot pattern than others, and that in many instances a specific plot pattern necessarily requires certain metaphors. Thus, the plot pattern 'sow-grow-harvest' requires unconditionally the use of either a sower or farmer as actor;[305] and the plot pattern 'commission-stewardship-reckoning' requires certain actors, which are then used as metaphors, such as kings, rich men, vineyard keepers, workers, servants.[306] The other plot patterns remain more open to the type of actors required, and thus the thematic determines the choice of metaphor. For instance, the thematic 'invite-celebrate' in the plot pattern 'plans made-plans accomplished' seems to require the pair of actors 'host and guests'.[307] The plot pattern 'need-call for help-outcome' is even more open to various kinds of actors because 'need' and 'calling for help' both belong to the human condition. According to Baasland, while a call for help may be addressed to anyone, it is more likely that it would be addressed to householders, judges, priests or

303. Baasland, 'Zum Beispiel der Beispielerzählungen', p. 204.

304. Baasland, 'Zum Beispiel der Beispielerzählungen', p. 205: 'For example, in the Old Testament God is represented as father, king, judge, shepherd. Israel is the vineyard, the grapevine, the flock, etc. The final judgment corresponds to the harvest, the vintage, and the eschatological final consummation to the marriage, the banquet'.

305. Baasland, 'Zum Beispiel der Beispielerzählungen', p. 205. Baasland points out that, perhaps apart from Mt. 13.24-30, the sower or farmer remains in the background, and that in the Old Testament neither 'sower' nor 'farmer' are used directly as metaphors for God. It should be noted that Baasland must add the actor 'fisherman' with regard to the parables which exhibit the plot pattern 'fish-catch' (see p. 206).

306. Baasland, 'Zum Beispiel der Beispielerzählungen', p. 206.

307. Baasland, 'Zum Beispiel der Beispielerzählungen', p. 206.

Levites, or simply to God; correspondingly, while anyone may come to find herself or himself in a situation of need, it is not uncommon to find widows and poor people in a perpetual state of need.[308]

Based upon the results of his analysis of plot patterns and actors in the synoptic parables, Baasland constructs a grid of four parable types. Each type of parable has a characteristic plot pattern and characteristic actors, the kinds of actors appearing in each type being dependent upon the plot structure.[309] The growth parables (*Wachstumsgleichnisse*) have the plot pattern 'sow-harvest' (or 'fish-catch'), and may have as actors a farmer, a gardener, a sower (or a fisherman): Mk 4.3ff., 4.26ff., 4.29ff., (13.28ff.); Lk. 13.6ff.; Mt. 13.24ff., 13.33, 13.47ff. The stewardship parables (*Verwaltungsgleichnisse*) have the plot pattern 'commission-stewardship-reckoning', and may have as actors a king, a servant, a householder, a vineyard keeper, a worker: Mk 12.1ff., 13.33ff.; Mt. 20.1ff., 21.28ff., 24.25, 25.1ff., 25.14ff.; Lk. 15.11ff., 16.1ff., 17.7ff. The operation parables (*Einsatzgleichnisse*)[310] have the plot pattern 'plans made-plans accomplished', and may have as actors a man, a woman, a king, a rich man, a merchant: Lk. 11.5, 11.11ff., 14.7-25 (Mt. 22.1-13), 14.28ff., 12.16ff., 14.30ff., 15.11ff., 16.3ff., 18.1ff.; Mt. 7.24ff., 13.44ff., (Lk. 15.3ff., 15.8ff.); Mk 3.27. The need/help parables (*Not/Hilfe-gleichnisse*) have the plot pattern 'need-call for help-outcome', and may have as actors a king, a servant, a judge, a widow, a householder, a steward, a father, a son, a shepherd, a flock: Mt. 18.21ff., 5.25ff.; Lk. 7.41ff., 16.3ff., 18.1ff., (15.11ff., [15.3ff.],

---

308. Baasland, 'Zum Beispiel der Beispielerzählungen', p. 206.

309. Baasland, 'Zum Beispiel der Beispielerzählungen', pp. 206-207. Baasland lists principally those actors that may be used as metaphors; note that he does not include, e.g. a priest, a Levite, a Samaritan, a Pharisee, a tax collector, God, Abraham, Lazarus. A word of caution about Baasland's chart is necessary: The actors he lists do not always correspond precisely to the group of parables on the same line. (Where in any *Beispielerzählung* does a shepherd or a flock appear?)

310. This translation of 'Einsatzgleichnisse' into English is rather inexact. I understand Baasland to mean by the term 'Einsatz' a bringing into operation, a bringing into action, or a bringing into effect the plans that are made and then accomplished. If one prefers to translate 'Einsatz' as an adjective, then perhaps either 'effective parables' or 'operational parables' may be a better rendering. Baasland observes that many *Einsatzgleichnisse* are τίς-ἐξ-ὑμῶν parables, but he argues (against Greeven) that these *Gleichnisse* do not comprise a specific *Gattung* (see 'Zum Beispiel der Beispielerzählungen', pp. 207-209).

15.8ff.), 10.30ff., 16.19ff., 18.9ff., (12.16ff.).[311] This, then, is Baasland's version of an accidence of the synoptic parables, and this accidence provides the framework for his consideration of the uniqueness of the example stories. Before he directs his attention to specific aspects of narrative technique evident in the example stories, Baasland makes an important concession about his scheme of parable types.

Baasland is aware that two types of parables display variations in their narrative frameworks (*Erzählgerüsts*) to the extent that the same formal construction cannot always be discerned, which is the case especially in the operation parables and the need/help parables. Although in the operation parables he lists six variations of narrative frameworks and in the need/help parables three, Baasland asserts that it is precisely the plot pattern (*Handlungsmuster*) that gives the parables in each group a similar structure. Nevertheless, Baasland must concede that a few of the narrative parables can be said to manifest two, or even three, different plot patterns.[312]

As a control to his classification of the parables, Baasland gives attention to the referential function of the plot pattern of each group. That certain plot patterns and actors are natural bearers of certain material concerns is no accident; thus, it follows, in Baasland's view, that drawing a distinct or fixed border between *Bildhälfte* and *Sachhälfte*—as Jülicher and others are wont to do—must be called into question. However, the alternative of maintaining an identity between those two planes in the parables is unacceptable to Baasland 'because an inference procedure [*Sclussverfahren*] *a minore ad majus*, from the immanent to the transcendent, from the part to the whole, must always

---

311. Baasland, 'Zum Beispiel der Beispielerzählungen', pp. 206-207. I reproduce the references to the parables as given by Baasland. Unfortunately, misunderstandings may unavoidably arise due to the manner in which Baasland charts his scheme.

312. Baasland, 'Zum Beispiel der Beispielerzählungen', pp. 207-208. It may be the case that the general nature of the plot patterns as identified by Baasland is what allows him to see a similarity in structure among the operation parables and among the need/help parables. Baasland himself points out that several parables (he gives Lk. 15.11ff. as the only sample) can be said to manifest two or three plot patterns. By my count, he lists four parables in two different groups (Lk. 12.16ff., 18.1ff., 15.3ff., 15.8ff.) and two parables in three groups (Lk. 15.11ff. and 16.1ff.). Note that The Foolish Rich Man, a *Beispielerzählung*, is listed primarily among the *Einsatzgleichnisse* and parenthetically with the other *Beispielerzählungen* as a *Not/Hilfe-gleichnisse* (p. 207).

be presupposed'.[313] That presupposition permits Baasland to postulate that the plot patterns of three types of parables intend the inference *a minore ad majus*: from actions in, and their effect upon, nature to the coming kingdom of God (growth parables); from actions in daily life to actions with reference to the kingdom of God (stewardship parables); or from the depiction of certain actions opposite other actions to actions of God or Jesus in relation to the actions of humans (operation parables).[314] It is at this point that Baasland detects what he regards as a peculiarity of the example stories.

Baasland issues a generalization about narrative parables, one which pertains to some operation parables and to some need/help parables: 'In general, the narrative parables which depict certain actions vis-à-vis others [other actions] presuppose an inference a minore ad majus to the actions of God/Jesus vis-à-vis us'.[315] According to Baasland, the example stories belong to the need/help type of parable, a type which as a whole often contains some sort of saving actions (*rettende Handlungen*) that, *a minore ad majus*, point to the actions of God or Jesus vis-à-vis us, or saving actions that can be a model (*Vorbild*) to serve as a contrast to our actions.[316] Baasland does not say the same for the example stories:

> On this point, the so-called example narratives appear to have a certain peculiarity. The deficiency of the actions (egoistical actions, self-satisfaction) that are represented here permit no inference *a minore ad majus*. No correspondence to the 'transcendent' plane is intimated or at all possible. Here, that is to say, the egoistic way of acting is set against the judgment (court) of God (Jesus). The 'court scene' is not located in the narrative itself, as is the case in the stewardship parables, rather in the application and always directly as the judgment of Jesus (God).[317]

313. Baasland, 'Zum Beispiel der Beispielerzählungen', p. 208.

314. Baasland offers a more detailed explanation; see 'Zum Beispiel der Beispielerzählungen', pp. 208-209.

315. Baasland, 'Zum Beispiel der Beispielerzählungen', p. 209: 'Im allgemeinen setzen die Gleichniserzählungen, die bestimmte Handlungen gegenüber anderen darstellen, einen Scluss a minore ad majus zu Gottes/Jesu Handlungen uns gegenüber voraus' (no italics appear in the original).

316. Baasland, 'Zum Beispiel der Beispielerzählungen', p. 209. As parables which present saving actions that can be a model (*Vorbild*), Baasland lists Mt. 18.21ff., 5.25; Lk. 15.3ff., cf. Mt. 18.10ff.; perhaps also Lk. 10.30ff. and Lk. 16.3ff.

317. Baasland, 'Zum Beispiel der Beispielerzählungen', p. 209: 'In diesem Punkt scheinen die sog. Beispielerzählungen eine gewisse Eigenart zu haben. Die Mängel

For this reason, in Baasland's opinion, negative 'examples' are predominant in the example narratives, the only positive 'examples' being the Samaritan and the toll collector.[318] In spite of all that, Baasland resists speaking of an identical nature of *Bildhälfte* and *Sachhälfte* in the example stories. His preference, as we have seen, is to regard at least two of the example narratives—The Merciful Samaritan and The Pharisee and the Toll Collector, parables in which the 'thematic love of God and love of neighbor' is clearly expounded—as synecdochical.[319]

Having noted this peculiarity of the example stories, Baasland proceeds to examine the formal aspects of their narrative framework (*Erzählgerüst*) in more detail.[320] Baasland previously identified the narrative framework of the example stories as 'situation of need-way out/request-outcome'. Now he simply remarks that in The Merciful Samaritan, and perhaps also in The Rich Man and Poor Lazarus, the emphasis falls on the 'situation of need'; in the remaining example stories, where the situation of need is not clearly identified, the stress lies on the 'outcome'.[321]

The relationships between actors next receives Baasland's consideration. According to him, in the parables the fundamental relationships among the actors are that of master-servant and that of two persons of equal rank. In the example stories, two actors are set against each other:

Luke 10.30ff.:	Priest and Levite–Samaritan
	Robber–Samaritan
Luke 18.9ff.:	Pharisee–Toll Collector
Luke 16.9ff.:	Rich Man–Lazarus
(Luke 14.7ff.:	A Proud Man–A Humble Man).[322]

der Handlungen (egoistische Handlungen, Selbstzufriedenheit), die hier dargestellt sind, erlauben keinen Schluss *a minore ad majus*. Keine Entsprechung auf der "transzendenten" Ebene ist angedeutet oder überhaupt möglich. Hier ist nämlich die egoistische Handlungsweise dem Urteil (Gericht) Gottes (Jesu) gegenübergestellt. Die "Gerichtszene" liegt nicht in der Erzählung selbst, wie es in den Verwaltungsgleichnissen der Fall ist, sondern in der Anwendung und immer direkt als Urteil Jesu (Gottes)'.

318. Baasland, 'Zum Beispiel der Beispielerzählungen', pp. 209-10.

319. Baasland, 'Zum Beispiel der Beispielerzählungen', p. 210.

320. Recall that for Baasland the *Erzählgerüst* does not hold much significance in terms of categorizing the parables, but it does give indications of the intended interpretations of the parables (see 'Zum Beispiel der Beispielerzählungen', p. 211).

321. Baasland, 'Zum Beispiel der Beispielerzählungen', p. 211; cf. p. 207.

322. Baasland, 'Zum Beispiel der Beispielerzählungen', p. 212.

These contrasts, Baasland asserts, point to two distinguishable standards of living, one characterized by riches and self-satisfaction and the other characterized by love of God and love of neighbor. He conjectures that The Foolish Rich Man may be ironic in that the farmer stands alone, without relation to God or neighbor.[323]

Baasland then returns to the issue of the metaphorical (or 'intended') language in the parables. He argues that many parables employ well-known metaphors which have clear intentions because they are familiar metaphors within the 'linguistic universe' of the speaker and hearer (for instance, against the background of the Hebrew scriptures, metaphors such as 'harvest', 'vineyard', 'father', 'son' would have rather clear meanings).[324] However, Baasland posits that in the example stories—with the possible exception of The Merciful Samaritan, in which the actions of the Samaritan might be analogous to the actions of Jesus—there is a dearth of intended language: 'The actions or states of affairs are so designed that the picture-world (*Bildwelt*) corresponds both to actual reality in the life of Jesus and also to the history of Israel or, as the case may be, to texts of the Old Testament brought to mind'.[325]

Finally, Baasland examines a few of the unusual or atypical features in the parables and offers his observations on them from the perspective of 'an aesthetics of reception', focusing specifically on features in the parables that are constructed in such a way as to function as signals for how the parable is to be received by the hearer.[326] He points out that the parables contain not only ordinary features (such as repetition and detail), but also unusual features (such as hyperbole and extravagance), both of which serve to guide the attention of the hearers.[327] According to Baasland, the parables do indeed persuade the hearer, but they also surprise and arouse the hearer. On the one hand, the parables engage the hearer in a certain way:

> As analogical speech, the parables structure a world which in decisive points is similar to that of the hearers. The hearer is *interwoven into this*

323. Baasland, 'Zum Beispiel der Beispielerzählungen', p. 212.
324. Baasland, 'Zum Beispiel der Beispielerzählungen', p. 212.
325. Baasland, 'Zum Beispiel der Beispielerzählungen', p. 213.
326. Baasland, 'Zum Beispiel der Beispielerzählungen', pp. 213-17. Baasland admits that this approach to the parables is really nothing new since many interpreters—e.g. Jülicher and several who come after him—have been interested in pragmatic or functional aspects of the parables (p. 214).
327. Baasland, 'Zum Beispiel der Beispielerzählungen', pp. 213-14.

world and must *take a position* towards *the actions of the (co-)actors.*[328]

On the other hand, the unusual features of the parables have an 'estrangement effect'. When confronted by 'atypical features' in the parables (such as hyperbole), the hearer is challenged to consider whether her or his world corresponds in an analogical way to the world structured by the parable.[329] Baasland submits that the example stories do not 'surprise' the hearer by means of various unusual features like those found in the other parables; rather, the example narratives surprise the hearer by means of the choice of actors depicted therein and by the application.[330] Baasland elaborates upon this feature of the example stories vis-à-vis the other parables as follows.

The example narratives, Baasland argues, provoke the hearer toward a special kind of engagement. He asserts that in all the parables which portray the actions of specific characters an identification process is unavoidable. The hearer must decide with which character to identify and which character serves as an example (*exemplum*) for the proper action: 'Here, the stewardship parables are more important than those named "example narratives" in the research'.[331] Nevertheless, the example stories demand a special engagement because, first of all, the plot pattern 'need-call for help-outcome' is extremely well-suited for inducing the hearer to identify with characters and, 'second, in three of the narratives of this genre [*Gattung*] the (contrasted) characters and groups are called by name'.[332] Baasland contends that the first hearers of these narratives would have identified themselves directly with the priest, the Levite and the Pharisee, not with the Samaritan, Lazarus or the toll collector. But, in Baasland's view,

> ...the parables are narrated so that one identifies with the wrong characters/groups; for this reason, the application comes as a surprise. God (Jesus) measures action differently than the hearer; the narratives are in this sense 'parables of reversal' (J.D. Crossan).[333]

328. Baasland, 'Zum Beispiel der Beispielerzählungen', p. 215; Baasland's emphasis.
329. Baasland, 'Zum Beispiel der Beispielerzählungen', p. 215.
330. Baasland, 'Zum Beispiel der Beispielerzählungen', p. 215.
331. Baasland, 'Zum Beispiel der Beispielerzählungen', p. 215.
332. Baasland, 'Zum Beispiel der Beispielerzählungen', p. 215.
333. Baasland, 'Zum Beispiel der Beispielerzählungen', pp. 215-16. It remains unclear whether Baasland intends for this to apply to all the *Gleichnisse* or to just the *Beispielerzählungen*: 'M.E. werden die Gleichnisse so erzählt, dass man sich

In summing up his analysis of the formal features of the example stories, Baasland attempts to put the putative peculiarities of those narratives in perspective.

> The research since Jülicher has viewed the peculiar connection between *Bildhälfte* and *Sachhälfte* as characteristic for the so-called example narratives. If, however, the boundary between *Bild* and *Sache* is not so sharply drawn in the remaining parables, this (relative) peculiarity must be determined differently. We have seen that in these parables the audience is 'in the narrative'. (How does the auditor act vis-à-vis one who requires help? Like the Samaritan or like the priest/Levite? Does he pray in the temple like the Pharisee or the toll collector?) However, in the so-called example narratives the *Sache* is also 'in the narrative'. Love of God and love of neighbor is directly the thematic of these narratives.[334]

Baasland concludes that the category '*Beispielerzählung*' cannot be retained for the Lukan parables ('10.30ff; 12.16ff; 16.19ff; 18.9ff [or also 14.7ff and 15.11ff?]') designated as such by researchers.[335] As he puts it, 'Neither by formal criteria nor by "examples" can this genre be established'.[336] Having stated this conclusion, Baasland immediately cedes that the *Beispielerzählungen* indeed have a peculiarity which has been emphasized by researchers, but he points out that the distinctive marks of the example narratives only rarely are evidenced in those narratives alone, for in fact they can be found in the other parables as well. To illustrate his point, Baasland lists the various attributes ascertained in the example narratives that purportedly establish the peculiarity of that category:

> —Contrast between two groups (not in Lk. 12.16ff.; also in Lk. 14.7ff. and in the stewardship parables).
> —The plot pattern (only limited in Lk. 18.9ff. and perhaps indirectly in Lk. 12.16ff.; also other parables have this pattern).
> —Synecdoche (*exemplum* as demand only in Lk. 10.37; positive and negative *exempla* also in the stewardship parables and the operation parables).
> —Coined metaphors are lacking (lacking also in other parables).

mit den falschen Personen/ Gruppen identifiziert; die Anwendung kommt deshalb als Überraschung. Gott (Jesus) misst die Handlung anders als die Hörer; die Erzählungen sind in diesem Sinne "Gleichnisse der Verkehrung" (J.D. Crossan)'.

334. Baasland, 'Zum Beispiel der Beispielerzählungen', p. 217.
335. Baasland, 'Zum Beispiel der Beispielerzählungen', p. 217.
336. Baasland, 'Zum Beispiel der Beispielerzählungen', p. 217: 'Weder durch formale Kriterien noch durch "Beispiele" kann man diese Gattung begründen'.

—God is directly addressed (not however in Lk. 10.30ff.; 18.9ff., perhaps in 15.18 and 16.8?).
—The judgment of Jesus/God in the 'application' (Lk. 10.37, 16.22ff., 18.14; also Lk. 12.20f., 14.11; but also Lk. 16.8).
—Love of God and love of neighbor is thematized in the narratives (in all, but—aside from Lk. 10.30ff.—very general).
—The application signifies a reversal (Lk. 16.19ff., 18.9ff.; also Lk. 12.16ff., 14.7ff.).
—Characters and groups are called by name.[337]

On the basis of this tabulation of attributes, Baasland posits that only a 'relative peculiarity of the so-called example narratives'—the scope of which is difficult to demarcate—can be discerned, but he re-emphasizes that this relative peculiarity must be viewed within the framework of an accidence of the parables.[338]

Baasland successfully demonstrates that the example narratives share a substantial number of features in common with other narrative parables in the synoptic tradition. His list of attributes said to be characteristic of the example narratives shows graphically that the distinction between *Beispielerzählung* and *Parabel* is tenuous because many of the formal characteristics identified in the *Beispielerzählungen* are also exhibited by the *Parabeln*. In addition, his analysis, which indicates that the example narratives do not exhibit the same plot pattern, lends support to his assertion that no common formal structure can be ascertained in the *Beispielerzählungen*.[339] Therefore, Baasland is quite

337. Baasland, 'Zum Beispiel der Beispielerzählungen', p. 218.
338. Baasland, 'Zum Beispiel der Beispielerzählungen', pp. 218-19.
339. See 'Zum Beispiel der Beispielerzählungen', p. 203, where Baasland states that The Foolish Rich Man must be viewed within the framework of the 'plans made-plans accomplished' plot pattern, and thus belongs to the *Einsatzgleichnisse* (cf. p. 207). He later remarks that the 'need-call for help-outcome' plot pattern is 'limited in 18.9ff.' (p. 218). Yet another study which focuses on aspects of plot in the synoptic parables shows that some *Beispielerzählungen* are very similar to some *Parabeln*. Tolbert (*Perspectives on the Parables*, p. 74) suggests that the surface patterns of the parables can be explored by determining how many actions are involved in the plot of the narrative. She states that 'among the parables that involve two actions there appear to be two major formal types of a very general nature: a concentric circle type and a parallel plot type'. In the concentric circle parables (e.g. 'the Wicked Tenants, the Unjust Steward, and the Unmerciful Servant') a first action begins, a second action begins and ends, and then the initial action ends. In the parallel plot parables (e.g. 'the Prodigal Son, the Workers in the Vineyard, the Pharisee and the Publican, and the Two Sons') a first action begins

justified in his conclusion that the genre *'Beispielerzählung'*, since it cannot be substantiated on the basis of formal criteria, cannot be maintained for the group of Lukan narratives designated as such by parable scholars.

Baasland is less successful in demonstrating that the example narratives manifest a 'relative peculiarity' because his notion of what constitutes that 'relative peculiarity' does not rest primarily upon formal criteria, rather it is dependent upon his assumption that in the parables 'an inference procedure *a minore ad majus*, from the immanent to the transcendent, from the part to the whole, must always be presupposed'. Baasland feels compelled to concede that the example narratives have a 'relative peculiarity' mainly for reasons that pertain to a putative 'peculiar connection' between their *Bildhälfte* and *Sachhälfte*. This is most evident when Baasland states that, unlike the other narrative parables which depict certain actions opposite other actions and presuppose an inference procedure *a minore ad majus* to God's or Jesus' actions vis-à-vis humans, the example narratives present actions so deficient that they preclude such an inference; in fact, as he puts it, in the example narratives 'no correspondence to the "transcendent" plane is intimated or at all possible'. Thus, Baasland claims that 'in the so-called *Beispielerzählungen* the *Sache* is also "in the narrative"', by which he means 'love of God and love of neighbor is directly the thematic of these narratives'—a curious claim in light of his contention that in the example narratives the actions depicted are deficient and that in them negative examples predominate. Even Baasland must admit later that this thematic, love of God and love of neighbor, is 'very general' in all of the example narratives except The Merciful Samaritan.[340]

and ends, then a second action begins and ends. Tolbert asserts that observations about the manner of discourse in the parable can assist in discerning patterns in the surface structure of the narrative, which in turn act as guides 'in noting the emphases and nuances of the plot' (p. 75). According to her analysis, The Two Sons (Mt. 21.28-31)—a *Parabel*—and The Pharisee and the Publican—a *Beispielerzählung*—exhibit remarkably similar patterns in plot and surface structure (see pp. 75-77).

340. Baasland, 'Zum Beispiel der Beispielerzählungen', p. 218. Baasland is inconsistent on this point, stating first (p. 204) that a clear situation of need is presupposed in only two example narratives (The Rich Man and Poor Lazarus and The Merciful Samaritan) and then secondly (p. 210) that the thematic 'love of God and love of neighbor' is clearly expounded in The Merciful Samaritan and the Pharisee and the Toll Collector. I leave aside the question of how The Foolish Rich Man,

The inference procedure presupposed by Baasland is not a formal feature of the narrative parables or the example narratives, and, consequently, his notion of the 'relative peculiarity' of the example narratives is relativized even further.

Baasland's analysis shows that the uniqueness of the example narratives is not that they alone, as a special group or genre of synoptic parables, provide positive or negative examples because the parables he calls operation parables and stewardship parables (and even other need/help parables) do so, too. Like those parables, according to Baasland, the example narratives portray actions of specific characters or groups, often posing contrasts between characters or groups, and require that the hearer decide which character or group serves as an example for the proper action. He suggests that the parables are narrated in such a manner that the hearer identifies with the wrong character or group, and thus the application surprises the hearer. Baasland points out that three of the example narratives, however, induce the hearer to identify with named characters or groups.[341] At this point, Baasland mentions—perhaps unwittingly—a single feature which is manifest in all four *Beispielerzählungen*: All four example narratives depict characters who are identified specifically by proper name or by the name of the group to which they belong. The last item in Baasland's list, which seemingly applies to all the example narratives and excludes all the other parables, calls attention to itself.

Naming People: An Aspect of Character in the Example Stories

That named characters or groups of characters appear in the example stories has not gone completely unnoticed, but it remains an issue that has received uneven notice. The name given to the poor man in one example story has attracted the most attention. Jones observes that the

which exhibits a different plot pattern ('plans made-plans accomplished') and a different thematic ('building-result') than the other *Beispielerzählungen*, can then be said to manifest the same thematic found in the other three *Beispielerzählungen*, which exhibit the plot pattern 'need-call for help-outcome'.

341. In the list of attributes identified in the *Beispielerzählungen*, the only item that does not have citations referring to other parables is the last: 'Characters and groups are called by name' (see 'Zum Beispiel der Beispielerzählungen', p. 218). Earlier, Baasland states that this applies to three *Beispielerzählungen* (p. 215), and from the ensuing comments there it can be surmised that he does not regard The Foolish Rich Man as having this feature.

characters in Jesus' parables are usually anonymous or nameless, and
remarks that 'only one of the parabolic characters is given a name:
Lazarus...'[342] Another authority on the parables, Jeremias, agrees:
'Lazarus is the only figure of a parable who receives a name...'[343]
Other scholars duplicate the comment that The Rich Man and Poor
Lazarus is the only parable in which a character, Lazarus, is called by
proper name.[344] Despite the unanimity of opinion, that observation is
only partially accurate, for in the very same parable—and only a few
sentences later (Lk. 16.22)—another character, Abraham, is identified
by his proper name. The issue of names in the synoptic parables, however, extends beyond the proper names given two personages in The
Rich Man and Poor Lazarus.

The Merciful Samaritan, as other scholars have noted, contains the
names of specific groups and the names of specific places. James
Breech, who considers The Good Samaritan to be one of 12 parables
authentic to Jesus, states that 'this is the only parable which includes
place names (Jerusalem, Jericho) or the identification of characters by
cultural code (Samaritan, priest, Levite)'.[345] Crossan also notices the
naming of specific groups and specific places in this parable:

> In 10:30 the *Jewish* traveller was specified as such indirectly by three
> topographical indices: Jerusalem, down, Jericho. We now have three

342. Jones, *The Art and Truth of the Parables*, p. 124.
343. Jeremias, *Die Gleichnisse Jesu*, p. 183. Hendrickx (*The Parables of Jesus*,
p. 200) makes a similar remark.
344. See Flusser, *Die rabbinischen Gleichnisse und der Gleichniserzähler Jesu*,
p. 293. Two more scholars agree, and they concur on another aspect of this parable
as well. Scott (*Hear Then the Parable*, p. 141) writes: 'In only one parable does a
character have a proper name, and in only one parable is a scene from the afterlife
depicted'. Donahue (*The Gospel in Parable*, p. 169) states: 'This parable has certain unique features: only here does a character have a proper name, Lazarus, and
only here is the action mythological, that is, taking place in both the earthly and
heavenly spheres'. (The phrase 'heavenly spheres' is an oversight; Donahue is
aware that Hades is not 'heavenly' [see p. 171].)
345. Breech, *The Silence of Jesus*, p. 162. He excludes all other example stories
from this core group of Jesus' authentic parables. Breech thinks that the place
names and the identification of characters by cultural code are 'secondary Christian
additions', and therefore he expunges them from this parable (see p. 163). His view
receives the endorsement of James Champion ('The Parable as an Ancient and
Modern Form', *Journal of Literature & Theology* 3 [1989], pp. 16-39 [30-32]),
who regards the geographical and cultural codes as interpolations that should be
bracketed.

further specifications, but of a socio-religious nature: Priest, Levite, Samaritan. These six rubrics are extremely important because, (i) they represent an intrusion from historical reality into what one assumes to be a fictional narration, and (ii) with regard to Jesus' parabolic system, such an extensive intrusion of 'reality' never occurs again.[346]

Crossan nevertheless points out that 'reality' does intrude again in other 'examples': 'Note, for example, Pharisee, publican, Temple in Luke 18:10; or (maybe) the name Lazarus in Luke 16:20, both of which I would argue are also parables become examples'.[347] Crossan's observation about 'an intrusion from historical reality into what one assumes to be a fictional narration', perhaps, is a factor that contributed to his decision to revise his view of three example stories—The Good Samaritan, The Rich Man and Lazarus, and The Pharisee and the Publican—as being metonymical parables in which 'parts-of-world' (that is, parts of the 'real' world) are used to subvert that world and reduce it to paradox.[348] Be that as it may, Crossan's remarks indicate that three of the example stories name specific characters or groups of characters and that two example stories name specific places; moreover, his remarks intimate that because of this 'intrusion from historical reality' these are a different kind of parable, or indeed 'parables become examples'. The 'intrusion' of specifically named places in the example stories calls for closer inspection.

Crossan identifies an interesting feature apparent in two example stories. In his terms, The Good Samaritan and The Pharisee and the Publican have 'topographical indices' (Jerusalem and Jericho in the former, the temple in the latter) which represent 'an intrusion from historical reality'. What of the other two example stories? The Foolish Rich Man provides no specific name for its setting; rather, it presupposes a general agrarian setting, as is also the case in a number of other parables.[349]

346. Crossan, 'Structural Analysis and the Parables of Jesus', p. 199; emphasis his.

347. Crossan, 'Structural Analysis and the Parables of Jesus', p. 216 n. 8.

348. See Crossan, *Raid on the Articulate*, p. 108. Drawing upon Roman Jakobsen's distinction 'between "the metaphoric and metonymic poles" in language' (p. 107)—metonymy being the pole with intimate ties to realism—Crossan modifies his opinion of these three so-called example stories, which he had earlier viewed as poetic metaphors.

349. The Foolish Rich Man mentions the χώρα (land) of the rich man, a general setting assumed in sections of other parables (Lk. 15.13-15, 19.12). A general agrarian setting is presupposed in The Sower (Mk 4.3-8//Mt. 13.3-8//Lk. 8.5-8),

The Rich Man and Poor Lazarus presupposes a general household setting in its first section, a setting which is assumed in other parables, too.[350] However, in the second section of The Rich Man and Poor Lazarus the characters are located in specific places: After he dies, the poor man is taken to 'the bosom of Abraham'; after his death, the rich man is in Hades (Lk. 16.22-23). While Hades is obviously not 'an intrusion from historical reality', it is a specific, named setting.[351] It can now be said, then, that the action in sections of three example stories transpires in specifically named settings, but it must be asked whether or not that is peculiar to these narratives. Although it is usually the case that the action in the synoptic parables takes place in rather nondescript or general settings, a 'topographical index', Capernaum, is specified in the first παραβολή uttered in the Gospel of Luke.[352] Therefore, specifically named settings, either historical or mythological, cannot be

The Seed Growing Secretly (Mk 4.26-29), The Mustard Seed (Mk 4.30-32 [Mt. 13.31 specifies a field, ἀγρῷ, while Lk. 13.19 makes it a garden, κῆπον]), and The Fig Tree (Mk 13.28//Mt. 24.32//Lk. 21.29-30). Other parables, as was just noted, mention a field, ἀγρός: The Wheat and the Tares (Mt. 13.24-30), The Treasure (Mt. 13.44), the Dutiful Servant (Lk. 17.7-10), and part of The Prodigal Son (Lk. 15.15, 25). A vineyard (ἀμπελών) is given as the setting for The Workers in the Vineyard (Mt. 20.1-15), The Two Sons (Mt. 21.28-30), The Barren Fig Tree (Lk. 13.6-9), and part of The Wicked Tenants (Mk 12.1-9//Mt. 21.33-41//Lk. 20.9-16).

350. The house of the rich man's father receive specific mention in 16.27. House (οἶκος or οἰκία) appears also in The Lost Sheep (Lk. 15.6), The Lost Coin (Lk. 15.9) and The Prodigal Son (Lk. 15.25). A household is assumed as the setting in The Friend at Midnight (Lk. 11.5-8), The Faithful Servant (Lk. 12.42-48) and The Dishonest Steward (Lk. 16.1-9). Obviously, a household setting lingers in the background of those parables that depict a householder (οἰκοδεσπότης) or a steward (οἰκονόμος).

351. If 'the bosom of Abraham' is a specific place, where is it? Speculation abounds, but perhaps the most that can be said, on the basis of Lk. 13.28, is that Abraham will be 'in the kingdom of God'. For a different view—that Abraham is in Hades—see Sellin, 'Lukas als Gleichniserzähler', p. 181.

352. See Lk. 4.23. Here Jesus puts a parable into the mouths of his hearers. The third evangelist clearly uses the word παραβολὴν, and I am of the opinion that this parable extends beyond the 'proverb' of three words, 'Physician, heal yourself'. After the imperative 'proverb', the parable continues, 'What we have heard you did at Capernaum, do here also in your own country' (RSV). The punctuation supplied by the RSV committee indicates that they agree. I note in passing that here is another place where imperative verbs, θεράπευσον and ποίησον, are used in parables other than the *Beispielerzählungen*, the latter verb being of the same root as the one said to be an 'imperative as demand' following The Merciful Samaritan.

said to be a unique feature of the example stories which unites them as a group and which can then be used to distinguish them as a special kind of parable because this feature is not exhibited in The Foolish Rich Man and because it is exhibited in a *Gleichnis*. At best, it can be said that the naming of specific places is a characteristic feature of some parables in the Gospel of Luke.[353]

The knowledge that named characters or groups of characters appear in three of the parables designated as *Beispielerzählungen* seems to solidify the position of some scholars who regard the example stories as either a different kind of parable or as something other than parables. Baasland, as we have seen, contends that the naming of characters or groups in three of the example stories is one of their distinguishing features, but he will only concede their 'relative peculiarity'. Jindřich Mánek, on the other hand, is inclined to make a firmer distinction between *Beispielerzählung* and *Parabel* on the basis of that feature. Mánek acknowledges that the *Beispielerzählung* and the *Parabel*—both freely invented narratives—are closely associated kinds of *Gleichnisse*, yet he posits this distinction:

> But while in the *Parabel* it is a matter of an analogy (correspondence), in the example story it is a question of an *Exempel* (example, model case). In contradistinction to the *Parabel*, in the example story the characters are readily specified or designated by name.[354]

Mánek does not elaborate, but apparently he, like Baasland, does not consider this claim applicable to The Foolish Rich Man.[355]

Three assumptions are implicit in Mánek's claim: first, the appearance of characters 'readily specified or designated by name' is a unifying feature of the *Beispielerzählungen*, one which they all share in common; secondly, this is a unique feature of the *Beispielerzählungen*, one which can be used to distinguish them from the *Parabeln*; and thirdly, this feature makes them 'examples' and not parables. In light of

---

353. The use of geographical names in parables is not unique to the Gospel of Luke: A rabbinic parable mentions Akko, Tyre, Sidon, Biri and Antioch (see Johnston, 'Parabolic Interpretations Attributed to Tannaim', pp. 261-62).

354. Mánek, ... *Und brachte Frucht*, p. 8.

355. Mánek, ... *Und brachte Frucht*, p. 8. Here Mánek refers specifically to only three example stories—The Merciful Samaritan, The Rich Man and Poor Lazarus, and The Pharisee and the Toll Collector. Heininger (*Metaphorik*, pp. 29-30) notes the appearance of named characters in all four example stories.

those assumptions, three questions deserve to be asked: If the appearance of characters 'readily specified or designated by name' is a unifying feature of the *Beispielerzählungen*, should it not also be manifest in The Foolish Rich Man? Is the appearance of characters or groups of characters designated by name unique to the *Beispielerzählungen*? Even if the appearance of named characters or groups of characters is unique to the *Beispielerzählungen*, does the manifestation of this feature necessarily mean that they are 'examples' and not parables? The answer to the first question can be provided almost effortlessly; the second and third questions will require more thought.

Each of the four *Beispielerzählungen* do, in fact, depict named characters or individual characters designated by the name of the group to which they belong. As we have seen, The Merciful Samaritan has three characters (a priest, a Levite, a Samaritan) identified by the name of the group to which they belong, and The Pharisee and the Toll Collector obviously has two (a Pharisee and a toll collector). Two characters in The Rich Man and Poor Lazarus are given proper names: Lazarus and Abraham. Parable scholars have avoided the recognition of this feature in The Foolish Rich Man, but there is a specifically named or designated character in this narrative: God (Lk. 12.20).[356] Thus, all four of the so-called example stories share in common a particular feature; that is, characters who are 'readily specified or designated by name'. This, then, is a collective feature of the *Beispielerzählungen* which unites them as a group, and so the answer to the first question is given. The question of whether or not that feature is unique to the *Beispielerzählungen* must still be pursued.

A study devoted to the rabbinic parables shows that the appearance of named characters is not peculiar to the example stories found in the Gospel of Luke. Although Robert Morris Johnston's study does not focus on the synoptic parables, his analysis of the rabbinic parables is pertinent here because he applies his findings with regard to the rabbinic parables to the synoptics parables and concludes that the *Beispielerzählungen* recorded in the Gospel of Luke are just that, example

---

356. God does not appear in the version of this parable found in the *Gospel of Thomas*: 'Jesus said, "There was a rich man who had much money. He said, 'I shall put my money to use so that I may sow, reap, plant, and fill my storehouse with produce, with the result that I shall lack nothing.' Such were his intentions, but that same night he died. Let him who has ears hear"' (Logion 63).

stories.[357] Johnston argues that the example stories in rabbinic literature are not *moshalim* in the strictest formal sense, rather 'example stories are formally *me'asim*...'[358] He accepts several criteria for distinguishing between example stories and *meshalim* from Jülicher and Bultmann, but he adds a criterion that can be used to differentiate between example stories and *meshalim* in those cases where some *meshalim* appear to be very similar to *me'asim*: The *mashal* does not involve itself with named personages, but the 'example-*ma'aseh* often does'.[359] While Johnston never states that the appearance of a named personage is a constitutive feature of example stories, he does state that the manifestation of that feature can serve to indicate whether a narrative is an example story or a *mashal*. However, Johnston weakens the viability of that criterion when he cites a *mashal* in which 'a named personage, the legendary "good Gentile" emperor Antoninus' appears.[360] An answer to the second question can now be given: The appearance of a named character is not unique to the example stories in rabbinic literature, nor is it unique to the *Beispielerzählungen* in the Gospel of Luke.

That answer is not entirely satisfactory because data has been obtained from parables outside the synoptic gospels and because Johnston deals with the issue of 'named personages' mainly in terms of whether a proper name is given to the character. Thus, as we return to the synoptic parables to examine the issue of characters who are 'readily specified or designated by name', let us note that an answer to the third question has been broached in this digression: Despite John-

---

357. See Johnston, 'Parabolic Interpretations Attributed to Tannaim', pp. 189, 251, 636.

358. Johnston, 'Parabolic Interpretations Attributed to Tannaim', p. 185. Johnston considers the example stories to be one of several 'marginal types and forms' found in rabbinic literature (see pp. 185-89). He asserts that 'rabbinic literature is filled with exempla of various kinds, but it should be evident that on terminological, formal, and content grounds they ought not to be classified as *meshalim*' (p. 189). Johnston points out that example stories are similar to anecdotes (see pp. 179-85). For anecdotes and example stories that give the names of characters, see pp. 379-80, 396.

359. Johnston, 'Parabolic Interpretations Attributed to Tannaim', p. 250. The influence of Jülicher and Bultmann (especially) can be seen in Johnston's description of the example story (see pp. 185-86).

360. Johnston, 'Parabolic Interpretations Attributed to Tannaim', p. 221. The *mashal* in question is identified by Johnston as 'Antoninus and His Sons, Mek. Beshallach 1:214ff.'.

ston's intention of invoking the appearance of 'named personages' as a criterion to distinguish between example story and *mashal*, his analysis suggests that the appearance of a character given a proper name is not a feature which, in and of itself, can be employed to make an absolute distinction between example story and parable. Indeed, only two characters in one of the four *Beispielerzählungen* under consideration here are called by proper name. The issue of specifically identified characters or groups of characters in the parables extends beyond the proper name.

The observation that characters in the synoptic parables are usually anonymous or nameless is quite accurate. However, the issue of characterization in the parables is not that simple. In the synoptic parables it is not uncommon for one of the main characters to be introduced in the opening line as 'a certain man' or as 'a man'. Despite the economy of narrative details given about the characters in the parables, more is often said about that 'man', for instance that the man is a king (Mt. 18.23, 22.2), or that the man is a merchant (Mt. 13.45), or that the man is rich (Lk. 12.16, 16.1, 16.19). Although the characters in the parables are nameless, they are customarily identified by a particular trait, or by the action in which they are engaged, or by their occupation. The characters in the parables are not fully developed individuals, rather they are 'typical'[361] or 'representative',[362] and their anonymity contributes to that.[363] When all of the synoptic parables are removed from their Gospel contexts and considered as a group, the depiction of named characters or groups of characters in the example stories—a priest, a Levite, a Samaritan, Lazarus, Abraham, God, a Pharisee, a toll collector—appears to stand out as a rather unique trait. The matter of how characters are identified in the synoptic parables ought to be pursued a bit further.

A perusal of the synoptic parables yields a sample of main and auxiliary (minor or mentioned) characters[364] which reflects a first-century

361. See Tolbert, *Perspectives on the Parables*, pp. 16-18, 90-91.
362. See Jones, *The Art and Truth of the Parables*, pp. 124-25.
363. For investigations of the roles and functions of anonymous characters in biblical literature, see Adele Reinhartz, 'Anonymity and Character in the Books of Samuel', *Semeia* 63 (1993), pp. 117-41; and David R. Beck, 'The Narrative Function of Anonymity in Fourth Gospel Characterization', *Semeia* 63 (1993), pp. 143-58.
364. Only human characters are of concern here, although a variety of flora and

Mediterranean social and cultural milieu.[365] Many characters are identified on the basis of their position or status in an agrarian economic and social structure: sowers, a vinedresser, harvesters, tenant farmers, householders, stewards, laborers, slaves and servants of several stripes.[366] Other characters are identified as members of a family or community: fathers, wives, sons, brothers, children, friends, neighbors, citizens.[367] Some characters in the parables might be said to be, in broad terms, government or bureaucratic functionaries: kings, a judge, envoys, troops.[368] And then there is a miscellany of other characters: women, maidens, a widow, prostitutes, a bridegroom, merchants, debtors, a creditor, rich men, poor men, robbers, a thief, torturers, enemies, an opponent, the lame, the maimed, the blind.[369] In general, as

fauna are mentioned in the parables, with some performing actions vital to the story. Types of flora include: wheat (Mt. 13.25, 30), fig trees (Mt. 24.32//Lk. 21.29; Lk. 13.6), weeds (Mt. 13.25-26), thorns (Mk 4.7//Mt. 13.7//Lk. 8.7), fruit or grain (Mk 4.7-8//Mt. 13.8//Lk. 8.8; Mk 4.29; Mt. 13.26, 21.34; Lk. 12.17, 13.6-9, 20.10), and a variety of seed (Mt. 13. 24, 27; Mk. 4.31//Mt. 13.31-32//Lk. 8.4; Lk. 13.19). Types of fauna include: birds (Mk 4.4//Mt. 13.4//Lk. 8.5; Mk 4.32//Mt. 13.32//Lk. 13.19), sheep (Mt. 18.12-13//Lk. 15.3-6), swine (Lk. 15.15-16), dogs (Lk. 16.21), a pack animal (Lk. 10.31), oxen (Mt. 22.4//Lk. 14.19), and fat calves (Mt. 22.4; Lk. 15.23).

365. See Scott, *Hear Then the Parable*, pp. 73-75, 79-80, 205-208.

366. The lists of characters in this note and the three which follow are intended to be representative, not exhaustive. Sowers (ὁ σπείρων): Mk 4.3-8//Mt. 13.3-8//Lk. 8.5-8. Vinedresser (ἀμπελουργός): Lk. 13.7. Harvesters (θεριστής): Mt. 13.30. Tenant farmers (γεωργός): Mk 12.1-9//Mt. 21.33-41//Lk. 20.9-16. Householders (οἰκοδεσπότης): Mt. 13.27, 20.1, 11, 21.33, 24.43; Lk. 12.39, 13.25, 14.21. Stewards (οἰκονόμος): Lk. 12.42, 16.1-9. Laborers (ἐργάτης): Mt. 20.1-16; day laborers (μίσθιος): Lk. 15.17-21. Slaves (δοῦλος): Mk 12.2-4//Mt. 21.34-36//Lk. 20.10-12; Mk 13.34; Mt. 13.27, 18.23-34, Mt. 22.2-14//Lk. 14.16-24; Mt. 25.14-30//Lk. 19.12-27; Lk. 12.36, 17.7-10, 15.22; servant (διάκονος): Mt. 22.13; boy slave (παῖς): Lk. 12.45, 15.26; girl slave (παιδίσκη): Lk. 12.45.

367. Fathers (πατήρ): Lk. 11.11-13, 15.11-32, 16.24-30. Wives (γυνή): Mt. 18.25; Lk. 14.20. Sons (υἱός): Mk 12.6//Mt. 21.37//Lk. 20.13; Mt. 7.9//Lk. 11.11; Mt. 22.2; Lk. 15.11-32; or (τέκνον): Mt. 21.28-31; Lk. 15.31, 16.25. Brothers (ἀδελφός): Lk. 15.27, 32, 16.28. Children (παιδίον): Mt. 11.16//Lk. 7.32; Lk. 11.7. Friends (φίλος): Lk. 11.5-8, 14.10, 15.6, 7, 9; or comrades (ἑταῖρος): Mt. 20.13, 22.12. Neighbors (γείτων): Lk. 15.6, 9. Citizens (πολίτης): Lk. 15.15, 19.14.

368. Kings (βασιλεύς): Mt. 18.23-24, 22.2-13; Lk. 14.31. Envoys (πρεσβεία): Lk. 14.32, 19.14. Troops (στάτευμα): Mt. 22.7. Judge (κριτής): Lk. 18.2-5.

369. Women (γυνή): Mt. 13.33//Lk. 13.21; Lk. 15.8-9. Maidens or virgins (παρθένος): Mt. 25.1-12. Widow (χήρα): Lk. 18.3-5. Prostitutes (πόρνη): Lk.

Flusser contends, the characters in the synoptic parables are not identified by proper name; rather, 'the figures of the *Gleichnisse* are designated only by their social position and their vocation, or by their family membership'.[370] Let us reflect upon the issue of named characters in the *Beispielerzählungen* in light of Flusser's contention.

If Flusser is correct, most of the named characters or groups of characters in the example stories seem to be identified in much the same way as characters in the other synoptic parables. The priest, the Levite, the Pharisee, and the toll collector are designated 'by their social position and their vocation'; or it might be said that the social position or vocation of these individual characters is specified by giving the name of the group to which they belong. Viewed from this perspective, the supposedly 'peculiar' feature of having characters designated by the name of the group to which they belong is not a feature that is unique to the example stories, and as a result it would be a feature of questionable value for the purpose of distinguishing between the *Beispielerzählungen* and the *Parabeln*. In addition, this feature is not one that unifies the example stories as group, for there are exceptions: The Rich Man and Poor Lazarus identifies two of its characters by proper name, the others remain anonymous; The Foolish Rich Man has one anonymous character and one specifically identified character, God, and the deity breaks the mold of being identified by group name or proper name.

We need not quibble over minutiae. It cannot be denied that scholars perceive something peculiar about the characters in the example stories. When the synoptic parables are analyzed *en bloc* outside their respective Gospel contexts, it is easy to understand why scholars might reach the conclusion that the *Beispielerzählungen* as a group are a different kind of parable since each one exhibits the apparently peculiar feature of having specifically named characters or characters identified by the name of the group to which they belong. A consideration of this feature

---

15.30. Bridegroom (νυμφίος): Mt. 25.1-12. Merchants (ἔμπορος): Mt. 13.45. Debtors (χρεοφειλέτης): Lk. 7.41, 16.5. Creditor (δανιστής): Lk. 7.41. Rich men (πλούσιος): Lk. 12.16, 16.1-9, 16.19-31. Poor [men] (πτωχός): Lk. 14.21, 16.20, 22. Robbers (λῃστής): Lk. 10.30; thief (κλέπτης): Lk. 12.39. Torturers (βασανιστής): Mt. 18.34. Enemies (ὁ ἐχθρός): Mt. 13.25, 28; Lk. 19.27. Opponent or accuser (ἀντίδικος): Lk. 18.3. Lame (χωλός): Lk. 14.21. Maimed (ἀνάπειρος): Lk. 14.21. Blind (τυφλός): Mt. 15.14// Lk. 6.39; Lk. 14.21.

370. Flusser, *Die rabbinischen Gleichnisse und der Gleichniserzähler Jesu*, p. 293. This statement applies to the rabbinic parables and the synoptic parables.

in relation to 'reality' and in relation to 'religion' will shed some light on some of the claims about the example stories made by parable scholars.

The parables are correctly considered to be fictional, or freely invented, narratives. The recognition that the parables are narrative fictions is evidenced in the celebration of parables as 'aesthetic objects' and in the application of literary-critical methodologies as a means of interpreting them.[371] As narrative fictions, the parables are assumed to recount fictional events or actions performed by fictional characters. The fictitiousness of the parables is strongly reinforced by the appearance of nameless or anonymous characters who go about their business in nondescript or generalized settings. For some, the fictional quality of the parables is disrupted when characters are given a proper name. Flusser, for instance, regards the appearance of a proper name in a parable to be a blemish which 'impairs intolerably the effectiveness of a *Gleichnis*'.[372] For others, the fictional quality of a parable is breached when characters are identified by specifications 'of a socio-religious nature', or when specific 'topographical indices' are given, both of which to Crossan 'represent an intrusion from historical reality into what one assumes to be a fictional narration'.

A majority of scholars accept the premise that the *Beispielerzählungen* are also freely invented narratives, but the appearance of characters 'readily specified or designated by name' in the example stories seems to obscure their fictional nature. The addition of details, such as proper names and the names of specific ('real') groups—and in some instances, the names of specific ('real') places—sharpens the vividness of the example stories; or better, it heightens the verisimilitude of the example stories. Verisimilitude in the example stories—or in any narrative, for that matter—should not be confused with 'reality', but it is not unusual to encounter the suggestion, even in this century, that one or more of the example stories, especially The Merciful Samaritan, arises out of an actual occurrence or is based upon a real incident.[373] Perhaps

371. On the parable as a 'short narrative fiction', see Scott, *Hear Then the Parable*, pp. 35-42; see also Hedrick, *Parables as Poetic Fictions*, esp. pp. 32-89.

372. Flusser, *Die rabbinischen Gleichnisse und der Gleichniserzähler Jesu*, p. 293.

373. As we saw in Chapter 2, van Koetsveld dealt with the question of whether the group of parables later known as example stories are 'real' stories or 'fictional' parables. The view that one or more of the parables in this group might be a 'real'

it is the case that because characters in each of the four example stories are identified by proper name or by the name of the group to which they belong, these narratives have been perceived by scholars as being 'more direct', or less 'figurative', or less 'symbolical', or 'non-metaphorical' or 'nonparabolical'. Does the appearance of characters identified in such a manner intensify the verisimilitude of the example stories to such a degree that it can be said that 'in them every element of the pictorial is missing'? Such perceptions can easily foster the argument that these four example stories are more direct, are less figurative, and thus are not really parables. Even if this line of reasoning is granted, is it necessary to deduce that the example stories are meant to be taken literally as 'examples'?

While most students of the parables do not argue explicitly that because the four so-called example stories contain named characters or groups of characters, they are therefore 'examples' and not 'parables', it is readily comprehensible how that feature could give rise to such a notion. The appearance of either characters who are identified by the name of the group to which they belong, groups which also exist in historical 'reality' outside the parables, or characters who are identified by proper name disrupts the fictional quality of the example stories and, as a result, they may seem to be a different kind of parable or, as some would have it, 'no longer parables'. Indeed, a student of the rabbinic parables, David Stern, posits a distinction between parable and example because the example makes a 'rhetorical claim to historicity', whereas the parable is 'self-admittedly fictional'.[374] Thus, according to Stern, the example story belongs among other 'nonparabolic narratives in rabbinic literature'.[375]

The appearance of a 'real' historical figure (Abraham) or members of groups which exist in 'reality' (a priest, a Levite, a Pharisee, a toll

story persists; see, e.g., Jones, *The Art and Truth of the Parables*, p. 115; Jeremias, *Die Gleichnisse Jesu*, p. 201 (Jeremias cites others who share this view [p. 201 n. 10], but he does not reserve this remark for The Merciful Samaritan alone; cf. p. 19 n. 2); Young, *Jesus and his Jewish Parables*, p. 239. Mánek (...*Und brachte Frucht*, p. 84) states that we do not know whether or not this is a real story.

374. Stern, *Parables in Midrash*, p. 324 n. 16; cf. pp. 13-15. While Stern does not deal specifically with the issue of character or named characters, his remarks are relevant to the perceived difference between example story and parable under consideration.

375. See Stern, *Parables in Midrash*, pp. 237-42.

collector) in three of the so-called example stories may give the
semblance of lessening the distance between the narrative world and
the 'real' world, but it must be admitted that narratives can and do
depict within their narrative world named people and members of
named groups who exist in the 'real' world and still be entirely
fictitious narratives. Readers of any fictional narrative ought to avoid
equating the verisimilar and the real.[376] In other instances when a
parable depicts characters by virtue of a position or an occupation—
such as kings, judges, troops—which also exists in 'reality' outside the
parable narrative, rarely is the verisimilar confused with the 'real'.
Nevertheless, it can be surmised that the difference in the degree of
verisimilitude in the example stories has exerted considerable influence
upon scholars who conclude that the *Beispielerzählungen* are different
in kind from the *Parabeln*. Interestingly, the appearance of a named
character, God, in The Foolish Rich Man has not weighed heavily in
the discussion of how the example stories relate to 'reality', but the
appearance of that character has entered into the discussion about the
relationship of the example stories to 'religion'.

'Religion' has been used as an index by some scholars to pinpoint the
peculiarity of the *Beispielerzählungen*, as we have seen. The familiar
claim is that the example stories, unlike the *Parabeln*, contain religion.
This purportedly unique aspect of the example stories has been
described in several ways, often in terms of the 'peculiar' relationship
between the 'two planes' (or spheres, or fields) in the example stories:
It has been alleged that the *Bildhälfte* of the example stories mention
the transcendent directly and thus there is a decrease in distance
between the *Bildhälfte* and *Sachhälfte*, or alternatively, that in the
example stories the *Sache* appears directly in the *Bildhälfte* and thus
there is no *Sachhälfte*. Either way, the conclusion is that the example
stories are a different kind of parable, or that they are not parables. The

---

376. See Scott, *Hear Then the Parable*, p. 41: 'Sometimes the fictional character
of the parables is laid aside as when Jeremias or others argue that a parable is based
on an actual event. That is beside the point and mistakes verisimilitude for reality.
Parables have high verisimilitude, as attested by their use of everydayness, but
everydayness has been fictionalized by being taken up into story'. Jonathan Culler,
in his discussion of 'convention and naturalization' (*Structuralist Poetics: Structuralism, Linguistics, and the Study of Literature* [Ithaca, NY: Cornell University
Press, 1975], pp. 131-60), distinguishes five levels of *vraisemblance* (see pp. 140-
60).

issue of 'religion' in the example stories has not been articulated succinctly, for we have also seen that some scholars dispute the putative appearance of religion in the example stories and thus this 'unique' aspect of the *Beispielerzählungen*. Another reason can be added for disputing the contention that the example stories are unique, or different in kind from the *Parabeln*, due to the appearance of religion or the transcendent in them. Things 'religious'—indeed, the transcendent—are mentioned directly in other *Parabeln*: The younger son in The Prodigal Son says that he has 'sinned against heaven' (Lk. 15.18, 21) and the judge in The Unjust Judge is described, and he repeats the description himself, as one who does not 'fear God' (Lk. 18.2, 4). Scholars rarely claim that these two *Parabeln* are example stories. The manner in which characters are identified in the example stories can also be brought to bear upon the issue of 'religion' in these narratives.

Each of the four example stories depicts directly or mentions, in addition to anonymous or nameless figures, characters or individuals as members of groups who play a role (positive or negative) in the religious traditions, the religious mythology or the religious lore of the Jewish people. In The Merciful Samaritan, we meet an anonymous man, robbers, an innkeeper, and also a priest, a Levite and a Samaritan. An anonymous rich man appears in The Foolish Rich Man, but so does God. The Rich Man and Poor Lazarus includes not only a named poor man and a nameless rich man, but also (Father) Abraham and angels; not only are the father and brothers of the rich man mentioned, but also 'Moses and the prophets' and 'someone from the dead'. Obviously, The Pharisee and the Toll Collector depicts its eponymous characters, but it also mentions God, extortioners, unjust people and adulterers. The mention or depiction of groups who are of obvious concern to segments of the Jewish people and their religion in (first-century) 'reality'—a priest, a Levite, a Samaritan, God, Abraham, angels, Moses and the prophets, a Pharisee, a toll collector and certain other undesirables—may magnify the perception that the example stories contain in them 'religion', and thus strengthen the conclusion that they 'lack a pictorial element', or that they are 'less symbolical', less 'figurative', 'nonmetaphorical', and thus are more 'direct' or 'literal'.[377] The impulse might be to conclude that the feature manifest in each of the

---

377. Moreover, the force of that perception may be increased by the mention in three *Beispielerzählungen* of specific 'religious' places—mythological (Hades) or 'real' (Jerusalem, the temple).

example stories that is unique to them as a group has at last been identified: Each of the four example stories contains the direct depiction or mention of characters or groups who play a role in the religious traditions, religious mythology or religious lore of the (first-century) Jewish people. Such a conclusion, however, would prove to be premature.

The selection of characters and their deliberate depiction in the so-called example stories has an aura of peculiarity or uniqueness when the example stories are excised from their narrative context in the Gospel of Luke and then compared to the other synoptic parables. Examined in that light, the *Beispielerzählungen* provide what is perceived to be a stark contrast to the *Parabeln*: The example stories, in contradistinction to the other synoptic parables, appear to manifest the singular feature of depicting or mentioning characters according to their position or status in a 'socio-religious structure' evident in 'reality' outside the parables. If this is a feature unique to this group of four example stories, it can be utilized as index to cement the singularity of that group since it would also disqualify other narratives identified by scholars as *Beispielerzählungen*. In fact, other narratives purported to be example stories—such as The Unjust Steward (Lk. 16.1-9), The Prodigal Son (Lk. 15.11-32), The Places at Table (Lk. 14.7-11), and The Dutiful Servant (Lk. 17.7-10)—can be eliminated on the basis of this feature, for none of those parables names or identifies characters according to its position or status in a socio-religious structure of the 'real' world. Upon closer inspection, however, the sheen of this 'unique' feature is not so brilliant.

When the example stories are situated firmly within their narrative context in the Gospel of Luke and then compared to other parables in that Gospel narrative, the lustre of their apparently peculiar feature is dulled somewhat because other Lukan parables name groups of characters which figure in the socio-religious structure established in that Gospel. It is almost a commonplace in New Testament scholarship that the Gospel of Luke champions the cause of groups which comprise the underclass of first-century Mediterranean society—such as the poor and widows—groups which do exist in the 'real' world and groups which are thought to be neglected or excluded by certain Jewish groups of influence in that milieu. Several other groups found in the Gospel of Luke—such as the lame and the blind—could be added. Members of each of those groups are also depicted or mentioned in the parables spoken by Jesus in the Gospel of Luke; for instance, The Unjust Judge (Lk. 18.2-5) depicts a widow and The Great Banquet (Lk. 14.16-24) includes mention of 'the poor and maimed and blind and lame'.[378] Note that another saying of Jesus often alleged to be an example story, The Proper Guests (Lk. 14.12-14), lists the same groups (v. 13: 'poor, maimed, lame, blind') as does The Great Banquet. 'Sinners', another group often shunned within the socio-religious structure of the 'real' world—and indeed shunned by some within the narrative world of the Gospel of Luke—are shown confessing their sin in a *Parabel* and a *Beispielerzählung*: The younger son in The Prodigal Son does so (Lk. 15.18, 21), as does the toll collector in The Pharisee and the Toll Collector (Lk. 18.13). Rather than focusing on the relation of named groups of characters to 'reality' or 'religion', a more productive avenue of investigation would be to examine how the depiction of characters identified by proper name or by the name of the group to which they belong in the example narratives relates to the depiction of those characters or groups in the larger narrative context of the Gospel of Luke.[379]

378. See v. 21. If Mt. 22.2-14 represents a genuine parallel to The Great Banquet (Lk. 14.16-24), the feature under consideration is put into greater relief. Note that in the Matthean parable, the king, angry at his previous invitees, gives his servants instructions to invite now 'as many as you find', and that the servants 'gathered all whom they found, both bad and good' (RSV). The householder in the Lukan parable is also angry at his previous invitees, but he gives specific instructions about whom the servants are to invite: 'the poor and maimed and blind and lame'.

379. An interpretation of the example stories as embedded narratives would, of course, attempt to analyze and assess the interplay between those narrative texts as spoken by the main protagonist in the larger narrative, Jesus, and the larger narrative text in which he also is a character. This study suggests that one avenue of exploration would be to determine how the characters or groups of characters depicted in the example stories relate to their counterparts in the larger Gospel narrative. Another way to describe the narrative strategy apparent in the example stories is this: The characters in some narrative parables are without an obvious syntagmatic relationship to the larger Gospel narrative, but the characters in those parables do have a clearer semantic relationship to the larger Gospel narrative; some of the characters in the example stories have both an obvious syntagmatic relationship and a clear semantic relationship to the larger Gospel narrative. This is not 'unique' to the example stories among the Lukan parables, for character groups such as the blind, the lame, the poor appear in parables and also have counterparts in the larger Gospel narrative. (Nor is this narrative strategy peculiar to the Gospel of Luke and its parables; see pp. 271-72 n. 382 below on 'kings' in the Gospel of

The aura of uniqueness that is often perceived as surrounding the four example stories disperses when these parables are left within their narrative context and considered in relation to other Lukan parables. 'Religion', it seems, impinges upon other Lukan parables in addition to the four so-called *Beispielerzählungen*. The third evangelist apparently had no qualms about including in his parables the direct mention of 'heaven' or 'God', no misgivings about depicting characters—even God—or groups of characters who play a role in the religious traditions, the religious mythology, or the religious lore of the Jewish people of his day. What appears to be a unique feature of the example narratives looks more like a particular narrative strategy employed by the third evangelist in his parables. The 'uniqueness' of the example stories is diminished, then, when they are examined and analyzed within their narrative context as parables of the Gospel of Luke.

Comments and Conclusions

This survey of research on the example stories conducted by parable scholars in the century since the publication of Jülicher's *Die Gleich-nisreden Jesu* is now ended. An answer to a particular question has been sought throughout: Is there any definitive feature or trait manifest in the example stories that necessarily makes them categorically—or essentially—different from the other narrative parables in the synoptic gospels? A quick and sure response in the affirmative is increasingly difficult to give in light of the preceding studies of the example stories. The sanction of the category '*Beispielerzählung*' is violated time and again in the findings of some scholars who address the question; yet that category, as part of the classification system of the parables popu-larized by Jülicher, remains almost a dogma (to paraphrase Sellin) in the work of other scholars. One of the striking things in the history of research on the example stories is this: The example stories are said to exhibit a particular trait or feature that makes them a unique or separate category of parable or that precludes them from being regarded as parables, but upon closer examination that peculiar feature or trait either is not exhibited by all four of the so-called example stories, or that putatively peculiar feature can be found in other parables (*Parabeln* or *Gleichnisse*)—if not by the very scholar who identified the trait and pronounced it peculiar to the example stories, then by other

Matthew and some of its parables.)

scholars who analyze the parables. At the very least, then, the preceding survey of scholarship on the example stories renders problematical the categorical distinction between example narrative (*Beispielerzählung*) and narrative parable (*Parabel*).

Some of the problems with maintaining a categorical distinction between *Beispielerzählung* and *Parabeln* are thrown into relief by Bultmann's brief treatment of the example stories. Bultmann accepts the distinction between *Parabel* and *Beispielerzählung* as separate *Gattungen* of parables. Against those who appeal to the ancient rhetorical tradition to categorize the synoptic παραβολαί, Bultmann argues that the *Beispielerzählungen* are not to be confused with the παραδείγματα of ancient rhetoric. Nevertheless, in what has been one of the most influential formulations of the category in this century, Bultmann maintains that the *Beispielerzählungen* 'offer examples=models for the right conduct'. According to Bultmann, the example narratives are not rhetorical examples; rather, they are 'moral examples'.

There are at least two problems with Bultmann's conception of the *Beispielerzählungen*, and the same problems are encountered in the work of others who hold that the example narratives are 'moral examples': first, Bultmann does not identify specific formal features in the *Beispielerzählungen* that can give support to his contention that they are 'moral examples'; secondly, he claims that other parables (*Parabeln*) offer positive or negative examples, while still other parables evoke a judgment about the morality of the action(s) depicted in them. Bultmann asserts that the *Beispielerzählungen* have 'a strong formal relationship to the *Parabeln*'—and his analysis of narrative technique in the synoptic parables attests to that—but he still detects something about the example narratives that makes them seem different from the *Parabeln*: In the *Beispielerzählungen* 'every element of the pictorial is missing'. It must be asked again whether it follows logically that because 'every element of the pictorial is missing' in the *Beispielerzählungen*, they must therefore be 'moral examples'. At any rate, Bultmann does not stand alone in suspecting that there is something peculiar about the comparative mechanism of the example narratives.

Various explanations of how the comparative mechanism of the *Beispielerzählungen* differs from that of the *Parabeln* have been given. Some scholars are content with Jülicher's description of the difference: The *Beispielerzählungen* already belong to the religious–ethical sphere and provide, by means of a particular case, an example of the proposi-

tion to be asserted. Others go beyond Jülicher to posit that the *Sache*—
some aspect of 'religion', or 'the transcendent'—is directly *in* the
narrative of the example story.

More recent attempts to defend or dispute the peculiarity of the comparative mechanism of the example stories are done in terms of a view
of the parable as metaphor. Scholars on both sides of the issue diverge
from the formulation of the category *Beispielerzählung* as set forth by
Jülicher. Via, for instance, is of the opinion that the example stories
lack the semantic tension between the narrative vehicle and the tenor
(the kingdom of God) evident in the metaphorical parables, and thus
the example stories 'can only be read morally'. Other scholars affirm
the notion that in the *Beispielerzählungen* the distance between the
Bildhälfte and *Sachhälfte* is less than in the *Parabeln*, or that the *Bildhälfte* and *Sachhälfte* overlap significantly, or even that the example
stories do not have two planes (or spheres or fields). Those sorts of
observations frequently result in the conclusion that the example stories
are not metaphors and thus are not parables, or that the example stories
are to be read literally or morally. Although such a conclusion seemingly upholds the distinction between *Beispielerzählung* and *Parabeln*
proposed by Jülicher, it often goes unrecognized that the line of argumentation leading up to that conclusion represents a departure from
Jülicher, who argued that all parables are to be dissociated from
metaphor and that all parables—*Gleichnisse*, *Parabeln* and *Beispielerzählungen*—are to be read as 'actual speech'. If the assumption
behind some of these claims is that the *Beispielerzählungen* are no
longer about the kingdom of God, then this is certainly a departure
from Jülicher, for he did not assert that the example narratives have
nothing to do with that in their *Sachhälfte*. Baasland, for instance, takes
leave of Jülicher when he contends that since the example stories
permit no conclusion *a minore ad majus*, they therefore admit no correspondence to the transcendent plane.

Other scholars challenge or reject the notion that the comparative
mechanism of the *Beispielerzählungen* is significantly different from
that of the *Parabeln*. Some argue that the example stories are not to be
read literally or morally; rather they are to be read figuratively as
metaphorical parables or metonymical parables, or they are to be read
'tropically' as synecdochical parables. While Boucher applies her
argument to all of the example stories, Funk does not contend explicitly
that *all* of the so-called example stories are metaphorical parables, and

Crossan does not assert that *all four* of the example stories are metonymical parables.[380] These scholars clearly oppose Jülicher, for he would not allow that any of the parables of Jesus are to be read as 'non-actual speech'.

Proponents on both sides of the debate over the propriety of the distinction between *Beispielerzählung* and *Parabel* strive to promote their respective positions by adducing evidence drawn from the characteristic features or traits of the example stories vis-à-vis the other narrative parables. If the *Beispielerzählungen* are 'formally quite distinct' from the *Parabeln*, one would naturally expect it to be demonstrated that the example stories manifest a common set of characteristics—or, minimally, one collective feature—which unites them as a group and which distinguishes them from the *Parabeln*. If that condition were to be met, then the conclusion that the *Beispielerzählungen* are a different kind (or *Gattung*, or genre) of παραβολή might be warranted. However, attempts to identify the peculiarity of the example stories in terms of formal features have been largely unsuccessful because, simply stated, the *Beispielerzählungen* and the *Parabeln* share in common a number of formal features. The introductory formulae of the *Beispielerzählungen* are not distinctively different from those of the *Parabeln*. Not all of the example stories contain imperative verbs and some parables do. The peculiarity of the example stories cannot be established definitely on the basis of plot (or plot pattern), for the example stories as a group do not exhibit the same plot and some of the example stories exhibit the same plot as other *Parabeln*. Relatedly, the motif of reversal has been identified in some or all of the *Beispielerzählungen*, depending upon the analyst, and in some of the *Parabeln*. Contrary to what might have been expected—that the *Beispielerzählungen* as a group would manifest a similar surface structure and a similar deep structure, both noticeably different from the *Parabeln*—it has not been established conclusively that all four of the example stories have the same surface structure and the same deep structure; instead, it has been shown that some of the example stories have both the same deep structure (Funk, Crossan) and the same surface structure (Via) as other 'authentic' parables. Several studies have suggested that the uniqueness of the example stories can be traced to one or another aspect of the formal feature character; yet we have witnessed that the *Beispielerzählungen*

---

380. However, recall that Crossan, in earlier works, argues that all of the *Beispielerzählungen* are poetic metaphors.

cannot be distinguished from the *Parabeln* on the basis of: the number of characters who appear; a 'three person scheme' (or triangular structure); a 'monarchic structure'; an actantial structure; or a contrast drawn between characters. The formal feature of setting cannot be said to distinguish the four example stories from the other narrative parables. Rather than proving that the *Beispielerzählungen* are unique in kind and 'formally quite distinct' from the *Parabeln*, or indeed that the example stories are not parables, the preceding analyses of the formal characteristics manifest in the *Beispielerzählungen* indicate rather clearly that they have 'a strong formal relationship to the *Parabeln*'.

Some may have already read enough to conclude that the example narratives (*Beispielerzählung*) are narrative parables (*Parabeln* or *Gleichniserzählungen*). Are not the numerous similarities between the *Beispielerzählungen* and the *Parabeln* of critical mass? Enough probative evidence may have been amassed to sustain the verdict that the example stories are narrative parables, that the *Beispielerzählungen* are not different in kind from the *Parabeln*. Nonetheless, some may still feel compelled to uphold the view that the example stories have about them a 'relative peculiarity', that the *Beispielerzählungen* are not different in kind from the *Parabeln* but in degree.

Those who opt for the position that the example stories have a 'relative peculiarity' may choose to side with Baasland. Although he argues that the example stories do not manifest a common formal structure and hence that the genre '*Beispielerzählung*'—since it cannot be established by means of formal criteria—cannot be maintained for the group of narratives identified as such by scholars, Baasland does notice one attribute of the example stories that leads him to concede their 'relative peculiarity': In at least three of the example stories, 'characters and groups are called by name'.[381] If this feature is to be used to substantiate the 'relative peculiarity' of the example narratives, it should be manifest in all of the *Beispielerzählungen*.

In the previous section, I went beyond the observations of Baasland,

---

381. It may be more accurate to say that the ramifications of this attribute encourage such a conclusion. Baasland, as we have seen, argues that other types of parables engage the hearer to identify with the character who serves as an *exemplum* for the proper action, whereas the *Beispielerzählungen* elicit a special kind of identification process in which the hearer identifies with the wrong character(s). Moreover, because the actions performed by the characters in the *Beispielerzählungen* are so deficient, an inference procedure *a minore ad majus* is precluded.

Mánek and others with regard to the issue of characters 'readily specified or designated by name' in the example stories by pointing out that specifically named characters or characters identified by the name of the group to which they belong are depicted in each of the four example stories. The value of that supposedly unique feature as a criterion to establish the uniqueness, or even the 'relative peculiarity', of the example stories decreased when it was noted that the designation of characters by the name of the group to which they belong may be considered as a variation of the identification of characters by social position or vocation common in other synoptic parables.

The feature of characters 'readily specified or designated by name' was submitted to further scrutiny. The suggestion was tendered that when the example stories are considered outside their narrative context in the Gospel of Luke and then compared to the other synoptic parables, this feature does give an aura of peculiarity to the example stories, particularly so when the characters depicted in the example stories are viewed in relation to 'reality' and 'religion', and especially so when the referent of all authentic parables is assumed to be the kingdom of God. This putatively peculiar feature of the example stories was considered in light of some of the claims made about how the comparative mechanism operative in the *Beispielerzählungen* is supposed to differ from that operative in the *Parabeln*.

If it is the case that parables are comprised of a fictional *Bildhälfte*, which depicts anonymous characters and deals with secular or profane circumstances that are then brought to bear figuratively upon a *Sachhälfte*, which has to do with the kingdom of God, then the example stories may give the appearance of being 'unique' or 'peculiar' in that they depict specifically named characters or members of specific groups who have what is thought to be a direct connection to 'reality' or 'religion' outside the narrative proper. The *Bildhälfte* of the example story—if, for a moment, it may be said to have one—is seemingly 'literal' because some of its characters appear in 'reality' outside the narrative. The apparent abrogation of the 'fictitiousness' of the *Bildhälfte* may lead to the supposition that the example story is not figurative or is not metaphorical. Does this mean that the example stories are to be read literally as 'moral examples'? If the *Bildhälfte* of the example story is said to contain 'religion' because some of its characters are connected to the religious traditions and lore of the Jewish people of that day, this may lead some to the conclusion that the example story already belongs to the 'religious-ethical sphere', or that it lacks 'semantic tension' between the narrative vehicle and the metaphorical tenor, and that, in turn, reinforces the notion that the example stories 'can only be read morally'. That feature helps explain why the example stories resist, in the judgment of some scholars, being defined as metaphorical parables. However, when the example stories are examined as parables of the Gospel of Luke—that is, as integral parts of that Gospel narrative—the 'uniqueness' of that feature dissipates because other Lukan parables depict characters who figure in the socio-religious structure assumed in that Gospel. Moreover, other Lukan parables contain the direct mention of the deity and things religious. Should this be taken to mean that those other parables 'can only be read morally'? A consistent application of criteria would seem to demand it.

What, then, are we to conclude about the example stories? The pre-ponderance of evidence indicates that the four so-called example narratives are narrative parables. These four *'Beispielerzählungen'* share a substantial number of formal features in common with other narrative parables recorded in the synoptic gospels, as has been shown repeatedly in the analyses performed by the parable scholars reviewed in this chapter. The cumulative effect of this history of research is the realization that the categorical distinction between parable and example story rests upon a precarious foundation. The *'Beispielerzählungen'* exhibit neither a collective set of features nor a singular, peculiar feature that can be utilized as a means of making an absolute distinction between example narrative and narrative parable. No compelling evidence has been submitted that leads inexorably to the conclusion that the four 'example stories' alone, among all the synoptic parables, are 'moral examples'. The *Beispielerzählungen*, therefore, do not appear to be categorically different from the *Parabeln*. This represents but one option in the debate on the problem of 'parable versus example'. Philosophers and theologians might well be better equipped to deter-mine when a difference in degree becomes a difference in kind. Doubtlessly, the debate will continue and scholars will put forth other options.

Some participants in the debate who perceive the *Beispielerzählung* as being different in kind from the *Parabel* will seize upon the feature that has been examined in some detail—that the example stories depict specifically named characters or characters identified by the name of the group to which they belong—as a formal feature which can be used to support the argument that the example stories are a 'unique' type of parable, or are not parables at all. In anticipation of that eventuality, the following observation will be reiterated: The supposedly peculiar feature identified here may give the semblance of uniqueness to the example stories when they are viewed outside their narrative context in the Gospel of Luke and then compared to other synoptic parables. What scholars perceive as a characteristic feature peculiar to the example stories and purported to make them an essentially unique kind of parable may be, rather, a characteristic feature of quintessential Lukan parables. If that is granted, then it need not be said that the *Beispielerzählungen* are different in kind from all the other synoptic *Parabeln*, and so even the claim that the example stories manifest a 'relative peculiarity' can be relativized further: The unifying feature of the example stories thought to bestow upon them a 'relative peculiarity' is relative to their narrative context in the Gospel of Luke.

If all of the 'authentic' parables of Jesus or all the parables recorded in the synoptic gospels are said to refer indirectly (or figuratively, or metaphorically) to the kingdom of God by means of a fictional narrative in which the sacred (or the transcendent, or religion) is neither mentioned nor depicted directly, then the comparative mechanism of the four Lukan *Beispielerzählungen* may seem to be different from all the other parables of Jesus and the synoptic parables. However, the third evangelist did not erect an impermeable partition between the sacred and profane, the religious and the secular, in his parables. In his parables, the third evangelist can have a son admit that he has 'sinned against heaven', and he can have a judge described as one who does not 'fear God'; in his parables, the third evangelist can depict specifically named characters—Abraham, Lazarus, God—and characters designated by the name of a specific group—a Pharisee, a toll collector, a priest, a Levite, a Samaritan—who figure largely in the religious traditions and religious lore of the Jewish people of his day. What is more important about the characters 'readily specified or designated by name' in the example stories is not that these characters appear in the 'real' world, but that they appear also in the narrative world of the Gospel of Luke;[382] not that the characters in the example stories are

---

382. Even in this regard the example stories are not 'unique'. Kings appear in some Matthean parables (Mt. 18.23-34, 22.2-13) and obviously kings exist in 'reality' outside the parables. Kings also appear in the narrative world of the Gospel

designated according to their position or status in the socio-religious structure prevalent in a first-century Mediterranean society, but that these characters figure in the socio-religious structure postulated in the Gospel of Luke.

The Lukan cast of characters in the example stories reflects a particularly Lukan cast upon the example stories. This feature may prove to be more important when considered not as a 'peculiar' feature of a group of parables in the synoptic gospels, but as a narrative strategy of parables embedded within a particular Gospel narrative.[383] Thus, more

of Matthew: Herod the Great (2.1, 9) and Herod the Tetrarch (14.9); another king, David, is mentioned in the genealogy (1.6); and, of course, the magi come to see the one born 'king of the Jews' (2.2), which is a label used with reference to Jesus near the end of the narrative (27.11, 29, 37, 42).

383. Although proper attention cannot be given here either to the interplay between the example stories—their characters and other textual elements—and the larger Gospel context in which they are embedded or to the issue of how the depiction of characters in the example stories contributes to the characterization of groups or individuals who appear in the larger narrative context, the following can be noted as a preliminary to such investigations. (1) The Merciful Samaritan depicts the actions of a priest, a Levite and a Samaritan. A specific priest, Zechariah, appears early in the narrative (Lk. 1.5 and thereafter), and priests are mentioned elsewhere (cf. 5.14; 6.4; 17.14). Additionally, priests appear in the Acts of the Apostles: Priests are part of a group angry at Peter and John for preaching in the temple (4.1-3), but priests are also said to be 'obedient to the faith' (6.7). (The 'chief priests' may also figure here; see Lk. 3.2; 9.22; 19.47; 20.1, 19; 22.2, 4, 50, 52, 54, 66; 23.4, 10 ,13; 24.20; Acts 4.6, 23; 5.17, 21, 24, 27; 7.1; 9.1, 14, 21; 19.14; 22.5, 30; 23.2, 4-5, 14; 24.1; 25.2, 15; 26.10, 12.) Levites do not receive frequent mention—indeed, not again in the Gospel of Luke; however, a particular Levite is shown acting favorably in the Acts of the Apostles (4.36-37). The first mention of Samaritans in the Gospel of Luke is negative—they do not receive Jesus and his entourage (9.52-53); but in 17.11-19 a Samaritan leper is shown thanking Jesus and praising God after he is healed (note that the entire group of ten lepers is told to go show themselves to a priest [v. 14]). In the Acts of the Apostles, Philip preaches in Samaria, and many Samaritans are healed, believe in the good news of the kingdom of God and in the name of Jesus Christ, are baptized and—after Peter and John arrive—receive the holy spirit (8.1-25). (2) The Rich Man and Poor Lazarus depicts two groups of characters who obviously figure in the larger Gospel narrative, the rich (see also The Foolish Rich Man) and the poor; yet a specific character is depicted who also plays a role in the larger Gospel narrative, Abraham. Abraham, in turn, mentions a person and a group of importance (as individuals, as groups, or as circumlocutions for 'scripture') in the larger Gospel narrative—Moses and the prophets—although neither Abraham, nor Moses, nor the prophets act as

consideration needs to be given to the four Lukan 'example narratives' as narrative parables in the Gospel of Luke.

The categorical distinction between the *Beispielerzählungen* and the *Parabeln*, as part of classification of the parables popularized by Jülicher, is near collapse. If this distinction does not hold, in what sense does the word 'example' apply? The 'strong formal relationship' between the *Beispielerzählungen* and the *Parabeln* has been affirmed. The claim has been made that the dichotomy of παραβολή (*Parabel*) and παράδειγμα (*Beispielerzählung*) is untenable. What is to be made of the assertion that the four *Beispielerzählungen* are *exempla* that give examples of behavior to be imitated or avoided? How is Bultmann's contention that the example stories 'offer examples=models for the right conduct' but that the example stories are not παραδείγματα to be assessed? If modern parable scholars are correct about the peculiarity

characters. In Mary's song of praise, Abraham is linked with God's mercy to Israel (1.54-55), and in Zechariah's prophecy Abraham is again linked to God's mercy promised to the fathers of Israel (1.72-73). Jesus is shown to be a descendent of Abraham in the genealogy (3.34). However, John the Baptist warns that it is not enough to claim Abraham as 'father' (3.8). Jesus says in a parable that those left outside will suffer when they see Abraham, Isaac and Jacob, and all the prophets in the kingdom of God (13.28)—which foreshadows The Rich Man and Poor Lazarus. In that parable, Jesus is made to have Abraham link Moses and the prophets to one raised from the dead, and the risen Jesus will later explain the scriptures concerning himself beginning with Moses and the prophets (24.25-27, 44-45). Elsewhere in the Gospel of Luke, Moses is linked to the raising of the dead (20.37). In the Acts of the Apostles, Moses and the prophets are linked to God's raising up a prophet (3.22; 7.37) and to convincing people about Jesus, one raised from the dead (28.23). For other references to Abraham, see Lk. 13.16; 19.5; Acts 3.13, 25; 7.2, 16-17, 32; 13.26. For the story of Moses in Stephen's speech, see Acts 7.17-44. (3) The Pharisee and the Toll Collector depicts members of two groups who have been involved in tension throughout the Gospel narrative, a tension which is summed up in 15.1-2: 'Now the tax collectors and sinners were all drawing near to him [Jesus]. And the Pharisees and the scribes murmured, saying, "This man receives sinners and eats with them"' (RSV). Indeed, after The Pharisee and the Toll Collector, Jesus receives and eats with a chief toll collector (19.1-10; cf. the reference to Abraham [v. 9]). For other references to the toll collectors in the Gospel, see 3.12; 5.27-30; 7.29-34. Although the Pharisees do not fare well in the Gospel narrative (see 5.17-33; 6.2, 7; 7.30-39; 11.37-54; 12.1; 13.31; 14.1-3; 16.14; 17.20; 19.39) and this trend follows them into the Acts of the Apostles, they, or some of their members, do appear in a better light in the Acts of the Apostles at times, with some Pharisees mentioned among the believers in Jerusalem (15.5); for other references to the Pharisees in Luke's second narrative, see 5.34; 23.6-9; 26.5.

of the example stories, would it be unreasonable to expect to find corroboration in the ancient rhetorical tradition? To answer those questions, we will have to examine what certain rhetoricians had to say about the παραβολαί and the παραδείγματα.

Chapter 5

PARABLE AND EXAMPLE IN THE ANCIENT RHETORICAL TRADITION

'Roman writers have for the most part preferred to give the name of *similitudo* to that which the Greeks style παραβολή, while they translate παράδειγμα by exemplum, although this latter involves comparison, while the former is of the nature of an exemplum. For my own part, I prefer with a view to making my purpose easier of apprehension to regard both as παραδείγματα and to call them exemplum.'

Quintilian,
Institutio Oratoria

The previous chapters elucidate some of the problems associated with attempts to distinguish between the *Parabeln* and the *Beispielerzählungen*. A particular problem encountered in the preceding conspectus of opinions on the example stories involves the invocation of ancient rhetoric as a means of classifying the παραβολαί—either as parables of Jesus, or as parables of the synoptic gospels—into various forms, or *Gattungen* or categories. The subject of concern in this study has been a particular category, the example story, and in the course of examining what parable scholars have had to say with respect to that group of four Lukan parables we have learned that scholars before and after Jülicher raised questions about the example stories: Are they parables or stories, parables or examples?

The latter question has garnered more notice, and in order to answer it some parable scholars, including Jülicher, have consulted directly the ancient rhetoricians, while others have either made vague reference to ancient rhetoric or ignored it altogether. Some parable scholars appeal to the ancient rhetorical tradition in order to uphold the categorical distinction between *Parabel* and *Beispielerzählung*, others in order to dispute it (as we saw in Chapters 2, 3 and 4). Regardless of whether direct reference is made to a specific rhetorician, it is not uncommon to find that the narrative parables are associated with the παραβολαί, the example narratives with the παραδείγματα or *exempla*. The task to be undertaken in this chapter is to canvass several ancient rhetoricians in order to determine what they have to tell us about the distinction between parable and example, παραβολή and παράδειγμα.

It is entirely appropriate that attention should be given to what ancient rhetoricians have to say about parable and example. An obvious reason for doing so is that Jülicher is thought to have derived his classification schema of Jesus' parables from Aristotle's *Rhetoric*, and, as we have seen, he has been chastised for that by some scholars. The suggestion was made earlier that Jülicher was more open to criticism for the manner in which he appropriated a section of Aristotle's *Rhetoric* than for the fact that he attempted to apply it to the parables recorded in synoptic parables. (To repeat, it is another question whether or not it was appropriate for Jülicher to apply Aristotle's *Rhetoric* to *Jesus'* parables.) Thus, we must attend to that section of Aristotle's *Rhetoric* in order to discern what he writes about parable and example. Here, Jülicher will not be rebuked for appealing to Aristotle, but his reading of Aristotle's *Rhetoric* will be subjected to critique.

A second reason for being attentive to ancient rhetoric is this: Knowledge of what ancient rhetoricians taught about parable and example can act as an instructive reminder that we need to safeguard against an ahistorical formalism with respect to the example stories. Since all four of the example stories are embedded within the Gospel of Luke, interpreters must be cognizant of the historical and cultural milieu in which that Gospel narrative was produced. Consulting ancient rhetoric may help interpreters determine better what conventional expectations might have been associated with a number of rhetorical techniques and strategies, and thereby prove invaluable as a propaedeu tic to modern readers of ancient literature. At the very least, a review of what ancient rhetoricians had to say about παραβολή and παράδειγμα might help interpreters avoid a mismatch of conventions, that is, approaching ancient rhetorical practices with modern preconceptions of 'parable' and 'example'. Such a mismatch of conventions may be a factor contributing to some of the conflicting views of the example stories held by some parable scholars.

We have met with a number of disparate, often contradictory, remarks made by some parable scholars not only with regard to what constitutes the 'uniqueness' of the example narratives, but also with regard to what ancient rhetoricians wrote about parable and example. Rather than rehearse those remarks now, several questions should be

kept in mind as we proceed: Do ancient rhetoricians make any statements that can serve as a basis for upholding the dichotomy between
Parabel conceived as παραβολή (or λόγος) and *Beispielerzählung* conceived as παράδειγμα? Do ancient rhetoricians identify particular
formal characteristics of the parables or the examples? Do ancient
rhetoricians differentiate between parable and example according to
form or according to function? Do ancient rhetoricians reserve the
terms παράδειγμα or *exemplum* exclusively for the 'historical example'? Do ancient rhetoricians maintain that the παράδειγμα, or *exemplum*, is a 'model for the right conduct' or that it offers an example of
behavior to be imitated or avoided? Do ancient rhetoricians issue prescriptive directives to the effect that in a παραβολή there can be mention of 'earthly circumstances' only? Do ancient rhetoricians supply
any probative evidence that can be utilized to maintain a categorical
distinction between *Beispielerzählung* and *Parabel*?

A few preliminary remarks are necessary before the ancient rhetoricians are consulted in order to find answers to those questions. Reference has been made to 'the ancient rhetorical tradition' in a manner that
may be misleading. The word 'ancient' as it is used here encompasses
an expansive period (roughly, the fourth century BCE through the first
century CE) which extends from the classical era through the Hellenistic era, a period in which rhetoric flourished. Although 'tradition' is a
singular noun, it must be recognized that there were competing schools
of thought among both Greek and Roman rhetoricians with regard to
the place and function of rhetoric in society and its discourse. During
the period in view, rhetorical theory was developed and refined by the
prominent rhetorical theorists of the day. And it should not be left
unsaid that Roman rhetoricians augmented and cultivated Greek rhetorical theory to meet the present needs of their culture; Roman rhetoricians did not merely repeat verbatim the precepts of the Greek
rhetoricians who preceded them. These remarks are not intended to
suggest that no agreement exists among ancient rhetoricians concerning
various aspects of rhetoric, for indeed common ground can be found
regarding certain matters of interest here; rather, these remarks simply
point out that 'the ancient rhetorical tradition' is not monolithic.[1] It

---

1.   Friedrich Solmsen points out that both Cicero and Quintilian speak of two
early traditions or systems of rhetoric, the Isocratean and the Aristotelian ('The
Aristotelian Tradition in Ancient Rhetoric', *AJP* 62 [1941], pp. 35-40, 169-90; repr.
in Keith V. Erickson (ed.), *Aristotle: The Classical Heritage of Rhetoric*,

should be stressed, then, that here 'ancient rhetorical tradition' is nothing more than a convenient phrase employed to refer to several extant rhetorical treatises written by classical Greek rhetoricians and later Greek and Roman rhetoricians.

The limitations of this chapter are clear. Answers to the questions raised about παραβολαί and παραδείγματα are conditioned by constraint and by choice. One constraint which automatically affects the outcome of this inquiry is the availability of ancient rhetorical treatises. The writings of several important teachers of rhetoric have not survived antiquity. Another constraint is self-imposed: The limited scope of this study precludes a comprehensive report on the details pertaining to parable and example in every rhetorical treatise that has survived. This limitation is not insurmountable because ancient views of parable and example have been examined by classical scholars in studies of far wider scope, and they will be enlisted as reliable guides.[2] Here, then, a

[Metuchen, NJ: Scarecrow Press, 1974], pp. 278-309 [278]; all references are to the reprint edition). Solmsen focuses on the latter and demonstrates how Aristotle's contributions are manifested and transformed in later rhetorical treatises, especially those of Cicero and Quintilian. For a comprehensive history of ancient rhetoric, see George A. Kennedy, *The Art of Persuasion in Greece* (Princeton, NJ: Princeton University Press, 1963); *idem, The Art of Rhetoric in the Roman World 300 B.C.– A.D. 300* (Princeton, NJ: Princeton University Press, 1972); and *idem, Greek Rhetoric under Christian Emperors* (Princeton, NJ: Princeton University Press, 1983). Kennedy states that 'though a practical and a philosophic tradition may be discerned, and though there were temporary vagaries, the history of ancient rhetoric is largely that of the growth of a single, great, traditional theory to which many writers and teachers contributed' (*The Art of Persuasion in Greece*, p. 9). For his description of the traditional features of ancient rhetorical theory, see pp. 3-25. To be sure, Kennedy does not view ancient rhetorical theory as monolithic; on the contrary, he observes that there were changes and revisions (see p. 13). Kennedy identifies some of the developments in rhetorical theory during the Hellenistic period and provides an instructive comparison of the different emphases in Greek rhetoric and Roman rhetoric (*The Art of Rhetoric in the Roman World*, pp. xv, 3-23, 264-68).

2.   The secondary literature on the ancient rhetorical tradition is vast and complex. I am not unaware that classicists also produce alternative readings of the ancient rhetorical tradition. Another constraint upon this study, therefore, is my choice of guides. For an overall view of the ancient rhetorical tradition, I have relied heavily upon Kennedy. On the specific subject of parable and example in the ancient rhetorical tradition, my indebtedness to the works of two classical scholars will become apparent; both of their studies have a scope far wider than this study,

selective review of what is written about parable and example in several extant rhetorical treatises, mainly the rhetorical handbooks, will be
conducted. The assumption underlying this choice is that an examination of παραβολή (or *similitudo*) and παράδειγμα (or *exemplum*) in a
τέχνη or *ars*—a handbook in which a teacher of rhetoric provides
instruction in rhetorical theory by means of an exposition of precepts—
might enable us to determine some of the conventional expectations
associated with parable and example as rhetorical techniques or strategies. In light of what has been said about the ancient rhetorical tradition, we should expect to find a range of opinions on parable and
example espoused by the rhetoricians, and indeed one will search in
vain for a unified theory of parable and example common to all ancient

---

both draw upon many ancient sources and both are informed by generations of
classical scholarship. Marsh H. McCall, Jr (*Ancient Rhetorical Theories of Simile
and Comparison* [LCM; Cambridge, MA: Harvard University Press, 1969]) presents a detailed analysis of various terms of comparison employed in ancient
rhetorical texts and other documents. Bennett J. Price ('Παράδειγμα and
Exemplum in Ancient Rhetorical Theory' [PhD dissertation, University of
California, Berkeley, 1975]) investigates the nature and function of examples
according to the precepts of five rhetoricians ('Anaximanes', Aristotle, Auctor
Rhetorica ad Herennium, Cicero, Quintilian). The former study is helpful for an
understanding of ancient views on the παραβολή and other techniques of
comparison; the latter, παράδειγμα and *exemplum*. My interest lies in the points
where those two studies converge. Kennedy, McCall and Price exhibit extensive
knowledge of the primary and secondary literature on the ancient rhetorical
tradition, and their books provide ample bibliographical information. A far less
helpful approach to ancient understandings of the παραβολή, due to a lack of
precision in detail, is that of W. Bedell Stanford, *Greek Metaphor: Studies in
Theory and Practice* (Oxford: Basil Blackwell, 1936). The study of the example is
by no means limited to the period of concern here. A number of studies investigate
the use of example in folklore and the various forms of examples throughout the
centuries; see, e.g., Hermann Bausinger, 'Zum Beispiel', in Fritz Harkort, Karel C.
Peeters and Robert Wildhaber (eds.), *Volksüberlieferung* (Festschrift für Kurt
Ranke zur Vollendung des 60. Lebensjahres; Göttingen: Otto Schwartz & Co.,
1968), pp. 9-18; *idem*, 'Exemplum und Beispiel', *Hessische Blätter für Volkskunde*
59 (1968), pp. 31-43; Karlheinz Stierle, 'Geschichte als Exemplum—Exemplum als
Geschichte: Zur Pragmatik und Poetik narrativer Texte', in *idem, Text als
Handlung: Perspektiven einer systematischen Literaturwissenschaft* (Munich:
Wilhelm Fink Verlag, 1975), pp. 14-48; Rudolf Schenda, 'Stand und Aufgaben der
Exemplaforschung', *Fabula* 10 (1969), pp. 69-85; Peter Assion, 'Das Exempel als
agitatorische Gattung: Zu Form und Funktion der kurzen Beispielgeschichte',
Fabula 19 (1978), pp. 225-40; and Gelley (ed.), *Unruly Examples*.

rhetorical treatises. Despite these limitations, what the writers of several ancient rhetorical treatises have to say about parable and example will be examined in order to establish parameters within which the distinction between *Parabel* and *Beispielerzählung* as proposed by some parable scholars can be assessed.

The evidence for παραβολή and παράδειγμα used as technical rhetorical terms prior to the fourth century BCE is quite sparse, and doubtless the paucity of extant rhetorical treatises written by the early teachers of rhetoric contributes to that. Although the words παραβολή and παράδειγμα occur in literature of the fifth and fourth centuries, the usage of both words is diverse, and it is difficult to discern a specific sense for either word that can be designated as a technical rhetorical meaning.[3] The first extensive discussions of παραβολή and παράδειγμα (of which we have knowledge) as technical rhetorical terms come in the late fourth century: The author of *Rhetorica ad Alexandrum* discusses παράδειγμα, and Aristotle discusses both παραβολή and παράδειγμα in his *Rhetoric*. These works provide a suitable starting point for a review of parable and example in the ancient rhetorical tradition.

Parable and Example in Rhetorica ad Alexandrum

This investigation of parable and example in ancient rhetorical theory begins with a cursory examination of *Rhetorica ad Alexandrum*, a rhetorical handbook approximately contemporaneous with Aristotle's *Rhetoric*.[4] The remarks of some scholars indicate that we should not

3.   For documentary evidence on παράδειγμα, see LSJ, pp. 1307-1308, and Price, 'Παράδειγμα and *Exemplum* in Ancient Rhetorical Theory', pp. 11-13, 220-21; on παραβολή, see LSJ, p. 1305, and McCall, *Ancient Rhetorical Theories of Simile and Comparison*, pp. 1-23.

4.   The text and translation of *Rhetorica ad Alexandrum* cited in this chapter is provided by H. Rackham in *Aristotle, Problems II, Books XXII–XXXVIII, Rhetorica ad Alexandrum* (trans. W.S. Hett and H. Rackham; LCL; London: Heinemann; Cambridge, MA: Harvard University Press, 1937). The authorship and date of this treatise, as well as whether it manifests Isocratean or Aristotelian influences, are matters of debate among classical scholars; see Rackham, *Rhetorica ad Alexandrum*, pp. 258-62; Kennedy, *The Art of Persuasion in Greece*, pp. 114-24; McCall, *Ancient Rhetorical Theories of Simile and Comparison*, pp. 20-22; Price, 'Παράδειγμα and *Exemplum* in Ancient Rhetorical Theory', pp. 14, 221-22; and Edward M. Cope, *An Introduction to Aristotle's Rhetoric with Analysis Notes and*

expect to learn much of importance about either παραβολή—and indeed the author does not use the noun παραβολή—or παράδειγμα from this treatise. The influence of *Rhetorica ad Alexandrum* upon the developing rhetorical tradition is reputed by Kennedy to be 'negligible'.[5] Bennett J. Price states that the classifications and definitions posited in *Rhetorica ad Alexandrum* '...were by and large ignored or abandoned in antiquity while Aristotle's views, however much altered, are clearly visible in later writers'.[6] Marsh H. McCall, Jr, finds little information of substance with regard to the use of technical terms of comparison in *Rhetorica ad Alexandrum*, except for a rather idiosyncratic use of παραμοίωσις in one chapter.[7] These comments are not to be taken lightly, and the opinions of those scholars will not be gainsaid. Still, even though the precepts expressed by 'Anaximanes' in *Rhetorica ad Alexandrum* do not carry such a weight of influence upon subsequent rhetorical theory as those expressed by Aristotle in his *Rhetoric*, a modicum of information about the παράδειγμα can be extracted from *Rhetorica ad Alexandrum* that is not entirely worthless.

The first mention of παράδειγμα in *Rhetorica ad Alexandrum* occurs in the opening chapter, but we do not learn a great deal about examples from it. Having identified three genera and seven species of public speeches, Anaximanes states that he will treat each species *seriatim* and will then discuss 'their qualities, their uses and their arrangement'.[8]

Appendices (London: Macmillan, 1867 [repr. Dubuque, IA: William C. Brown Reprint Library]), pp. 401-64. While Aristotelian authorship has been ruled out by many scholars, other scholars deem it plausible that the handbook is either the work of the author suggested by Quintilian (*Institutio Oratoria* 3.4.9), Anaximanes (of Lampsacus), or is based upon his work. As a matter of convenience, I refer to the author as 'Anaximanes'. For quotations and references to particular sections of *Rhetorica ad Alexandrum*, I cite the nearest numbered line in Rackham's edition.

5. Kennedy, *The Art of Persuasion in Greece*, p. 115.

6. Price, 'Παράδειγμα and *Exemplum* in Ancient Rhetorical Theory', p. 14.

7. McCall, *Ancient Rhetorical Theories of Simile and Comparison*, pp. 20-22; on παρομοίωσις, see *Rhetorica ad Alexandrum* 11.1430b10.

8. See *Rhetorica ad Alexandrum* 1.1421b15. The three genera are legislative, ceremonial (epideictic) and forensic (judicial); the seven species are exhortation, dissuasion, eulogy, vituperation, accusation, defense and investigation. Although Anaximanes makes it clear that 'in their practical application' the species of rhetoric overlap (5.1427b30-35), exhortation and dissuasion are prevalent in legislative speeches, eulogy and vituperation in ceremonial speeches, accusation and defense in forensic speeches.

Turning to exhortation and dissuasion, he defines both species and shows how a list of common topics applies to each.[9] Following a definition of each topic, Anaximanes discusses the sources to which the speaker can turn for pertinent material: the definition of each topic; analogies to or opposites of each topic; and previous judgments made about each topic (1.1422a20-30). A demonstration of the argument from analogy to the just is provided and then one from the opposite to the just. Between the two, παράδειγμα receives mention: 'This is the way in which we must take the analogous [ὅμοιον] to the just; and we must illustrate the actual example [παράδειγμα] given from its opposites [ἐναντίων]...' (1.1422a35). This particular section of the first chapter assumes a knowledge of παράδειγμα. Anaximanes is careful to provide more details about the example in later chapters. Prior to a consideration of those chapters, a section of an intervening chapter may prove to be of interest with regard to the parable.

Although the word παραβολή is not found in *Rhetorica ad Alexandrum*, the author does use παραβάλλειν and ἀντιπαραβάλλειν during the course of his discussion of the species eulogy and vituperation. Amplification, while useful in vituperation, is especially effective in eulogy. Anaximanes suggests several methods by which a matter or topic brought forward for eulogy can be amplified; the second and third are of interest here.

> A second method is to introduce a previous judgment—a favourable one if you are praising, an unfavourable one if you are blaming—and then set your own statement beside it and compare [παραβάλλειν] them with one another, enlarging on the strongest points of your own case and the weakest ones of the other and so making your own case appear a strong one. A third way is to set in comparison [ἀντιπαραβάλλειν] with the thing you are saying the smallest of the things that fall into the same class, for thus your case will appear magnified... (3.1426a20-30).

This mention of παραβάλλειν in conjunction with previous judgments is even more intriguing in light of Price's perceptive observation that there is an unmistakable similarity between previous judgments and παραδείγματα in this treatise, especially in the samples of previous judgments given in the first chapter.[10] However, we should not make

9. See *Rhetorica ad Alexandrum* 1.1421b25. The list includes that which is just, lawful, expedient, honorable, pleasant and easily practicable. We learn later (6.1427b40-1428a5) that this list of topics is common to all species of rhetoric.

10. See Price, 'Παράδειγμα and *Exemplum* in Ancient Rhetorical Theory',

too much of this interesting curiosity, for no explicit mention is made of either παραβολή or παράδειγμα here. We learn more about examples in the discussion of proofs.

We are told that proofs are necessarily employed in all species of speeches, but that they are particularly useful in accusation and defense (6.1428a5-10).[11] According to Anaximanes, there are two modes of proof. Some proofs—such as probabilities, examples, tokens, enthymemes, maxims, signs, refutations—'are drawn from words and actions and persons themselves'; other proofs—such as the opinion of the speaker, the evidence of witnesses, evidence extracted by means of torture, oaths—'are supplementary to what the persons say and do' (7.1428a15-20).[12] In chs. 7–14, attention is given to each of the proofs; they are defined, sources are identified and the differences between the proofs are explained.

Chapter 8 of *Rhetorica ad Alexandrum* is devoted to the παραδείγματα. A formal definition of example is followed by prescriptions for the use of examples:

> Examples are actions [πράξεις] that have occurred previously and are similar [ὅμοιαι] to, or the opposite [ἐναντίαι] of, those which we are now discussing. They should be employed on occasions when your statement of the case is unconvincing and you desire to illustrate it, if it cannot be proved by the argument from probability, in order that your

pp. 31-34. Although, according to Price, the three samples of previous judgments given in the first chapter of *Rhetorica ad Alexandrum* 'seem to be quite proper *paradeigmata*', he points out that there is an implicit distinction between previous judgments and παραδείγματα (p. 33). He also notes that 'κρίσις and παράδειγμα often overlap' and gives reference to Aristotle's *Rhetoric* (p. 234 n. 57).

11. In *Rhetorica ad Alexandrum*, proofs are discussed explicitly in sections which deal with accusation and defense, exhortation and dissuasion. The use of proofs is not ruled out in eulogy and vituperation since these species also deal with the list of topics common to all species of rhetoric (cf. 3.1425b40) and since, as we have seen, examples are used in arguments from analogy to the just.

12. Price ('Παράδειγμα and *Exemplum* in Ancient Rhetorical Theory', p. 15) states that 'the difference between the two types of proof is not quite clear but the distinction seems to be that of the invention of arguments versus the use of evidence...' Thus, Price refers to the proofs 'drawn from words and actions and persons themselves' as 'argumentative' or 'inventive' proofs. He notes that this distinction between arguments and evidence is found in Aristotle and later rhetoricians (p. 223 n. 25); other scholars refer to these two types of proofs as artificial and inartificial proofs. Unlike later rhetoricians, Anaximanes does not treat the example as 'an ornamental or stylistic device' (p. 35).

audience may be more ready to believe your statements when they realize that another action resembling [πρᾶξιν ὁμοίαν] the one you allege
has been committed in the way in which you say that it occurred
(8.1429a20-30).[13]

Anaximanes then indicates that there are two modes of examples, and
he gives samples of each.

> There are two modes of examples. This is because some things happen
> according to reasonable expectation, others against reasonable expecta-
> tion; and those happening according to expectation cause credit, those
> not according to expectation incredulity. I mean, for instance, if some-
> body asserts that the rich are more honest than the poor, and produces
> cases of honest conduct on the part of rich men: examples of this sort
> appear to be in accordance with reasonable expectation, because most
> people obviously think that those who are rich are more honest than
> those who are poor. If, on the other hand, one were to produce instances
> of rich men acting dishonestly for money, by employing this example of
> something that has happened contrary to probability he would cause the
> rich to be discredited... (8.1429a25-39).

Other samples involving the numbers of combatants in war are adduced
to show how a speaker can use examples to argue according to general
expectation or to argue against probability (8.1429b1-25). In those
examples, reference is made to particular battles fought by specific
countries, and some leaders are named. Additional comments on the
use of both modes of example follow,[14] and the chapter ends with a
remark on the available supply of examples:

> The events of the past and those occurring now will supply you with
> many examples; most actions are partly like [ὅμοια] and partly unlike
> [ἀνόμοια] one another, so that for this reason we shall be well supplied
> with examples, and also shall have no difficulty in countering those put
> forward by the other side (8.1430a5-10).[15]

---

13. Price indicates that there may be textual corruptions in this passage (see
'Παράδειγμα and *Exemplum* in Ancient Rhetorical Theory', pp. 17, 223-25 n. 29).
   14. See *Rhetorica ad Alexandrum* 8.1429b25-1430a5. Price ('Παράδειγμα and
Exemplum in Ancient Rhetorical Theory', pp. 19-22, 227-28 nn. 36-38) states that
there are difficulties in this section, some of which may be attributable to the
manuscript tradition of this treatise.
   15. Other sources for examples are tacitly excluded, for, as Price remarks,
'Anaximanes nowhere states or implies that mythological or fabulous events may
be used as paradigms' ('Παράδειγμα and *Exemplum* in Ancient Rhetorical
Theory', p. 34).

Although this concludes the chapter in which Anaximanes focuses on the παραδείγματα, other remarks on examples are scattered throughout the treatise. A cursory glance at those remarks will round out an understanding of the conception of παράδειγμα advanced in *Rhetorica ad Alexandrum*.

The example is closely related to other proofs, specifically, probabilities and tokens. According to the delineation of two modes of παραδείγματα in ch. 8, one mode of example makes reference to things that happen according to probability. Indeed, in the chapter immediately preceding the discussion of examples, Anaximanes defines probability in terms involving the example: 'A probability [Εἰκὸς] is a statement supported by examples [παραδείγματα] present in the minds of an audience' (7.1428a25). Later, Anaximanes distinguishes between probability and example, and between examples and tokens; unfortunately, a lacuna in the text obscures our understanding of those distinctions, although the extant portion suggests that examples 'can be drawn both from contrary things [ἐκ τῶν ἐναντίων] and from similar things [ἐκ τῶν ὁμοίων]'.[16]

Examples receive mention again in the discussion of the arrangement of the parts of speeches. Anaximanes states that in legislative speeches proofs can be effectively employed in the confirmation. Among the most appropriate proofs named are 'the customary course of events, examples, considerations [ἐνθυμήματα], and the opinion of the speaker' (32.1438b30-35).[17] The order prescribed here requires that examples follow the opinion of the speaker:

> Next we must adduce examples, and employ any available similarity [ὁμοιότης] to support the statements we are making. We must take examples that are akin to the case and those that are nearest in time or place to our hearers, and if such are not available, such others as are most important and best known. After these we must cite maxims. Also at the end of sections devoted to probabilities [εἰκότων] and examples we must frame the conclusions in the form of considerations

16. See *Rhetorica ad Alexandrum* 14.1431a25-30. On the textual problems in this section, see Price, 'Παράδειγμα and *Exemplum* in Ancient Rhetorical Theory', pp. 31, 233-34 n. 56. The extant portion here is in accord with what is said about examples earlier in 8.1429b35: 'And we must draw examples not only from similar cases but also from the opposite...'

17. 'Considerations' is Rackham's translation of ἐνθυμήματα, customarily rendered as 'enthymemes'. I have added the Greek word here.

[ἐνθυμηματώδεις] and maxims. This, then, is how we must introduce proofs as to matters of fact (32.1438b40-1439a10).

Proofs can be omitted entirely if the statement of the facts by itself is convincing, in which case the policies in question should be confirmed on the basis of the list of topics common to all species of public speeches (32.1439a5-10). Justice is the initial topic, and Anaximanes rehearses how that plea may be entered:

> We should place the plea of justice first, if it is available, going through the topics of absolute justice, approximate [ὁμοίου] justice, the opposite [ἐναντίου] of justice, and justice as decided by a previous judgment [τοῦ κεκριμένου]. You must also produce examples [παραδείγματα] conforming [ὅμοια] with the principles of justice that you assert (32.1439a10-15).[18]

Examples, according to Anaximanes, can be used to good effect in forensic speeches both by the prosecution and the defense. In accusatory speeches, proofs are used in the confirmation. If either evidence obtained from witnesses or confessions extracted by means of torture are available, these proofs come first.

> Next this evidence must be confirmed by means of maxims and general considerations, if it be convincing, or if not entirely convincing, by probability, and then by examples, tokens, signs and refutations, and by considerations and the enunciation of maxims to finish with (36.1442b35-1443a5).

In defense speeches, examples are to be used in the refutation of charges against the accused. After offering suggestions for the refutation of other proofs, Anaximanes writes: 'In dealing with an example, first show if you can that it does not resemble [ὅμοιόν] the act of which you are accused, or else yourself produce another example to the contrary [ἐκ τῶν ἐναντίων] that has occurred against probability [παρὰ τὸ εἰκὸς]' (36.1443b35-40).[19] This marks the end of the precepts on the παράδειγμα as given by Anaximanes.

Rhetorica ad Alexandrum does not furnish a great deal of information that can be applied directly to the questions raised in this study on the distinction between *Parabel* and *Beispielerzählung*. That is so

---

18. Given what was said earlier about the similarity between previous judgments and examples, the proximity of the terms ὁμοίου, παραβολή, κεκριμένου, παραδείγματα, ὅμοια is to be noted.

19. See also *Rhetorica ad Alexandrum* 8.1429b20-25.

because Anaximanes neither discusses nor defines παραβολή. Even
though the words παραβάλλειν and ἀντιπαραβάλλειν are employed in
the context of remarks on previous judgments, and despite the similarity between previous judgments and παραδείγματα noticed by Price,
anything that might be inferred from that with regard to a relation
between παραβολή and παράδειγμα would be conjecture.[20] On the
basis of the precepts of rhetorical theory espoused in *Rhetorica ad
Alexandrum*, it is reasonable to assume that at least in one sector of the
rhetorical tradition in the fourth century BCE not much emphasis was
placed upon the παραβολή as a rhetorical device or strategy. We will
soon see that another sector of the rhetorical tradition in that period, as
represented by Aristotle, devoted more attention to the παραβολή.
Before turning to Aristotle, some of the main features of the
παράδειγμα according to Anaximanes can be highlighted as follows.

In *Rhetorica ad Alexandrum* the παραδείγματα are treated mainly
within the context of a discussion of proofs, which are divided into two
modes. The example is listed among the mode of proof which is 'drawn
from the words and actions and persons themselves'; among this mode
of proof, the examples are related to tokens, but even more closely
related to probabilities. Proofs, and by implication examples, are said to
be useful in forensic speeches of accusation and defense, but Anaximanes allows that in practice proofs are employed in all species of
speeches.

Examples are formally defined as 'actions that have occurred previously and are similar to, or the opposite of, those which we are
now discussing'. Anaximanes offers a rather idiosyncratic distinction
between two modes of examples, παραδείγματα κατὰ λόγον and
παραδείγματα παρὰ λόγον; the former can be employed to enhance
arguments from probability, the latter to discredit. Both modes of
examples may be employed in speeches as a means of confirmation or
of refutation. The parts of speeches devoted to probabilities and examples should end with conclusions framed in the form of enthymemes or
maxims.

Although a formal definition of example is given, a specification of
the formal characteristics of examples is lacking; for instance, no limits
are set on the length of the example, and the samples provided by
Anaximanes vary according to length and the amount of detail. The

20. The lines of that relation could perhaps be developed in terms of comparison, which would include both similarity and contrast.

definition suggests that παραδείγματα—'actions [πράξεις] that have occurred previously'—are 'historical examples' drawn from the past, but we are told later that 'events of the past and those occurring now' are sources for examples. Thus, there is a degree of latitude with regard to the temporality of the event, but the event itself apparently must have taken place in history (that is, the 'real' world, as opposed to the worlds of myth or fable).[21] While some of the samples of παραδείγματα proffered by Anaximanes do make reference to specific individuals and places by name, he does not require that an example must give the names of the persons involved in the action or the name of the geographical locale of the action. In fact, as Price demonstrates, Anaximanes exhibits a proclivity for referring to the persons in the samples of παραδείγματα by means of τις and not by name.[22] Nevertheless, Anaximanes encourages reference to events or actions that are well known to the audience, especially to those events and actions nearest in time and place to the audience. The matter of importance with regard to this aspect of examples, it would appear, is the 'action', for Anaximanes defines the παραδείγματα in terms of πράξεις.

The formal definition of example makes reference to a more notable feature of the παραδείγματα according to the precepts advanced in *Rhetorica ad Alexandrum*: 'Examples are actions that have occurred previously and are similar [ὅμοιαι] to, or the opposite [ἐναντίαι] of, those which we are now discussing'. As we have seen, Anaximanes frequently mentions the similar, ὅμοιον (or related terms), and the opposite, ἐναντίον (or related terms), in conjunction with παραδείγματα. While Price is certainly correct in his assertion that Anaximanes does not define ὁμοιότης as a technical term,[23] it is fairly clear nonetheless that Anaximanes regards the παράδειγμα as a mode of proof that can be employed effectively in speeches as a comparative technique or strategy to show, depending on the purpose at hand,

21. For more on the temporality of the example, see Price, 'Παράδειγμα and *Exemplum* in Ancient Rhetorical Theory', pp. 23-26, 229-30 n. 44.

22. See Price, 'Παράδειγμα and *Exemplum* in Ancient Rhetorical Theory', pp. 27-28, esp. p. 231 n. 48. Price concludes that 'despite a fondness for τις in his illustrations, it is clear that the practicing speaker must be fairly specific; he must have definite events or people in mind' (p. 28; cf. p. 34).

23. See Price, 'Παράδειγμα and *Exemplum* in Ancient Rhetorical Theory', p. 233 n. 53. Although this is true, *Rhetorica ad Alexandrum* has more to say about comparison than the brief section on παρομοίωσις in ch. 7.

similarity or dissimilarity. In this respect, *Rhetorica ad Alexandrum* is not in discord with other important treatises in the ancient rhetorical tradition.

Parable and Example in 'Art' of Rhetoric

This investigation of parable and example in ancient rhetorical theory continues with another rhetorical handbook of the late fourth century written by one of the preeminent thinkers in antiquity. Aristotle, a prodigious writer, mentions παραβολή and παράδειγμα in several of his volumes devoted to ethics, politics, logic, dialectic and rhetoric, but it is fair to say that the παράδειγμα is of more interest to him and thus receives more of his attention.[24] The focus here will be upon Aristotle's discussion of parable and example as provided in his *Rhetoric* because aspects of that discussion exert influence upon precepts issued by other important rhetoricians in antiquity and because parable scholars have appealed to the *Rhetoric* for various reasons, not infrequently in order to classify the parables of Jesus as recorded in the synoptic gospels. As this section unfolds, a word of caution should be kept in mind: Aristotle's treatment of the παράδειγμα in the *Rhetoric* presents terminological and conceptual difficulties which have bedeviled classical scholars, not all of which can be attributed to the composition history of the treatise. The same difficulties will confront us, the most obvious difficulty being that not only does Aristotle use the technical term παράδειγμα in two ways, he employs the same term in a non-technical sense as well.[25] An attempt to resolve those difficulties is unnecessary

24. A partial list of references to παραβολή outside of the *Rhetoric* would include: *Topica* 1.10.104a28, 8.1.156b25-27, 8.1.157a14-15, 8.14.164a15; *Politics* 2.5.1264b4-6; *Metaphysics* H.11.1036b24; *Eudemian Ethics* 7.12.1244b23, 7.12.1245b13; *On Sophistical Refutations* 17.176a33. A partial list of references to παράδειγμα outside of the *Rhetoric* would include: *Topica* 8.1.157a14-15; *Metaphysics* A.9.991b1, H.5.1079b35; *Prior Analytics* 2.24.68b38-69a13, 2.24.69a14-16; *Posterior Analytics* 1.1.71a9-11; *Problems* 18.3.916b26-27, 32-34.

25. On the date and composition history of the *Rhetoric*, see George A. Kennedy, *Aristotle, On Rhetoric: A Theory of Civic Discourse* (Oxford: Oxford University Press, 1991), pp. 299-305. Some scholars argue that Aristotle is inconsistent in his treatment of the παραδείγματα in the *Rhetoric*, or that the treatment of the παραδείγματα in the *Rhetoric* contradicts what Aristotle says about the παραδείγματα in other treatises; conversely, other scholars argue that Aristotle offers a unified view of παραδείγματα in the *Rhetoric*, one that does not contradict

here; a simple and brief review of a few important sections of the *Rhetoric* which treat the παράδειγμα and the παραβολή will provide an adequate basis for the assessment of the views espoused by parable scholars regarding the distinction between the *Parabel* and the *Beispielerzählung*.

Aristotle treats παραδείγματα in all three books of the *Rhetoric*, which is an indication of their importance in his rhetorical theory. The most extensive discussion of παραδείγματα comes in Books 1 and 2, which deal broadly with the means of persuasion available to public speakers. Brief mention of παραδείγματα is made in Book 3, which is concerned with matters of style and arrangement. As important as the παράδειγμα is in the *Rhetoric*, it is not as important as the enthymeme, the fulcrum of the rhetorical theory advanced by Aristotle. Although for obvious reasons the focus of attention will be on the παράδειγμα— which means that the παραβολή will also come into view—we should be observant of the context in which Aristotle discusses the παράδειγμα.

In Book 1 of the *Rhetoric*, where we first find mention of the παράδειγμα, Aristotle introduces the subject of rhetoric as the 'counterpart' of dialectic (1.1.1) and then provides some basic definitions and distinctions. In a critique of other rhetorical handbooks (τέχνας), Aristotle faults his predecessors for concerning themselves with external matters and for neglecting proofs. These censures are not negligible because, according to Aristotle, 'only proofs [πίστεις] are artistic [ἔντεχνόν]'.[26] His most pointed stricture is that previous

other treatises. On this debate, see Cope, *An Introduction to Aristotle's Rhetoric*, pp. 99-108; Price, 'Παράδειγμα and *Exemplum* in Ancient Rhetorical Theory', pp. 37-83, 235-54; McCall, *Ancient Rhetorical Theories of Simile and Comparison*, pp. 24-27; Gerard A. Hauser, 'The Example in Aristotle's *Rhetoric*: Bifurcation or Contradiction?', *Philosophy and Rhetoric* 1 (1968), pp. 78-90 (repr. in Erickson [ed.], *Aristotle: The Classical Heritage of Rhetoric*, pp. 156-68); *idem*, 'Aristotle's Example Revisited', *Philosophy and Rhetoric* 18 (1985), pp. 171-80; Scott Consigny, 'The Rhetorical Example', *The Southern Speech Communication Journal* 41 (1976), pp. 121-34; William Lyon Benoit, 'Aristotle's Example: The Rhetorical Induction', *Quarterly Journal of Speech* 66 (1980), pp. 182-92; Michael McGuire, 'Some Problems with Rhetorical Example', *Pre/Text* 3 (1982), pp. 121-36; Carlo Natali, 'Paradeigma: The Problems of Human Acting and the Use of Examples in Some Greek Authors of the 4th Century B.C.', *Rhetoric Society Quarterly* 19 (1989), pp. 141-52.

26. *Rhetoric* 1.1.3; my translation. The Greek text cited throughout this study is

rhetorical handbooks say nothing about enthymemes, which are 'the body of proof [πίστεως]', indeed 'the strongest of rhetorical proofs [πίστεων]'.[27] Aristotle redresses this situation by presenting rhetoric as an artistic method (ἔντεχνος μέθοδος) concerned with proofs (πίστεις), and in particular artistic proofs (ἐντέχνων πίστεων), because it is by means of artistic proofs that a speaker becomes 'enthymematic' (ἐνθυμηματικός).[28] His formal definition of rhetoric reads: 'Let rhetoric be [defined as] an ability, in each [particular] case, to see the available means of persuasion' (1.2.1). Having introduced and defined rhetoric, Aristotle immediately directs his attention to proofs.

Aristotle distinguishes between two kinds of proof (1.2.2). Some proofs are not provided by the speaker but already exist for the speaker to use; these proofs (such as 'witnesses, tortures, contracts') are called 'nonartistic' (or inartificial, atechnic: ἄτεχνοι). Other proofs are invented by the speaker, that is, constructed by method or by the efforts of the speaker; these proofs are called 'artistic' (or artificial, entechnic:

Aristotle, *'Art' of Rhetoric* (trans. John H. Freese; LCL; London: Heinemann; Cambridge, MA: Harvard University Press, 1926 [repr. 1982]). However, I prefer Kennedy's translation in *Aristotle, On Rhetoric*; therefore, all translations of the *Rhetoric* cited in this study, unless stated otherwise, will be Kennedy's. For information pertaining to the critical editions upon which Freese and Kennedy rely, see *Aristotle, 'Art' of Rhetoric*, p. xxxi; *Aristotle, On Rhetoric*, pp. xi-xii. For details on the 'external matters' named by Aristotle, such as appeals to the emotions (1.1.4) and arrangement (1.1.9), see 1.1.3-10. Aristotle also criticizes other writers (1.1.4-14) for their fixation on judicial rhetoric at the expense of epideictic rhetoric and deliberative rhetoric, the latter judged by Aristotle to be the nobler or finer species of rhetoric (1.1.10). Aristotle defines the species of rhetoric in 1.3.1-9 and then considers each species individually: deliberative rhetoric in 1.4.1–1.8.7; epideictic rhetoric in 1.9.1-41; judicial rhetoric in 1.10.1–1.15.33.

27. *Rhetoric* 1.1.3 and 1.1.11; Freese's translation. For more on the enthymeme, see James H. McBurney, 'The Place of the Enthymeme in Rhetorical Theory', *Speech Monographs* 3 (1936), pp. 49-97 (repr. in Erickson [ed.], *Aristotle: The Classical Heritage of Rhetoric*, pp. 117-40): and Lloyd F. Bitzer, 'Aristotle's Enthymeme Revisited', *Quarterly Journal of Speech* 45 (1959), pp. 399-408 (repr. in Erickson [ed.], *Aristotle: The Classical Heritage of Rhetoric*, pp. 141-55).

28. See *Rhetoric* 1.1.11 and 1.1.9. Aristotle takes pains to describe rhetoric as an art which, like dialectic, is not concerned with a single genus of subject, an art which functions 'not to persuade but to see the available means of persuasion in each case, as is true of all the other arts' (1.1.14). Aristotle's desire to describe rhetoric both as an artistic method and as the counterpart to dialectic is obvious in 1.1.11.

ἔντεχνοι). Aristotle's main concern is with the latter, which he divides into three species: Some proofs provided through speech (διὰ τοῦ λόγου) derive from the character of the speaker, some from disposing the audience to react emotionally in a certain way, and some from the argument itself (αὐτῷ τῷ λόγῳ) by means of showing or seeming to show something (διὰ τοῦ δεικνύναι ἢ φαίνεσθαι δεικνύναι).[29] The group mentioned last, which shall be called 'logical arguments' (following Kennedy[30]), are subdivided into two modes, which can be designated as enthymematic and paradigmatic. Thus, we come to the first discussion of the παράδειγμα in the *Rhetoric*.

Aristotle makes several important comments on the modes of logical arguments, and it will allay confusion if the section (1.8-10) is quoted in full. He takes up the discussion of the artistic proof which derives from the argument itself by repeating the phrase διὰ τοῦ δεικνύναι ἢ φαίνεσθαι δεικνύναι:

> 8. In the case of persuasion through proving or seeming to prove something, just as in dialectic [1356b] there is on the one hand induction [ἐπαγωγή] and on the other the syllogism and the apparent syllogism, so the situation is similar in rhetoric; for the παράδειγμα ['example'] is an induction [ἐπαγωγή], the ἐνθύμημα a syllogism. I call a rhetorical syllogism an enthymeme, a rhetorical induction a paradigm [παράδειγμα δὲ ἐπαγωγὴν ῥητορικήν]. And all [speakers] produce logical persuasion by means of paradigms [παραδείγματα] or enthymemes and by nothing other than these. As a result, since it is always necessary to show something either by syllogizing or by inducing (and this is clear to us from the *Analytics*), it is necessary that each of these be the same as each of the others. 9. What the difference is between a paradigm [παραδείγματος] and an enthymeme is clear from the *Topics* (for an account was given there earlier of syllogism and induction [ἐπαγωγῆς]): to show on the basis of many similar instances [πολλῶν καὶ ὁμοίων] that something is so is in dialectic induction [ἐπαγωγῆς], in rhetoric paradigm [παράδειγμα]; but to show that if some premises are true, something else [the conclusion] beyond them results from these because they are true, either universally or for the most part, in dialectic is called syllogism and in rhetoric enthymeme. 10. And it is also apparent that either

29. *Rhetoric* 1.2.3. Aristotle explains further what he means by these three kinds of artistic proofs—commonly referred to as ethos, pathos and logos—and continues the discussion of how rhetoric and dialectic relate to each other in 1.2.3-7. Nonartistic proofs are given consideration in 1.15.1-33, where Aristotle adds laws and oaths to this type of proof.

30. See Kennedy, *Aristotle, On Rhetoric*, pp. 14, 30 n. 9.

species of rhetoric has merit (what has also been said in the *Methodics* is true in these cases too); for some rhetorical utterances are paradigmatic [παραδειγματώδεις], some enthymematic; and similarly, some orators are paradigmatic [παραδειγματώδεις], some enthymematic. Speeches using paradigms [παραδειγμάτων] are not less persuasive, but those with enthymemes excite more favorable audience reaction.[31]

Aristotle states that he will discuss later the ways in which each mode of logical argument, the enthymematic and the paradigmatic, should be employed, and he does so in Book 2. At this juncture, however, Aristotle wishes to explain more clearly the two modes of logical argument. The remaining points about the παράδειγμα made in Book 1 will be pursued here.

Aristotle continues his explanation of the two modes of logical argument by identifying the sources of enthymemes and examples, and by describing the movement of their logic. He asserts that both the enthymeme and the example necessarily are 'concerned with things that are for the most part capable of being other than they are—the paradigm inductively, the enthymeme syllogistically...' (1.2.13).[32] Depending upon whether an enthymeme is drawn from a probability (εἰκός) or from signs (σημείων), the statement about human actions

31. *Rhetoric* 1.2.8-10. I have replaced Kennedy's transliteration with the Greek words and have added πολλῶν καὶ ὁμοίων, which could be translated literally as 'the many and the similar'. Kennedy (*Aristotle, On Rhetoric*, pp. 40-41) provides references to the works alluded to by Aristotle in this section. Kennedy consults other documents in Aristotle's oeuvre and compiles a helpful overview of the levels of reasoning, the processes of reasoning common to all levels, and the relation of each to absolute truth and probable truth; see *The Art of Persuasion in Greece*, pp. 96-99.

32. These remarks take place within a discussion of the things about which rhetoric deliberates and of how one may deliberate rhetorically (see *Rhetoric* 1.2.11-14). Aristotle posits that something is persuasive to particular people because that which is persuasive is 'either immediately plausible and believable in itself or seems to be shown by statements that are so' (1.2.11). No art investigates the particular, and so with rhetoric: Rhetoric does not theorize about each opinion held by a particular person, but about what seems true to certain people. Moreover, people debate about 'things that seem to be capable of admitting two possibilities' (1.2.12) and not about things that are incapable of being other than they are, 'necessary things'. Human actions, the subject of rhetoric's examination and deliberation, are not necessary, but can be other than they are: '...things that happen for the most part and are possible can only be reasoned on the basis of other such things...' (1.2.14).

that can be other than they are will be related either 'as a universal [καθόλου] is related to a particular [μέρος]' or the reverse.[33] The example makes a statement based upon a different relation; Aristotle explicates the difference and offers a sample:

> It has been explained that a paradigm [Παράδειγμα] is an induction [ἐπαγωγὴ] and with what kinds of things it is concerned. It is reasoning neither from part [μέρος] to whole [ὅλον] nor from whole to part [nor from whole to whole] but from part to part, like to like [ὅμοιον πρὸς ὅμοιον], when two things fall under the same genus [γένος] but one is better known than the other. For example [οἶον], [when someone claims] that Dionysius is plotting tyranny because he is seeking a bodyguard [φυλακήν]; for Peisistratus also, when plotting earlier, sought a guard [φυλακὴν] and after receiving it made himself tyrant, and Theagenes [did the same] in Megara, and others, whom the audience knows of, all become examples [παράδειγμα] of Dionysius, of whom they do not yet know whether he makes this demand for this reason. All these actions fall under the same καθόλου: that one plotting tyranny seeks a guard [φυλακὴν].[34]

33. See *Rhetoric* 1.2.14-18.

34. *Rhetoric* 1.2.19. The sample παράδειγμα given here by Aristotle is commonly referred to as a 'historical example'; we will return to this momentarily. Note the mention of 'bodyguard' in this sample. Although I provide Kennedy's translation, it has been modified in several places: I have added a phrase that was apparently overlooked ('[whole to whole]'), and I added some Greek words for the sake of clarity. Also, I left καθόλου untranslated. Kennedy translates καθόλου as '[genus]', while Freese translates it as 'universal proposition'. To be sure, καθόλου is the same word used just prior to this section with reference to the enthymeme. On this, see also Edward M. Cope's remarks in *The Rhetoric of Aristotle with a Commentary* (3 vols.; rev. and ed. John E. Sandys; Cambridge: Cambridge University Press, 1877 [repr. Dubuque, IA: William C. Brown Reprint Library]), I, p. 48. There has been considerable debate on the issue of whether the example relates to a 'universal'. McGuire ('Some Problems with Rhetorical Example', p. 121; emphasis his) summarizes in this way the debate of late: 'There is not clear agreement among rhetorical theorists about the rhetorical example. Hauser, Consigny, and Benoit all have offered interpretations of Aristotle's concept of rhetorical example, but they fail to agree about either the logical or the epistemological qualities of example. All three interpretations raise the question whether example actually moves from part to part, unmediated, or from part to whole to part. It is, of course, possible that example *moves verbally* from part to part, but is understood, *moves epistemically* in terms of a part to whole to part motion'. Natali ('Paradeigma', pp. 141-52) examines other literature of the fourth century BCE and contends that the *paradeigma* was put to other uses than the one prescribed by Aristotle (induction): In some

For the moment, Aristotle ends his discussion of examples and resumes the discussion of enthymemes, now bringing up the matter of the topics of syllogisms and enthymemes (1.2.20-22). Next, he defines the species of rhetoric (1.3.1-6), identifies the topics common to all species of rhetoric (1.3.7-9) and the specific topics with which each species of rhetoric deals (1.4.1–1.14.7), and then discusses the use of nonartistic proofs in judicial rhetoric (1.15.1-33). The παράδειγμα does not figure largely throughout the remainder of Book 1, but examples do resurface with the use of the word παράδειγμα in what appears to be a non-technical sense[35] and with the use of the word in a technical sense slightly different than what we have met with so far. The latter usage can be treated briefly.

Aristotle comments on the παράδειγμα in the chapter devoted to epideictic rhetoric, a chapter in which he discusses topics useful in this species of rhetoric, defines several virtues and that which is honorable as sources of praise available to the speaker, and offers advice on how the speaker can amplify praise. The view of proofs just reviewed becomes more complicated because amplification (αὔξησις) is now placed on a level with enthymemes and examples as an εἴδη common to all species of rhetoric. Aristotle's purpose is clear enough, nonetheless. He remarks on the suitability of each of the κοιναὶ εἴδη with respect to a particular species of rhetoric.

> In general, among the classes of things common [κοινῶν εἰδῶν] to all speeches, amplification [αὔξησις] is most at home in those that are epideictic; for these take up actions that are agreed upon, so that what

instances 'the whole life of one person assumes an emblematical character' (p. 147), and here Natali cites Isocrates; in other instances 'both single events and entire lives' are proposed as models, and here Natali cites some historiographers of the period (p. 149). It is interesting that in this section (1.2.19) Aristotle mentions several specific historical figures who, along with all other known tyrants, may serve as an example of Dionysius (παράδειγμα πάντες γίγνονται τοῦ Διονυσίου), but it is rather evident that Aristotle is maintaining here that the actions of these persons, and not the persons themselves, constitute the example employed inductively.

35. See *Rhetoric* 1.5.2: 'Let us, then, for the sake of giving an example [παραδείγματος] [of what might be more fully explored], grasp what happiness is, simply stated, and the sources of its parts...'; and also 1.9.2: 'Thus, only for the sake of giving an example [παραδείγματος] [of what might be more thoroughly explored] let us speak about these propositions also' (Kennedy's translation [Greek added]). Freese translates παραδείγματος in both places as 'illustration'.

remains is to clothe the actions with greatness and beauty. But paradigms [παραδείγματα] are best in deliberative speeches; for we judge future things by predicting them from past ones [προγεγονότων]; and enthymemes are best in judicial speeches, for what has happened in some unclear way is best given a cause and demonstration [by enthymematic argument].[36]

Interestingly, both amplification and example are mentioned later in conjunction with the use of a nonartistic proof (tortures) in judicial rhetoric (1.15.26).

> Tortures [βάσανοι] are a kind of testimony and seem to have credibility because some necessity [to speak] is involved. It is thus not difficult about them either to see the available [means of persuasion] from which it is possible to provide amplification [αὔξειν] if they are in favor [of the speaker]...There is [also] need to cite examples that the judges know, which have [actually] happened [γεγενημένα παραδείγματα].[37]

We will have cause to return to amplification, but for the present two observations can be made. First, amplification and παράδειγμα and enthymeme are taken up together as classes of things common to all species of rhetoric. Secondly, the παραδείγματα are characterized in the latter sections of Book 1 not as induction but as things past or things that have happened. These two technical senses of παράδειγμα converge in Book 2.

In Book 2 of the *Rhetoric*, Aristotle revisits and expands upon the means of persuasion introduced in Book 1 (1.2.3-6), the specific emphasis now resting upon the artistic proofs. Before that, he defines the pertinent emotions and offers propositions on them so that a speaker might arouse the emotions of an audience in order to persuade the auditors to render the desired judgment (chs. 2–11). Next, Aristotle treats

---

36. *Rhetoric* 1.9.40; Kennedy's translation (Greek added). The obscurities surrounding what constitutes and separates the κοινά, the τόποι and the ἴδια are formidable; see the explanatory notes provided by Kennedy, *Aristotle, On Rhetoric*, pp. 45-47, 50-52, 87, 173, 189-90, 213-14, 281. Cope (*The Rhetoric of Aristotle*, I, pp. 186-87; cf. pp. 182-83) contends that amplification is a κοινὸς τόπος and also one 'of the three universal kinds of persuasion' (p. 186). On τῶν κοινῶν εἰδῶν in this section, he makes this comment: 'This seems to be a division, for the nonce, of rhetorical πίστεις as a γένος, into three εἴδη or species, each specially adapted to one of the three branches of Rhetoric. The division has no pretension to a regular scientific character: αὔξησις is not a logical kind of argument at all, and the three members of the division are not coordinate' (p. 187).

37. Kennedy's translation (Greek added).

various kinds of character (chs. 12–17), knowledge of which is important if a speaker is to adapt his or her character to that of the audience
so that the audience might be better disposed toward the speaker.
Finally, Aristotle resumes his discussion of logical arguments (chs. 18–
26), and it is within this context that the famous section on example and
parable occurs.[38]

Aristotle, having treated the κοινά, subjects of argument useful in
each species of rhetoric, in 2.18.3–2.19.26, now turns to the κοιναὶ
πίστεις, common proofs—the basic modes of logical argument useful
in each species of rhetoric, which he referred to as demonstrative in
1.2.19 and which he will refer to again as demonstrative in 2.20.9.
Aristotle discusses the παράδειγμα first, and we will examine carefully
the entire section, for here he provides additional details on the example
as induction by delineating the species of παραδείγματα and by stating
how and when they should be used. The section on the common proofs
begins in this way:

> It remains to speak about the proofs that are common to all [species of
> rhetoric], since the specifics have been discussed. These common proofs
> are of two genera, example and enthymeme (for the maxim is part of an
> enthymeme). First, then, let us speak of example, for the example is
> similar to induction, and induction is a beginning.[39]

Note that Aristotle divides the common proofs into two genera,
example and enthymeme; he will now speak on the species of the
παραδείγματα.

> There are two species of examples; for one species of example is to tell
> of things [or events] that have happened before, and one [species is] to
> make them [πράγματα] up [or create them]. Of the latter, parable
> [comparison or juxtaposition] is one [species], one [species] tales [or
> fables], such as the Aesopic and [the] Libyan.[40]

38. Kennedy (*The Art of Persuasion in Greece*, p. 101) is perhaps more accurate in saying that 'chapter twenty reintroduces enthymeme and example as forms
of proof common to all kinds of oratory'.

39. *Rhetoric* 2.20.1-2; my translation: Λοιπὸν δὲ περὶ τῶν κοινῶν πίστεων
ἅπασιν εἰπεῖν, ἐπείπερ εἴρηται περὶ τῶν ἰδίων. εἰσὶ δ' αἱ κοιναὶ πίστεις δύο τῷ
γένει, παράδειγμα καὶ ἐνθύμημα. ἡ γὰρ γνώμη μέρος ἐνθυμήματος ἐστίν.
πρῶτον μὲν οὖν περὶ παραδείγματος λέγωμεν. ὅμοιον γὰρ ἐπαγωγῇ τὸ
παράδειγμα, ἡ δ' ἐπαγωγὴ ἀρχή. On the significance of ἀρχή, see Cope, *The
Rhetoric of Aristotle*, II, p. 196.

40. *Rhetoric* 2.20.2-3; my translation: Παραδειγμάτων δ' εἴδη δύο. ἓν μὲν γὰρ

To reiterate: According to Aristotle, there are two genera of common proofs, the example and the enthymeme, and there are two species of examples, one species which relates events that have happened before (commonly called 'historical' examples), and one species which makes up or creates events (commonly called 'fictitious' examples). Moreover, the 'fictitious' examples are divided into two subspecies, parables and tales.

Aristotle then provides samples of each species and subspecies of examples.

> To tell of things [that have happened before] is of this kind, as if someone were to say that it is necessary...[41]

ἐσι παραδείγματος εἶδος τὸ λέγειν πράγματα προγεγενημένα, ἕν δὲ τὸ αὐτὸν ποιεῖν. τούτου δ᾽ ἕν μὲν παραβολή ἕν δὲ λόγοι, οἷον οἱ Αἰσώπειοι καὶ Λιβυκοί. On the 'tales' (λόγοι) and their relation to αἶνοι, see Cope, *The Rhetoric of Aristotle*, II, pp. 196-97, and *An Introduction to Aristotle's Rhetoric*, pp. 255-56 n. 1. According to Cope, there are two kinds of λόγοι: 'When λόγος and μῦθος are distinguished, λόγος is a "tale," real or fictitious; μῦθος is "a fable," and more especially one of Æsop's' (p. 255 n. 1). See Aristotle's remarks on μυθολογεῖν in 2.21.9. Gregory Nagy (*The Best of the Achaeans: Concepts of the Hero in Archaic Greek Poetry* [Baltimore: The Johns Hopkins University Press, 1979], pp. 239, 281) indicates that the formal designation of the Aesopic fable in many ancient sources is αἶνος. Nagy furnishes a number of interesting insights on the αἶνος, such as the relation of the αἶνος to the derivative noun αἴνιγμα and the compound verb παραινέω, in his chapter 'Poetry of Praise, Poetry of Blame', pp. 222-42; see also his chapter 'Ancient Greek Epic and Praise Poetry: Some Typological Considerations', in John Miles Foley (ed.), *Oral Tradition in Literature: Interpretation in Context* (Columbia, MO: University of Missouri Press, 1986), pp. 89-102. Theon, who wrote a rhetorical treatise in the first century CE, points out that the ancients called the 'fable' αἶνος, μῦθος and λόγος, among other things (*Progymnasmata* 4.1-42), and contends that it is simplistic to make a distinction among fables based upon whether they depict animals or people (4.14-18). According to Theon (4.34-36), some choose to call the fable an αἶνος because it contains instruction (παραίνεσίν). For the text of Theon's *Progymnasmata*, see James R. Butts, 'The "Progymnasmata" of Theon: A New Text with Translation and Commentary' (PhD dissertation, Claremont Graduate School, 1986).

    41. *Rhetoric* 2.20.3; my translation: ἔστι δὲ τὸ μὲν πράγματα λέγειν τοιόνδε τι, ὥσπερ εἴ τις λέγοι ὅτι δεῖ... I have given the reading based upon L. Spengel's alteration of the eleventh century MS (Aᶜ), which reads παραδείγματα λέγειν instead of πράγματα λέγειν. Spengel's alteration is accepted by Cope (*The Rhetoric of Aristotle*, II, p. 197), Freese (*Aristotle, 'Art' of Rhetoric*, p. 272) and Kennedy (*Aristotle, On Rhetoric*, p. 179).

The manner in which Aristotle refers to the 'historical' example here is obscured by alternative readings in various manuscripts of the *Rhetoric*, but Aristotle obviously intends to offer a sample of the species of example in which the speaker tells of things or events that have happened before. Such an example

> ...is if someone were to say that it is necessary [δεῖ] to make preparations against the king [of Persia] and not allow Egypt to be subdued; for in the past Darius did not invade [Greece] until he had taken Egypt, [1393b] but after taking it, he invaded; and again, Xerxes did not attack [Greece] until he took [Egypt], but having taken it, he invaded; thus if [οὗτος] he [the present king] takes [Egypt], he will invade [Greece]; as a result it must not be allowed.[42]

Following the sample of the species of ('historical') example which relates events that have happened before, Aristotle gives samples of the species of ('fictitious') examples which relate events that are fabricated, the parable and the tale.

> 4. Socratic sayings are an instance of comparison [παραβολή], for example [οἷον], if someone were to say that officials should not [οὐ δεῖ] be chosen by lot (for that would be as if [ὅμοιον γὰρ ὥσπερ] someone [τις] chose athletes randomly—not those able to contest, but those on whom the lot fell); or [as if] choosing by lot any one [τινα] of the sailors to act as pilot rather than the one who knew how.[43]
>
> 5. An example of the fable [Λόγος δέ, οἷος] is what Stesichorus said about Phalaris and Aesop about the demagogue. When the people of Himera had chosen Phalaris as dictator and were about to give him a bodyguard [φυλακὴν], after saying other things at some length, Stesichorus told them a fable about how a horse had a meadow to himself. When a stag came and quite damaged the pasture, the horse, wanting to avenge himself on the stag, asked a man [τινὰ ἄνθρωπον] if he could

---

42. *Rhetoric* 2.20.3. For the sake of clarity, I provide Kennedy's translation (Greek added), in which he supplies details to facilitate comprehension.

43. *Rhetoric* 2.20.4; Kennedy's translation (Greek added). The appearance of ὅμοιον is suppressed in Kennedy's rendering of this section on the parable. Cope (*The Rhetoric of Aristotle*, II, p. 198) translates this section as follows: 'Of παραβολή the Socratic practice or method is an example; as for instance if one were to say, that the magistrates ought not to be chosen by lot: for this is analogous to the case of choosing for the athletes (who were to enter the lists) not those who are fitted for the combat, but those upon whom the lot falls; or to choosing the steersman out of a crew of sailors on the principle that it was the man who won the toss, and not the man of knowledge and skill (the man who knows his business), that ought to be chosen'.

help him get vengeance on the stag. The man said he could, if the horse were to take a bridle and he himself were to mount on him holding javelins. When the horse agreed and the man mounted, instead of getting vengeance the horse found himself a slave to the man. 'Thus you too [οὕτω δὲ καὶ ὑμεῖς],' said Stesichorus, 'look out [ὁρᾶτε], lest while wishing vengeance on your enemies you suffer the same thing as the horse. You already have the bridle [in your mouth], having appointed a general with absolute power; if you give him a bodyguard and allow him to mount, you will immediately be slaves to Phalaris.' 6. Aesop, when speaking on behalf of a demagogue who was on trial for his life in Samos, told how a fox, while crossing a river, was carried into a hole in the bank. Not being able to get out, she was in misery for some time and many dog-ticks attacked her. A hedgehog came wandering along and, when he saw her, took pity [κατοικτείραντα] and asked if he could remove the ticks. She would not let him and, when he asked why, [said], 'These are already full of me and draw little blood, but if you remove these, other hungry ones will come and drink what blood I have left.' 'In your case too [ἀτὰρ καὶ ὑμᾶς], O Samians,' said [Aesop], 'this man [οὗτος] will no longer harm you; for he is rich. But if you kill him, other poor ones will come who will steal and spend your public funds.'[44]

After identifying the species of examples and providing samples of each, Aristotle discusses when and how examples are to be used.

7. Fables are suitable in deliberative oratory and have this advantage, that while it is difficult to find similar historical incidents that have actually happened [πράγματα μὲν εὑρεῖν ὅμοια γεγενημένα], it is rather easy with fables. They should be made in the same way as comparisons [ποιῆσαι γὰρ δεῖ ὥσπερ καὶ παραβολάς], provided one can see the likenesses [ὅμοιον], which is rather easy from philosophical studies. 8. Although it is easier to provide illustrations through fables, examples from history [τὰ διὰ τῶν πραγμάτων] are more useful in deliberation; for generally, future events will be like [ὅμοια] those of the past [τοῖς γεγονόσιν].[45]

---

44. *Rhetoric* 2.20.5-6; Kennedy's translation (Greek added). Note that the tale told by Stesichorus concerns the issue of Phalaris being granted a bodyguard (φυλακὴν) by the people of Himera.

45. *Rhetoric* 2.20.7-8; Kennedy's translation (Greek added). Note that Kennedy does not translate γὰρ; if it is translated, the sentence would read '...it is easier with fables, for they should be made [or constructed] in the same way as parables...' (my translation). In addition, εὑρεῖν can be translated as 'invent' (see Kennedy, *Aristotle, On Rhetoric*, p. 37 n. 39). Aristotle's remark in 2.20.8 is not completely unlike a statement made by Isocrates (*To Demonicus* 34), which reads, 'When you are deliberating, regard things which have happened as examples of

The appropriate uses of the species of examples in relation to deliberative rhetoric now established, Aristotle explains when to use the genera of common proofs.

> 9. If one does not have a supply of enthymemes, one should use paradigms [παραδείγμασι] as demonstration [ἀποδείξεσιν]; for persuasion [then] depends on them. But if there are enthymemes, paradigms should be used as witnesses [μαρτυρίοις], [as] a supplement [ἐπιλόγῳ] to the enthymemes. When the paradigms are placed first, there is the appearance of induction [ἐπαγωγῇ], but induction [ἐπαγωγὴ] is not suitable to rhetorical discourses except in a few cases; when they are put at the end [ἐπιλεγόμενα] they become witnesses [μαρτυρίοις], and a witness [μάρτυς] is everywhere persuasive. Thus, too, when they are first, it is necessary to supply many of them [but] when they are mentioned at the end [ἐπιλέγοντι] one is sufficient; for even a single trustworthy witness [μάρτυς] is useful. This concludes the discussion of how many species of paradigms [εἴδη παραδειγμάτων] there are and how and when they should be used.[46]

This chapter in the *Rhetoric* represents Aristotle's explanation of the specific relation between parable and example. Sporadic references to examples are made throughout the remainder of the treatise, but the noun παραβολή reappears only once.

Aristotle's preferred common proof captures his attention in most of the subsequent chapters in Book 2, and he initiates the discussion of enthymemes by treating the maxim, which he considers to be part of an enthymeme.[47] Next, Aristotle identifies two species of enthymemes and enumerates 28 topics (or elements) of enthymemes.[48] Induction enters

what will happen. For the unknown may be learned most quickly from the known' (as cited by Kennedy, *The Art of Persuasion in Greece*, p. 98).

46. *Rhetoric* 2.20.9; Kennedy's translation (Greek added).

47. Aristotle's definition of 'maxim' is as follows: 'A maxim is an assertion—not, however, one about particulars, such as what kind of person Iphicrates is, but of a general sort [καθόλου], and not about everything [περὶ πάντων καθόλου] (for example, not that the straight is the opposite of the crooked) but about things that involve actions [πράξεις] and are to be chosen or avoided in regard to action' (*Rhetoric* 2.21.2; Kennedy's translation [Greek added]). The ensuing discussion of maxims includes the παροιμία (see 2.21.12). Aristotle later asserts that a maxim is a statement of the general (2.21.15), and that one advantage of using maxims is they make the speaker ethical in that they indicate the moral preferences of the speaker (2.22.15-16).

48. See *Rhetoric* 2.22.12–2.25.14. On 'topics' and 'elements', see Kennedy, *Aristotle, On Rhetoric*, pp. 189-90.

the discussion as a topic of enthymemes (2.23.1), and even though it is curious that there is no direct mention of examples here, Aristotle nonetheless relates how other speakers have utilized things that have happened before.[49] Other than what seems to be a non-technical usage of the word παράδειγμα,[50] the final mention of examples in this book occurs in the discussion of the refutation (λύσις) of enthymemes, where Aristotle names the example as one of four sources of enthymemes.

> Since enthymemes are drawn from four sources and these four are probability [εἰκὸς], paradigm [παράδειγμα], τεκμήριον [or necessary sign], and σημεῖον [or fallible sign] (enthymemes from probabilities are drawn from things that either are, or seem for the most part [to be], true; others come from example by induction of what is like [τὰ δὲ δι' ἐπαγωγῆς διὰ τοῦ ὁμοίου], whether one thing or more, whenever a general [τὸ καθόλου] statement is made and then supported [συλλογίσηται] by a particular instance [τὰ κατὰ μέρος διὰ παραδείγματος]; others are derived from a necessary and always existing sign [τεκμηρίου]; others from signs [σημείων] of what is generally or in part true or not)...[51]

Moving ahead to Aristotle's prescription for refuting an example, we read:

> The refutation of examples is the same as that of probabilities; for if we cite an example that does not accord [with the generalized] conclusion, the argument is refuted because it is not 'necessary,' even if something else is more often true or true in more cases. But if the larger number of instances is usually as the opponent says, one should contend that the present case is not similar [ὅμοιον] or not in the same way [ὁμοίως] or has some difference.[52]

In Book 3, where Aristotle takes up the issues of style (λέξις) and

49. On the difficulties posed by this section (that is, now induction is a topic of enthymemes, whereas earlier induction and enthymeme were correlative as logical arguments), see Price, 'Παράδειγμα and *Exemplum* in Ancient Rhetorical Theory', pp. 65-76, 247-53, and the articles mentioned on pp. 289-91 nn. 25 and 27.

50. See *Rhetoric* 2.23.13, where Aristotle provides an example of the topic 'from the parts' by citing the *Socrates* of Theodectes (παράδειγμα ἐκ τοῦ Σωκράτους τοῦ Θεοδέκτου).

51. *Rhetoric* 2.25.8; Kennedy's translation (transliterated words replaced by Greek words and other Greek words added).

52. *Rhetoric* 2.25.13; Kennedy's translation (Greek added). Freese translates οὐχ ὁμοίως as 'did not take place in the same way'. Here, Aristotle's prose is dense and difficult to render in English; cf. also Cope, *The Rhetoric of Aristotle*, II, p. 327.

arrangement (τάξις), not much space is granted to either the παράδειγμα or the παραβολή. The παραδείγματα, excluding several non-
technical uses of the word,[53] are mentioned once, and the παραβολή
once. The reference to examples, made within the course of remarks on
proofs as part of an oration, repeats a point made earlier about the
suitability of the use of παραδείγματα in deliberative speeches.

> Examples [παραδείγματα] are most appropriate in deliberative oratory,
> enthymemes more appropriate in judicial oratory; for the former is con-
> cerned with the future, so it is necessary to tell examples from the past
> [ὥστ᾽ ἐκ τῶν γενομένων ἀνάγκη παραδείγματα λέγειν]...[54]

The noun παραβολή appears in the final chapter of the *Rhetoric*, a
chapter in which Aristotle treats the epilogue of a speech. The epilogue,
according to Aristotle, is comprised of four parts: the first is to dispose
the audience favorably toward the speaker and unfavorably toward the
opponent; the second is to amplify (αὐξῆσαι) and to minimize
(ταπεινῶσαι); the third is to arouse the emotions of the audience; the
fourth is to recapitulate (3.19.1). The beginning of the recapitulation
should be a statement by the speaker to the effect that the speaker has
performed according to promise (3.19.4). The speaker should then state
what has been said and why it has been said. Remarks in this section of
the epilogue, that is, the recapitulation, may derive from a direct comparison of the speaker's case with that of the opponent (λέγεται δὲ ἐξ
ἀντιπαραβολῆς τοῦ ἐναντίου)—which may be accomplished by a
comparison or juxtaposition of what both speakers have said on the
same point (παραβάλλειν δὲ ἢ ὅσα περὶ τὸ αὐτὸ ἄμφω εἶπον)—or
may derive from irony (ἢ ἐξ εἰρωνείας), or from interrogation (ἢ ἐξ
ἐρωτήσεως). Thus, the speaker can recapitulate by means of a comparison (ἐκ παραβολῆς) of points or by giving the statements according to
the order in which they were made, the speaker's first and then, if
desirable, the opponent's separately (3.19.5). The important require-
ment is that in the recapitulation the speaker should conduct a review of
what has been said by whom and why, and then the speaker should
solicit the audience for a judgment (3.19.6).

---

53. See *Rhetoric* 3.14.1 (an example from the prooemium of Isocrates' *Helen*),
3.16.7 (examples from Homer [*Odyssey*], Phaÿllus and Euripides [*Oeneus*]), and
3.16.9 (an example from Sophocles [*Antigone*]).

54. *Rhetoric* 3.17.5; my translation.

Aristotle's last chapter in Book 3 of the *Rhetoric* presents an intriguing complication with respect to the παραβολή. Aristotle, it appears,
does not employ the noun παραβολή here (Book 3) in a fashion entirely
consistent with his usage of the same noun in Book 2; that is to say, the
παραβολή in Book 3 consists of the points made by one orator in a
speech put into juxtaposition with, or compared to, the points made by
the opposing orator, whereas the παραβολή in Book 2 consists of
fictional events put into juxtaposition with, or compared to, an event at
issue or a matter at hand. McCall notes the appearance of παραβολή in
Book 3 and indicates one way of approaching its use there:

> Both ἐξ ἀντιπαραβολῆς and ἐκ παραβολῆς refer to the same thing,
> comparison of one's own case with the opponent's, but ἀντιπαραβολή
> may better be regarded as a subspecies of παραβολή than as synony-
> mous with it. παραβολή denotes more than mere comparison of *opposite*
> viewpoints; ἀντιπαραβολή is restricted to this one sphere.[55]

McCall's suggestion is not entirely satisfactory because there is no
overt correlation of the usage of παραβολή here and the apparently
different usage in Book 2. The issue is complicated even further if we
go beyond a consideration of only the noun forms παραβολή and
ἀντιπαραβολή.

As McCall correctly notes, the other two instances of the noun
ἀντιπαραβολή occur in a single passage at the beginning of the discussion of the parts of a speech, which Aristotle seeks to limit to two,
although he will admit at most four (the prooemium, the statement of
the proposition, the proof, the epilogue).[56] According to Aristotle, the
'necessary parts' of a speech are the statement of the proposition
(πρόθεσις) and the proof (πίστις). Aristotle compresses the additional
parts of a speech identified by other rhetoricians into these two
'necessary parts'; thus, for instance, he relegates the refutation and the
reply to the opponent by means of a comparison of arguments—
ἀντιπαραβολή—to the proof: 'For replies to the opponent belong to the
proofs; and reply by comparison is amplification of the same [καὶ ἡ
ἀντιπαραβολὴ αὔξησις τῶν αὐτοῦ], so it is a part of the proofs'

---

55. McCall, *Ancient Rhetorical Theories of Simile and Comparison*, p. 29; his
emphasis. McCall's observation raises a question about his contention that
'Aristotle's regular understanding of the term' παραβολή is 'illustrative comparison' or 'analogy' (p. 28).

56. See *Rhetoric* 3.13.4.

(3.13.4).[57] Aristotle's prescriptions here set the stage for the discussion of the epilogue, in which he identifies amplification and recapitulation as two of its parts, with ἀντιπαραβολή, παραβάλλειν and παραβολή mentioned in the treatment of the latter.

Whether or not ἀντιπαραβολή is a subspecies of παραβολή, as McCall contends, it is clear that in Book 3 the noun παραβολή is employed with respect to a direct comparison of points made about a case in speeches delivered by opposing orators. This παραβολή takes place in the second part of the speech, referred to by Aristotle as the proof, and specifically, the recapitulation in the epilogue—something we would not expect based upon the treatment of the παραβολή in Book 2, where παραβολή is a subspecies of the παράδειγμα. The suspicion that the use of the noun παραβολή in Book 3 differs from that of παραβολή in Book 2 is reinforced by the appearance of παραβολή in conjunction with the noun ἀντιπαραβολή and that, in turn, in conjunction with the verb παραβάλλειν—all in proximity to remarks about amplification. If these terms of comparison were to appear in association with amplification, it would suggest that amplification has to do with comparison. These terms do, in fact, appear in a discussion of amplification; however, if we return to a section of the *Rhetoric* in which Aristotle treats amplification and in which we find παραβάλλειν and ἀντιπαραβάλλειν, it would seem that Aristotle might not set strict limits on either ἀντιπαραβολή or παραβολή as a 'comparison of opposing arguments' or 'reply by comparison'.

We have already seen that the παράδειγμα is mentioned as a κοιναὶ εἴδη and that, according to Aristotle, example is most suitable to deliberative rhetoric, amplification to epideictic rhetoric (1.9.40). Aristotle repeats elsewhere that amplification is suitable to epideictic rhetoric (2.18.5; cf. 3.17.2), but it must be pointed out that amplification is not restricted to epideictic rhetoric, for one of the subjects of propositions common to all species of rhetoric, greatness or magnitude, can and should be amplified.[58] In addition, Aristotle recommends the use of

57. Kennedy's translation (Greek added). The epilogue is subsumed into the proof, thus the remarks on the epilogue in 3.19.5. Cope translates ἀντιπαραβολὴ here as 'counter-comparison (a comparative statement of your own views and arguments placed in juxtaposition with them to bring them into contrast)' (*The Rhetoric of Aristotle*, III, p. 160).

58. See *Rhetoric* 2.18.4-5, 2.19.27, and 1.3.9 (by implication; note the use of ἀντιπαραβάλλειν).

'many means of amplification' in conjunction with several nonartistic proofs employed in judicial rhetoric.[59] Amplification remains, for all of that, especially characteristic of epideictic rhetoric, as Aristotle makes clear in Book 1.

Within the context of a discussion of epideictic rhetoric, amplification is recommended as particularly useful in situations where the purpose is to praise someone. First, Aristotle offers advice on how to use the accomplishments of a person or honors bestowed upon that person in order to amplify the praise of that person, and then he tenders suggestions on what to do in other situations.

> 38. [In epideictic] one should also use many kinds of amplification [αὐξητικῶν]... And if you do not have material enough with the man himself, compare him with others [ἄλλους ἀντιπαραβάλλειν], which Isocrates used to do because of his lack of experience in speaking in court. One should make the comparison with famous people [ἐνδόξους συγκρίνειν]; for the subject is amplified [αὐξητικὸν] and made honorable if he is better than [other] worthy ones.
>
> 39. Amplification [αὔξησις], with good reason, falls among forms of praise; for it aims to show superiority, and superiority is one of the forms of the honorable. Thus, even if there is no comparison with the famous, one should compare [the person praised] with the many [πρὸς τοὺς ἄλλους δεῖ παραβάλλειν], since superiority [even over them] seems to denote excellence.[60]

Observe that three terms of comparison appear here as verbs: συγκρίνειν, ἀντιπαραβάλλειν and παραβάλλειν. Although it is difficult to pin down the precise meaning of these terms, it is obvious that amplification has to do with comparison. The παραβολή is associated with two κοιναὶ εἴδη—παράδειγμα and αὔξησις—and in both cases the παραβολή is treated within the context of a discussion of

---

59. See *Rhetoric* 1.15.20-21 (contracts), 1.15.26 (tortures) and 1.15.33 (oaths).

60. *Rhetoric* 1.9.38-39; Kennedy's translation (Greek added). Recall that in *Rhetorica ad Alexandrum* ἀντιπαραβάλλειν and παραβάλλειν occur within the context of a discussion of amplification. It is interesting that Aristotle also uses συγκρίνειν in the discussion of amplification. We meet this trio of comparative terms (ἀντιπαραβάλλειν, παραβάλλειν, συγκρίνειν) again in Theon's chapter Περὶ Συγκρίσεως (*Progymnasmata* 10.1-80). To my knowledge, this is the only occurrence of συγκρίνειν in the *Rhetoric*, although Aristotle uses σύγκρισις three times in his *Topica* (see McCall, *Ancient Rhetorical Theories of Simile and Comparison*, p. 136). McCall does not examine σύγκρισις because, in his opinion, it does not refer to figures of comparison (pp. 135-36).

comparison. The result of having borne witness to this complication with regard to the παραβολή in Book 3 is a rather comprehensive view of Aristotle's precepts on the παράδειγμα and the παραβολή as set forth in the *Rhetoric*.

Aristotle's *Rhetoric* furnishes information that can be applied directly to some of the questions raised in this study on the distinction often made between *Parabel* and *Beispielerzählung*. The *'Art' of Rhetoric* represents a sector of the rhetorical tradition in the fourth century in which—as opposed to *Rhetorica ad Alexandrum*—more attention is given to the παραβολή, but still—as in *Rhetorica ad Alexandrum*—far more emphasis is placed on the παράδειγμα than upon the παραβολή. It should be recalled, nonetheless, that Aristotle places even greater emphasis on the enthymeme ('the strongest of rhetorical proofs') than he does on the παράδειγμα. Indeed, Aristotle claims at one point that the example should be used if a supply of enthymemes is not available, and that if enthymemes are available, then the example should be used as an epilogue to the enthymeme. That priority notwithstanding, the παράδειγμα occupies a prominent place in Aristotle's rhetorical theory, enough so that he deems it necessary to discuss the παράδειγμα in all three books of his *Rhetoric*. Some of the main aspects of the παράδειγμα and the παραβολή according to Aristotle's *Rhetoric* will now be underscored, and information retrieved from the *Rhetoric* will then be brought to bear upon the distinction between *Parabel* and *Beispielerzählung*.

In the *Rhetoric*, Aristotle treats both the παράδειγμα and the παραβολή mainly within the context of a discussion of proofs, which he separates into two groups, nonartistic proofs and artistic proofs. The artistic proofs are divided into three species, traditionally referred to as ethical proofs, pathetical proofs and logical proofs. According to Aristotle, there are two modes of logical proofs, the enthymematic and the paradigmatic, and these modes of logical proofs are later treated as κοιναὶ πίστεις, the two genera of logical arguments that are employed in all species of rhetoric. Both the enthymematic and the paradigmatic modes of logical arguments are used to show something, or to seem to show something as so—that is, both are used as a means of demonstration.

As a genera or mode of logical argument, the παράδειγμα is defined in terms of induction, a type of proof in which the intent is to show something to be so 'on the basis of many similar instances'. The logic of the παράδειγμα as a mode of logical argument moves from 'part to part, like to like, when two things fall under the same genus but one is better known than the other'. The παράδειγμα, then, may be described (in non-Aristotelian language) as a comparative technique or strategy. Given Aristotle's purpose of bringing dialectic to bear upon rhetoric, he describes the logic of this comparative technique or strategy in terms of induction, and this may account, in part, for Aristotle's treatment of the παράδειγμα as a matter of proof and not as a matter of ornament or style.[61]

That the παράδειγμα is a comparative technique or strategy can be demonstrated by a brief rehearsal of some of Aristotle's remarks on both the παράδειγμα as a genus of logical argument and as a species ('historical' example). Aristotle states that 'to show on the basis of many similar instances [πολλῶν καὶ ὁμοιῶν] that something is so is in dialectic induction, in rhetoric paradigm'. He describes the logic of the παράδειγμα as 'reasoning neither from part to whole nor from whole to part nor from whole to whole but from part to part, like to like [ὅμοιον πρὸς ὅμοιον], when two things fall under the same genus but one is better known than the other'. Some enthymemes, according to Aristotle, come from 'example by induction of what is like [διὰ τοῦ ὁμοίου]'. He suggests that one way to refute an example is to contend that 'the present case is not similar [ὅμοιον] or not in the same way [ὁμοιῶς] or has some difference'. With specific reference to the species of παραδείγματα, Aristotle admits that it is 'difficult to find similar historical incidents that have actually happened [πράγματα εὑρεῖν ὅμοια γεγενημένα]'. He instructs that tales (fables) and parables are to be constructed in the same way, 'provided one can see the likeness [ὅμοιον]'. Indeed, the sample of παραβολή cited by Aristotle makes specific use of ὅμοιον ('for that would be like [ὅμοιον]'). Finally, Aristotle counsels that 'historical' examples are more useful in deliberative oratory, 'for generally, future events will be like [ὅμοια] those of the past'. One aspect of Aristotle's treatment of the genus παράδειγμα and

61. As Price observes ('Παράδειγμα and *Exemplum* in Ancient Rhetorical Theory', p. 83). Price offers a different understanding of the παράδειγμα and its relation to induction (see pp. 46-76, 239-53), concluding that while the παράδειγμα can be correctly regarded as rhetorical induction, the παράδειγμα cannot be considered a κοιναὶ πίστεις because it contains a more basic element, i.e. ἐπαγογή (p. 76). See especially his discussion of 'The Inductive-Deductive Paradigm vs. the Analogical Paradigm', pp. 63-76.

its species that remains consistent throughout the *Rhetoric* is the frequent mention of the similar (ὅμοιον) in conjunction with the παράδειγμα.

Aristotle makes even finer distinctions with respect to both genera of logical arguments, the enthymematic and the paradigmatic, by identifying two species of each genera. The distinction between the species of παραδείγματα is made on the basis of whether the παράδειγμα relates events that have happened before or whether the παράδειγμα relates events that have been made up or created. The former species of παράδειγμα is traditionally referred to as 'historical' example, the latter as 'fictional' example—but both species are examples. The 'fictional' examples are divided into two species, parables and tales (fables)—but both are examples. The 'historical' example, the 'fictional' example and its two subspecies, παραβολή and λόγος, are all παραδείγματα. Therefore, according to Aristotle's precepts in Book 2 of the *Rhetoric*, not all παραδείγματα are 'historical' examples,[62] but the παραβολή is a παράδειγμα. An examination of the species of παραδείγματα will make it possible to determine if any definitive distinction can be made between 'historical' example, παραβολή and λόγος on the basis of formal elements.

Aristotle does not issue prescriptive regulations with respect to the formal elements that might be peculiar to each species of παραδείγματα. Consequently, the following remarks are the result of inference from the samples of each species provided by Aristotle (2.20.3-7). There are obvious differences between the species; for instance, although the λόγοι cited by Aristotle are lengthier than either the παραβολή or the 'historical' example, and only the λόγοι contain direct dialogue, neither of those elements determines the species. However, the species share a number of elements in common. The 'historical' example and the παραβολή are prefaced with a statement of the event or issue at hand (the former: 'it is necessary to...' [δεῖ plus infinitive verb]; the latter: 'it is not necessary to...' [οὐ δεῖ plus infinitive verb]), and then follow with the narration of two similar events (the former: what Darius did and what Xerxes did; the latter: choosing athletes by lot and choosing a helmsman by lot) marked by γάρ (the former: καὶ γάρ; the latter: ὅμοιον γάρ). The similarity

---

62. In addition, as we have seen, παράδειγμα is also used in a non-technical sense.

between the event or issue at hand and the events narrated is more evident in the 'historical' example (subduing Egypt and then crossing over to Greece) and the παραβολή (choosing by lot) than in the λόγοι. Aristotle specifies the occasion of the λόγοι told by Stesichorus and Aesop, the two speakers tell their tales, and both mark the similarity between the tale and the occasion in the conclusion by uttering nearly identical phrases (οὕτω δὲ καὶ ὑμεῖς; ἀτὰρ καὶ ὑμᾶς). (Note that in this section of the *Rhetoric* [2.20.5] Aristotle can give a sample of a fable that is brought to bear upon the matter of giving a demagogue a bodyguard, whereas in an earlier section he gives a sample of a 'historical' example that is brought to bear upon the matter of a tyrant asking for a bodyguard [1.2.19].) The παραβολή and the λόγοι do not have specifically named characters, but some of the characters are referred to by τις (the παραβολή: τινα; the first λόγος: τινὰ ἄνθρωπον); characters in the 'historical' example, however, are given names (Darius, Xerxes). Relatedly, the παραβολή and the λόγοι do not mention named geographical locations, while the 'historical' example does (Egypt and Greece). In their applications, the 'historical' example and the second λόγος refer to the person with respect to whom the events are narrated as οὗτος, and both the 'historical' example and the λόγοι have ἐὰν plus subjunctive verbs in their applications. All three species relate past events: the 'historical' example tells of events that have happened in the 'real' world of history, the παραβολή and the λόγοι tell of events that have happened in hypothetical or fabulous worlds of fiction. None of the samples of the three species provided by Aristotle deal with the world of myth. Some of the elements of the species are apparently interchangeable, which points to the obvious: The 'historical' example, the parable and the fable are closely related species of παραδείγματα.[63]

63. Some scholars go further in describing the difference between παραβολή and λόγος, arguing on the basis of Aristotle's samples here that whereas the παραβολή depicts hypothetical situations, events or actions that might occur in the real world, the λόγος depicts situations or events that are purely fictitious. As a result, the παραβολή would possess a higher degree of probability than the λόγος. McGuire ('Some Problems with Rhetorical Example', pp. 124-26) briefly discusses the issue of probability with respect to the parable and fable. Price ('Παράδειγμα and *Exemplum* in Ancient Rhetorical Theory', p. 42) says of the parable: 'It is an analogy whose *illustrantia* are drawn from the real everyday world'. He observes that the παραβολή differs from the 'historical' example in that it 'describes the activities of types of people rather than specific individuals' and 'may describe a

By now it should be exceedingly clear that according to the *'Art' of Rhetoric* (2.20) the παραβολή is a παράδειγμα, the parable is an example. As with the genus παράδειγμα, so with the species παραβολή. This means that the παραβολή is an artistic proof, and more precisely that the παραβολή is a mode of logical argument designated by Aristotle as paradigmatic, which in turn means that the logic of the παραβολή moves from 'part to part, like to like, when two things fall under the same genus but one is better known than the other'. Both the παραβολή (species) and the παράδειγμα (genus) are comparative techniques or strategies.[64] Both the παραβολή and the παράδειγμα can be employed to show, or to seem to show, that something is so; both can be used as a means of demonstration. This aspect of Aristotle's discussion of the παράδειγμα and the παραβολή in Book 2 of the *Rhetoric*—specifically, that the παραβολή is a species of the παράδειγμα—poses a serious problem to those who attempt to maintain a categorical distinction between the *Parabel* and the *Beispielerzählung* based upon the premise that the example (παράδειγμα) is not a parable,

---

fictitious, hypothetical, and imaginary situation' (pp. 42-43). Freese (*'Art' of Rhetoric*, p. 274 n. *a*) contends that 'the παραβολή as understood by Aristotle is a comparison and application of cases easily supposable and such as occur in real life, for the purpose of illustrating the point in question; the fable, on the other hand, is pure fiction'. Cope, in a critique of Trench, posits that '*Aristotle*, to whom Dr Trench does not refer, distinguishes parable *in general* from fable by this: that the former depicts *human* relations (in which the N.T. parable coincides with it); it *invents* analogous cases, which are not *historical*, but always such as *might* be so; always probable, and corresponding with what actually occurs in real life. The fable is *pure fiction*, and its essential characteristic is, that it invests beasts, birds, plants, and even things inanimate with the attributes of humanity' (*The Rhetoric of Aristotle*, II, p. 198 n. 1; his emphasis). These remarks are indeed plausible and *might* find support in a passage from Aristotle's *Politics* (2.5.1264b4-6), where in criticism of Plato's view of the ideal state Aristotle writes: 'It is absurd to argue, from the analogy of the animals [ἄτοπον δὲ καὶ τὸ ἐκ τῶν θηρίων ποιεῖσθαι τὴν παραβολήν], that men and women should follow the same pursuits, for animals have not to manage a household' (B. Jowett's translation, cited by McCall, *Ancient Rhetorical Theories of Simile and Comparison*, p. 28). McCall points out that 'the *Republic* passage to which Aristotle refers is 451d4ff, where Socrates poses a series of questions to Glaucon in order to force an admission that no dissimilarity should exist between the lives of lower animals and human beings' (p. 28). It is interesting that Aristotle refers to a 'parable' told by Socrates that has to do with animals.

64. This statement applies in a limited sense to the usage of the noun παραβολή in Book 3; it also applies to the παράδειγμα as species ('historical' example).

for according to this witness to the ancient rhetorical tradition the parable *is* an example. Before this issue is pursued further, a review of the species of παραδείγματα as delineated by Aristotle in Book 2 of the *Rhetoric* may prove helpful.

As we have seen, Aristotle identifies one genus of logical argument as paradigmatic, and then identifies two species of παραδείγματα. Aristotle does not make distinctions among the species of παραδείγματα on the basis of formal elements manifest in each species; rather, the species of παραδείγματα are distinguished on this basis: 'There are two species of examples; for one species of example is to tell of things [or events] that have happened before [πράγματα προγεγενημένα], and one [species is] to make them [πράγματα] up [or create them: τὸ αὐτὸν ποιεῖν]'. The reference to a species of παράδειγμα that tells of events that have happened before is clear enough, for Aristotle previously made reference to this species of example, recommending it as best suited for deliberative oratory.[65] The reference to a species of παράδειγμα that 'makes up' events is not as clear, so Aristotle immediately clarifies by identifying two of its species: 'παραβολή is one, and one λόγοι, such as the Aesopic and Libyan'. All three species are suitable for use in deliberative oratory, although Aristotle acknowledges that λόγοι (and by implication παραβολαί) possess an advantage over 'historical' examples: '...while it is difficult to find similar incidents that have happened [πράγματα μὲν εὑρεῖν ὅμια γεγενημένα], it is easier [to find] fables, for it is necessary to make them up [ποιῆσαι γὰρ δεῖ] in the same way as parables, if one is able to see the likeness [ὅμοιον]...'[66] Nevertheless, according to Aristotle, 'historical' examples (τὰ διὰ τῶν πραγματῶν) are more useful in deliberative oratory, 'for the future for the most part is like [or

65. Although it is not named as such, the sample of παράδειγμα as induction in *Rhetoric* 1.2.19 is a 'historical' example. The species 'historical' example is referred to regularly as things or events that have happened before; compare 2.20.2 (πράγματα προγεγενημένα) to 1.9.40 (παραδείγματα...ἐκ γὰρ τῶν προγεγονόν-των), 3.17.5 (ὥστ' ἐκ τῶν γενομένων ἀνάγκη παραδείγματα λέγειν), and 1.15.26 (γεγενημένα παραδείγματα). Cf. 3.16.11 on the narration (διήγησις) in deliberative speeches, which, if there is one at all, will be of things past (γενομένων).

66. *Rhetoric* 2.20.7; my translation. Price thinks it odd that Aristotle devotes so much space to 'fables' when so few extant speeches from antiquity contain the use of fables (see 'Παράδειγμα and *Exemplum* in Ancient Rhetorical Theory', pp. 43-46, 237-39).

resembles: ὅμοια] the past [τοῖς γεγονόσιν]'.[67] Aristotle's distinction between the 'historical' example and the 'fictional' examples, then, rests upon whether the event actually took place or whether the event is fabricated.

The significance of Aristotle's discussion of the species of παραδείγματα, in McCall's opinion, does not lie in details about the form of either the παραβολή or the παράδειγμα, but in the close association of two species of παραδείγματα, the 'historical' example and the παραβολή.

> The identifying features of παραβολή do not, in Aristotle's mind, seem to include a particular form. This is indicated both by the careless phrasing of the illustration of the παραβολή and by the similar form given to the surrounding illustrations of historical example and fable (λόγοι)...These resemble the παραβολή in being similarly comparative. Form, therefore, is a relatively interchangeable feature of historical example, παραβολή, and fable: all serve as means of persuasion and differ not so much in form as in content.[68]

McCall contends that Aristotle utilizes 'two essential terms of comparison', παραβολή and εἰκών (simile), and he makes a perceptive remark on Aristotle's use of those two comparative terms: In the *Rhetoric*, παραβολή is closely connected to παράδειγμα, while εἰκών is closely connected to metaphor (repeatedly in Book 3).[69] Thus, McCall states his opinion on the significance of Aristotle's treatment of the species of παραδείγματα (in 2.20):

> The importance of the passage lies in the collocation of historical example and fictional comparison as closely related forms of persuasion or proof. In Theodorus a term of comparison, εἰκών, was associated with metaphor, and this connection recurs frequently in Aristotle and elsewhere. Probably the most common association of comparison in ancient rhetoric, however, is with historical example, and the first moderately full statement is in the present passage. The collocation receives only limited emphasis from Aristotle when compared to the repeated pairing of εἰκών and metaphor in Book III; but in subsequent works

---

67. *Rhetoric* 2.20.8; my translation.

68. McCall, *Ancient Rhetorical Theories of Simile and Comparison*, p. 27.

69. McCall, *Ancient Rhetorical Theories of Simile and Comparison*, pp. 24-26; on the εἰκών, see pp. 29-53. McCall's observation would not benefit Jülicher, who wants to establish an essential distinction between parable and allegory by arguing that the former is based upon simile, the latter upon metaphor (see Chapter 3).

such as the *Rhetorica ad Herennium*, Cicero's *de Inventione*, Quintilian's *Institutio Oratoria*, and the late technical treatises historical
example and fictional comparison are coupled in a fixed rhetorical
canon, while metaphor and comparison are connected less frequently.[70]

The collocation of παράδειγμα and παραβολή will be revisited shortly.
Before moving on to a consideration of parable and example in later
Roman rhetorical treatises, let us reflect upon the implications of what
Aristotle has to say about the παράδειγμα and παραβολή in his
Rhetoric.

An examination of παράδειγμα and παραβολή in Aristotle's *'Art' of
Rhetoric* indicates that the distinction made by some parable scholars
between *Parabel* and *Beispielerzählung*, parable and example, must be
rethought, for Aristotle regards the παράδειγμα and παραβολή as very
closely related means of persuasion. The problems inherent in some
attempts to extract a classificatory grid from Aristotle's *Rhetoric* for
categorizing according to form the παραβολαί of Jesus as recorded in
the synoptic gospels should be evident. Aristotle's *Rhetoric* poses a
severe problem to those who wish to maintain a categorical distinction
between *Parabel* and *Beispielerzählung* by arguing along these lines:

Major Premise:	The parables are not examples.
Minor Premise:	The *Beispielerzählungen* are examples.
Conclusion:	Therefore, the *Beispielerzählungen* are not parables.

Such reasoning is, of course, valid mechanically, but the argument is
based on a premise that cannot be found in the *Rhetoric* of Aristotle.
No such dichotomy between parables and examples exists in the
Rhetoric, for there the παραβολή is a species of the genus παράδειγμα.
Aristotle does distinguish between the species 'historical' example and
the species 'fictional' example (and its subspecies παραβολή and
λόγος), but both are species of the genus παράδειγμα. This aspect of
Aristotle's treatment of the παράδειγμα and the παραβολή in Book 2
of the *Rhetoric* is either overlooked, ignored or suppressed by Jülicher
in his attempt to correlate two kinds of παραβολαί *Jesu*, the *Gleichnis*
and the *Parabel*, to the παραβολή and the λόγος (respectively)—both
of which are species of the 'fictional' example, which is a species of

70. McCall, *Ancient Rhetorical Theories of Simile and Comparison*, pp. 25-26;
but cf. p. 31 n. 24. McCall notes that the same collocation of παράδειγμα and
παραβολή occurs in *Topica* 8.1.157a14-15.

παράδειγμα. Whereas Aristotle's intent is to identify the species of the παραδείγματα, Jülicher's intent is to classify the παραβολαί of Jesus; whereas Aristotle identifies the παραβολή as a species of παράδειγμα, Jülicher identifies the example (narrative) as a kind of παραβολή. To his credit, Jülicher did not ultimately exclude the *Beispielerzählungen* from among Jesus' παραβολαί; however, his appeal to Book 2 of Aristotle's *Rhetoric* in order to solidify his classification of Jesus' παραβολαί has caused a fair amount of confusion among subsequent generations of parable scholars, for Jülicher apparently failed to notice that Aristotle makes a distinction between two genera of proofs (enthymeme and παράδειγμα) and between two species of παραδείγματα.[71]

Quite obviously, there is no exact correspondence between Jülicher's categories of παραβολαί *Jesu—Gleichnis, Parabel* and *Beispielerzählung*—and Aristotle's species of παραδείγματα—'historical' example, 'fictional' example παραβολή and 'fictional' example λόγος (see Figures 1 and 2). Jülicher went so far as to correlate *Gleichnis* and παραβολή, *Parabel* and λόγος, and went no further.[72] If he were to complete the correlation of his categories of παραβολαί in a fashion consistent with Aristotle's species of παραδείγματα, then Jülicher would be compelled to correlate the *Beispielerzählung* and the 'historical' example, which is something he steadfastly sought to avoid, as we saw in Chapter 3. A correlation of the *Beispielerzählung* and the 'historical' example would force Jülicher to accept the untenable position that the *Beispielerzählungen* relate historical 'events that have happened before'.

Scholars before Jülicher addressed the question of whether the group of four παραβολαί which he designated as *Beispielerzählungen* were parables or stories of 'real' events, as we saw in Chapter 2. It seems plausible that Jülicher reacted against such a view, although doubtlessly his main concern was to squelch the view of Jesus' parables as allegories, for which reason he appealed to ancient rhetorical treatises, and

71. My critique differs somewhat from Baasland's comment: 'Jülicher seems to have overlooked the difference between the actual rhetorical proofs (enthymeme) and examples/paradigms, which was precisely the decisive point for Aristotle' ('Zum Beispiel der Beispielerzählungen', p. 198 n. 23).

72. Of course, given the other similarities between the *Parabeln* and *Beispielerzählungen* observed by Jülicher, it is possible that he would also correlate the *Beispielerzählungen* to the λόγοι; however, I regard that as unlikely.

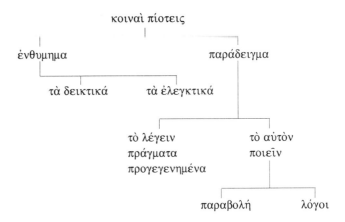

Fig. 1. Aristotle's classification of the κοιναὶ πίστεις.

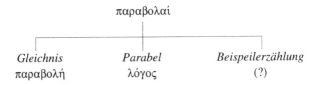

Fig. 2. Jülicher's classification of the παραβολαί *Jesu*.

especially Aristotle's *Rhetoric*. This critique of Jülicher's appropriation of Aristotle's precepts on παράδειγμα and παραβολή should not be construed as suggesting that Jülicher was wrong to turn to Aristotle's *Rhetoric* in order to understand better the parables of Jesus *as recorded in the synoptic gospels*, and in particular those found in the Gospel of Luke. However, Jülicher restricted himself to a limited use of a brief—albeit important—section of Aristotle's *Rhetoric*. A more comprehensive reading of what Aristotle wrote in his *Rhetoric* with regard to the παράδειγμα and the παραβολή might have yielded a different understanding of parable and example, but one that would still have permitted Jülicher to accomplish his purposes in *Die Gleichnisreden Jesu*. Be that as it may, the distinction between *Parabel* and *Beispielerzählung* as posited in *Die Gleichnisreden Jesu* certainly does not derive from Aristotle's *Rhetoric*. Jülicher accepted the distinction between (narrative) parable and example (narrative) as proposed by those who preceded him, and he passed that distinction on to those who follow him.

Aristotle's *'Art' of Rhetoric*, an eminent representative of one sector of the ancient rhetorical tradition in the fourth century, provides invaluable information that can serve to establish some of the conventional expectations associated with the παραβολή and the παράδειγμα in antiquity. For Aristotle, the παράδειγμα is a means of persuasion, a genus of proof and mode of logical argument that employs a comparative technique or strategy—exhibited in all of its species—in order to show, or to seem to show, that something is so 'on the basis of many similar instances', a means of persuasion that can be used effectively in all species of rhetoric. Even though the term παραβολή is apparently used in a somewhat different manner in Book 3 of the *Rhetoric*, and even though the verb παραβάλλειν is used in association with amplification, it is equally apparent that Aristotle conceives of the παραβολή as a species of παράδειγμα, and thus as a comparative technique or strategy that can be employed effectively as a means of persuasion in rhetorical speeches of all kinds.

We leave Aristotle's *Rhetoric* and the classical Greek rhetorical tradition in order to move on to Roman rhetorical treatises so that we can examine what is written there about parable and example. We would do well to remember that in so doing we are crossing a divide of both centuries and cultures. As McCall states, '...a lacuna exists from Aristotle to the first century B.C., and the treatises that mark the reappearance of rhetorical literature are, geographically, not products of the Greek world but of Rome'.[73] The discussion will be limited to four important Latin rhetorical treatises: *Rhetorica ad Herennium, De Inventione, De Oratore* and *Institutio Oratoria*.

Parable and Example in Rhetorica ad Herennium

This investigation of parable and example in the ancient rhetorical tradition now moves from representatives of the classical Greek rhetorical tradition of the fourth century to representatives of the Roman rhetorical tradition of the first century. Although such a move requires that we traverse centuries, cross cultures and change languages, the subject of concern remains the same. Attention will be directed to what is written about parable and example in three of the earliest Roman rhetorical treatises: *Rhetorica ad Herennium*, the first complete rhetorical handbook (*ars*) written in Latin that has survived antiquity; *De Inventione* and *De Oratore*, two rhetorical treatises written by Cicero, one of the dominant Roman rhetoricians in all of antiquity. Rhetorical

73. McCall, *Ancient Rhetorical Theories of Simile and Comparison*, p. 56.

theory underwent change in the period from Aristotle to Cicero—it was modified, developed and adapted to the exigencies of practitioners of rhetoric in new eras and different cultures—and some of those changes are reflected in both *Rhetorica ad Herennium* and *De Inventione*.[74] Therefore, different emphases with respect to parable and example in the later rhetorical treatises should be expected.[75] While *Rhetorica ad Herennium* and *De Inventione*, written by authors who were contemporaries, share more in common than their era, they do not offer identical precepts on either parable or example.[76] The *ars* will be treated first,

74. For a description of Greek rhetorical theory during the Hellenistic period, see Kennedy, *The Art of Persuasion in Greece*, pp. 264-336; *idem, The Art of Rhetoric in the Roman World*, pp. 103-48; *idem, Classical Rhetoric*, pp. 86-99. Although in a narrow sense both *Rhetorica ad Herennium* and *De Inventione* are Roman rhetorical treatises, they reflect certain Hellenistic developments of rhetorical theory (see Kennedy, *The Art of Rhetoric in the Roman World*, pp. 114-26). With reference to *Rhetorica ad Herennium*, Harry Caplan states: 'Like Cicero's incomplete *De Inventione*, which belongs close to it in time, this work reflects Hellenistic rhetorical teaching. Our author, however, gives us Greek art in Latin dress, combining a Roman spirit with Greek doctrine'; see his introduction to *[Cicero] Ad C. Herennium de ratione dicendi (Rhetorica ad Herennium)* (trans. Harry Caplan; LCL; London: Heinemann; Cambridge, MA: Harvard University Press, 1954 [repr. 1981]), p. vii. Unless stated otherwise, all references will be to this edition of *Rhetorica ad Herennium* and all translations will be those provided by Caplan.

75. Given the scarcity of rhetorical documents from the two-century period from Aristotle to Cicero, very little can be known of the developments with regard to the parable and example. Price ('Παράδειγμα and *Exemplum* in Ancient Rhetorical Theory', pp. 85-87, 255-56) points out that during this period *exempla* and λόγοι collections began to appear.

76. Although the chronological order of the two treatises is uncertain, *De Inventione* is thought to have preceded *Rhetorica ad Herennium* by several years (see Caplan, *[Cicero] Ad C. Herennium*, pp. xxv-xxvi; Kennedy, *The Art of Rhetoric in the Roman World*, pp. 103-13; McCall, *Ancient Rhetorical Theories of Simile and Comparison*, pp. 58, 88). Both treatises are thought to stand within the same tradition of rhetorical theory and to be dependent upon the same source(s)—perhaps even based upon the teachings of the same Roman rhetorician (see Caplan, *[Cicero] Ad C. Herennium*, pp. xxiii-xxxii; Kennedy, *The Art of Persuasion in Greece*, pp. 264-65; *idem, The Art of Rhetoric in the Roman World*, pp. 103-13). McCall (*Ancient Rhetorical Theories of Simile and Comparison*, p. 57) describes the relationship between the two documents in this way: 'The two works appear not at all interdependent but rather mutually dependent upon an earlier Hellenistic source or sources...' On the sources of the two treatises, see Kennedy, *The Art of*

Cicero's *De Inventione* second, his *De Oratore* third.

The main discussion of parable and example in *Rhetorica ad Herennium* is reserved for the latter chapters of Book 4, in which the author[77] furnishes a lengthy treatment of style (*elocutio*). Prior to the discussion of style, the author covers many issues relevant to the matter of speaking in public about which he would have Gaius Herennius know. The *auctor ad Herennium* expounds upon those topics which he deems 'pertinent to the theory of public speaking' (1.1.1) in four books. A cursory review of those topics is necessary.

In Book 1, after stating the task of the public speaker, the genera of causes (epideictic, deliberative, judicial) which the public speaker must treat, and the faculties (invention, arrangement, style, memory, delivery) which the public speaker should possess, the author indicates how the speech may be adapted to the speaker's task (1.1.1–1.2.3). His main concern for the remainder of the first book is to explain the use of invention in the six parts of a speech (introduction, statement of facts, division, proof, refutation, conclusion) that treats a judicial cause, 'the most difficult' of the three causes (2.1.1). Book 2 continues the discussion of the judicial cause and the speaker's most important and difficult task, invention.[78] More details are then provided on three parts of the speech: the proof and the refutation, including types of issues and epicheiremes (2.2.3–2.29.6), and the conclusion (2.30.47–2.31.50). In Book 3, the author deals with invention as it relates to the deliberative

---

Rhetoric in the Roman World, pp. 126-48. For a discussion of the similarities and dissimilarities between the two with regard to content, see Kennedy, *The Art of Rhetoric in the Roman World*, pp. 113-48; *idem, The Art of Persuasion in Greece*, pp. 304-18; Caplan, *[Cicero] Ad C. Herennium*, pp. xv-xxxii.

77. For a discussion of matters on the author and date of *Rhetorica ad Herennium*, see Caplan, *[Cicero] Ad C. Herennium*, pp. vii-xxvi; Kennedy, *The Art of Rhetoric in the Roman World*, pp. 111-13, cf. pp. 103-10; McCall, *Ancient Rhetorical Theories of Simile and Comparison*, pp. 57-58. Early on, and throughout the Middle Ages, *Rhetorica ad Herennium* was attributed to Cicero, but Ciceronian authorship has been ruled out in recent scholarship. Cornificus has been nominated as author, but that has also been disputed. Given the uncertainties involving attribution of this treatise to a specific author, I follow Caplan in referring to an *auctor incertus*. There is less debate on the date of the treatise. Caplan fixes the date of *Rhetorica ad Herennium* between 86 and 82 BCE. Kennedy establishes a date for *De Inventione* between 91 and 89 BCE (p. 110).

78. *Rhetorica ad Herennium* 2.1.1; cf. 3.8.15 where *inventione* is called 'the most difficult part of rhetoric'.

cause (3.2.2–3.5.9) and the epideictic cause (3.6.10–3.8.15). The treatment of invention complete, the author turns his attention to three other faculties, referred to now (3.8.15) as parts of rhetoric: arrangement (3.9.16–3.10.18), delivery (3.11.19–3.15.27) and memory (3.16.18–3.24.40). Book 4 is devoted to 'the fifth part of rhetoric' (3.24.40), style.[79] After a severe critique of the Greek 'theory of examples' (*exemplorum rationem*), that is, the manner in which examples are chosen to illustrate principles of style in Greek rhetorical handbooks (4.1.1–4.7.10), the author moves on to discuss the kinds of style (grand, middle and plain) to which a speech must conform (4.8.11–4.10.16) and the qualities of style (taste, artistic composition, distinction) which a speech should always have (4.12.17–4.55.69).

As this examination of parable and example in *Rhetorica ad Herennium* continues, certain terminological complications arise. As McCall indicates, the *auctor ad Herennium* employs several different terms of comparison—such as *similitudo, simile, comparatio, collatio, imago*—in a variety of contexts throughout the treatise; in some contexts the terms are used technically to refer to 'figurative' comparisons, and in other contexts the terms are used non-technically to refer to 'non-figurative' comparisons.[80] Moreover, the term 'exemplum' is employed technically and non-technically in a variety of contexts. As Price observes, the section at the beginning of Book 4 deals with *exempla* as quotations from other orators and authors used to illustrate precepts on style and not with *exempla* as 'historical' examples.[81] Given this situation, each term of comparison will not be examined, nor will every

---

79. The author informs us that he will treat style in Book 4 'because it seems to require a fuller treatment' (3.1.1). He does indeed offer a full treatment of style, one which comprises nearly half of the entire treatise (Kennedy, *The Art of Rhetoric in the Roman World*, p. 118). Caplan notes that 'in the Peripatetic order of the *officia oratoris* Style followed Invention in second place, Arrangement being third...' (*[Cicero] Ad C. Herennium*, p. 184 n. *a*.). Delivery, then, would be fourth, memory fifth.

80. McCall, *Ancient Rhetorical Theories of Simile and Comparison*, pp. 58-62, 79-80.

81. Price, 'Παράδειγμα and *Exemplum* in Ancient Rhetorical Theory', p. 93; cf. pp. 257-58: 'The beginning of book 4 discusses at great length whether the instructor of rhetoric should illustrate his precepts by making up his own examples or by quoting suitable lines from various notable authors. *Exemplum* here is much closer to "grammatical paradigm" than it is to "historical example"' (p. 257 n. 17).

mention of *exemplum* be treated. Another obvious terminological complication involves translating Greek rhetorical terms into Latin, as the author himself states (4.7.10). These complications will obviate any hard and fast conclusions with regard to the issues of concern in this study. Although the focus here will be upon the section in Book 4 of *Rhetorica ad Herennium* in which it is rather evident that the terms *similitudo* and *exemplum* are used in a technical sense, we would do well to glance at a few of the remarks made with reference to both scattered throughout the first three books.

The first mention of *similitudo* occurs in Book 1 where the author explains the subtle approach to introducing a cause. If the audience is experiencing fatigue as a result of listening to previous speeches, our author advises opening with something that might provoke laughter, and he lists *similitudine* (which Harry Caplan translates as 'comparison') among the several options.[82] Little can be divined about the *similitudo* from this list, and the author will not provide specific details on the *similitudo* for three more books.[83]

The author makes an intriguing reference to *simile* and *exemplum* in Book 2 in his explanation of how to develop a (judicial) argument. According to the author, 'the most complete and perfect argument' has five parts: the proposition, the reason, the proof of the reason, the embellishment and the summation (2.18.28). He provides a sample of a model argument (2.19.28-30), and then identifies faults and weaknesses

82. *Rhetorica ad Herennium* 1.6.10. The list also includes *fabula* and *historia* (cf. 1.8.13).

83. *Similitudo* also occurs in the discussion of the proof and the refutation, with specific reference to the types of issues (conjectural, legal, juridical) presented by the cause (here, the judicial); see 1.10.18–1.11.18. The legal issue is divided into six subtypes (1.11.19), the last being 'reasoning by analogy' (*ratiocinationem*). The author states that 'the controversy is based on Analogy when a matter that arises for adjudication lacks a specifically applicable law, but an analogy is sought from other existing laws on the basis of a certain similarity [*similitudine*] to the matter in question' (1.13.23). The author returns to this subtype of legal issue in 2.12.18 and again uses the term *similitudinem*. Comparison (*comparatio*) also comes up for discussion as one of the subtypes of the assumptive type of juridical issue (1.14.24 and 1.15.25; cf. 2.14.21-22). Comparison (*collatio*) is listed as one of the six subdivisions of the conjectural issue in a judicial cause (2.2.3; cf. 2.4.6) McCall (*Ancient Rhetorical Theories of Simile and Comparison*, p. 159) regards these instances of *comparatio* and *collatio* as referring to 'a broad and nonfigurative kind of comparison'.

that can occur in each part of the argument.[84] After enumerating the components of the embellishment (*exornatio*), certain flaws of each component are discussed:

> Since Embellishment consists of similes [*similibus*], examples [*exemplis*], amplifications, previous judgments, and the other means which serve to expand and enrich the argument, let us consider the faults which attach to these.

The concern here is with the first two.

> A Simile [*Simile*] is defective if it is inexact in any aspect, and lacks a proper ground for the comparison [*conparationis*], or is prejudicial to him who presents it.
> An Example [*Exemplum*] is defective if it is either false, and hence refutable, or base, and hence not to be imitated [*imitandum*], or if it implies more or less than the matter demands.[85]

McCall is of the opinion that *simile* here should not be rendered as 'simile'—and it is true that the figure simile is referred to as *imago* in Book 4 (4.49.62). The significance of this section, according to McCall, is 'the collocation of *simile* and *exemplum* (fictional comparison and historical example), which recalls Aristotle's equivalent collocation of παραβολή and παράδειγμα...'[86] Whether or not *simile* refers to

---

84. *Rhetorica ad Herennium* 2.20.31–2.29.46. The author deals specifically with faults in making a comparison (conparandis) in the proof of the reason (2.28.45).

85. *Rhetorica ad Herennium* 2.29.46. This is not the first time that *exemplum* is mentioned in Book 2; see 2.8.12 and 2.10.14. On embellishment, see 2.18.28: 'Embellishment we use in order to adorn and enrich the argument, after the Proof has been established'.

86. McCall, *Ancient Rhetorical Theories of Simile and Comparison*, p. 61. McCall correlates the remarks on *simile* here with the sample of an argument given in 2.19.29 (p. 60). He adds that 'here, as in Aristotle, fictional comparison and historical example form part of a juridical argument, primarily to provide proof. In Book IV the author will use the same collocation more than once but always within the context of style rather than argument' (p. 61). While I do not disagree with McCall's statement, I would qualify it by recalling that Aristotle recommends the παράδειγμα as especially useful in deliberative speeches. The example is not limited to judicial rhetoric in *Rhetorica ad Herennium*, for the author asserts that the conclusions in deliberative speeches are nearly the same as conclusions in judicial speeches, except that in the conclusions of deliberative speeches it is especially useful 'to present examples from the past in the greatest possible number' (3.5.9). See also 3.3.4, where the example appears as a topic of wisdom in deliberative

παραβολή, it is fairly certain that *exemplum* should be taken to mean 'historical' example. Price locates the significance of this section in its contribution to the refutation of an example, that is, '...that the *illustrans* may be unworthy of emulation or that it may be simply untrue'.[87]

The preceding assessments of this section are accurate. However, one aspect of the author's treatment of *simile* and *exemplum* in this section that has received insufficient emphasis is this: The author explains how to develop arguments (*argumentationes*) in a judicial cause (2.18.27); earlier he states that these *argumentationes* were called *epicheiremata* by the Greeks, and thus belong to the proof and the refutation.[88] (Let us not forget that the epicheireme is a development of the enthymeme into a more complicated form.[89]) The embellishment (*exornatio*) and its components, therefore, are part of a quinquipartite epicheireme.[90] Consequently, the *exemplum* and the *simile* are not merely stylistic embellishments in *Rhetorica ad Herennium*.[91]

Since the main treatment of *similitudo* and *exemplum* occurs in the discussion of style (*elocutio*) in Book 4, it is easy to understand why some scholars submit that both the *similitudo* and the *exemplum* are regarded by the author of *Rhetorica ad Herennium* as stylistic ornaments and not as components of proof. However, the author does not isolate style from all other parts of rhetoric; indeed, *elocutio* is defined (1.2.3) as 'the adaptation of suitable words and sentences [*verborum et*

speeches. The relationship between style and argument is dealt with below.

87. Price, 'Παράδειγμα and *Exemplum* in Ancient Rhetorical Theory', p. 101; cf. pp. 90-92.

88. *Rhetorica ad Herennium* 2.2.2: 'It remained for me, as it seemed, to show by what method we can adapt the means of invention to each type of issue or its subdivision, and likewise what sort of technical arguments (which the Greeks call *epicheiremata*) one ought to seek or avoid; both of these departments belong to Proof and Refutation' (Caplan's emphasis). Thus, the treatment of the development (*tractatio*) of an argument here is the *tractatio* of an epicheireme.

89. Kennedy (*The Art of Persuasion in Greece*, p. 273) notes that 'epicheireme' gradually replaced 'enthymeme' as the term 'for the basic rhetorical argument' (cf. pp. 316-17).

90. Caplan (*[Cicero] Ad C. Herennium*, pp. 106-107 n. *b*) indicates that the view of epicheireme described in *Rhetorica ad Herennium* is somewhat idiosyncratic, and he doubts that this view of epicheireme was very influential in rhetorical practice (cf. also pp. 60-61 n. *c*).

91. This adds balance to some of the comments made by Price (e.g. 'Παράδειγμα and *Exemplum* in Ancient Rhetorical Theory', p. 88) and McCall (e.g. as in n. 86 above).

sententiarum] to the matter devised [*inventionem*]'. Style is obviously
related to invention, and we shall see that style is also related to proof
(*confirmatio*), which is defined as 'the presentation or our arguments
[*argumentorum*], together with their corroboration' (1.3.4). We press
forward, then, to the discussion of style in Book 4.

The *auctor ad Herennium* provides his most extensive treatment of
similitudo and *exemplum* in the section of Book 4 where he treats
embellishments of thought (*exornationes sententiarum*). Over three
chapters are devoted to *similitudo* and *exemplum* (4.45.59–4.49.62),
with more space allocated to the former than the latter. Both terms are
employed prior to those chapters, and it is important to cover some of
those instances. As we have seen, the author criticizes Greek authors
who wrote rhetorical handbooks for the manner in which they select
examples from orators, poets and historians in order to demonstrate
precepts on how to embellish style (4.1.1–4.7.10). Moreover, he critiques the view that examples 'serve the purpose of testimony'.[92] The
author would have it that 'first and foremost, examples are set forth, not
to confirm or to bear witness, but to clarify [*demonstrandi*]'.[93] It is
rather apparent that in this section—and in other sections of Book 4—
the term '*exemplum*' does not refer directly to 'historical' example,
which becomes the concern in ch. 49.[94] The author's use of the term
'*similitudo*' prior to ch. 45 is even more complicated. In order to appreciate more fully the author's use of both terms, a few additional
remarks on style are necessary.

The author divides his precepts on style into two parts (4.7.10). After
he treats the genera of styles—grand, middle and plain (4.7.11–
4.11.16)—he treats the qualities of style—taste, artistic composition,
distinction (4.12.17–4.56.69)—but the emphasis is on distinction (43
chapters); for, as the author states in 4.11.16, each genus of style 'gains
distinction from *exornationes*'. Thus,

---

92. *Rhetorica ad Herennium* 4.1.2; cf. 4.3.5.

93. *Rhetorica ad Herennium* 4.3.5; cf. 4.3.6—but see Caplan's comment
(*[Cicero] Ad C. Herennium*, p. 237 n. *e*).

94. Price ('Παράδειγμα and *Exemplum* in Ancient Rhetorical Theory', pp. 257-
58 n. 17) contends, against Alewell and Caplan, that this section does not concern
the 'historical' example. For other instances of *exemplum* used in a non-technical
sense (i.e. where 'exemplum' does not refer to 'historical' example), see 4.3.5,
4.10.15, 4.27.37, 4.42.54, 4.45.58.

To confer distinction upon style is to render it ornate, embellishing it by variety. The divisions under Distinction are Figures of Diction and the Figures of Thought. [*Haec in verborum et in sententiarum exornationes dividitur*]. It is a figure of diction [*Verborum exornatio*] if the adornment is comprised in the fine polish of the language itself. A figure of thought [*Sententiarum exornatio*] derives a certain distinction from the idea [*in ipsis rebus*], not from the words (4.13.18).

Note that the word 'exornatio', translated by Caplan here as 'figure', is the same word used by the author to identify embellishment as a component of 'the most complete and perfect argument', that is, the epicheireme. As we will soon see, the *auctor ad Herennium* himself links the various 'figures' to 'embellishment'. Therefore, the 'figures' will be referred to as 'embellishments'.

Although the extended discussion of *similitudo* takes place in conjunction with other embellishments of thought, *similitudo* is mentioned in conjunction with several embellishments of diction—paronomasia (*adnominatio*), hyperbole (*superlatio*), metaphor (*translatio*) and allegory (*permutatio*). Paronomasia (a play on words) is an embellishment which modifies sound or changes letters and produces a resemblance in words 'so that similar words express dissimilar things' (4.21.29), and it can be accomplished in several ways. Some kinds of paronomasia are such 'in which the words lack so close a resemblance [*similitudinem*], and yet are not dissimilar' (4.22.30); two samples based upon this sort of resemblance (*similitudo, similitudinem*) are provided.[95]

The author treats hyperbole, metaphor and allegory among a set of ten embellishments of diction in which 'the language departs from the ordinary meaning of the words and is, with a certain grace, applied in another sense' (4.31.42).[96] Hyperbole exaggerates the truth, 'whether for the sake of magnifying or minifying something', which can be accomplished separately or with comparison (*conparatione*).[97] The author states that 'hyperbole with comparison [*conparatione*] is formed from either equivalence [*similitudine*] or superiority', and samples of

95. The author's use of *similitudo* here is not unlike his use of the term in a section on memory in Book 3; there he discusses the resemblance or likeness which can be set up between words and images (see 3.21.34 and 3.22.37).

96. The ten embellishments of this class (*genere*) are: onomatopoeia, pronomination (*antonomasia*), metonymy, periphrasis, hyperbaton, hyperbole, synecdoche, catachresis, metaphor, allegory (see 4.31.42–4.34.46).

97. *Rhetorica ad Herennium* 4.33.44. *Similitudo* is used in the discussion of *comparatio*.

each follow (4.33.44). Metaphor, an embellishment 'used for the sake of creating a vivid mental picture' (*Ea sumitur rei ante oculos ponendae causa*), also involves *similitudo*: 'Metaphor occurs when a word applying to one thing is transferred [*transferetur*] to another, because the similarity [*similitudinem*] seems to justify this transference' (4.34.45).[98] Metaphor and *similitudo* both appear in conjunction with another embellishment, allegory. According to the author,

> Allegory [*Permutatio*] is a manner of speech denoting one thing by the letter of the words, but another by their meaning. It assumes three aspects: Comparison [*similitudinem*], argument [*argumentum*], and contrast. It operates through a comparison [*Per similitudinem*] when a number of metaphors [*translationes*] originating in a similarity [*simile*] in the mode of expression are set together, as follows: 'For when dogs act the part of wolves, to what guardian, pray, are we going to entrust our herds of cattle?' An Allegory is presented in the form of argument [*Per argumentum*] when a similitude [*similitudo*] is drawn from a person or place or object in order to magnify or minify, as if one should call Drusus a 'faded reflection of the Gracchi.'

The author goes on to provide an instance of allegory drawn from contrast, noting that in it and in allegory drawn from a *similitudine* one can make use of argument through the metaphor, and again he provides samples of each.[99] Having completed the discussion of allegory, the last of the embellishments of diction, the author directs his attention to embellishments of thought.

Similitudo and *exemplum* receive more detailed comment in the section on embellishments of thought. Apart from the discussion of each as an embellishment in its own right, both *similitudo* and *exemplum* are

98. In terms of modern scholarship, the author here espouses what can be described as a view of metaphor based upon transference. Jülicher obviously would not appeal to *Rhetorica ad Herennium* to buttress his argument on the essential distinction between simile and metaphor, for the author employs *similitudo* in his discussion of metaphor and simile (*imago*; see 4.49.62). Jülicher would no doubt wince at what follows on *permutatio*.

99. *Rhetorica ad Herennium* 4.34.46. For more on the discussion of hyperbole, metaphor and allegory in the treatise, see McCall, *Ancient Rhetorical Theories of Simile and Comparison*, pp. 61-64. McCall advises that although some of the samples of allegory 'are built *on similitudo*, it must be kept in mind that they are not examples *of similitudo* but of allegory. Hence, the meaning "likeness, resemblance" is as dominant here as "comparison"' (p. 64; his emphasis). Moreover, McCall wants to keep metaphor and *similitudo* separate (see pp. 61, 64 n. 28).

mentioned in conjunction with other embellishments of thought: *simile* and *exemplum* in conjunction with refining (*expolitio*), and *similitudo* in conjunction with simile (*imago*) and emphasis (*significatio*). The author's treatment of *expolitio* gives valuable information relevant not only to *similitudo* and *exemplum*, but also on the relationship of style and its embellishments of thought and diction to the embellishment as part of a speech.

The author defines *expolitio* and tells how it can be accomplished (4.42.54).

> Refining [*Expolitio*] consists in dwelling on the same topic [*loco*] and yet seeming to say something ever new. It is accomplished in two ways: by merely repeating the same idea, or by descanting upon it. [*Ea dupliciter fit: si aut eandem plane dicemus rem, aut de eandem re.*] We shall not repeat the same thing [*rem*] precisely—for that, to be sure, would weary the hearer and not refine the idea [*non rem expolire*]—but with changes [*sed commutate*]. Our changes [*Commutabimus*] will be of three kinds: in the words, in the delivery, and in the treatment [*tractando*].

The author explains further the two ways of accomplishing an *expolitio*, adding later (4.44.58) that refining consists of these types (*generibus expolitio*).

The first *expolitio*, repeating the idea (with changes), can vary the theme by making changes in wording, in delivery and in treatment; and the theme can be varied in the treatment (*tractando*) by dialogue and by arousal (4.43.55, 56). The variations of the first *expolitio*, with the exception of delivery, are illustrated by the author (4.43.55). The second *expolitio*, descanting upon the same theme, makes use of many variations, which are described by the author in this way:

> Indeed, after having expressed the theme [*rem*] simply, we can subjoin the Reason, and then express the theme in another form, with or without the Reasons; next we can present the Contrary (all this I have discussed under Figures of Diction); then a Comparison and an Example [*simile et exemplum*] (about them I shall say more in their place); and finally the Conclusion... (4.43.56–4.44.56).

This sort of refinement, we are told, will consist of many embellishments of diction and thought (*exornationibus verborum et sententiarum*), and they can be ornate. The author then provides a seven-part treatment (*tractabitur*) to show 'how easily, by the precepts of rhetoric, a simple idea is developed [*tractetur*] in a multiple manner' (4.44.56).

What follows, as Caplan points out, is a *tractatio* of a *chria* that includes each of the seven components—*simile* (comparison) and *exemplum* included—enumerated previously by the author.[100] McCall and Price concur that here *simile* is equivalent to *similitudo*,[101] and thus *Rhetorica ad Herennium* provides another instance of the collocation of fictional comparison (*simile/similitudo*—παραβολή) and historical example (*exemplum*—παράδειγμα).[102] After the *tractatio*, the author identifies two important advantages of *expolitio* (4.44.58): first, practicing the principles of refining provides a 'means of training for skill in style'; secondly, in actual speeches refining 'gives force and distinction' to the speech and can be put to use 'in the Embellishment of an argument' (*exornabimus argumentationem*), which—as we saw earlier—is one of the five parts of 'the most complete and perfect argument', the epicheireme.[103]

The author fulfills his promise of speaking further on the comparison and the example in the very next chapter. The *similitudo* is treated first

100. My understanding of this section of *Rhetorica ad Herennium* differs somewhat from that of Caplan and McCall. Caplan indicates in his explanatory note on 4.42.54 that *expolitio*, which he translates as 'refining', is 'a χρεία, a thought (usually ethical) developed in detail in accordance with definite rules; a favourite type of *progymnasma*' (*[Cicero] Ad C. Herennium*, p. 365 n. *c*; his emphasis). Later, he remarks on the illustration in 4.44.47 that 'the *tractatio* (ἐξεργασία) of the *chria* is freer than that of the epicheireme in 2.xix.28 ff. This is our oldest extant illustration of a *chria*' (p. 370 n. *d*; his emphasis). McCall (*Ancient Rhetorical Theories of Simile and Comparison*, p. 64) follows Caplan. With reference to the second *expolitio*, I concur that the illustration of the seven-part *tractatio* in 4.44.57 is an ἐξεργασία of a *chria*. However, the author indicates that he speaks of two types of *expolitio*. My question is this: Is the illustration of the first kind of *expolitio*—repeating the same theme with variations—also an ἐξεργασία of a *chria*?

101. McCall, *Ancient Rhetorical Theories of Simile and Comparison*, pp. 64-65; Price, 'Παράδειγμα and *Exemplum* in Ancient Rhetorical Theory', p. 259 n. 23.

102. See Caplan, *[Cicero] Ad C. Herennium*, p. 372 n. *c*; McCall, *Ancient Rhetorical Theories of Simile and Comparison*, pp. 64-65; Price, 'Παράδειγμα and *Exemplum* in Ancient Rhetorical Theory', p. 258 n. 20.

103. Note that in his initial remarks on the *tractatio* of an argument (epicheireme), the author states that 'it is very difficult to refine what has been invented' (*difficillimum vero est inventum expolire*), and that it is this—refining what has been invented—that enables a speaker to refrain from dwelling on the same topic longer than is necessary (2.18.27; my translation).

in a lengthy discussion, the example second in a more abbreviated discussion. The main points made by the author with regard to each of these embellishments of thought will be attended to now.[104]

The treatment of the *similitudo* begins with a definition; the author then states the uses of *similitudo* and identifies its modes of presentation.

> Comparison is a manner of speech that carries over an element of likeness from one thing to a different thing. This is used to embellish or prove or clarify or vivify. Furthermore, corresponding to these four aims, it has four forms of presentation: Contrast, Negation, Detailed Parallel, Abridged Comparison. To each single aim in the use of Comparison we shall adapt the corresponding form of presentation.[105]

Each of the four modes of presenting a *similitudo* are dealt with individually, and samples of each are furnished.

The *similitudo per contrarium* can be used to embellish, as in this sample (4.45.59):

> 'Unlike what happens in the palaestra, where he who receives the flaming torch is swifter in the relay race than he who hands it on, the new general who receives command of an army is not superior to the general who retires from its command. For in the one case it is an exhausted runner who hands the torch to a fresh athlete, whereas in this it is an experienced commander who hands over an army to an inexperienced.'

The author concedes that a straightforward statement might express the idea 'simply, clearly, and plausibly', but he asserts that the use of a comparison for embellishment gives a certain distinction to the style. The *similitudo* in the mode of contrast, the author adds, 'is used when we deny that something else is like [*similem*] the thing we are asserting to be true' (4.46.59).[106]

104. McCall (*Ancient Rhetorical Theories of Simile and Comparison*, pp. 65-79) deals with the minutiae of this section on *similitudo* and *exemplum*.

105. *Rhetorica ad Herennium* 4.45.59: 'Similitudo est oratio traducens ad rem quampiam aliquid ex re dispari simile. Ea sumitur aut ornandi causa aut probandi aut apertius dicendi aut ante oculos ponendi. Et quomodo quattuor de causis sumitur, item quattuor modis dicitur: per contrarium, per negationem, per conlationem, per brevitatem. Ad unam quamque sumendae causam similitudinis adcommodabimus singulos modos pronuntiandi'. McCall suggests that the text of the last sentence quoted here may be corrupt since the third and fourth purposes do not correspond exactly to the third and fourth modes of presentation as described by the author later (*Ancient Rhetorical Theories of Simile and Comparison*, p. 66 n. 33).

106. McCall (*Ancient Rhetorical Theories of Simile and Comparison*, pp. 67-68)

The *similitudo per negationem* can be used for proof, as follows (4.46.59):

> 'Neither can an untrained horse, however well-built by nature, be fit for the services desired of a horse, nor can an uncultivated man, however well-endowed by nature, attain to virtue.'

This *similitudo*, according to the author, contributes to the proof by making the idea more plausible since the verisimilitude is greater (*magis est veri simile*).[107]

Per brevitatem, the third mode of presenting a *similitudo* (referred to here as *simile*), can be used to clarify, and a sample is given to show how such a purpose can be accomplished (4.47.60).

> 'In maintaining a friendship, as in a footrace, you must train yourself not only so that you succeed in running as far as is required, but so that, extending yourself by will and sinew, you easily run beyond that point.'

The author explains that the *simile* in an abridged mode of presentation, unlike the other modes of presenting a *similitudo*, does not separate the term of the comparison from the subject, but conjoins and intermingles both in the presentation (4.47.60).

The fourth mode of presenting a *similitudo* is *per conlationem*, 'detailed parallel', and is used for vividness (*Ante oculos ponendi negotii causa sumetur similitudo*). This mode of *similitudo* embellishes both terms (the subject and the comparative part), relates both terms in parallel description and correlates items that are expressed in both terms, as the author shows in an extended sample (4.47.60).

> 'Let us imagine a player of the lyre who has presented himself on the stage, magnificently garbed, clothed in a gold-embroidered robe, with purple mantle interlaced in various colours, wearing a golden crown illumined with large gleaming jewels, and holding a lyre covered with golden ornaments and set off with ivory. Further, he has a personal

deals with what he perceives to be difficulties in this section. For instance, if this mode of *similitudo* serves to embellish, then do the other three modes of presentation not serve to embellish? If not, then in what sense can they be 'embellishments' of thought?

107. McCall (*Ancient Rhetorical Theories of Simile and Comparison*, pp. 69-70) also perceives a difficulty in the treatment of the *similitudo per negationem*: 'Its purpose, proof (*probatio*), would seem quite alien to embellishment. Should this type of *similitudo* then be considered essentially different from *similitudines* that are embellishments?' (p. 69; his emphasis). My answer to McCall's question should become apparent later.

beauty, presence, and stature that impose dignity. If, when by these means he has roused a great expectation in the public, he should in the silence he has created suddenly give utterance to a rasping voice, and this should be accompanied by a repulsive gesture, he is the more forcibly thrust off in derision and scorn, the richer his adornment and the higher the hopes he has raised. In the same way, a man of high station, endowed with great and opulent resources, and abounding in all the gifts of fortune and the emoluments of nature, if he yet lacks virtue and the arts that teach virtue, will so much the more forcibly in derision and scorn be cast from all association with good men, the richer he is in the other advantages, the greater his distinction, and the higher the hopes he has raised.'

The author completes his treatment of *similitudo* as an embellishment of thought with remarks on establishing and maintaining resemblance between the things set in correspondence, and with a list of sources for the invention of comparisons.

In Comparisons we must carefully see to it that when we present the corresponding idea for the sake of which we have introduced the figure we use words suited to the likeness. The following is an example: 'Just as the swallows are with us in summer time, and when driven by the frost retire,...' Keeping the same comparison [*similitudine*], and using Metaphor [*translationem*], we now say: 'so false friends are with us in a peaceful season of our life, and as soon as they have seen the winter of our fortune, they fly away, one and all.' But the invention of Comparisons [*inventio similium*] will be easy if one can frequently set before one's eyes everything animate and inanimate, mute and articulate, wild and tame, of the earth, sky, and sea, wrought by art, chance, or nature, ordinary or unusual, and can amongst these hunt out some likeness [*similitudinem*] which is capable of embellishing or proving or clarifying or vivifying. The resemblance [*similis*] between the two things need not apply throughout, but must hold on the precise point of comparison [*similitudinem*].[108]

With these remarks, the discussion proper of *similitudo* as an embel-

108. *Rhetorica ad Herennium* 4.48.61. The Latin text of the first sentence quoted here reads: 'In similibus observare oportet diligenter ut, cum rem adferamus similem cuius rei causa similitudinem adtulerimus, verba ad similitudinem habeamus adcommodota'. The mention of metaphor together with *similitudo* recalls the previous treatments of metaphor and allegory. These sections are not entirely supportive of McCall's position on metaphor and comparison in *Rhetorica ad Herennium*, in which he maintains a distinction between metaphor and *similitudo* (see *Ancient Rhetorical Theories of Simile and Comparison*, pp. 61-63, 78, 85-86). Note further that *translatio*, *similitudo* and *exemplum* are said to create 'vividness'.

lishment of thought ends, and the author proceeds to another related embellishment, the *exemplum*. These are not, however, the final remarks made on *similitudo* in *Rhetorica ad Herennium*.

The next embellishment of thought treated by the author is the *exemplum* (4.49.62). His definition of *exemplum* is succinct, his discussion brief.

> Exemplification [*Exemplum*] is the citing of something done or said in the past, along with the definite naming of the doer or author [*est alicius facti aut dicti praeteriti cum certi auctoris nomine propositio*]. It is used with the same motives as a Comparison [*similitudo*]. It renders a thought more brilliant when used for no other purpose than beauty; clearer, when throwing more light upon what was somewhat obscure; more plausible, when giving the thought greater verisimilitude [*cum magis veri similem facit*]; more vivid, when expressing everything so lucidly that the matter can, I may almost say, be touched by the hand. I would have added individual specimens [*exempla*] of each type had I not under Refining [*expolitione*] demonstrated the nature of Exemplification [*exemplum*], and, under Comparison [*similitudine*], made clear the motives of its use.

Several points need to be emphasized. The author explicitly correlates the functions of *exempla* to the functions of the *similitudines*. Although he does not give *exempla* of the individual genera of examples, he implies that the modes of presenting examples would correlate to the modes of presenting *similitudines*.[109] The author alludes to the earlier section on the *tractatio* of the second *expolitio* and therefore reminds us that the *exemplum* is related to proof, but he treats two other embellishments of thought in which reference is made to *similitudo*.

Similitudo is mentioned in conjunction with simile (*imago*). That *imago* and *similitudo* are related is evident in the definition of *imago* (4.49.62): 'Simile [*Imago*] is the comparison [*conlatio*] of one figure with another, implying a certain resemblance [*similitudine*] between them'. Here, both *conlatio* and *similitudine* appear together, as was the case in the treatment of *similitudo* immediately preceding the treatment of *exemplum*.[110]

---

109. The author refers to the sample of 'historical' example involving Decius provided in the treatment of the *tractatio* of the second *expolitio* (4.44.57). Recall that in the conclusion of that *tractatio* the example is said to have 'confirmed' (*exemplo conprobatum*) the thesis. Price does not fancy the correlation of *similitudines* and *exempla*; the fourfold classification of *exempla* here is, in his words, 'grossly inaccurate' ('Παράδειγμα and *Exemplum* in Ancient Rhetorical Theory', p. 98).

110. McCall wants to keep *imago* and *similitudo* separate; see *Ancient Rhetorical*

Similitudo is also identified as one of several ways of producing emphasis (*significatio*) and embellishment, 'which leaves more to be suspected than has been actually asserted' (4.54.67). Emphasis is produced *per similitudinem*, the author explains,

> ...when we cite some analogue [*re simile*] and do not amplify it, but by its means intimate what we are thinking, as follows: 'Do not, Saturninus, rely too much on the popular mob—unavenged lie the Gracchi.'[111]

Note that the *re simile* both involves named characters and also seemingly refers to an event in the past. A *similitudo* expressed in this manner, then, produces *significatio*, an embellishment which 'permits the hearer himself to guess what the speaker has not mentioned' (4.54.67).

After a brief treatment of two other embellishments, the discussion of how to embellish style is finished. The author then makes a few personal remarks to Gaius Herennius, encouraging him to practice diligently according to the principles of rhetoric expressed throughout the treatise, and thus concludes the *ars* on rhetoric *ad Herennium*.

What we have learned about *similitudo* and *exemplum* from a first-century Roman rhetorical treatise can now be brought to bear upon the distinction made between parable and example, *Parabel* and *Beispielerzählung*, but caution is a must so as to avoid hasty conclusions. While it is evident that *Rhetorica ad Herennium* gives more attention to *similitudo*—indeed, it provides a discussion of four kinds of *similitudo* according to aim and mode of presentation—than either *Rhetorica ad Alexandrum* or *'Art' of Rhetoric* give to παραβολή, it would be premature to conclude that the parable is accorded a more prominent place in the Roman rhetorical tradition than in the Greek rhetorical tradition. Although it is true that *similitudo* is used frequently in *Rhetorica ad Herennium*, rivaled only by *simile*, which is said to be synonymous with *similitudo*, to construe every reference to *similitudo* as a reference to parable would be problematical because, as we have seen, the *auctor* does not employ *similitudo* solely as a technical rhetorical term to refer to a particular embellishment of thought. *Similitudo* is used in a variety of contexts (non-technically) to mean 'likeness' or 'resemblance'. Moreover, *similitudo* is used in conjunction with a number of other

Theories of Simile and Comparison, pp. 78-86.

111. Caplan translates *per similitudinem* here as 'through Analogy'. The author refers to Saturninus and the Gracchi also in 4.22.31.

embellishments, and it is uncertain whether or not some of these references to *similitudo* are technical. The problem of taking every instance
of *similitudo* to be a reference to parable is compounded by the
difficulty of discerning whether *similitudo* is, according to the author,
the exact equivalent of παραβολή. We are on firmer ground with
exemplum since the *auctor ad Herennium* mentions the Greek rhetoricians and 'their theory of examples', but again we encounter problems
because *exemplum* does not mean only 'historical' example in this treatise. Nevertheless, if we are mindful of these problems and confine
ourselves to those sections where it is reasonably safe to assume that
the author is speaking about *similitudo* and *exemplum* in a technical
rhetorical sense—and if the assumption is granted that in those places
the Latin term *similitudo* is equivalent to the Greek term παραβολή—
we may venture to assess the distinction between parable and example
in light of *Rhetorica ad Herennium*.

According to *Rhetorica ad Herennium*, the *similitudo* and the *exemplum* are closely related. We have witnessed the collocation of
simile/similitudo and *exemplum* here, which parallels the collocation of
παραβολή and παράδειγμα in Aristotle's *Rhetoric*. However, unlike
the situation in *'Art' of Rhetoric*, where παραβολή as 'fictional' example and παράδειγμα as 'historical' example are species of the genus of
proof παράδειγμα (rhetorical induction), in *Rhetorica ad Herennium*
the *similitudo* and the *exemplum* are not collocated as species of the
rhetorical proof induction.[112] The *similitudo* is not a species of *exemplum* and the *exemplum* is not a species of *similitudo*. Nevertheless,
similitudo and *exemplum* are closely bound together as embellishments—both are components of embellishment as part of 'the most
complete and perfect argument', the epicheireme, and both are embellishments of thought. While it is certainly the case that the main
treatment of *similitudo* and *exemplum* occurs in the discussion of style,
neither the *similitudo* nor the *exemplum* are merely stylistic embellishments, for the *auctor ad Herennium* does not leave the discussion of
style dangling at the end of his *ars*. On the contrary, the author explicitly relates certain embellishments of thought, including the *similitudo*
and the *exemplum*, to his discussion of proof: the *tractatio* of the
second *expolitio* can be put to use in the embellishment of an argument

112. Kennedy observes that a discussion of induction is lacking in *Rhetorica ad
Herennium*; see *The Art of Persuasion in Greece*, p. 316, and *The Art of Rhetoric in
the Roman World*, pp. 134-35.

as part of the *tractatio* of an epicheireme. Therefore, it can be said that in *Rhetorica ad Herennium*, as in earlier handbooks in the rhetorical tradition, the *similitudo* and the *exemplum* are of service to the speaker as a 'means of proof', although admittedly *Rhetorica ad Herennium* advances a rather idiosyncratic view of proofs.[113]

The *similitudo* and the *exemplum* are manifestly linked to each other as embellishments of thought in *Rhetorica ad Herennium*. The author says that the *similitudo* and the *exemplum* are to be used for the same four motives—to embellish, to prove, to clarify, to vivify—and thus he indicates that neither *similitudo* nor *exemplum* are limited to a single function.[114] Apparently, the author would have it that the *similitudo* and the *exemplum* share the same four modes of presentation, although Price warns against a facile acceptance of the correspondences between *similitudo* and *exemplum*.[115] While the author does delineate four modes of presentation with regard to the *similitudo*, he does not issue dicta on the form of the *similitudo*, as McCall asserts.[116] For instance, the samples provided by the author indicate that a *similitudo* can be lengthy or brief. The same holds true for the *exemplum*. While no formal characteristics are prescribed for either the *similitudo* or the *exemplum*, some observations about their characteristics can be made.

That the *similitudo* and the *exemplum* share common characteristics is rather apparent. Both are drawn from the 'real' world and thus render a thought (*res*) more plausible by giving it greater verisimilitude. It can be inferred that both of these embellishments exclude myth or fable. The main difference between the two embellishments under consideration seems to be that the *similitudo* relates a 'fictional' (or hypothetical)

---

113. Compare this with the earlier remarks on the epicheireme. Note also that *Rhetorica ad Herennium* does not explicitly distinguish between artistic proofs and nonartistic proofs, although the discussion of confirmatory proofs in 2.6.9–2.8.12 has elements that vaguely resemble Aristotle's nonartistic proofs.

114. Price, 'Παράδειγμα and *Exemplum* in Ancient Rhetorical Theory', p. 101: 'While the quadripartite division of *exemplum* in terms of modes of presentation and function appears to be a case of *divisio ad absurdum*, yet it shows an awareness that the functions of an *exemplum* may be manifold'.

115. Price, 'Παράδειγμα and *Exemplum* in Ancient Rhetorical Theory', pp. 99-101. Price contends that the only example explicitly labelled '*exemplum*' (the one involving Decius in 4.44.57) does not fit precisely any of the four modes of presentation outlined in 4.45.59.

116. McCall, *Ancient Rhetorical Theories of Simile and Comparison*, p. 78; cf. p. 84.

event or happening, whereas the *exemplum* relates a 'historical' event
or happening that actually took place in the past. The formal definition
of *exemplum* stipulates that an example cites 'something done or said in
the past, along with the definite naming of the doer or author'.[117] Thus,
the difference between *similitudo* and *exemplum* as embellishments of
thought would appear to be that the *exemplum* alone recounts a past
('historical') occurrence (*facti aut dicti*) involving specifically named
individuals. No absolute distinction between *similitudo* and *exemplum*
can be made on this basis, however, since the author himself provides
a brief *similitudo* that refers to a past ('historical') event involving
named characters, as we saw above in the sample of *significatio per
similitudinem*.

The treatment of *similitudo* and *exemplum* as embellishments of
thought in *Rhetorica ad Herennium* emphasizes their similarities. Even
if one were to equate parable (παραβολή) with *similitudo* and *exemplum* with *Beispielerzählung*—in which case the parable would be a
fictional comparison and the example narrative would be a historical
example—the precepts on *similitudo* and *exemplum* in *Rhetorica ad
Herennium* preclude making a fixed, categorical distinction between
parable and example, for *similitudo* and *exemplum* share the same
functions, the same modes of presentation and other features in
common.[118] As embellishments of thought, both the *similitudo* and the
exemplum are comparative strategies that can be used for a variety of
purposes in the argument of a speech.[119] Parable scholars could con-
ceivably appropriate the fourfold division of *similitudines* according to
purpose and mode of presentation in order to classify the parables
recorded in the synoptic gospels, but they would face sizeable difficulties if they were to appeal to *Rhetorica ad Herennium* in order to
validate the categorical distinction between parable and example story.

117. This definition, referring to things said in the past and to authors, might not
exclude *exempla* of the sort discussed in 4.1.1–4.7.10.

118. Although in the discussion of the refutation of an example the author states
that an *exemplum* is defective if it is base 'and hence not to be imitated', the *exemplum* in *Rhetorica ad Herennium* is not presented primarily as a 'model for the right
conduct'.

119. It is evident that the *similitudo* is conceived of by the author as a comparative strategy; however, the *exemplum* is discussed between two embellishments that
are comparative in nature, and the functions of one of those comparative strategies,
the *similitudo*, are correlated to the *exemplum*.

Parable and Example in De Inventione *and* De Oratore

This investigation of parable and example in the ancient rhetorical tradition now approaches one of the most famous orators in antiquity, M. Tullius Cicero, author of numerous rhetorical and philosophical treatises. The aim of this chapter has been to determine what is written about parable and example in the ancient rhetorical tradition, and several rhetorical handbooks have been consulted as a means toward that end. Cicero presents a situation that requires a modified approach: Although several of Cicero's rhetorical treatises have survived antiquity, a complete *ars* is not to be found among them. *De Inventione*, one of Cicero's earliest rhetorical works, is the first part of an *ars*, but he did not complete the project.[120] This, then, precludes an examination of Cicero's treatment of *similitudo* and *exemplum* within a systematic explication of rhetoric in all its parts.

Several avenues of approach are possible. We could, of course, pass Cicero by and go straight to Quintilian's *Institutio Oratoria*. That approach is entirely unsatisfactory given Cicero's stature among ancient rhetoricians. The investigation could be confined to a consideration of *De Inventione*, but that option is not without problems, for *De Inventione* was written so early in his career that we would discover only what the younger Cicero wrote about *similitudo* and *exemplum*, leaving unexplored what the more mature Cicero had to say about the subjects of interest in this study.[121] The best approach would be to examine all of Cicero's treatises, both rhetorical and philosophical, in order to obtain specific information on *similitudo* and *exemplum*, and then attempt to fashion a comprehensive view of *similitudo* and *exemplum* according to Cicero. In terms of this study, the obvious

120. In *De Inventione* 1.7.9 and 2.59.178, Cicero gives indication that he envisioned writing a complete *ars*.

121. Cicero himself was not entirely pleased with his efforts in *De Inventione* judging from *De Oratore* 1.2.5, where he refers to *De Inventione* as inchoate essays taken from the notebooks of his boyhood and adolescence. On the life and career of Cicero, see Kennedy, *The Art of Rhetoric in the Roman World*, pp. 103-10. If *De Inventione* was written between 91 and 89 BCE, as Kennedy surmises, then Cicero would have been 15 or 17 years old at the time. McCall (*Ancient Rhetorical Theories of Simile and Comparison*, p. 87) speaks against limiting his investigation of Cicero's views of comparison to *De Inventione* because, as he puts it, that treatise is 'youthful and incomplete', 'early and derivative'.

problem with that option is the enormity of such an undertaking. Fortunately, McCall and Price have conducted studies of comparison and example which take into account a number of Cicero's treatises.[122] Their approach will not be reduplicated here, but the results of their analyses will be utilized.

Another approach may prove adequate for the purposes of this study. The present intent is to determine what Cicero has to say about *similitudo* and *exemplum*, but all of Cicero's writings will not be consulted. The scope of this investigation will be limited to sections of two rhetorical treatises in which Cicero discusses *similitudo* and *exemplum*, but other treatises will be given a glance if the situation warrants. Admittedly, such an approach will not yield a comprehensive understanding of Cicero's views on *similitudo* and *exemplum*, but a report on relevant sections of *De Inventione* and *De Oratore* will provide a representative, if partial, understanding of his views on *similitudo* and *exemplum*, one which is sufficient for the purposes of this study. Since Cicero uses the terms *similitudo* and *exemplum* non-technically in both *De Inventione* and *De Oratore*, here an effort will be made to concentrate on those instances in which Cicero employs *exemplum* and *similitudo* in a technical sense to refer to a particular 'figure' (embellishment or ornament) or rhetorical strategy, although his usage of *similitudo* adds a measure of difficulty to such an endeavor.[123] I begin with *De Inventione*.

De Inventione represents young Cicero's systematic treatment of the

---

122. Besides *De Inventione* and *De Oratore*, both McCall and Price consult other rhetorical treatises written by Cicero during a span of half a century, such as *De Partitione Oratoria*, *Topica*, *Brutus* and *Orator*. For a more thorough examination of *similitudo* in Cicero's works, see McCall, *Ancient Rhetorical Theories of Simile and Comparison*, pp. 87-129; for a more thorough study of *exemplum*, see Price, 'Παράδειγμα and *Exemplum* in Ancient Rhetorical Theory', pp. 103-29, 262-73.

123. For instances of *exemplum* used to refer to an illustration or sample of some precept of rhetoric, see *De Inventione* 1.30.49, 1.33.55, 1.41.76, 2.1.3, 2.1.4, 2.1.5, 2.4.14, 2.19.57, 2.20.59, 2.29.87, 2.33.102, 2.33.103, 2.51.156; and *De Oratore* 1.19.88, 1.20.91, 1.42.190, 2.64.264, 3.55.208. (In *De Inventione* 2.37.110 and *De Oratore* 1.40.181, the term seems to refer to legal precedents.) Cicero's use of *similitudo* is more varied. The term is employed frequently to mean 'resemblance', 'likeness' or 'similarity'; in addition to the instances treated in this chapter, see *De Inventione* 2.7.33 and *De Oratore* 1.33.153, 2.12.53, 2.23.96, 2.23.98, 2.36.152, 2.51.209, 2.53.212, 2.60.244, 2.61.249, 2.88.359, 3.15.56, 3.49.191. *Similitudo* carries the sense of 'monotony' in *De Inventione* 1.41.76, 2.51.177; *De Oratore* 2.41.177; and *De Partitione Oratoria* 13.48.

first part of rhetoric, *inventio*, which—after a general introduction (1.1.1–1.6.8)—is defined as 'the discovery of valid or seemingly valid arguments [*rerum verarum aut veri similium*] to render one's case plausible [*probabilem*]'.[124] Following a treatment of *constitutio* (στάσις), in which four possible issues of a case are defined and discussed (1.8.10–1.14.19), Cicero turns his attention to the parts of an oration (exordium, narration, partition, proof, refutation, digression, peroration) for the remainder of Book 1. In Book 2, Cicero treats the invented arguments appropriate to each genus of speech (judicial, deliberative, epideictic), with emphasis on the judicial (2.4.14–2.51.154). The last few chapters provide precepts on the presentation of arguments in deliberative speeches and epideictic speeches (2.52.157–2.59.178). As McCall shows, several terms of comparison—*comparatio, collatio, similitudo, simile, imago*—appear throughout *De Inventione*, with *similitudo* being the term used most frequently and broadly.[125]

The first mention of *similitudo* occurs in the treatment of a part of the speech Cicero identifies as *narratio*, which is 'an exposition of events that have occurred or are supposed to have occurred' (1.19.27). Three kinds of narration are listed, and *similitudo* is mentioned under the second, a digression, which can be made for four purposes. The second *narratio*, then, is that '...in which a digression is made beyond the strict limits of the case for the purpose of attacking somebody, or of making a comparison [*aut similitudinis*], or of amusing the audience in a way not incongruous with the business in hand, or for amplification'.[126] Not much information on the *similitudo* is imparted in these remarks on *narratio*, so we proceed to Cicero's remarks on that part of speech he calls *confirmatio*, proof.

---

124. *De Inventione* 1.7.9. The texts and translations of *De Inventione* and *Topica* used in this study can be found in *Cicero, De Inventione, De Optimo Genere Oratorium, Topica* (trans. H.M. Hubbell; LCL; London: Heinemann; Cambridge, MA: Harvard University Press, 1949).

125. See McCall's analysis of these terms in *Ancient Rhetorical Theories of Simile and Comparison*, pp. 88-100.

126. *De Inventione* 1.9.27. Cicero's discussion of the third kind of *narratio* is interesting, for one of its subdivisions deals with expositions of events and has three parts: 'fabula', 'a narrative in which the events [*res*] are not true and have no verisimilitude [*nec verae nec veri similes*]'; 'historia', 'an account of actual occurrences [*gesta res*] remote from the recollection of our own age'; and 'argumentum', 'a fictitious narrative [*ficta res*] which nevertheless could have occurred'.

Cicero defines *confirmatio* as 'the part of the oration which by mar-shalling arguments lends credit, authority, and support to our case' (1.24.34). After a discussion of the material from which arguments can be drawn (1.24.34–1.28.43), he turns to the forms of argumentation to be derived from that material. According to Cicero, all arguments drawn from the topics discussed must be either probable or irrefutable (1.29.44). The example and several terms of comparison are found in the discussion of probable arguments. *Similitudo* occurs in the defi-nition of probability: 'That is probable [*Probabile*] which for the most part usually comes to pass, or which is a part of the ordinary beliefs of mankind, or which contains in itself some resemblance [*similitudinem*] to these qualities, whether such resemblance be true or false' (1.29.46). With respect to resemblance, Cicero states: 'Resemblance [*Similitudo*] is seen mostly in contraries [*in contrariis*], in analogies [*ex paribus*], and in those things which fall under the same principle' (1.30.46). Samples of each of these three subdivisions of *similitudo* are provided (1.30.46-47).

Cicero makes further subdivisions of probability which are of con-cern here. Everything probable used in argument is, according to Cicero, 'either a *sign*, or something *credible*, or a point on which *judg-ment* has been made, or something which affords an opportunity for *comparison* [*comparabile*]'.[127] Each subdivision is treated in order, *comparabile* last.

> Lastly, probability which depends on *comparison* [*Comparabile*] involves a certain principle of similarity [*similem*] running through diverse material. It has three subdivisions, similitude [*imago*], parallel [*collatio*], example [*exemplum*]. A *similitude* [*Imago*] is a passage [*oratio*] setting forth a likeness [*similitudinem*] of individuals or charac-ters. A *parallel* [*Collatio*] is a passage putting one thing beside another on the basis of their resemblances [*ex similitudine*]. An *example* [*Exem-plum*] supports or weakens a case by appeal to precedent or experience, citing some person or historical event. Instances [*exempla*] and descrip-tions of these principles will be given with the rules for style.[128]

Unfortunately, no examples or descriptions of these subdivisions of the *comparabile* are forthcoming since Cicero never finished writing his

---

127. *De Inventione* 1.30.47; Hubbell's emphasis.

128. *De Inventione* 1.30.49; Hubbell's emphasis. Price comments that this is 'the earliest definition in Latin of *exemplum*...' ('Παράδειγμα and *Exemplum* in Ancient Rhetorical Theory', p. 103).

ars. That being the case, it cannot be determined with certainty whether Cicero's triad of the *comparabile—imago, collatio, exemplum*—is equivalent to the triad *similitudo, exemplum, imago* in *Rhetorica ad Herennium*, as H.M. Hubbell's translation suggests and as McCall argues.[129] While it is true that Cicero plainly collocates *similitudo* and 'historical' example in Book 2, we are not constrained to read it into this section.[130] Cicero's tripartite division of the *comparabile* will be left intact and note will be made that *imago* and *collatio* have to do with *similitudo* and that the *exemplum* ('historical' example) is listed among other comparative devices which can be used in probable arguments as part of the section of the speech concerned with proof.[131] Cicero is not yet finished with his discussion of argumentation, however, and *similitudo* appears in conjunction with a particular form of argumentation.

129. See McCall, *Ancient Rhetorical Theories of Simile and Comparison*, pp. 95-98. His conclusion is that 'the triad of terms, *imago, collatio, exemplum* ("similitude, parallel, example"), must be equivalent to the triad *similitudo, exemplum, imago* in *ad Herennium*, despite the fact that only two terms are common to both triads and that the terms in *ad Herennium* are among the embellishments of thought while in *de Inventione* they are elements of probable truth' (p. 95). In the section where Cicero tells how to refute the *comparabile* (1.44.82), the three subdivisions are not mentioned, but the phrase '*per similitudinem*' appears twice. It remains unclear whether or not this is a technical use of the term *similitudo*. Cicero states further that the ability to refute the *comparabile* is critical in opposing arguments that have been developed by means of induction. According to Price ('Παράδειγμα and *Exemplum* in Ancient Rhetorical Theory', p. 263 n. 7), it is in this section that Cicero comes closest to linking the *exemplum* and induction in *De Inventione*. Compare the remarks made in 1.44.82 with Cicero's comments in the section on a conflict arising in legal disputes when a law is applied *per ratiocinationem* (2.50.148-53, esp. 2.50.153).

130. In a discussion of issues of fact, Cicero points out that the prosecutor can maintain that a crime was committed on impulse by someone suffering from 'mental agitation', and that it is not so strange that such a person could commit a crime: 'This can be done by citing examples [*exemplorum*] of those who have done something under a similar [*simili*] impulse and by collecting parallels [*similitudinum collatione*] and by explaining the nature of mental disturbance' (2.5.19). The defense counsel can counter by either denying any impulse or by contending that the emotion was too weak to give rise to the particular crime, and the defense 'will have to offer examples and parallels [*exempla et similitudines*]' (2.8.25).

131. That examples can be employed to show similarity is also evident in 2.32.100; cf. the previous note as well.

'All argumentation, then', Cicero states (1.31.51), 'is to be carried on [*tractanda*] either by induction [*per inductionem*] or by deduction [*per ratiocinationem*]'. Here, Cicero employs *similitudo* both in his definition of *inductio* and in his discussion of it.[132]

> Induction is a form of argument which leads the person with whom one is arguing to give assent to certain undisputed facts; through this assent it wins his approval of a doubtful proposition because this resembles [*similitudinem*] the facts to which he has assented (1.31.51).

The sample of induction given here is a rather lengthy dialogue composed by Aeschines Socraticus; in this dialogue, Socrates recounts the manner in which Aspasia reasoned with Xenephon and his wife (1.31.51-52). At the close of this sample (1.31.53), Cicero observes:

> In this instance, because assent has been given to undisputed statements, the result is that the point which would appear doubtful if asked by itself is through analogy [*similitudinem*] conceded as certain, and this is due to the method employed in putting the question.

Socrates, Cicero adds, used this method frequently.

Cicero issues precepts for inductive argumentation, the first being that the statement introduced as the basis for induction *per similitudinem* should be one that will be granted as true (1.32.53). Other suggestions for leading the interlocutor in the desired direction ensue. Cicero also gives advice on what to do if the interlocutor either refuses to answer the question, or concedes the point, or denies the point: 'If he denies it, you must show that it resembles [*similitudo*] the points which have previously been conceded, or use another induction' (1.32.54). Before providing another example (*exemplo*) of induction (in 1.32.55-56), Cicero characterizes *inductio* in this way:

> Thus this style of argument [*genus argumentandi*] is threefold: the first part consists of one or more similar cases [*pars ex similitudine*], the second of the point which we wish to have conceded, for the sake of which the similar cases [*causa similitudines*] have been cited; the third is the conclusion which reinforces the concession or shows what results follow from it (1.32.54).

Although in this section we may hear the faint echo of Aristotle's remarks on παραβολή (such as told by Socrates), it is more important

---

132. Later, Cicero employs *similitudo* and *collatio* in his discussion of *ratiocinationem* in a legal dispute (2.50.148-53).

simply to note that Cicero's remarks indicate rather clearly that part of the genus of argument referred to here as induction consists of 'similar cases'.[133]

De Inventione cannot be mined for a treasure of information with regard to either *similitudo* or *exemplum* used technically. The word *similitudo* occurs a number of times throughout the treatise, especially in discussions involving aspects of comparison, but usually with the sense of 'resemblance' or 'likeness'. Moreover, subdivisions of *similitudo* as resemblance are enumerated in the treatment of probability. We can be fairly confident that *similitudo* refers to a particular 'figure' of comparison, 'similar cases', as part of the inductive argument; perhaps the reference to *similitudo* in the second kind of *narratio* is a technical usage as well. *Similitudo* and *exemplum* appear in collocation, and both are used for comparative purposes in the proof of an argument. The *exemplum* is identified as a subdivision of the *comparabile* in a probable argument, but beyond that, and rather surprisingly, *exemplum* as 'historical' example does not receive much attention in *De Inventione*. Cicero will have more to say about the *exemplum* 40 years later in *De Oratore*.

Cicero presents *De Oratore* in the form of a dialogue—with L. Licinius Crassus and Marcus Antonius as the main participants—which is fabricated to permit Cicero to expound upon his notion of the ideal orator.[134] Although not an *ars*, *De Oratore* offers a sweeping view of Cicero's conception of rhetoric as an art; thus, most of the topics

133. Price argues that Cicero is wrong about ἐπαγωγή in Aristotle (see 'Παράδειγμα and *Exemplum* in Ancient Rhetorical Theory', pp. 135-47). The mainstay of Price's argument is that παραβολή = τὰ Σωκρατικά in Aristotle's *Rhetoric*. Based upon his analysis of passages from Cicero, Price states: '...we see that all knowledge and understanding of Aristotle's technical term παραβολή (i.e. τὰ Σωκρατικά), has vanished as has all knowledge of the logical difference between παραβολή and ἐπαγογή. Τὰ Σωκρατικά, Socrates' method, now means "ask leading questions" and has become almost synonymous with *inductio*, the Latin equivalent of ἐπαγωγή' (p. 144).

134. Kennedy provides a summary of *De Oratore* in *The Art of Rhetoric in the Roman World*, pp. 205-30. All citations and translations of *De Oratore* and *De Partitione Oratoria* come from *Cicero, De Oratore, Books I–II* (trans. E.W. Sutton and H. Rackham; LCL; London: Heinemann; Cambridge, MA: Harvard University Press, 1942 [repr. 1979]) and *Cicero, De Oratore, Book III, De Fato, Paradoxa Stoicorum, De Partitione Oratoria* (trans. H. Rackham; LCL; London: Heinemann; Cambridge, MA: Harvard University Press, 1942 [repr. 1992]).

usually found in an *ars* can also be found in one of its three books. As in *De Inventione*, a plurality of comparative terms are utilized in *De Oratore*. The focus will remain on *similitudo* and *exemplum*, both of which are treated in two important sections of *De Oratore* where the discussion turns toward matters pertaining to proof and style. This examination of *similitudo* and *exemplum* will be restricted to those two sections after note is made of a few other remarks scattered throughout *De Oratore* that are pertinent to the issues raised in this study.

The *exemplum* as 'historical' example is not slighted by Cicero in *De Oratore*, although in many places *exemplum* is employed with reference to an instance, illustration or sample of some precept of rhetoric. Cicero and his characters emphasize that the orator must have a thorough knowledge of history and a store of *exempla* at hand.[135] Cicero has more to say about the use of examples, as we shall see, but first an interesting use of *similitudo* in *De Oratore* needs to be mentioned.

Two references to *similitudo* in *De Oratore* are worthy of note because both involve a named and well-known person, the renowned actor Roscius. Antonius makes the initial reference to Roscius in his complaint that practitioners of other arts who fail to perform according to their abilities are subjected to less severe criticism than orators, who face a 'sterner judgment' (1.27.123-25). Crassus is untroubled by such criticism and argues that orators should indeed exercise care in the practice of their art, 'which is admittedly the greatest' (1.28.129). Crassus relates how Roscius says he finds it difficult to approve of his students because their blunders remain fixed in his memory; Crassus then takes up 'this comparison [*similitudinem*] with this player as our standard of an orator's merit', contending that Roscius, the consummate actor who excels in his art, is to be held up as a standard of 'absolute perfection', something which Crassus demands of the orator (1.28.129-30). Antonius disfavors holding up Roscius, an actor, as the standard for orators (1.59.251), but he will use Roscius for his own

---

135. See *De Oratore* 1.5.18, 1.46.201, 1.55.256, 2.30.131. On the value of history, see 2.9.36; cf. the exchange on various historians in 2.12.51–2.15.64. The first reference to *exemplum* as 'historical' example comes in Q. Mucius Q.F. Scaevola's suggestion that he could 'use examples from our own and other communities' of damage done by men of eloquence (1.9.38). See also the use of example by Antonius in 1.48.210-12; he defines what he means by 'general', 'statesman' and 'jurisconsultant', and then gives examples of prominent men, identified by name, who fit those definitions.

purposes. Indeed, Antonius later disputes a point made by Crassus with these words: 'And yet, as we are taking from a single artist a number of details for our likeness [*similitudinem*] of an orator, that same Roscius is fond of saying...' (1.60.254).[136] In both of these references to *similitudo*, one by Crassus and the other by Antonius, something said by Roscius is seized upon and used to make a point with regard to rhetoric. In *De Inventione* Cicero considers *similitudo* as useful and effective in making arguments, and the same holds true in *De Oratore*.

In *De Oratore*, Cicero has Antonius expound upon matters pertaining to proof. The materials of proof are distinguished in a manner that is familiar (2.27.116-18):

> For purposes of proof...the material at the orator's disposal is twofold, one kind made up of things which are not thought out by himself, but depend upon the circumstances and are dealt with by rule, for example documents, oral evidence, informal agreements, examinations, statutes, decrees of the Senate, judicial precedents, magisterial orders, opinions of counsel, and whatever else is not produced by the orator, but is supplied to him by the case itself or by the parties: the other kind is founded entirely on the orator's reasoned argument. And so, with the former sort, he need only consider the handling of his proofs [*tractandis argumentis*], but with the latter, the discovery [*inveniendis*] of them as well.

Antonius elects to treat the invention of arguments himself and to leave the treatment of the embellishment of arguments to Crassus (2.28.121-23). *Similitudo* and *exemplum* are discussed by both Antonius and Crassus in their respective sections.

Antonius devotes a section of his treatment of the invention of arguments to the commonplaces (*loci*), or topics, 'the sources from which the whole argument for every case and speech is derived'.[137] At the outset, Antonius warns that if a speaker is a stranger to the *exemplum*, among other things, then the commonplaces from which arguments are derived will be of little use.[138] That being said, and after several

---

136. Roscius is mentioned elsewhere in *De Oratore*, especially with reference to his manner of delivery; see 2.57.233, 2.59.242, 3.25.102, 3.69.221.

137. *De Oratore* 2.30.130; cf. 2.34.146.

138. *De Oratore* 2.30.131: 'For bring me a man as accomplished, as clear and acute in thinking, and as ready in delivery as you please; if, for all that, he is a stranger to social intercourse, precedent [*in exemplis*], tradition, and the manners and disposition of his fellow-countrymen, those commonplaces [*loci*] from which proofs [*argumenta*] are derived will avail him but little'.

digressions, Antonius makes a distinction between intrinsic *loci* and extrinsic *loci*, and then correlates the *loci* with the types of arguments derived from them. Intrinsic arguments are 'derived from the essential nature of the case'; extrinsic arguments are 'adopted from without':

> Intrinsic arguments, when the problem concerns the character of the subject [*res*] as a whole [*tota*], or of part [*pars*] of it, or the name [*vocabulum*] it is to bear, or anything whatever relating [*attingat*] to the subject [*rem*]; extrinsic arguments, on the other hand, when topics are assembled from without and are not inherent in the nature of the case.[139]

The focus here will be upon the extrinsic arguments, for that is where the terms *similitudo* and *exemplum* are to be found.[140]

Cicero, to reiterate, has Antonius correlate arguments and commonplaces. If the problem concerns the whole subject (*res tota*), definition (*definitione*) is to be used; if it concerns part (*pars*) of the subject, distribution (*partitione*); and so on (2.39.164-66). The interest here is with what Antonius recommends if the problem has to do with something related to the subject (2.39.166):

> If it turns on something correlated [*attingat*] with the subject [*rem*], the proofs [*argumentorum*] come from several sources or common-places [*loci*]; for we shall investigate connected terms, and general heads with their sub-divisions, and resemblances and differences [*similitudines et dissimilitudines*], and opposites, and corresponding and concurrent circumstances, and so-called antecedents, and contradictories, and we shall track down the causes of things, and the effects proceeding from causes, and investigate things of relatively greater, equal or lesser significance.

Samples of arguments drawn from each commonplace are provided (2.40.167-72), but only those drawn from *similitudines et dissimilitudines* (2.40.168-69) will be considered:

---

139. *De Oratore* 2.39.163. Sutton's translation does not help dispel confusion concerning *loci* and arguments. Cicero defines both terms in *Topica* 2.8: 'Accordingly, we may define a topic as the region of an argument, and an argument as a course of reasoning which firmly establishes a matter about which there is some doubt'.

140. Other terms of comparison appear. A sample of arguing from the greater is given 'to show how we shall compare [*comparabimus*] things of relatively greater, lesser and equal significance' (2.40.172). See also the precepts issued by Antonius in his brief discussion of *tractatio* (2.41.177), where he tells how to produce a comparison (*simile*).

> *Ex similtudine autem*: 'If the wild beasts cherish their young, what ten-
> derness ought we to bear to our children!' *At ex dissimilitudine*: 'If it be
> the mark of uncivilized folk to live but for the day, our own purposes
> should contemplate all time.'

Then we read:

> And, in cases involving both [similarity] and dissimilarity, [*exempla*] are
> found in the deeds or the words or the fate of other people, and [fictitious
> narratives] must often be cited.[141]

To sum up, *similitudo* is listed among extrinsic *loci*; specifically, *similitudo* is a subdivision of the *locus* in which something is related to the
subject at hand.[142] In arguments derived from either the *locus similitudo*
or the *locus dissimilitudo*, 'historical' examples—drawn from the
words, deeds or fate of people—and fictitious narratives can be used.

Cicero includes *similitudo* among intrinsic *loci* in two other treatises,
Topica and *De Partitione Oratoria*. While the distribution of the *loci* in
which something is related to the subject at hand is virtually the same
in *De Oratore*, *Topica* and *De Partitione Oratoria*, in a chapter of
Topica devoted entirely to the *locus similitudo* Cicero identifies its
genera in a somewhat different fashion. We learn there (*Topica* 10.41-
45) that there are several genera of *similitudines*. One genus of
similitudo—which Cicero tells us is called 'inductio, in Greek
ἐπαγωγή'—attains the desired proof 'by several comparisons [*ex
pluribus collationibus*]', and this genus was used by Socrates in his
dialogues; a second genus of *similitudo* 'rests on comparison
[*collatione*], when one thing is compared to one, equal to equal'; a third
genus of *similitudo* is the citing of *exempla*; a fourth genus of
similitudo is referred to as fictitious examples.[143] In Cicero's *Topica*,

---

141. *De Oratore* 2.40.169: 'Atque utroque in genere et similitudinis et dissimili-
tudinis exempla sunt ex aliorum factis aut dictis aut cventis, et fictae narrationes
saepe ponendae'. My alterations of Sutton's translation are bracketed. Earlier,
Antonius shows the effectiveness of adducing *similitudines* in an argument by
recounting an incident involving Crassus and Servius Galba (1.56.240).
142. Cicero uses both *similitudo* and *exemplum* in other discussions of definition;
see *De Partitione Oratoria* 36.126 and *Topica* 7.32.
143. See *Topica* 10.41-45. Cicero makes an extremely intriguing remark about
the last genus of *similitudo*, fictitious examples: 'Under this topic of similarity orators and philosophers have licence to cause dumb things to talk, to call on the dead
to rise from the world below, to tell of something which could not possibly happen,
in order to add force to an argument or lessen it: this is called ὑπερβολή

then, we find mention of fictitious examples rather than fictitious narratives.

In what we have seen so far, we can be sure that Cicero regards 'historical' *exempla* and fictitious narratives as useful in arguments drawn from the *locus similitudo*. In this context, *similitudo* is used technically to identify a *locus* of argument that has to do with comparison, but *similitudo* is not used technically to refer to a specific 'figure' of comparison. We will have to turn to the discussion of embellishment given by Crassus to learn about *similitudo* as a rhetorical 'figure'.[144]

The lecture given by Crassus on issues involving style in *De Oratore* comprises the bulk of Book 3. Cicero has Crassus accept the division of labor proposed by Antonius, but Crassus will not speak on the embellishment of arguments alone because the matter of a speech should not be separated from the language of the speech (3.5.19). Crassus explains the requisites of style, which are '...that our language should be correct, lucid, ornate and suitably appropriate to the particular matter under consideration' (3.10.37). *Similitudo* occurs repeatedly in the section that has to do with the third requisite of style, that the speech be

(hyperbole)' (10.45). McCall (*Ancient Rhetorical Theories of Simile and Comparison*, pp. 116-18) regards ὑπερβολή as a fifth type of argument *a similitudine*. Price, ('Παράδειγμα and *Exemplum* in Ancient Rhetorical Theory', p. 266 n. 26) disputes the classification of ὑπερβολή as a genus of the argument derived from *similitudo*, and I tend to agree with Price. Still, Price illustrates that the number of genera listed under the *locus similitudo* is a matter open to debate (see his detailed analysis, pp. 106-19).

144. Between the discussion of the invention of arguments by Antonius and the discussion of the embellishment of arguments by Crassus, *similitudo* comes up for discussion in a section where Caesar treats the use of laughter in oratory (*De Oratore* 2.58.235–2.71.290). In his analysis of the section (2.66.264-65) where Caesar gives attention to the 'types of pleasantry' that depend upon facts—which includes *narratio*, 'fables', material derived from history (*aliquid ex historia*), material derived from resemblance (*ex similitudine*), including comparison (*aut collationem*) and caricature (*aut tanquem imaginem*)—McCall argues that Cicero presents the common rhetorical triad consisting of *imago*, *collatio* and *exemplum* (*Ancient Rhetorical Theories of Simile and Comparison*, pp. 102-106). Price, though appreciative of McCall's insights, doubts that Cicero recommends the *exemplum* as a source of jokes in 2.66.264-65 (see 'Παράδειγμα and *Exemplum* in Ancient Rhetorical Theory', pp. 120-26). Note the description of the peculiar function of *narratio* in this section (2.66.264): '...it must describe [*exprimenda*], and present to the mind's eye [*ponenda ante oculos*], such things as bear the semblance of truth [*videantur et verisimilia*]...'

ornate (3.37.148–3.44.208). After a discussion of general principles to which a speaker should adhere in order to confer distinction upon the speech (3.25.96–3.31.126), Crassus deals with matters that pertain to rendering orations ornate through embellishment. He treats words in isolation first, words in combination second.[145]

Crassus speaks of three ways in which an orator can embellish a speech simply in terms of vocabulary: the speaker can employ rare words, new words or metaphorical words (3.38.152). The discussion of metaphorical words 'is of wide application', and Crassus has quite a bit to say about such words (3.38.155–3.43.170). A concentrated use of *similitudo* is easily perceived in the discussion of metaphor, as the following remarks demonstrate.

Crassus asserts that words are employed metaphorically for the sake of necessity and for the sake of entertainment: '...when something that can scarcely be conveyed by the proper term is expressed metaphorically, the meaning we desire to convey is made clear by the resemblance [*similitudo*] of the thing that we have expressed by the word that does not belong' (3.38.155). A formal definition—but one regarded as spurious by some scholars[146]—is given:

> A metaphor is a short form of simile, contracted into one word; this word is put in a position not belonging to it as if it were its own place, and if it is recognizable it gives pleasure, but if it contains no similarity it is rejected.[147]

Crassus advises that metaphorical words should be used to make the matter clearer, gives a sample and then comments: '...to make them clearer almost all the details are expressed by metaphors based upon resemblance [*translatis per similitudinem*]...'[148] Crassus notes that

145. See *De Oratore* 3.36.149.

146. See Rackham's note on *De Oratore* 3.39.157. See also McCall's discussion of the issues weighing in favor of the passage and against it (*Ancient Rhetorical Theories of Simile and Comparison*, pp. 107-11); he concludes that this passage 'should be retained as genuine' (p. 111).

147. *De Oratore* 3.39.157: 'Similitudinis est ad verbum unum contracta brevitas, quod verbum in alieno loco tanquam in suo positum si agnoscitur, delectat, si simile nihil habet, repudiatur'. The last clause of this sentence repeats a point made earlier (3.13.49) on correct Latin style ('non valde productis eis quae similitudinis causa ex aliis rebus transferuntur').

148. *De Oratore* 3.39.157-58; cf. in the same sentence: 'translatis verbis similitudine ipsa indicat'.

metaphors drawn from the sense of sight are more vivid:

> For there is nothing in the world the name or designation of which cannot be used in connexion with other things; with anything that can supply a simile [*simile*]—and a simile can be drawn from everything—a single word supplied by it that comprises the similarity [*similitudinem*], if used metaphorically [*translatum*], will give brilliance to the style (3.40.161).

Crassus warns that the speaker should avoid the use of a metaphor in which there is dissimilarity,[149] and should take precaution so that the comparison (*similitudo*) or resemblance (*similitudinis*) does not lead the hearers' minds to things unseemly or ugly.[150]

Within the context of this discussion of the embellishment of a speech by means of metaphorical words, the prevalent sense of *similitudo* is 'resemblance' or 'likeness'. *Similitudo* should not be taken as a reference to a particular 'figure', especially since Crassus contemplates instances in which a single word is used metaphorically.[151] However, *similitudo* does refer to a specific 'figure' in the ensuing discussion of embellishments of thought, where Crassus merely lists such embellishments.

Crassus prefaces his catalogue of embellishments with a few summary statements to remind his hearers of the important aspects of style discussed previously (3.52.200-201). Embellishments of thought are enumerated first, embellishments of diction second (3.54.206-208). Crassus gives neither definitions nor examples, as C. Aurelius Cotta points out to him (3.55.208). As Crassus sprints through the list of embellishments of thought, this is all he has to say about the embellishments of interest in the present study: '...then two extremely effective figures, comparison and example [*similitudo et exemplum*]'.[152] This

---

149. *De Oratore* 3.40.162. A sample is given and Crassus criticizes it because 'a sphere possesses no possible resemblance to a vault'.

150. *De Oratore* 3.41.163-64. Samples are provided. Crassus is not made to use *similitudo* in the brief mention of 'a valuable stylistic ornament' which, though it is left unnamed, can be surmised to be allegory (see 3.41.166–3.48.169). The word 'simile' does appear here.

151. For more on the discussion of metaphor in *De Oratore*, see McCall, *Ancient Rhetorical Theories of Simile and Comparison*, pp. 106-11. McCall notes that Cicero, like Aristotle, couples comparison and metaphor but that Cicero reverses Aristotle by 'making comparison the principal, metaphor the subordinate, figure' (p. 111).

152. *De Oratore* 3.53.205.

brief remark—the last mention of *similitudo* and *exemplum* in *De Oratore*—is significant because of the collocation of *similitudo* and *exemplum* as embellishments of thought.

Although Cicero's entire corpus of rhetorical and philosophical treatises has not been surveyed in order to discover what he wrote about *similitudo* and *exemplum*, in this examination of *De Inventione* and *De Oratore* we have encountered what can be regarded as some of his representative views of *similitudo* and *exemplum*. It should be underscored that we have encountered 'some' of his 'views' of *similitudo* and *exemplum*, for Cicero does not express a single, unified view of either. As a means of injecting a dose of clarity to the preceding, the conclusions of two scholars who have conducted far more comprehensive studies of comparison and example in Cicero's writings will be rehearsed.

McCall observes that Cicero is not overly concerned with consistency in his use of technical vocabulary, especially in some philosophical treatises where *similitudo* and *collatio* are employed in a manner that is 'by no means absolutely uniform'.[153] With respect to Cicero's rhetorical works, McCall asserts:

> Certain usages and ideas, however, recur quite consistently. *Similitudo* (with *simile* on occasion used synonymously) clearly embraces the widest scope of the various terms of comparison. Its use is split between a general sense of 'similarity,' 'resemblance,' and a figurative sense of 'comparison,' and the two are at times juxtaposed. *Collatio*, a less frequent term, is usually a subdivision of *similitudo* and often means a figure of comparison in which both parts are developed equally and with corresponding detail. *Comparatio* regularly refers to the process of comparison but on occasion denotes an actual figure of comparison. *Comparabile* occurs once, in *de Inventione*, as a major heading of rhetorical figures of comparison and historical example. *Imago* is hard to classify. It slips in and out of the triad of historical example and two terms of comparison. It is rarely illustrated, but when it refers to a type of comparison the focus is on personal characteristics and description. The

---

153. McCall, *Ancient Rhetorical Theories of Simile and Comparison*, p. 129; cf. pp. 119-29. In one philosophical treatise, Cicero uses both *similitudo* and *collatio* with reference to things religious in his reply to an imaginary opponent: 'I shall speak of lots presently; although you really do not strengthen the cause of sacrifices by comparing [*similitudine*] them to lots; but you do weaken the cause of lots by comparing [*conlatione*] them with sacrifices' (*De Divinatione* 2.17.38, as cited by McCall, p. 128).

different terms of comparison are couched on occasion in the form of simile, but verbal form is never the essential ingredient of any of them.[134]

Thus, McCall is led to conclude that, according to Cicero,

Comparison belongs to every section of oratory, and to philosophy as well; it serves as an embellishment of style, as an element of proof, as a type of argument, and it can be used to advantage in all the various parts (for example, exordium, peroration) of a speech.[155]

Price concludes his analysis of example in Cicero's writings in this way:

The most striking feature of Cicero's view of the *exemplum* is that he has no one view. The *exemplum* is variously a constituent of *comparabile*, a type of *similitudo*, a *locus*, and a Figure of Thought. It is used for Proof, Amplification, and Ornament by philosophers, orators, and legal experts.[156]

It is not necessary to add much to the remarks of McCall and Price. Cicero has a high estimation of both *similitudo* and *exemplum*. Neither *similitudo* nor *exemplum* are merely stylistic embellishments according to Cicero; both are treated as rhetorical figures of comparison predominantly within the context of a discussion of proofs (induction) and (probable) arguments.[157] Although there are numerous instances in which Cicero uses the term *exemplum* non-technically, it is evident that *exemplum* frequently refers to 'historical' example. It bears repeating that *similitudo* is used in a variety of contexts and with a range of meanings; thus, it is difficult to ascertain when *similitudo* should be taken as a reference to a specific rhetorical figure of comparison, and even more difficult to determine when *similitudo* is the equivalent of παραβολή. There is, however, one passage in *De Partitione Oratoria* where Cicero appears to duplicate the triad 'historical' example, parable and fable:

154. McCall, *Ancient Rhetorical Theories of Simile and Comparison*, pp. 118-19.
155. McCall, *Ancient Rhetorical Theories of Simile and Comparison*, p. 119.
156. Price, 'Παράδειγμα and *Exemplum* in Ancient Rhetorical Theory', p. 128.
157. That *similitudo* and *exemplum* can be used for purposes of amplification is made clear in *De Partitione Oratoria*: 'Amplification of the facts is obtained from all the same topics [*locis*] from which were taken the statements made to secure credence; and very effective are accumulations of definitions...and especially analogies and instances [*maximeque similitudines et exempla*]; and also imaginary persons and even dumb objects must speak' (16.55).

But the greatest corroboration is supplied to a probable truth [*ad simili-tudinem veri*] by first an example [*exemplum*], next the introduction of a parallel case [*rei similitudo*]; and also sometimes an anecdote [*fabula*], even though it be a tall story [*incredibilis*], nevertheless has an effect on people.[158]

That being said, it must be noted that some of Cicero's remarks effectively blur the line between *similitudo* and *exemplum*, two terms that appear in collocation on occasion.

In some sections of Cicero's treatises, the line between *similitudo* and *exemplum* is thin indeed. As we have seen, Cicero makes it patently clear that the *exemplum* as 'historical' example—which involves 'citing some person or historical event', or involves 'the deeds or the words or the fate of other people'—is a rhetorical figure of comparison. The *exemplum* is a subdivision of the *comparabile* in probable arguments; it is a genus of the *locus similitudo* in extrinsic arguments. One of the most remarkable aspects of Cicero's treatment of the *exemplum* is that he allows for fictitious examples (as a genus of the *locus similitudo* in *Topica*). Given that, when we recall that in *De Oratore* Cicero provides an instance in which a *similitudo* depicts the saying of a named and real person, Roscius, the line between *similitudo* and *exemplum* virtually vanishes. Despite the uncertainty about whether and where Cicero equates *similitudo* and παραβολή, it is fair to say that Cicero's views on *similitudo* and *exemplum* provide at best a most tenuous warrant for upholding an absolute or categorical distinction between parable and example. In this respect, Cicero prefigures Quintilian.

Parable and Example in Institutio Oratoria

This investigation of parable and example in the ancient rhetorical tradition concludes with a lengthy treatise published during the last decade of the first century CE, *Institutio Oratoria*, in which Marcus Fabius Quintilianus, an official teacher of rhetoric in Rome, advances his program for the education of the ideal orator.[159] Although not an *ars*

158. *De Partitione Oratoria* 11.40. Earlier, Cicero defines 'the term "probable" [*verisimile*] as "that which usually occurs in such and such a way"' (10.34).

159. For biographical information on Quintilian, see Kennedy, *The Art of Rhetoric in the Roman World*, pp. 487-96; on the date of *Institutio Oratoria*, see p. 493. The text of *Institutio Oratoria* used in this study is *The Institutio Oratoria*

in the strictest sense, *Institutio Oratoria* provides a systematic and thorough exposition of rhetoric in all its parts that comprises the bulk of the treatise's 12 books. Included in that exposition of rhetoric is what has been recognized as perhaps the most detailed and intricate analyses of comparison and example in all of antiquity.[160] Obviously, the desire here is to examine Quintilian's comments on comparison and example—which are indeed numerous and diffuse—especially those that have a bearing on the distinction made between parable and example; however, given the magnitude of *Institutio Oratoria* and the purposes of this study, some limits must be imposed on this investigation.

To that end, every instance in which Quintilian employs the term *exemplum* non-technically will not be of concern.[161] Moreover, even though Quintilian uses several terms for comparison, the focus will be on *similitudo*, which is the term for comparison that he employs most often.[162] Finally, every remark made with reference to either *similitudo* or *exemplum* in *Institutio Oratoria* will not be examined, and it is not necessary to do so since Quintilian provides a concentrated treatment of both in a section of his discussion of the invention of proofs in Book 5 and then again in a section of his discussion of the ornamentation of style in Book 8. If those sections are attended to with care, and if brief notice is given to other salient remarks dispersed throughout *Institutio Oratoria*, an adequate understanding of Quintilian's views on *similitudo* and *exemplum* can be had.

Although Quintilian treats both *similitudo* and *exemplum* at length in his discussion of the third part of a speech, the proof (*probatio*), the *similitudo* and the *exemplum* are mentioned in discussions of other parts of a speech. Before the discussion of the *similitudo* and *exemplum*

of Quintilian (trans. H.E. Butler; LCL; 4 vols.; London: Heinemann; Cambridge, MA: Harvard University Press, 1920–22). Unless specified otherwise, all translations are Butler's.

160. See McCall, *Ancient Rhetorical Theories of Simile and Comparison*, p. 236; and Price, 'Παράδειγμα and *Exemplum* in Ancient Rhetorical Theory', p. 131.

161. See, e.g., *Institutio Oratoria* 4.2.116, 5.10.64, 5.10.77, 5.10.92, 5.10.97, 5.10.110, 5.10.120, 6.3.65, 8.3.54, 8.3.66, 8.4.1, 8.4.4, 8.4.28, 8.6.15, 8.6.52, 9.2.61, 9.3.31, 9.3.50, 9.3.67, 9.3.70, 10.1.2, 10.1.46, 10.2.1, 10.2.2, 10.2.4, 10.2.11.

162. McCall, *Ancient Rhetorical Theories of Simile and Comparison*, p. 178: '*Similitudo, simile, imago, comparatio*, and *collatio* are all used, but it is soon apparent that, as in Cicero, *similitudo* is the basic term of comparison'. For more on Quintilian's use of these terms, see McCall's excellent analysis, pp. 178-236.

in Book 5, Quintilian makes a few noteworthy remarks that can be reviewed summarily. At the beginning of Book 3, which begins the expansive and systematic exposition of rhetoric in all its parts (invention, arrangement, style, memory, delivery), Quintilian apologizes to the reader because what follows may seem to be a dry development of principles; he indicates that he would have preferred to provide a more attractive and pleasant statement of precepts on the constituent parts of rhetoric in order to lure the young into a study of rhetoric and not to repulse them. Quintilian observes that Lucretius set forth his philosophical system in verse with the same thoughts in mind, and then he quotes a *similitudo* used by Lucretius (3.1.4):

> 'And as physicians when they seek to give
> A draught of bitter wormwood to a child,
> First smear along the edge that rims the cup
> The liquid sweets of honey, golden-hued,'...

Quintilian then applies this *similitudo* to *Institutio Oratoria*: 'But I fear that this book will have too little honey and too much wormwood, and that though the student may find it a healthy draught, it will be far from agreeable' (3.1.5). Little about the *similitudo* is learned from this, except that it may be composed in verse.[163]

Quintilian makes two brief remarks about the *exemplum* in his discussion of deliberative oratory. While, as we shall see, the *exemplum* can be employed in any of the three genera of oratory (panegyric, deliberative, judicial[164]), Quintilian asserts that 'examples are of the greatest value in deliberative speeches' (3.8.36).[165] He soon indicates

163. McCall demonstrates that another rhetorical treatise quotes samples of παραβολαί in verse (e.g. from Sappho); see his illuminating treatment of [Demetrius] *On Style* (*Ancient Rhetorical Theories of Simile and Comparison*, pp. 137-55).

164. See *Institutio Oratoria* 3.3.14–3.4.16 (cf. 3.6.104) for Quintilian's handling of the debate over whether or not there are three or more 'parts' of rhetoric, 'genera' of rhetoric, or genera of 'causes'.

165. The importance of 'historical' examples for deliberative oratory is not unexpected given Quintilian's remark that 'the *deliberative* department of oratory (also called the *advisory* department), while it deliberates about the future, also enquires about the past, while its functions are twofold and consist in advising and dissuading [*suadendi ac dissuadendi*]' (3.8.6; Butler's emphasis). Comparison plays an important role in deliberative oratory as well: 'Consequently as a rule all *deliberative* [*suasoria*] speeches are based simply on comparison [*comparatio*]...' (3.8.34; Butler's emphasis). Authority [*auctoritas*]—pre-eminently, the authority of

why the *exempla* are of value in deliberative speeches: 'As regards the use of examples [*exemplorum*] practically all authorities are with good reason agreed that there is no subject [*materiae*] to which they are better suited, since as a rule history seems to repeat itself [*videantur respondere futura praeteritis*] and the experience of the past is a valuable support to reason' (3.8.66). Another comment involving *similitudo* and *exemplum* in Book 3 deserves a glance.

Quintilian mentions both *similitudo* and *exemplum* in the same sentence later in Book 3 when he ridicules other writers who include division, proposition and digression as parts of a judicial speech (3.9.1-4). Quintilian sides with many authorities who divide the judicial speech into five parts: exordium, statement of facts (*narratio*), proof, refutation and peroration (3.9.1). He argues that if digression lies outside the case, it cannot be part of the case, and that if digression lies within the case, it is an argument or ornament and not part of the case: 'For if anything that lies within the case is to be called part of it, why not call *argument, comparison* [*similitudo*], *commonplace, pathos, illustration* [*exempla*] parts of the case?'[166] Here, *similitudo* and *exemplum* are included in a list of devices employed in digression; Quintilian explicitly mentions the *exemplum* again in the discussion of *narratio*.[167] Prior to that, however, he makes a short remark about the use of *similitudo* and *exemplum* in another part of a speech.

Quintilian spends a chapter on the exordium of a speech in Book 4. He advises that the exordium should be simple and that it should contain little evidence of artifice (4.1.55-71). Quintilian is well aware of the rule that no unusual words, no audacious words, and so on should be detected in the exordium (4.1.58), and he discusses several problems

the speaker (3.8.12)—is an issue that must be given consideration in deliberative oratory, even with respect to the use of *exempla*: 'Consequently, though examples are of the greatest value in deliberative speeches, because reference to historical parallels is the quickest method of securing assent, it matters a great deal whose authority is adduced and to whom it is commended' (3.8.36).

166. *Institutio Oratoria* 3.9.4; Butler's emphasis. Digression may be used in any part of a speech (4.3.12).

167. See *Institutio Oratoria* 4.2.17: 'There are also statements [*narrationes*] which do not set forth the facts of the case itself, but facts which are none the less relevant to the case: the speaker's purpose may be to illustrate the case by some parallel [*exempli*], as in the passage in the *Verrines* about Lucius Domitius who crucified a shepherd...'

that might result from the use of such in the exordium. Quintilian, however, compromises that rule; he maintains that a speaker may make use of ornament in the exordium but should avoid the display of art. Indeed, Quintilian cites instances in which great orators have used figures, such as apostrophe, in the exordium, and points out that Cicero employed examples (*exemplis*) in the exordium of one of his famous speeches (4.1.69). Thus, according to Quintilian, the speaker can employ ornaments in the exordium if there is reason to do so, but not indiscriminately:

> The same remark applies to *simile* [*similitudine*] (which must however be brief), *metaphor* and other *tropes*, all of which are forbidden by our cautious and pedantic teachers of rhetoric, but which we shall none the less occasionally employ...[168]

We should not fail to note that *similitudo* is referred to in conjunction with metaphor, for later Quintilian will mention *similitudo* in his discussion of that trope.[169] Again, it can be observed that *exemplum* and *similitudo* appear in proximity to each other, here in the context of discussion of certain figures and tropes that a speaker may be employ with caution in the exordium (4.1.65). It is not uncommon for Quintilian to mention *similitudo* and *exemplum* together, and he does so in his discussion of yet another part of the speech, the proof.

Quintilian's detailed treatment of *similitudo* and *exemplum* takes place within the context of his discussion of the proof in Book 5. He accepts Aristotle's division of proofs into ἄτεχνοι, or inartificial proofs, and ἔντεχνοι, or artificial proofs (5.1.2). Quintilian classifies the species of inartificial proofs and discusses each in turn.[170] Both *similitudo* and *exemplum* receive mention in the section on previous judgments, one of the inartificial proofs. There are three kinds of previous judgments, and the concern here is with the first one.

168. *Institutio Oratoria* 4.1.70; Butler's emphasis. Compare this to what Quintilian says in 11.1.6.
169. Quintilian discusses metaphor among tropes (8.6.4-18). McCall deals with some of the problems brought about by the mention of *similitudo* alongside other tropes in 4.1.70 (e.g. is the *similitudo* a figure of thought or a trope?); see *Ancient Rhetorical Theories of Simile and Comparison*, pp. 185-87.
170. As species of the genus inartificial proof, Quintilian lists the following: previous judgments, rumors, evidence extracted by torture, documents, oaths and witnesses (5.1.1-2); see his treatment of each species in 5.2.1–5.7.37.

> First, we have matters on which judgment has been given at some time
> or other in cases of a similar nature [*ex paribus causis*]: these are, how-
> ever, more correctly termed precedents [*exempla*], as for instance where
> a father's will has been annulled or confirmed in opposition to his sons
> (5.2.1).

All previous judgments are confirmed in two ways: '…by the authority
of those who gave the decision and by the likeness [*similitudine*]
between the two cases'.[171] Although *similitudo* in this context does not
seem to be used in a technical sense, *exemplum* does. The *exemplum*,
then, is first treated among inartificial proofs; but Quintilian more consistently treats *exempla* among artificial proofs.[172]

Artificial proofs, according to Quintilian, 'are wholly the work of art
and consist of matters [*rebus*] specially adapted to produce belief'
(5.8.1). After a summary statement of features common to all kinds of
proofs (5.8.4-7), Quintilian proceeds to classify the genera and species
of artificial proofs. He identifies the genera of artificial proofs in this
assertion: 'Every artificial proof consists either of indications [*signis*],
arguments [*argumentis*] or examples [*exemplis*]'.[173] The signs and their
species are discussed first (5.9.3-16), then the arguments. In his discussion of arguments, Quintilian deals with the various terms for arguments (such as ἐνθυμήματα, ἐπιχειρήματα, ἀποδείξεις) and the
meanings attached to those terms by others (5.10.1-11), certainty and
degrees of credibility (5.10.12-19) and the *loci* from which arguments
are derived (5.10.20-125).[174] Having dispensed with the first two genera
of artificial proofs, Quintilian turns to the third.

Quintilian, as we have seen, gives the name '*exemplum*' to the third
kind of artificial proof. Quintilian's explanation of what he means by
'exemplum' begins with these words:

171. *Institutio Oratoria* 5.2.2. Conversely, one way of refuting previous judgments is by demonstrating dissimilarity between the two cases (5.2.3).

172. Price ('Παράδειγμα and *Exemplum* in Ancient Rhetorical Theory', pp. 185-
88) points out that Quintilian is not entirely consistent in maintaining his position
that examples are artificial proofs.

173. *Institutio Oratoria* 5.9.1.

174. Quintilian claims that all arguments fall into two classes, those concerned
with persons or those concerned with things (5.10.23). Several *loci* of arguments of
related interest are *locus similibus* (to which belongs ἐπαγωγή), *locus dissim-
ilibus* (5.10.73), and arguments drawn from fictitious suppositions (5.10.95-99),
which also involve a demonstration of similarity or resemblance to the case under
consideration.

The third kind of proof, which is drawn into the service of the case from without, is styled a παράδειγμα by the Greeks, who apply the term to all comparisons of like with like, but more especially to historical parallels. Roman writers have for the most part preferred to give the name of comparison to that which the Greeks style παραβολή, while they translate παράδειγμα by example, although this latter involves comparison, while the former is of the nature of an example. For my own part, I prefer with a view to making my purpose easier of apprehension to regard both as παραδείγματα and to call them examples. Nor am I afraid of being thought to disagree with Cicero, although he does separate comparison from example. For he divides all arguments into two classes, induction and ratiocination, just as most Greeks divide it into παραδείγματα and ἐπιχείρηματα, explaining παράδειγμα as a rhetorical induction.[175]

Quintilian makes it clear that he considers his own view of *exemplum* as artificial proof to be a synthesis of precepts with regard to the *exemplum* as proof issued by some earlier Greek and Roman writers, mainly Aristotle and Cicero, although he is aware that some will think his view is at odds with Cicero. Quintilian's opening remarks are not without problems, but whether or not Quintilian successfully justifies his view of *exemplum* as a genus of artificial proof, whether or not Quintilian successfully reconciles Cicero's terminology with Aristotle's terminology, whether or not Quintilian sufficiently comprehends Aristotle's view of παράδειγμα as a genus of artificial proof, all that is necessary here is a summary and clarification of some of the basic points Quintilian endeavors to make at the outset of his discussion of *exemplum* as an artificial proof.[176]

175. *Institutio Oratoria* 5.11.1-2: 'Tertium genus ex iis, quae extrinsecus adducuntur in causam, Graeci vocant παράδειγμα, quo nomine et generaliter usi sunt in omni similium adpositione et specialiter in iis, quae rerum gestarum auctoritate nituntur. Nostri fere similitudinem vocari maluerunt, quod ab illis παραβολή dicitur, alterum exemplum, quanquam et hoc simile est et illud exemplum. Nos, quo facilius propositum explicemus, utrumque παράδειγμα esse credamus, et ipsi appellemus exemplum. Nec vereor, ne videar repugnare Ciceroni, quanquam collationem separat ab exemplo. Nam idem omnem argumentationem dividit in duas partes, inductionem et ratiocinationem, ut plerique Graecorum in παραδείγματα et ἐπιχειρήματα, dixeruntque παράδειγμα ῥητορικὴν ἐπαγωγήν'. The accentuation of the Greek words has been reproduced here exactly as it appears in the Loeb text and translation.

176. Price deals with these and other issues in his analysis of example in *Institutio Oratoria* ('Παράδειγμα and *Exemplum* in Ancient Rhetorical Theory', pp. 131-

Quintilian's remarks in this section serve notice that he is moving away from the differentiation between *similitudo* and *exemplum* common among some Roman rhetoricians and that he is moving toward the Aristotelian view of example as a genus of proof. In his retrieval of the Aristotelian tradition with respect to example as a genus of proof, Quintilian retains fictional comparison and 'historical' example as two of its species. He attempts to reconcile Latin terminology with Greek terminology, which means that he necessarily must make dual use of the terms *exemplum* and *similitudo*.

Quintilian, then, decides to call the third genus of artificial proof 'exemplum'. In subsequent comments on this genus of proof and its species, Quintilian publicizes his awareness that certain Greeks designate the genus *exemplum* as παράδειγμα and that they employ the term παράδειγμα both in a wider sense to refer to 'all comparisons of like with like' (genus) and in a narrower sense to refer to 'historical' examples (species). Quintilian observes a preference among certain Romans who reserve the term '*similitudo*' (species) for the Greek term παραβολή (species), and the term '*exemplum*' (species) for the Greek term παράδειγμα (species). Quintilian's own view of the two species is this: *exemplum* 'involves comparison', and parable 'is of the nature of an *exemplum*'. Quintilian's preference, then, is to regard both the *similitudo* and the *exemplum* as species of the genus 'παραδείγματα and to call them examples'. Thus, Quintilian's term *exemplum* in the wider sense refers to a genus of artificial proof, one that is comprised of *exemplum* in the narrower sense of 'historical' example and *similitudo* in the narrower sense of fictional comparison.

Next, Quintilian attempts to bring his view of *exemplum* into alignment with Cicero, who separates the species fictional comparison (*collatio*) from the species 'historical' example (*exemplum*). Quintilian's tactic here is to correlate Cicero's argument of induction to παραδείγματα and Cicero's argument of ratiocination to ἐπιχειρήματα. By this means, Quintilian establishes to his satisfaction that his own view of *exemplum* in the wider sense as a genus of proof (παράδειγμα) is equivalent to rhetorical induction (ῥητορικὴν ἐπαγωγήν), and thus that he is not at odds with Cicero.

210, 274-98). Price argues that the conceptions of example as artificial proof espoused by Aristotle, Cicero and Quintilian exhibit substantial differences. Quintilian, according to Price, either glossed over those differences or remained unaware of them.

Then Quintilian states that Socrates made extensive use of rhetorical induction, which is characterized as follows:

> The method of argument chiefly used by Socrates was of this nature: when he had asked a number of questions to which his adversary could only agree, he finally inferred [*inferret*] the conclusion of the problem under discussion from its resemblance [*simile*] to the points already conceded. This method is known as induction [*Id est inductio*], and though it cannot be used in a set speech, it is usual in a speech to assume that which takes the form of a question in a dialogue.

Quintilian provides a sample of *inductio* in a dialogue and shows how it can be used in a speech (5.11.4-5) before resuming his discussion of proofs.[177]

Quintilian continues his discussion of the genus of artificial proof that he has identified as *exemplum* and made equivalent to induction with this statement:

> All arguments of this kind [*genere*], therefore, must be from things like [*similia*] or unlike [*dissimilia*] or contrary [*contraria*]. Comparisons [*Similitudo*] are, it is true, sometimes employed for the embellishment of the speech [*orationis ornatum*] as well, but I will deal with them in their proper place; at present I shall pursue what relates to proof [*probationem*].[178]

This remark indicates that the *similitudo* can be used for purposes of embellishment, and Quintilian will treat the *similitudo* in his discussion of embellishment in Book 8. Thus, the *similitudo* can be used for purposes of proof and for purposes of embellishment. McCall refers to this as a 'dual classification of *similitudo*', and asserts:

> The classification is an important one. Quintilian's promise is fulfilled at 8.3.72-81, which deals with *similitudo* not as an element of *probatio* but of *ornatus*, and for the first time in (extant) ancient criticism these two

---

177. On the relationship between ἐπαγωγή, induction, παραβολή and 'the Socratic method' in Aristotle's *Rhetoric* vis-à-vis *Institutio Oratoria*, see McCall, *Ancient Rhetorical Theories of Simile and Comparison*, pp. 187-90; and Price, 'Παράδειγμα and *Exemplum* in Ancient Rhetorical Theory', pp. 131-47. McCall asserts that Quintilian 'deviates only slightly' from Aristotle (p. 190), while Price contends that Quintilian, heavily influenced by Cicero, lacks a clear understanding of Aristotle's precepts on ἐπαγωγή as rhetorical induction, παράδειγμα as a genus of artificial proof, and the species of the genus παράδειγμα.

178. *Institutio Oratoria* 5.11.6; McCall's translation (*Ancient Rhetorical Theories of Simile and Comparison*, p. 191).

purposes of comparison are clearly proposed as elements of a single term, with each purpose analyzed under a separate rubric of oratory.[179]

Quintilian will discuss the *similitudo* as a species of artificial proof later in this chapter (5.11.22-31), but for the moment he intends to discuss the most important species of artificial proof. As we read further, it becomes apparent that Quintilian begins to use the term *exemplum* in its narrower sense.

Quintilian identifies the most important species of the third genus of artificial proof and offers a definition:

> The most important of proofs of this class [*generis*] is that which is most properly styled example [*exemplum*], that is to say the adducing of some past action real or assumed [*rei gestae aut ut gestae*] which may serve to persuade the audience of the truth of the point which we are trying to make (5.11.6).

Quintilian locates the action of the 'historical' example in the past, but elsewhere he suggests that the 'historical' example may be old or new.[180] One aspect of Quintilian's definition of 'historical' example is, in Price's opinion, novel: 'The addition of *ut gestae* to the definition enables Quintilian to subsume poetic fictions and Aesop's fables under the rubric of historical example'.[181] While it is true that Quintilian's definition makes provision for adducing past actions that are 'real or assumed', and while it is evident that Quintilian treats poetic fictions and types of fables as species of the genus of artificial proof called *exemplum*, it is not as certain that Quintilian considers poetic fictions and fables to be species of the 'historical' example.[182] Nevertheless,

---

179. McCall, *Ancient Rhetorical Theories of Simile and Comparison*, p. 192.

180. *Institutio Oratoria* 12.4.1: 'Above all, our orator should be equipped with a rich store of examples [*exemplorum*] both old and new: and he ought not merely to know those which are recorded in history or transmitted by oral tradition or occur from day to day, but should not neglect even those fictitious examples [*poetis ficta*] invented by the great poets. For while the former have the authority of evidence or even of legal decisions, the latter also either have the warrant of antiquity or are regarded as having been invented by great men to serve as lessons to the world. He should therefore be acquainted with as many examples as possible'.

181. Price, 'Παράδειγμα and *Exemplum* in Ancient Rhetorical Theory', p. 149.

182. Price ('Παράδειγμα and *Exemplum* in Ancient Rhetorical Theory', p. 190) later makes a more moderate claim: 'His definition of *exemplum*, "rei gestae aut ut gestae...commemoratio" (V 11.6), allows him to treat "untrue" stories under the rubric of *exemplum* but the relationship between historical example, poetic fiction,

subsequent to the definition of the 'historical' *exemplum* in 5.11.6, Quintilian does discuss five types of 'historical' examples in 5.11.6-16.

In a somewhat haphazardly arranged section, Quintilian identifies five types of 'historical' examples and gives samples of each. For the purpose of this study, it will suffice to list the types of 'historical' examples, to highlight some of Quintilian's remarks, and to make a few observations about some of the samples provided. The five types of 'historical' examples as identified by Quintilian are: *exemplum ex simile, exemplum ex dissimile, exemplum ex contrario, exemplum ex maioribus ad minora* and *exemplum ex minoribus ad maiora*.[183] One of the most remarkable aspects of Quintilian's classification of 'historical' *exempla* is, as Price puts it, that he divides 'examples into five distinct kinds of comparisons'.[184] The samples of examples given by Quintilian in this section vary in length—some are brief (as in 5.11.6-8) and some are longer (as in 5.11.11-12)—which is in accord with his remark that 'such parallels will be adduced at greater or less length according as they are familiar or as the interests of adornment [*decor*] of our case may demand' (5.11.16). This remark also suggests that the 'historical' example may be used for the purpose of adornment. Most of the samples refer to named characters, but some do not.[185] One sample of *exemplum ex contrario*, an excerpt from Virgil's *Aeneid*, is in verse (5.11.14).[186] Quintilian suggests an interesting use for *exempla imparia*:

and Aesop's fable is never made clear…It is consequently impossible to determine whether Quintilian sees any hierarchy among these types of examples, e.g., that historical example, poetic fiction, and Aesop's fable are all species of the genus *exemplum*, the third genus of artificial proof, or that poetic fictions and Aesop's fables are subspecies of historical examples'.

183. For a detailed analysis of the five kinds of 'historical' *exempla* in 5.11.6-16, see Price, 'Παράδειγμα and *Exemplum* in Ancient Rhetorical Theory', pp. 148-73, esp. pp. 148-54. According to Price, the five types of 'historical' *exempla* are distinguished on the basis of 'relations of similarity between *illustrans* and *illustrandum*' (p. 154).

184. Price, 'Παράδειγμα and *Exemplum* in Ancient Rhetorical Theory', p. 209; cf. pp. 154-56.

185. See the samples of *exemplum ex maioribus ad minora* and *exemplum ex minoribus ad maiora* in 5.11.9.

186. Price ('Παράδειγμα and *Exemplum* in Ancient Rhetorical Theory', p. 283 n. 37) writes: 'This illustration from the *Aeneid*…is particularly interesting since it is the first verse illustration of *paradeigma* or *exemplum* to be encountered in the rhetors…'

'Arguments from unlikes [*imparia*] are most useful in exhortation [*exhortationem*]'.[187] Finally, Quintilian recommends the *exemplum ex simile*, the *exemplum ex dissimile* and the *exemplum ex contrario* as useful forms of proof in 'panegyric or denunciation'; the *exemplum ex simile* is also said to be useful 'when we are speaking of what is likely to happen'.[188]

When the discussion of 'historical' examples ends, the discussion of another species of the artificial proof *exemplum* begins.[189] Quintilian states that 'a similar method is to be pursued in quoting from the fictions of the poets [*ex poeticis fabulis*], though we must remember that they will be of less force as proofs' (5.11.17). A crafty use of fictitious narrative (*fictis fabulis*) in one of Cicero's speeches is offered as a sample (5.11.18). Another kind of fictitious example, recommended as persuasive for a particular audience, receives brief mention:

> Again those fables [*fabellae*] which, although they did not originate with
> Aesop (for Hesiod seems to have been the first to write them), are best

187. *Institutio Oratoria* 5.11.10. As Price suggests ('Παράδειγμα and *Exemplum* in Ancient Rhetorical Theory', pp. 167-68), the term *imparia* may refer to another category of 'historical' example; however, the term may apply to both *exemplum ex maioribus ad minora* and *exemplum ex minoribus ad maiora*. Price points out that other taxonomies of this section could be proposed (see pp. 171-72, 288 nn. 57, 58). Further, Price notes that not all of the samples given in this section are 'hortatory' (p. 173). Much later, Quintilian makes comments of related interest. First, Quintilian argues that more important than a study of philosophy is knowledge of 'all the noblest sayings and deeds that have been handed down to us from ancient times' (12.2.29). He champions Roman history as the best source for such examples: 'For if the Greeks bear away the palm for moral precepts, Rome can produce more striking examples [*exemplis*] of moral performance, which is a far greater thing' (12.2.30). Secondly, Quintilian rejects the notion that in a written speech, which will be read by the learned, the ἐνθύμημα is more suitable, whereas in an actual speech the παράδειγμα is more suitable (12.10.51).

188. *Institutio Oratoria* 5.11.7-8. Price infers from this section that Quintilian allows for the use of 'historical' examples in judicial, epideictic and deliberative speeches ('Παράδειγμα and *Exemplum* in Ancient Rhetorical Theory', p. 173). McCall observes that the samples of *exemplum ex simile* are not 'regularly in the form of a simile'; the sample in 5.11.8 is conditional, the sample in 5.11.11 is declarative (see *Ancient Rhetorical Theories of Simile and Comparison*, p. 194). Note that the *exemplum can* be expressed as a simile.

189. See Price's analysis of this section under the heading 'Non-historical Examples' ('Παράδειγμα and *Exemplum* in Ancient Rhetorical Theory', pp. 190-94).

known by Aesop's name, are specially attractive to rude and uneducated minds, which are less suspicious than others in the reception of fictions [*ficta*] and, when pleased, readily agree with the arguments from which their pleasure is derived (5.11.19).

Menenius Agrippa's fable of the limbs and the belly is referred to as a sample of fable, and then a line from Horace is quoted as another sample (5.11.19-20). Quintilian notes that fables go by various Greek and Roman appellations (αἶνοι, αἰσωπείους, λόγους, λιβυκούς, *apologationem*) and then adds:

Similar to these is that class of proverb [παροιμίας] which may be regarded as an abridged fable and is understood allegorically: 'The burden is not mine to carry,' he said, 'the ox is carrying panniers' (5.11.21).

More space is allocated to another species of the artificial proof *exemplum*. Quintilian shifts between various views of the *similitudo* in 5.11.22-31; thus, Quintilian's line of thought in this section needs to be followed carefully, and McCall's insightful analysis will help us do so.[190] Quintilian first states his own view of the *similitudo* of proof and provides a sample of it.

Next to example [*exempli*], comparison [*similitudo*] is of the greatest effect, more especially when drawn from things nearly equal without any admixture of metaphor, as in the following case: 'Just as those who have been accustomed to receive bribes in the Campus Martius are specially hostile to those whom they suspect of having withheld the money, so in the present cases the judges came into court with a strong prejudice against the accused.'[191]

Quintilian's sample, expressed as a simile, contains no metaphorical terms and draws upon Roman public life in both its parts, and thus the resemblance is clear.[192]

In the next section, Quintilian digresses from his own view of the *similitudo* to discuss a more common view of the *similitudo* used as proof, for which he employs the Greek term παραβολή (perhaps to

190. See McCall's analysis of 5.11.22-31 in *Ancient Rhetorical Theories of Simile and Comparison*, pp. 196-210. McCall's perceptive observation that this section is structured chiastically (p. 205) lends strength to his analysis.

191. *Institutio Oratoria* 5.11.22; McCall's rendering (*Ancient Rhetorical Theories of Simile and Comparison*, p. 196), in which he combines the translations of Butler and J.S. Watson.

192. McCall, *Ancient Rhetorical Theories of Simile and Comparison*, p. 196.

avoid confusion): 'For παραβολή, which Cicero translates by "compar-ison" [*collationem*], is often apt to compare [*comparentur*] things whose resemblance is far less obvious' (5.11.23). According to McCall, what distinguishes Quintilian's own view of *similitudo* as proof from the more common view of *similitudo* as instanced in Cicero's speech is that in the common *similitudo* the comparison is drawn from subjects that are more disparate (*longius res*), and there is metaphorical lan-guage in the subject part, a combination which yields an attenuated aid to proof.[193] The common *similitudo*-παραβολή, as Quintilian states, not only compares 'the actions of men as Cicero does in the *pro Mure-na*...[;] [o]n the contrary, similitudes [*simile*] of this kind are some-times drawn from dumb animals and inanimate objects'.[194] Although the common *similitudo*-παραβολή may draw a comparison between human activities and either animals or inanimate objects, as the samples cited by Quintilian will show, Quintilian still favors the use of the common *similitudo*-παραβολή over the use of the εἰκών in oratory:

> Further, since similar objects often take on a different appearance when viewed from a different angle, I feel that I ought to point out that the kind of comparison which the Greeks call εἰκών, and which expresses the appearance of things and persons (as for instance in the line of Cassius—
>
> 'Who is he making that contorted face of an old, barefooted dancer?') should be more sparingly used in oratory than those comparisons which help us to prove our point.[195]

Quintilian's point here, as surmised by McCall, is that the term εἰκών is used to describe a stylistic embellishment in which a descriptive likeness, and not a specific comparison of two situations, is expressed.[196] This digression within a digression complete, Quintilian resumes the discussion of the common view of *similitudo*-παραβολή.

Quintilian had mentioned that the common *similitudo*-παραβολή, in which disparate subjects are compared, may sometimes be 'drawn from

---

193. McCall, *Ancient Rhetorical Theories of Simile and Comparison*, pp. 198-99.

194. *Institutio Oratoria* 5.11.23; text and translation from McCall, *Ancient Rhetorical Theories of Simile and Comparison*, pp. 198-99.

195. *Institutio Oratoria* 5.11.24; text and translation from McCall, *Ancient Rhetorical Theories of Simile and Comparison*, p. 201.

196. McCall, *Ancient Rhetorical Theories of Simile and Comparison*, p. 202. As McCall notes, in 8.3.72 Quintilian gives a definition of *similitudo* as an embellish-ment in language much like the remark on εἰκών here.

dumb animals and inanimate objects', and he now furnishes samples to show what he means.

> For instance, if you wish to argue that the mind requires cultivation, you would use a comparison [*similitudine*] drawn from the soil, which if neglected produces thorns and thickets, but if cultivated will bear fruit; or if you are exhorting [*horteris*] someone to enter the service of the state, you will point out that bees and ants, though not merely dumb animals, but tiny insects, still toil for the common weal. Of this kind is the saying of Cicero: 'As our bodies can make no use of their members without a mind to direct them, so the state can make no use of its component parts, which may be compared to the sinews, blood and limbs, unless it is directed by law' (5.11.24-25).

Cicero, Quintilian adds, also drew one *similitudo* from horses, one from stones. In these samples, the disparity between subject parts and comparative parts is evident, and metaphor is present in some. Moreover, McCall notes, these samples of the common *similitudo*-παραβολή indicate that 'Quintilian regards the common *similitudo* as adhering to no set form'.[197] In addition, it can be observed that, like the *exemplum*, the common *similitudo*-παραβολή may be used to exhort.

Next, Quintilian contrasts his preferred *similitudo* of proof to the common *similitudo*-παραβολή: 'Those [*similitudines*], as I have said, are closer, "as rowers without a pilot, so soldiers without a general are useless"'.[198] This sample, as McCall indicates, conforms to the stipulations Quintilian made earlier with regard to his preferred *similitudo* of proof: 'There is no metaphorical admixture; the two parts of the comparison are "equal" in their parallel structure; and the subjects, rowers without a pilot and soldiers without a general, are also completely "equal" in that both refer to the same human condition of underlings without a leader'.[199] To reinforce the point that the matter of similarity in a *similitudo* is critical, Quintilian adduces faulty *similitudines*.[200]

Quintilian concludes his discussion of *similitudo* with curious

---

197. McCall, *Ancient Rhetorical Theories of Simile and Comparison*, pp. 204-205.

198. *Institutio Oratoria* 5.11.26; McCall's translation (*Ancient Rhetorical Theories of Simile and Comparison*, p. 205).

199. McCall, *Ancient Rhetorical Theories of Simile and Comparison*, p. 205.

200. See *Institutio Oratoria* 5.11.26-29. One of the samples involves Socratic questioning, and here Quintilian reintroduces the sample given earlier (5.11.3) in the context of his discussion of the genus *exemplum* as *inductio*; on this section, see McCall, *Ancient Rhetorical Theories of Simile and Comparison*, pp. 206-208.

remarks on what he considers irrelevant to an analysis of the *similitudo* as proof, namely 'pedantic zeal in making a minute classification' of *similitudines*.[201] In the remaining section of this chapter on the genus of artificial proof designated as *exemplum*, Quintilian treats arguments 'drawn from similar, opposite, and dissimilar points of law' (5.11.32-33), then the relation of ἀναλογίαν and *simile* (5.11.34-35), then extrinsic sources of authority that may be employed to support a case (5.11.36-44).[202] This ends Quintilian's first concentrated analysis of the *similitudo* and the *exemplum*.

Two chapters later, Quintilian begins his discussion of the fourth part of a speech, the *refutatio*. The *similitudo* and the *exemplum* are treated serially in the section where Quintilian gives consideration to the manner in which an opponent's arguments are to be refuted. He states that since most accusatory arguments are based upon similarity (*similibus*), the defense counsel should endeavor to show that the argument is discrepant due to dissimilarity (5.13.23). Quintilian deems it relatively easy to refute points of law and certain *similitudines* in this way; however, refuting *exempla* will require deftness on the part of the speaker.

> As to parallels [*similitudines*] drawn from dumb animals or inanimate objects, they are easy to make light of. Examples [*Exempla*] drawn from facts, if damaging to our case, must be treated in various ways: if they are ancient history, we may call them legendary [*fabulosa*], while if they are undoubted, we may lay stress on their extreme dissimilarity [*dissimilia*]. For it is impossible for two cases to be alike in every detail...In the last resort, if all else prove unavailing, we must see if we can show that the action adduced as a parallel was itself unjustifiable. These remarks as to examples [*exemplis*] apply also to previous decisions in the courts.[203]

---

201. *Institutio Oratoria* 5.11.30. As McCall states, 'It is somewhat strange that Quintilian should scoff at this "minute classification," since it turns out essentially to be divisions of *similitudo* into *simile* (what is like), *dissimile* (what is unlike), and *contratium* (what is contrary), and in section 5 he himself has said of *exemplum* in its broad sense (*similitudo* being a part of this type of *exemplum*) that "all arguments of this kind, therefore, must be from things like or unlike or contrary"' (*Ancient Rhetorical Theories of Simile and Comparison*, pp. 208-209).

202. On ἀναλογίαν, see McCall, *Ancient Rhetorical Theories of Simile and Comparison*, pp. 209-10. On the relationship between the statements that confer *auctoritas* and the various types of *exempla*, see Price, 'Παράδειγμα and *Exemplum* in Ancient Rhetorical Theory', pp. 196-208.

203. *Institutio Oratoria* 5.13.23-26.

In this excerpt from Quintilian's discussion of the *refutatio* of a speech, *exemplum* and *similitudo*, two species of the artificial proof *exemplum*, are treated together, but the 'historical' example is once again linked to an inartificial proof, previous judgments. Quintilian's remarks on the refutation of a certain kind of *similitudo*, one which can be eluded with relative ease, suggest that it is not a particularly strong proof. To refute the 'historical' example requires more effort. Now that several of Quintilian's precepts on *similitudo* and example issued in the treatment of invention (*inventio*) have been examined, with specific attention given to the details provided concerning the use of both in various parts of a speech,[204] attention can be given to some of the precepts on *similitudo* and example Quintilian issues in his treatment of style (*elocutio*), a part of oratory discussed in Books 8 and 9 of *Institutio Oratoria*.

The second concentrated treatment of the *similitudo* comes in Book 8, where Quintilian's concern is with rhetorical ornament (*orationis ornatus*). Quintilian stresses that the skillful use of ornament both increases the likelihood that the speaker will gain the enthusiastic approval of the audience or judge (8.3.1-4) and also contributes to the furtherance of the speaker's case (8.3.5-6). The requirements of ornament with respect to individual words are given consideration first (8.3.15-39); the requirements of ornament with respect to groups of words are given consideration for the remainder of the book. After a discussion of faults to be avoided (8.3.42-60), Quintilian defines ornament:

> The ornate [*Ornatum*] is something that goes beyond what is merely lucid and acceptable. It consists firstly in forming a clear conception [*concipiendo*] of what we wish to say, secondly in giving this adequate expression [*exprimendo*], and thirdly in lending it additional brilliance [*nitidiora faciat*], a process which may correctly be termed embellishment [*cultum*].[205]

Among the ornaments that effect vividness, Quintilian places ἐνάργεια (or *repraesentatio*). Next, he discusses 'one form [*genus*] of vividness

---

204. References to *similitudo* in Quintilian's discussion of how the speaker can make effective use of wit to evoke laughter from a judge or audience have been passed over here; see *Institutio Oratoria* 6.3.56-62 and McCall's analysis (*Ancient Rhetorical Theories of Simile and Comparison*, pp. 210-14).

205. *Institutio Oratoria* 8.3.61. Butler has emended this passage, as he indicates in his explanatory note. I have added the Latin in order to add some precision to Butler's translation.

which consists in giving an actual word-picture of a scene'.[206] After that, another genus of ornament, the *similitudo*, occupies Quintilian for several sections.

Quintilian advises that, since the *similitudo* can make a description of things even more vivid, the invention of *similitudines* affords the speaker an excellent way of illuminating the subject matter brought forward for consideration. He alerts the reader to the fact that he is now speaking of the *similitudo* as a genus of ornament, not as a genus of proof—although the two are not unrelated.

> The invention of *similitudines* has also provided an admirable means of illuminating our descriptions. Some of these are designed for insertion among our arguments [*argumenta*] to help our proof [*probationis*], while others are devised to make our pictures [*imaginem*] yet more vivid...[207]

The *similitudo*, then, can be used for purposes of proof and for purposes of embellishment. Quintilian states that his concern in this section is with the *similitudo* used for embellishment, and he offers two samples of the comparative part of the *similitudo*, both taken from the *Aeneid*: 'Thence like fierce wolves beneath the cloud of night' and 'Like the bird that flies//Around the shore and the fish-haunted reef,//Skimming the deep'.[208] Quintilian expands upon his view of the *similitudo* as *ornatus* and offers another *similitudo* in verse, again from Virgil.

Quintilian stipulates that the comparative part of a *similitudo* should be clearer than the subject part, as McCall explains: 'Quintilian does here what he will do elsewhere [8.3.77] in his discussion of the *similitudo* of *ornatus*: he breaks a comparison into its two parts, subject and comparative, and for the lack of another word he uses the term of the whole comparison (*similitudo*) for the comparative part only'.[209] Thus, according to Quintilian,

206. See *Institutio Oratoria* 8.3.62-71. Butler's translation leaves it unclear whether 'word-picture' is a genus of '*repraesentatio*'. The text reads: 'Est igitur unum genus, quo tota rerum imago quodammodo verbis depingitur...' (8.3.63).

207. *Institutio Oratoria* 8.3.72. As McCall contends (*Ancient Rhetorical Theories of Simile and Comparison*, p. 215), there is good reason for not translating *similitudo* as 'simile' in this section. Like McCall, I will leave this Latin term untranslated. On the relationship between Quintilian's view of *similitudo* as embellishment and εἰκών, see p. 216.

208. *Institutio Oratoria* 8.3.72.

209. McCall, *Ancient Rhetorical Theories of Simile and Comparison*, p. 217.

In employing this form [*genere*] of ornament we must be especially careful that the subject chosen for our *similitudinis* is neither obscure nor unfamiliar: for anything that is selected for the purpose of illuminating [*illuminat*] something else must itself be clearer [*clarius*] than that which it is designed to illustrate [*illustrandae*]. Therefore while we may permit poets to employ such [*exempla*] as:—

> 'As when Apollo wintry Lycia leaves,
> And Xanthus' streams, or visits Delos' isle,
> His mother's home,'

it would be quite unsuitable for an orator to illustrate [*demonstret*] something quite plain by such obscure allusions.[210]

Quintilian now begins to impose certain restrictions upon the *similitudo* suitable for use in oratory in that he requires the comparative part to be clearer (*clarius*) than the subject part ('that which it is designed to illustrate').[211] Certain *similitudines* invented by poets may provide vivid descriptions—all three of the samples from Virgil's *Aeneid* do so—but they do not contribute to clarity if they contain obscure allusions. Quintilian does not fault the third Virgilian *similitudo* because it is in verse, or because it mentions geographical locations, or because it contains reference to a deity; rather, Quintilian faults it because, in his estimation, it contains 'obscure allusions'. Quintilian, then, does not advocate an unrestricted use of verse *similitudines* in oratory, and he then turns to a type of *similitudo* that may be used more effectively in oratory.

As we have seen, Quintilian previously discussed various types of *similitudines* and their uses in the proof of a speech. He now recalls one type of *similitudo* and assesses its effectiveness as an ornament.

> But even the type [*genus*] of *similitudo* which I discussed in connexion with arguments [*argumentis*] is an ornament to oratory [*ornat orationem*], and serves to make it sublime, rich, attractive or striking, as the case may be. For the more remote [*longius*] the *similitudo* is from the subject to which it is applied, the greater will be the impression of novelty and the unexpected which it produces.[212]

210. *Institutio Oratoria* 8.3.73. Note that Quintilian uses the word 'exempla' to refer to examples of *similitudines* that illustrate the point he wishes to make.

211. McCall (*Ancient Rhetorical Theories of Simile and Comparison*, p. 218) thinks that Quintilian vacillates in his attempt to separate the practical side of oratory from its stylistic side: 'If the purpose of an embellishing *similitudo* is vivid illumination it should make no difference whether the comparative part is plain or obscure, so long as a certain brilliant atmosphere is created'.

212. *Institutio Oratoria* 8.3.74-75. I concur with McCall (*Ancient Rhetorical*

Quintilian provides two samples of such a *similitudo*, with qualifying remarks:

> The following type may be regarded as commonplace and useful only as helping to create an impression of sincerity: 'As the soil is improved and rendered more fertile by culture, so is the mind by education,' or 'As physicians amputate mortified limbs, so must we lop away foul and dangerous criminals, even though they be bound to us by ties of blood.' Far finer [*sublimius*] is the following from Cicero's defence of Archias: 'Rock and deserts reply to the voice of man, savage beasts are oft-times tamed by the power of music and stay their onslaught,' and the rest (8.3.75).

An important point emerges in this section: a *similitudo* of proof becomes 'an ornament to oratory'; and, as McCall puts it, 'the lines between the two have for the moment virtually disappeared'.[213] The clear distinction between the *similitudo* of proof and the embellishing *similitudo* will become even more ambiguous when Quintilian discusses the arrangement of the comparative and the subject parts of the *similitudo*. Before he speaks on arrangement, however, Quintilian bemoans the degeneration of embellishing *similitudines* at the hands of 'declaimers', and he offers samples of faulty *similitudines*, blemished because the comparative part either makes a false comparison or does not apply to the subject part (8.3.76).

In describing the arrangement of the comparative part and the subject part of a *similitudo*, Quintilian faces a terminological difficulty. We saw earlier that Quintilian employed the same term, *similitudo*, with reference to the comparative part and to the comparison as a whole.

Theories of Simile and Comparison, pp. 219-20) that Quintilian refers back to his analysis of the common *similitudo*-παραβολή in 5.11.23-25, where the word *longius* was used to distinguish between the common *similitudo*-παραβολή and his preferred type of *similitudo*. According to McCall, in 5.11.23 *longius* was employed to mean that the two parts of the common *similitudo*-παραβολή (the comparative part and the subject part) '...were not "equal" and that there might be an admixture of metaphor. All three examples here [8.3.75] illustrate both traits: they compare mute or inanimate objects (the soil, diseased limbs, stones and beasts) to active human qualities (the mind, wicked people, a jury). In addition, they all contain metaphor: the application of "more fertile" to the mind, of "lop away" to criminals, and (less strongly) of "reply" to rocks and deserts' (p. 219). Moreover, the first sample of *similitudo* in 8.3.75 is 'almost identical' to a *similitudo*-παραβολή mentioned in 5.11.24 (pp. 219-20).

213. McCall, *Ancient Rhetorical Theories of Simile and Comparison*, p. 220.

Now, Quintilian will refer to the comparative part as *similitudo* and to the comparison as a whole as 'parabole', a transliteration of παραβολή into Latin.[214] Thus, according to Quintilian, the component parts of a *similitudo* (a whole comparison) can be arranged as follows: 'In every comparison [*parabole*] either the *similitudo* precedes and the subject [*res*] follows, or the subject [*res*] precedes and the *similitudo* follows'.[215] Two other options of arrangement are possible, and Quintilian makes his preference known:

> But sometimes it [the *similitudo*] is free and detached, and sometimes, a far better arrangement, is attached to the subject [*re*] which it illustrates [*cuius est imago*], the correspondence between the resemblances being exact [*collatione invicem respondente*], an effect produced by *reciprocal representation* [*redditio contraria*], which the Greeks style ἀνταπόδοσις.[216]

As a sample of comparison (*similitudo* or *parabole*) in which the comparative part precedes the subject, Quintilian refers again to the first *similitudo* he quoted from the *Aeneid*; as a sample of a comparison in which the comparative part follows the subject, he quotes some lines from the first *Georgic* (8.3.78). However, according to Quintilian, there is no ἀνταπόδοσις in either of these samples.

Redditio, Quintilian's preference for arrangement, puts the subject part and the comparative part side by side before the eyes and displays both parts simultaneously (8.3.79). Quintilian could, he admits, find splendid examples (*exempla*) in the writings of Virgil, but he chooses to provide samples of *redditio* from Cicero's *pro Murena*.

> In the *pro Murena* Cicero says, 'As among Greek musicians (for so they say), only those turn flute-players that cannot play the lyre, so here at Rome we see that those who cannot acquire the art of oratory betake themselves to the study of the law.' There is also another *similitudo* in the same speech, which is almost worthy of a poet, but in virtue of its *redditione* is better adapted for ornament [*ornatum*]: 'For as tempests are generally preceded by some premonitory signs in the heaven, but often, on the other hand, break forth for some obscure reason without any

214. See further, McCall, *Ancient Rhetorical Theories of Simile and Comparison*, pp. 221-22.

215. *Institutio Oratoria* 8.3.77; my translation.

216. *Institutio Oratoria* 8.3.77; Butler's emphasis. On the 'flurry' of terms is this section, see McCall, *Ancient Rhetorical Theories of Simile and Comparison*, pp. 223-24.

warning whatsoever, so in the tempests which sway the people at our
Roman elections we are not seldom in a position to discern their origin,
and yet, on the other hand, it is frequently so obscure that the storm
seems to have burst without any apparent cause.'[217]

As McCall asserts, Quintilian's comments in this section 'effectively
unite *similitudines* of proof and embellishment'.[218]

The samples of *similitudines* that exhibit *redditio contraria* are rather
lengthy, but Quintilian indicates that embellishing *similitudines* may be
quite brief, and short samples are provided (8.3.81). Of the shorter
embellishing *similitudines*, Quintilian writes: 'Such comparisons reveal
the gift not merely of placing a thing vividly before the eye [*aperte
ponendi rem ante oculos*], but of doing so with rapidity and without
waste of detail' (8.3.81). Indeed, Quintilian recognizes brevity as a
virtue, although he warns that certain attempts at brevity (specifically,
with respect to brachylogy) may be unsuccessful and result in obscurity
rather than clarity.[219] After the remarks on the virtue of brevity, Quintilian discusses another virtue, ἔμφασις, and then other ways of embellishing (8.3.83-90). As he finishes this chapter, Quintilian foreshadows
the next topic of interest in the discussion of style with these words:
'But the real power of oratory lies in enhancing or attenuating the force
of words' (8.3.89). Quintilian treats amplification in the ensuing
chapter, and there we learn that the *exemplum* can be used for
amplification.

The chapter on amplification begins with a consideration of how a
word used to describe something can be employed as a means of
amplification or attenuation (8.4.1-3). Quintilian's main concern is with
four methods of amplification, which he identifies as augmentation,
comparison, reasoning and accumulation (*incremento, comparatione,
ratiocinatione, congerie*).[220] *Amplificatio per comparationem* is of

217. *Institutio Oratoria* 8.3.79-80. I have modified Butler's translation by leaving in the Latin terms.

218. McCall, *Ancient Rhetorical Theories of Simile and Comparison*, p. 226.
McCall observes that the poetic elements in the second sample from the *pro
Murena*—'disparate subject matter and metaphorical admixture'—are the marks of
the common *similitudo*-παραβολή of proof: 'Thus, Quintilian comes near suggesting that the *similitudo* of embellishment is at its finest when it is most similar to a
similitudo of proof'.

219. See *Institutio Oratoria* 8.3.81-82.

220. *Institutio Oratoria* 8.4.3.

interest here, for Quintilian states that a 'historical' example can be used in this method of amplification.

> At times, again, we may advance a parallel to make something which we desire to exaggerate seem greater than ever [*Interim proposito velut simili exemplo efficiendum est, ut sit maius id quod a nobis exaggerandum est*], as Cicero does in the *pro Cluentio*, where, after telling a story of a woman of Miletus who took a bribe from the reversionary heirs to prevent the birth of her expected child, he cries, 'How much greater is the punishment deserved by Oppianicus for the same offence! For that woman, by doing violence to her own body did but torture herself, whereas he procured the same result by applying violence and torture to the body of another' (8.4.11).

Quintilian then emphasizes that using the 'historical' example for amplification is not the same as using the 'historical' example for proof.

> I would not, however, have anyone think that this method is identical with that used in argument [*ex argumentis loco*], where the greater is inferred from the less [*maiora ex minoribus*], although there is a certain resemblance between the two. For in the latter case we are aiming at proof [*probatio*], in the former at *amplification*; for example, in the passage just cited about Oppianicus, the object of the comparison [*comparatione*] is not to show that his action was a crime, but that it was even worse than another crime.[221]

Quintilian reiterates that there is an affinity between the 'historical' example used for proof and the 'historical' example used for amplification, and he will quote again an *exemplum* cited in the section on proof (5.8.24) in order to demonstrate how a 'historical' example can be used to amplify.

> For what I have now to demonstrate is that when amplification [*augendi*] is our purpose we compare [*comparari*] not merely whole with whole [*non tota modo totis*], but part with part [*partes partibus*], as in the following passage: 'Did that illustrious citizen, the pontifex maximus, Publius Scipio, acting merely in his private capacity, kill Tiberius Gracchus when he introduced but slight changes for the worse that did not seriously impair the constitution of the state, and shall we as consuls suffer Catiline to live, whose aim was to lay waste the whole world with fire and sword?' Here Catiline is compared to Gracchus, the constitution of the state to the whole world, a slight change for the worse to fire and sword and desolation, and a private citizen to the consuls…[222]

221. *Institutio Oratoria* 8.4.12; Butler's emphasis.
222. *Institutio Oratoria* 8.4.13-14.

Whether or not Quintilian is successful in differentiating the 'historical' example of proof from the 'historical' example of amplification, he shows an awareness that the 'historical' example (as a species of the genus of artificial proof *exemplum*) can be used for proof and that it (as a species of the method of amplification identified as '*comparatio*') can be used for the ornamentation of oratory.[223]

Quintilian's detailed treatments of *similitudo* and *exemplum* in *Institutio Oratoria* are complete by the end of the fourth chapter of Book 8. Nevertheless, he makes further comments that should not be ignored. Several sections in which either the *similitudo* or *exemplum* are mentioned will be reviewed briefly.

Within the context of a discussion of rhetorical ornaments, Quintilian turns his attention to the matter of tropes. He defines trope as 'the artistic alteration of a word or phrase from its proper meaning to another' (8.6.1). The first trope to receive consideration is what he regards as 'the commonest and by far the most beautiful' of tropes, namely metaphor (*translatio*, or μεταφορά in Greek).[224] Before he divides metaphor into four classes, Quintilian states:

> On the whole, *metaphora* is a shorter form of *similitudo*, while there is this further difference, that in the latter we compare [*comparatur*] some object [*rei*] to the thing which we wish to describe [*exprimere*], whereas in the former this object is actually substituted for the thing. It is a comparison [*Comparatio*] when I say that a man did something *like a lion*, it is a metaphor when I say of him, *He is a lion*.[225]

As McCall notes, the examples of comparison [*comparatio*] and metaphor given by Quintilian here are clearly in the Aristotelian tradition; however, Quintilian inverts the Aristotelian subordination of

223. For an opposing view, see Price, 'Παράδειγμα and *Exemplum* in Ancient Rhetorical Theory', p. 292 n. 68. For a more thorough analysis of the relationship between *similitudo* and *comparatio*, see McCall, *Ancient Rhetorical Theories of Simile and Comparison*, pp. 229-35.

224. *Institutio Oratoria* 8.6.4. The following may be intended as a definition of metaphor: 'A noun or a verb is transferred from the place to which it properly belongs to another where there is either no *literal* term or the *transferred* is better than the *literal*' (8.6.5; Butler's emphasis). Quintilian remarks later that '...*metaphor* is designed to move the feelings, give special distinction to things and place them vividly before the eye [*rebus ac sub oculos subiiciendis reperta*]...' (8.6.19; Butler's emphasis). A similar remark was made earlier about the shorter embellishing *similitudines* (8.3.31).

225. *Institutio Oratoria* 8.6.8-9; Butler's emphasis.

simile (εἰκών) to metaphor.[226] The first sentence in this passage would seem to suggest, at first glance, that for Quintilian the term *similitudo* can also mean 'simile', yet Quintilian switches to another term, *comparatio*, in the next sentence. We need not linger to give consideration to the vexing challenges this passage presents—such as, whether *similitudo* or *comparatio* is used to mean 'simile'—rather, we move forward to a later section in which Quintilian treats another trope.[227]

The term *similitudo* appears in conjunction with *translatio* again in Quintilian's discussion of *allegoria*. He defines allegory and identifies one of its genera as follows:

> *Allegory*, which is translated into Latin by *inversio*, either presents one thing in words and another in meaning, or else something absolutely opposed to the meaning of the words. The first type [*genus*] is generally produced by a series of metaphors [*continuatis translationibus*].[228]

Quintilian gives samples of what he regards to be the different types of allegory along with analytical comments, and then we read: 'But far the most ornamental effect is produced by the artistic admixture of *similitudo*, metaphor, and allegory...'[229] Thus, not only does Quintilian mention the *similitudo* of embellishment in conjunction with metaphor, but he also mentions it in conjunction with allegory as well.

Similitudo and *exemplum* appear in collocation twice in Book 9. The first instance of that collocation is in Quintilian's quote of a lengthy section from *De Oratore* in which, as we saw earlier, Cicero lists a multitude of figures of thought.[230] Following the quote from Cicero, Quintilian indicates that his view of what constitutes a figure of thought represents a departure from Cicero, for Quintilian intends 'to speak only of those figures of thought [*sententiarum figuris*] which depart from the direct method of statement' (9.2.1). Quintilian asserts that many share a similar view, but he adds quickly:

226. See McCall, *Ancient Rhetorical Theories of Simile and Comparison*, pp. 229-30.

227. On the relationship between the *similitudo* and *comparatio*, *similitudo* and *translatio*, see McCall, *Ancient Rhetorical Theories of Simile and Comparison*, pp. 229-35.

228. *Institutio Oratoria* 8.6.44; Butler's emphasis.

229. *Institutio Oratoria* 8.6.49: 'Illud vero longe speciosissimum genus orationis, in qou trium permixta est gratia, similitudinis, allegoriae, translationis...' Jülicher would not concur with such a remark.

230. *Institutio Oratoria* 9.1.31 (cf. *De Oratore* 3.53.205).

> On the other hand, all those embellishments which differ in character
> from these are none the less virtues whose importance is such that with-
> out them all oratory will be little less than unintelligible. For how can the
> judge be adequately instructed unless lucidity characterise our perfor-
> mance of the following tasks: explanation, proposition…introduction of
> comparisons [*similitudo*] or precedents [*exemplum*]…(9.2.2).

Neither samples nor analyses are given with this mention of *similitudo*
and *exemplum*, but we do learn that Quintilian, contra Cicero, will not
include the *similitudo* and the *exemplum* in his discussion of figures of
thought. With that, this examination of Quintilian's precepts on the
similitudo and the *exemplum* within the context of his systematic exposition of rhetoric in all its parts comes to a close.

Attention must be given to yet another section of *Institutio Oratoria*
in which *similitudo* and *exemplum* are mentioned together, though not
in collocation. It is fitting that this examination of *similitudo* and
exemplum in *Institutio Oratoria* should end with a cursory glance at a
sentence in which both terms appear, for in the surrounding context
Quintilian uses the term *exemplum* in two senses. Both senses of *exemplum* in that section have a bearing on the subject of concern in this
study, for we have been instructed by some parable scholars that the
Beispielerzählungen offer examples of behavior to be imitated or
avoided, but we have yet to encounter a precept on the *exemplum* to
that effect issued by any of the rhetoricians consulted here. Quintilian
does speak of *exempla* and imitation, but not in the manner that might
be expected.

In Book 10, Quintilian resumes his discussion of a number of issues
that pertain to the education of the ideal orator, and these issues will
occupy him for the next two books. In the opening remarks of Book 10,
Quintilian contends that while the precepts of rhetoric (*eloquendi prae-
cepta*) are necessarily part of a student's theoretical knowledge, the
ability to speak forcefully cannot be procured from a knowledge of precepts alone (10.1.1). Quintilian maintains that '…eloquence will never
attain to its fullest development or robust health, unless it acquires
strength by frequent practice in writing, while such practice without the
models supplied by reading [*lectionis exemplum*] will be like a ship
drifting aimlessly without a steersman' (10.1.2). According to Quintilian, eloquence is the first essential element in the formation of the ideal
orator, imitation is the second and 'diligent practice in writing' is the
third (10.1.3).

Quintilian extols the value of reading widely and copiously as a means of accumulating a store of resources. Thus, he recommends reading speeches, history, poetry, philosophy, tragedies and comedies (10.1.20-131). Quintilian lavishes praise upon one author, whose works are esteemed as especially worth reading:

> I shall, I think, be right in following the principle laid down by Aratus in the line, 'With Jove let us begin,' and in beginning with Homer. He is like his own conception of Ocean, which he describes as the source of every stream and river; for he has given us a model [*exemplum*] and an inspiration for every department of eloquence (10.1.46).

Quintilian mentions many of Homer's admirable qualities, both poetical and oratorical; several of the latter are listed in this sentence: 'Then consider his *similitudines*, his amplifications, his *exempla*, digressions, indications of fact, inferences, and all the other methods of proof and refutation which he employs' (10.1.49). Obviously, in this sentence the terms *similitudines* and *exempla* are used in their technical senses, with *exempla* meaning 'historical' examples. However, in 10.1.46 *exemplum* is quite properly taken to mean 'model'.

In the next chapter, Quintilian issues precepts on imitation (*imitatio*). In the discussion of imitation, the word *exemplum* occurs several times and it consistently means 'model', as in the introduction to the chapter:

> It is from these and other authors worthy of our study that we must draw our stock of words, the variety of our figures and our methods of composition, while we must form our minds on the model [*exemplum*] of every excellence. For there can be no doubt that in art no small portion of our task lies in imitation [*imitatione*], since, although invention came first and is all-important, it is expedient to imitate whatever has been invented with success (10.2.1).

Further on, Quintilian observes that imitation is inferior to that which it imitates, and that this holds true for a shadow, a portrait and an actor (10.2.10).

> The same is true of oratory. For the models [*exemplum*] which we select for imitation have a genuine and natural force, whereas all imitation [*imitatio*] is artificial and moulded to a purpose which was not that of the original orator.[231]

Quintilian demands an exacting assessment of the material chosen

---

231. *Institutio Oratoria* 10.2.11.

for imitation in order to determine if it is proper and suitable. More-over, he insists that the student or orator must consider whom to imitate first because 'there are many who have aspired to a resemblance [*similitudines*] with the worst and the most corrupt' of authors.[232] Later in this section on imitation, Quintilian stresses that the orator should strive for nothing less than perfection '...when there are before us so many more models of oratorical excellence [*exempla bene dicendi*] than were available for those who have thus far achieved the highest success' (10.2.28).

Much more could be said about Quintilian's views on the value of reading, imitation and practice, but we have seen enough to know that Quintilian uses the word '*exemplum*' in this context—with one excep-tion (10.1.49)—predominately in the sense of 'model' or even 'exemplar', and with reference to an eloquent author, an eloquent orator, or some admirable department of eloquence. Thus, the '*exem-plum*' recommended by Quintilian as worthy of imitation is someone (such as an orator or poet) who, or something (such as an exordium, vocabulary or figures) which, embodies excellence in oratory.

This examination of Quintilian's views on *similitudo* and *exemplum* expressed in *Institutio Oratoria* is now ended. Ever mindful that Quin-tilian's every remark about either the *similitudo* or the *exemplum* in his extensive treatise on the education of the ideal orator has not been scrutinized, the preceding review of some of the more important sec-tions of *Institutio Oratoria* in which *similitudo* and *exemplum* enter the discussion has introduced us to some of the lessons the eminent teacher of rhetoric in Rome provides on the topics of concern. As we can now attest, Quintilian's analyses of *similitudo* and *exemplum* are intricate and complex. Although neither term is used exclusively in a technical sense—thus, *similitudo* does not always mean 'comparison' or 'parable', *exemplum* does not always mean 'historical' example—it is not exceedingly difficult to recognize those instances in which *simili-tudo* and *exemplum* are used technically. Thus, some of Quintilian's precepts on *similitudo* and *exemplum* can be highlighted as follows.

According to Quintilian, both the *similitudo* and the *exemplum* are comparative techniques or strategies that can serve a variety of func-tions in several parts of a speech. Although *similitudo* and *exemplum*

---

232. *Institutio Oratoria* 10.1.14; my translation. Note that here *similitudo* is used non-technically; i.e. it does not refer to a specific figure of comparison. *Similitudo* appears also in 9.1.12, and there it carries the sense of 'monotony'.

are mentioned in conjunction with other proofs, ornaments, figures and tropes, we have seen that *similitudo* and *exemplum* are not infrequently collocated. That Quintilian conceives of the *similitudo* and the *exemplum* as closely related comparative techniques comes to the fore in the discussion of the third genus of artificial proof, the purpose of which is to produce belief, and which is designated by Quintilian as *exemplum*. Quintilian makes it clear that he prefers to regard both the *similitudo* and the *exemplum* as παραδείγματα and to call them *exempla*. The basis for his preference is his view that the *exemplum* 'involves comparison' and that the *similitudo* 'is of the nature of an example'. Cicero's identification of five types of *exempla* used for proof, a classification based upon relations of similarity, reinforces his contention that the *exemplum* 'involves comparison'.

Quintilian leaves little doubt that the 'historical' example is the 'most important' of the artificial proofs called *exempla*, and that the example is of greatest value in deliberative oratory. A certain degree of latitude with regard to what constitutes a 'historical' example is evident in some of Quintilian's remarks, however. In his formal definition of 'historical' example, Quintilian stipulates that it adduces 'some past action real or assumed which may serve to persuade the audience of the truth of the point which we are trying to make', but later he indicates that such *exempla* may be old or new, and he intimates that sayings and deeds are suitable sources for such *exempla*. Moreover, poetic fictions—including fables of various sorts—can be used for a purpose similar to that of the 'historical' example, although the force of the former is less than that of the latter. The *similitudo* is closer to the *exemplum* in terms of force, and especially *similitudines* of the kind Quintilian prefers. Nevertheless, both the *similitudo* and the *exemplum* can be used by orators for purposes other than proof; both the *similitudo* and the *exemplum* are useful in exhortations, and both are useful in the ornamentation of oratory.

If the 'historical' example is more important than the *similitudo* as an aid to proof, the *similitudo* may be said to be more important than the *exemplum* as a descriptive ornament. Quintilian devotes more attention to the *similitudo* and how it may be employed as an ornament to oratory than he does to the *exemplum*, which is mentioned only briefly as one of several means of amplification—but even there Quintilian regards the 'historical' example as a comparative technique or strategy.

Quintilian does not issue precepts on the form of the *similitudo* or the *exemplum* that can be used to distinguish between the two. He allows that both the *similitudo* and the 'historical' *exemplum* can be short or long, depending upon the requirements of the situation. In addition, Quintilian cites samples of both *similitudines* and 'historical' *exempla* in verse. Although most of the samples of 'historical' examples mention characters by name, some do not; correspondingly, although most of the samples of *similitudines* do not mention characters by name, one does—and a god at that. To this can be added an insightful observation made by Price about the samples of *similitudines* and *exempla* in *Institutio Oratoria*: 'The *exempla* are generally paratactic and self-contained, the *similitudines* are not'.[233] That observation, however, does not promise much as a means of distinguishing between *Parabeln* and *Beispielerzählungen*, for as Price points out, Quintilian does not stipulate that this should be the case; had Quintilian done so, then the all narrative parables in the synoptic gospels would seem to be more like the *exempla* than like the *similitudines*. Quintilian does not issue dicta on the form of either the *similitudo* or the 'historical' *exemplum*; indeed both share a number of features in common.

Quintilian's *Institutio Oratoria*, then, provides little incontrovertible evidence that can be used to establish a secure foundation for the distinction made by some parable scholars between *Parabeln* and *Beispielerzählungen*. Quintilian's precepts on the *similitudo* and the 'historical' example cannot be appealed to as warrants to sustain the verdict that the *Parabeln* are categorically different from the example stories. According to Quintilian, the *similitudo* and the 'historical' example are so closely related as comparative techniques or strategies, especially as species of the third genus of artificial proof, that he proposes calling them both '*exemplum*'. In fact, Quintilian's definition of '*exemplum*'—'the adducing of some past action *real* or *assumed* which may serve to persuade the audience of the truth of the point which we are trying to make'—seems to allow for 'real historical' examples and

233. Price, 'Παράδειγμα and *Exemplum* in Ancient Rhetorical Theory', p. 151; see further, pp. 149-52. The fund of *exempla* upon which Price bases this observation includes poetic fictions and Aesop's fables, for Price regards both as species of the 'historical' example. Since Price makes several prudent qualifications of this assertion, it should not be taken as a rigid standard. Another of Price's valuable insights has to do with the 'remarkable similarity between Quintilian's definition of historical example and his definition of *narratio* as one of a speech's five *partes*' (p. 150).

'fictional historical' examples, or perhaps better, 'feigned historical' examples. Not a few of the synoptic παραβολαί could meet the requirements of that definition. Since Quintilian makes no attempt to define either the *similitudo* or the *exemplum* in terms of form, since the *similitudo* and the *exemplum* share so many characteristics in common—characteristics manifest in both the narrative parables and the example stories as well—and since the *similitudo* and the *exemplum* can be employed for many of the same purposes, it is difficult to appeal to Quintilian's precepts on *similitudo* and *exemplum* for warrants to uphold a categorical distinction between *Parabel* and *Beispiel-erzählung*.

Comments and Conclusions

The preceding examination of parable and example in the ancient rhetorical tradition has not produced indisputable evidence that can be employed to provide a definitive solution to the problems associated with some attempts to distinguish between parables and example stories. Had it been possible to discover a unified theory of parable and example in the ancient rhetorical tradition, then perhaps I would be in a position to render a resounding verdict from an ancient perspective on the modern distinction between *Parabel* and *Beispielerzählung*. In this review of several rhetorical treatises written by important representatives of the ancient rhetorical tradition, we have been introduced to a plurality of perspectives on parable and example. Thus, the results of this review do validate one conclusion: There is no unified theory of parable and example in the ancient rhetorical tradition, for the ancient rhetoricians do not speak with one voice on matters pertaining to παραβολαί or *similitudines*, παραδείγματα or *exempla*. Nevertheless, we have learned a good deal about parable and example that can be brought to bear upon the distinction made by parable scholars between *Parabel* and *Beispielerzählung*. Further comment is justified if at least two points made at the beginning of this chapter are kept firmly in mind.

First, only a selective review of what is written about parable and example in several extant rhetorical treatises has been conducted in this chapter. Every rhetorical document to survive antiquity has not been consulted, and as a result the delusion that what has been discovered about parable and example here represents 'the ancient rhetorical tradition' in its entirety should not be endured. Therefore, the temptation to overgeneralize ought to be withstood. Still, it is not unreasonable to assume that representative views on parable and example prevalent in the ancient rhetorical tradition have been encountered here, for no less than three prominent rhetoricians have been consulted (Aristotle, Cicero and Quintilian) whose precepts on rhetoric, though not universally accepted, were widely disseminated. Since this review has been limited to what is written about parable and example in just a few rhetorical treatises—*Rhetorica ad Alexandrum*, '*Art*' *of Rhetoric*, *Rhetorica ad Herennium*, *De Inventione*, *De Oratore*, *Institutio Oratoria*—this rightfully cannot be considered a comprehensive report on parable and example in the ancient rhetorical tradition; yet it is fair to say that no study of parable and example in the ancient rhetorical tradition can be deemed comprehensive if these rhetorical treatises are not taken into account.

Secondly, this review of what is written about parable and example in several rhetorical treatises has not been conducted with the intention of condensing or correlating precepts in order to produce either a distilled or unified view of parable and example, and no attempt will be made to do so now. Therefore, the temptation to be reductive ought to be avoided. The aim of this chapter, as stated at the outset, has been to examine what is written about parable and example in several ancient rhetorical treatises in order to establish parameters within which the distinction between *Parabel* and *Beispielerzählung* as proposed by some parable scholars can be assessed. If it is granted that this aim has been achieved, and if I guard against the danger of overgeneralizing, on the one hand, and the danger of being reductive, on the other hand, then I may proceed to answer the questions raised at the beginning of this chapter.

One outcome of this survey of several ancient rhetorical treatises is the realization that the terms παραβολή and *similitudo*, παράδειγμα and *exemplum* are not univocal. Neither παραβολή nor *similitudo* can be taken as a reference to a figure of comparison in the strictest technical sense in every occurrence; sometimes παραβολή means 'comparison' or 'juxtaposition' in a wider sense, and sometimes *similitudo* can mean 'comparison', or 'likeness' or 'resemblance' (or even 'monotony'). Correspondingly, neither παράδειγμα nor *exemplum* can be taken as a reference to 'historical' example in every occurrence; sometimes both παράδειγμα and *exemplum* are employed to name a genus of artificial proof, and sometimes both terms refer to an instance or sample of a particular precept or principle under consideration. Further, we saw that Quintilian, in one section of *Institutio Oratoria*, uses the term 'exemplum' in the sense of a 'model'. The important point that needs to be made in light of some of the remarks made about παράδειγμα and *exemplum* by some parable scholars is this: The terms παράδειγμα and *exemplum* do not refer exclusively to 'historical' example; or, stated another way, not all παραδείγματα and *exempla* are 'historical' examples.

More attention needs to be given to some of the additional information about παράδειγμα and *exemplum* obtained here. Several of the rhetoricians identify a number of species of παραδείγματα and *exempla*, such as 'historical' examples, παραβολαί, fables, fictitious narratives and even fictitious *exempla*. Although they do not always concur on either the particular species or the number of species of παραδείγματα or *exempla*, the rhetoricians one and all agree on this point: The example, παράδειγμα or *exemplum*, is a comparative device, and this holds true for each species of example, including the 'historical' example. This particular point should be underscored because several parable scholars show little or no awareness that the example, according to our representatives of the ancient rhetorical tradition, is a comparative device. Some rhetoricians may speak in more detail about the use of an example to show similarity, dissimilarity or contrariety, but those uses are strategies that fall under the rubric of comparison. Quite obviously, the rhetoricians also conceive of the parable (παραβολή or *similitudo*) as a comparative device. Both the parable and the example, then, are comparative devices; in this respect, no thick line is drawn between parable and example in the ancient rhetorical treatises reviewed here. Some of the rhetoricians consider the παραβολή and παράδειγμα, *similitudo* and *exemplum*, to be closely related in other ways as well. It is not uncommon to find parable and example collocated either as proofs, or as figures (embellishments) or as ornaments. Indeed, the main functions of both παραβολή (*similitudo*) and παράδειγμα (*exemplum*) are proof and embellishment.

In several of the rhetorical treatises reviewed here, both the parable and the example are seen as species of the proof designated variously as artistic, artificial or extrinsic. Even the *auctor ad Herennium*, who treats the *similitudo* and *exemplum* mainly as embellishments of style, does not isolate *similitudo* and *exemplum* from purposes of proof, for both the *similitudo* and *exemplum* are said to increase verisimilitude and thus contribute to proof by making the idea more plausible. In some of the rhetorical treatises we consulted, both the parable and the example as species of artificial (or artistic, extrinsic) proofs are associated with induction. Aristotle stipulates that as artistic proofs, the παραβολή and the παράδειγμα ('historical' example) can be used to show that something is so on the basis of similar instances. Two of our rhetoricians, Aristotle and Quintilian, went on to identify this type (genus) of artificial proof as 'example' (παράδειγμα and *exemplum*, respectively). Quintilian explicitly proposed using the same term, *exemplum*, to refer to both species. Although the parable and the example are not used exclusively for purposes of proof, it is especially as artificial proofs that the parable and the example are closely related. Within that context the assertion could be made that the παραβολαί are παραδείγματα, that the *similitudines* are *exempla*, that the parables are examples—and two influential rhetoricians could be invoked as authorities. Parables and 'historical' examples are paradigmatic in function.[234] However, the parables and the examples do not have only one purpose or function.

On the contrary, in several of the rhetorical treatises reviewed in this chapter, the parable and the example are said to function as stylistic devices. According to the precepts of our Roman rhetoricians, the parable and the example are two of many figures or embellishments of thought. In their function as embellishments of thought, the *similitudo* and the *exemplum* elucidate a thought, they 'put things before the eye' vividly, although Quintilian modifies this view so that the *similitudo* elucidates as an ornament, while the *exemplum* amplifies as an ornament.[235] Cicero and the *auctor ad Herennium*, on the other hand, do not appear to think such a modification necessary; for both of those rhetoricians, the *similitudo* and the *exemplum* are effective embellishments of thought.

Some of the ancient rhetoricians, then, do not make an absolute distinction between parable and example with respect to function. Furthermore, several of them limit neither the parable nor the example to a

234. Sellin, as we saw in Chapter 4, is a proponent of the view that the *Beispielerzählungen* and other Lukan parables are paradigmatic in function.
235. We should recall that Anaximanes does not discuss the παραβολή specifically, and that Aristotle does not treat the παραβολή as an embellishment. However, both Anaximanes and Aristotle employ the verb παραβάλλειν in their discussions of amplification.

single function; both can serve several functions, and frequently both are said to serve the same functions. As the *auctor ad Herennium* would have it, both the *similitudo* and the *exemplum* embellish, prove, clarify and vivify.

One function often attributed to the 'example' by some parable scholars is not to be found in this chapter, and this function is conspicuous in its absence. At no point in this examination of parable and example in several rhetorical treatises have we witnessed one of the rhetoricians issue the precept that the παραδείγματα or *exempla* offer examples of behavior to be imitated or avoided. This, then, should serve as a corrective to the view espoused by some parable scholars that the sole purpose of παράδειγμα or *exemplum* is to offer an example of behavior to be imitated or avoided. And yet just as soon as that remark is made, it must be qualified, for we have come across faint adumbrations of a view of the *exemplum* that seems to presuppose, or at least does not preclude, its use in advocating behavior to be imitated or avoided. Recall that the *auctor ad Herennium* deems an *exemplum* defective if it is base and consequently not to be imitated. We have seen Quintilian indicate that the *exemplum* can be used in exhortations, but he also makes it known that the *similitudo* can be used in exhortations; therefore, Quintilian makes no categorical distinction between *similitudo* and *exemplum* based upon the tenet that the *exemplum* alone can be used in exhortations. We paused to examine a section of *Institutio Oratoria* in which Quintilian does recommend the imitation of *exempla*, but saw that '*exemplum*' in Book 10 does not refer to 'historical' example or to any other species of *exemplum* treated in his exposition of rhetoric in all its parts; rather, in that section of Book 10 'exemplum' is used with reference to the teacher of rhetoric as a model for students and with reference to a particularly excellent part of a speech or figure (and so on) that can serve as a model for students to imitate in their practical exercises.[236]

Given the limited number of rhetorical treatises examined in this chapter, it cannot be asserted unequivocally that the ancient rhetorical tradition does not advocate the use of παραδείγματα or *exempla* to

---

236. For more on the role of *exempla* as models in rhetorical instruction, see Lausberg, *Handbuch der literarischen Rhetorik*, I, pp. 25-26, 365-66, 457-58. See also Fiore's section on 'The Place of Example in Rhetorical Education' (*The Function of Personal Example*, pp. 33-37) and the bibliography he provides there.

offer examples of behavior to be imitated or avoided.[237] Indeed, the recommendation that 'historical' examples are especially effective in deliberative oratory, which has as one of its purposes to persuade or dissuade an audience with respect to a particular course of action, may be related indirectly to a recognition of the value of 'historical' examples in depicting commendable or reprehensible actions. That notwithstanding, and cognizant of the fact that practice does not always comply with precept, it can only be said that the ancient rhetoricians reviewed in this chapter do not identify and then emphasize as one of the functions of παραδείγματα and *exempla* the offering of examples to be imitated or avoided.

The ancient rhetoricians consulted here, then, do not provide discrete criteria with respect to the functions of the parable and the example that can be seized upon to solidify a categorical distinction between the *Parabeln* and the *Beispielerzählungen*. The same holds true with respect to form. As a matter of fact, the *auctor ad Herennium* explicitly correlates the *similitudo* and the *exemplum* with respect to function and mode of presentation. Although we have encountered several formal definitions of 'historical' example, prescriptions relative to its formal characteristics are lacking. Little or no space is devoted to a discussion of formal characteristics of either the parable or the 'historical' example; and we have not met with any attempt to delimit the 'historical' example as one 'genre' and the parable as another 'genre' on the basis of formal elements peculiar to each. On several occasions we have observed that the samples of parables and 'historical' examples provided by the rhetoricians share many features in common. The ancient rhetoricians reviewed here do not define either the parable or the 'historical' example on the basis of 'form'. It can be said, in light of

237. Fiore provides an important study in which the exhortative and dissuasive uses of *exempla* as protreptic and apotreptic devices is established. In his survey of several of the same rhetorical treatises that we have reviewed in this chapter, Fiore is unable to amass much impressive evidence to demonstrate that our rhetoricians regard either exhortation or admonition as the primary purpose of examples (see *The Function of Personal Example*, pp. 26-33). However, Fiore does show that another important rhetorician, Isocrates, both emphasizes the hortatory use of examples as patterns for imitation (pp. 50-51, 64) and makes extensive use of examples for such a purpose in several of his discourses (pp. 45-67). In addition to the documents already mentioned, Fiore investigates the variety and functions of exempla in treatises written by Plutarch and Seneca, in the eponymous epistles, and in the Pauline epistles.

what we have read in several rhetorical treatises, that both the parable and the 'historical' example may be species of proofs or embellishments, but neither the parable nor the 'historical' example is a 'genre'. 'Example' is the term employed by both Aristotle and Quintilian to designate not a 'genre' but a 'genus' of artificial proof, and for them 'example' is a term that encompasses a variety of 'forms'.[238]

How, then, are we to assess Bultmann's claims that the example stories 'offer examples=models for the right conduct', but that the example stories are not παραδείγματα? Based upon this review of parable and example in several ancient rhetorical treatises, it can be said that Bultmann is right and wrong. It is correct to say that the example stories are not 'historical' examples (a species of the artificial proof called 'example'), which is what Bultmann means by παραδείγματα; but it is incorrect to say that the example stories are not a species of the genus of artificial proof designated as παράδειγμα. An exact assessment of the accuracy of Bultmann's assertion that the example stories 'offer examples=models for the right conduct' cannot be provided, except to remark that a view of the παραδείγματα—and 'historical' examples, at that—as offering examples of conduct to be imitated or avoided lies on the periphery of some of the treatments of the example in the ancient rhetorical treatises consulted in this chapter. Having said all this, we must remember that it was precisely Bultmann's point that the example stories are not παραδείγματα. In other words, his view of the *Beispielerzählungen* as a *Gattung* is not grounded in the ancient rhetorical tradition.

By now it should be increasingly apparent that the ancient rhetorical treatises reviewed here do not yield much in the way of evidence that can be used to maintain a categorical distinction between the *Parabeln*

238. This finding is in accord with the results of other studies of the *exemplum* that take into account a wider range of texts from different periods, as Schenda remarks in his survey of research on the example: 'Exemplum is therefore both a collective concept for the most diverse genres, and also at the same time a function concept, by no means is it a self-standing genre designation' ('Stand und Aufgaben der Exemplaforschung', p. 81); cf. Assion ('Das Exempel als agitatorische Gattung', pp. 234-39). Two parable scholars express similar views: see Sellin, 'Lukas als Gleichniserzähler', pp. 168, 178; and Baasland, 'Zum Beispiel der Beispielerzählungen', pp. 200, 218-19. For more on 'die literarische Form' of the *exemplum* according to Quintilian, see Lausberg, *Handbuch der literarischen Rhetorik*, I, pp. 229-30.

and the *Beispielerzählungen*.[239] On the contrary, the precepts issued by
the rhetoricians with respect to parable and example render the distinction between narrative parable and example story even more problematic. Few parable scholars who wish to maintain a categorical distinction between the *Parabeln* and the *Beispielerzählungen* do so on the
basis of the formal characteristics manifest in the samples of
παραβολαί and *similitudines*, παραδείγματα and *exempla*, provided by
the rhetoricians.[240] If such an attempt were made, then the formal characteristics evident in the *Parabeln* would need to be correlated with the
formal characteristics evident in the παραβολαί or *similitudines*, and
the formal characteristics evident in the *Beispielerzählungen* would
need to be correlated with the formal characteristics evident in the
'historical' examples—and a rather discomfiting problem would arise:
Such a procedure would be tantamount to making the example stories
equivalent to 'historical' examples, something both Jülicher and Bultmann sought to avoid. It is true that the *Beispielerzählungen* manifest
some of the appurtenances of 'historical' *exempla*, but then so do the
Parabeln, for both the *Parabeln* and the *Beispielerzählungen* recount
the words and deeds of persons in the past, and usually in narrative.
Some of the problems inherent in an attempt to correlate the example
stories and the 'historical' *exempla* on the basis of their formal characteristics need to be explored further.

In Chapter 4 of this study, we saw that some parable scholars
endeavor to establish the 'uniqueness' of the example stories, and
thereby maintain a categorical distinction between *Parabeln* and
Beispielerzählung, by identifying formal characteristics peculiar to the
example stories. According to some scholars, the appearance of things
divine or 'religious' in the example stories is the differentium that
marks the distinction between *Parabeln* and *Beispielerzählungen*. We
cannot appeal to the ancient rhetoricians to adjudicate the matter, for
they issue no precepts to the effect that parables can be drawn only

---

239. It would be difficult to employ length as a criterion to distinguish between
Parabeln and *Beispielerzählungen* because (a) there are long and short samples of
both parables and examples in the ancient rhetorical treatises surveyed here, and (b)
both the *Parabeln* and *Beispielerzählungen* are approximately equal in length. The
use of length as a criterion would be more applicable to the distinction between
Gleichnisse and *Gleichniserzählungen*, but again ancient rhetoricians provide
samples of longer and shorter parables.

240. Recall that Jülicher correlates the *Parabeln* to fables (λόγοι).

from earthly circumstances (or material) and that the 'historical' examples must be drawn only from religious circumstances (or material) or things divine. (What a strange 'historical' example would the latter directive create.) In fact, two rhetoricians, Cicero and Quintilian, introduced us to two *similitudines* which did have to do with things religious or things divine, one involving sacrifices and one involving a god.[241] Those two Roman rhetoricians, then, do not unfailingly and punctiliously avoid the mention of things religious or divine in their *similitudines*, and they certainly do not make a distinction between *similitudo* and *exemplum* on the basis of whether there is mention of deities or matters pertaining to religion.[242]

Another apparently peculiar feature of the example stories fares little better in light of the samples of 'historical' examples and parables furnished by our rhetoricians. Named characters or groups of characters do appear in the example stories and many of the 'historical' *exempla*; but even though both the example stories and the 'historical' examples share this feature in common, it cannot provide the foundation for a categorical distinction between the *Parabeln* and the *Beispielerzählungen*. We have encountered samples of 'historical' examples with and without specifically named characters; some 'historical' examples do refer to famous historical persons by name, yet others do not supply the names of the persons involved.[243] We have also encountered samples of parables with and without named characters; while most of the samples of parables refer to characters by means of some characteristic having to do with occupation or status or gender, two *similitudines* (one in *Rhetorica ad Herennium*, one in *De Oratore*) refer to a specific and famous person or god by name. Even if it could be established that, according to the rhetorical treatises reviewed in this chapter, the appearance of named characters or groups of characters constitutes an essential formal element peculiar to the 'historical' *exempla* and that

241. Fiore alludes to examples from Isocrates and Plutarch that involve the gods or God; see *The Function of Personal Example*, pp. 49, 69.

242. Thus, the greater or lesser proximity of *Sachhälfte* to *Bildhälfte* fares poorly as a criterion that can be employed to distinguish between *Parabeln* and *Beispielerzählungen*. Indeed, Quintilian recommends his preferred παραβολή-*similitudo* precisely because its comparative part and its subject part are more closely related.

243. In his samples of 'historical' examples, Anaximanes frequently referred to the persons involved not by name but by τις. Fiore indicates that Isocrates does the same thing in some of his examples; see *The Function of Personal Example*, p. 49.

could then be used to certify the distinction between the *Parabeln* and the *Beispielerzählungen*, the problem of equating 'historical' examples and example stories would return to confront us.

These comments are not intended to suggest that there is no difference at all between the παραβολαί or *similitudines* and the παραδείγματα or *exempla* in the ancient rhetorical treatises surveyed in this chapter. The simple fact that separate words for 'parable' and 'example' are used in both the Greek and the Latin rhetorical treatises implies a distinction between the two.[244] Indeed, Quintilian—who, more than any other rhetorician consulted in this study, seeks to make παράδειγμα, παραβολή, *exemplum* and *similitudines* coterminous as artificial proofs—employs both *similitudo* and *exemplum*, and he devotes sections of *Institutio Oratoria* to discussions of one apart from the other. The basis for a distinction between parable and example, though not stated as overtly by our rhetoricians as we might like, is easy enough to discern.

Although several rhetoricians explicitly indicate that there are various species of examples, such as 'historical' examples, parables and fables, to name but three, we have seen that the 'historical' example is regularly regarded as more probable or credible than either the parable of the fable. While the *auctor ad Herennium* and Quintilian allow that even a fictional narrative increases verisimilitude, Quintilian avers that a fictional narrative carries less force as a proof than the 'historical' example. Cicero establishes a hierarchy: The greatest corroboration of a probable truth comes from a 'historical' example first, then from a *similitudo*, then from fable. Two species of artificial proof, parable and 'historical' example, deserve more consideration.

The parable and example, according to the ancient rhetoricians, are comparative devices that can be used for purposes of proof and for purposes of embellishment. A tacit presupposition with respect to the parable held by some of the rhetoricians is expressed succinctly by Aristotle: The parable is a species of example (the genus of artificial proof) that involves 'made up' events or actions. The presupposition

---

244. In light of this remark, the omission of παραβολή in *Rhetorica ad Alexandrum* can be taken in one of several ways: either Anaximanes regards παραβολή and παράδειγμα as coterminous without informing us, or he employs another Greek word to refer to the comparison most other Greek rhetoricians refer to as παραβολή, or he places little emphasis on the value of the παραβολή as a comparative device. The latter scenario strikes me as being the most plausible one.

with respect to the 'historical' example is more overt: The 'historical' example is a species of example (the genus of artificial proof) that involves 'things that have happened before' or 'past actions'.[245] The parable and the 'historical' example, then, are species of the genus of artificial proof that two of the rhetoricians call 'example', but the παραβολή or *similitudo* is a fictional comparison, whereas the παράδειγμα is a 'historical' comparison. Some of the rhetoricians would have it that comparisons drawn from the real world of history and which involve the sayings and actions of historical persons are more probable or credible, and thus are more forceful as proofs than comparisons drawn from a fictional world and which involve fabricated characters. Why? The answer can be inferred from Aristotle and Quintilian: History repeats itself, the future resembles the past, future actions can be predicted from past actions.[246] Past actions, then, can be adduced in order to persuade a judge or an audience of the truth or probable truth of the point being made. However, not all the rhetoricians erect such a neat boundary between fictional comparison and 'historical' example; Cicero makes provision for fictional examples, and Quintilian permits that the 'historical' example may be the 'adducing of some past action real or assumed'.

For the moment, I keep Cicero and Quintilian in abeyance in order to determine whether the distinction between παραβολή or *similitudo* as fictional comparison and the παράδειγμα or *exemplum* as 'historical' example can be applied directly in support of the categorical distinction between *Parabel* and *Beispielerzählung*. If it were to be established that the ancient rhetorical treatises employed a classificatory criterion based upon lesser or greater degrees of verisimilitude, which in turn contribute to lesser or greater degrees of probability, to categorize species of a genus of artificial proof; and if that criterion were appropriated in

245. It should be reiterated that there is no uniform definition of 'historical' example found in each of the rhetorical treatises reviewed here. One rhetorician contends that a 'historical' example is an action from the past, another that the 'historical' example recounts the sayings and deeds of famous persons from the past, another that the 'historical' example involves past actions 'real or assumed'; moreover, one rhetorician requires that the names of the persons involved must be given, while another allows that the event to which reference is made does not have to be in the past.

246. These remarks are taken from sections already examined in which Aristotle and Quintilian recommend the use of 'historical' example as very effective in deliberative speeches.

order to uphold the categorization of two species of παραβολαί *Jesu* as *Parabeln* and *Beispielerzählungen*, that distinction could not be applied unless one were willing to argue that the example stories are 'historical' examples. This would entail claiming that the *Beispielerzählungen* are comparisons drawn from the real world of history which recount the sayings and actions of historical persons, and that the example stories therefore are unlike the *Parabeln*, which are fictional comparisons. Few are the parable scholars who would grant that the four example stories are 'historical' examples. Even though, as I remarked earlier, the example narratives depict named characters or groups of characters who have counterparts in the 'real' world, and that increases the verisimilitude of the *Beispielerzählungen*, the example narratives are still—like the *Parabeln*—fictional comparisons, that is, παραβολαί.

This examination of parable and example in several ancient rhetorical treatises has not established unequivocal evidence to support the categorical distinction between the *Parabeln* and the *Beispielerzählungen* as advanced by some parable scholars, and this is so because the criteria invoked by parable scholars to justify the distinction between *Parabeln* and *Beispielerzählungen* are rendered problematic by those very ancient rhetorical treatises. In the ancient rhetorical treatises reviewed in this chapter, the παραβολαί or *similitudines* and the παραδείγματα or *exempla* share not only several functions in common, but also many formal characteristics in common. Thus, it is not surprising that we have encountered difficulties in utilizing what is written in those treatises about the parable and the example to separate the constituent members of the category '*Parabel*' from the constituent members of the category '*Beispielerzählung*'. Those difficulties stem from what is perhaps a more fundamental problem. The species *Beispielerzählung* as conceived and identified by several parable scholars does not correspond to the species 'historical' example as conceived by the ancient rhetoricians consulted in this chapter. One of the underlying reasons for that is this: Whereas some of the rhetoricians are concerned with identifying the parable and the 'historical' example as species of a particular genus of artificial proof, designated as 'example' by Aristotle and Quintilian, some of the parable scholars are concerned with identifying the *Parabel* and the *Beispielerzählung* as species of the genus παραβολαί *Jesu*. If the genera do not correspond to each other, it is unlikely that the species of those genera will correspond to each other. It would not be inordinately difficult to rectify the situation. If we follow two prominent rhetoricians in antiquity, Aristotle and Quintilian, the παραβολαί *Jesu*, including all its species as identified by parable scholars, would be a species of the genus of artificial proof 'example'—and then all the παραβολαί *Jesu* would be examples, and the *Parabeln* would also be 'example stories'. The same holds true with respect to the parables of the synoptic gospels. If, from a rhetorical perspective, the term 'example' applies to *all* of the parables of Jesus (whether the Jesus of history or the Jesus[es] of the synoptic gospels), does that not render the categorical distinction between 'parable' and 'example story' ineffectual? Does that not make the category 'example story' a hollow one?

The questions raised at the beginning of this chapter about parable and example in the ancient rhetorical tradition have been answered, and the answers to those questions, in turn, call into question the distinction between *Parabel* and *Beispielerzählung*. The ancient rhetorical treatises reviewed here supply us with a plurality of perspectives on the parable and the example that do not restrict the potentiality of either. The ancient rhetoricians do not debate directly the issue of 'parable versus example', but they do issue precepts on parable and example that provide parameters for assessing the categorical distinction made by some parable scholars between *Parabel* and *Beispielerzählung*. In light of this examination of parable and example in a number of ancient rhetorical treatises, several formulations of the category 'example story' as proposed by parable scholars are increasingly suspect. The more we read about parable and example in ancient rhetorical treatises, the more readily we can call each one of the four so-called example stories what another ancient author, the one who recorded them for posterity, called two of them: a παραβολή.[247] But having read Aristotle and Quintilian, we are forced to acknowledge that all of the parables (παραβολαί) of Jesus recorded in the synoptic gospels are examples (παραδείγματα).

---

247. See Lk. 12.16 and 18.9.

Chapter 6

CONCLUSION: A PERSPECTIVE ON FOUR PARABLES IN THE GOSPEL OF LUKE

'Genre-critically, the category *'Beispielerzählung'* cannot be retained for the Lukan *Gleichnisse*. Neither by means of formal criteria nor by means of 'example' can this *Gattung* be established. The so-called *Beispiel-erzählungen* indeed have a peculiarity, which has been accentuated by the research, but the distinguishing marks of these narratives are only seldom encountered in all of these *Gleichnisse*; they also apply to other *Gleichnisse*...From these traits only a relative peculiarity of the *Beispielerzählungen* (whose scope is difficult to delimit) can be perceived.'

Ernst Baasland,
'Zum Beispiel der Beispielerzählungen'

The author of the Gospel of Luke might be perplexed to discover that some of his readers could assert that four of the παραβολαί in his narrative are not 'parables' but 'example stories'. A perusal of some of the narrative introductions to the parables in Luke indicates that the third evangelist did not make an obvious distinction between 'parable' and 'example story'.[1] In fact, two of the so-called example stories are prefaced with narrative introductions which state clearly that Jesus, the protagonist, is about to tell a παραβολή.[2] In the story told by the third evangelist The Merciful Samaritan, The Foolish Rich Man, The Rich Man and Poor Lazarus, and The Pharisee and the Toll Collector are

---

1.　See, e.g., Lk. 5.36, 6.39, 8.4, 13.6, 14.7, 15.3, 18.1, 19.11, 20.9 and 21.29.

2.　Prior to The Foolish Rich Man we read: Εἶπεν δὲ παραβολὴν πρὸς αὐτοὺς λέγων (Lk. 12.16). Prior to The Pharisee and the Toll Collector we read: Εἶπεν δὲ καὶ πρός τινας τοὺς πεποιθότας ἐφ' ἑαυτοῖς ὅτι εἰσὶν δίκαιοι καὶ ἐξουθενοῦντας τοὺς λοιποὺς τὴν παραβολὴν τυάτην (Lk. 18.9). In an ancient textual witness, codex Bezae (D), The Rich Man and Poor Lazarus is obviously considered to be a παραβολή, as the introduction indicates (Εἶπεν δὲ καὶ ἑτέραν παραβολήν; Lk. 16.19).

apparently to be taken as παραβολαί *Jesu*; nevertheless, in the history of parable research these four parables in the Gospel of Luke have become 'example stories'. Indeed, against the contention that Luke transformed four of Jesus' parables into 'example stories', the findings obtained in this study provide the basis for a counterclaim: *Luke* did not transform those four parables into 'example stories', rather *parable scholars* did.

A Review: Findings and Implications

This study contains the story of the transformation of four parables in the Gospel of Luke into 'example stories', and that story began before the publication of *Die Gleichnisreden Jesu*. Although it would be interesting to know the identity of the first scholar to argue that The Merciful Samaritan, The Foolish Rich Man, The Rich Man and Poor Lazarus, and The Pharisee and the Toll Collector belong to a particular group of parables and to know the rationale given to justify conceiving of these four parables as members of that group, we may well never know.

We now know, on the basis of van Koetsveld's testimony, that for some time scholars have perceived something different about that group of parables, and that early on the question was whether those four parables are (real) stories or (fictional) parables. After van Koetsveld, who regarded that group as 'moral sketches', several scholars—including Weiss, Göbel, Stockmeyer and Jülicher—advanced the notion that those four parables are different from the other parables because they are not 'emblematic', or because they already move on the 'higher plane' of religion. Yet these parable scholars of the nineteenth century, who endeavored to make finer discriminations among the parables of Jesus, assumed that—they did not debate whether—those four parables are authentic parables of Jesus. Debate over the authenticity of that group of parables, known famously as 'example stories' after Jülicher, was not long in coming, and it has continued well into this century. Another development in the debate over the example stories is this: Some parable scholars of the twentieth century assume that Jesus did not utter mere 'examples', or 'moral examples', and thus some attempts at making finer discriminations among the parables of Jesus have become platforms for discrimination against the 'example stories'. The story of the transmutation of those four parables into something other than a group of παραβολαί *Jesu* can also be found in this study.

To be sure, I have done more in this study than simply recount the history of scholarship on the example stories. The category 'example story' has been subjected to scrutiny from a variety of angles. A number of perspectives on the example stories have been introduced so that my evaluation of that category might be proper and just. Both the questions raised about the example stories and the answers given by other scholars have been examined in light of a set of specific questions. While I certainly have not provided answers to every question raised about the example stories, I have provided certain answers that call into question not only the category '*Beispielerzählung*' itself, but also the categorical distinction between *Parabeln* and *Beispielerzählungen*. This study, then, has placed the category 'example story' within the history of parable research only to displace it. However, only after the results obtained here have been evaluated by other scholars can the determination be made as to whether this study yields a 'just assessment' of the category 'example story'.

The focus of this study in its entirety has been upon the problems, real and perceived, posed by a group of παραβολαί classified by Jülicher as '*Beispielerzählungen*'. I have shown (1) that some of the problems associated with the example stories are the effluence of a misunderstanding or misconception of what Jülicher himself said about the *Beispielerzählungen*; (2) that other problems associated with the example stories emanate from a conflation of Jülicher's conception of the *Beispielerzählungen* and Bultmann's conception of the *Beispielerzählungen*; and (3) that still other problems associated with the example stories result from confusion over what is meant by 'example'. Moreover, those problems are compounded by a mismatch of conventions, that is, by approaching ancient rhetorical techniques—παραβολή or *similitudo*, παράδειγμα or *exemplum*—with modern preconceptions about the form of the parable and the example. Thus, in an attempt to add a measure of clarity to the debate over 'the problem of parables versus examples', I have (1) furnished a careful exposition of Jülicher's formulation of the category '*Beispielerzählung*' within the context of the whole of *Die Gleichnisreden Jesu*; (2) demonstrated that Bultmann's conception of that category is not identical to Jülicher's; and (3) surveyed several perspectives on the parable and the example as advanced in a number of ancient rhetorical treatises. My findings suggest that it is not the four parables classified as 'example stories' that pose a problem; rather, the very classification of those four parables as 'example stories' constitutes the problem.

The results of this study, in turn, pose a serious problem to those who wish to uphold the classification of four parables in the Gospel of Luke as 'example stories'. It bears repeating: The *Beispielerzählungen* cannot be distinguished as a unique group of παραβολαί on the basis of form (since those four parables do not share identical attributes), nor can they be differentiated from the *Parabeln* on the basis of form (since those four parables share a number of attibutes in common with the *Parabeln*). Baasland's conclusions, as cited in the epigraph to this chapter, find corroboration here, for a common formal structure has not been discerned in the example stories. Attempts to establish the uniqueness of the example stories on the basis of tangible formal features manifest in the example stories have not enjoyed success, largely because the *Beispielerzählungen* share a multitude of formal features in common with the *Parabeln*.

A review of various attempts to distinguish between the example stories and the narrative parables made by scholars who employ diverse methods rendered the distinction between *Beispielerzählung* and *Parabel* even more problematic. The categorical distinction between example story and narrative parable is suspect because, to reiterate, not only do the example stories share a number of formal features in common with other narrative parables in the synoptic gospels, but also because the example stories have not been shown to exhibit either a collective set of features or a singular, peculiar feature that can be invoked as a means of making an absolute (essential) distinction between *Beispielerzählung* and *Parabel*. Thus, the difference between the example stories and the parables, if indeed there is any substantive difference, must be seen as a difference of degree and not a difference of kind. Momentarily, then, this study corroborates Baasland's conclusion that the example stories, when viewed within an accidence of the synoptic parables, exhibit a 'relative peculiarity'.

During the course of this study, however, the 'relative peculiarity' of the example stories diminished. When the example stories as a group are viewed apart from their narrative context in the Gospel of Luke and then compared to other parables in the synoptic gospels, they may give the semblance of being a unique or peculiar group of παραβολαί because they manifest features that seem to be unique—for instance, characters or groups of characters specified by name, or the direct mention of things 'religious'—but when the example stories are viewed within their narrative context they seem less than unique because, upon closer examination, other parables in the Gospel of Luke also manifest those features. Moreover, an examination of parables and examples in several ancient rhetorical treatises revealed that those same features—characters specified by name and the direct mention of things 'religious'—are to be found in other parables as well. This suggests, then, that the threat of dissolution looms over one bond shared by four parables in the Gospel of Luke for over 100 years—the category 'example story'.

As the centennial of the publication of the revised edition of *Die Gleichnisreden Jesu* approaches, it is fitting that we acknowledge again Jülicher's substantial contributions to research on the parables of Jesus. A significant part of Jülicher's legacy, a part that Jülicher himself would perhaps deem dubious, is that the program for interpreting the parables of Jesus as proposed in *Die Gleichnisreden Jesu*, which toppled the prevailing interpretive approach to and understanding of those parables, cleared the way for scholars to avail themselves of new interpretive approaches in their endeavors to plumb the depths of Jesus' parables for meaning and relevance. However, as we have seen, one part of Jülicher's bequest to subsequent generations of parable scholars, the classification of four parables in the Gospel of Luke as example stories, has posed problems for those who wish to interpret the parables of Jesus.[3] That category in Jülicher's classification of the παραβολαί *Jesu* has served its usefulness, and we should recognize that the very categorization of four parables in the Gospel of Luke as 'example stories' has called special attention to some parables that otherwise might not have garnered as much notice. Nonetheless, scholars have been unable to discover a common characteristic shared by those four parables which leads inexorably to the conclusion that they, and they alone among all the synoptic parables, are 'examples'. As a means of distinguishing either a unique group of παραβολαί *Jesu* or a unique group of παραβολαί *Lukas* distinct from all the other parables attributed to Jesus in the synoptic gospels, the category 'example story' is otiose. That category is one part of Jülicher's legacy which does not merit defense and preservation. If that is so, then this study has made a chip in the marmoreal classification of Jesus' parables which has been dominant in parable research for over a century. We may well wish to divest ourselves of the category 'example story' as part of our heritage from

---

3.   As I have pointed out, Jülicher cannot be held accountable for all of the problems associated with that category.

Jülicher, to relinquish that category and rid parable scholarship of it forever, but we will not, for debate over 'the problem of parables versus examples' will continue at least as long as the view that the example stories are 'moral examples' persists. One ramification of this study should, rather than put an end to the debate over 'the problem of parables versus examples', spur that debate and move it forward.

The results of this study call into question the view that only the example stories—either as a unique group of παραβολαί *Jesu*, or as a group of inauthentic parables imputed to him, or as a group of peculiarly Lukan parables—are 'moral examples'. Mark well that I do not rule out the possibility that the narrative parables (*Parabeln*) and the example narratives (*Beispielerzählungen*) have to do with moral concerns, rather I would rule out the certainty that *only* the example narratives have to do with moral concerns. At this point, the narrow focus of this study repays a dividend: A concentrated examination of over a century of parable research reveals that scholars have been unsuccessful in their efforts to identify either a collective set of features shared in common by the example stories as a group or a singular feature exhibited by all four example stories that can be advanced as proof that they are 'moral examples'. An examination of parable and example in a number of ancient rhetorical treatises indicated that several ancient rhetoricians do not make a distinction between parable and example on the basis of whether one or the other is to be used for 'hortatory' purposes; indeed, one ancient rhetorician suggests that both the parable and the example can be useful in exhortations. The findings obtained here make the dichotomy between parable and example story as maintained by some participants in the debate over 'the problem of parables versus examples'—which is based upon the supposition that the example stories, in contradistinction to the parables, are 'moral examples'—increasingly untenable.

If the last remark is valid in the least, then it carries with it several implications for a number of related issues which have been kept at bay throughout this study, and certain important, complex issues which have been dealt with by parable scholars in this century now begin to reassert themselves. The restrictions imposed at the outset of this study do not authorize me to go beyond the established parameters to issue pronouncements on all of those issues, but it may not be illegitimate for me to make a few observations and to raise a few questions about some of them.

The preceding chapters of this study, in which a detailed examination of a variety of scholarly perspectives on the example stories has been conducted, entitle me to offer this observation: A certain irony is evident in the arguments of some modern parable scholars who, in the debate over 'the problem of parables versus examples', take umbrage with Jülicher's classification of four parables in the Gospel of Luke as 'example stories' and who vigorously oppose the notion that any of Jesus' parables are 'moral examples'. We have encountered at least three approaches adopted by scholars to avoid including 'moral examples' among Jesus' authentic parables. One approach rehabilitates the example stories to a more noble status so that they can stand with dignity among the authentic parables of Jesus; accordingly, the so-called example stories, like all of Jesus' authentic parables, are shown to be 'metaphors'. Another approach, a variation of the first, concedes that the example stories as they appear in the Gospel of Luke are 'moral examples', but then proceeds to demonstrate that these four parables in their original form as spoken by Jesus are 'metaphors'. Yet another approach regards the situation as irremediable: The example stories 'can only be read morally', they are not metaphors, and thus are not to be included among Jesus' authentic parables. The irony is this: Jülicher did not differentiate between the *Parabeln* and the *Beispielerzählungen* on the grounds that the example narratives alone are 'moral examples', nor did he finally exclude the example narratives from among the genuine παραβολαί *Jesu*; rather, Jülicher argued that all of Jesus' παραβολαί—*Gleichnisse*, *Parabeln* and *Beispielerzählungen*—have a deeply moral or ethical purpose and evidence the *Sache* 'the kingdom of God'. That irony is heightened by this: Bultmann, who did conclude that 'the "example narratives" offer examples=models for the right conduct', did not maintain that only the example stories evoke a moral judgment. What is to be made of the claim that the example stories are 'moral examples' and therefore not authentic parables of Jesus and the counterclaim that the example stories are metaphors and therefore authentic parables of Jesus? I will make this comment and move on: Any approach to the example stories which excludes them from among Jesus' authentic parables if, or because, they are 'moral examples' not only presupposes that Jesus' authentic parables have nothing to do with moral or religious concerns directly, but also simultaneously manifests an uneasiness with the view that any of Jesus' parables might have ethical, moral or religious concerns.

Another observation is in order. Whereas Jülicher admonished those who would allegorize Jesus' parables, Jülicher is now admonished for 'moralizing' Jesus' parables. The impetus behind some modern attempts to define and delimit the form of Jesus' parables in a manner that excludes 'moral examples' provides an interesting parallel to the impetus behind Jülicher's attempt to define and delimit the essence of Jesus' παραβολαί in a way that excludes allegories:[4] Both attempts cordon off the form of Jesus' parables as 'parable inviolate', and both attempts appeal to that form as a means of establishing a guide for the 'correct' interpretation of Jesus' parables. If, as I have shown, it is exceedingly difficult to differentiate the *Beispielerzählungen* from the *Parabeln* on the basis of form or formal characteristics, and if, as Bultmann and others have shown, the *Beispielerzählungen* manifest a 'strong formal relationship' to the *Parabeln*, what then? Is it consistent to exclude any moral concern whatever from the *Parabeln Jesu* and to reserve that concern exclusively for the *Beispielerzählungen* as inauthentic παραβολαί or as peculiarly Lukan παραβολαί? We may suspect, with some justification, that the view that Jesus' authentic parables according to their essence or form lack any moral concern rests upon either a particular view of Jesus or a particular view of his 'message'. To pursue that suspicion much further would quickly lead beyond the parameters of this study, for I would need to discuss an issue that has been of critical importance in twentieth-century parable research but which has been touched upon only briefly in this study, and that issue is the relationship of eschatology to the parables of Jesus. Given some of the findings of this study and the implications that those findings may be perceived to entail, it may not be inappropriate to comment on what may be a recurring trend in parable research. At this point, a portion of the *Nachleben* of Jesus research comes back into view, and a certain historical figure emerges from the background.

A Recurrent Trend in Parable Research

If we reflect for a moment on one of the predominant views of Jesus' parables in this century—that the parables are paramount components

---

4.   The preceding examination of parable and example in the ancient rhetorical tradition suggests that an easy opposition to Jülicher on the basis of 'essences'— that Jülicher views the essence of the παραβολή as simile, whereas the essence of the παραβολή is really metaphor—is problematic.

in Jesus' eschatological proclamation of the kingdom of God—we may better understand why some modern parable scholars are reluctant to admit that Jesus' authentic parables may have had a moral concern; and that, in turn, may help us to comprehend the stigma attached to the so-called example stories as 'moral examples'. Although several distinctive versions of Jesus' view of eschatology have been advanced in this century,[5] the view expressed by Jeremias has been highly influential, especially in American parable scholarship. According to Jeremias, the evangelists and the 'primitive church', in their appropriation of Jesus' parables, shifted the emphasis away from the eschatological crisis announced by Jesus and settled for a 'hortatory' interpretation of his parables.[6] Jeremias states:

> The primitive Church saw itself, and increasingly with the passage of time, standing midway between two crises, of which one belonged to the past, the other to the future. Standing thus between the Cross and the *Parousia*, the Church, looking for the guidance of Jesus, found itself forced by the altered conditions to interpret those parables of Jesus which were intended to arouse the crowd to a sense of the gravity of the moment, as directions for the conduct of the Christian community, thus shifting the emphasis from the eschatological to the hortatory interpretation.[7]

Given the prestige that Jeremias has enjoyed among American scholars in this century, and in light of the strictures he heaped upon Jülicher, whom he castigated for advancing the jejune view that 'the parables

---

5. To provide an adequate account of the different proposals for interpreting the parables of Jesus in light of his eschatological proclamation of the kingdom of God would take us far beyond the scope of this study. For a helpful discussion of some of the developments in twentieth-century parable research that pertain to the eschatological interpretation of Jesus' parables, see I.H. Marshall, *Eschatology and the Parables* (London: Tyndale Press, 1963); Perrin, *Jesus and the Language of the Kingdom*, pp. 32-40, 65-80, 90-107; and Kissinger, *The Parables of Jesus*, pp. 89-173.

6. Jeremias, *The Parables of Jesus*, pp. 42-48, 113-14. Similar claims are made by Dibelius (*From Tradition to Gospel*, pp. 231-65) and Dodd (*The Parables of the Kingdom*, pp. 6-16, 130-39). Against those claims it should be pointed out that the evangelists and the early church did not stand alone in understanding parables as 'hortatory', for indeed a prominent first-century rhetorician recommended the use of the *similitudo* when the speaker's purpose was hortative (see above p. 367; cf. pp. 381, 387).

7. Jeremias, *The Parables of Jesus*, p. 44; emphasis in the translation.

announce a genuine religious humanity', a view which effectively strips away the 'eschatological import' of Jesus' parables,[8] it is not surprising that some scholars balk at the notion that any of Jesus' parables might have expressed moral concerns.[9]

A panoramic view of the history of parable research conducted in the last two centuries seems to indicate that there is an inverse relationship between an emphasis on the moral (ethical or religious) aspect of Jesus' proclamation of the kingdom of God in parables and an emphasis upon the eschatological aspect of Jesus' proclamation of the kingdom of God in parables. If the eschatological aspect of Jesus' parables is prioritized, then the moral aspect of his parables is commonly depreciated; conversely, if the moral or ethical aspect of Jesus' parables is elevated, then the eschatological aspect of his parables is inhibited or obscured.[10] Brad H. Young critiques the eschatological emphasis in the interpretation of Jesus' parables in this way:

> The main thrust of Jesus' eschatological message is in need of reinterpretation. One can only question to what extent this hypothetical situation can be imposed upon so many of Jesus' parables. Is Jesus to be perceived as an end times radical proclaiming imminent catastrophe? While not neglecting the eschatological aspects of Jesus' teaching, it must be observed that much of his great ethical instruction deals with practical issues of everyday life. Jeremias rightly emphasized that the parables of Jesus must be understood in light of all that can be known concerning his message. But if Dodd and Jeremias have wrongly understood the central theme of the parables, then Jesus' career is only obscured by an obsession to create an eschatological crisis.[11]

Is it time, then, to recall from exile an approach to the interpretation of Jesus' parables which emphasizes their moral aspects? That question is not as outlandish as it may first appear given recent developments in parable research, for despite the angst exhibited by some parable

8.   Jeremias, *The Parables of Jesus*, p. 19.
9.   In Chapter 4 we encountered remarks to the effect that Jesus' parables do not inculcate moral principles (see the section on 'The example stories as moral examples', pp. 166-77). See also Stein, *An Introduction to the Parables of Jesus*, pp. 55-58; and Baudler, *Jesus im Spiegel seiner Gleichnisse*, p. 65.
10.   This has been recognized by others; see, e.g., Young, *Jesus and his Jewish Parables*, pp. 26-27: 'Albert Schweitzer's work also contended that Jesus' moral instruction had been overemphasized to the great neglect of his eschatological teaching which was the primary thrust of the historical Jesus' message'.
11.   Young, *Jesus and his Jewish Parables*, p. 28.

scholars at the suggestion that any of Jesus' parables might have moral concerns, other parable scholars acknowledge that Jesus' parables, and not just the example stories, have to do with moral concerns, and rightly so.[12] Although it is likely that the re-emphasis of the moral aspect of Jesus' parables represents a move toward a more balanced view,[13] this development in parable research may be symptomatic of a larger trend in life of Jesus research which Helmut Koester incisively speaks of as 'the tendency in recent scholarship toward a noneschatological Jesus'.[14] Koester certainly does not champion that tendency; on the contrary, he finds it troubling that contemporary life of Jesus research manifests several atavistic features, one of which is this: '...the renaissance of the quest of the historical Jesus has returned full circle to a position that is not unlike that of Albrecht Ritschl and of the portraits of Jesus drawn by the nineteenth-century authors of a "life of Jesus"'.[15] Is there an emergent renaissance in parable research which parallels the renaissance of the quest for the historical Jesus as characterized by Koester? If, as this study suggests, a 'moral concern' cannot be reserved for the example stories alone, does this mean that the future of the example stories and the other parables attributed to Jesus in the synoptic gospels necessarily entails a return to 'moralizing' interpretations?

The results of this study do *not* legitimate a call for moralizing interpretations of the parables of Jesus (or the parables of the synoptic gospels). I affirm with Paul Ricoeur that we kill Jesus' parables by 'trivial moralizing'.[16] Yet I ask: Do we enervate Jesus' parables if we

---

12. Such views were encountered in Chapter 4. See also Etienne Trocmé, *Jesus and his Contemporaries* (trans. R.A. Wilson; London: SCM Press, 1973), pp. 92-96; Perkins, *Hearing the Parables of Jesus*, pp. 154-77; Kjärgaard, *Metaphor and Parable*, p. 198; Gerhardsson, 'The Narrative Meshalim in the Synoptic Gospels', pp. 361-63; Young, *Jesus and his Jewish Parables*, pp. 6, 26-33, 320; Culbertson, *A Word Fitly Spoken*, pp. 68-72; and Ivor Harold Jones, *The Matthean Parables: A Literary and Historical Commentary* (NovTSup, 80; Leiden: E.J. Brill, 1995), p. 3.

13. The resurgence of an emphasis on the moral aspect of Jesus' parables might possibly be linked to the 'New Hermeneutic' and the existential hermeneutical approaches to the interpretation of Jesus' parables, but that possibility will need to be investigated in another study.

14. Helmut Koester, 'Jesus the Victim', *JBL* 111 (1992), pp. 3-15 (7).

15. Koester, 'Jesus the Victim', p. 5.

16. Paul Ricoeur, 'Listening to the Parables of Jesus', *Criterion* 13 (Spring, 1974), pp. 18-22 (21).

remove any possibility that they may manifest a concern for virtuous behavior or a critique of ignominious behavior? Does this leave us at an impasse? Must the eschatological aspect of Jesus' parables be divorced from their moral aspect? These questions, of course, point to issues that demand further inquiry, and the following suggestion may serve as a catalyst.

A Digression: The Parables as Utopian Fictions

A conception of the parables of Jesus (and the parables of the synoptic gospels, for that matter) as utopian fictions might facilitate maintaining an appropriate degree of tension between their eschatological aspect and their 'moral' aspect. Few scholars would deny that the parables of Jesus as recorded in the synoptic gospels communicate values. The telling of parables in each of the synoptic gospels is not an innocent act; to be sure, the one who speaks the parables in the synoptic gospels is a character with a point of view.[17] The parables attributed to Jesus by the synoptic evangelists are brief narrative fictions which depict the words and deeds of certain characters—indeed, the economy of narrative details in the parables draws attention to what the characters say and do—and those words and deeds are valorized. The outcome of the parable invites the hearer to make a value judgment, to accept or reject the axiology of values communicated in and by the parable. (The problem confronting those interested in interpreting the parables of Jesus is that the parables attributed to him are embedded in narrative texts and the axiology of values expressed in those parables is usually in alignment with the values of the texts in which they are embedded, which values may or may not be those of Jesus of Nazareth.) This much covers the 'moral' aspect of the parables as utopian fictions and also points toward the eschatological. The values of the parables of Jesus are 'utopian' values to the extent that they are based upon a vision of ideal perfection in a place which is no place (οὐ τόπος), a time which is not yet, a place and a time in which the political, social and religious values of the existing world are not regnant, but are often reversed and always subjected to the 'reign of God'.

We can avail ourselves of certain insightful observations made by three scholars from different fields in order to thicken the texture of a

---

17. As Ivor Jones remarks, 'So the argument cannot be that the parables are free from ideology and cultural values' (*The Matthean Parables*, p. 141).

conception of the parables of Jesus recorded in the synoptic gospels as utopian fictions. Suleiman, a literary critic, makes a remark which can be used to give voice to the 'moral' aspect of the parables as utopian fictions. She argues that the project of all 'exemplary' narratives— parables, fables and the *roman à thèse*—is 'utopian: to modify the actions of men (and women) by telling them stories'.[18] Koester, a biblical scholar who is fully aware that Jesus' own eschatological views are inscribed in sources that display 'a bewildering variety of traditional eschatologies',[19] makes remarks which can be employed to supply the eschatological aspect of the parables as utopian fictions. Koester maintains that 'the only eschatological term that can be assigned to Jesus with certainty is "rule of God" (βασιλεία τοῦ θεοῦ)...'[20] The specifics of Jesus' own eschatology, however, are refracted in the eschatologies

18. Suleiman, *Authoritarian Fictions*, p. 54.

19. Koester, 'Jesus the Victim', p. 14. Koester indicates that there were, in addition, other competing utopian concepts of eschatology in Hellenistic societies; see pp. 10-13. Moreover, Doyne Dawson (*Cities of the Gods: Communist Utopias in Greek Thought* [Oxford: Oxford University Press, 1992]) documents that there were competing utopian traditions in antiquity. 'The main aim of [Dawson's] book is to provide an outline account of one of the most distinctive traditions of ancient Greek political thought: the literary depiction of imaginary ideal societies practicing communal property and communal family life' (p. 3). However, Dawson demonstrates that the Greek utopian tradition was not monolithic. He proposes the following typology: (1) utopian works of myth, fantasy and messianism; (2) a 'low' political utopianism; and (3) a 'high' political utopianism (see p. 7; cf. p. 5). According to Dawson: 'The first tradition goes back to some misty Indo-European past and has analogies the world over. The second, a peculiarly Greek tradition that appeared in the late fifth century B.C., had no evident connection with the first. The third was apparently invented by Plato ca. 375 B.C. and drew on both the earlier traditions' (p. 7). The second and third utopian traditions receive the bulk of Dawson's attention—indeed, the 'higher' utopian tradition is the focus of his study— although he is careful to treat facets of the first utopian tradition that possibly contributed to the political utopian thought of the philosophers (see pp. 13-52). Thus, Dawson's emphasis is on the political utopias advanced by philosophers who flourished in the fifth through the third centuries BCE. Dawson provides no significant treatment of utopian themes in religious literature of that period, but he does trace the history of utopian ideas in the Christian literature of the Roman Empire (see his chapter on 'The Ghosts of Utopia', pp. 258-90). Dawson treats the New Testament briefly, but enough to suggest that the phantasm of communist utopian thought appears most vividly in the writings of the third evangelist (see pp. 258-63).

20. Koester, 'Jesus the Victim', p. 14 n. 32.

of his followers, who had to contend with the problem posed by a specific event: the death of Jesus.

> The church had to respond to political and metaphysical systems based on ideologies of eschatological fulfillment. This response had to be given in the terms of whatever these ideologies proclaimed and could not simply be informed by whatever Jesus had said and done. After Jesus' death, continuity was no longer possible.[21]

As Koester points out, the vexing problem is whether or not the eschatological values of Jesus of Nazareth correspond to the eschatological values proclaimed by his followers. For the followers of Jesus,

> The coming of the new age through 'Jesus the victim' implied a complete reversal of all political, social, and religious values that were held sacred and holy in the world of ancient Judaism as well as in the Roman system of realized eschatology. How did the reversal of traditionally accepted values, which became the very basis of the founding of communities of the new age and the new world, correspond to the ministry of Jesus of Nazareth?[22]

Koester's response, which is quoted in full, should be given pensive review.

> Critical historical inquiry may be able to establish that in the earliest tradition of Jesus' sayings he himself proclaimed and lived such a reversal of values, that serving others rather than lording over them was the order of the rule of God, that lending to those who cannot repay their loan was the way of the new age (Luke 6.34), that loving one's enemy was the only possible response to hostility (Luke [Q] 6.27-28), that people from all the nations of the world would be invited to the feast of the kingdom (Luke [Q] 13.28-29), and that those who had nothing to lose—the poor, those who were hungry, and those who weep—would inherit it (Luke [Q] 6.20-21). Perhaps there is a vision of the community of the new age, of the rule of God, in whatever fragments of Jesus' preaching can be discerned. It is a vision that is eschatological, albeit often expressed in words that must be classified as wisdom sayings. It is a vision that reckons with God's coming, a coming that begins to be realized in the community of those who dare to follow him. And it is a universalistic vision of a banquet in which privileges of status, wealth, and religious heritage are no longer relevant. But there is no guarantee that such sayings or the inaugural sermon of Q (Luke [Q] 6.27-49) represent the preaching of the historical Jesus. Moreover, it is interesting that sayings

---

21. Koester, 'Jesus the Victim', p. 14.
22. Koester, 'Jesus the Victim', pp. 14-15.

of highly charged mythical content are rarely assigned to this Jesus by modern interpreters. In any case, the fragmentary character of these texts, even if some sayings originate with the historical Jesus, does not permit the writing of the story of his life and message—not to speak of a 'reconstruction' of the historical Jesus. Such an attempt only reveals once more the preoccupation with the search for the great human personality. It may bypass the real challenge that arises from early Christian texts, namely, to understand our world on the basis of criteria that have their origin in the proclamation of Jesus the victim. We have enough talk about great personalities of religious traditions. After Jesus died, his followers recognized that Jesus as a great human person would mean nothing, but that the kingdom of God had to be proclaimed as the utopia of a new community, a new political order, and indeed a new world.[23]

In his examination of fictional utopias in antiquity, Doyne Dawson, a classicist, makes remarks which should inform an approach to the parables as utopian fictions. One of Dawson's basic insights is that in ancient Greek cultures it was 'difficult to separate the notions of property and family',[24] and that the notions of property and family were inseparably intertwined in the household (*oikos*) as a social institution.[25] Greek utopian visions of the ideal society revolved around the concept of *koinonia* of property and the implications that had for the household.[26] If one were to pursue an investigation of the parables as utopian fictions, a good starting point would be to focus on those parables in which there is mention of households, families and property.[27]

23. Koester, 'Jesus the Victim', p. 15.

24. Dawson, *Cities of the Gods*, p. 21.

25. Dawson, *Cities of the Gods*, p. 41. We should exercise caution with this point, for, as Dawson suggests, ancient Greek economies were not 'regulated by palace and temple bureaucracies, as in the Middle Eastern civilizations' (p. 41); see his section on 'Household and City: The Social and Political Background of Greek Utopianism' (pp. 40-43).

26. Dawson points out that *koinonia* was already an ideal in Greek society, but that the philosophers extended that ideal in their utopias to total *koinonia* (*Cities of the Gods*, pp. 42-43). The basis of the 'higher' utopias was complete communism in property and family. Indeed, 'the distinguishing mark of utopian communism', according to Dawson, was that sex, marriage and family life were communal (p. 18). The basic ideals of communistic utopias included a break with separate housholds and the elimination of family ties.

27. See, e.g., the references given previously on p. 251 n. 350 and p. 256 nn. 366, 367. Herzog's study would complement such an approach nicely; see his chapter on 'The World of Agrarian Societies and Traditional Aristocratic Empires' in *Parables as Subversive Speech*, pp. 53-73.

Such an investigation should not ignore the fact that in constructing their utopias, the philosophers expressed a concern for *arete*—virtue, excellence or (if proper care is taken with the word) morality.[28] Therefore, an approach to the parables as utopian fictions ought not rule out that dimension as irrelevant.

To be sure, one of Dawson's remarks about the fictional utopias of the philosophers would hold true for the parables as utopian fictions; that is, '...one of the main purposes of the utopian method was to shock its audience into an awareness of new possibilities in human nature and society'.[29] However, even though we might well discover utopian themes and motifs manifest in the parables of the synoptic gospels, we should anticipate a different nuance vis-à-vis the fictional utopias of the philosophers. According to the testimony of the Gospels, Jesus obviously did not offer a theoretical construct of the ideal city-state, which Dawson refers to as 'cities of the gods';[30] rather, Jesus expressed a distinctive vision of facets of ideal political, societal and religious orders under the 'rule of God', and that vision had a prophetic edge. As one part of a shrewd rhetorical strategy, Jesus employed the parables to elucidate, to amplify, to vivify, to clarify aspects of his utopian vision of a new world and a new age, in which he offered a critique of the prevailing values of the society of his day by envisioning an ideal 'rule' (which is thus no place) in a future (eschatological) time (which is thus not yet). Would anyone really care to argue that Jesus did not intend for the values inherent in his vision to impinge upon the real world of the time in which he lived?

The challenge for parable scholars is to determine the place of Jesus' parables in the proclamation of the kingdom of God as a 'utopia of a new community, a new political order, and indeed a new world', while remaining aware that utopian fictions—and the manifold interpretations of them—are not necessarily and always egalitarian in essence; on the

28. See Herzog, *Parables as Subversive Speech*, pp. 41, 55-56, 95, 128, 145, 162-64, 193-95, 224-25.

29. Dawson, *Cities of the Gods*, p. 195.

30. There is a certain irony about Dawson's designation for the ideal political utopias of the philosphers, which he derives from a remark in Plato's *Laws* (739d): 'Perhaps some of the gods, or children of the gods, dwell in such cities as this' (as quoted by Dawson in the epigraph to *Cities of the Gods*; cf. p. 73). If I understand Dawson correctly, the philosophers were content, by and large, to exclude the gods and religion from their ideal city-states.

contrary, utopian fictions—and their interpretations—can become
coercive, authoritarian and totalitarian.[31] Even in utopia an economy of
power is in force.

The preceding digression should not only serve to disabuse anyone of
the notion that the results of this study lead ineluctably to the conclusion that all of the parables attributed to Jesus in the synoptic gospels,
and not just the example stories, are to be read 'only morally', but it
should also serve to circumvent such interpretations of those parables.
This digression also serves as a reminder that several important matters
pertaining to the parables of Jesus recorded in the synoptic gospels
merit further consideration and that several tasks remain to be carried
out by others in the next century of parable research. While this study
may have clarified some issues in the debate that centers on the category 'example story', it does not signal the end of all debate on the
problems posed by the classification of four parables in the Gospel of
Luke as 'example stories'. Future research will add even greater clarity
to some of the issues addressed in this study, and a rehearsal of the
findings obtained here might serve to indicate some of the issues others
may wish to pursue.

The Future of the Example Stories

The examination of various views on the parable and the example in
the ancient rhetorical tradition conducted in Chapter 5 of this study
produced enough evidence to suggest that some of the problems in the
debate over 'the problem of parables versus examples' are the result of
a mismatch of conventions and that some of those problems are compounded by confusion over what is meant by 'example'. Some biblical
scholars have erroneous conceptions of what several ancient rhetoricians mean by 'example'; other biblical scholars remain unaware that
the παράδειγμα and *exemplum*, like the παραβολή and *similitudo*, are
comparative devices; still others do not realize that certain rhetoricians
valued the *similitudo*, and not just the *exemplum*, as useful in achieving
a hortative effect.

31. Throughout *Authoritarian Fictions*, Suleiman points to the very real possibility that utopian fictions can become coercive, authoritarian and totalitarian.
Dawson proves the point in his analysis of Plato's utopia, which does have its
egalitarian side, but which also has a hierarchichal, authoritarian and totalitarian
side; see *Cities of the Gods*, pp. 77-91.

The ancient rhetorical tradition does not support Jülicher's classification of the παραβολαί *Jesu* into *Gleichnisse*, *Parabeln* and *Beispielerzählungen*; indeed, in light of a review of parable and example in the ancient rhetorical tradition, both the category 'example story' as proposed by a number of parable scholars and the categorical distinction between *Parabeln* and *Beispielerzählungen* are, if not indefensible, then certainly problematic. According to the last four ancient rhetoricians consulted in the preceding chapter, there is no dichotomy stated in terms of 'parable versus example', rather, as embellishments there are parables and there are examples; and according to two rhetoricians, as proofs the parables *are* examples. If, according to Aristotle and Quintilian, the term 'example' (παράδειγμα) applies to the 'parable' (παραβολή), then the categorical distinction between parable and example story as proposed by a number of parable scholars must be regarded as superfluous. Those findings, however, are provisional because I consulted but a few of the many rhetorical treatises available to us. An examination of parable and example in other ancient rhetorical treatises might well uphold the findings of this study, but it could also necessitate a revision of some of the findings obtained here.

Quite a bit of work on the parable and example in the ancient rhetorical tradition obviously remains to be done. Although I have shown that in several ancient rhetorical treatises the parable and the example are comparative devices that can be used for a variety of purposes, a comprehensive understanding of the conventional expectations associated with the parable and the example has not been furnished here.[32] An investigation of parable and example in the progymnasmata would certainly contribute to our understanding of the conventional expectations associated with both of those comparative devices in ancient rhetoric.[33] While the focus of this study has been on the relationship between the parable and the example, we have seen nonetheless that the

---

32. The direct application of rhetorical theory to the synoptic gospels presents problems, for the Gospels are narrative texts, not rational arguments in carefully planned speeches spoken by skilled orators. Wolfgang Harnisch sounds the proper note of warning in 'Die Sprachkraft der Analogie: Zur These vom "argumentativen Charakter" der Gleichnisse Jesu', *ST* 28 (1974), pp. 1-20 (repr. in Harnisch [ed.], *Gleichnisse Jesu*, pp. 238-55).

33. This work has already begun; see Mack and Robbins, *Patterns of Persuasion in the Gospels*, pp. 1-68. The late date of the progymnasmata is a matter that must be taken into account.

παραβολή is mentioned in conjunction with a variety of other comparative devices—for instance, σύγκρισις, simile, metaphor and allegory—and an investigation of those relationships would be illuminating,[34] for in several of the ancient rhetorical treatises consulted here the relationships between parable, simile, metaphor and allegory are more involved than Jülicher and others have led us to believe.[35] The ancient rhetorical tradition offers up a variety of precepts on the many facets and components of rhetoric. Although an appeal to the ancient rhetorical tradition can safeguard against a mismatch of conventions with respect to the parable and the example, the precepts of a single rhetorician should not be absolutized and then employed to make rigid claims about the parables recorded in the synoptic gospels. Perhaps, modern interpreters of the parables could learn from the ancient rhetoricians not to countenance a restrictive view of the parable.

For nearly two thousand years The Merciful Samaritan, The Foolish Rich Man, The Rich Man and Poor Lazarus, and The Pharisee and the Toll Collector have shared the bond of a common narrative context in the Gospel of Luke, and that bond remains as firm as ever. Of all the many characteristics and features identified in attempts to establish the peculiarity of the 'example stories', only one feature unites them as a group: Those four parables depict specifically named characters or groups of characters, and moreover characters or groups of characters who appear in the larger narrative context of the Gospel of Luke. However, that feature does not establish the uniqueness of the example stories, for named characters also appear in some rabbinic parables and in parables quoted by some ancient rhetoricians, and other synoptic parables depict groups of characters who also appear in the larger narrative contexts of their respective Gospels.

We have seen that several scholars, including Jülicher, are vaguely aware that something about the characters in the 'example stories' appears to be distinctive. I offered an explanation for that: The appearance of named characters or groups of characters in the 'example stories' may be a contributing factor to several claims advanced with

34. As Price indicates ('Παράδειγμα and *Exemplum* in Ancient Rhetorical Theory', p. 280 n. 24), 'Παραβολή is also used very broadly as a rhetorical term meaning "comparison"…Unfortunately there is no one source where the various definitions and uses of *parabole* have been collected…'

35. Do Cicero and Quintilian maintain that the *similitudo* and the metaphor differ in essence? Do they allow for the use of *similitudo* and metaphor in allegory?

respect to their uniqueness, or even their 'relative peculiarity'; for instance, that the 'example stories' present a more particular case, that they are 'more direct', that they make a 'rhetorical claim to historicity', or even that they are 'real stories'. The fictional quality of these four parables is perceived as being disrupted by the depiction of characters identified by proper name or groups of characters designated by name, especially when those characters or groups of characters have counterparts in the 'real' world. This feature does heighten the verisimilitude of the example stories, but that does not mean that these narratives are 'less figurative' or 'literal'—indeed, from an ancient rhetorical perspective, an increase in the verisimilitude of parables and examples makes them more plausible. I have also offered the explanation that the appearance of characters and places identified by specifications 'of a socio-religious nature' in the example stories may contribute to the view that they are peculiar because they already move on 'the higher plane of religion', or because the distance between their *Bildhälfte* and *Sachhälfte* is decreased significantly, or even because they 'lack any element of the pictorial'.[36] However, the force of the claim that the '*Beispielerzählung*' are unique because they have 'religion' as their content is weakened by the observation that other Lukan *Parabeln* contain mention of things religious, and by the observation that some parables in ancient rhetorical treatises mention things religious and beings divine. The uniqueness or 'relative peculiarity' of the 'example stories' cannot be established on the basis of the fact that they depict named characters or groups of characters.

Nevertheless, as I have suggested, the peculiarly Lukan cast of characters in The Merciful Samaritan, The Foolish Rich Man, The Rich Man and Poor Lazarus, and The Pharisee and the Toll Collector gives a

---

36. If the premise that the parables are comprised of two planes (or levels) and always reference the kingdom of God is accepted for a moment, we could take a different angle of approach and ask this: Does the decreased distance between the earthly sphere and the heavenly sphere in the 'example stories' indicate only that the 'example stories' already move on the higher plane, or might it suggest that the boundary between those two spheres is permeable? What if, as the so-called 'example stories' would then seem to intimate, the heavenly sphere irrupts into the earthly sphere? What if that irruption materializes in the religious activities of those who inhabit the earthly sphere? If, as we have been told, the parables of Jesus envision the inbreaking of the kingdom of God, does anyone really wish to hold to the position that Jesus' vision of the rule of God has no ramifications for the religions of the world?

peculiarly Lukan cast to those four parables. I do not take this to mean that those four parables are Lukan creations.[37] The fact that a version of The Foolish Rich Man can be found in the *Gospel of Thomas* rules out the conclusion that the third evangelist created that parable, and it is not implausible that the third evangelist had access to a source containing other parables spoken by Jesus of Nazareth. Those four parables, however, are clearly Lukan productions—or, if it makes the notion more palatable, Lukan (re)productions—to the extent that the third evangelist supervised and controlled the manner in which they were to be presented to the public. I have shown that one particular thing the third evangelist did in his presentation of those four parables was to have Jesus, the one who narrates those parables, depict characters or groups of characters who also play a role in the larger Gospel narrative of which he himself is a part. Thus, a particularly interesting avenue of approach to those four parables would be to conduct a sustained study of how the characterization of the named individuals or groups in those narratives embedded in the Gospel of Luke contributes to the characterization of those individuals or groups in the larger Gospel narrative.[38] If the economy of narrative details in the parables draws attention to what the characters do or say, then the added detail of names in the four Lukan parables that have been identified as 'example stories' draws attention to what specific characters do or say; if the parables invite the hearer or reader to make a value judgment about the words and deeds of unnamed characters, then the so-called 'example stories' invite the hearer or reader to make a value judgment about the words and deeds of specific characters. An exploration of the interplay between the fictional world of those parables and the narrative world of the text in which they are embedded could yield provocative results. Such a study

37. In agreement with Heininger, who makes the claim that it is not necessary to conclude that Luke wrote the 'L' parables (*Metaphorik*, p. 219).

38. A number of recent studies treat characters and characterization in the Gospel of Luke; see, e.g., Robert L. Brawley, *Centering on God: Method and Message in Luke–Acts* (Literary Currents in Biblical Interpretation; Louisville, KY: Westminster/John Knox Press, 1990), pp. 107-58; Jack Dean Kingsbury, *Conflict in Luke: Jesus, Authorities, Disciples* (Minneapolis: Fortress Press, 1991), pp. 9-34; David B. Gowler, *Host, Guest, Enemy and Friend: Portraits of the Pharisees in Luke and Acts* (Emory Studies in Early Christianity, 2; New York: Peter Lang, 1991); and John A. Darr, *On Character Building: The Reader and the Rhetoric of Characterization in Luke–Acts* (Literary Currents in Biblical Interpretation; Louisville, KY: Westminster/John Knox Press, 1992).

might demonstrate that those four parables are thoroughly Lukan productions which serve purposes thoroughly Lukan.[39]

A Name for the Example Stories

The prize for this extensive and detailed examination of the 'example stories' in over a century and a half of parable research is the knowledge that there is little in the way of probative, incontrovertible evidence to warrant (1) categorizing four parables in the Gospel of Luke—The Merciful Samaritan, The Foolish Rich Man, The Rich Man and Poor Lazarus, The Pharisee and the Toll Collector—as example stories, or (2) maintaining a categorical distinction between the *Parabeln* and the *Beispielerzählungen*. The classification of those four parables in the Gospel of Luke as 'example stories' does not withstand scrutiny. This outcome may be perceived as predominately negative, for I have not only called into question many of the reasons given for conceiving of these four Lukan παραβολαί as 'example stories', but I have also called into question the category itself. If this study takes away, it also gives back in return, for now scholars—according to their interests and without compunction—should feel free to interpret the four erstwhile 'example stories' as parables, either as parables of Jesus or as parables of the Gospel of Luke.

This study does not issue a call for the end of all attempts to classify the parables attributed to Jesus in the synoptic gospels. Classifying the parables of Jesus recorded in those Gospels is not a 'fruitless labor', a valueless exercise; on the contrary, classifying or grouping those parables can serve productive and useful purposes.[40] A number of classifications of the parables of Jesus have been introduced in this study, and doubtlessly other classification schemes will be constructed in the future. This study suggests, however, that as parable research moves into the twenty-first century, it should move forward without the classification of four parables in the Gospel of Luke as 'example stories'. The codification of '*Beispielerzählung*' as a form-critical *Gattung*

39. One of those purposes, evident in each of the four so-called example stories, is treated thoroughly by John O. York, *The Last Shall Be First: The Rhetoric of Reversal in Luke* (JSNTSup, 46; Sheffield: JSOT Press, 1991), pp. 62-80, 104-106, 126-33.

40. On the benefits of grouping or clustering the parables, see Tolbert, *Perspectives on the Parables*, pp. 83-89.

needs to be reassessed, rethought, revised or perhaps—if the findings of this study are deemed to have undermined the validity of the *Gattung* 'example story'—relinquished. My own opinion is that the categorical distinction between 'parables' and 'example stories' is superfluous, that the category 'example story' is vacuous and should be abandoned. Nevertheless, it must be emphasized that my perspective on those four parables in the Gospel of Luke is but one among many. Even if future generations of parable scholars reject the conclusions of this study, it will have contributed to a situation in which an informed choice can be made from among the many perspectives on the 'example stories', as well as from among other classifications of the parables attributed to Jesus in the synoptic gospels. Those choices should be made with Suleiman's words in mind, for what she says of genres obtains also for categories, forms, classes and *Gattungen*:

> ...the perception and the naming of the genre are interpretive and evalu-ative acts, which indicate, prior to any commentary, a certain attitude on the part of the reader or critic. One can probably say the same thing about all genres: to name them is already to interpret them by half.[41]

If we choose to be consistent with the findings of this study and thus renounce the category and the name by which The Merciful Samaritan, The Foolish Rich Man, The Rich Man and Poor Lazarus, and The Phar-isee and the Toll Collector have been bound for over a century— 'example story' or '*Beispielerzählung*'—then how shall we refer to them? We might opt to refrain from using the term 'example story', but that term will not be effaced easily for it has been inscribed, perhaps indelibly, in parable scholarship for generations of interpreters to read. We could choose to employ the name 'example story' and then put it under erasure, for indeed the trace of that category has been impressed firmly upon those four parables in the Gospel of Luke, so firmly per-haps that even if the name remains unspoken, the words unwritten, the name of that category will continue to track them down in the century to come. In the end, to prepare the way for the future of those four parables in the Gospel of Luke, it might be best to opt for a name from the past and elect to call each one what an ancient authority, the writer who (re)produced all four, chose to call two of them, and then each one will always be, as it already was, a παραβολή.

---

41. Suleiman, *Authoritarian Fictions*, p. 4.

BIBLIOGRAPHY

Achtemeier, Paul J., '*Omne verbum sonat*: The New Testament and the Oral Environment of Late Western Antiquity', *JBL* 109 (1990), pp. 3-27.

Alewell, Karl, 'Über das rhetorische ΠΑΡΑΔΕΙΓΜΑ: Theorie, Beispielsammlungen, Verwendung in der römischen Literatur der Kaiserzeit' (PhD dissertation, University of Kiel, 1913).

[Anaximanes], *Rhetorica ad Alexandrum*, in *Aristotle, Problems II, Books XXII–XXXVIII, Rhetorica ad Alexandrum* (trans. W.S. Hett and H. Rackham; LCL; London: Heinemann; Cambridge, MA: Harvard University Press, 1937).

Aristotle, *'Art' of Rhetoric*, in *Aristotle, 'Art' of Rhetoric* (trans. John H. Freese; LCL; London: Heinemann; Cambridge, MA: Harvard University Press, 1926; [repr. 1982]).

Assion, Peter, 'Das Exempel als agitatorische Gattung: Zu Form und Funktion der kurzen Beispielgeschichte', *Fabula* 19 (1978), pp. 225-40.

Baasland, Ernst, 'Zum Beispiel der Beispielerzählungen: Zur Formenlehre der Gleichnisse und zur Methodik der Gleichnisauslegung', *NovT* 28 (1986), pp. 193-219.

Bailey, Kenneth E., *Poet and Peasant: A Literary-Cultural Approach to the Parables in Luke* (Grand Rapids: Eerdmans, 1976).

—*Through Peasant Eyes: More Lukan Parables, their Culture and Style* (Grand Rapids: Eerdmans, 1980).

Baudler, Georg, *Jesus im Spiegel seiner Gleichnisse: Das erzählerische Lebenswerk Jesu— Ein Zugang zum Glauben* (Stuttgart: Calwer Verlag; Munich: Kösel, 1986).

Bausinger, Hermann, 'Exemplum und Beispiel', *Hessische Blätter für Volkskunde* 59 (1968), pp. 31-43.

—'Zum Beispiel', in Fritz Harkort, Karel C. Peeters and Robert Wildhaber (eds.), *Volksüberlieferung* (Festschrift für Kurt Ranke zur Vollendung des 60. Lebensjahres; Göttingen: Otto Schwartz & Co., 1968), pp. 9-18.

Beardslee, William A., 'Recent Literary Criticism', in Eldon Jay Epp and George W. MacRae (eds.), *The New Testament and its Modern Interpreters* (SBLBMI, 3; Atlanta: Scholars Press, 1989), pp. 175-98.

Beck, David R., 'The Narrative Function of Anonymity in Fourth Gospel Characterization', *Semeia* 63 (1993), pp. 143-58.

Benoit, William Lyon, 'Aristotle's Example: The Rhetorical Induction', *Quarterly Journal of Speech* 66 (1980), pp. 182-92.

Berger, Klaus, *Formgeschichte des Neuen Testaments* (Heidelberg: Quelle and Meyer, 1984).

—'Hellenistische Gattungen im Neuen Testament', in *ANRW*, 25.2, pp. 1031-432.

—'Materialien zu Form und Überlieferungsgeschichte neutestamentlicher Gleichnisse', *NovT* 75 (1973), pp. 1-37.

Bitzer, Lloyd F., 'Aristotle's Enthymeme Revisited', *Quarterly Journal of Speech* 45 (1959), pp. 399-408 (repr. in Keith V. Erickson [ed.], *Aristotle: The Classical Heritage of Rhetoric* [Metuchen, NJ: Scarecrow Press, 1974], pp. 141-55).

Black, Matthew, 'The Parables as Allegory', *BJRL* 42 (1960), pp. 273-87.

Blackman, E.C., 'New Methods of Parable Interpretation', *CJT* 15 (1969), pp. 3-13.

Blomberg, Craig L., *Interpreting the Parables* (Downers Grove, IL: InterVarsity Press, 1990).

Booth, Wayne C., *The Rhetoric of Fiction* (Chicago: University of Chicago Press, 2nd edn, 1983).

Boucher, Madeleine, *The Mysterious Parable: A Literary Study* (CBQMS, 6; Washington, DC: Catholic Biblical Association, 1977).

—*The Parables* (New Testament Message, 7; Wilmington, DE: Michael Glazier, rev. edn, 1983).

Bovon, François, *Luc le théologien: Vingt-cinq ans de recherches (1950–1975)* (Neuchâtel: Delachaux & Niestlé, 1978).

Brawley, Robert L., *Centering on God: Method and Message in Luke–Acts* (Literary Currents in Biblical Interpretation; Louisville, KY: Westminster/John Knox Press, 1990).

Breech, Earl, 'Kingdom of God and the Parables of Jesus', *Semeia* 12 (1978), pp. 15-40.

Breech, James, *The Silence of Jesus: The Authentic Voice of the Historical Man* (Philadelphia: Fortress Press, 1983).

Brodie, Thomas Louis, 'Greco-Roman Imitation of Texts as a Partial Guide to Luke's Use of Sources', in Charles H. Talbert (ed.), *Luke–Acts: New Perspectives from the Society of Biblical Literature Seminar* (New York: Crossroad, 1984), pp. 7-46.

Brown, Frank Burch, and Elizabeth Struthers Malbon, 'Parabling as a *Via Negativa*: A Critical Review of the Work of John Dominic Crossan', *JR* 64 (1984), pp. 530-38.

Brown, Raymond E., 'Parable and Allegory Reconsidered', *NovT* 5 (1962), pp. 36-45.

Bruce, Alexander Balmain, *The Parabolic Teaching of Christ: A Systematic and Critical Study of the Parables of Our Lord* (New York: Armstrong & Son, 3rd rev. edn, 1898).

Bugge, Christian August, *Die Haupt-Parabeln Jesu* (Giessen: J. Ricker'sche Verlagsbuchhandlung, 1903).

Bultmann, Rudolf, *Die Geschichte der synoptischen Tradition* (FRLANT, 29; Göttingen: Vandenhoeck & Ruprecht, 8th edn, 1970).

—'Gleichnis und Parabel. II. In der Bibel', in Hermann Gunkel and Leopold Zscharnack (eds.), *Die Religion in Geschichte und Gegenwart: Handwörterbuch für Theologie und Religionswissenschaft* (Tübingen: J.C.B. Mohr [Paul Siebeck], 2nd rev. edn, 1928), II, pp. 1238-42.

—*The Historical Jesus and the Kerygmatic Christ* (trans. and ed. Carl E. Braaten and Roy A. Harrisville; Nashville: Abingdon Press, 1964).

—*History of the Synoptic Tradition* (trans. John Marsh; New York: Harper & Row, rev. edn, 1963).

Butts, James R., 'The "Progymnasmata" of Theon: A New Text with Translation and Commentary' (PhD dissertation, Claremont Graduate School, 1986).

Buzy, P. Dionisio, *Introduction aux paraboles évangéliques* (Paris: J. Gabalda, 1912).

Cadoux, A.T., *The Parables of Jesus* (New York: Macmillan, 1931).

Carlston, Charles E., 'Changing Fashions in Interpreting the Parables', *ANQ* 14 (1974), pp. 227-33.

—'Parable and Allegory Revisited: An Interpretive Review', *CBQ* 43 (1981), pp. 228-42.

—*The Parables of the Triple Tradition* (Philadelphia: Fortress Press, 1975).

Champion, James, 'The Parable as an Ancient and Modern Form', *Journal of Literature & Theology* 3 (1989), pp. 16-39.

Cheyne, T.K., and J. Sutherland Black (eds.), *Encyclopædia Biblica* (4 vols.; New York: Macmillan, 1899–1903).

Cicero, *De Inventione*, in *Cicero, De Inventione, De Optimo Genere Oratorium, Topica* (trans. H.M. Hubbell; LCL; London: Heinemann; Cambridge, MA: Harvard University Press, 1949).

—*De Oratore*, in *Cicero, De Oratore, Books I–II* (trans. E.W. Sutton and H. Rackham; LCL; London: Heinemann; Cambridge, MA: Harvard University Press, 1942 [repr. 1979]).

—*De Oratore*, in *Cicero, De Oratore, Books III, De Fato, Paradoxa Stoicorium, De Partitione Oratoria* (trans. H. Rackham; LCL; London: Heinemann; Cambridge, MA: Harvard University Press, 1942 [repr. 1992]).

[Cicero], *Rhetorica ad Herennium*, in [Cicero] *Ad C. Herennium de ratione dicendi (Rhetorica ad Herennium)* (trans. Harry Caplan; LCL; London: Heinemann; Cambridge, MA: Harvard University Press, 1954 [repr. 1981]).

Clark, Donald L., *Rhetoric in Greco-Roman Education* (New York: Columbia University Press, 1957).

Consigny, Scott, 'The Rhetorical Example', *The Southern Speech Communication Journal* 41 (1976), pp. 121-34.

Conzelmann, Hans, and Andreas Lindemann, *Interpreting the New Testament: An Introduction to the Principles and Methods of N.T. Exegesis* (trans. Siegfried S. Schatzmann; Peabody, MA: Hendrickson, 1988).

Cope, Edward M., *An Introduction to Aristotle's Rhetoric with Analysis Notes and Appendices* (London: Macmillan, 1867 [repr. Dubuque, IA: William C. Brown Reprint Library]).

—*The Rhetoric of Aristotle with a Commentary* (3 vols.; rev. and ed. John E. Sandys; Cambridge: Cambridge University Press, 1877 [repr. Dubuque, IA: William C. Brown Reprint Library]).

Crespy, Georges, 'La parabole dite: "Le bon Samaritan": Recherches structurales', *ETR* 48 (1973), pp. 61-79.

—'The Parable of the Good Samaritan: An Essay in Structural Research' (trans. John Kirby), *Semeia* 2 (1974), pp. 27-50.

Crossan, John Dominic, 'A Basic Bibliography for Parables Research', *Semeia* 1 (1974), pp. 236-73.

—*The Dark Interval: Towards a Theology of Story* (Allen, TX: Argus Communications, 1975).

—'The Good Samaritan: Towards a Generic Definition of Parable', *Semeia* 2 (1974), pp. 82-112.

—*In Parables: The Challenge of the Historical Jesus* (New York: Harper & Row, 1973).

—'Parable and Example in the Teaching of Jesus', *NTS* 18 (1972), pp. 285-307 (repr. in *Semeia* 1 [1974], pp. 63-104).

—*Raid on the Articulate: Comic Eschatology in Jesus and Borges* (New York: Harper & Row, 1976).

—Review of *Metaphor and Parable: A Systematic Analysis of the Specific Structure and Cognitive Function of the Synoptic Similes and Parables qua Metaphor* (ATDan, 29; Leiden: E.J. Brill, 1986), by Mogens Stiller Kjärgaard, *JBL* 108 (1989), pp. 148-50.

—'Structuralist Analysis and the Parables of Jesus: A Reply to D.O. Via, Jr., "Parable and Example Story: A Literary-Structuralist Approach"', *Semeia* 1 (1974), pp. 192-221.

Culbertson, Philip L., *A Word Fitly Spoken: Context, Transmission, and Adoption of the Parables of Jesus* (Albany, NY: State University of New York Press, 1995).

Culler, Jonathan, *Structuralist Poetics: Structuralism, Lingusitics, and the Study of Literature* (Ithaca, NY: Cornell University Press, 1975).

Darr, John A., *On Character Building: The Reader and the Rhetoric of Characterization in Luke–Acts* (Literary Currents in Biblical Interpretation; Louisville, KY: Westminster/John Knox Press, 1992).

Dawson, Doyne, *Cities of the Gods: Communist Utopias in Greek Thought* (Oxford: Oxford University Press, 1992).

Derrida, Jacques, *Of Grammatology* (trans. Gayatri Chakravorty Spivak; Baltimore: The Johns Hopkins University Press, 1976).

Dibelius, Martin, *From Tradition to Gospel* (trans. Bertram Lee Woolf; Cambridge: James Clark and Co., 1971).

Dodd, C.H., *The Parables and the Kingdom* (New York: Charles Scribner's Sons, rev. edn, 1961).

Donahue, John R., *The Gospel in Parable: Metaphor, Narrative, and Theology in the Synoptic Gospels* (Philadelphia: Fortress Press, 1988).

Drury, John, *The Parables in the Gospels: History and Allegory* (New York: Crossroad, 1985).

Dundes, Alan, (ed.), *The Study of Folklore* (Englewood Cliffs, NJ: Prentice–Hall, 1965).

Dupont, Jacques, *Pourquoi des paraboles? La méthode parabolique de Jésus* (Lire la Bible, 46; Paris: Cerf, 1977).

Eaton, David, 'Jülicher on the Parables', *ExpTim* 11 (1899–1900), p. 300.

—'Professor Jülicher on the Parables of Jesus', *ExpTim* 10 (1898–99), pp. 539-43.

Eichholz, Georg, *Gleichnisse der Evangelien: Form, Überlieferung, Auslegung* (Neukirchen–Vluyn: Neukirchener Verlag, 1971).

Epp, Eldon Jay, and George W. MacRae (eds.), *The New Testament and its Modern Interpreters* (SBLBMI, 3; Atlanta: Scholars Press, 1989).

Erickson, Keith V. (ed.), *Aristotle: The Classical Heritage of Rhetoric* (Metuchen, NJ: Scarecrow Press, 1974).

Farmer, William R., 'Notes on a Literary and Form-Critical Analysis of Some of the Synoptic Material Peculiar to Luke', *NTS* 8 (1962), pp. 301-16.

Fascher, Erich, *Die formgeschichtliche Methode: Eine Darstellung und Kritik: Zugleich ein Beitrag zur Geschichte des synoptische Problems* (Beihefte zur Zeitschrift für die neutestamentliche Wissenschaft und die Kunde der älteren Kirche, 2; Giessen: Alfred Töpelmann, 1924).

Fiebig, Paul, *Altjüdische Gleichnisse und die Gleichnisse Jesu* (Tübingen: J.C.B. Mohr [Paul Siebeck], 1904).

—*Die Gleichnisreden Jesu im Lichte der rabbinischen Gleichnisse des neutestamentlichen Zeitalters: Ein Beitrag zum Streit um die 'Christusmythe' und eine Widerlegung der Gleichnistheorie Jülichers* (Tübingen: J.C.B. Mohr [Paul Siebeck], 1912).

Fiore, Benjamin, *The Function of Personal Example in the Socratic and Pastoral Epistles* (AnBib, 105; Rome: Biblical Institute Press, 1986).

Fitzmyer, Joseph A., *The Gospel According to Luke (I–IX): Introduction, Translation, and Notes* (AB, 28; Garden City, NY: Doubleday, 1981).

—*Luke the Theologian: Aspects of his Teaching* (Mahwah, NJ: Paulist Press, 1989).

Flusser, David, *Die rabbinischen Gleichnisse und der Gleichniserzähler Jesus. I. Das Wesen der Gleichnisse* (Judaica et Christiana, 4; Bern: Peter Lang, 1981).

Foakes-Jackson, F.J., and Kirsopp Lake (eds.), *The Beginnings of Christianity. Part 1: The Acts of the Apostles* (5 vols.; London: Macmillan, 1920–33).

Foley, John Miles (ed.), *Oral Tradition in Literature: Interpretation and Context* (Columbia, MO: University of Missouri Press, 1986).

Forbes, Christopher, 'Comparison, Self-Praise and Irony: Paul's Boasting and the Conventions of Hellenistic Rhetoric', *NTS* 32 (1986), pp. 1-30.

France, R.T., and David Wenham (eds.), *Gospel Perspectives II* (Sheffield: JSOT Press, 1981).

Funk, Robert W., 'Critical Note', *Semeia* 1 (1974), pp. 182-91.

—'Foreword', in Warren S. Kissinger, *The Parables of Jesus: A History of Interpretation and Bibliography* (American Theological Library Association Bibliography Series, 4; Metuchen, NJ: Scarecrow Press, 1979).

—'The Good Samaritan as Metaphor', *Semeia* 2 (1974), pp. 74-81.

—*Parables and Presence: Forms of the New Testament Tradition* (Philadelphia: Fortress Press, 1982).

—*Language, Hermeneutic, and Word of God: The Problem of Language in the New Testament and Contemporary Theology* (New York: Harper & Row, 1966).

—'Structure in the Narrative Parables of Jesus', *Semeia* 2 (1974), pp. 51-73.

Funk, Robert W., Bernard Brandon Scott and James R. Butts, *The Parables of Jesus: Red Letter Edition: A Report of the Jesus Seminar* (The Jesus Seminar Series; Sonoma, CA: Polebridge Press, 1988).

Gasque, Ward, *A History of the Criticism of the Acts of the Apostles* (BGBE, 17; Tübingen: J.C.B. Mohr [Paul Siebeck], 1975).

Gelley, Alexander, 'The Pragmatics of Exemplary Narrative', in *idem* (ed.), *Unruly Examples: On the Rhetoric of Exemplarity*, pp. 142-61.

—(ed.), *Unruly Examples: On the Rhetoric of Exemplarity* (Stanford, CA: Stanford University Press, 1995).

Gerhardsson, Birger, *The Good Samaritan—The Good Shepherd?* (*ConNT*, 16; Lund: C.W.K. Gleerup, 1958).

—'The Narrative Meshalim in the Synoptic Gospels: A Comparison with the Narrative Meshalim in the Old Testament', *NTS* 34 (1988), pp. 339-63.

Göbel, Siegfried, *Die Parabeln Jesu methodisch ausgelegt* (2 vols.; Gotha: Friedrich Andreas Perthes, 1879).

—*The Parables of Jesus: A Methodological Exposition* (trans. Professor Banks; Edinburgh: T. & T. Clark, 1883).

Goulder, M.D., 'Characteristics of the Parables in the Several Gospels', *JTS* 19 (1968), pp. 51-69.

Gowler, David B., *Host, Guest, Enemy, and Friend: Portraits of the Pharisees in Luke and Acts* (Emory Studies in Early Christianity, 2; New York: Peter Lang, 1991).

Granskou, David M., *Preaching on the Parables* (Philadelphia: Fortress Press, 1972).

Grässer, Erich, 'Acta-Forschung seit 1960', *TRu* 41 (1976), pp. 141-94.

—'Acta-Forschung seit 1960', *TRu* 42 (1977), pp. 1-68.

Example Stories

424   *Example Stories*

Greeven, Heinrich, '"Wer unter Euch...?"', *Wort und Dienst*, NS, 3 (1952), pp. 86-101 (repr. in Wolfgang Harnisch [ed.], *Gleichnisse Jesu: Positionen der Auslegung von Adolf Jülicher bis zur Formgeschichte* [Wege der Forschung, 366; Darmstadt: Wissenschaftliche Buchgesellschaft, 1982], pp. 238-55).

Grimm, Jacob, and Wilhelm Grimm, *Deutsches Wörterbuch* (16 vols.; ed. Deutschen Akademie der Wissenschaften zu Berlin; Leipzig: Verlag von S. Hirzel, 1854–1954).

Groupe d'Entrevernes, *Signes et paraboles: Sémiotique et texte évangélique* (Paris: Seuil, 1977).

—*Signs and Parables: Semiotics and Gospel Texts* (trans. Gary Phillips; PTMS, 23; Pittsburgh: Pickwick Press, 1978).

Gunkel, Hermann, and Leopold Zscharnack (eds.), *Die Religion in Geschichte und Gegenwart: Handwörterbuch für Theologie und Religionswissenschaft* (5 vols.; Tübingen: J.C.B. Mohr [Paul Siebeck], 2nd rev. edn, 1927–31).

Güttgemanns, Erhardt, 'Einleitende Bemerkungen zur strukturalen Erzählforschung', *LB* 23/24 (1973), pp. 2-47.

—'Introductory Remarks Concerning the Structural Study of Narrative' (trans. William G. Doty), *Semeia* 6 (1976), pp. 23-126.

—'Die linguistische-didaktische Methodik der Gleichnisse Jesu', in *idem, Studia linguistica neotestamentica: Gesammelte Aufsätze zur linguistischen Grundlage einer neutestamentlichen Theologie* (BEvT, 60; Munich: Chr. Kaiser Verlag, 1971), pp. 125-37.

—'Narrative Analyse synoptischer Texte', *LB* 25/26 (1973), pp. 50-72 (repr. in Wolfgang Harnisch [ed.], *Die neutestamentliche Gleichnisforschung im Horizont von Hermeneutik und Literaturwissenschaft* [Wege der Forschung, 575; Darmstadt: Wissenschaftliche Buchgesellschaft, 1982], pp. 179-223).

—'Narrative Analysis of Synoptic Texts' (trans. William G. Doty), *Semeia* 6 (1976), pp. 127-79.

—*Studia linguistica neotestamentica: Gesammelte Aufsätze zur linguistischen Grundlage einer Neutestamentlichen Theologie* (BEvT, 60; Munich: Chr. Kaiser Verlag, 1971).

Harkort, Fritz, Karel C. Peeters and Robert Wildhaber (eds.), *Volksüberlieferung* (Festschrift für Kurt Ranke zur Vollendung des 60. Lebensjahres; Göttingen: Otto Schwartz & Co., 1968).

Harnisch, Wolfgang, 'Die Sprachkraft der Analogie: Zur These vom "argumentative Charakter" der Gleichnisse Jesu', *ST* 28 (1974), pp. 1-20 (repr. in *idem* [ed.], *Gleichnisse Jesu: Positionen der Auslegung von Adolf Jülicher bis zur Formgeschichte* [Wege der Forschung, 366; Darmstadt: Wissenschaftliche Buchgesellschaft, 1982], pp. 238-55).

Harnisch, Wolfgang (ed.), *Gleichnisse Jesu: Positionen der Auslegung von Adolf Jülicher bis zur Formgeschichte* (Wege der Forschung, 366; Darmstadt: Wissenschaftliche Buchgesellschaft, 1982).

—*Die neutestamentliche Gleichnisforschung im Horizont von Hermeneutik und Literaturwissenschaft* (Wege der Forschung, 575; Darmstadt: Wissenschaftliche Buchgesellschaft, 1982).

Harrington, Wilfred J., 'The Parables in Recent Study (1960–1971)', *BTB* 2 (1972), pp. 219-41.

Harris, William V., *Ancient Literacy* (Cambridge, MA: Harvard University Press, 1989).

Hauck, Friedrich, 'παραβολή', in *TDNT*, V, pp. 744-61.

Hauser, Gerard A., 'Aristotle's Example Revisited', *Philosophy and Rhetoric* 18 (1985), pp. 171-80.

—'The Example in Aristotle's *Rhetoric*: Bifurcation or Contradiction?', *Philosophy and Rhetoric* 1 (1968), pp. 78-90 (repr. in Erickson [ed.], *The Classical Heritage of Rhetoric*, pp. 156-68).

Hedrick, Charles W., 'Parables and the Kingdom: The Vision of Jesus in Fiction and Faith', in Kent Harold Richards (ed.), *Society of Biblical Literature 1987 Seminar Papers* (Atlanta: Scholars Press, 1987), pp. 368-93.

—*Parables as Poetic Fictions: The Creative Voice of Jesus* (Peabody, MA: Hendrickson, 1994), pp. 142-63.

Heininger, Bernhard, *Metaphorik, Erzählstruktur und szenisch-dramatische Gestaltung in den Sondergutgleichnissen bei Lukas* (NTAbh, NS, 24; Münster: Aschendorff, 1991).

Hendrickx, Herman, *The Parables of Jesus* (Studies in the Synoptic Gospels; London: Geoffrey Chapman; San Francisco: Harper & Row, rev. edn, 1986).

Herzog, William R., II, *Parables as Subversive Speech: Jesus as Pedagogue of the Oppressed* (Louisville, KY: Westminster/John Knox Press, 1994).

Hughes, Philip Edgcumbe, 'The Languages Spoken by Jesus', in Richard N. Longenecker and Merrill C. Tenney (eds.), *New Dimensions in New Testament Study* (Grand Rapids: Zondervan, 1974), pp. 127-43.

Hunter, A.M., *Interpreting the Parables* (London: SCM Press, 1960).

Jeremias, Joachim, *Die Gleichnisse Jesu* (Göttingen: Vandenhoeck & Ruprecht, 8th edn, 1970).

—*The Parables of Jesus* (trans. S.H. Hooke; New York: Charles Scribner's Sons, 2nd rev. edn, 1972).

Johnston, Robert Morris, 'Parabolic Interpretations Attributed to Tannaim' (PhD dissertation, The Hartford Seminary Foundation, 1977).

Jones, Geraint Vaughan, *The Art and Truth of the Parables: A Study in their Literary Form and Modern Interpretation* (London: SPCK, 1964).

Jones, Ivor Harold, *The Matthean Parables: A Literary and Historical Commentary* (NovTSup 80; Leiden: E.J. Brill, 1995).

Jordan, G.J., 'The Classification of the Parables', *ExpTim* 45 (1933–34), pp. 246-51.

Jülicher, Adolf, *Die Gleichnisreden Jesu* (Freiburg i.B.: J.C.B. Mohr [Paul Siebeck], 1888).

—*Die Gleichnisreden Jesu* (Zwei Teile in einem Band; Tübingen: J.C.B. Mohr, 1910).

—*Die Gleichnisreden Jesu* (Zwei Teile in einem Band; Nachdruck der Ausgabe Tübingen 1910; Darmstadt: Wissenschaftliche Buchgesellschaft, 1963).

—*Die Gleichnisreden Jesu. Erste Hälfe: Allgemeiner Theil* (Freiburg i.B.: J.C.B. Mohr [Paul Siebeck], 1886).

—*Die Gleichnisreden Jesu. Erster Teil: Die Gleichnisreden Jesu im Allgemeinen* (Freiburg i.B.: J.C.B. Mohr [Paul Siebeck], 2. bearb. Aufl. 1899).

—*Die Gleichnisreden Jesu. Zweiter Teil: Auslegung der Gleichnisreden der drei ersten Evangelien* (Freiburg i.B.: J.C.B. Mohr [Paul Siebeck], 1899).

—*An Introduction to the New Testament* (trans. Janet Penrose Ward; London: Smith, Elder & Co.; New York: Putnam's Sons, 1904).

—'Parables', in Cheyne and Black (eds.), *Encyclopædia Biblica*, III, pp. 3563-67.

Jüngel, Eberhard, *Paulus und Jesus: Eine Untersuchung zur Präzisierung der Frage nach dem Ursprung der Christologie* (Tübingen: J.C.B. Mohr [Paul Siebeck], 3rd edn, 1967).

Kennedy, George A., *Aristotle, On Rhetoric: A Theory of Civic Discourse* (Oxford: Oxford University Press, 1991).

—*The Art of Persuasion in Greece* (Princeton, NJ: Princeton University Press, 1963).

—*The Art of Rhetoric in the Roman World 300 B.C.–A.D. 300* (Princeton, NJ: Princeton University Press, 1972).

—*Classical Rhetoric and its Christian and Secular Tradition from Ancient to Modern Times* (Chapel Hill, NC: University of North Carolina Press, 1980).

—*Greek Rhetoric under Christian Emperors* (Princeton, NJ: Princeton University Press, 1983).

—*New Testament Interpretation through Rhetorical Criticism* (Chapel Hill, NC: University of North Carolina Press, 1984).

Kingsbury, Jack Dean, *Conflict in Luke: Jesus, Authorities, Disciples* (Minneapolis: Fortress Press, 1991).

—'Ernst Fuchs' Existentialist Interpretation of the Parables', *LQ* 22 (1970), pp. 380-95.

—'Major Trends in Parable Interpretation', *CTM* 42 (1971), pp. 579-96.

—'The Parables of Jesus in Current Research', *Dialog* 11 (1972), pp. 101-107.

—*The Parables of Jesus in Matthew 13: A Study in Redaction-Criticism* (Richmond, VA: John Knox Press, 1969).

Kinneavy, James L., *Greek Rhetorical Origins of Christian Faith: An Inquiry* (Oxford: Oxford University Press, 1987).

Kissinger, Warren S., *The Parables of Jesus: A History of Interpretation and Bibliography* (American Theological Library Association Bibliography Series, 4; Metuchen, NJ: Scarecrow Press, 1979).

Kjärgaard, Mogens Stiller, *Metaphor and Parable: A Systematic Analysis of the Specific Structure and Cognitive Function of the Synoptic Similes and Parables qua Metaphor* (ATDan, 29; Leiden: E.J. Brill, 1986).

Klauck, Hans-Josef, 'Adolf Jülicher: Leben, Werk und Wirkung', in Georg Schwaiger (ed.), *Historische Kritik in der Theologie: Beiträge zu ihrer Geschichte* (Studien zur Theologie und Geistesgeschichte des neunzehnten Jahrhunderts, 32; Göttingen: Vandenhoeck & Ruprecht, 1980), pp. 99-150.

—*Allegorie und Allegorese in synoptischen Gleichnistexten* (NTAbh, NS, 13; Münster: Aschendorff, 1978).

—'Neue Beiträge zur Gleichnisforschung', *BibLeb* 13 (1972), pp. 214-30.

Klemm, Hans Gunther, *Das Gleichnis vom barmherzigen Samariter: Grundzüge der Auslegung im 16./17. Jahrhundert* (BWANT, 3; Stuttgart: W. Kohlhammer, 1973).

—'Die Gleichnisauslegung Ad. Jülichers im Bannkreis der Fabeltheorie Lessings', *ZNW* 60 (1969), pp. 153-74 (repr. in Harnisch [ed.], *Gleichnisse Jesu*, pp. 343-68).

Koester, Helmut, 'Jesus the Victim', *JBL* 111 (1992), pp. 3-15.

Kümmel, Werner Georg, *The New Testament: The History of the Investigation of its Problems* (trans. S. Maclean Gilmour and Howard Clark Kee; Nashville: Abingdon Press, 1972).

Kurz, William S., 'Hellenistic Rhetoric in the Christological Proof of Luke–Acts', *CBQ* 42 (1980), pp. 171-95.

Lambrecht, Jan, *Once More Astonished: The Parables of Jesus* (New York: Crossroad, 1981).

Lanham, Richard A., *A Handlist of Rhetorical Terms: A Guide for Students of English Literature* (Berkeley: University of California Press, 1968).

Lausberg, Heinrich, *Handbuch der literarischen Rhetorik: Eine Grundlegung der Literaturwissenschaft* (2 vols.; Munich: Hueber, 1960).

Linnemann, Eta, *Gleichnisse Jesu: Einführung und Auslegung* (Göttingen: Vandenhoeck & Ruprecht, 4th edn, 1966).

—*Parables of Jesus: Introduction and Exposition* (trans. John Sturdy; SPCK Large Paperbacks, 25; London: SPCK, 1966).

Little, James C., 'Parable Research in the Twentieth Century. I. The Predecessors of J. Jeremias', *ExpTim* 87 (1976), pp. 356-60.

—'Parable Research in the Twentieth Century. II. The Contributions of J. Jeremias', *ExpTim* 88 (1976), pp. 40-44.

—'Parable Research in the Twentieth Century. III. Developments since J. Jeremias', *ExpTim* 88 (1976), pp. 71-75.

Lohmeyer, Ernst, 'Vom Sinn der Gleichnisse Jesu', *ZST* 15 (1938), pp. 319-46.

Longenecker, Richard N., and Merrill C. Tenney (eds.), *New Dimensions in New Testament Study* (Grand Rapids: Zondervan, 1974).

Lyons, John D., *Exemplum: The Rhetoric of Example in Early Modern France and Italy* (Princeton, NJ: Princeton University Press, 1989).

Mack, Burton L., *Rhetoric and the New Testament* (Guides to Biblical Scholarship Series; Minneapolis: Fortress Press, 1990).

Mack, Burton L., and Vernon K. Robbins, *Patterns of Persuasion in the Gospels* (Foundation and Facets: Literary Facets; Sonoma, CA: Polebridge Press, 1989).

Mánek, Jindřich, *...Und brachte Frucht: Die Gleichnisse Jesu* (trans. Joachim Dachsel; Stuttgart: Calwer Verlag, 1st edn, 1977).

Marrou, Henri-Irénée, *Histoire de l'education dans l'antiquité* (Paris: Seuil, 3rd edn, 1955).

—*A History of Education in Antiquity* (trans. George Lamb; New York: Sheed and Ward, 1956).

Marshall, I.H., *Eschatology and the Parables* (London: Tyndale Press, 1963).

Mattill, A.J., and Mary Bedford Mattill, *A Classified Bibliography of Literature on the Acts of the Apostles* (Leiden: E.J. Brill, 1966).

Mazamisa, Llewellyn Welile, *Beatific Comradeship: An Exegetical–Hermeneutical Study on Lk 10:25-37* (Kampen: Kok, 1987).

McBurney, James H., 'The Place of Enthymeme in Rhetorical Theory', *Speech Monographs* 3 (1936), pp. 49-97 (repr. in Erickson [ed.], *The Classical Heritage of Rhetoric*, pp. 117-40).

McCall, Marsh H., Jr, *Ancient Rhetorical Theories of Simile and Comparison* (LCM; Cambridge, MA: Harvard University Press, 1969).

McFague, Sallie, *Speaking in Parables: A Study of Metaphor and Theology* (Philadelphia: Fortress Press, 1975).

McGuire, Michael, 'Some Problems with Rhetorical Example', *Pre/Text* 3 (1982), pp. 121-36.

Mees, M., 'Die moderne Deutung der Parabeln und ihre Probleme', *Vetera Christianorum* 11 (1974), pp. 416-33.

Mills, Watson E., *A Bibliography of the Periodical Literature on the Acts of the Apostles 1962–1984* (Leiden: E.J. Brill, 1986).

Monselewski, Werner, *Der barmherzige Samariter: Eine auslegungsgeschichtliche Untersuchung zu Lukas 10, 25-37* (BGBE, 5; Tübingen: J.C.B. Mohr [Paul Siebeck], 1967).

Morgenthaler, Robert, *Lukas und Quintilian: Rhetorik als Erzählkunst* (Zürich: Gotthelf Verlag, 1993).

Mowry, Lucetta, 'Parable', in *IDB*, III, pp. 649-54.

Nagy, Gregory, 'Ancient Greek Epic and Praise Poetry: Some Typlogical Considerations', in Foley (ed.), *Oral Tradition in Literature*, pp. 89-102.

—*The Best of the Achaeans: Concepts of the Hero in Archaic Greek Poetry* (Baltimore: The Johns Hopkins University Press, 1979).

Natali, Carlo, 'Paradeigma: The Problems of Human Acting and the Use of Example in Some Greek Authors of the 4th Century B.C.', *Rhetoric Society Quarterly* 19 (1989), pp. 141-52.

Olrik, Axel, 'Epic Laws of Folk Narrative', in Alan Dundes (ed.), *The Study of Folklore* (Englewood Cliffs, NJ: Prentice–Hall, 1965), pp. 129-41.

—'Epische Gesetze der Volksdicthung', *Zeitschrift für deutsches Altertum* 51 (1909), pp. 1-12.

Patte, Daniel, 'An Analysis of Narrative Structure and the Good Samaritan', *Semeia* 2 (1974), pp. 1-26.

—*The Religious Dimensions of Biblical Texts: Greimas's Structural Semiotics and Biblical Exegesis* (SBLSS; Atlanta: Scholars Press, 1990).

—'Structural Analysis of the Parable of the Prodigal Son: Towards a Method', in *idem* (ed.), *Semiology and Parables*, pp. 71-149.

Patte, Daniel (ed.), *Semiology and Parables: An Exploration of the Possibilities Offered by Structuralism for Exegesis* (PTMS, 9; Pittsburgh: Pickwick Press, 1976).

Payne, Philip Barton, 'The Authenticity of the Parables of Jesus', in R.T. France and David Wenham (eds.), *Gospel Perspectives II* (Sheffield: JSOT Press, 1981), pp. 329-44.

Perkins, Pheme, *Hearing the Parables of Jesus* (New York: Paulist Press, 1981).

Perrin, Norman, *Jesus and the Language of the Kingdom: Symbol and Metaphor in New Testament Interpretation* (Philadelphia: Fortress Press, 1976).

—'The Modern Interpretation of the Parables of Jesus and the Problem of Hermeneutics', *Int* 25 (1971), pp. 131-48.

—*Rediscovering the Teaching of Jesus* (New York: Harper & Row, 1967).

Petersen, Norman R., 'On the Notion of Genre in Via's "Parable and Example Story: A Literary-Structuralist Approach"', *Semeia* 1 (1974), pp. 134-81.

Poland, Lynn M., *Literary Criticism and Biblical Hermeneutics: A Critique of Formalist Approaches* (American Academy of Religion Academy Series, 48; Chico, CA: Scholars Press, 1985).

Polk, Timothy, 'Paradigms, Parables, and Měšālîm: On Reading the Māšāl in Scripture', *CBQ* 45 (1983), pp. 564-83.

Praeder, Susan Marie, 'Luke–Acts and the Ancient Novel', in Kent Harold Richards (ed.), *Society of Biblical Literature 1981 Seminar Papers* (Chico, CA: Scholars Press, 1981), pp. 269-92.

Price, Bennett J., 'Παράδειγμα and *Exemplum* in Ancient Rhetorical Theory' (PhD dissertation, University of California, Berkeley, 1975).

Quintilian, *Institutio Oratoria*, in *The Institutio Oratoria of Quintilian* (trans. H.E. Butler; LCL; 4 vols.; London: Heinemann; Cambridge, MA: Harvard University Press, 1920–22).

Reinhartz, Adele, 'Anonymity and Character in the Books of Samuel', *Semeia* 63 (1993), pp. 117-41.

Rese, Martin, 'Das Lukas-Evangelium: Ein Forschungsbericht', in *ANRW*, 25.3, pp. 2258-328.

Richard, Earl, 'Luke—Writer, Theologian, Historian: Research and Orientation of the 1970s', *BTB* 13 (1983), pp. 3-15.

Richards, Kent Harold (ed.), *Society of Biblical Literature 1981 Seminar Papers* (Chico, CA: Scholars Press, 1981).

—(ed.), *Society of Biblical Literature 1987 Seminar Papers* (Atlanta: Scholars Press, 1987).

Ricoeur, Paul, 'Biblical Hermeneutics', *Semeia* 4 (1975), pp. 29-148.

—'Listening to the Parables of Jesus', *Criterion* 13 (Spring 1974), pp. 18-22.

Robinson, James M. *A New Quest of the Historical Jesus* (Philadelphia: Fortress Press, 1983).

—(ed.), *The Nag Hammadi Library: In English* (San Francisco: Harper & Row, 1981).

Sanday, W., 'A New Work on the Parables', *JTS* 1 (1900), pp. 161-80.

Sanders, E.P., and Margaret Davies, *Studying the Synoptic Gospels* (London: SCM Press; Philadelphia: Trinity Press International, 1989).

Satterthwaite, Philip E., 'Acts Against the Background of Classical Rhetoric', in Bruce W. Winter and Andrew D. Clarke (eds.), *The Book of Acts in its First Century Setting*. I. *The Book of Acts in its Ancient Literary Setting* (Grand Rapids: Eerdmans, 1993), pp. 337-79.

Schenda, Rudolf, 'Stand und Aufgaben der Exemplaforschung', *Fabula* 10 (1969), pp. 69-85.

Schierling, Stephen P., and Marla J. Schierling, 'The Influence of the Ancient Romances on *Acts of the Apostles*', *The Classical Bulletin* 54 (1978), pp. 81-88.

Schneider, Gerhard, *Parusiegleichnisse im Lukas-Evangelium* (SBS, 74; Stuttgart: Katholisches Bibelwerk, 1975).

Schramm, Tim, and Kathrin Löwenstein, *Unmoralische Helden: Anstössige Gleichnisse Jesu* (Göttingen: Vandenhoeck & Ruprecht, 1986).

Schwaiger, Georg (ed.), *Historische Kritik in der Theologie: Beiträge zu ihrer Geschichte* (Studien zur Theologie und Geistesgeschichte des neunzehnten Jahrhunderts, 32; Göttingen: Vandenhoeck & Ruprecht, 1980).

Schwartz, Regina M. (ed.), *The Book and the Text: The Bible and Literary Theory* (Oxford: Basil Blackwell, 1990).

Scott, Bernard Brandon, 'Essaying the Rock: The Authenticity of the Jesus Parable Tradition', *Forum* 2.1 (1980), pp. 3-54.

—*Hear Then the Parable: A Commentary on the Parables of Jesus* (Minneapolis: Fortress Press, 1989).

—*Jesus, Symbol-Maker for the Kingdom* (Philadelphia: Fortress Press, 1981).

—'The Prodigal Son: A Structuralist Interpretation', *Semeia* 9 (1977), pp. 45-73.

Sellew, Philip, 'Interior Monologue as a Narrative Device in the Parables of Luke', *JBL* 111 (1992), pp. 239-53.

Sellin, Gerhard, 'Allegorie und "Gleichnis": Zur Formenlehre der synoptischen Gleichnisse', *ZTK* 75 (1978), pp. 281-335 (repr. in Harnisch [ed.], *Die neutestamentliche Gleichnisforschung im Horizont von Hermeneutik und Literaturwissenschaft*, pp. 367-429).

—'Gleichnisstrukturen', *LB* 31 (1974), pp. 89-115.

—'Lukas als Gleichniserzähler: Die Erzählung vom barmherzigen Samariter (Lk 10 25-37)', *ZNW* 65 (1974), pp. 166-89.

—'Lukas als Gleichniserzähler: Die Erzählung vom barmherzigen Samariter (Lk 10 25-37)', *ZNW* 66 (1975), pp. 19-60.

Sider, John W., *Interpreting the Parables: A Hermeneutical Guide to their Meaning* (Grand Rapids: Zondervan, 1995).

—'The Meaning of *Parabole* in the Usage of the Synoptic Evangelists', *Bib* 62 (1981), pp. 453-70.

—'Nurturing our Nurse: Literary Scholars and Biblical Exegesis', *Christianity and Literature* 32 (1982), pp. 15-21.

—'Proportional Analogies in the Gospel Parables', *NTS* 31 (1985), pp. 1-23.

—'Rediscovering the Parables: The Logic of the Jeremias Tradition', *JBL* 102 (1983), pp. 61-83.

Smith, B.T.D., *The Parables of the Synoptic Gospels: A Critical Study* (London: Cambridge University Press, 1937).

Snodgrass, Klyne, *The Parable of the Wicked Tenants: An Inquiry into Parable Interpretation* (WUNT, 27; Tübingen: J.C.B. Mohr [Paul Siebeck], 1983).

Solmsen, Friedrich, 'The Aristotelian Tradition in Ancient Rhetoric', *AJP* 62 (1941), pp. 35-40, 169-90 (repr. in Erickson [ed.], *The Classical Heritage of Rhetoric*, pp. 278-309).

Stanford, W. Bedell, *Greek Metaphor: Studies in Theory and Practice* (Oxford: Basil Blackwell, 1936).

Stein, Robert H., *An Introduction to the Parables of Jesus* (Philadelphia: Westminster Press, 1981).

Stern, David, *Parables in Midrash: Narrative and Exegesis in Rabbinic Literature* (Cambridge, MA: Harvard University Press, 1991).

—'Rhetoric and Midrash: The Case of the Mashal', *Prooftexts* 1 (1981), pp. 261-91.

Stewart, G.W., 'Jülicher on the Nature and Purpose of the Parables', *The Expositor* 1 (1900), pp. 232-40, 311-20, 461-72.

Stierle, Karlheinz, 'Geschichte als Exemplum—Exemplum als Geschichte: Zur Pragmatik und Poetik narrativer Texte', in *idem*, *Text als Handlung*, pp. 14-48.

—*Text als Handlung: Perspektiven einer systematischen Literaturwissenschaft* (Munich: Wilhelm Fink Verlag, 1975).

Stockmeyer, Immanuel, *Exegetische und praktische Erklärung ausgewählter Gleichnisse Jesu* (ed. Karl Stockmeyer; Basel: Verlag von R. Reich, 1897).

Stowers, Stanley Kent, *The Diatribe and Paul's Letter to the Romans* (SBLDS, 57; Chico, CA: Scholars Press, 1981).

Suleiman, Susan, *Authoritarian Fictions: The Ideological Novel as a Literary Genre* (New York: Columbia University Press, 1983).

—'Le récit exemplaire', *Poétique* 32 (1977), pp. 468-89.

Talbert, Charles H. (ed.), *Luke–Acts: New Perspectives from the Society of Biblical Literature Seminar* (New York: Crossroad, 1984).

Tolbert, Mary Ann, 'The Gospel in Greco-Roman Culture', in Regina M. Schwartz (ed.), *The Book and the Text: The Bible and Literary Theory* (Oxford: Basil Blackwell, 1990), pp. 258-75.

—*Perspectives on the Parables: An Approach to Multiple Interpretations* (Philadelphia: Fortress Press, 1979).

—'The Prodigal Son: An Essay in Literary Criticism from a Psychoanalytic Perspective', *Semeia* 9 (1977), pp. 1-20.

—*Sowing the Gospel: Mark's World in Literary-Historical Perspective* (Minneapolis: Fortress Press, 1989).

Trench, Richard Chenevix, *Notes on the Parables of Our Lord* (New York: D. Appleton & Co., 8th edn, 1856).

Trocmé, Etienne, *Jesus and his Contemporaries* (trans. R.A. Wilson; London: SCM Press, 1973).

Tucker, Jeffrey T., 'A Class unto Themselves: The Scholarly Myth of Adolf Jülicher's Example Narratives' (Paper delivered at the annual meetings of the Society of Biblical Literature, New Orleans, November 1996).

—'Four Parables in the Gospel of Luke: Perspectives on the Example Narratives' (PhD dissertation, Vanderbilt University, 1994).

Van Koetsveld, C.E., *De Gelijkenissen van den Zaligmaker* (2 vols.; Utrecht: A.H. Ten Bokkel Huinink, n.d.).

Van Segbroeck, Frans, *The Gospel of Luke: A Cumulative Bibliography 1973–1988* (BETL, 88; Collectanea Biblica et Religiosa Antiqua, 2; Leuven: Peeters, 1989).

Via, Dan Otto, Jr, 'Parable and Example Story: A Literary-Structuralist Approach', *Semeia* 1 (1974), pp. 105-33.

—'The Parable of the Unjust Judge: A Metaphor of the Unrealized Self', in Patte (ed.), *Semiology and Parables*, pp. 1-32.

—*The Parables: Their Literary and Existential Dimension* (Philadelphia: Fortress Press, 1967).

—'The Prodigal Son: A Jungian Reading', *Semeia* 9 (1977), pp. 21-43.

—'The Relationship of Form to Content in the Parables: The Wedding Feast', *Int* 25 (1971), pp. 171-84.

—'A Response to Crossan, Funk, and Petersen', *Semeia* 1 (1974), pp. 222-35.

Wagner, Günther (ed.), *An Exegetical Bibliography of the New Testament*. II. *Luke and Acts* (Macon, GA: Mercer University Press, 1985).

Wailes, Stephen L., *Medieval Allegories of Jesus' Parables* (Berkeley: University of California Press, 1987).

Weder, Hans, *Die Gleichnisse Jesu als Metaphern: Traditions- und redaktionsgeschichtliche Analysen und Interpretationen* (FRLANT, 120; Göttingen: Vandenhoeck & Ruprecht, 1978).

Weiss, Bernhard, *The Life of Christ* (3 vols.; trans. M.G. Hope; Edinburgh: T. & T. Clark, 1894).

—'Ueber das Bildliche im Neuen Testamente', *Deutsche Zeitschrift für christliche Wissenschaft und christliches Leben* NS 4 (1861), pp. 309-31.

Weiss, Johannes, 'Jülichers "Gleichnisreden Jesu"', *TRu* 4 (1901), pp. 1-11 (repr. in Harnisch [ed.], *Gleichnisse Jesu*, pp. 11-19).

Westermann, Claus, *The Parables of Jesus in the Light of the Old Testament* (trans. Friedemann W. Golka and Alastair H.B. Logan; Minneapolis: Fortress Press, 1990).

—*Vergleiche und Gleichnisse im Alten und Neuen Testament* (Calwer Theologische Monographien, Series A, 14; Stuttgart: Calwer Verlag, 1984).

Wilcox, Max, 'Jesus in the Light of his Jewish Environment', in *ANRW*, 25.1, pp. 131-95.

Wilder, Amos N., *Early Christian Rhetoric: The Language of the Gospel* (Cambridge, MA: Harvard University Press, 2nd edn, 1971).

Winter, Bruce W., and Andrew D. Clarke (eds.), *The Book of Acts in its First Century Setting*. I. *The Book of Acts in its Ancient Literary Setting* (Grand Rapids: Eerdmans, 1993).

Wittig, Susan, 'Meaning and Modes of Signification: Toward a Semiotic of the Parable', in Patte (ed.), *Semiology and Parables*, pp. 319-47.

—'A Theory of Multiple Meanings', *Semeia* 9 (1977), pp. 75-103.

York, John O., *The Last Shall Be First: The Rhetoric of Reversal in Luke* (JSNTSup, 46; Sheffield: JSOT Press, 1991).

Young, Brad H., *Jesus and his Jewish Parables: Rediscovering the Roots of Jesus' Teaching* (New York: Paulist Press, 1989).

INDEXES

INDEX OF REFERENCES

BIBLE

JOURNAL FOR THE STUDY OF THE NEW TESTAMENT
SUPPLEMENT SERIES